NO PLAN B

THE ADVENTURES OF A CARBON UNIT
IN SILICON VALLEY

NO PLAN B

THE ADVENTURES OF A CARBON UNIT IN SILICON VALLEY

or

How I Made a Million Dollars in Hi-Tech Startups Basically by Just Showing Up (Don't Try This At Home)

NO PLAN B:
The Adventures of a Carbon Unit in Silicon Valley
or, How I Made a Million Dollars in Hi-Tech Startups Basically by Just Showing Up (Don't Try This At Home)

Published by The Impermanent Press

First Ebook Edition: May 2020
First Print Edition: July 2020

v04

ISBN 978-1-886404-40-3

Cover Design by D. Scott Apel
Cover Photo by Catherine Inslee

“What is the purpose of the carbon units?”
—V’Ger, *Star Trek: The Motion Picture*

DEDICATION

To Piph,
who always trusted that there was a plan.

A Note About the Cast of Characters

My so-called career in Silicon Valley was aided by a number of individuals. In most cases, the names of the innocent have been preserved, because they deserve the recognition. They are all heroes. In a very few cases, out of respect for their privacy, only their first name has been used, or their name has been changed at their request to a pseudonym of their choosing.

For those peripheral to the story, I've used only their first names. They'll know who they are, but I don't want to intrude on their privacy, or embarrass them by their association with me (or by my occasionally less than flattering portraits of them). When no co-workers are mentioned, it's because they were so unexceptional, or so exceptionally uninteresting, that squandering any brain cells on remembering or documenting them seems unwarranted.

The names of the guilty—those who hindered my alleged career—have been comically altered, because they don't deserve the recognition. Also because they are the shitheels most likely to sue. You bastards know who you are.

CONTENTS

PART I: ANALOG

PART II: DIGITAL

PART III: A BITE OF THE APPLE

PART IV: 2020 HINDSIGHT

PREFACE

First, what this book is *not*.

It is *not* a history of Silicon Valley. If you're looking for a scholarly and objective accounting of how Silicon Valley came into being, there are several excellent books that cover this subject in depth, foremost among them Michael S. Malone's 1985 chronicle *The Big Score: The Billion Dollar Story of Silicon Valley*.

No Plan B is *not* a Silicon Valley overview. It is an *under*-view. It is a report from ground level; a memo sent from the trenches, not the penthouse—notes from the break room, not the boardroom. It is dispatches from the belly of the beast.

It is *not* the story of a struggling startup that went on to rule the world. It is the far more common story of a few startups that tried but tanked, as witnessed by a cubicle dweller who went down with those ships, often without a life preserver.

It is *not* a success story of one of the handful of pioneers who became internet godzillionaires, or of a ragtag band of disruptive engineers and entrepreneurs who bet everything by founding a tech company that took over the world. It is the simple story of a middle-class, middle-aged, arrow-straight, lily-white male of middling intelligence trying to survive in the cutthroat culture that evolved around him in his own home town. *No Plan B* is not a business book. It's a *work* book.

There are more than enough books about Silicon Valley that concentrate on The Big Picture: the epic struggles of a startup to survive, and the outrageous and outsized egos of their larger-than-life founders. But for every successful startup, there are nearly a hundred that go belly-up in the first 18 months, and for every Jobs or Ellison or Zuckerberg, there are 10,000 nameless, faceless workers who toil in obscurity to make the vision of these visionaries a success...if only just to hold onto their jobs.

Nobody tells their stories. But here's one...

INTRODUCTION

Charles Dickens opened his masterpiece *David Copperfield* with these words: *"Whether I shall turn out to be the hero of my own life, or whether that station will be held by anybody else, these pages must show."*

I shall open my minorpiece by paraphrasing that memorable quote: *Whether I shall turn out to be the hero of my own life, or whether that station will be held by anybody else...* Ah, fuck it. I'm the hero.

No Plan B is the story of my experiences working in Silicon Valley. Since it's a personal journal, it includes no boring tutorials on electronics or economics. It's a record of a small cog in the great machine of hi-tech (who often ended up like Charlie Chaplin in *Modern Times*) attempting to navigate the minefields of employment and office politics. Ultimately, *No Plan B* is an attempt to shake off the layers of soot accumulated through decades of work deep in the tech mines and to condense and compress it into a diamond. Whether the resultant rock is rough or multifaceted, a gem or merely a cubic zirconium...well, "these pages must show."

Everyone who works for a living occasionally comes home and complains about their day—the petty slights; the tedious, frequently meaningless work; the idiot boss. Clearly, only a narcissistic egotist (or a literary novelist) would expend the effort to chronicle these trivial experiences at book length. Nice to meet you.

Some might question the accuracy or veracity of these events. My reply is that these incidents are related as honestly as memory allows. If anyone takes issue with my memory or perspective, they are advised to write their own damn book. Or even better, they are invited to sit the hell down and shut the fuck up. And to bite me.

Chapter Zero

PLAN A

"I hate Plan B. Forget Plan B.
If you have Plan B then you can never truly focus on Plan A, and that's a big mistake. To test yourself and grow, you have to operate without a safety net."
—Arnold Schwarzenegger

"There's no reason to have a Plan B
because it distracts from Plan A."
—Will Smith

"If God has given you a Plan A, do you really need a Plan B?"
—Stephen Colbert, "The Colbert Report," May 11, 2006

There was always a Plan A.

Plan A was to become what I had discovered I was: a writer. And it *was* a discovery, not a decision. Once that revelation crystallized in my mind—not "I want to be a writer," but "I *am* a writer"—the meaning of many experiences, opinions, and attractions fell into place like iron filings around a magnet. And the more writers I met, the more I realized how much we had in common psychologically—much more in common than with, say, actors (of whom I met many), or fine artists, or scientists, or engineers, or, God help me, corporate managers.

By 1974, at age 23, I was so deeply invested in Plan A that it never occurred to me that a backup plan might be necessary, or even desirable. I was committed to persist with Plan A no matter how long it took. That's the American way, right? The American Dream? That's what we've always been told, that hard work and persistence is a guarantee of success. As Will Smith said above, any backup plan, any Plan B, could only be a distraction —as well as a clear indication of lack of confidence in Plan A... and by extension, lack of confidence in myself. Implementing a Plan B would mean just one thing: Failure. Defeat. Giving up.

But I discovered, as George Carlin put it, "they call it the American Dream because you have to be asleep to believe it." And my wake-up call would not occur until I was too deeply immersed in Plan A to extricate myself without significant effort.

Until then, I concentrated on Plan A: honing my craft until such time as I could attain my goal of making at least a moderate living by writing what I wanted to write—novels, mostly. Kurt Vonnegut said it takes a novelist twenty years to become known. *OK,* I told myself at the beginning of Plan A (and while clenching my sphincter), *I'll put in the twenty years.*

My aspirations as a writer were not particularly high. I never once considered writing the archetypal "Great American Novel," for example—or that I even could. After all, what did I know? I was a straight, white, non-substance-abusing male; a child of the American suburban Baby Boomer middle class. I never suffered. I was never an addict, or a recovered addict. I never went to jail, or to war, or hungry. I never fronted a rock band or starred in a Major Motion Picture. I never painted, heisted or forged a masterpiece. I never became a refugee, or felt the sting of oppression in any way that might inspire deep, heartrending Timeless Literature. White? Straight? Male? Hell, it was people like me that *ruled the world!* What did we know about suffering? So my goals as a writer were modest: I wanted to write what interested me, which was mainly genre tales—science fiction and mysteries. The literature of ideas. If I could use what I'd learned reading the Great Literature of the masters—Shakespeare, Joyce, Borges—I might be able to write stories that interested me, in a style a cut above the pulp fiction ghetto to which genre fiction had been consigned in the dark days prior to the 1970s.

Edison's formula for success was one percent inspiration and 99 percent perspiration. I thought I'd discovered the formula for literary success: 50 percent talent and 50 percent persistence. After a decade of writing prolifically and submitting assiduously while remaining unpublished, however—and while simultaneously watching a steady stream of what I considered to be lesser works by lesser authors populate bookstore shelves—I was forced to recalculate that formula. Literary success, I determined, was about five percent talent, forty-five percent persistence, and fifty percent sheer goddamn *luck*. If you were persistent enough

—that is, *observant* enough—you might at some point spot a potential lucky break in which you'd have a brief opportunity to display whatever talent you possessed, however meager.

This reformulation did not change my work habits. I continued writing and submitting, hoping I'd catch the right agent or editor on the right day in the right mood, in a market that could support what I'd produced. That day has yet to come.

My Plan A was an all-or-nothing, balls-to-the-wall, go-for-broke career decision. I would settle for nothing else.

Until I did.

Cut to the chase: Plan A failed. But a man must eat, and pay rent and taxes. And drink. And buy nice things for his girlfriend. And drink some more. Thus, while there was never a backup plan, a Plan B emerged from necessity and virtually organized itself. (I will, however, take all the credit.)

This is the story of From There to Here.

PART I:

ANALOG

"Why should I be constrained to work for a living?
I have committed no crime."
—Javier K. Caneeditu

Chapter 1

THE SECRET HISTORY OF SILICON VALLEY

"Silicon Valley runs on stories."
—Tim O'Reilly, investor and founder of O'Reilly Media, quoted in *Wired,* November 2016

Once upon a time—before 1955, specifically—there was a pristine agricultural region at the southern end of the San Francisco Bay Area in Northern California known as the Santa Clara Valley. Surrounded by mountains, the temperate climate made the geographic bowl an agricultural paradise, and it became famous for its apricots, prunes, cherries, peaches and nuts, among other crops. Del Monte grew fruit and canned it in its factory in Sunnyvale; Paul Masson and the Mirassou family worked vast tracts of vineyards and bottled distinctive wines and champagne; Sperry grew acres and acres of flowers in San Jose—solely to harvest the seeds for packaging.

And lo, the Lockheed Aircraft Company in Calabasas, deep in the bowels of Southern California, looked upon the face of the Valley and said, "Yea, let us build our new strategic missile facility there. Yeah, right *there*, next to the Navy's Moffett Field air station. Right next to that big-ass blimp hanger." And so they did. And IBM likewise gazed upon the unmolested Valley and said, "Let us also build our newest facility in this delightful valley—even if we have to put it in South San Jose," and so they did. And, like anchor stores in some immense megamall, these job magnets drew employees to the Valley in record number, creating an economic boom the likes of which this sleepy region had never seen—and for which it was hardly prepared.

In the 1960s, everyone who lived in The Valley had a relative or neighbor who worked for one of these two corporate giants. And this rich source of labor drew other companies to the area, names that were or would become legendary even before the Coming of the Silicon: Hewlett Packard. Eastman Kodak.

Xerox. General Electric. But the electronics developed at Stanford began creeping into the surroundings like silicon kudzu—so quickly and pervasively that in 1971 journalist Don Hoefler coined the moniker "Silicon Valley," and it stuck. No longer did we live in "The Valley of Heart's Delight."

Lest we forget, there were sinister foreshadowings of the soul-deadening side of this new "Silicon Valley." Santa Clara Valley was the site of the 1886 Supreme Court decision ("Santa Clara County v. Southern Pacific Rail Road" [sic]) that resulted in corporations being declared "individuals" and granted the same legal rights as "natural persons" under the 14th Amendment, for instance. And in 1933, San Jose, the self-appointed capital of Silicon Valley, was the site of one of the last public lynchings in the United States.

But things were simpler then. People were honest, hard-working and God-fearing. Checks were in the mail. Dinosaurs ruled the earth.

And me? Well, our family moved to The Valley in 1960, when I was only nine years old, so I was basically just standing there minding my own business (high school, college) when Silicon Valley sprang up around me in the 1970s. I watched it mushroom, and ultimately—like so many other residents—I was sucked up into its vortex of employment. Electronics firms overran my lovely agricultural valley like an alien invasion—something that, as Stephen Hawking reminded us, is never good for the natives. And the composition of the invaders was: Silicon.

Chapter 2

A JOB OF WORK
or, Work is for the Dogs

Moe: "Get a job!
Curly: "No, please… Not that! Anything but that!"
—*The Three Stooges*

"Heigh-ho, heigh-ho, it's off to work we go."
—The Dwarfs, *Snow White and the Seven Dwarfs*

During a lull in conversation at a dinner party a few years ago, one of our guests broke the silence by asking a clever question: "What was the worst job you ever had?" (Ultimately, this icebreaker proved to be a ploy for him to describe his own worst job, which he knew would trump anyone else's—it had something to do with wearing hip boots and shoveling sludge out of oil tanks—but it did serve its purpose for dinner party conversation: it inspired us all to share our horror stories.)

While each person around the table related the story of his or her Job From Hell, I was doing what everyone else was doing: paying scant attention while mentally organizing my own story and impatiently awaiting my turn to talk. I decided to talk about my first, and worst, job of work.

The indignity occurred during the summer of 1968. I was 17, between junior and senior years of high school. I had a driver's license but no car. And I was caught in a classic Catch-22 faced by countless middle-class teens: in order to own a car, I needed a job to buy the car and pay for gas, oil, and insurance. But in order to get a job, I needed a car to get me to work and back. "That's some catch, that Catch-22," Joseph Heller wrote. "Yep. The best there is."

Without any viable public transportation, the solution was, of course: Mom. She would drive me to my job. And pick me up. Every workday. All. Summer. Long. More than half a century later, I understand what this kind of pre-soccer mom sacrifice meant to her. At the time, however, I couldn't think of anything beyond my own humiliation. What 17-year-old wants to spend half an hour twice a day in a car *with his mom?*

Frankly, I'm not sure how I even got the job—probably through the network of parents and friends of parents. This was the pre-social networking social network; adults asking around among friends and co-workers. "You know anyone hiring teens this summer?" All I recall is that I was going to work in a dog kennel. Me, a cat person. Oh joy.

Before Silicon Valley absorbed every square inch of land in the South Bay, Santa Clara Valley was a loose affiliation of towns of various sizes, from the central city of San Jose to small-town outliers like Los Gatos to the south and Mountain View to the north. The kennel was located in a (then) rural neighborhood of Campbell, about eight miles away from home. The place was essentially a large barn, holding about 25 or 30 cages, each connected to a cement-pad dog run. It was owned and operated by an old guy and his wife, who lived in the house in front of the barn. Their names are irrelevant to the story. I don't remember them anyway.

Oh, it was a job all right—and an eye-opening introduction to working life. I was due at the kennel every morning at 7:00 AM—an hour earlier than my earliest high school class. I rarely saw the owner once he trained me. I have no idea where he was at 7 AM. Probably sleeping. I know I would have been, if I owned the place and could get a sub-minimum wage teen to open the facility at 7 AM.

My routine was invariable, because dogs are schedule-oriented animals. First, open the doors separating the individual cages from the individual dog runs. The entire dog run was essentially a huge cement pad separated by a series of parallel chain link fences so each dog had a long, narrow, vertical runway connected to his cage. And while the dogs were doing their business in their runs, I cleaned the cages, removing and replacing the newspaper linings. (There were always huge stacks of old editions of the San Jose *Mercury News* on hand. I don't know where they came from and don't recall ever asking, or even being curious about how they showed up. Twenty-some years later, while working as the video columnist for the *Merc*, I occasionally visualized my newspaper page being used as a dog's toilet. Maybe the dogs deserved better. I'm not sure my column did—it might have been just good enough, as Triumph the Insult Comic Dog used to say, "for me to poop on!")

Once the canine accommodations were cleaned, I prepared and delivered bowls of dog food to all the empty cages. Occasionally, we did a "special request" diet for the owners (there was never a Kosher option, however). At this point I let the dogs back into their cages—they were more than eager to return for their breakfast—and dropped the trap doors that led outside.

Then the real fun began: I donned my rain boots and went out to the dog runs, bucket and shovel in hand, where I assumed the function of Canine Waste Disposal Engineer. I collected the day's deposits and hosed down the runs. By 11 AM, my workday was done.

Actually, only the first *half* of my workday was done. Mom showed up at 11 AM and drove me home, where I occupied myself in some fashion until 3:30. (What I recall of that time half a century later is reading Shakespeare and masturbating. Not simultaneously, you understand, although if any writer was worth it…) Then it was time to return to the kennel for the second half of my split shift. And from 4 PM until 7 or 8 PM, I repeated the above functions. My entire day was *déjà vu*, and every day was, to quote Yogi Berra, "*déjà vu* all over again."

So this was my first, and worst, job: Start at 7 AM; finish at 8 PM; work a split shift; and specialize in canine feces disposal ...all for a sub-minimum wage, because it was just a summer job for a teenager. A summer job which, I was frequently reminded, *I was lucky to have*. Many of my friends had no summer job at all and were forced to spend the entire summer *having fun*.

I endured this endeavor from June 10 through September 9, 1968. As it turned out, however, this literal shit job did have one long-term advantage: for the rest of my working life, no matter how bad things got, no matter how much metaphorical bullshit or horseshit I had to endure, I could always put things in perspective by reminding myself, "Well, at least you aren't shoveling shit in a kennel!"

Chapter 3

1969: FRONTIER VILLAGE

"Return with us now to those thrilling days of Yesteryear..."
—from the narrative introduction to *The Lone Ranger*

My career trajectory did not begin by barreling toward the future. Before I was thrust face-first into the Silicon Valley hi-tech workforce, I took a retrograde trip to the Wild West. So… saddle up!

In the spring of 1969, I was a senior in high school, looking for a summer job. This time I was determined to find one on my own, and not rely on the Parental Network. My primary motivation for self-starting was the memory that, the previous summer, the ParentalNet™ found me a job shoveling shit in a dog kennel. I thought I could perhaps do better on my own, so I scoured the Want Ads in the San Jose *Mercury News*, where I found a job that sounded perfect: summer employment at a local amusement park, Frontier Village.

Frontier Village was the brainchild of Joe Zukin, a Santa Clara Valley carwash magnate who took his kids to Disneyland in 1959 and became convinced that San Jose could support a smaller version of this clean, wholesome, family-friendly entertainment venue. He decided to base his modest empire on just one quadrant of Disneyland: Frontierland, Uncle Walt's squeaky-clean recreation of the Wild West.

Zukin purchased a 40-acre parcel of land in south San Jose that had once been the formal gardens of the Hayes Estate, a sprawling 600-acre domain with a 64-room mansion built in 1889. A couple of decades after its construction, the Hayes house would become the weekend destination of a generation of Hollywood silent film stars.

Zukin broke ground for his park in August 1960—just one month before my family relocated to the area from a Chicago suburb—and opened the massive timber entrance gates to the public in late 1961. The park proved immediately popular. It was a sanitized and spacious recreation of a generic Old West town, complete with two-story buildings housing food services and souvenir shops, an ornate Victorian train station (suspiciously similar to Disneyland's Frontierland train station), and acres of tall, stately oaks, cypress, eucalyptus and pepper trees.

And rides. Lots of rides, including such period-appropriate attractions as a mule train, a stagecoach, a Merry-Go-Round, a shooting gallery, a canoe ride, and a small scale train, as well as anachronisms like a Ferris Wheel (which did not debut until 1893, at the Columbian Exposition in Chicago) and other mild, carnival-style thrill rides.

Every summer the park employed between 300 and 400 teens as ride operators and food concession vendors in these "30 fun-filled acres." According to the *Images of America* history of the park by Bob Johnson, "Frontier Village employees were the cream of the crop, facing rigorous screening to get hired and then meticulously trained in their duties. FV [sic] cowboys and cowgirls were attractive, polite, wholesome, and friendly. They enjoyed their jobs and shared their enjoyment with the guests." I managed to fool them on all counts and land a job. In the 20 years the park was open, I estimate that over 5,000 kids between the ages of 17 and 22 worked there. I was merely one of them, and would inadvertently become one the management either doesn't remember or wishes they could forget.

In April 1969, I interviewed with the Operations Manager—we'll call him "Warden Pretzel"—one of a pair of brothers who managed the park on a day-to-day basis. (Spoiler alert: I could hardly suspect that six months later, I'd be sitting in the same chair in the same office listening to him fire me.) Warden was a gangly, chinless guy, hardly older than his employees, sporting a close-cropped crew cut. I later discovered he'd been a Marine. (One of the older employees laughed when I asked him about this. "Yeah," he said. "Warden once shot a leaf in Vietnam.")

Warden's final interview question was, "If you could spend an afternoon doing anything, what would you do?" I was too young and naive to give the answer I would have given any time post-college ("Get high and screw") but I was not so young and naive that I knew that "read a book" would not be an appropriate response. That would be far too introverted for someone expected to interact with guests and work outside all day. So I said, "I'd go to Disneyland." I like to think that's what clinched the interview; by the time I'd made the 20-minute drive home, he'd called twice offering me a job. I'd start on Saturday, May 3.

For guests, Frontier Village was an amusement park. But I soon found out that for employees, it was more of an abusement park. For starters, it was mandatory to wear the "FV costume": blue jeans and a powder blue, short-sleeved shirt for cowboys; blue denim skirts and a powder blue blouse for the cowgirls; a cowboy hat and a red neck scarf, always hung to the right, for both genders. (This taught me that some people simply cannot differentiate between the concepts of "costume" and "uniform.") We had to purchase our costumes, for $48.50 (via payments deducted from our paychecks).

The park opened at 10 AM, but there was always a crew scheduled to arrive at 7 AM to rake leaves, sweep up, and clean and polish the rides. If you fell out of Warden Pretzel's graces, you'd find yourself on the early shift, sometimes for a 12-hour day. And due to a legal loophole (similar to the one that allowed 12-hour days), we were paid a starting wage of $1.10 an hour—far below minimum wage, since we were classified by the State of California as "park workers" rather than "employees." Welcome to the wonderful world of working for a living!

In addition, we were indoctrinated in idiosyncratic idioms: instead of "Hi," for instance, we were instructed to greet everyone with a hearty "Howdy!"—a habit that stuck with me for years afterward—and guests were always to be referred to as "pardner." For many of us, *pardner* quickly became the ultimate insult. I heard one fellow employee sputter once, for instance: "That jerk! That idiot! That... that... *pardner*!" We reframed the definition so we could call the public "pardner" to their faces and they took it as a compliment.

A RICH SENSE OF HUMOR

"No way to delay
That trouble comin' every day."
—The Mothers of Invention, "Trouble Every Day" (1966)

The trouble started early, but I swear to God it wasn't my fault. It was never my intention to be a troublemaker. Quite the opposite, actually. I wanted to succeed. I didn't want the embarrassment and humiliation of fucking up. After all, this was my first real job. If I fucked up, what would I tell my next employer? Besides, I was a polite, responsible lad. (I would not cultivate a "question authority" streak until college.)

I blame Rich Chadwick, who cornered me during our new employee orientation and kept up a steady stream of hilarious whispered commentary about the process, the rules, the speaker, and whatever else entered his head. He hit me from my blind side humor. I couldn't resist. Hell, I knew that if it wasn't him making these *sotto voce* comments, it could easily have been me, since the same sarcastic, subversive and anti-authoritarian mockery that came out of his mouth was already running through my head. Maybe it was my fault for not discouraging him. Maybe I should have moved away from him on the Group W bench and tried to be attentive, serious, committed. But I didn't. And all I got out of it was a good friend—one who lasted far longer than the job.

THE DATING GAME

For a hundred kids between the ages of 17 and 20, Frontier Village was a breeding ground for, well, *breeding*. What could you expect, throwing together that many young, attractive teens?

During that summer, there were, on average, three parties a week. Everyone was expected to host a party at some point. (I threw mine the week my parents took my siblings on vacation. "I can't go with you this year, Mom and Dad—I have to *work*!") The few 21-year-old employees were always in great demand since they were the only ones among us who could buy liquor.

We changed partners and dates as rapidly as a square dance. The dating scene grew so complicated that Rich and I actually drew up a chart of who was dating who during any given week. And I know for a fact that the appropriately named summer of '69 spawned at least four marriages (including Rich and Jan).

Even though I had limited dating experience, I realized this was an opportunity that might never occur again and was determined to hone my dating skills before I was confronted with College Women, so I jumped into the Village dating pool—cautiously, but hopefully. Lauren was a good place to start. She was a confidence builder—she never said no to a date request, so there was no fear of rejection. (She was also tall, sweet, and attractive. She was a win-win.) During that summer I went out with a great many girls, including one who gave me a lecture on Mormonism instead of a goodnight kiss. I also went out with Marsha for the sole reason that she had pouty, "bee-sting" lips... and I simply *had* to know what it was like to chew on them. (Answer: Awesome!) All told, I went on more dates during that summer than in any other three-month period before or since.

THE WORK

Warden Pretzel started me out on my first day on the security detail for the "Lost Frontier Mine," a popular dark ride. Rowdy teens sometimes attempted to vandalize the ride, he explained, and Mine Security was there to prevent that damage. He led me into the dark, cavernous ride and once our eyes adjusted to the gloom he showed me the secret passageways. Being able to see in the dark (somewhat) when the riders couldn't made the Mine Security guy effectively The Invisible Man. I got quite a kick out of walking directly behind cars full of riders knowing they literally could not see me. This might have led to some mischief, and of course, it did...but only once. A car full of "tween" girls was mocking the ride: how fake it all seemed, how it wasn't scary at all—until I reached out and squeezed the shoulders of the two girls riding in the back seat. "Janie?" I heard a voice quake. "Was that you?" *"Noooooo...."* Janie replied. And they screamed until they hit daylight. I suppose in these days that would be an HR violation, and I'd be fired, or a #MeToo violation, and I'd be arrested, but at the time, my only goal was to provide these non-believers with a thrill ride they'd never forget. (I discovered years later that one of the concepts for the original Haunted Mansion ride at Disneyland was for a hidden employee to reach through a hole in the wall and grab a guest. They abandoned that gimmick, but my escapade, I realized, was "proof of concept.")

The next weekend, both Rich and I were promoted to Grounds. We each took half the park and made constant rounds, sweeping up and picking up detritus dropped and spilled by careless and slovenly guests. On the Sunday morning after our Saturday debut, Warden Pretzel took us into his office to give us a pep talk. He told us a story about how, after the bombing of Pearl Harbor decimated much of the Pacific Naval fleet, the six remaining battleships were sent on high-speed patrols through the Pacific to convince the Japanese that we had more ships than we actually did because they were sighted so often in so many different places. I listened quietly and grasped the analogy —if there were only two groundskeepers, we had to keep moving at flank speed to make it appear as though there were many more. Duh. Rich, on the other hand, waited until Warden was done, then took him to task on the historically inaccurate details of his tale. "In December 1941," he told Warden, "there were, in fact, *nine* battleships in the fleet, not six, and three aircraft carriers. There were also fifty destroyers, thirty-three submarines and one hundred patrol bombers." And so on. I had to bite my tongue to keep from laughing.

The following weekend, Warden promoted me to Ride Operator. I ran the "Antique Autos" ride, which essentially consisted of pressing a button to start the cars on the track, then stopping the rolling cars at the end of the ride—with my foot. And on Memorial Day weekend I was promoted to operating the Ferris Wheel. This was a ride that actually required some skill, if only the skill of keeping out of the way of the wheel as it swung around and brushed my cowboy hat. Ferris Wheel operation depended on the eye of the operator to "guess the weight" of guests in line, and balance the wheel so it didn't burn out its miniscule motor. *1, 7, 8, 2, 3, 9, 10, 4, 5, 11, 12 and 6*—that was the load sequence, the equation to balance the 12-seat Wheel. (I can still count that way at the drop of a cowboy hat.)

Once the Wheel was fully loaded with riders, you let 'er rip for about three minutes—while standing on the operator's platform and leaning to the left so you didn't get your head ripped off by the "elephant ears" (i.e., cable guides). My most memorable moment: a pair of chunky-style, supersized guests insisted on riding together, which threw the entire balance of the Wheel off so much that it actually went backward, returning them to the loading platform a few seconds after they'd been seated. I didn't even have to fat-shame them by telling them I'd have to split them up—red-faced, they knew it immediately.

After a few weeks on the Wheel, on June 24th I was promoted once again, this time to Relief Man. This was a position of great respect: there were only three of us, working in teams of two per day. And since the Relief Man ran the ride while operators took their breaks and lunches, the operators were always glad to see me coming. It did mean that I had to learn to operate every ride in the park, but that was compensated for by the idea that the position perfectly matched my short attention span: running any one ride for an eight-hour shift was like prison, but as a Relief Man, I never had to spend longer than half an hour on any one ride any day. I was in my element.

So within a couple of months I had climbed the Frontier Village corporate ladder high enough to be given a position of responsibility—to the point where, one summer afternoon, when Founding Father Joe Zukin showed up to take the management team out to dinner, I was left in charge. I was left in charge of the entire amusement park full of people. And during the three hours the bosses were away eating, drinking and celebrating, *every single ride* in the park broke down and was repaired by Rich (who'd been promoted to Maintenance). When the execs returned, Warden asked me how it went. I just shrugged and smiled. "Business as usual," I said.

Even after half a century, I still recall the occasional 18-hour day, beginning at 7 AM raking eucalyptus leaves and ending at 1 AM hauling the day's garbage to the dumpster; the grueling summer heat, intensified by the park's blacktop streets; the constant pressure to smile, to be polite, to look clean and happy and busy. But it's the good memories that stand out: the cheering faces of my fellow employees at the train station as I broke the speed record for driving the train around the park after hours; the excitement of engineering the train one hot summer evening and discovering that the tinderbox back-of-the-park "badlands" were ablaze, powering the little engine through a literal Wall of Fire (and I wasn't even an OT3!); sitting in the bleachers of the Puppet Theater on the sultry evening of July 20, 1969, watching a tiny portable black and white TV placed on the stage as Neil Armstrong took one small step for (a) man onto the moon.

IN WHICH I AM FIRED–FOR THE FIRST TIME

And so went the summer of '69: hard but fun work; endless parties; an almost inexhaustible dating pool. But every summer ends with a fall...

November 1969

Following the summer season, the park remained open on weekends for several months. This ensured steady employment that worked excellently around employees' college class hours. On Halloween weekend, however, while groups of Villagers were out partying on that Friday night, someone made the grave error in judgment of TP'ing—"toilet papering"—Warden Pretzel's house. Let me be clear: it was not my friends or me who committed this heinous act. In fact, I never found out who performed this dastardly deed. But when we arrived at work at 7 AM the following morning, Saturday, the first of November, we found a typed message posted above the time clock addressed TO ALL EMPLOYEES and signed by Warden Pretzel. It recounted this inexcusable act of vandalism and reminded us (in all caps) that "YOUR CONDUCT AWAY FROM THE VILLAGE DOES AFFECT YOUR STATUS AT THE PARK." *What a humorless tool*, I thought. Evidently, I wasn't alone: someone had already amended his posted note with a hand-written comment: "Wise up, Pretzel." I thought this was both hilarious and appropriate, so I checked around to make sure I was totally alone in the break room, then added my own comment: "*Grow* up, Pretzel."

Later that day I was summoned to Warden Pretzel's office. He showed me the memo with the handwritten comments. "I know it was you who wrote that," he said.

"I *didn't* write that," I lied, confident there were no witnesses.

"I have a witness who saw you," he continued.

Well, that put me in a bind. My only defense would be to call him on his lie; to say, "There *couldn't* be a witness. I made sure no one saw me when I wrote that." It was a Catch-22 (even though I hadn't read that book yet). In the words of Homer Simpson (who wouldn't first utter this for 20 years): *"D'oh!"*

And so I was fired. The specific charge was that I had violated the "moral turpitude" clause of my employment contract, and I was fired for insubordination. For years I was ashamed of that. But given some time and perspective, I realized that for the anti-establishment radical I'd become this was in fact a point of pride.

At the time, however, I could only think: *This is horrible*. My future was circumcised, if not completely emasculated. I couldn't use Frontier Village on my résumé. I was banished from my social circle of Village employees. And worst of all... *I'd have to find another job*. Bloody hell.

Dramatis Personae

Rich Chadwick – The cocky joker who set me on the course of being a cocky joker. Rich was one of the most naturally funny people I've ever known, and could pivot from sarcastic to absurd in the space of a single sentence. We became fast friends and stayed so until he married one of our co-workers and moved to the East Coast.

During our summer in The Village, Rich and I developed a dating technique we called SNATO, an acronym for "Saturday Night at the Orgy." We'd get one of the 21-year-old employees to buy us some booze (I hazily recall bottles of Passport brand Scotch), then invite our current favorite girls out for a drive in the country to, you know, "watch the submarine races." I was embarrassed at the time to be driving my mother's old Rambler station wagon, but we quickly discovered that if you dropped the back seats and threw in a couple of sleeping bags, there was just enough room for a pair of wrestling couples.

Pete Smith – Yeah, I know, it sounds like a made-up name, but swear to God, that's his real name. He was an "older guy"—21—who worked at the park during summers away from college. Pete was laid back, goofy—and the first real stoner I'd ever met. We became immediate friends, even though in those days I had no familiarity with "the certain substances."

One day I saw that Pete was the engineer on the little train that circled the park, and I jumped in the cab as he was pulling out of the station, just to hang out with him on the ride. About three-quarters of the way around the park, the train ran through a long, straight corridor, fenced in on both sides to prevent guests from accidentally wandering onto the track. There was literally nothing to see in this segment of the ride, so the engineer often put the pedal to the metal (the engine of this faux "steam locomotive" was actually appropriated from a Chevy Chevelle, so the idiom in this case was literal) and sped through the boring segment, which is exactly what Pete did on our ride. We spotted the rock on the track simultaneously—a rock clearly placed there deliberately by one of the brats that terrorized the park during the summer, and a rock certainly big enough to derail the mini-engine. We looked at the rock. We shared one intuitive thought: "There's not enough time to stop. We're gonna be derailed." We looked at each other. "Oh, shit," Pete sighed resignedly. It was incredibly fatalistic, and, at the time, the single coolest response to an unavoidable catastrophe I'd ever seen. I vowed to be like Pete when I grew up.

Deniece Walters – One of the heroes. The blackest name for the whitest woman. Tall, rail-thin, gawky, with perfectly sculptured Swedish cheekbones, Denny shared a sense of humor with Rich and me. We became an almost inseparable trio, hanging out even on our days off. If there had been any romance involved, it could have become a *Jules et Jim* story, but there simply wasn't. We were friends: "The Three Muscatels." (I still have some 8mm footage of Denny dressed up as the Easter Bunny for a Frontier Village event.) At some point she married her invisible fiancé in Ft. Collins, Colorado. We corresponded for a while. I hope she's well and happy and surrounded by dozens of fun-loving grandkids who inherited her perfectly sculptured cheekbones.

THE LAST ROUNDUP

Unbelievably, Frontier Village continued to get along just fine without me...for a while. Partially in response to the opening of Marriott's Great America—a newer, larger amusement park, a few miles away in Santa Clara—Arrow Development, the new owners of Frontier Village, decided to double down—literally—and double the size of the little park. They planned to invest $10 million over the next five years—a move they estimated would triple attendance.

Their grandiose plans were thwarted, however, by groups in the neighborhoods that had sprung up during the previous decade and now surrounded the park. The locals vehemently protested the expansion, citing threats of noise, crime and increased traffic. And when the City of San Jose demanded nearly $2 million in upgrades to alleviate these potential problems, the owners balked and decided to shutter the park. So after nearly twenty years of operation, on September 28, 1980, Frontier Village closed its massive wooden gates forever. A few years later, a complex of high-end condominiums was erected on the land.

Former Frontier Village employees who fared better than I did still have a website and hold annual reunion picnics. For some reason, I've never been invited.

FRONTIER VILLAGE TAKEAWAYS:

1) Don't make your job the center of your social life. When you move on—whether by choice or not—your social circle will evaporate along with your employment.

2) No one is indispensable. You can be one of three key employees in a corral of 200 and they'll still dump your ass if they want to be rid of you.

3) Whoever said "Don't get your meat where you get your potatoes" was an idiot. Tell it to a couple of hundred horny teens.

Chapter 4

1970: INFORMATION STORAGE SYSTEMS (ISS)

Say Hello to Your Future

"640 Kb [of memory] ought to be enough for anyone."
—Bill Gates *(although he denies ever saying this)*

November 1969

"Only 30 more Nothings until the Great Big Nothing!"

This was the tiny sign I had on the bulletin board in my bedroom. I felt it appropriately expressed my despair at being fired from my job and ostracized from my social circle.

I was crushed. I was devastated. Fired by—and banished from—my first real job, I was without employment, without resources, and almost without friends. So I devoted myself to my freshman year of college, making new friends—and living off spare change from my spare change jar.

February 1970

A few months later, I found a job. Or it found me. Or someone found it for me. Who remembers? I can't recall how it happened—probably through the Parental Network once again. Whatever the story, I was invited to interview at a company called Information Storage Systems—"ISS" for short. They were looking for a college student who could work afternoons and evenings in the Reprographics Department, running the Xerox machines after hours to keep up with the overflow. *What the heck,* I figured. *Even* I *can run a Xerox machine!*

On the appointed day (February 24, precisely), I set out for my interview. In those dim, dark, pre-internet days of 1970, there was no Google Maps; we used Rand McNally foldable paper maps. I located Tantau Ave. in Cupertino and drove there —only to find a vacant lot. What the hell? Was this some kind of cruel hoax? I drove around until I found a payphone (no cell phones in 1970. We were still only one step away from telegraphs and carrier pigeons.) I called the main number for the company and told the operator my plight. "Oh!" she laughed. "There's the problem. You're on *South* Tantau. We're on *North* Tantau." Huh? I checked the map again...and sure enough, there was, in fact, a North Tantau—unconnected to its other half, and bisected by Highway 280. After some time, I found the building and connected with my contact. I had to apologize for the confusion—and hope he didn't think I was simply an idiot who couldn't read a map. Even though I was.

Despite my late arrival and lack of any job skills whatsoever —I could run a Ferris Wheel, but they didn't have one—I got the job. I'd work 4 to 8 PM every weekday, overlapping the fulltime staff by an hour so they could inform me what needed to be done during my after-hours shift.

I had no idea what ISS did. I worked there two for years and had only a vague understanding that they designed and manufactured computer hard drives. These storage devices (Oh, I get it! Information *Storage*!) were about the size of a washing machine —and held less information than a thumb drive or your iPhone holds today. At the time, however, these devices were The Shit.

Day 1: My boss, Al Neuer, a short, soft-spoken, self-effacing, slightly ruddy forty-ish guy, instructed me on how to use the giant blueline machine, a bizarre contraption that took original schematic drawings and copied them as blueprints. The typical schematic was hand-drawn by an engineer on translucent vellum paper—a process that took dozens of hours in itself. The typical ISS schematic was 24 by 36 inches: two feet high by three feet wide. And unwieldy. To make a blueprint using the blueline machine, one needed to take the original drawing and lay it on top of a piece of yellow, chemically coated paper of the same dimensions. Once you fed this pair of papers into the machine, an arcane chemical development process using ammonia vapors (yeah, you could definitely smell it) exposed the copy paper, turning it blue everywhere that was not drawn on, as part of the schematic. It only took a few seconds. Easy-peasy.

And so, on my first evening alone, I ran my first blueprint—and watched in horror as the bloody blueline machine *ripped it to shreds. Tore it up.* Caught it in its gears and *ate the entire original.*

Now I was really fucked. For life. It took some engineer *hundreds of hours* to draw that original schematic—and I destroyed it. I could work at ISS for *years*, every penny of my salary being withheld as compensation for the damages, and still never pay off the cost of that single document. Clearly, I'd be fired—just like I'd been fired from Frontier Village. I could never use either job on my résumé. I was almost 19 years old, and *I had no résumé.* I had *no job experience* that I could present to future employers. *I would never work again*—I was fated to be a gas station attendant in a world that was rapidly moving towards self-service stations.

I left the detritus of the schematic—now little more than confetti—in a manila envelope addressed to my boss, along with a note of apology, in which I informed him I completely understood if I was fired. I returned the following afternoon to face the music, only to be met by Al, who was holding my envelope. And smiling. "Don't worry about it," he chuckled. "Everybody in this department has done exactly the same thing. I've done it. No big deal." Now *this* was a guy I could work for!

At times, this was the proverbial "dream job": when there was little or no work for me, I'd put in my hours (or my after hours) and get paid $2.25 an hour to study. Well, occasionally study. There were temptations that often seduced me away from my boring textbooks. With access to Xerox machines and a small printing press, I was always busy with my own projects. One example: In 1970, California was still issuing black and white driver's licenses, and the birthdate field consisted of type-written numbers set against a background of tiny black dots. I realized that I could draw a large (12 x 18 inch) pattern of black dots with a magic marker, draw large numerals in a typewriter font on top of that, and run the page through the Xerox 1800 reducing machine, again and again and again, until I had a miniscule image the same size and appearance as the birthdate field on the license. Recursive reductions hid any flaws that might be visible in the full-size version of the date-and-dots field. All that was required to create a fake ID was to carefully cut the little image from the final reduction and paste the miniscule slip onto a legitimate license, then insert the entire CDL into a plastic cover so the date field wouldn't appear raised. I provided fake IDs for all my friends, allowing us to drink with impunity long before we turned 21—the legal drinking age in California at the time.

I had no clue in those days that this "electronics" stuff would ever amount to anything, much less that it would ultimately remake my home turf and define my work life. It was none of my concern. I went to school and I ran a Xerox machine; that was my world. It was just a job. I had no indication that as Silicon Valley blossomed around me like a triffid, I'd find myself pulled deeper and deeper into its malignant clutches, caught like a misaligned schematic in a blueline machine.

Dramatis Personae:

Al Neuer—My boss, a middle-aged middle manager. Think "blonde Bill Bixby" and you won't be far off. Al was relaxed in an industry that I came to discover rewarded anxiety and hyperactivity. The more I think about Al the more I admire him. He hired misfits and fringe dwellers, like the 60+-year-old lady in tennis shoes who lived on Advil and outperformed all of us. And like me. Al entered the D. Scott Apel Hall of Heroes in March 1976: Years after I'd worked for him, he "loaned" me his printing press and an operator for an entire weekend so I could print 100 copies of my first novel. Al, if you ever see this...thank you.

May—A 20-something single mom, dark-haired, big-eyed. We became fast friends, and something like a couple, including territorial spats. Long before the concept of "work wife" was defined, my friendship with May was often my favorite thing about this job.

Meredith—Mid-20s; a beautiful, sexy redhead with a broad, cat-like face (always a weakness for me). Meredith was a *professional*: an adult woman with a job, when I was just a teenage college freshman. She was clearly (and clearly entirely) out of my league—but a boy can dream, can't he? She was a friend of May's, and my life became nearly complete when May confided in me that Meredith thought I was "smart." If only she'd thought I was "sexy." A boy can dream, can't he?

Those two snarky, gum-chewing, middle-aged Oklahoma women—I told them repeatedly that they'd better be nice to me since someday I was gonna write a book about my work life. Now I can't even remember their names. Payback's a bitch, bitches.

Jim Rose—When I first saw Seth Rogan in a movie, I was convinced that Jim Rose had had himself cloned. Jim was hired to run our small printing press. He was in his late twenties, and possessed one of the foulest mouths I've ever had the pleasure to encounter—he could have made Richard Pryor blush. I learned a shitload of creative profuckingfanity from that wonderful cocksucker. Unfortunately for him, he was determined to share his taboo form of creativity, loudly, whenever the printing press fucked up—which was frequently. Al had to have a talk with him about toning down the language. I missed his outbursts of creative profanity, goddamn it.

ISS: AFTERMATH

I stayed at ISS for nearly two years, working after hours during school months and full-time during the summer. And I never entirely understood what the fuck we were manufacturing.

In January 1972, I moved to Virginia to spend a semester at a branch of the University of Virginia and had to say good-bye to Al, May, Jim and the gang at ISS. As a going-away present, they gave me an artist's rendition of me as a turkey in running shoes, making a break for it. (In those days, calling someone a "turkey" was a non-obscene insult. I used it frequently enough that they ultimately applied it to me.) In 2020, I still have that caricature.

ISS was purchased by Sperry Rand and was absorbed so completely that a Google search today yields no specific results for the company. If I was the guy who founded ISS—James J. Woo—and if I was still alive…I'd be a little pissed.

Chapter 5

1972: CORDON BLEU & JC PENNEY

I'm A Salesman Now—One Day Only!

"WORK!"
—Maynard G. Krebs, *The Many Loves of Dobie Gillis*

March 1972

I needed a job. I was living with friends in Springfield, Virginia, attending a semester at the George Mason College of the University of Virginia. And although I had a small allowance from my parents, it was barely enough to cover gas and food. If I ever wanted to buy anything like an LP, or weed (and I desperately wanted to buy both), I needed a source of income. I checked the bulletin boards at the college and my attention was drawn to a flyer that promised "Weekend Work; Large Commissions." That would fit my college lifestyle nicely. And so I arrived one Saturday morning at a sales rally for a company with the classy name Cordon Bleu. They were a company that sold "hope chest" items to young women: linens, quilts, lace and china, for example. But that was simply a cover story to get a foot in the door and pitch these unsuspecting girls a line of waterless cookware.

(Let's not even get into what "waterless cookware" is. You can Google it nowadays; in those days, the only place you could find out was by hitting the huckster's tent at the County Fair.)

These Cordon Bleu guys were enthusiastic, if nothing else. The rally included chants to pump up the salesmen and encourage action: "If you want money and a new car too / Go to work for Cordon Bleu!" *OK*, I thought. *I'm not a joiner or a mindless drone, but I need the money, so I'll hear them out.*

The job consisted of two parts: in Part One, you hit the city streets during the weekday lunch hour and handed out four-by-six cards to potential suckers—uh, *customers*—coercing them into giving up their personal information (name, address, phone number) with the vague promise: "Would you like to take a short survey and win a prize?" Since our line of products was pitched to young, single women, the company taught us how to spot a wedding ring from 100 paces—and to ignore those girls. The good news was that most of this canvassing was done in downtown Washington, D.C., which is simply crawling with young secretaries during lunch hour. The bad news was that this was weekday, noon-hour work—not something a college student could accomplish easily, and hours that were in direct opposition to the flyer's claim of "weekend work."

I was excused from the weekday work, however, since I was a trainee. I was instructed to arrive at the office at 9 AM on Saturday when the real sales work began. I was assigned a mentor—a guy barely older than I was, but a real go-getter. We sorted through the cards he'd collected during the week and started making calls. "You've won a prize!" he'd gush to the girl who answered. "We'll come by about 2 PM and deliver it!" Maybe one in ten fell for this. And once all the cards were called and the appointments were set, we'd organize them by area and call them again. "Looks like we won't be able to make it until about 4 PM," or whatever time we'd determined based on the most efficient route from one appointment to another. Oddly, most of them agreed.

And we set off to our meetings. "What's the prize we're gonna give them?" I asked my hotshot mentor. "Oh, we'll figure it out," he replied, smiling enigmatically. And figure it out he did! Before our first appointment, we stopped at a Roy Rogers fast food joint for lunch. (These still exist—they're like cut-rate Arby's.) On our way out, Hotshot swung by the counter and snagged a handful of autographed color photo prints of Roy Rogers, "The King of the Cowboys," then rolled them up and stuck them in his jacket. "You really need fifty photos of Roy Rogers?" I asked.

"Idiot," he enlightened me. "These are our *prizes*!"

I think we made two or three calls that day. I was there to observe, not participate, and thank The Great Whoever for that. We'd sit in the suburban living room of some young working woman, always with her mother by her side, and pitch hope chest items—particularly (you guessed it) waterless cookware.

My mentor was a dynamo, an expert hustler, an encyclopedia of flattery and lies and sales tricks and slick bullshit. I was embarrassed to be there.

We didn't make a sale that day, but Hotshot was undeterred. "Buncha stupid cunts this week," he explained to me. "We're gonna rob 'em blind next weekend!"

I laughed. I agreed, so he didn't kill me.

And I never returned.

I'M A SALESMAN NOW—THE SEQUEL

Fall 1972

Following my semester at UVA in northern Virginia and a summer spent camping around the Caribbean on the cheap, I returned home—to my parents' house in Silicon Valley (Los Gatos, to be precise). I was preparing for my senior year at Santa Clara University. And while my room and board were guaranteed by mom and dad, if I ever wanted to buy an ounce (which I definitely wanted to do, with ever-increasing frequency), or a book, or an album, I needed money. I was too old for an allowance—room and board were about the most I could mooch off the 'rents.

Eventually, I had to face the horrible inevitable: I needed a job.

Once again, Mom came to the rescue—although I suspected she figured that if I had a job, I could contribute to the household...at least by enough to cover the electricity, water and food I consumed while living in her house. Fair enough. Mom was the Personnel Director at a JCPenney store by this time, so she sent me to interview with one of her peers—a Personnel Director at a different Penney's store, this one in Eastridge Mall, an enormous (1.4 million square feet!), sprawling mall in East San Jose that had opened just a year earlier.

I dressed nicely, didn't slouch, and endured a perfunctory interview with a gruff middle-aged guy. I refused to be enthusiastic, since it was a foregone conclusion that he'd hire me, as a favor to my mom—his peer. The one question he asked that sticks in my mind to this day (probably because of the wording) was this: “You’re not particularly enamored of that beard, are you?” A couple of years of increasing radicalism had prompted me to express my disdain of everything Amerikkkans hold sacred by growing a goatee. And now this conservative, right-wing, fascist asshole was subtly implying that JCP had a clean-shaven employee policy. I was incensed that he would make such a demand, and expressed my contempt for the whole Imperialist Capitalist Authoritarian Oligarchy by immediately replying, “What, this? Nah, I can shave it off. No problem.” Once again, I capitulated to The Man and his outrageous demands, sigh. At least he didn’t demand that I cut my hair, which I hadn’t cut since I started college three years earlier. I’m gonna let my freak flag fly, motherfucker!

I got the job. (Duh.) And I spent several evenings a week between October ’72 and May ’73 standing behind a counter in the Photography Department doing...nothing. Literally, precisely nothing (and making $2.50 an hour for doing it… which is not a bad salary for just being a warm body on site.) The store was almost always empty. I didn’t know jack squat about cameras and would have been worse than useless to anyone who ever wanted to ask a question about the shit we sold. Not that anyone ever did. No customer ever interrupted my four-hour evening shift—The Shift When Time Stood Still—to ask a question. No Supervisor ever checked in on me. No co-worker ever wandered over to say hi.

I don’t recall who my Supervisor was, or what he did to train me. I have no memory of clocking in or out, although I must have done this a hundred times. I have no memory of quitting. My outstanding memory of months of employment as a part-time sales associate was of selling a roll of film to a local news anchor. I was essentially being paid to be a mannequin—to stand around in a dress shirt and tie and be bored. And that was just fine with me.

It was a ghost job, and I was a ghost employee in a ghost town.

Chapter 6

1973: PLAN A: THE EARLY YEARS

"Out of college, money spent
See no future, pay no rent..."
— The Beatles, "You Never Give Me Your Money,"
Abbey Road

PRINTER'S DEVIL

Fall 1973

The Beatles quote? True dat...except for the "pay no rent" part. But I was indeed out of college. And definitely broke.

It was time once again to face the execrable inevitable: I needed a job—particularly since I'd decided to return to Santa Clara University for an additional undergrad year to earn a second bachelor's degree. I'd just graduated with a B.S. in Psychology, and I had enough additional credits that I could finish a B.A. in English with just a few more classes. No doubt you're wondering, *Why would anyone want two bachelor's degrees?* One reason is that I never knew anyone with two Bachelor's degrees. I would be unique, which appealed to me. Another reason was that I had no interest in going to graduate school—especially not in Psychology. If I couldn't go deep, I'd go wide. And I certainly had no interest whatsoever in leaving the comfy nest of college and attempting to join the workforce.

But first I needed money to pay for the expensive private university courses—not to mention rent for my half of the apartment I'd moved into with my college friend Kevin C. Briggs, and food and utilities, as well as my recent vices, cheap beer and The Chronic.

I found an ad on the SCU Work/Study bulletin board: *Press Operator for the City of San Jose.* Three-month contract; experience required. Well, damn—I actually *had* some experience running a small printing press, at ISS. Recent experience, too (although at age 22, virtually everything qualifies as "recent experience").

I landed the job. And I made some friends at work by volunteering for the long-run jobs—printing thousands of copies of whatever document was in the hopper. Once these jobs were running, they required only occasional spot checks for quality and occasional refills of the paper tray and ink trough. To the guys who did this for a living, long runs meant one thing: terminal boredom. But for me, I could sit hidden behind the churning press and read the assignments for my English classes. And since I'd assumed the burden of boredom, my co-workers turned a blind eye to the fact that twice a week I took a two-hour lunch so I could attend my noon class.

My one claim to fame at this job was that I printed all the Miranda Rights cards ("You have the right to remain silent...," etc.) carried by San Jose police officers for years. I always thought that if I was ever pulled over and arrested, I might gain a slight edge by telling the officer, "I printed that card, y'know." Fortunately, any circumstances in which that would be necessary never arose, as I was never caught.

B. DALTON, BOOKSELLER—PART 1

April 1974

The printing job was temporary. After that, I needed another job. And how I got that job was a mystery to me. Literally.

My roommate Kevin Briggs and I were living in a mediocre apartment on Washington St. in Santa Clara, having been evicted from our previous digs (which is another story for another time, but involves an absolutely epic party Briggs threw for the entire incoming Freshman class of SCU, so you can probably fill in the blanks). One morning I woke up... OK, full disclosure, one *afternoon* I woke up...and when I walked into the living room, I spotted an envelope on the floor—not mail, just an unsealed envelope with my name written on the front. *Another eviction notice*, I figured, although I couldn't think of any reason why we should be given the boot. But no. Inside was a handwritten note from the manager of the B. Dalton, Bookseller, bookstore at Valley Fair mall, about a mile away: an employment invitation.

The manager wanted me to come to work for him. I had no idea why, or how he knew me (or how he got into our locked apartment). But I had no hesitation in jumping at his offer of employment (even at $2.65 an hour). And I worked there from April through November. There's no sense in detailing the work, however. I mean, how interesting is it to read about someone shelving books or building a display or running a cash register? Exactly.

PLAN A: INSPIRATION AND DESPERATION

Sometime during this period, the idea for my first novel gelled in my alleged brain. It grabbed me and wouldn't let go. Since then I've discovered this is how I write novels (and I've written seven): intuit an idea that keeps generating more ideas; a plot that magnetically constellates details around itself—often without any effort. Sure, it's an obsession—but it's an obsession that is self-inspiring and self-perpetuating.

I started researching and plotting. After several months, I knew the beginning, the ending, and all the major plot points in between. I had a file card box full of notes detailing incidents, lines of dialog, descriptions, and so on. I felt like I was ready to begin writing. But I knew there was no way I could carve out the hundreds of hours necessary to write a novel as long as I was living in a house with several roommates who interrupted every potential writing session with the diversions of pot, beer, TV, and hanging out with friends whose lives centered around pot, beer and TV. If I was going to devote myself to this novel, if I was going to make it the central intent of my life, I had to distance myself from these temptations to focus on nothing but the book.

And so, late in 1974, I arranged to move back to northern Virginia. I'd rent a room from the people who'd housed me during my junior year in college, and I'd transfer my job to the B. Dalton, Bookseller, branch in the nearby Springfield Mall.

My hosts were happy to see me return. And the manager of the B. Dalton store gave me the thumbs up to start work as soon as I arrived.

So this would be my life for as long as it took to finish the novel: freed from the distractions of a dissolute peer group and with a small but assured income, I'd write. All my ducks were in a row...

B. DALTON, BOOKSELLER—PART 2

December 1974

...except that one of those ducks turned out to be in a shooting gallery. When I reported to the bookstore, I was met with a confused manager—and not the manager I'd talked to. Not the manager I'd made arrangements with. "I'm the new manager," he said. "I've only been here a couple weeks. I don't know anything about any arrangements the previous manager made."

"I just moved cross-country on the strength of his approval of my transfer," I explained. "I moved *three thousand miles* because he said he had a job for me."

He just shrugged. "I don't."

And that was that.

Chapter 7

1975: NVTCMR

My Career Moves Forward Even Though Retarded

February 1975

There are plenty of stories of artists creating masterpieces while living in abject poverty—so many, actually, that the so-called "starving artist" has become a cliché.

I was not one of those guys. I was at best only the worst half of that cliché: living in poverty. And what I discovered is that it's difficult to concentrate on creating Art when: a) you've never done it before; and b) you are hungry.

There was only one solution: I needed a job.

I don't recall the specific circumstances (I forgot that pot affects your memory, which in itself is rather ironic), but I did indeed find a job a few weeks later at the Northern Virginia Training Center for the Mentally Retarded. My B.S. in Psychology came in handy as a calling card qualifying me to work there. My wage: a whopping $3.65 an hour.

NVTCMR was a large facility in Fairfax, just a few miles from where I was living, and just a few miles away from the branch of the University of Virginia where I'd spent a semester of my junior year of college. (It was also only a few miles from the Manassas/Bull Run Civil War battlefield. Not that that matters to this narrative, but, you know... "lest we forget.")

The facility was built to house low-functioning retarded people—the unfortunate few who were so severely or profoundly retarded that they required institutionalization to provide the extensive level of maintenance that their families could not. The campus itself was lovely—low-slung, single-story red brick buildings in the middle of a meadow set back far from the road and bordering on a forest. The complex had several wings, including one for adults who were both crippled and retarded, and a heartbreaking unit for babies who were not even expected to reach childhood. I visited that unit once and was so devastated that I never returned.

A note about language: In today's world (circa 2020), the term "retarded" has become a slur; a degrading and offensive insult—in other words, Politically Incorrect. The PI police insist the word be replaced with terms like "special," or "developmentally challenged." In 1975, however, "retarded" was an innocuous word that no one thought of as injurious or demeaning—"retarded," was, in reality, a polite euphemism for offensive words from a previous generation, like "idiot," and was, in fact, a technical medical term, free of any value judgment. Since I'm recounting events of 1975, I've chosen to retain the language of the time. Any other approach would be, well... special.

I was assigned to a ward that housed about 20 higher-functioning teens, and after a couple of weeks of training on the day shift, I transferred to the graveyard shift and quickly fell into a comfortable routine. I'd arrive at 11 PM, count the meds in the locked cabinet with a member of the swing shift (to document that no one was stealing drugs) then read through the daily log, which included staff notes about the day's events: who was acting up and who was acting out; who was out for a parental overnight visit; any changes to policy, and so on. By 11:30, the swing shift was long gone, and my co-worker and I would begin the laundry. Each unit had its own industrial-strength washer and dryer, and every kid's clothes (and sheets) were laundered every night, so there were always two or three huge loads (think 30-gallon waste cans on wheels). Washing, drying and folding took most of the night—but only for a few minutes every hour or so.

Each unit's graveyard shift consisted of a pair of attendants. Our ward had three regular graveyard shift employees; on any given night two of us were on and one was off. I worked with two women, an elderly, grandmotherly type and a young single mom who worked two jobs. And they were a blessing. Every night, once the day staff had left, they put on the first load of laundry…and promptly fell asleep. The sweet old lady curled up on the couch in our dimly lit office overlooking the ward; Suzanne sat in a desk chair, put her feet up, and conked out. They loved me because I never insisted they stay awake or assist with the laundry; I loved them because they both were dead asleep long before midnight, providing me with hours of quiet time to write without interruption (except to switch out the laundry once an hour). The ward had a TV, but I only ever turned it on once, to watch the premiere of NBC's *Saturday Night* (which we know today as *Saturday Night Live).* I was thrilled to see my old friend Michael O'Donoghue appear in the opening sketch.

At 5:30 AM, I'd have my lunch, and at 6 o'clock I'd wake my co-worker. We'd spend the next hour rousting the kids out of bed and getting them dressed, so the day shift could take them to breakfast when they arrived at 7 AM. We had a record player on the ward, but only two LPs, which we played over and over again every morning. (I'm tempted to steal a Steven Wright punchline here: "Sure wish I could remember what they were.") So aside from the laundry and the early morning muster, I could usually scare up a solid six hours of uninterrupted writing time, five nights a week. And get paid to do it.

And write I did. Over the course of the next nine months. I finished the first draft of my (still unpublished) Magnum Opus. The irony of writing a utopian novel about consciousness expansion while surrounded by a sea of sleeping slowbirds was not lost on me.

B. DALTON, BOOKSELLER—PART 3

Sometime in June, I got a phone call from the manager of the B. Dalton store in Springfield—not the same guy who refused to honor his predecessor's agreement to hire me, but an even newer manager.

"I've been reviewing some old paperwork," he said, "and it looks like you kinda got screwed out of a job here months ago. But if you still want a part-time position, I have an opening."

I did some quick mental calculations and realized that the graveyard shift hours I worked would never overlap with any hours the bookstore was open. I could, it seems, have two jobs and squirrel away even more money for my eventual (jobless) return to California. So I took the position. The bonus was that this was a "fuck you" to the previous B. Dalton manager (in my mind, at least. He'd probably never know).

Although the hours never overlapped, I discovered that on occasion I was in for some very long days. I'd work Saturday nights at NVTCMR, for instance, get off at 7 AM, then report to B. Dalton at 10 AM—just long enough to go home, shower, eat and catch the bus to the Springfield Mall. If I was scheduled for a full eight-hour shift at the bookstore on Sunday, I'd get off work about 6 PM with just enough time to have a shower, eat, and maybe, *maybe*, grab a nap before I had to report back to NVTCMR at 11 PM, for a full eight-hour shift. By 7 AM on Mondays, I was ready to sleep until it was time to rise and go back to the nightshift job.

But, as I'd calculated, the hours never conflicted. And while working 60 hours a week oddly didn't bother me, the whack-a-doodle schedule played havoc with my biorhythms, man. (This was the '70s, remember. Biorhythms were a thing then, like wide belts, paisley shirts, bell-bottoms and mood rings. If you don't believe me, just watch an episode of *The Brady Bunch*.) My one hedge against stress was this consolation: I knew that if either job ever pissed me off too much, I could just yell, "Fuck you! I don't need this shit!" and walk out, knowing I had a fall-back job—a Plan B.

That scenario never happened. And I kept up this 60-hours-a-week pace for several months. By mid-December, however, I'd finished the novel. My mission was accomplished; living in Virginia and working two jobs was no longer necessary (or desirable). I quit both jobs and took Amtrak back home to NorCal.

As I walked out of the San Francisco train station, a van pulled up in front of me and screeched to a halt. The side panel slid open. I thought perhaps I was being kidnapped, until my former roommate Briggs and our mutual friend Jim Ferrigan jumped out, grabbed my arms, and yanked me into the van. The door slammed shut and the van sped away. Briggs stuck a joint in my mouth and Jimmy slapped a bottle of beer in my hand.

"A year passes like nothin' for the Fabulous Furry Freak Brothers," Briggs exclaimed.

I was home.

Chapter 8

1976: RANCHO VERDE MANOR

"One flew east, one flew west,
One flew over the cuckoo's nest."
—Children's nursery rhyme

March 1976

Yeah, I was home. But I needed a job.

I was 25 and living in my old bedroom at my parents' house in San Jose. I'd spent the first couple months of 1976 typing up the novel I'd written the previous year, and by March, I'd spent my savings down to next to nothing. Mom encouraged me to find employment, as only a mom can: I could live in her house, and I could have my meals there...but if I ever wanted to carouse with my friends, or indulge in my vices, I'd need money —and, by extension, a way to make money.

I needed a job. Sad but true.

I knew too well that I had no marketable job skills. All I was suited for was physical labor. But as an intellectual—and now a goddamned *author*, goddamn it—that was right out. So when I saw a newspaper ad in April for "Weekend Psych Tech" at a local private mental asylum, I applied, albeit reluctantly. I had, I believed, some experience—not only recently, working with severely to profoundly retarded teens at NVTCMR, but I'd also done a college Psych major internship at a local asylum (and worked on the ward where Ken Kesey had written *One Flew Over the Cuckoo's Nest* while he worked the graveyard shift. I hoped to hell I was following in his footsteps.) Turns out I probably didn't even need the experience; it appears that the only qualifications for the job were that you: a.) were sane, and b.) had a Psych degree. I could easily fake one of those requirements. And I had a Psych degree.

Rancho Verde Manor in San Jose was a 100-bed locked psychiatric facility; a one-story ranch-style building with three main wings converging on a central lobby and staff station. It was old and a bit worn, but hardly the "snake pit" of horror movie lore. On the other hand, it was no utopia, either.

Most of the residents were there for short term stays. Some were even voluntary. I asked one sweet, constantly smiling middle-aged woman why she was there voluntarily (and why she seemed so happy about psychiatric incarceration). "I have ten children," she replied. "I check myself in here for a couple of months every year. This is my only vacation." I would imagine her situation was a Catch-22: if she'd ever told the truth to her doctor, he'd know she wasn't insane, and kick her out. On the other hand...ten kids? That'd drive anyone crazy.

On my first day, I attended a staff meeting. When I was assigned a high-functioning group, one of my fellow weekend warriors growled, "You took my group, you rat." I didn't want her mad at me. She was a vision—tall, dark hair, freckles, violet rings around her pupils...and to this day, the prettiest women I've ever met, and the sexiest. And very soon after she'd forgiven me for being assigned her group, Alexandra became my first True Love. (But that's a story for another book. Which will never be written.)

Weekend work consisted, essentially, of babysitting the nuts. We didn't do any therapy. We weren't qualified. We mostly handed out cigarettes, took the patients out for walks, or wandered around making sure they weren't doing anything crazy. Piece of cake.

Sure. Turns out the old cliché is correct: You can't have your piece of cake and eat it too.

On my first day, a warm Saturday afternoon, I took my group out for a walk, which I figured was a rather low-stress, low-maintenance activity. We walked around the perimeter of Alexian Bros. Hospital, a block away. And as we passed the Emergency entrance, one of my charges, who looked like a young Doris Day, decided she needed a heart transplant…right then, right there, and she'd throw a fit if I didn't take her inside and get her a heart transplant *right now.* After some time, I managed to calm her down while corralling the other four or five patients from wandering away once they saw how busy I was and sensed a chance to escape. (As Pink Floyd put it, "Got to keep the loonies on the path.")

This was my first day? What future horrors awaited me?

Not many, it turned out. Life in the asylum was actually fairly low-key—downright dull most of the time. Often the most entertaining event was watching the drugged-up patients scraping their feet along the hallway as they ambled, zombie-like, to some uncertain destination. (We called it "The Thorazine Shuffle," years before that term came into vogue.) And much as in a prison (or so I've heard), cigarettes were currency. There was a big storage closet stocked with cartons of cheap cigs, and all the Psych Techs kept a couple packs in our pockets to hand out as rewards, or to calm down tense situations. Occasionally this resembled tossing brain bits to hungry zombies —as soon as they got their coffin nails, the angry mobs stumbled away, pacified. For a while.

One thing I learned in the asylum is that not all insanity is sad or horrible. The patient who signed himself in as "Abraham Lincoln," for instance, approached me his first weekend in the place and announced that he was a woman. Fine by me; I wasn't going to argue with a loony. The next weekend, he claimed he was a woman and that he'd been raped. Sorry to hear that, I replied. The next weekend he cornered me and informed me that he was a woman, he'd been raped, and now he was pregnant. I had nothing but sympathy—and cigarettes (even though pregnant women are not supposed to smoke). The next weekend passed without an update, so the following Saturday I asked him how the pregnancy was going. "Oh," he replied offhandedly, "I got an abortion."

A couple of weeks later the same guy approached me and announced, "I have a radio in my head, you know." OK, I replied. "I have a stereo in there, too," he continued. He stopped for a moment, and, with a thoughtful look, sighed, "Sure wish I could get a tape deck."

This same kooky loon decided to play his guitar in the Talent Show the weekday staff had organized. His guitar had two strings, which was twice the number of lyrics as his song had. He honored us with a performance of Paul McCartney's "Too Many People" that began thus:

"Too many people going underground,
Too many people going underground.
Too many people going underground,
Too many people going underground."

For the refrain, his lyrics were:

"Too many pe-EEE-ple / Go-o-ing underground.
Too many people / Go-o-i-ing underground.
Too many people."

He remained faithful to the tune and quite creative in fitting this single line of lyric to the changes in the melody. The horrifying aspect is that this reimagining of a classic song became an earworm for me. To this day, I still sing his version occasionally, and have infected many other people with this insane viral meme—too many people.

One Saturday, I was poking around a storeroom and discovered a 16mm projector (this was a year or two before VCRs hit the consumer market) and a copy of Buster Keaton's classic silent film, *The General*. I quickly organized a screening for that evening...and 100 institutionalized mental patients watched this timeless comedy in rapt attention, laughing in all the appropriate places. I was impressed by the healing power of comedy.

Perhaps the most memorable character I met in the loony bin was Mr. K.C. Bragg (not his real name, of course). Mr. Bragg was a big, rock-solid black man from the streets of Oakland. He'd been diagnosed as schizophrenic, but he convinced me that not all alleged insanity is truly crazy. I caught him talking to a tree in the yard one day, for instance, and cautioned him against that kind of behavior if he ever wanted to leave this place. "That ain't no tree, man," he explained. "I'm practicing talking to my brother." *Of course*—if he ever wanted to leave, he'd have to convince whoever checked him in that he was sane. I understood his rational rationale for this unusual behavior immediately. And then he added this coda that blew my mind: *"The facts are spiritual, man."* Since Mr. K.C. Bragg shared that bit of crazy wisdom with me, I have encountered the same idea repeatedly in the writings of some of the most brilliant men who ever lived.

For instance: "The spirit does not dwell in concepts, but in deeds and in facts" (C.G. Jung). Or this: "We must bear in mind that the facts are spiritual facts" (Rudolph Steiner). Or this: "...the Spirit is truth" (1 John 5:6).

It wasn't all fun and games, of course. It was, after all, a fucking insane asylum. And one of the most tragic things I witnesssed was our patient Angelica (not her real name, naturally). Angelica was Chinese, quiet and withdrawn, and perhaps the most beautiful woman I'd ever encountered. She'd been an artist, studying at UC Berkeley, but had some kind of emotional breakdown and was institutionalized by her mother. I read through her files and was horrified. I'd been studying handwriting analysis as a psychological tool for several years by that time, and as I looked through her case file it became abundantly clear that not only was Angelica an ethereal artist, but that she was surrounded by people who were in reality truly insane—an overcontrolling harridan of a mother, a kinky psychiatrist, and so on. Angelica's handwritten notes were logical, aesthetic and guileless. The handwriting of those surrounding her consisted of scattered, harsh scribbles; sharp and illegible. It was clear to me that she was not insane, merely excessively sensitive, and subject to the whims of the true lunatics who insisted on controlling her and defining her fate. And there was nothing I could do about it, except to let her know I understood her situation, and suggest that once she was released she should do everything in her power to escape this circle of insanity that literally held her captive. I don't know her fate. I hope she fared well.

During this weekend babysitting, I would often sit with my patients and do unauthorized, informal "group therapy." I'd occasionally take some of their suggestions and complaints to the director of the institution. And some of my patients began to show improvement, even to the point of being discharged or voluntarily checking themselves out of the facility.

July 1976

That's when I was fired. The official reason: "Giving out too many cigarettes."

Chapter 9

1976: RECYCLE BOOKSTORE

A Recycled Career

September 1976

I needed a job. But where to go, and what to do? I began by assessing my miniscule work experience. Already I'd worked twice with machines (printing presses), and twice with damaged human beings (the insane and the retarded). Those experiences prompted me to make a couple of decisions. Decision One: No more machines. Machinery did not respond to reason and was often frustrating to work with. Decision Two: No more loonies. They did not respond to reason and were often frustrating to work with. My only other work experience was as a ride operator at Frontier Village, and even though a new amusement park, Marriott's Great America, had just opened in Santa Clara, I didn't really consider the life of a carny was one I wanted to pursue. Not to mention that if I listed Frontier Village on my résumé as my amusement park work experience, I would probably not get an unqualified endorsement from the Village management when my claim was checked out.

There was only one other field in which I had any actual work experience: bookstores. Fate or Chance seemed to reward my insight. One day I was in a big used bookstore in downtown San Jose and I ran into a girl I'd worked with at B. Dalton a couple of years earlier. She didn't like me, and I didn't like her, but I asked her if they were hiring and she made the mistake of saying yes. (One of the reasons I didn't like her was that she was stupid. If she'd just said no, I would have gone away and she'd never have had to work with me again.) I chatted up the owner and was hired on the spot. (I found out later that my former co-worker had voted against me. But they hired me anyway. So there.)

Recycle Bookstore had been around for several years, and had grown to become one of the three largest used bookstores in the Bay Area, and the biggest in the South Bay. I used it as a location in my first mystery novel, *The Uncertainty Principle?* and described it like this:

The Recycle building was an old-fashioned monster; brown, squat and boxy... I stepped inside the warehouse-sized store. The inner walls were lined with ten-foot tall shelves which didn't even reach halfway to the two-story ceiling. A square block of floor space was furrowed with row after row of pine shelves: seven feet tall, unfinished, leaning crookedly against one another, back to back and head to head, like drunken couples bracing each other to stand almost upright. I peered down one of the aisles to its vanishing point, a wall so far to the back of the store that the colored spines filling the shelves looked like a pointillist painting.

I worked at Recycle Bookstore for nearly three years, although "work" is probably too strong a word to describe what I did there. And there's virtually nothing interesting to write about bookstore work. How fascinating is it to describe shelving books, for example, or alphabetizing your sections, or operating a cash register? Or dealing with the public, who were often looking for "that book by that guy—you know, he was on that TV show?"

While working at this job I developed the firm belief that—not unlike universal conscription to military service—everyone should be forced to work retail for at least six months. This would impart two valuable life lessons: first, they'd discover just how stupid the average person is (and, as J.R. "Bob" Dobbs reminds us, "statistically, half of them are even dumber than that"); and second, that, as a customer, you should always treat retail clerks politely and with a little respect. And that goes double for waitstaff. (Thus endeth the rant.)

Bookstore employment was a good, if minimum-wage, job. The work was easy; the hours were flexible; the attitude was loose and casual. And there were benefits. I built a personal library at a massive discount. I educated myself about books and authors in almost every category and genre, which seemed somehow an adequate substitute for not obtaining that second Bachelor's degree in English. But the high point of employment at Recycle was its employees. I made several friends there with whom I still communicate (and even collaborated on a screenplay with one, years later). And a few months after I hired in, an adorable young female co-worker with blue eyes and curly blonde hair asked me out and soon became my girlfriend—for five years.

During my Recycle days I remained dedicated to Plan A, completing my second novel as well as performing interviews with several top-level science fiction writers in association with my friend and former roommate, Kevin Briggs, for a book which would not see publication for 35 years. (*Science Fiction: An Oral History* is currently available in both ebook and print editions.)

Chapter 10

1980: DOWN AND OUT IN SILICON VALLEY

June 1979

The blonde and I left Recycle to go backpacking through South America for six months. But that's another book altogether (and yet another book that will never be written, regardless of my copious notes, detailed travel journal and an abundance of photos). And during that trip, I completed my third novel (and first mystery novel), which would not see publication for 35 years. Plan A dies hard. (*The Uncertainty Principle?* is currently available in both ebook and print editions.)

January 1980

We returned from our South American sojourn completely devoid of resources—broke and homeless. (Clearly, we were too young to know about planning for the future—even though I was pushing 30.) We took up residence in my parents' house in Los Gatos—a house so huge that we occupied the entire second story, except for my teenage brother's bedroom. He was just out of high school and started working on the production line at an electronics firm in nearby Sunnyvale—another beneficiary (or victim) of creeping Siliconvalleyism. My sweetheart found employment in the shipping department of Hewlett-Packard, after proving in an interview that she could memorize and recite ten-digit shipping codes without error (something that only the highest one percent of IQs can do consistently). But I needed an income as well so we could move into our own apartment and she could go on to college.

In other words: I needed a job.

I felt a bit depressed that I was 28 and had to "move in with the parents" once again—this time with a girlfriend in tow. But this was common for the time, and my parents were happy to have us close by. Still, I feared becoming a “man-child” who couldn’t hold a job and ends up living in his ‘rent’s basement. (This in itself would have proven problematic, since the house didn’t have a basement.)

ALPHA BETA-TESTING

In Which I Become a Grocery Clerk: One Day Only!

February 16, 1980

I needed a job. Desperately.

We didn’t even have a car, so any employment I could get would have to be within walking distance—a tough requirement to fill, given that we were deep in the heart of suburbia. But then employees of the Alpha Beta supermarket chain went on strike. And—miracle of miracles—there was an Alpha Beta just two blocks from my parents’ house. Walking distance.

This presented me with a moral dilemma, however. I was young and liberal. I grew up boycotting California grapes in solidarity with Caser Chavez, and was in agreement with John Lennon’s pronouncement that “a working-class hero is something to be.” I also remembered how significant and beneficial a force the Union was in my own dad’s blue-collar career. How could I in all good conscience cross a picket line and be a *scab*?

But a man must work. And this potential work—both immediate and close—was simply too tempting to ignore. So I swallowed hard, sacrificed ethics for expedience, and sold my soul. For the first time. I walked to the store, crossed the picket line, and asked for a job. The manager was more than happy to put me on, starting the next day.

I arrived at 8 AM the following morning. I’d shopped at this Alpha Beta before, so I knew the required costume: white dress shirt and blue pants. I wore the shirt and a pair of jeans. “Oh...” the manager said, looking me over when I arrived and shaking his head. “We don’t wear jeans. Do you have a pair of blue slacks?” I said I thought I did, and he sent me home to change. Yeah, I did have a pair of blue slacks. But I hadn’t worn them since high school, and I’d gained a bit of weight in the dozen years since I’d last worn them—so much weight, in seems, that I could barely squeeze myself into them. And in addition to the inches I'd grown around my waist, I'd clearly grown an inch or so taller since then as well, as these pants now rose far above my sock line. *Floods*, is what we used to call pants that were *waaaaaaay* too short. But I sucked in my gut, wedged myself into the straight-jacket pants, and somehow managed to get them zipped and buttoned. And I stumbled back to the store like Frankenstein. I looked like ten pounds of sausage stuffed into a five-pound casing...but the pants were slacks, and blue, and passed muster. The manager handed me over to one of the two assistant managers for a thorough five-minute training.

The snotty young assistant manager immediately took me to the back of the store, which was kept at a temperature near Absolute Zero. "No matter what else we tell you to do," he said imperiously, through clouds of breath-smoke, "you have *got* to come back here at least once an hour and push the milk forward." If you've ever gone grocery shopping, you know what he meant: the various sized containers of various kinds of dairy were lined up on rollers set at an angle so that when a customer removed a container, the one behind it should roll forward by gravity. But they never seemed to roll. So by the time the first few cartons had been removed, the shoppers were forced to reach deep into the refrigerated case to grab one—if they could even reach that far. (It seems strange to me that some forty years later this is still the case. Didn't anyone think to improve this obvious design flaw of rollers that don't roll?) They needed a minimum-wage slave to push the containers forward so shoppers didn't suffer the frustration of the milk container they wanted being tantalizingly just out of reach of their fingertips.

My next task was to assist a fellow strikebreaker in stocking the shelves with...whatever. Who remembers? But if you've ever seen the movie *Repo Man* (and I highly recommend it), you've seen exactly how I spent my next hour. My partner—an old hand, since he'd worked there the entire previous day—was totally gung-ho about this golden opportunity. He confided that he was going to work so hard, and do such a bang-up job, that they would certainly hire him full-time once the strike was over. I didn't have the heart to inform him that that would never happen. Never, ever. Once the strike was settled, he (and I) would be kicked to the curb without a second thought. But who was I to pop his optimistic, delusional bubble?

At some point in the day, I was tasked with building an endcap display—a pyramid of coffee cans or cereal boxes or some such nonsense at the end of an aisle. I accomplished the task while the two young assistant managers assisted me by leaning on a counter, sipping their coffee and watching. Now, you'd think that during a strike, the management would be doing their damnedest to keep store operations running smoothly. But no—supervisors-in-training Beavis and Butt-head were content to watch the temporary help work. I finished the display and turned to the guys.

"Whattaya think?" I said.

"Nice," one replied—although I detected a note of sarcasm. I knew I was right when he taunted, "Next time could you do it faster?"

"Hey, c'mon, guys," I said in a self-deprecating tone. "Cut me some slack. It's my first day."

"Well, if you want a second day," the other snot jeered, "you'll work faster."

I have few regrets in life, but one of them is that I didn't step up to that smarmy asshole and just deck him. But I needed the job. I needed the job. I needed the goddamn job. So I simply smiled and let it go. To this day, however, I still regret not punching that sneering snakefucker in the face.

My shift was finally over about 5 or 6 PM, and I staggered home like Robby the Robot in my iron maiden slacks. I was due back the following morning at 8 AM—but by the time I'd walked home, the manager had already called the house and left a message that he wanted me in at 7 AM. Groan. An hour later, he called again and told me he wanted me there at 5 AM. "You bet!" I said, dying inside. And at 10 PM, he called yet again, telling me he wanted me back at midnight to unload delivery trucks all night. I'd gotten off at 6 and he wanted me back in six hours? With two hours' notice? He'd called three times in four hours and bumped my schedule up each time? I knew what I had to do. "You got it, boss," I said enthusiastically. "See you at midnight!"

I never saw him—or went into that store—again.

Thus endeth my career as a grocery store worker. The good news is this also ended my career as a scab.

IN WHICH I BECOME A SMOOTH OPERATOR

March 1980

I still needed a job. And I found one, kind of—a one-month gig working for Pacific Bell, the phone company. An entire quadrant of the Santa Clara Valley was being broken out into a new area code, and all calls to this new area code were first detoured to our call center. Our job was to inform the caller that this number now had a new area code, and they should make a note of it. About 50 of us sat in tiny cubicles in a bullpen, wearing headsets and answering up to 700 calls in an eight-hour shift. It didn't occur to me until years later that we were perhaps the last of the "live operators" to perform this kind of service, which was automated soon after that.

All I remember about this month was that our call center was overseen by a few middle-aged women with double-wide asses —probably from sitting around as phone operators for decades —who were Nazi-ish in their strict adherence to the rules... particularly the schedule. If you were five minutes late, you were fired. We were temp workers. We were expendable. We were not employees. We were not even people—we were the human version of the automation that they really wanted...the automation that would soon replace us, and, if there is any justice in the world, them. They sat imperiously in their glass booth watching us and randomly monitoring our calls to make sure we weren't goofing off or fucking up—like a high school language lab run by the Gestapo.

What they heard was all 50 of us repeating the same phrase hundreds of times a day— "That area code has changed to 510. Please make a note of it"—before the calls were re-routed to their intended destination. Most people just replied "OK," or grunted and hung up. But one day, a woman caller responded to my stock phrase saying, "My, you sound awfully chipper for a Friday afternoon." Before I could bite my tongue, I heard myself replying (chipperly), "That's because I'm high on drugs!" I was glad that that call, at least, was not being monitored.

And I remembered a bit of wisdom from the 1967 comedy *The President's Analyst*, in which one character proclaims, "I've never been in a country where everyone didn't hate The Phone Company." Now I knew why.

Chapter 11

1980: MONOLITHIC MEMORIES

April 1980

I needed a job.

Being the last of the live telephone operators was only a temp gig. And so, by early April, I needed a job—again. But when you're a guy who can't do anything, what kind of job can you qualify for?

In the pre-digital age, looking for a job meant one thing: searching the newspaper Want Ads. At length, I found a life-changing job—a job that would hurl my work life into a new trajectory, even though that wouldn't become clear for over a decade. I took advantage of the rampant growth of Silicon Valley and—like my girlfriend and my brother as well as many friends—I got a job in the burgeoning electronics industry.

It was an Entry Level position (which always sounded to me vaguely sexual, like "Missionary is an entry level position") in *Wafer Fab*. Whatever that was. But how bad could that be? It even had "fab" in the title, which fans of '60s British pop culture knew was short for "fabulous"!

There were two details about this job listing that piqued my interest. One was the schedule, something called the "Weekend Shift"—Friday, Saturday and Sunday, 6 AM to 6 PM. The odd hours came with a ten percent "shift differential" pay bonus: work 36 hours, get paid for 40. I did the wage math, then I did the time math: I could have a full-time job working just three days a week...leaving four days a week to spend on Plan A: my writing. Sure, I'd miss "the weekend," but I didn't like going out on weekends anyway—every venue was always crowded with Monday through Friday workers who had *only* the weekend to go out. And with four days off, technically, I'd have the equivalent of *two* weekends *every week*!

The second detail that caught my attention was the name of the company: *Monolithic Memories*. The initial image that leapt to mind was the alien monolith in Kubrick's classic film *2001: A Space Odyssey*. If you're an ape and you touch the Monolith, your consciousness is catapulted into becoming a human. And if you're a human and touch the monolith (like astronaut Dave Bowman), you become a god...or at least a Starchild. I wanted to touch that monolith—and have that experience etched into my memory. My second association: Who wouldn't want to have a monolithic memory? I could barely remember my phone number most days. And I just loved the sound of the company name. For the rest of my life, I could say, "I worked at [in a deep, portentous announcer's voice, with an echo effect] *Monolithic Memories*."

So I applied. I interviewed. I got the job. No detail is worth recounting—or remembering, apparently, since I don't. (So much for the monolithic memory.) And one Friday morning at 6 AM, I reported to my supervisor, Dave Mooney, and he taught me how to run an aligning machine.

Pay attention here, damn it, kids—Grandpa's telling tales of the primitive days of the hi-tech world we all live in now.

In the prehistoric days of electronics, computer chips were created by literally photographing electrical pathways onto wafers of pure silicon—shiny, thin, silvery disks about three-quarters of a millimeter thick that looked like big drink coasters, or mirrors from a lady's compact (albeit a rather large compact). The wafers arrived at my station in slotted plastic carriers—"boats"—of 50. My job was to sit at a console that consisted of a scope, two knobs, and a button. I'd load a boat of wafers into the machine, peer through the scope and align the current "mask" over the previously etched paths, then press a button, and the machine would work its photographic magic. One minute later I'd do it again. And so on, for twelve hours a day, three days a week. A monkey could do it. Evidently my *Space Odyssey* association was far from correct: by touching that Monolith, I'd devolved from human being to console monkey.

The task was a bit more complicated than this, of course, or they would have hired actual monkeys (if the monkeys could get H1 visas). Those circuits, those electron pathways that were photographed onto the wafers, had to come from somewhere, and that somewhere was "masks," or glass plates with the pattern printed on them. There were seven levels of mask, each more complicated than the previous, and each more difficult to align with the pathways previously imprinted onto the disks. "First mask" was simple—there was nothing to align, since this was the initial image printed onto the *tabula rasa* disks. You load the boat into the machine, fire it up, and walk away. Automation did all the work. Aligners could, in fact, operate as many as four separate aligning machines simultaneously if all they were aligning was first mask. It helped the production stats, cranking out hundreds of wafers in a 12-hour shift. This was the mask task we aligners requested when we were hungover.

Aligning subsequent masks become increasingly difficult. The final layer—seventh mask—required the equivalent of a black belt in karate or a ninja-level of skill. To successfully complete seventh mask, your kung fu needed to be strong. Fortunately, seventh mask was one of the rare instances in which Management understood the difficulty: no Aligner was ever punished or even questioned if they reported that they'd ruined all 50 wafers (or however many were left in a run after breakage) with a poorly-aligned seventh mask, or if they took an entire shift to lay the seventh mask on a handful of wafers. Expected yields of finished wafers were shockingly, almost comically low in the industry at that time.

These wafers underwent several other steps before and after aligning, like being coated with a photoresist before the alignment lithography, and washing away the remaining photoresist after aligning. There was also acid etch, testing, and other pit stops I never took the trouble to learn. But I did discover that I had an enviable job. Aligners got to sit down all day, for one thing. We didn't have to dress up in cleanroom suits or hazmat suits or wear protective latex finger cots or deal with vats of sulfuric and hydrofluoric acid or toxic chemicals like arsenic and phosphorus. And the job didn't really require any actual skill beyond what one could pick up as a three-year-old with an Etch-A-Sketch. I took to laying a pocket notebook and pen at my station so I could write, one minute at a time, during the interval when the machine was performing its portion of our joint effort.

(Speaking of joints, it occurred to me that this kind of seated, solitary, repetitive task was the perfect environment for working stoned to prevent boredom. I never did, however...there was always the risk of feeling stuck in one of those endless repetitive hells. Besides, who gets stoned at five in the morning? At the request of a journalist friend who was writing an article on drug use in the hi-tech workplace, however, I did interview most of my co-workers about their favorite substances to abuse on the job. Not surprisingly, the people who worked around acid baths preferred nothing other than coffee, to stay sharp and focused so they didn't burn their hands or faces off. And *nobody* drank. "You don't wanna puke in the acid bath," I was informed. A valuable life lesson, I suppose, whether taken literally or metaphorically.)

The Weekend Shift required a mental shift as well—a restructuring of internal schedules. In order to get enough sleep to work 12 hours on Friday, for instance, I had to go to bed about 8 PM on Thursday night—not an easy task for a night owl. (This was years before Ambien.) And simple arithmetic indicates that returning to work after four days off is twice as hard as coming back after only two. Friday was my Double Monday. Saturday was my Wednesday: all I could recall in short term memory was working, and all I had to look forward to was working. Sunday, however, was my Friday—a long, extended, will-it-never-end Friday.

The screaming didn't usually begin until Sunday afternoon. Sure, there were mere hours to go until the end of our three-day workweek, but some of us simply couldn't hold it together after two-and-a-half 12-hour days. We began to get silly: giggling in the lunchroom; blowing up finger cots with nitrogen guns to make balloons; sucking helium and spouting out orders in a Mickey Mouse voice. The management came up with one solution: if we met our quota, we were eligible for early release. (If that sounds like parole, you're beginning to understand the philosophy behind this book.)

My co-workers came up with a novel solution as well: the Virtual Gas Leak. The first actual gas leak occurred one Sunday morning and required that we all file out into the lobby and wait until the engineers fixed it and gave us the "all clear" to return to our stations. And that's when Management made their big mistake: they sent a couple of us out to McDonald's to buy breakfast for the crew—35 to 50 people at that time. After that, the Sunday morning "gas leak"—as well as a free Sunday morning McDonald's breakfast—became something of a tradition. (What substances did we all abuse? Maple syrup.)

Dramatis Personae

Dave Mooney – Dave was Supervisor of the weekend shift. He was my immediate superior—my boss. Nice guy; regular joe. I'd borrowed a car to get to work for the first week or two, but I finally had to return it. I asked Dave if there was a carpool in our area; we discovered he drove right past my house on the way to work every day and he offered to pick me up. On the first Friday we carpooled, he pulled up about 5:30 AM and I climbed into his VW with my cup of tea. "That smells great!" he said. (He was correct; it was Bigelow's Constant Comment.) So on Saturday, I climbed into his car with *two* cups of tea. "Now all we need is some cookies, and we'd have a tea party!" he joked. So on Sunday, I climbed into his car carrying a tea tray with china cups and saucers, a plate of cookies, cloth napkins, and a freshly brewed pot of hot Constant Comment. And for the next couple of months, until I got my own car, we had our breakfast tea party during every commute. It was, I figured, the least I could do for the guy who was carpooling me. Thanks, Dave!

José – Actually, I don't remember the guy's name. He was a tall, reed-thin Filipino who worked alone and kept to himself. He ran some kind of machine that sprayed shit onto wafers. I learned from him that he—and many of our co-workers—took this weekend shift because they had another full-time job, often 10 hours a day Monday through Thursday. These people were working nearly 80 hours a week?

"Why?" I asked him, baffled.

"I have a wife and kids and a mother-in-law in the Philippines," he explained. "I'm saving up to bring them over."

"I notice you're driving a new Cadillac," I said. "And wearing a Rolex. You must be making enough to bring them over."

"I'm in no hurry," he shrugged, smiling.

I wonder if his family isn't still in the Philippines.

The Engineer – She was a breathtakingly beautiful blonde. Both her grandfathers were Irish, she told me, and both her grandmothers were American Indian. So she ended up with the perfectly sculptured cheekbones of the Native Americans, but with the blonde hair and fair, milky complexion of her Irish ancestors. She could have been a supermodel. I initiated my A-game and threw my best lines and best moves on her. The only reaction I ever got, however, was an amused, Mona Lisa smile. Sure, she was out of my league, but I had to try. I didn't realize she was playing in a different league altogether until she moved in with the other engineer, Joan. I felt like Groucho Marx when he wrote, "I chased a girl for two years only to discover that her tastes were exactly like mine. We were both crazy about girls."

Narine – A pixie-ish blonde with a Peter Pan haircut, a perfectly chiseled nose and a world-class sense of humor. We went to lunch with a group of co-workers and discovered we were the only straight people in the bunch. We bonded over that, and bonded on and off regularly for a decade after that. But this is the story of my work life, not my love life. (For the story of my love life—which is significantly shorter and even more wretched than the story of my work life—see my upcoming book, *You Are My Nothing*, which will never be written.)

By December, I was ready to move on, having scored a much better job (see the next chapter). In my exit interview, the HR rep asked the standard question on her checkout sheet: "Is there anything we could do to make you stay?"

"Sure," I said. "Pay me triple what you're paying, and I'll be glad to stay."

She just looked at me, brow furrowed, and replied, "You're kidding, right?"

Ah...no. And *buh-bye*.

Chapter 12

1981:
LOCKHEED MISSILES & SPACE CO.
PART I

LOCKHEED MISSILES & SPACE CO.
PART I

"How come I gotta get up early and go to work, how come?"
—Canibus, "How Come"

December 1980

I didn't need a job. I had a job. But working the weekend shift making wafers for chips was...just a job. It was hardly a career. What I needed was a *better* job—meaning higher-paying. Since it was my mother who'd gotten me my first job, it seems only appropriate that she was the one who also got me my first white-collar position in the corporate world.

After having been a Sales Associate at JCPenney for many years, my mother had worked her way up to become Director of Personnel at the JCP store in Cupertino, California—which, if it isn't exactly the heart of Silicon Valley (that would be Sunnyvale), was at least one of its main ventricles. Once mom became middle management at JCP, however, it became abundantly clear to her that she would never advance beyond that point—not because of incompetence, but because of the as-yet-to-be-named "glass ceiling." (The *Wall Street Journal* wouldn't coin that term until 1986.) JCP was an old school, old world, Old Boys Club (White Boys Only). No woman had yet risen in JCP management beyond the level my mother had attained. And rather than fight the system, she took a more practical route: she left. She hired into Lockheed Missiles and Space Company, the Silicon Valley branch of the Lockheed Corporation, located in Sunnyvale, the heart of—well, you know.

From the early '60s through the '80s, the biggest employers in the Santa Clara Valley were IBM and LMSC. So, once she was deeply entrenched in the belly of the beast, Mom figured thus: "I'm working in Personnel at LMSC. Why shouldn't I get my family jobs here?"

Mom had an advantage in attempting to attain this goal of high-salary employment for her family, namely first-look access at all employment requests from every department at LMSC. She'd call me and say, "Come in and apply for this job." Given my lack of experience, I was looking forward to a job that involved, oh, running a Xerox machine, say, or some such nonsense, so I was the opposite of thrilled. But when a request for a Technical Editor crossed her desk, she insisted I apply. "I have no job skills or corporate experience," I said. Her reply: "You have a bachelor's degree. That's all you need to get in here." So in December 1980, I interviewed with the Lead and the Supervisor of a Technical Publications unit (Tech Pubs, in LMSC parlance). I put on my best suit, a white dress shirt and a conservative tie and met with them for a few minutes.

They seemed impressed that I'd written three novels and had (nearly) gotten a second bachelor's degree in English. And they revealed the secret to being a Tech Pubs editor: "We discovered it's a lot easier to find someone who knows English and teach them some engineering than it is to try to teach the engineers how to write coherent English." They were also impressed that I'd worked in an insane asylum. "That'll prove very valuable here," they agreed.

Whatever I said in the interview must have passed muster, because they made me an offer and I accepted. My starting salary would be $350 a week—more money than I had ever seen before. We set my start date as January 12, 1981—a week after they all returned from Lockheed's annual "Christmas break," a paid week off between Christmas and New Year's. I could have started on January 5th, the previous Monday, but I asked for the extra week because I was dragging my feet: this was going to be a major change of lifestyle, and I wanted an extra week of freedom and vacation, now that I was going to have some money for a change—not to mention that I also wanted a final week of sleeping till noon.

I had no idea what to expect, but I did have a clue how to dress for success: in 1980, one of the most popular shows on TV was *Lou Grant*, an hour-long dramatic series about the gruff newsman of the title (played by Ed Asner), spun off from the '70s sitcom, *The Mary Tyler Moore Show*. One *Lou Grant* character, "Art Donovan," played by Jack Bannon, was an avowed clotheshorse—and he worked as an editor in a corporate environment. So I paid close attention to what he wore in a couple of episodes—then went out and recreated that wardrobe for myself. *I might not know what I'm doing in this job*, I told myself, *but at least I'll look good doing it.*

January 12, 1981: Day One

And so, at 7:00 AM on that fateful day, I walked into the jaws of The Beast. I would not emerge unscathed.

Just to add a touch of historical context, on January 12, 1981, Jimmy Carter was still President—but only for one more week, when the White House would be turned over to Ronald Reagan. No wonder Lockheed was hiring: they knew the hawkish Reagan would increase the defense budget, and the entire military-industrial complex was ramping up its workforce to compete for as many of these defense contracts as possible. The '80s would come to be known as the Greed Decade, and this was the opening salvo. Since I was still living in the Me Decade, all I could see at the time was how this would benefit...me.

I went to Personnel and signed my paperwork. They took me to the Badging Unit, where I was issued my photo badge. And sometime later that morning, I walked into the Tech Pubs unit that supported the Program Office of the Missile Systems Division.

The unit was a big open bullpen. Ten Editor's desks—five rows of two side-by-side desks in two columns—occupied one side of the room, and a dozen Technical Illustrators' drafting tables were arranged in a similar layout on the opposite side of the room. Between them were the two typist's stations. (Yeah, typists. This was 1981, long before personal computers, desktop printers or PowerPoint.) The coffee machine occupied a place of honor at the front of the room. And at the far back of the room was our Lead's desk. We all sat with our back to her, and from her vantage point she could see everything that everyone was doing (or shirking). The layout reminded me of a classroom, except that our desks were Navy surplus: huge, rectangular, battleship gray metal boxes. Lu, our Lead, sat me in the back row—right in front of her desk—and suggested that my first task should be to clean my desk. So there I was, in my brand new, hundred dollar three-piece pinstripe suit and white silk tie, swabbing dirt, pencil shavings, and rusty old paper clips out of my desk. Welcome to the Big Time.

The guy sitting in front of me turned around and introduced himself. Thin, young, wireframe glasses, crooked smile. He said something funny and I replied with something I hoped was funny. This guy was Jeff Hopkins, and he would quickly become one of my best friends. He will figure prominently in the LMSC chapters of this wanker diary.

YOU ONLY HAVE ONE CHANCE TO MAKE A BAD FIRST IMPRESSION

Near the end of the day, our heavyset Supervisor, Jeanette, waddled into the unit and stopped at my desk. "So how was your first day?" she asked. "I don't know," I replied enthusiastically. "I've never held a job this long!" What I expected was laughter. What I got was a wide-eyed, jaw-dropped look of horror. I knew in an instant that I'd made a terrible, terrible mistake in assuming that she had any vestige of a sense of humor. I did bite my tongue, however, before asking, "Do we hafta do this again tomorrow?"

My first impressions of LMSC were that it was a city within a city, and that our building was a town in and of itself. Our unit, for instance, was located in perhaps the biggest building I'd even been in. It was only a single story, but it had two-story ceilings and aisles wide enough to hold golf carts races without fear of collisions. The bulletin boards told a story as well: every one of them held numerous flyers for retirement parties. *How many people work here?* I wondered. *And how many were old enough to retire?* Lots, apparently. Little did I realize that I was witnesssing the last gasp of a corporate environment that provided lifetime stability and job security. That ship was sailing ...or, more accurately, sinking.

Our Tech Pubs unit was just one of many similar units scattered throughout LMSC, but it did have the distinction of serving the Program Office of the Missile Systems Division (MSD)—the alleged "brains" behind the entire division. Because of this, we were exposed to many top MSD execs, and our work was expected to live up to their professional standards and high expectations.

And the work? Completely forgettable. We'd read documents, edit them, and send them back for retyping. (Word processing was still a *leeeetle* bit in the future.) We'd read handwritten bullet-point slide presentations, polish them, request that the typists type them up, then proofread them for accuracy. Occasionally we'd be assigned a larger project, like a manual, or a spreadsheet in which numbers had to be typed on a separate sheet of paper, then cut and pasted—with scissors, X-Acto knives, and rubber cement or actual glue—onto a larger grid. Golly, it was all just so goddamned *exciting*. I felt like Indiana Jones. When he was grading papers. (This is literary license, as that movie wouldn't be released for another couple of months.)

SECURITY—OR INSECURITY?

It's hard to believe, in this post-9/11 world, that pseudo-government facilities like LMSC had strict security measures. And it is perhaps even harder to believe given my experience with Security. Soon after I started at Lockheed, I found a small image of a poster of Jane Fonda sitting naked on a beach. I cut it out and taped it over my official portrait on my Lockheed badge. It took two years before any of the Security personnel stationed in every lobby of every building ever noticed.

DON'T FEAR THE REAPER

"They all hate us anyhow
So let's drop the Big One now."
—Randy Newman, "Political Science"

Working at a major corporation was a major change of lifestyle—and not just in the hours. College had radicalized me to the point where my two culture heroes were Marx and Lennon (Groucho and John). A working-class hero was something to be, and the worst possible fate was to *sell out*. And here I was, doing exactly that: selling out to the corporate world… selling out to *The Man*. I had become a cog in the Great Machine of the

Military-Industrial complex—the same mutant leviathan that gave birth to Silicon Valley (Lockheed was here first) and forever changed its nature.

I did find a few ways to assuage my guilty twinges. I quickly discovered, for instance, that just because you have to dress straight doesn't mean you can't still think twisted. With that epiphany, my three-piece suit became a costume rather than a uniform—a disguise for the inner anti-corporate hippie. I found a drawing in the *National Lampoon* that precisely illustrated my double life: in detailed Norman Rockwell style, a guy in his twenties stands looking in a full-length mirror. On one side of the mirror he has long hair, a beard, wireframe glasses, and is wearing jeans and a paisley shirt. His immaculately groomed reflection wears a three-piece suit and '70s-style aviator glasses with huge lenses and thick black frames. And in each version, he sports a shocked look at his reflection. Curiously, not only did the clothes on both sides of the looking glass mirror my own modes of dress, separated by a decade—right down to hair color, the black pinstripe suit and the glasses styles—but the guy even *looked* like me. I framed the drawing and put it on my desk. And since I worked in the Missile Systems Division, I added the caption, "From LSD to MSD."

In a larger sense, I realized that not only was I a corporate sell-out, but I was selling out to the worst possible corporate environment: the War Machine. Shame on me. I did, in truth, feel an occasional pang of guilt. I was, after all, working for a company whose main task was the design, production and maintenance of the U.S. Navy's Submarine Launched Ballistic Missiles (SLBMs): Fleet Ballistic Missiles tipped with nuclear warheads (I could tell you how many, but then I'd have to kill you), the sole purpose of which was to rain nuclear death down on our enemies should they attack us. So there I was: a corporate sellout, but not *just* a corporate sellout—an actual running dog flunky of the Military-Industrial Complex. I'd not only turned my back on my hippie beliefs, but I was also, in some small way, enabling the thermonuclear destruction of the entire human race. What an asshole.

There were, of course, any number of employees who believed that what we were doing—providing a nuclear deterrent against aggression by the Soviet Union—was of inestimable benefit to the security of America and Our Way Of Life. I wasn't one of them. I'd understood the insanity of the policy of "Mutually Assured Destruction" (MAD) since I'd seen *Dr. Strangelove*, years earlier. But whether one believed in Lockheed's mission or not, the allure was, of course, the money...and LMSC paid some of the highest wages in Silicon Valley. A little money assuages a lot of moral dilemmas.

But still I wondered: How could anyone with a conscience remain sane working here, knowing that they were supporting the end of the world? At some point, I realized that there were only a few ways to deal with these feelings: get out, get cynical, or simply get stupid and ignore reality.

And I discovered that the most pervasive attitude among the majority of my peers was Door Number 3: it wasn't that they thought they were helping defend the American Way of Life from the Godless Commies, but that they were simply not bothered by the implications of their work. They had no crisis of conscience weighing on them. The majority of people I met at LMSC just didn't care. They didn't ponder the Big Picture or their role in it. We were simply office drones, doing our paperwork, engaging in office politics, bucking for raises, waiting for the weekend. We might as well have been working for an insurance company or a car manufacturer. When you worked for Lockheed, you just put those larger concerns out of your mind and went about your assigned tasks. After all, that plan was to build these weapons as a defense, not to ever actually use them. We were working for deterrence, to maintain peace…and our government sanctioned this approach, so by definition we couldn't be doing anything wrong.

I wondered if we weren't perhaps like those Jehovah's Witnesses in the Nazi concentration camps who every day typed up a list of names of the Jews who were to be gassed, never stopping to question the ethics but just doing as they were told, since what they were doing didn't violate any of their religious principles. But I couldn't see LMSC employees as evil scoundrels, or as morally bankrupt, or as cynical villains who'd struck a Faustian bargain trading their souls for a big paycheck. We were just ordinary dumbass people trying to make a living. Still, during that first year I had more than one nightmare of nuclear bombs raining down on us. And awake, I knew that if we were ever attacked in an all-out atomic war, the big Blue Cube—the top-secret Air Force satellite tracking facility on our campus that looked like a giant Rubik's Cube with all the faces painted powder blue—would be Ground Zero for any first strike. We'd never have any warning. We'd be sitting at our desks one minute, sipping crap coffee, thinking about where to go for lunch, figuring out new ways to avoid work...and in the next moment we'd be radioactive vapor. Dust in the wind.

My inner rebel was activated when I got my first business cards, however. The cards were not well designed—all the text was left-justified, giving them a lop-sided look and leaving an entire quadrant of empty space on the right-hand side of the card. Inspiration struck. I knew how to fill that blank space. I went to a printer and ordered a small rubber stamp, with this text in 4 point type: "Subverting the system from the inside since 1980." (It should have read "since 1981," but since I was hired in December of 1980, I gave my subversion a promotion and backdated it to my hiring date.) I stamped this motto on a few cards and handed them out to a select few people I knew would appreciate the sentiment.

The single best lesson I learned in those early months: If you carry a piece of paper and walk with determined intent, people will think you're working—maybe even on something important—and won't bother you. You can walk around for hours doing nothing if you look like you're carrying out an important, time-sensitive mission.

DOES HUMOR BELONG IN THE WORKPLACE?
(Part 1 of a Nearly Infinite Series)

Once my pesky conscience was wrestled into submission (Satan wins again!), I discovered the fun side of working in a giant corporation. And decades later (since we never did have a nuclear Armageddon), it's the laughs I remember best.

For instance: Throughout the Valley, Lockheed was referred to as "The Lazy L Ranch," or simply "The Lazy L." I found out why when I noticed that no one ever seemed to be working too hard. Many of the people I met there had entire second careers, from selling real estate to producing teddy bear videos—"side hustles," in 2020 parlance. (Whenever I was asked how many people worked at Lockheed, my standard answer was, "About half.") Just coming up with new interpretations of the "LMSC" acronym was always a fun way to kill a few minutes. A partial list of those I remember include:

Let's Make Some Coffee
Let's Move Some Chairs
Let's Murder Some Commies
...and so on.

We used to tell a joke that illustrates the Lockheed Lifestyle of that era: Three young schoolboys are playing together at recess. The first boy says to his friends, "My dad is the fastest man in the world. He works at IBM. He gets off work at five o'clock every day, and he's home by five-thirty." The second kid replies, "No, *my* dad is the fastest man in the world. He works for the Post Office. He gets off work at four o'clock every day and he's home by four-fifteen." The third kid scoffs and sets them straight: "That's nothin'," he brags. "*My* dad works at Lockheed. He gets off at two-thirty, and he's home every day by noon." It's funny because it's true.

Our work in Tech Pubs depended on what others wanted us to do, and there was frequent downtime. We never worked too hard to begin with, and there was often time to kill. Jeff and I relied on humor to fill the empty hours. One major source of amusement for us was the President of LMSC at that time, Bob Fuhrman. By cutting and pasting text in the company newsletter, for instance, I retitled an article "Fuhrman: The Man Behind the Fuhr." Fuhrman was a tall man with an extremely high forehead and a magnificent mane of white hair. We agreed he looked like Exeter, the high-domed alien in the 1955 sci-fi flick *This Island Earth*. Or like a poodle. We'd take turns addressing one another in a deep, growling Fuhrman-poodle voice: *"Woof!"* My single actual close encounter with Bob Fuhrman occurred one morning as I was walking up the stairs to our building. I noticed to my horror that he was right behind me. I held the door open for him politely, smiled, and said pleasantly, "Good morning, Mr. Fuhrman." Here—and I swear this is true—is what he said to me:

"Woof!" I was dumbfounded. Were we being bugged? Was he really a telepathic alien? Or were we ironically on the right track about his poodle-tude?

Bob Fuhrman once sent out a motivational photo of himself giving a big "thumbs up" to his employees. But his hand was cocked at an odd angle, so when I added my own word balloon, his pose took on a new, even more appropriate, meaning: "Do your job or *hit the road!*" This became the motto Jeff and I shared for the next several years.

The other side of our sense of humor was aptly illustrated by one of our co-workers, a young woman with a perpetual scowl. One day soon after I began, we engaged in the following conversation:

Her: So...your name is "D. Scott Apel"?

Me: Yep.

Her: That's really odd. I have a friend—a woman friend—whose name is C. Scott Zimmerman.

Me: Wow. Hey, you should introduce us. Maybe we'll fall in love and get married and have a couple of kids. Then I could introduce my family by saying, "Hi! I'm D. Scott Apel. This is my wife, C. Scott Apel. And these are our kids, A. Scott Apel and B. Scott Apel."

Her (shaking her head perfunctorily): She's a feminist. She'd never take your name.

And the Award for Excellence in Point-Missing goes to...

April 1981

In April, I was the first editor assigned to a brand new word processing unit for a one-month rotation. The unit had recently installed state-of-the-art word processing equipment from the Wang Corporation. Great name—but did no one ever inform them, I wondered, that in America, "wang" is a euphemism for "penis"? There was a lapel button stuck in the wall above my workstation: *Wang First*. I couldn't help completing the thought: *Wang First. Ask Questions Afterward.* (I thought of suggesting an alternate corporate slogan: *Get Your Hands on a Wang*. But I refrained.) I'd finish editing most of the documents by 10 AM, and then spent the rest of the day working on my fourth novel.

Each project we worked on had a timecode, so we could charge the appropriate Lockheed department, or the Navy, for our work. We were required to keep timecards that tracked our projects in fifteen-minute increments. This often took so long that I once asked if there was a timecode for time spent updating our timecards. Only Jeff appreciated the meta-irony.

I had a dream around that time that pretty accurately sums up my perception of LMSC: In my dream, Jeff and I were walking down one of the immense hallways in our building, and when we turned a corner into another corridor, we spotted in the distance a swarm of clowns, acrobats, aerialists, wild animal trainers and even a ringmaster, heading right toward us. I turned to Jeff and said, in my best Jack Nicholson impersonation, "It's the circus, Jeff. It's the goddamn circus." I related this dream to him, and it became an inside-joke shorthand for the insanity that surrounded us.

ALL YOU NEED IS LUNCH

There was, however, one extremely serious and existentially vital task that consumed much of our mental effort on a daily basis: deciding where to go for lunch. One option was to stay on campus, since Lockheed had several cafeterias, each with its own daily specials. Tuesday was $1.49 New York steak day in one, for instance; on Wednesdays, the huge cafeteria in our own building served up slabs of prime rib at a ridiculously low price. Years—decades, even—before the idea of free company food became one of Silicon Valley's hallmarks, Lockheed was serving up government-subsidized meals designed to keep us all fat and happy. I can attest that it half-worked for me.

The area surrounding Lockheed also sported some great places to eat on those days when the LMSC cafeterias had nothing special to offer, and everyone had a favorite spot. Lunch was such an overriding concern that even a decade later, I'd start calling my people with this message: "It's 9 AM—time to start figuring out where to go to lunch." (One day in 1993—my final year at LMSC—I found myself eating lunch alone at my desk, which made me consider that perhaps my life had been a failure.)

Jeff was one of my regular lunch companions in the early days. And when we weren't going to lunch and talking about comedy, we were sitting at our desks, working and talking about comedy. Jeff was one of the funniest people I've ever met, and I'd met the founders of the *National Lampoon* (but that's another story for another book. And that book is *Famedroppings: Close Encounters with 100+ Celebrities*). His deadpan, dry wit and twisted, absurdist take on the world meshed precisely with mine, and he was a never-ending source of amusement.

...AND SUDDENLY THE ENTIRE WORLD BLEW UP IN HIS FACE

Perhaps too much so. Sometime later that year, our Supervisor called the two of us into her office. She was concerned that we were being too disruptive, disturbing the other editors and distracting them from their work. This was a patently false claim—we made sure that our comic dialogs didn't disturb any of our co-workers. I asked if our work was unacceptable; she said no. I asked if anyone had complained; again, no. But Jeanette announced she was going to "separate our desks." Jeff and I looked at one another quizzically. When we discussed this later, we realized we'd had precisely the same thought at that moment: *"What is this, third grade?"* I suggested that perhaps she should move our desks *next* to one another—if we were closer, we could talk even more quietly and not disturb anyone (not that anyone had claimed to be disturbed in the first place). But her word was final.

Almost final, anyway. A couple of months later, she decided I was a Bad Influence on her Golden Boy, Jeff. (Since we'd already determined this was grade school, I was tempted to whine, "He started it!") She simply did not want me around, so she transferred me to a completely different Tech Pubs unit. In another building. Halfway across the campus. This did not bode well for my career. I'd already been fired from my first two real jobs. Would my Salaryman career end ignominiously as well?

I can't say I was entirely blameless in being banished. I delighted no end in mocking Jeanette, for instance (never to her face, of course). But when she saw Jeff and me walking down the hall one day and sneered, "Well there they are—Heckle and Jeckle," I couldn't stop myself from replying, "That's *Doctor* Jekyll to you." A snide retort like this makes for a good laugh... but not for a great relationship with a humorless boss.

The day before I shipped out, my Tech Pubs unit served Jeanette a slap in the face by stopping work for an hour to throw me a good-bye party. There was cake. There were gag gifts. Jeff stood on his desk and sang a Talking Heads song, "Don't Worry About the Government." Most of our co-workers were baffled about his gift. I was touched.

"HOME OF THE RECTAL PROBE"

And so, one morning in the fall of 1981, I reported to a Tech Pubs unit in an outlying building. If you've seen the movie *Joe Vs. the Volcano* (which no one has, but all men should), I don't need to describe this new unit. It looked much like the basement office that Tom Hanks worked in early in the film—like a crypt, but less cheerful. The area was both damp and cold, for instance —a combination that created clammy conditions. The only lighting came from bare florescent bulbs set high in the ceiling—lamps that were always blinking and buzzing. No one could work without an individual desk lamp. The unit was stuck away in the butt end of an engineering building, as far away from any action as Luke Skywalker's home planet was from the galactic center. And it was a third-rate unit, devoted to low-level engineers rather than prominent Program Directors. I realized immediately that I'd been demoted as well as exiled. And once I met the personnel, I felt like I'd been shipwrecked on the Isle of Lost Toys.

One editor, for example, was a middle-aged minister who'd quit the church and was confused by everything about our job. (It was no mystery why he left the ministry—it appears that even God had forsaken him.) The single typist—upon whom all our work depended—was, technically, clinically insane. This I knew for certain, having previously worked in asylums. How she managed to navigate the real world outside work was a mystery—and I prayed it remained that way. She never actually refused to do her work—she could be fired if she did. But she couldn't be fired for throwing your finished work on your desk, most often accompanied by the comment "Here's your shit." All the editors kept scissors and X-Acto knives away from her...for our own safety.

In all fairness, I grew to like these people. Stan the crippled midget, in particular, was one of the most independent, sharpest, funniest people I've ever known, and a first-rate graphic artist. He used crutches to get around, but I had to hurry to keep up with him when we walked down the hall. He was bald, bearded, and had a handicapped van specially outfitted so he could drive with his hands instead of his feet. The van doubled as a mobile DJ station, and he DJ'd parties nearly every weekend. He had a deep, gravelly voice and a dark, wicked sense of humor. Most people let him get away with verbal murder because if they objected they'd look like assholes for abusing a poor cripple. When our lead came in one Monday and told us she'd been to a Bar Mitzvah over the weekend, for instance, Stan asked her what a Bar Mitzvah was. "You know," she replied. "Big party, lots of food." "Like a luau?" Stan shot back.

Even the insane typist grew on me, and evidently, vice versa. I always treated her with respect and took the time to talk to her. And when she inevitably got in trouble with HR, she insisted I be present at the hearing as a witness. "He's the only one I trust," she growled to her interrogators.

Pammy June grew on me as well. Tall, dark and goofy, she became my "work wife"—again, long before that term existed. We'd go to breakfast in the cafeteria next door every morning, bemoan our fate, and commiserate about being stuck in this hellhole. A few years later, I hired into the unit where her boyfriend worked, so we saw each other regularly for years.

I also warmed up to a little redheaded Graphic Artist, although her warming up to me was an uphill battle. But in the space of just a few months, we went from her debating whether or not to report me to HR for sexual harassment to living together. For five years. My HR takeaway: It's not harassment if they like it.

So it wasn't all bad.

And, unbeknownst to me, escape was waiting...

MEET THE WORLD'S NICEST MAN

One of my favorite clients while I was working in the Program Office Tech Pubs unit was Robert E. "Bob" Springer. He was one of two men on staff to the Director of Operations for the active Fleet Ballistic Missile programs, so he handled most of the paperwork for the guy who was in charge of the disposition and status of every single submarine-launched ballistic missile currently deployed by the U.S. Navy. The exact number is a secret. But I can reveal this: it was a lot.

Bob was a little guy, sixtyish and ruddy with a head of thick, lustrous, silver hair, a Mr. Magoo squint and a Letterman front tooth gap. He was always immaculately groomed and tailored. Lockheed had been his home for the past quarter of a century. I don't think we ever discussed any jobs he might have had prior to Lockheed—it was as if this was the only place he'd ever worked. He'd served in the Army with several guys who hired into Lockheed after the war, and eventually he followed them to this new job and career. Several of Springer's associates became top execs in LMSC or even in the Lockheed corporation. Bob Springer wasn't that ambitious, however, and certainly not that aggressive. He worked his way up to this Staff position and it suited him perfectly.

Springer was also an inveterate and unrepentant raconteur. He had a story for every occasion, and he often created the occasion just so he could spin one of his yarns. Jeff and I joked that he had a mental Rolodex that he'd twirl whenever a key word was mentioned. If I said I'd purchased a new pair of shoes, for instance, he'd cock his head and say, "Shoes? That reminds me of a time I bought a pair of alligator loafers to impress a girl..." and off he'd go on his story...anecdotes that were always long, always drawn out, and unfailingly amusing.

The day after I was informed that Jeanette was banishing me from the Tech Pubs unit where I often served Springer, he showed up and asked me if I could be assigned to a job he had pending. "I wish I could do that, Bob," I said, "but Jeanette just transferred me." His response was immediate and emphatic. "That cow!" he growled. "We'll see about *that*!" I believe that in the five years I knew Bob Springer, this was the only time he ever had anything bad to say about anyone, or ever lost his temper. I was touched.

A few months later Springer summoned me to his office. "How'd you like a job?" he said. "Working for you?" I replied. "Working *with* me," he explained. "You know Jamie, my assistant. He just earned an engineering degree and got himself a new job. So I need somebody to replace him. You'd basically be our liaison with Tech Pubs, and oversee all the paperwork we run through them."

"I can do that!" I said.

February 1982

Thus, one Friday in February, a year after I'd hired into LMSC, my second Tech Pubs unit threw me a going away party (no singing this time, unfortunately), and the following Monday I reported to Springer. Jamie, Bob's departing assistant, spent a week with me going over the regular and frequent reports and presentations I'd be overseeing, and introducing me to the personnel in the Program Office. And on my first week alone on the job—the week the monthly reports had to be created—I got the flu. There was no way in hell that I could take a sick day—much less a sick week, as my doctor laughingly suggested. That would not send a positive message to my new peers. So I rallied and focused and bulled my way through a sweaty, vertiginous week. It might not have been a trial by fire, but it was certainly a trial by 103-degree temperature. By Friday afternoon, all reports were completed to everyone's satisfaction. I went home and slept the entire weekend. (Seriously—I set a Personal Best by sleeping 23 consecutive hours. When I woke and checked the clock, I tried desperately to sleep for just one more hour to make it a full day of unconsciousness, but I was simply too awake to accomplish that final hour.)

Once my health returned I began to enjoy my new position. I was working with my old Tech Pubs unit again—only this time, I was the client rather than the editor. I was a surrogate Springer. And every time I showed up in the unit it galled Jeanette. It was now her job to make sure her people made me happy. Revenge is sweet.

Working with Springer was unlike working with anyone I've ever worked with, before or since. He was always calm and low-key—his outburst against Jeanette was the one time I ever saw him lose his cool. He believed that if you had to rush to get something done, you weren't suited for the job. I quickly learned that this laid-back attitude was a way of life with Bob. And I adjusted myself to the idea that it took at least fifteen minutes every morning just to say "good morning," sitting in his office and chatting about...anything and everything. This is not to imply that Springer was slow or dull. He was far sharper than most of his colleagues, and far sharper than most of them gave him credit for. In more than one meeting, for instance, someone would make an amusing comment and Bob was always the first to laugh. He "got it" more quickly than anyone else. Sharp. Yet he cultivated the image of a slow, spacey old man so that people in a rush would simply leave him alone. I knew Springer was not educated in things like philosophy, but I often thought he was a living example of Nietzsche's aphorism, "Only give seventy-five percent."

Bob Springer had a story about *everything*, and his delivery was half the fun. He spoke in a slow whine—not an annoying, grating nasal whine, more like a tenor W.C. Fields. ("*Ahhhh, yehhhhhs...*") He had a couple of stories that I found particularly amusing. He'd been in a nightclub in Dallas in the early '60s, for example, and the owner of the bar bought him a drink. No big deal, until the punchline: "Guy named *Jaaaaack Ruuuby*," he'd say, drawing out the name. Another time I answered a question using a Bogart voice. Springer sat back in his chair and smiled his gap-toothed, squint-eyed grin. I knew I was in for some kind of Springer mischief. "*Humphrey Bogarrrrrt*," he purred savoring the words. "D'I ever tell you about the time I knocked him out?" The time you...*what?* He proceeded to tell the story of how one night, decades earlier, his future in-laws had taken him and his fiancé out to dinner in Santa Monica. At one point he excused himself to go to the men's room, and when he pushed the swinging door to go in, Bogart was coming out. The door hit Bogart on the chin and knocked him out cold. OK, maybe not the most earthshattering celebrity encounter story... but do *you* know anyone who knocked Bogart out? I thought not.

Springer became my low-key mentor, my "Folksy Wan Kenobi." He taught without teaching, merely by dropping a casual idea here and there, and letting me figure out for myself how it applied—and its relative importance. "We're all professionals here," he told me one day, as we drove off campus to do a little grocery shopping. "That means you do your job and the rest of your time is your own." This was clearly an Old School principle, which would become obsolete by the time I started working in hi-tech startups, where work was never finished, where there were never enough hours in the day, and where your time (in and out of the office) was *always* supposed to be devoted to work. But in 1982, this was The Way of The Lazy L.

Springer disguised himself as a boring corporate clone, but he was full of surprises. One day, for instance, I found myself in a bind: a Navy Captain wanted me to get him a copy of a secret document before he left for D.C.—in ten minutes. Copying any kind of delicate document was a red-tape nightmare to begin with, involving paperwork and multiple signatures by those authorized to release sensitive materials. There was simply no way to fulfill the Captain's demands—but I didn't want to be the one to tell him that. I went to Springer and explained my dilemma. "Let's see the document," he said. I handed him the one-page artist's rendition of a submarine firing a missile. At the top and bottom of the page were SECRET markings, added to the vellum paper using strips of adhesive tape marked SECRET. Bob pondered the sheet for a moment, then fished an X-Acto knife from his desk drawer and stripped off the SECRET tape. "Not secret anymore," he said, matter-of-factly, handing me the document. "Just walk this down to Repro and get a quick Xerox." Problem solved! Of course, it was unconventional, a violation of national security, and possibly even illegal. But it was an exemplary example of thinking outside the box.

Bob Springer taught me a great many lessons, but his best advice was on display at every moment of the workday: a fortune cookie fortune he'd taped over his desk lamp, so it was always in his line of sight. The fortune read: "The smart man knows everything. The wise man knows everyone." Robert E. "Bob" Springer was a wise man.

Case in point: When he hit 64, he began to talk about retirement, and how he'd spent 25 years with Lockheed and had never taken a sick day. In those days, we were granted a dozen sick days a year...and he'd never taken a *single one*? Maybe, I thought, it was time to return the favor of his mentorship and teach him a lesson about something I knew well: subversion. "Bob," I admonished him, "those days were days the company approved of you taking off. It's not like you're cheating to take a sick day." I did some quick calculations. "Do you realize that by working an extra dozen days for 25 years that you've given this company 300 extra days of work? That's more than an *entire extra year* of work that you *did not need* to put in." He furrowed his brow. Apparently, he'd never weighed the loyalty against the math. "If I were in your position," I said, "I'd start taking every Wednesday or Friday off to play golf."

"Oh, I couldn't do that," he demurred. But when I went to his office the following Wednesday to say good morning, the departmental secretary (lovely, sweet Elaine) informed me that Bob had called in sick. "Sorry to hear that," I said. But I wasn't sorry. And I knew he wasn't sick. And I knew I'd never see Bob on a Wednesday again. Unless I became a caddy.

Bob Springer announced his retirement a year or so later, and I was determined to give him some sort of unique gift that would be meaningful to him. I wrote a short letter to a dozen or more of the highest executives at Lockheed who I knew had known Springer most of their careers. I informed them of his upcoming retirement, and asked if they would be kind enough to write Bob a short note of appreciation for his lifetime of service to the corporation. To their credit, every one of them complied, and many even included anecdotes from their long-term relationship. I slipped all these letters into plastic sheet protectors, collected them in a nice leather binder, and presented it to Bob on his last day in the office. It was, I thought, the least I could do for the guy who rescued my career and who was the best boss I've ever had.

A SIMPLE COUNTRY BOY WHO BECAME A GOD

I was the junior member of the Program Office staff. Bob was one of the two senior members. The other was Carl Doss. Tall and lanky, tan and fit, Carl was also quiet and calm...and unbelievably, spectacularly brilliant. I soon began referring to him among my friends as "a simple country boy who became a god." Doss singlehandedly wrote the annual contract between the Navy and LMSC, for instance—the schedule, and payments for performance. One year, he asked me to make some copies of the slides he'd drawn up to present the Navy. "Drawn up" is a precise term: he'd hand-drawn a series of charts, graphs and calculations. I took one look at them and said, "Carl, you've done your job. Now let me do mine. Let me take these over to Tech Pubs and have an artist redraw them and type them and pretty them up." He demurred. "No, no," he said. "If they look too good, they might believe 'em."

In the days before computer files, when everyone in business had a filing cabinet (or ten), Doss had his own unique filing system: a stack of papers on one end of the table in his office, shoved up against the wall—a column at least three feet high. I wondered how he ever found anything. And then I found out. One morning my phone rang. It was Doss, calling from Washington, D.C., where he was discussing something with the Navy. "I want to you go to my desk," he said, "and I'll call you there." I went to his office and the phone rang. "Are you sitting in my chair?" he asked. Yes. "OK, turn around and face the table. To your left is a stack of papers. I want you to dig down about seven and three-quarters inches and find a page marked CEP." I spotted a ruler on his desk and measured seven and three-quarters inches from the top of the stack, then lifted that pile. The exact page he wanted was precisely there.

While Springer had actively taken me under his wing to mentor me, Doss also became a mentor, however inadvertently. When we were discussing a test failure of one of the newer missile upgrades, for instance, I mentioned that it must be frustrating to have so many trials literally blow up in their faces. He just shrugged. "Not really," he said. "If you're meeting all your goals, you're not pushing the state of the art." There is a concept in philosophy called Truth Revealed, which says essentially that when you encounter a profound truth, you recognize it immediately. It hits you right in the face and you know without a doubt that it is Truth. That's how I felt when I heard Carl Doss casually toss off this bit of his personal philosophy. I had his statement made into a small poster, which I framed and hung on my cubicle walls for years. *If you're meeting all your goals, you're not pushing the state of the art*: as wise a justification for striving and failing—and overcoming failure—as I've ever encountered.

There were many times when Springer, Doss and I would end up in Bob's office—never for formal meetings, simply for wide-ranging discussions that often turned from work to nostalgia—theirs. They'd wax rhapsodic about Big Bands from the '30s and '40s that I'd never heard of, and movies from the '40s I'd never seen, and how music today was crap and movies today were all sex and violence. One day I finally had enough. I was in my early thirties and they were twice my age, but I knew how great the music of the '60s and the films of the '70s were. "OK, Carl," I challenged. "If the world has gone to hell like you keep claiming, what is it that made the world go to hell?" To his credit, he took me seriously, and sat in deep thought for a minute or two, pondering the question. And he had an answer.

"Two things," he replied. "Television and The Pill. Before television, people used to do things with their evenings. Spend time with their family. Read. Build things in their workshops. Play music. Socialize over cards with friends and neighbors. Use their imagination, listening to the radio. But TV made everybody hypnotized and passive. And The Pill—well, that should be obvious. The Pill is responsible for the decay of morals in society, since everybody can have licentious sex with no consequences, so there's no sense of responsibility."

I respected Carl Doss far too much to argue with him, particularly since he was specific in his critique of the (then) current culture, and had clearly given his answer some deep reflection. But I could hardly explain to him that the things he thought were destroying society were the very cornerstones of my existence. I'd never known a world without television, for instance—and TV figures from Superman, Roy Rogers and The Lone Ranger to Shari Lewis and Patrick McGoohan in *The Prisoner* pretty much defined who I was and wanted to be. (I also had no idea that very soon I'd be on TV myself, and would remain a local staple on Silicon Valley's PBS station for more than a decade.) And as for The Pill—hooray! It made sex slightly more available, and slightly less risky. The world the Old Farts lived in was over, thank The Goddess. I determined never to become so old and ossified as to not appreciate the changes the juggernaut of a dynamic society would bring to my life. Of course that was before rap music and *Family Guy*...

THE PIVACEK PRINCIPLE

In the early days of working for Springer, I was seated in a bullpen with other Program Office guys—about a dozen of us in a big open area surrounded by their supervisor's offices. I was lucky enough to have a desk next to Fred Pivacek, a gawky, gangly, good-natured guy about 50 with a deep voice, a pencil-thin mustache, and a constant ironic smile. At least once a week, Fred's boss Tom would rush up to his desk and frantically inform him that he needed to investigate one thing or another *right away*. "I'm on it, boss," Fred would declare—but as soon as Tom walked away, Fred would go back to his newspaper or, occasionally, his paperwork. This scenario occurred often enough that I had to find out what the hell was going on.

"Fred," I said after one of Tom's frantic requests, "every week Tom comes by and gives you an assignment, and then you just go back to doing whatever it was you were doing. How does that work?" He smiled and explained. "I've been working for Tom for a long time," he explained. "He gets these bugs up his ass, but they usually pass as quickly as he thinks them up. I just assure him I'm on it and wait to see if he even remembers what it was he wanted. If he comes back and asks me how the investigation is going, then I know it's real, and I get started on it. Saves me a lot of unnecessary effort." He clearly knew his boss and had figured out a way to manage his expectations.

The work might have been simple, but the hours were brutal. Not the number of hours, which rarely exceeded a standard 40-hour workweek, but the time of day. In the '80s, LMSC had just two start times: 7 AM and 7:30 AM. These start times were holdovers from the 1950s, when Lockheed personnel needed to be in contact and communication with Navy brass in D.C. Given a three-hour time difference, even 7 AM in California was 10 AM—late morning—in Washington. The good news was that we were out every day by 2:30 or 3 PM—early enough to beat traffic (which, even in the '80s, was slowing down and becoming gridlock-like). These hours might be fine for a biological "morning person." But for a night owl like me, 7 AM was *the middle of the fucking night.* It was only when I started working at LMSC that I switched from tea to coffee, out of sheer necessity. To rise at 6 AM and be at my desk by 7 AM meant a 10 PM bedtime to get eight hours sleep. 10 PM: No late TV dramas, no 11 PM news broadcasts, no Johnny Carson, and certainly no late night Letterman. Jeff the insomniac used to tell me stories of Letterman's nocturnal antics, but I despaired of ever seeing them for myself.

My commute route took me past a rescue mission in downtown San Jose, and I found myself eyeing the bums smoking out front, envying them for their freedom—until I realized that if they were up and dressed and out on the street even earlier than I was, the job of being a bum had even worse hours than mine.

I always assumed I would adjust to this unholy schedule, eventually. Then one morning, about three years into my employment, while walking from the parking lot to my building, I hit a wall, in the figurative, distance-runner sense. I stopped dead in my tracks as though I had literally run into a brick wall as the realization hit me: *I will* never *get used to these hours*. This was hardly the first depressing thought that crossed my mind during my years at Lockheed, and it would hardly be the last.

DYING TO LEAVE LOCKHEED

Another depressing thought—this one recurrent—was that now I was embedded in a "company-for-life" environment, I would probably die at my desk. Not a cheery thought for a 30-year-old, but even that fate was more pleasant than the thought of hunting for a new job. Clearly, I didn't die at my desk...but I did witness the fate of someone who did.

I never knew the guy; although he was one of the dozen or so men in our Program Office bullpen, he sat on the other side of the room and our paths never crossed. One Monday we were informed that he'd passed away over the weekend. Sad—but, as I said, I didn't know him. I didn't even know his name. Following his demise, I'd enter our bullpen and see his vacant desk and think that was probably going to be my fate. I looked at his desk often enough, actually, that I knew the contents of his desktop, which rested in peace, unmolested, as though it were a shrine and his co-workers were paying him some respect…or as though they were loathe to disturb it in case death was contagious and they would suffer a similar fate. A few days later, however, I noticed that his stapler was missing. A day or two after that, his tape dispenser was gone. His in/out box, telephone, penholder and calendar went AWOL in rapid succession, and soon his desktop was empty. A few days later I walked into the bullpen to discover that his entire desk had been removed, and the two desks next to his had been pushed closer together to close up the empty space. The guy had simply evaporated. All evidence of his ever having worked in this space—or even of ever having existed—had been erased. A chill crawled up my spine. There but for the grace of... Well, you know the rest. Later, I found myself hoping that his stapler, tape dispenser and so on, were haunted and would seek their revenge against the office supply-stealing grave robbers who'd desecrated his existence.

THE WIT AND WISDOM OF TOM TUCCI

On the lighter side, I met one of the most charismatic people I've ever known during this period. Tom Tucci was maybe 40, small but wiry; an olive-skinned Italian with thick black hair everywhere except the top of his head. Tom worked—although that's far too strong a word to describe what he did—in the Program Office of the US/UK (or, as we pronounced it, "YouSuck") Missile Systems. Lockheed had provided the British Navy with its first-generation SLBMs, the outmoded A2 model, once the U.S. Navy upgraded to a newer model, and Tucci worked in the office that oversaw the maintenance of these creaky old relics of the early days of the Cold War. Tucci's job was about as low-profile and low-importance a position as existed in MSD, and he often had nothing to do. Literally. I'd stop by his office and most often catch him in his characteristic position: feet up on his desk, reading a newspaper. But he was one of the quickest-witted and most joyously sarcastic people I'd ever met. Some might describe him as a smartass or as acid-tongued, but both Jeff and I thought of him as a role model. He was an endless source of edgy amusement as well, if only because he would not suffer fools gladly and always had a stinging comment that many of us might think but never dare utter. At one point we even assembled a small pamphlet we titled "The Wit and Wisdom of Tom Tucci." Although my notes are long gone, a few of the entries I recall include:

- When a co-worker suggested that Tom take his date out boating, he responded, "Boating, hell. I'll take her for a week's cruise on my waterbed."
- When he was asked to settle an argument about whether red wine should be imbibed chilled or at room temperature, his response was, "I don't give a shit. I'll drink it fucking boiled if I want to."
- Driving with Tom to lunch one day, I mentioned that there were too many people moving into the Valley, and that there had never been this much pollution before. He revealed his priorities by replying, "Yeah, but there's never been this much *pussy* before, either."

CHANGE IS GOOD… BUT LARGE DENOMINATION BILLS ARE BETTER

During my first couple of years at LMSC, I was getting raises hand over fist. I got a ten percent raise after my first six months, for instance—just for lasting, I guessed—and another ten percent raise after my first year. When Springer hired me in February, he gave me another ten percent bump (my promotion to Program Plans Assistant brought me up to $473 a week) and another six months later (just for being so damn good, I guessed), which brought me up to $518 a week. So after less than three years at the Lazy L, I was making nearly half again as much as the relatively high salary of $350/week at which I'd hired in. I crunched some numbers and figured that at this rate, I'd be a millionaire in about a decade and could retire.

It would be years before I'd read this saying by some wise Greek: "The only time the gods laugh is when you ask for money." But it certainly applies. Clearly, this trajectory could not last, and of course it didn't. Sometime in 1984, when an outsider launched a hostile takeover bid to purchase the Lockheed Corporation, belts got tightened, and the standard ten percent raises twice a year were gutted; cut back to a mere two to four percent per year—less than inflation (not to mention that four percent raises were granted only for outstanding, exceptional performance, so I knew I'd never see one of those). We would from now on work harder and be paid less.

The gravy train had pulled into the station.

NOT ALL EXECUTIVES ARE HUMORLESS PRICKS: AN EXAMPLE

My job as Staff to the Program Director of the Operational Missile Systems Division occasionally put me in contact with one of the best people I met at LMSC, a vice president named Don Jones. Don—like many top LMSC execs—had been an engineer who showed a flair for management and moved up to an executive position. He could not only talk to engineers in the highly technical language they used, but understood it as well. (I would discover much later, working in various startups, how unusual it was for employees to be guided by a person who actually understood what they were doing.) When my wanderings occasionally took me to his office, I always came prepared with a joke, and he was always prepared to listen. (I figured it couldn't hurt my status if I had an ally in the upper echelon of management.)

I ran into Don Jones on the front steps of our building one day when we were both sneaking out early. "Don," I said, "I just came back from a trip to POMFLANT" —the Atlantic Polaris Missile Facility in Charleston, South Carolina, where I'd been sent for some training—"and I noticed they had a display of all the ballistic missiles we'd built."

He nodded. "Oh, yes, I've been there many times. I've seen that."

"I think we should get something like that here in Sunnyvale," I continued. "Only we construct it out of actual working missiles. Then the next time it looks like Boeing or Rockwell is going to get a contract we should get...we nuke 'em!"

He stared off into the distance. "We could rule the industry," he whispered.

"We could rule the *world*," I suggested.

He shook his head. "I'm just not ready for that kind of responsibility," he said, apologetically.

GOVERNMENT INSECURITY

My three years with Springer were perhaps the best three years of my alleged career. I had easy work, a boss I adored, the status (if only by association) of the Program Office, revenge against my enemies, and a campus full of friends...not to mention full of eligible, single, intelligent, professional women. But all good things come to an end. Springer retired, and the Operational Systems Program Office began cutting budget and personnel, as the brand new D5 ballistic missile was about to replace the C4 missile program our office oversaw.

When the Program Office budget could only justify keeping me on half time, I found an additional part-time position in what seemed to me the most unlikely of places for a '60s radical ex-hippie wannabe like myself: the Government Security Training Department. (While this might sound impressive, like many job titles, it was simply a way to make a shit job sound important on a résumé.)

Government Security Training was the domain of "Anne Oyed." She was small, blonde, very attractive, and an Empire Builder. Not satisfied with whatever crap job she'd previously held at LMSC, she found a niche and created her own job position, convincing her superiors that this new job function she'd dreamed up was a vital necessity to the company—and that she was the person best suited to establish and run it. In this position, she gave security orientation lectures to new hires and designed materials to explain security procedures and raise awareness of these procedures and of the importance of security measures at LMSC.

When she got a budget to expand her department of one, she hired me on a half-time basis to write security materials, and also hired Rick, a graphic artist, to illustrate them. We began with a series of calendar posters highlighting some aspect of corporate security. And we developed a comic strip we'd negotiated to get into LMSC's twice-monthly campus newspaper, featuring an Indiana Jones-style hero who engaged in security-related adventures, like using security procedure binders to slice through snake-like red tape threatening to literally wrap him up like a mummy. The calendars were created. The comic strip never saw the light of day.

Anne Oyed was not only an Empire Builder, she was also a complete loon. She'd regularly go ballistic (an apt metaphor for a company that manufactured missiles) and berate my artist coworker and me for the most trivial transgressions. When Rick forgot to pick up a job from the print shop, for instance, she told us that "between the two of you, you don't have the brains of a dead armadillo!" Rick and I just looked at each other quizzically. If I'd seen this in a workplace sitcom, I would have broken up with laughter. But this was real life, she was dead serious—and our fates lay in her crazy hands.

Artist Rick and I talked about this at length one day.

"Have you noticed that she goes completely nuts about once a month?" he asked tentatively.

"Oh, don't even go there," I cautioned. "That's a stereotype that'll only cause us grief and make us look like sexist pigs if we ever mention it to anybody, you sexist pig."

He pulled a calendar out of his desk drawer—a calendar on which he'd marked the three days out of every 28 that Anne had gone completely berserk. He'd worked with her longer than I had, but I could verify the most recent dates.

"That's good science," I admitted. "Can't argue with observation. Or with the math, or the conclusion. But we have *got* to keep this to ourselves."

And keep it to ourselves we did—although we both knew which days to call in sick each month, if Anne didn't do so herself.

Anne Oyed's world-building plans finally collapsed, but whether this was because her self-created function was unnecessary or because she was...*difficult*...is hard to say.

"JOHNNY, TELL HIM WHAT HE'S WON!"

So I was out of work in Government Security Training. And soon afterward, I was informed that I'd no longer be needed in the Program Office either, and should find other employment. As a consolation prize, my management sent me to a Florida facility to deliver some documents. (I checked to make sure my plane ticket was round-trip.) They encouraged me to take a week's vacation in Florida and to take my girlfriend to Disney World. Which I did.

But I still had to find another job. And I wasn't ready to leave the nest of Mother Lockheed and seek employment in the real world, where they make you work hard and demanded that you have some actual skills. Heaven forbid! So I asked around and poked around and sniffed around and eventually got some recommendations and referrals and landed a spot in a reporting unit. How bad could that be?

THE 80-20 RULE

All Lockheed departments were identified by a unique numerical code. The unit I landed in was designated 80-20. I later learned that this was an ironically appropriate description, given the industry-wide rule of thumb called the "80/20 rule" (technically, "the Pareto principle"), which says that at a miserable job, 80 percent of your work takes about 20 percent of your time, but the remaining 20 percent of your job consumes the remaining 80 percent of your time. My new department was dedicated to grinding out the remaining 20 percent of MSD's work.

80-20 functioned (or, more appropriately, dysfunctioned) as an in-house reporting unit. It was our job to attend the staff meetings of other Missile Systems Division departments and report on their problems and progress, or lack thereof, to the upper management of MSD and to the Navy personnel assigned to LMSC. Since we were the authorized tattletales, alerting both our senior management and our "customer," the Navy, about difficulties, delays, and fuckups, no one in any department was ever happy to see us show up at their staff meetings. Our job was thankless, and our crew was ostracized by every other department in MSD. ("Snitches get stitches," is the current expression of this attitude.)

80-20, it turned out, was also a very high-profile department. Since we reported on middle management to upper management, middle managers kept a close watch on our activities—and our personalities. A good 80-20 employee—smart, ambitious, a team player—would sooner or later be offered a better job by virtue of having exhibited intelligence, energy and integrity. A prime example was Mike Inman, a sharp, charismatic Southern ginger with a full red beard who passed through his 80-20 exile in about six months before he was hired away by the very de-partment he'd been reporting on—perhaps under the Machiavel-lian dictum to keep your friends close and your enemies closer.

(Just to illustrate the small-town nature of LMSC, during my tenure in 80-20, Inman—no one ever called him "Mike"—started dating Pammy June, my old "work wife" from Tech Pubs, so we all saw one another regularly. In 1986, it was my pleasure to play referee to their relationship when they engaged in a heated, potentially relationship-nuking argument about how time travel worked, based on their viewing of the recently-released *Back to the Future*. I convinced them that as a sci-fi trope, time travel was fiction—a *fantasy*—and could therefore follow any set of rules a writer creates. They stayed together... but if that's the kind of thing they argued about, I don't know for how long.)

Another 80-20 co-worker who moved on to bigger and better things was Laurel Rematore, a diminutive blonde with a big brain and an admirable attitude. Laurel had a button—buttons were big in the '80s—pinned outside her cubicle that read: "51% Sweetheart, 49% Bitch. Don't push it." In my estimation, she underestimated her sweetheart component, which I proved by dating her occasionally over the following years (after my time with the redhead didn't work out.) I still have a soft spot in my heart for that smart little snow bunny.

80-20 was staffed with people on the way up—or on the way out. Alongside the ambitious youth were a handful of legacy leftovers—older guys who just couldn't cut it in any other department and who used the unit as a rest home, counting the hours until they could retire and die. Once I recognized that the nature of the unit was "move on or move out," I was more depressed than ever. I'd always known I wasn't a "corporate clone"; that I was an outsider who was (to steal the title of a Mothers of Invention album) "Only In It For The Money." And if I was not moving on, that left only one other direction. I became so depressed, in fact, that I actually considered jobhunting outside LMSC, despite my lack of any marketable job skills, and the attitude that (as I hope I've made clear in this narrative) there is no single task in one's work-life more repulsive than job-hunting.

It wasn't just my own lack of marketable skills that made me consider seeking other employment, however. My co-workers—those who fell into the "move out" category, anyway—provided much of my incentive. When I hired into 80-20, for instance, my immediate superior was a guy I'll call "John Burshit." JB was a little guy, and he attempted to compensate for it by being the biggest badass in the department. He wore cowboy boots (with lifts) with his three-piece suit, for instance, and bragged constantly about his prowess as a hunter. A common refrain among our co-workers was: "Hey, John, you gonna go shoot Bambi this weekend?" He refused to admit this was an insult.

In 1985, the idea of "anger management" was a concept yet to be conceived—people who flew off the handle with little provocation were simply dismissed as "assholes." But if that particular psychological dysfunction had been identified and acknowledged at that time, Burshit would have been a prime candidate for anger management therapy. He had the annoying habit of "going postal" (another '80s term for losing one's temper in a major way over minor events) at the slightest provocation, and then slinking back a few hours later to beg forgiveness—possibly because his poor, patient, put-upon wife was a Born-Again Christian and demanded that he seek forgiveness from those whom he trespassed against. I endured his wrath several times—always followed by support from my more insightful co-workers, who counseled me with advice like "Just forget about it" and "He doesn't mean it" and, of course, "Fuck him. He's an asshole." But working with Burshit was still like sitting on a stick of dynamite—uncomfortable at best, and potentially lethal if his fuse was lit.

At some point, I decided that his outbursts simply weren't worth enduring. I determined to confront him, and if he decided to get me fired, that would actually be a relief. And so the next time he ripped me a new rectum, I just waited him out. I knew he'd come crawling back in a couple of hours, begging forgiveness for his tantrumy temper. And when he did, I told him this: "John, you claim you're a Christian, and you ask me for forgiveness for your anger. Well, I'm *not* a Christian. I don't *have* to forgive you. So I don't forgive you. But if you *really are* sorry for what you did, you won't do it again. That's the only way I'll know you're sincere." He walked away in a daze. No one had ever responded to him like that. And the next time he was about to boil over, I reminded him: "If you're serious about apologizing for losing your temper, you won't do it again." I'd deflated him. Maybe emasculated him. I didn't care, as long as he left me alone. I just wish I could have found a way to stop him from murdering Bambi, the asshole.

At some point, the Business Gods must have determined that I'd endured sufficient suffering for some unknown corporate crime, and my prayers were answered: I was reassigned to report to a woman who turned out to be one of my favorite people at LMSC. Tricia Pruitt was a diminutive redhead who was not only sharp, but also a live wire—a bundle of energy. Words like "spitfire," "pistol" and "firecracker" come to mind whenever I think of Pruitt. (No one called her "Tricia.") I was very fond of her and her "take no prisoners" attitude, even though she made me work far beyond my comfort zone of innate laziness. She'd regularly pull me out of my cubicle, insisting that we go to some other department to get some information, for instance. When I'd groan and suggest we simply call them, her reply was always, "*Nooooo!* We have to get out there and *beat 'em up*!"

And so we frequently zoomed off to some supervisor or manager or director's office to "beat 'em up" about some aspect of their domain. Pruitt was a constant source of chatter and amusement during our field trips. She'd often point to some tall, good looking guy in a business suit roaming the campus, then nudge me and exclaim, "Oooh, look at *that* guy! He'd make a *great* ex-husband!" One of our regular stops was to an engineer who spoke in a peculiar Southern whine that I found particularly amusing. When we'd leave his office, I'd imitate his unique nasal twang, and Pruitt would laugh raucously and encourage me. It wasn't until much later that I discovered she'd been living with him for years…

A couple of brief asides: At some point during my days reporting on missile production I realized that I knew more about how ballistic missiles work than about how my car worked. And another: In those days, I'd taken to keeping a bouquet of dead roses in a vase on my desk. Only a few people ever commented on it, but when they did, I gave this justification: "Live roses die after a few days. These will last forever."

NOW APPEARING ON STAGE...

All efforts by all 80-20 personnel were directed toward a single goal: the weekly Friday morning assembly, in which we briefed top execs from the Missile Systems Division and their Navy counterparts on the status of ongoing programs. The location was a small theater seating perhaps 200 people, and the room was usually SRO, full of various directors, managers and supervisors anxious to hear us pass judgment on their current work. (Thus the high-profile nature of 80-20. If you were on stage, you were seen—and judged—by everybody who was anybody in MSD.) At the front of the room was a stage with two large side-by-side screens and a podium off to one side. Directly in front of the stage was a long conference table seating ten or twelve men (yes, always all men)—key MSD execs and Navy personnel. Although I diligently attempted to avoid having to present at these meetings, it was perhaps inevitable that I was finally tapped to start delivering the data I'd gathered.

If you google "Personal Anxieties," there is one that always ranks at or near the top of every list: Public Speaking. Fortunately, my time on the Lockheed stage proved to me that I do not suffer from that fear. In the years following this very high-profile exposure at 80-20, I addressed groups as small as a handful of people and as large as 2,000 attendees of a local sci-fi convention. I've done panels and interviews in front of audiences large and small, taught classes of 10 to 100 people, and have never suffered a moment of anxiety. (I later realized that even though I *could* do live public speaking without anxiety, it was never something I enjoyed—and that my preferred medium was video, where there's always the safety net of a second take.)

DOES HUMOR BELONG IN THE WORKPLACE?
(Part 2 of a Nearly Infinite Series)

So when I was finally informed that next week was my turn in the barrel, I thought: *Yeah, I'll present. I'll public speak the shit out of that crowd.* I wasn't about to embarrass myself in front of the upper echelon of MSD—not to mention in front of my own co-workers. And so I rehearsed until I felt I was prepared, even to the point that I'd memorized the "Good Question" response. The one thing presenters were cautioned against in these meetings was attempting to bullshit the execs. If the suits asked a question we hadn't investigated, the sole acceptable response was: "Good question. I don't know, but I'll find out and get back to you." (And we were actually expected to find out and get back to them, ASAP. The Pivacek Procrastination Principle did not apply here.)

And so, like any Toastmaster graduate, on my first appearance on stage, I opened with a joke to break the ice. The presentation went well—at least, no one asked any questions. Afterward, my boss's boss approached me. "Lou DiZombie" was a tall, dark, gaunt, taciturn guy who always looked to me like a stick of beef jerky with glasses, or like an unwrapped mummy about to pass into an alcoholic coma. I knew that if he was giving feedback, I must have done something wrong, otherwise he'd never open his mouth and make the enormous effort to form an alleged thought into words. This was his decree: "Don't be funny on stage." "But, Lou," I replied, "opening with a joke to break the ice is the first lesson they teach you in any public speaking class." He considered this without blinking. "Don't be funny on stage," he said. "Lou," I said, "you might as well ask me not to breathe on stage. It's who I am. It's what I do." He pondered this with his blinkless zombie gaze. "Don't be funny on stage," he said.

Over the course of several months of presenting, I discovered a couple of hacks—workarounds to Lou's Prime Directive. One was to make a spontaneous witty comment...even if it had to be pre-arranged. Months of missiles blowing up during test launches, for instance, resulted in a massive engineering effort to determine the cause of the problem and solve it. And when the cause was finally discovered and the problem finally solved, I reported on the fix to the Friday morning crowd with a timely trope, stating that, "You don't have to be a rocket scientist to understand why... But then again, in this case, you actually *do* have to be a rocket scientist to understand what went wrong." It sounded spontaneous. It got the laugh. And it didn't land me in hot water with the boss.

I knew that if I were to—totally inadvertently, you understand—make a comic comment on stage, I needed only one person to laugh: Don Jones, VP of MSD...and the highest-ranking guy in the room. And the guy whose office I'd stop by every few weeks to tell the latest jokes. I knew what made Don laugh. And if Don laughed, everyone laughed. Even Lou. He *had* to—his boss had pre-approved the response.

I deliberately took advantage of this loophole only once. Just before the meeting began, I cornered Don Jones and said, "Hey, I got a new joke. When I get up on stage, ask me what I've heard about the stealth fighter." In 1987 or '88, Lockheed's stealth fighter had just been revealed to the public, and was a hot topic around the company. And when I took the stage and introduced myself and my topic, Don gamely interrupted, saying, "Scott, I understand you have some news about the stealth fighter?" "Yes, I do, Don," I replied. "They went looking for it last week and couldn't find it." Don laughed. So everyone laughed, following the alpha dog.

There was only one time when I totally flaunted Lou's prohibition against being funny on stage—although it didn't turn out exactly as I'd intended. April 1, 1988, was a Friday, and I was scheduled to present. But since it was April Fool's Day, I was literally incapable of passing up an opportunity to attempt some kind of gag. Such is my curse. And so, along with my standard, straight informational review, I prepared a secondary presentation—a series of slides consisting solely of phrases like, "He's lying"; "He has no idea what he's talking about"; and "Please don't tell Scott his fly is open." My intention was to display these slides on the secondary screen—the screen to my back—as I faced the primary screen containing the real data. I would assume the role of the April Fool, and everyone would be in on the joke except me.

in 1988, no one used computer-based presentations. In 1988, PowerPoint had barely been invented, and had just recently been renamed "PowerPoint." At LMSC, we used *slides*—and not 35mm slides, either, but 8-1/2 by 11-inch sheets of clear plastic, onto which our typed pages of information were xeroxed. These "vufoils" were attached to plastic frames with masking tape, and were rear-projected onto the conference room screens by a guy sitting in the backroom, following a numbered script. The presenter held a buzzer; pushing it alerted the guy sitting in a cramped room behind the stage to change the slides.

The guy who had this task of enormous skill and responsibility was Braindead Bob—a 50ish Lockheed "lifer" who'd reached the end of his limited capacity to perform any task requiring him to rub more than two brain cells together. Rather than fire Braindead Bob, his previous years of loyal service were rewarded by setting him out to pasture in 80-20, where he would patiently wait out the remainder of his worklife. Like several of the permanent 80-20 staff, he'd drifted down to the bottom of the barrel and would probably die at his desk unless someone decided it was time for him to retire.

Or unless someone decided to murder him, which I almost did on April 1, 1988. Just before my presentation, I handed Braindead Bob my stack of vufoils, and as he thumbed through them he came to the first funny foil.

"The hell is this?" he growled.

"Hey, Bob," I chuckled, "it's a gag. It's April Fool's Day, so I have a couple of funny foils in there for the second screen. It'll be hilarious."

Braindead Bob was unconvinced. Worse, he was livid, as though this was some sort of personal affront.

"You can't do this!" he yelled at me. "I won't do this! This is totally unprofessional! I'm telling Lou!" And he proceeded to remove every one of my gag slides.

There was nothing I could do. He was right, of course—and Lou DiZombie had literally prohibited me from "being funny on stage." I couldn't win this one, and my carefully planned gag was going right down the toilet. I sat in the back of the auditorium, waiting for my turn to present, stewing. How *dare* Braindead Bob tell me what I could and could not present? Who the hell was he? He wasn't the boss of me. But he was in charge of changing the displays, so if he decided to remove my slides, there was not a goddamn thing I could do about it.

Or was there? Fortunately for me, I was scheduled as the final presenter, and the meeting ran way overtime that day. I had nearly two hours to subdue my rage, recover my equilibrium... and consider my alternatives. (The first decision was that I would never again depend on prop comedy.) But goddamn it, it was April Fucking Fool's Day—the one day of the year when some goofy gag not only gets a free pass, it's expected…virtually mandatory. I was not going to let this once-in-a-life-time opportunity pass...and I was not about to let Braindead Bob dictate what I could or could not do with my alleged career.

When I took the stage, I introduced myself and my topic, as usual. But then I went off-script and addressed the audience thus: "As you might be aware, today is April Fool's Day. I had an elaborate gag ready to present to you, but at the last minute, my management deemed it inappropriate. However, since it *is* April Fool's Day, I feel compelled to engage in some kind of mischief. And so I have no choice but to deliver the rest of my presentation...in Chinese." I aimed my pointer at the first line of data, and said, *"Gung hey fat choi..."*

I didn't need to fake any additional Chinese, because the entire room burst out in laughter. They didn't even wait for Don Jones to laugh first. I'd done it. I'd pulled off my gag—not the one I wanted, but one that got the laugh I wanted to gift them.

I was in 80-20 for another year and a half, and I never spoke another word to Braindead Bob. He was not only braindead, he was dead to me as well.

FOOL FOR LUNCH

The only good thing about working in 80-20 was that once we'd delivered our Friday morning presentations, we were done for the week. Done. There was simply nothing to do until we began gathering data again the following Monday morning—except, of course, go to lunch. Often for hours. I fell in with a collegial group of three or four other yuppies in our department, and we'd most often head over to the St. James Infirmary in Mountain View. The Infirmary was a rowdy "burger & beer" joint with peanut shells littering the floor, license plates nailed to the walls, and quirky antiques (like a 12-foot Wonder Woman statue and a 19th-century hearse) hanging precariously from the ceiling. (It was also the roadhouse where my One True Love from a decade earlier had once worked, so I got a pang of heart-break every time I entered—a pang that could only be assuaged by beer. Lots of beer.)

In *Cannery Row*, John Steinbeck wrote about drinking beer, saying that the first one's for thirst, and the next one's for taste. True enough. But here's the thing about drinking beer at lunch: If you have one beer, it just washes down your food. If you have two beers, all you really want is another beer. And if you go ahead and have three beers, all you really want after that is to sit around all afternoon drinking beer.

We often did. And when we did, at some point one of us would draw the short straw and call our supervisor to let him know we were a danger on the road and would not be returning that afternoon. As an ex-alcoholic himself, he understood where we were coming from. "Have a nice weekend," was his response on those occasions, although he'd often add, "Sounds like you've already got a good start."

Chapter 13

1988: INTERMISSION
Plan A: Episode IV: A New Hope

"I laboured hard at my book … It is not my purpose, in this record, though in all other essentials it is my written memory, to pursue the history of my own fictions. … when I refer to them, incidentally, it is only as a part of my progress."
—Charles Dickens, *David Copperfield*

Although *No Plan B* is a chronicle of my work life in Silicon Valley, there are certain side stream details that require inclusion if only to indicate how they shaped the jobs I was able to attain. How does one go from being the Prince of Paperwork at a missile factory (aka, "Lord of the Files," aka "Master of Administrivia") to becoming the Movie Guru for iTunes, for instance? And so we take this brief sideways excursion to detail a few of the activities outside the corporate universe in which I was engaged at that time—activities that ultimately altered the trajectory of my corporate career.

My original plan on hiring into LMSC, for instance—call it Plan A-Prime, if you wish (but please, not Plan A-Minus)—was to use Lockheed as a resource, not as a career. The plan was to work at a high rate of pay for three or four years, during which time I would diligently save up enough cash to support myself to write full-time for a year or two, and by which time, I assumed, I'd have sold at least one novel and landed contracts for one or two more, to keep the momentum going, keep the money coming in, and make the writing career self-sustaining. But by 1984, the exact opposite was occurring: I was hooked on the massive missile moolah, for one thing...and I'd made precisely zero progress on selling any of my fiction. I was still committed to Plan A, however; still writing evenings and weekends (and, whenever possible, at work). By 1988, I had four novels, two non-fiction books, two screenplays...and a file cabinet drawer full of rejection slips.

I knew I'd never be happy in 80-20. Or at LMSC. Or in the corporate world at all. I knew I didn't belong there and probably couldn't fool them forever. I needed an escape route, and Plan A was simply not happening—not to mention that I'd fallen into the trap of having a few dollars for the first time in my life, and was not willing to give that up. And what did I do with the few dollars? I bought a new car! I got a girlfriend who liked dinners out and weekend getaways! How could I give up an enviably easy job and go back to being a starving artist—particularly when no one whatsoever was interested in my alleged art?

I thought I'd found a loophole in the situation when I applied for a position that required a Top Secret clearance. I was informed that a clearance at this level often took a year or more to research and approve; during that time, I'd be assigned to a special unit called "The Icebox," full of people waiting for their clearances...with *no work assignments*. People in this position often went berserk, I was cautioned: one employee reportedly keyboarded the entire Bible onto computer disks during his period of suspended animation, for instance. But I chomped at the bit. An entire year to work on my novels while being paid the same big nuclear bucks? What could be better than Federally subsidized fiction? I thought I could absolutely turboboost my career if I had the twin resources of time and money.

Alas, I did not get the job. The supervisor was afraid I was "just too darn talented" and that I'd leave the position as soon as I attained my destined fame...or at least got published. A few years later, when I was still at LMSC, I resisted the temptation to call him and report that I was *still* unpublished and *still* at Lockheed, and ask him, "Who's too darn talented *now*, asshole?"

BIRTH OF A NOTION: PLAN A-PLUS

So there I was, stuck in a shit job in the bowels of Lockheed, and developing my own neurotic psychopathology (call it a military-industrial complex). In the summer of 1984, however, inspiration struck. VCRs had been around for about seven years, and hundreds of video rental stores both large and small had sprung up like mushrooms as VCR ownership in U.S. homes grew at the rate of a million a month, or about ten percent per year.

(Did you know anyone in the late '80s who *didn't* own a VCR?) I knew I could never break into the "movie critic" brotherhood... but I thought that perhaps I knew enough about movies to write about movies and related material released on video.

I sent a query letter to the Arts & Entertainment editor at the San Jose *Mercury News*, Silicon Valley's largest newspaper, with this opening line: "Everyone reviews videos. Who reviews video stores?" I pitched an article in which I'd list the best video stores in the Valley in several categories: largest stock, best prices, best special offers, and so on. Lee Grant, the section editor, liked the idea and gave me the green light. And in August 1984, I became a published writer when the *Merc* ran my piece —on the front page of the Friday Entertainment section, no less.

I must have made an impression of some sort on Lee, as he invited me in to discuss additional articles. I pitched him several ideas, and we decided on a version of the "desert island disks" trope; in this case, the ten movies currently available on video that one would want to have if stranded on a desert island (a desert island which, it seems, also had electricity, a VCR and a TV set...but I digress). The piece—another front-page feature article—ran in January 1985. And the ball was rolling.

March 1985

Lee Grant asked me to come in to discuss future features—and something more. He showed me a column on new video releases that had just started running in the Los Angeles *Times*. Lee wanted something similar for the *Merc* and asked if I'd be interested in writing it on a freelance basis. Well, duh. A few weeks later, I became the Video Columnist for the San Jose *Mercury News*, with a Friday column that would run for over ten years—532 consecutive weekly columns.

About the same time, I noticed a tiny entry in the daily gossip column written by another of the *Merc*'s columnists, Leigh Weimers. The entry mentioned a vanity license plate owned by a local restauranteur: KAR120C—the license plate of the Lotus driven by Patrick McGoohan's character in the classic 1968 TV series *The Prisoner*. I was intrigued, as I owned an almost identical license plate, precisely because it belonged to my TV role model. Leigh (who would become a friend during the next decade) went on to mention that KTEH-TV, the PBS station for Silicon Valley, would be airing the series in a month or so.

The Prisoner was perhaps the single biggest influence on my life at that point. I loved the show. I collected articles about it and—long before VCRs became available—audiotaped episodes and transcribed key scenes for my own reference. I would discover that the series had a huge cult following worldwide—at one time, second only to the cult following of *Star Trek*. I knew I had to be a part of any broadcast on my home turf, and I knew how to sell myself to whoever was in charge of the show when it aired on KTEH.

Flashback: In 1977, when *The Prisoner* was first syndicated to PBS (where it always belonged in the first place), San Francisco's PBS station, KQED, had aired it. Since the show was originally broadcast on network TV (CBS), each episode ran only about 51 minutes once the commercials were removed. So PBS had about nine minutes of airtime to fill when airing each episode. KQED held panel discussions hosted by a genial hippie named Stan Tenen. I was his most frequent guest. I figured that this credential, plus my uber-geek scrapbook of articles and transcriptions, might impress whoever was in charge at KTEH.

I called the station and set up a meeting with Danny McGuire, the producer who oversaw the show's broadcasts on KTEH. I showed him a tape of my KQED appearances and my *Prisoner* scrapbook full of articles and transcripts. I casually mentioned that I'd just been appointed Video Columnist for the *Merc*. He decided we should shoot some wraparounds, or "wraps," for local broadcast: a minute or so at the front end of each episode, to introduce it, and a seven- or eight-minute segment following each episode, where I could discuss themes, production details, trivia, cast bios, and so on. I'd write and host; Danny would do everything else. (Nearly four decades after this initial collaboration, this remains one of my favorite projects, and Danny remains one of my closest friends.)

There was a period when I was working for LMSC's Government Security Training during the day then driving out to KTEH one afternoon a week to shoot these "wraparounds" for *The Prisoner*. By day, I created material intended to browbeat employees into following anally strict government security procedures; by night, I encouraged viewers to think for themselves and never to trust any secretive, oppressive government. One *Prisoner* episode is entitled "The Schizoid Man," and I realized: *This is me*. How could I reconcile the fact that by day I was a member of the military-industrial complex's Government Security Training while by night I appeared on the liberal mass media biting the hand that literally fed me by denouncing the very institutions that signed my paycheck? This dual life did not make me crazy, however—it did little more than provide me endless amusement…and revealed to me my high tolerance for ambiguity. The punchline to this potential conflict of interests is this: no one at Lockheed ever noticed that I led a double life.

(I was even more amused by this Janus-faced irony than I had been during the summer of 1969, when *The Prisoner* was being broadcast a second time and I spent most days working at Frontier Village...or as we referred to it, "The Village.")

So now I was the Video Columnist for the "paper of record" of Silicon Valley, and the host of a classic TV series on Silicon Valley's PBS station. And if this weren't enough, I made a deal with the San Francisco *Examiner* to write a monthly feature article on a theme of my choice about movies on video. (I could hardly know that a couple of decades later I'd be working once again for the publisher of the *Examiner*.)

My writing career was taking off—but hardly in the manner or direction I'd imagined. And—sorry to say—not in any financial manner that could even come close to the Big Bucks I was still pulling in at Lockheed. Even adding up the checks from four columns and two feature articles a month amounted to less than a week's worth of nuclear bucks. And—spoiler alert —this side career of freelance writing about movies never paid off in any financial manner remunerative enough that it would allow me to exit the corporate world (although an active freelance career did help tide me over in times of unemployment).

As I mentioned, these are side stream stories, briefly noted, and included here to indicate the roots of future developments, as my freelance writing career would later significantly alter—and become integrated into—my Silicon Valley startup life.

We now return to our narrative, which is already in progress.

Chapter 14

1989: LOCKHEED MISSILES & SPACE CO. PART II

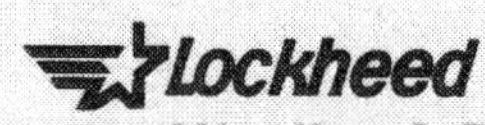

Missiles & Space Company, Inc.

D. Scott Apel
Writer/Director
Video/Film Productions

Orgn. 19-52, Bldg. 534
151 Gibralter Ct., Sunnyvale, CA 94089-3504
(408) 742-3410

1989: LOCKHEED MISSILES & SPACE CO. PART II

July 1989

PLAN A REVISITED (AND REVISED)

I'd been in the status reporting group of LMSC for four interminable years. My workload was minor and I'd spent as much office time as I could get away with concentrating on growing my freelance writing business. I was writing feature articles on film and video on a regular basis for two national magazines, *Video* and *Video Review*, as well as for the San Jose *Mercury News* and numerous other newspapers nationwide, from Alabama to Alaska.

I knew that the key to independence from the corporate world was to syndicate my weekly video column. If I could just get it into even fifty newspapers at the low, low, bargain-basement price of just ten dollars a week each, I'd be matching my Lockheed salary and could quit. A few hours' work per week would equal my salary...and give me six days a week to work on Plan A: my fiction. All attempts at syndication had come to naught, however. My freelancing work was making me an extra few hundred bucks a month, which was nice...but nothing close to that nuclear detonation-sized Lockheed paycheck.

In the meantime, I was stuck in 80-20, with no skills to buy my way into another position. The only way I could figure to get out of 80-20 was to leave Lockheed altogether, which presented its own set of problems: What job skills did I possess, for instance, beyond what I'd picked up at Lockheed—which was essentially nothing? Wherever could I go to make this much money for knowing as little as I knew and doing as little as I did? And what kind of job could I get except, perhaps, a similar position—still pushing paperwork, just at a different company? And so I muddled along, trying to figure out some way to cut this frustrating Gordian knot.

DESTINY CALLS (COLLECT)

And then one day I got a call from Lorin Fink, the Supervisor of the Video/Film department of LMSC's Information Services division. (*Note:* As mentioned earlier in *No Plan B*, throughout this book I've used the real names of people who were helpful to my alleged career, and changed the names of the bastards who sabotaged it. But what do I do about a guy who eventually did both? I'll leave it as an exercise for the reader to determine whether "Lorin Fink" was in fact his real name or a comically appropriate pseudonym, since his eventual role in my career was as a Rat Fink.)

This wasn't the first time I'd heard from Lorin. A year or so earlier, when he discovered I was the Video Columnist for the *Merc*, he called me up and asked if I could perhaps promote the teddy bear videos he was producing and selling as a side gig. I occasionally wrote columns about the local film and video scene, so I was more than happy to accommodate him. This call, however, was a vice versa: he wanted to do something for me. Would I be interested in writing a short script for his department? Of course I would. In those days, I turned down no opportunity. (I even ended up at one point interviewing Nancy Kwan, who'd starred in the 1961 film *Flower Drum Song*, but whose career since then mostly consisted of Hong Kong action flicks and guest star roles on TV shows like *Hawaii 5-0, Wonder Woman, Kung Fu* and *The A-Team*. Less than stellar, clearly. But I still took the assignment, if only because—as Phil says in *Groundhog Day*—"Anything different is good.")

I don't have any recollection what the script was about. But it must have passed muster, because soon afterward, Lorin asked if I'd like to transfer to his Video/Film Department as a writer. My first thought was: *There is a God, and Lorin Fink is his prophet.* I told him I'd think about it, and suggested we talk again. Soon.

We talked. I agreed to the transfer. Years later, I'd hear the Dalai Lama say, "I can't reach down into the Hell Worlds and pull someone up." Maybe he can't. But clearly Lorin Fink could, because he did it for me.

It's important to this narrative to note precisely why Lorin wanted me on his team: not just for my writing skills, which he'd followed through my newspaper column and articles, but also specifically for my sense of humor. "Industrial videos are mostly just boring," he told me. "Your job is to spice them up with some humor."

I had, at that juncture, no idea of the tribulations and agitation that fulfilling this mandate would rain down upon me.

I COACH A TEAM OF ONE

Another side stream—but stay with me; it does pay off.

When my younger sister Gail became pregnant with her first child in 1981, she wanted to do "natural childbirth," with her husband as her birthing coach. But her hubby Richard worked for PG&E, the Northern California power company, and at that time he was assigned to a field project more than two hours drive away. PG&E would bus the employees up to the site every Monday morning, where they'd work and live in camps until they were bussed back home to Silicon Valley on Friday afternoon. The upshot is that Richard would not be around to take the Lamaze childbirth classes—and couldn't even guarantee he could rush back home in time to coach my sister when she went into labor. She gave this some thought and decided she wanted her big brother to be her coach. I was flattered and honored that she chose me—and since I didn't plan on ever having a family myself, I knew this was my one shot at ever participating in one of life's major events: childbirth.

So we went through the birth-coaching class together. The other couples found it very amusing that we were brother and sister (after they realized that it was not me who got her pregnant, at any rate). And when the time came, she gave birth to the first member of the next generation of our family: a son, Anthony. (Since then I have delighted in occasionally warning my nephew with artificial irritation, "I brought you *into* this world, and I can *take you out of it!")* And even though Richard was around when my sister became pregnant again a few years later, he asked if I would be her coach once again. "You know how I am around blood," he confided. That time I coached her into giving birth to my niece, Jamie.

By my sister's third pregnancy, in 1989, no one even asked or wondered: we all simply assumed I'd be her coach. After all, we'd proven ourselves to be a winning team. "Just one rule," I joked to Gail. "Do *not* give birth on August 14th, because that's my first day at my new job." And we both laughed.

August 14, 1989

When the phone rang at 3 AM, I knew immediately what was happening. I raced to the hospital where my sister was in labor and where the family had gathered. And while I was coaching her to "Breathe! Breathe! Now push! *Push*!" I glanced up at the clock. 7 AM. I was supposed to be reporting for my first day at my new job at that exact minute. Two thoughts passed through my preoccupied mind. The first was that my new boss, Lorin Fink, would probably be pretty irritated when I didn't show up and didn't even bother to call. ("And he seemed so excited about the position," I could hear him muttering under his breath.) My second thought: I have the world's greatest excuse for not showing up or even calling.

A couple of hours later, once my beautiful niece Valerie was born and everyone's excitement had turned to exhaustion, I found a payphone and rang Lorin.

"We were expecting you hours ago," he said. "Where are you?"

I played my trump card: "I'm in the hospital," I exclaimed. But then I told him why—not because I was ill, but because I was coaching a birth.

"Well, we'll see you tomorrow then, I guess," Lorin said.

Free pass!

VIDEO/FILM

August 15, 1989

He guessed right. After we had a good laugh about the previous day's unscheduled event, Lorin showed me around the

Video/Film Production building on Gibraltar Court, a cul-de-sac a couple of blocks from the main campus. The department was housed in its own standalone, two-story building specifically designed for film and video production. The layout included a large, two-story studio and editing bays on the first floor. The second floor was devoted to offices, a big conference room, a kitchen and a bullpen.

Lorin had arranged a desk for me in a small office I would share with Tom Conrad, one of the other writers. Tom was in his late 50s and looked like the cartoon Droopy Dog with Einstein's hair. I began to think of him as possibly the most informed man on the planet, since he read every page of at least three newspapers every day. We got along just fine as roomies, however; he kept a radio tuned low to the classical station, which I found soothing...as well as an inadvertent source of humor, as when, for instance, they ran an endorsement of a local antique store by a woman who praised them for "restoring a piece I got on my honeymoon."

Video/Film had about 25 employees at that time, and would expand to include more than 35 people, all locked away in our own building. The mix of people ran the gamut from ultraconservative to my end of the spectrum, the crazy-ass, troublemaking creative types. (Guess which end of the spectrum caused trouble later. Wrong.) Somewhere in the normal middle was Steve, the quiet editor who had a two-hour commute each way... and who would continue to make that commute for the next *25 years*. There was Ruth, a slender editor with a British accent who classed up the joint, and her co-editor, Bruce, a big "bear" gay guy with a snarky attitude. There were a couple of computer animation guys, but they had their own room and didn't hang out much with the rest of us. There was Ken, the enormous videographer who, even in his 60s, rode his bike to work every day and ate sardines directly from the tin, so he smelled like sweat and fish all day...but he was too nice a guy for anyone to confront him about this. Then there was Bill, a writer/ producer/ director who insisted on doing his own camera work. He scoffed at tripods to the point where we referred to his technique as "unsteadycam." (Bill was also adamant that escalators were stairs to be walked up, not elevators to stand on. Takes all kinds.)

I quickly fell in with my favorite crowd, the videographers —Curt Brown, Mike Weaver and Dave "Davo" Lee—all three of whom have remained close friends to this day. Since they are all still close friends, I find it uncomfortable describing or dissecting them here, although mentioning them occasionally is unavoidable.

My early days in Video/Film were kind of a blur—mostly of boredom rather than overactivity. I wrote a few scripts, refined my alleged style, and reviewed some earlier videos the department had produced. Lorin was right—they were a drag. I kept my eyes open for an opportunity to write a script that might hold peoples' interest by amusing them.

AN EARTHSHAKING DEVELOPMENT, BUT NOT CAREER-WISE

October 17, 1989

I'd only been on the job a couple of months when the Loma Prieta earthquake hit the Bay Area. I walked into my apartment a little after 5 PM that day and tossed my briefcase on the hall table. And the table began to shake. I thought immediately of Bullwinkle's line: "Don't know mah own strenth"—until the entire apartment started shaking. As a California native, I knew immediately that this was an earthquake. I'd laughed through many quakes as strong as 5.4 on the Richter scale, so I just stood in the hallway, waiting for the shivering to stop.

But it didn't stop. Instead, it got worse—bad enough for long enough that I did something I'd never before done in an earthquake: I stepped into a doorway for protection. And still it shook —a waving, rolling motion that had the entire apartment building swaying. I watched, slack-jawed, as the walls listed in one direction and cabinet doors on one side of the kitchen swung open, spitting out cans and bottles, at which point the building swayed in the opposite direction, and cabinet doors on the opposite side of the kitchen swung open and tossed out more cans and bottles. I looked behind me, into my bedroom, which doubled as a home office, and saw my precious Macintosh computer "walking" toward the edge of the desk—at which point I gave up any thought of personal safety and moved from the doorway to grab the 'puter and save it from crashing to the floor.

Eventually, the shaking stopped. I could hear car alarms going off all over the apartment complex. I estimated that—given what I'd observed with the cabinets and the computer—about a minute had elapsed. I later discovered the quake lasted a mere 15 seconds. I still don't believe that it was over that quickly—I know what I experienced, and how long it took for everything I saw to occur.

The Loma Prieta quake was felt—and did damage—from its origin point, near Santa Cruz, about 35 miles to the south of the Valley, all the way to San Francisco, about 75 miles to the north. It was originally estimated to be a 7.1, although it was later downgraded to a 6.9. But if that was a 6.9, I don't ever want to feel a 10—or even a 7.1, for that matter. I'd lived in Northern California for nearly 30 years by then, and Loma Prieta is still the largest (and only scary) quake I've ever experienced.

I was lucky: nothing broke. But naturally, the power went out. I used the adrenaline rush to help my neighbor clean up and to pick up the stuff that had spilled out of my own cabinets and littered the kitchen. I found a few candles and a flashlight. And I had an advantage over everyone else whose power was out: I owned a tiny, battery-powered TV set—a plastic cube about two inches on a side, with a screen that measured about an inch and a half per side. I settled in to eat some ice cream (so it didn't melt in the non-functioning freezer) and watch the news. Clearly, power was out in many locations, since only one channel was broadcasting. But KRON did a great job of covering what they knew, what they found out, and of soothing their shaken (um, sorry) viewers. They even provided us with helicopter video footage of the burning neighborhoods in San Francisco and the collapsed segment of the Bayshore Freeway.

WHAT KIND OF COMPANY WAS LMSC TO WORK FOR? *Part 1*

Once the extent of the damage was pretty well known and reported, KRON began broadcasting information they'd received about closures for the following day. Federal government offices from San Francisco to Santa Cruz: Closed. State government offices: Closed. County and city government offices for all nearby counties: Closed. They listed each school district in the Bay Area; all closed the following day. And they listed information they'd received about major businesses: IBM: Closed. Hewlett-Packard: Closed. Kaiser Permanente: Closed. Lockheed: Open.

Whoa—what? "Lockheed: OPEN"? Every government office, school, and business in a 75-mile radius would be closed. But "Lockheed: OPEN"? Mother*fuckers!*

Being a good corporate serf, I dutifully showed up to work the following morning (after driving through less traffic congestion than I'd ever seen before or since). Posted on the front door of our building was a note from Facilities instructing us to: 1) enter the building with caution; 2) check for damage; 3) report any damage, and if there was none, then 4) get to work, goddamn it. (I added that "goddamn it," but it was certainly implied.) I found it annoyingly ironic that this company whose sole mission was to protect the citizens of America did not consider its own employees worth protecting.

Turns out the joke was on Lockheed. Even though we all showed up, not a single molecule of work was accomplished during the rest of the week. Our closed building, with its contingent of 30 or so people, turned into a giant exercise in group therapy, as every one of us exchanged detailed stories with everyone else in the building about what we experienced—over and over again. Several of us were so committed to our therapy sessions that we even continued them after work at a local pub over pitchers of beer. (These liquid therapy sessions lasted for several months—long after the earthquake was forgotten.)

This inconsiderate attitude toward employees was hardly an isolated incident. In February 1988, for example, a disgruntled ex-employee of a company named ESL entered his old building, which was located across the street from a complex of Lockheed buildings. Armed to the teeth, he shot and killed seven people and wounded four others, then held a SWAT team at bay for five hours before surrendering.

My mother was working in a Lockheed building across the street at the time. She told me that word came down from Management that she and her co-workers would be allowed to leave the building and go home...but The Company would not be not responsible if any of the employees who chose to leave were shot in the parking lot when exiting. What a swell corporation!

IN WHICH I BECOME A FILMMAKER (OF SORTS)

I'd only been on the job a few months when Supervisor Fink decided the current producers had too much work and that I should become a writer/producer rather than just a writer. Fine by me (although the new job description did not come with a raise or a promotion). My trial run was a rather dull interview film in which I failed to get enough coverage to mask some awkward transitions. I learned then to shoot a lot of extra video —what the heck; it's cheap—in case something needed to be saved in the editing room or in post-production. This became my prime rule in producing video: *All's well that posts well.*

I learned other valuable lessons with my first efforts as well. For instance: no one wants to sit through an industrial video longer than seven minutes. And if you can get people to walk away remembering even *one point* made in a video presentation, you've fulfilled your mission. (If they remember two points, you can be assured you've created something incredible.)

IN WHICH I ATTAIN THE ULTIMATE CORPORATE GOAL (KIND OF)

Sometime in 1990, with the addition of new personnel, the Video/Film office space was reorganized. I bid a fond farewell to my roommate Tom and was relocated into a cubicle in the corner of the second-floor maze of cubicles, next to a window overlooking our main stage on the first floor.

So I'd finally attained the corporate goal of a corner office with a window—but not exactly as the cliché was understood.

WHAT KIND OF COMPANY WAS LMSC TO WORK FOR? *Part 2*

In January 1991, I—well, I guess the word is "celebrated"— my tenth year at Lockheed. As a ten-year anniversary gift I received an LMSC "shooting star logo" lapel pin with a diamond chip embedded in it—it took a jeweler's loupe to find it—and a certificate of congratulations. On which my name was misspelled. Keep up the good work, D.S. Apex!

IN WHICH I BECOME A SERIAL KILLER (KINDA SORTA)

A confusion of identities became more than just a punch line in October 1991, when I received a letter from the California EDD (Employment Development Department) that had been sent to LMSC's personnel division then forwarded to me. The letter informed us—Lockheed and me—that due to an error, my Social Security number had been assigned to another person. The name of the person my SSN had been reassigned to rung a bell. And a bit of research indicated that this particular guy had recently murdered his wife and children and was currently imprisoned for life. And he had my Social Security number. OK…

The letter further indicated to LMSC that "your employee *is the true holder* of that SSN" (emphasis theirs)—but went on to say that even so, I—the *true holder* of that SSN—would be held responsible for any illegal activity committed by the other guy. Uhh… OK?

The bottom line is that nothing untoward ever occurred, so it's just a frivolous anecdote rather than a career-destroying tragedy. But since this letter was a *form letter*, with blank spaces to fill in the names, it did make me wonder just how often this kind of potentially life-destroying accident occurs. Clearly, it occurred often enough that the state had a form letter to address the issue.

"LEELOO DALLAS, MULTI-PASS"

As early as 1991, once I felt like I had some rudimentary handle on what I was doing as a writer/producer/director, I realized that a seismic shift had occurred in my work life: I didn't hate coming to work anymore. It took 20 years, but I finally had a job I actually liked...sometimes.

One reason was the atmosphere. The Video/Film Department was "a band apart" in several ways, unlike most other units in this massive, conservative corporation. We worked for the entire company, for one thing, including the Space division of Lockheed Missiles and Space, so some of the guilt I felt about supporting the production of nuclear missiles was assuaged: we made movies, not missiles. We had our own separate building as well, and treated it like an asylum, in both senses of the word. (My co-worker Davo told us he'd overheard one of our more conservative customers refer to us as "that bunch of free-thinkers," for instance—as though that was an insult.)

And we had carte blanche—a *Fifth Element*-style "Multi-Pass" (even though that movie would not be released until a few years later)—to go virtually anywhere Lockheed operated if we had an assignment there, from the office of the President to various secret programs in locked buildings. We shot video in engineering buildings, in massive factory spaces, in enormous satellite cleanroom facilities and in executive offices. We shot from helicopters and at the secret explosives testing facility in the Santa Cruz Mountains (where we were actually snowed on). One of my co-workers wrote a show that featured an amusement park ride; half a dozen of us volunteered to appear in the show and spent the day riding Great America's newest ride, over and over again, without ever getting off or standing in line, *wheee!*

We shot at the Kennedy Space Center at Cape Canaveral, recording the landing of a Space Shuttle ferried from California on the back of a 747, and we shot in the enormous Vertical Assembly Building, the world's tallest single-story building. We shot in NASA's Mission Control in Houston, something even Ron Howard didn't do (he built his own clone of Mission Control for *Apollo 13*). In December 1992, we were tasked with ushering the President of LMSC, the avuncular, pixie-ish John McMahon, around the campus as he spread holiday cheer among the troops. He was fun to hang out with, although the entire day reminded me of an old *Playboy* cartoon that depicted a chest-puffed executive striding through a sea of desks, announcing to the workers, "Keep up the good work, whatever it is, whoever you are."

DOES HUMOR BELONG IN THE WORKPLACE?
(Part 3 of a Nearly Infinite Series)

After cutting my teeth on a few simple, low-profile shows, I decided to step up and Release the Beast, aka my alleged sense of humor. It was, after all, my mandate. A medley of the hits I produced during the next couple of years includes:

* My college recruiting film, which LMSC reps would show on college campuses to convince the "best and brightest" to hire into Lockheed when they graduated. This show opened with a short segment entitled "The Job Interview From Hell," in which a fresh-faced young interviewee is subjected to an interrogation by a trio of horrid corporate cogs. Mike Weaver filmed the segment on a darkened stage with ample Kubrickian bottom lighting and clouds of floor-level smoke to give the entire set a sinister, hellish ambiance. The trio of interrogators included Dave Lee as an uber-nerd, dressed in a sweater vest and bow tie, his hair parted in the middle, who whined the line "Why should we hire you?" over and over again. Supervisor Fink assaulted the candidate with questions like "What does your father do? What does your mother do?" while I, as a belligerent and bellicose boss in a forest green leisure suit, stabbed my cigar at the kid while pelting him with a series of absurd questions: "What's the square root of pi? What's the infield fly rule? Who wrote the book of love?" We verbally assaulted the candidate simultaneously until his head exploded. (For the record, this show won me an award from the National Merit Scholarship Corporation. So less than a year after I began producing videos, I was competing for—and winning—the same honors as my peers, some of whom had been doing this for over twenty years.)

* A sales pitch for a Lockheed "secure" telephone opened with an illustration of the ultimate *non*-secure phone: a series of scratchy black-and-white shots of people outfitted in 1920s costumes listening in on an antique hand-crank wall phone's "party line" while a distressed wife detailed the misadventures of her drunken husband "down at the licensed saloon."

* An instructional video about Computer Security opened with an illustration of what would happen on a real-world scale if people were as lax about security as they were about securing their computer. Mr. Doofus (me again, in my forest green leisure suit and white belt—which turned out to be a great investment as a costume—as well as Eisenhower-era glasses held together by tape) leaves his house unlocked, leaves his car unlocked, and yells his password to his wife at the ATM, among other "security" violations.

* For a show about where paychecks come from, I wrote and produced "Farewell, My Paycheck" in a film noir style. When a worker drone (me) is distressed that his paycheck is not delivered by the departmental secretary (played by our departmental secretary), a '40s era P.I. (superbly played by our departmental scheduler, Dave Whaley) is brought in to investigate. This was my homage not only to Raymond Chandler but also to *Dragnet*. My favorite line is when the P.I. introduces himself in voice-over: "My name is Thursday. I carry a badge," as he clips his Lockheed employee badge to his trench coat. But the line that always got the biggest audience laugh occurs as the private eye interviews the supervisor of the Accounting Division (played, in brilliant typecasting, by the supervisor of the Accounting Division). When this "money maven" explains how the differences in pay grade, hours, and various deductions factor into an employee's pay, he informs the detective that "every paycheck is unique," to which the private eye deadpans, "Like snowflakes, sir?" But I gave myself the final line of the film: When the P.I. finds the missing check and delivers it to the distressed worker drone (me, in brilliant typecasting), I sigh, "You know the really ironic thing? It's already spent." Cue the *Dragnet* sting and fade to black.

* In the early 1990s, most major corporations were dedicated to trying new theories of management, in part to boost productivity in our war against the rising Japanese economy of the '80s. One such program that Lockheed adopted was called TQM: Total Quality Management. (As Jeff's gruff boss at the time growled, "We don't need TQM. All we need is GFM: *Good*

Fuckin' Management.") I was tasked with creating a video that explained the key components of the program to our workforce. Rather than produce a dry, didactic tutorial, I wrote a script entitled "The Quality Café," in which a quartet of Lockheed employees exits a lecture on TQM, all confused and with many questions. They go to lunch to discuss their concerns. At the Quality Café, they are served by a waitress who exhibits all the main concepts of the program—things like "anticipating the customer's needs" by delivering a glass of water just before one of the diners asks for one; "correcting mistakes immediately," by returning a dish no one ordered; and the "value-added" aspect by comping them a dessert because of the delay in getting their lunch. Dave Lee (in brilliant typecasting) played the clueless dork who didn't grasp any of these points until they were (often literally) shoved right in front of his face; Norman Leigh (who will be introduced later) played the wise old employee (one-third anti-typecasting) who was the first to recognize that the waitress embodied the details of TQM; the lovely Stacey, a "friend of the department," played the tack-sharp female lead (in brilliant typecasting); and I cast myself as the smartass idiot who delighted in teasing the others and missing the point (OK, I admit it—typecasting). My favorite line was when Stacey cautioned me to "quit acting like such a baby." When I responded, "Hey, I'm 39 years old," she shot back, "Yeah, but you're as much trouble as 13 three-year-olds."

Watching this video nearly 30 years later, I am struck by the fact that everyone moves the "plot" forward except me, who does nothing but crack jokes. Brilliant typecasting...and a prime example of my motto from a decade earlier: "Subverting the system from the inside since 1980."

* For an update on LMSC's research on Artificial Intelligence, I created a video that took place a hundred years in the future, in which crazy, wild-haired scientist Eli (that would be me, channeling *Back to the Future*'s Doc Brown) reports to his supervisor—a talking teddy bear—on the early days of AI research being performed by Lockheed's R&D lab in Palo Alto. I took a popular toy of the time, Teddy Ruxpin (a rudimentary audio-animatronic teddy bear whose mouth moved in synch with

a storytelling audiotape inserted in his back), dressed him up with a pair of glasses, a lab coat and a goatee, and dubbed the voice so he'd appear to be having a conversation with his assistant (me). At the end, when "Dr. Theodore" gives his assistant a condescending "A for Effort" on his research, an irritated Eli turns to the camera and whispers to the viewer, "We should never have given them the vote!" (FYI: Yes, Lockheed was indeed researching AI in the early '90s, long before it became smarter than humans and enslaved all Humankind, if you're reading this anytime after 2049 A.D.)

* One non-comic show I produced concerned an Assured Crew Return Vehicle (ACRV) proposed for the International Space Station. The mushroom-shaped ship would attach to the exterior of the ISS; in a medical emergency, an injured crew member could be loaded aboard and shot back to earth for treatment. Illustrating how this "lifeboat" would be used posed a challenge, namely that the crew in the ISS is weightless—and I was budgetless. A lovely engineer on the ACRV program and I donned blue jumpsuits and a dead-serious demeanor as we "floated" the unconscious "injured" crewmember through Lockheed's mockup of one corridor of the ISS and loaded him into an on-site, life-size mockup the rescue vehicle (constructed mainly of plywood). Ultimately, I wove together live-action, computer graphic animation, and NASA footage into a short show about how the proposed vehicle would be used. The final video was shown to Congress (but the ACRV was never built).

All told, during my four years in LMSC's Video/Film department, I would produce over 100 programs. The above are a few of the most memorable—to me, anyway.

AN AWARD-WINNING VIDEO PRODUCER…OR NOT

The previous year, in my capacity as Video Columnist for the *Mercury News*, I'd been invited to be a judge for the San Jose Film and Video Commission's "Joey" Awards, and when Joe O'Kane, the founder and President, discovered I wrote and produced videos, he suggested I submit my best work in the

Corporate Video category the following year. It wasn't until the final day submissions would be accepted that I decided this ACRV show was worth a shot and submitted it with literally minutes to spare. I submitted the paperwork to clear the show for public viewing to LMSC's Legal department the following week and they approved it.

The day before the Joey Awards were to be announced, I got an angry call from Legal demanding that I withdraw the show from the competition since I hadn't requested clearance until after I'd submitted it. "But you cleared it," I replied, "like, two days later."

"Yeah, but not until *after* you'd submitted it, which violates procedure," the legal eagle replied. "So you have to pull it from the competition."

There was no way around this, so I called my contact at the Commission and explained the situation.

"Are you sure you want to withdraw it?" she asked.

"Well, no, I don't *want* to withdraw it," I explained. "I *have* to withdraw it. I've been *ordered* to withdraw it."

"Are you *sure*?" she repeated. Now I was getting irritated. It was bad enough that I was being forced to withdraw the show from competition against my will. How many times did I have to argue with people about it? Before I could respond, however, she continued in a whisper, "If you withdraw it, we're gonna have to change the name on the First Place statuette."

Oh, fuck me. I'd won. I'd won the award, but I couldn't accept it. It's not like I placed any value on external trivia like awards. But I'd *won* the award, goddamn it, and I *could not accept it!*

Fucking Lockheed! Fucking lawyers!

IN WHICH I AM SENT INTO ORBIT

Another incident concerning this program seemed almost to counterbalance the frustration of winning an award but being prevented from accepting it. A year or so after I finished this show, our Video/Film unit had a visit from one of the Skylab astronauts—Joe Kerwin, who at that time was the American astronaut who had spent the most time in space. I'd met him on a work trip to Houston a few months earlier, when we were shooting a different show in Mission Control. He told me he specifically wanted to look me up when he was in Sunnyvale to ask me how I got such realistic zero-G effects. I had to laugh. "Those were my zero-budget zero-G effects," I confessed. "We laid the unconscious astronaut on top of a rolling garbage can, hidden from the camera, so it looked like he was floating horizontally. And the woman and I just faked weightlessness by moving in slow-motion and bobbing gently up and down." To this day, I consider his amazement as one of the highest compliments I've ever received.

IN WHICH I AM SPEECHLESS

The show I am most proud of, however, is one I would nominate into any competition for Weirdest Industrial Video of All Time (and I'd probably win, but would be barred from accepting the award). When the Director of Facilities came to us to produce a short film about what his division did, he specifically requested that it be funny...so naturally, I drew the assignment. "I've been told I don't have a sense of humor," he confessed to me in our initial interview, "so I'm going to leave it up to you as to what you want to do." Miracle of miracles: I'd been given a blank check to create whatever I wanted. I'd found the Golden Ticket. I heard the angels singing.

"Trust me," I told him, smiling.

What I finally landed on was very simple. Mr. Facilities Director would perch on the edge of a desk in an office setting and introduce himself and the presentation. As a stagehand rolled in a monitor on a cart beside him, he'd explain that since his topic was rather dry, he'd invited a guest to help illustrate his points: "the famous French mime, Jacqueaux." Enter Jacqueaux on the monitor: a classic mime in white face, black tights, and black-and-white striped shirt. (This, of course, was me—I didn't trust anyone else to give the precisely-timed comic performance this gag demanded.) The Director began listing the duties for which his department was responsible, like new construction, which the mime illustrated by air-hammering and air-sawing, or "developing budgets for future construction and maintenance," which Jacqueaux demonstrated by punching keys on an invisible adding machine, pulling the handle, and scanning the invisible paper tape. So far so good. But eventually, the departmental tasks began to include items like, "assessing future requirements for continued expansion"—leaving Jacqueaux at a loss. As the Director rambled along through his list of increasingly esoteric functions ("creating forecasting strategies for various alternative Facilities scenarios"), poor Jacqueaux just stopped dead in his tracks. From the monitor, he looked at the Director, looked at the audience, gestured toward the Director, and shrugged in the exaggerated body language of mimes to express his "WTF?" confusion. The more intangible the list of activities became, the more irked poor Jacqueaux grew, until he finally just waved the Director off in frustrated disgust and began performing classic mime routines like "Trapped in a Box," "Tug-o'-War," and "Walking Against the Wind." And at some point, Jacqueaux just gave up altogether and lumbered ungracefully off-screen.

I considered this my masterpiece: a cascading comedy unlike anything I'd ever seen in any industrial video. And be honest with yourself: if you were a wage slave at a soul-crushing, megalithic corporation and were ordered to stop working and attend a seminar about (insert the Business Trend Of The Week here), wouldn't your stomach drop, and maybe even reflux a little? Wouldn't it be a pleasant surprise to discover that the meeting opened with a comic video?

Of course it would. But not everyone shared my sense of humor, or had one. The most caustic criticism of this particular show came from a clueless viewer who, ironically, intuited my central intention when she wrote this remark on her comment card: "The mime distracted me from the information." If I were actually a mime, you'd see me slowly shaking my head now.

We occasionally made shows for internal use as well as for our "customers." When I was tasked with making a comic tribute to one of our Directors, for example, I scanned through his numerous appearances in other videos, cherry-picked specific statements and responses, and wove them into a fake interview by a panel in a show called "Stress for Success." I played Sherman Shepard, one of a trio of interviewers asking leading questions that used his out-of-context remarks as answers. As one example, I used the Director's original comment about hiring top scientists—"It would cost us an arm and a leg to hire those people"—as his answer to my query, "Lockheed has been accused of not being diverse enough in its workforce. Why, for instance, have we not hired any cannibals?"

And I was always happy to blow off my own work and appear in my co-workers' shows, including a role as a Doc Brown-style mad scientist (Great Scott...are you beginning to sense a pattern developing here?) for a show about the importance of filling out time cards. I didn't care what the show was about—I only cared that I got to demonstrate my character's newest invention, "Spam in a Can": an aerosol can of pink Silly String that I shot into my mouth from arm's length. (It took nearly an hour to learn exactly where and how to hold the can so that the stream of Silly String shot directly into my mouth without looking. Acting is *hard*.)

There is one show I regret was never produced, as it would have been my crowning glory. Sometime in 1991 I finally got around to watching a movie I'd missed during its 1988 release: *Rain Man*, starring Dustin Hoffman and Tom Cruise. I was blown away. It was one of the best movies I'd ever seen, and one of the funniest. I was not alone in this opinion, it seems, since it won Best Picture, Director and Actor Oscars. Hoffman's brilliant performance as the high-functioning autistic savant Raymond Babbitt worked its way under my skin and I soon began imitating him in conversations. And the impersonation went viral among my friends in Video/Film. Within a couple of weeks, half a dozen of us were imitating Rain Man in meetings, or stumbling down the hall in a Rain Man gait, mumbling to ourselves (which baffled many of our visiting clients).

Eventually, I put together a script for a short video I wanted to shoot solely for our own amusement, entitled "Rain Manager." Word worked its way up the management chain and soon our real manager, Dexter—Supervisor Fink's boss—wanted to know what this was all about. So I acted it out for him.

The scene was a meeting in a conference room, and some of the dialog went like this:

Worker: So, Ray, what's the per diem on this project?

Rainmanager: About a hundred dollars.

Worker: And what's the total budget for the project?
Rainmanager: About a hundred dollars.
Worker: Who's the driver on this project?
Rainmanager: I'm an excellent driver.

And so on. We never got around to making the short, but Dexter seemed amused. Years later I discovered that ever since my command performance, he'd been signing all his memos "Rainmanager."

WHAT KIND OF COMPANY WAS LMSC TO WORK FOR? *Part 3*

I only found out much later that I never produced any humorous video that did not get a complaint from someone somewhere in the company. I must credit my boss Lorin Fink with protecting me from this negative feedback, and to living up to his initial mandate that I add some humor to the dry industrial videos, even if he had to take some flack.

On the other hand, this same supervisor tipped his hand about what he thought of my work in my 1992 employee evaluation. Since a potential raise was dependent on a good review, I'd done my due diligence and had compiled an impressive list of statistics, including the number of shows I'd produced in the previous year, the number of the scripts I'd written and/or directed, commendations I'd received, and so on. As the cherry on my slave-labor sundae, I topped off my recital by pointing out that I'd also saved the company literally thousands of dollars by appearing in our videos instead of hiring professional actors. Lorin physically recoiled. "I can't give you any credit for *that*," he insisted. "Why not?" I asked. "You *enjoyed* it!" he replied.

NEW CHARACTERS ENTER

As Lockheed expanded, so did our little Video/Film unit. I was glad I was fully entrenched as new personnel were added, for better or for worse. (Meaning, for better *and* for worse.)

We welcomed Chris, for instance, a rail-thin guy with prematurely white hair, as our new Executive Producer. Even though I was a bit miffed about having another layer of management inserted above me, Chris proved to be an intelligent, talented and amiable co-worker. We spent the better part of a year working together, off and on, for instance, on a show highlighting the bleeding edge research being performed at Lockheed's Palo Alto Research Lab, and bonded over the frustration that those fucking eggheads insisted on revising every one of the multiple iterations of the brilliant script we wrote.

We welcomed Vicki as well, who came to us with a background in television production. She was a Midwestern gal, tall, blonde and solid, and had grown up with numerous brothers, so she was not put off by the male camaraderie and hijinks prevalent among our otherwise all-male production crew. I was impressed that she was one of the few women I'd worked with for whom gender was never an issue.

And we got Howard van Zandt, with his perpetually sunny disposition, who Davo quickly dubbed "Mr. Touchy-Feely" for his habit of communicating his expansive warmth with a hand on your shoulder or (if you could handle it), a bro-hug. I got a classic example of Howard's glass-half-full outlook on life one Friday afternoon when we were driving to a theater to meet our gang for a movie. The movie started at 5:00 and we were stuck in traffic at 4:55. When I began grousing about how we'd never make it on time, Howard just smiled and said, "Well, we're not late yet." If I'd been a lesser man, I might have pushed him out of the car. But his response was so sweet, so innocent, and so fucking stupid, it just made me laugh. We continued to socialize years after we both left Lockheed. And even in the face of his divorce, losing his lovely house, and a quadruple bypass, he maintained a cheery outlook. Howard passed away in 2016. I miss that sweet, innocent bastard.

We were also saddled with a couple of people who might never have joined us if their own little video unit hadn't been shuttered, forcing us to assimilate them. We were, after all, the A-Team: the main video unit for LMSC, tasked with producing a corporate video newsmagazine, making commercials that aired nationally on cable channels, and creating compelling product pitches for Congress and the military (see the ACRV and secure telephone stories above, in my Greatest Hits summary, for instance). *They* came from some pissant, bush-league unit called

"Industrial Video Training," where they made shows like "How to Screw an Aluminum Plate to a Standard Issue Navy Desk." But we were saddled with people like "Biff" anyway. (Seriously, who names their kid "Biff" besides Arthur Miller? And the Tannens?)

We also lost people in the early '90s—not to death, thank the FSM, but for various other reasons. Sandra, for instance, whose cousin was a rising film star, left to go to work for film director Alan Rudolph. We never heard from her again. No one noticed. Ken the Giant Cameraman retired, taking his bicycle, his horrifying Spandex bike shorts and his reeking sardine tins with him. The only absence I really felt was when Mike Weaver left to seek fame and fortune in Hollywood. (Spoiler alert: he found them both, as well as a beautiful, talented wife or two.)

By 1992, LMSC's Video/Film Department not only had about 35 people in our locked asylum, but we were a model of modern diversity, with two African-Americans, two Asians, an openly gay man (and a closeted gay man) and two redheads. Yep, that constituted diversity in Silicon Valley in the '90s.

NORMAN LEIGH: A TRIBUTE

My favorite new addition was Norman Leigh, a small, wire-thin, wiry old guy with a long, proboscis-prominent face and a head of thick white hair. Norman was Old Hollywood, and had a war chest full of war stories about working in The Industry (like the time director William Friedkin threatened to break both Norman's legs if he didn't get the shot Friedkin wanted). He'd produced a couple of movies himself, had worked as a gaffer (chief electrician) on films like *Midnight Cowboy, The Wiz* and *Network* (where he created the lightning effects by standing on a New York rooftop and jamming live high-power electrical cables together), and was Line Producer for the New York scenes in Robert Zemeckis' 1984 action comedy *Romancing the Stone*. He moved up from gaffing to cinematography, where he was Director of Photography for several films and the first season of ABC's Dirty Harry lampoon, *Sledge Hammer!* in 1986.

If the words "New York" appear frequently in that career rundown it's only because Norman Leigh was the archetypal

"New *Yaw*-kuh," complete with the requisite Hell's Kitchen accent and attitude. Norman was 60 when he joined us—when most of us were still in our 30s. My guess is that he'd had enough of Hollywood and decided to opt out for the comparatively cushy job of making industrial videos. No budget, no pressure, better pay, better hours. He considered it a point of honor, however, not just to keep up with our other, younger videographers, but to outperform them.

Several people in our outfit simply *did not like* Norman. But I did, and I pressed them to explain why he rubbed them the wrong way. Some time later, it became clear: the people who didn't like him were laid-back locals, who simply did not understand and could not adjust to his *New Yawk* style of communication, which is no-nonsense, no bullshit, blunt and direct, as opposed to California's easy-going, non-confrontational style. I'd lived on both coasts and understood both methods of communication. The NY "in your face" method didn't bother or intimidate me—I understood that it was just the way these people learned to communicate and converse. But my California compadres simply could not see past the surface irritation. The manner in which his thoughts were delivered distracted them from the thoughts themselves. Their loss.

Once I figured this out, I attempted to welcome Norman into our little clique by inviting him to our Friday nights at the Tied House in Mountain View—my favorite microbrewery. He returned the favor by inviting me to the monthly film screenings at the San Francisco branch of the Director's Guild, where he was a member. We'd go up to The City, gorge ourselves on Mexican food and beer, swap stories, then attend the screening.

Occasionally I'd catch Norman sitting in a meeting, shaking his head slowly and fingering a pendant he wore on a gold chain. I confronted him about this out of curiosity, and he showed me his pendant, which consisted simply of the letters KMS. "What's that stand for?" I asked. And he told me: "I sit in these fucking meetings listening to them shovel their fucking bullshit and my first impulse is to call 'em on it. But I've learned over the years that doing that only ever got me in trouble. So when I feel the urge to speak up, I remind myself not to make waves by touching the pendant."

"Yeah," I said. "But what does KMS *mean*?"

And he told me: "*Keep Mouth Shut.*"

My favorite Norman Leigh story was an incident that occurred sometime in 1993. He was producing a show set in a World War I trench (for reasons known only to him). He'd built the set, rented the costumes (in this case, uniforms—which are the exact opposite of costumes, but let's not let that throw us off track), and had even obtained some (allegedly) non-functional WWI-era rifles for authenticity. Late one afternoon, I heard an odd sound emanating from Norman's cubicle—*clunk, clunk, click; clunk, clunk, click*—and I went over to investigate. I found him sitting at his desk, oiling and testing the slide action and trigger of one of the prop rifles—*clunk, clunk, click.*

"Norman," I said, interrupting his reverie, "we're friends, right?"

"Of course we are, Scotty," he said, continuing his cleaning.

"Then can you do me a favor?"

"Sure," he said, cradling the rifle like a beloved baby doll. "What do you need?"

I pointed at his prop. "Can you please just tell me what day I should call in sick?"

He pulled the trigger—*click.* "You'll be the only one," he chuckled.

Norman passed away in 1996, but not before he married a long-time female friend, so she could continue to collect his Lockheed pension long after he was gone. Gotta admire that parting shot; he died as he lived, with a final, genuine New York "fuck you" gesture to Lockheed.

If this book is a way to celebrate the heroes of my career and castigate the villains, it can also hopefully serve as a tribute to co-worker friends who are no longer with us, like Howard and Norman.

WITH A LITTLE HELP…

What's difficult to quantify is just how much many of us enjoyed working together, and how tight a little clique we developed. Mike, Davo and I went drinking two or three nights a week for a year or more, for instance. And every Friday since about 1987 I'd been assembling a loose group of (mostly) co-workers—anywhere from two to 20 people—to go see whatever big movie was opening that week, followed by beers at the Tied House and dinner at one of Mountain View's many fine restaurants. We were all single, and this gave us the opportunity to have a casual "date night" without the burdensome social requirements of actually having a date.

Even on the rare times I had to travel for work, a road trip with my crew was more like going on a working vacation than being forced together with a group of strangers. On a trip to Cape Canaveral in late June 1991, for instance, I arranged for us to miss our Friday night flight to our next stop, Houston, where we weren't expected until Monday, which gave the three of us the opportunity to spend the weekend at Walt Disney World... with a per diem. As Robin Williams put it, "*Carpe per diem!*"

I'd determined early in my work life (like right after being fired from Frontier Village) not to make friends with co-workers, since as soon as you (or they) left the job, they'd no longer be part of your social circle. Despite my original instincts, however, I couldn't help but form friendships with a few people who I knew would be friends, regardless of our work circumstances —and several of the friends I made in LMSC's Video/Film Department remain friends to this day, even after numerous changes in jobs, or retirement.

WHAT KIND OF COMPANY WAS LMSC TO WORK FOR? *Part 4*

One day in 1992, I received two pieces of mail in the interoffice mail delivery. The first was a letter to All Employees, signed by LMSC President John McMahon. It began something like, "In order to remain viable in the highly competitive aerospace market, it is necessary to enact the following cost-cutting measures," and went on to detail how we'd be getting smaller raises as well as fewer benefits. The second piece of mail that arrived that day was the LMSC Quarterly Report to Stockholders: a slick, full-color pamphlet that opened with a letter from LMSC President John McMahon. His message to the stockholders began, "We are proud to announce that LMSC is showing record profits for the 17th consecutive quarter..."

Does this cognitive dissonance "disconnect" even require comment or analysis?

IN WHICH I SAVE THE WORLD. NO, SERIOUSLY

Sometime in late 1991, all employees received an email from LMSC President John McMahon announcing a new joint venture with Motorola—series of up to 77 interconnected communications satellites that would provide voice and data coverage for the entire globe. They called the new system "Skynet."

Uh-oh. I took a chance that John McMahon might actually read an email sent by one of his 28,000 employees and replied, suggesting that he might want to reconsider that program name, as "Skynet" was the name of the satellite system that became conscious and destroyed all of Humankind in the recent blockbuster movie *Terminator 2: Judgment Day*.

A few weeks later, all employees received an email from Mr. McMahon informing us that the joint venture recently announced as "Skynet" had changed its name to "Iridium" (after element number 77, the proposed number of satellites).

There would be no Skynet. And that, kids, is how I saved the world and everyone in it. You're welcome.

IN WHICH I GET REVENGE AGAINST MY MOTHER

One day in 1991 or '92, I had an epiphany. My mother was still working at LMSC then, and I called her to share my insight.

"Hey, Mom," I said. "Do you remember when I was a kid how I used to watch TV all the time?" I knew precisely the two responses I'd get, since I'd heard them so frequently as a child.

"You let that box run your life," she replied, right on cue—followed, as always, by: "You were frittering your life away."

"Well," I said. "Now I'm making videos for Lockheed. I have a weekly column on video in the *Merc*. And I'm on PBS every Sunday night hosting the evening's programs. So all that time I spent in front of the TV as a kid? *It was all research*!"

She didn't buy it, but at least she laughed.

THE OXYMORONIC WORLD OF "CORPORATE ETHICS"

Sometime around 1990, Lockheed began requiring mandatory training for all employees on topics beyond the security training given during their orientation. In 1992, for instance, in the wake of several Pentagon budget scandals—including one in which Lockheed was discovered to have charged the Navy several hundred dollars for a fucking *hammer*—all employees were mandated to attend weekly Ethics Training sessions. Much of each hour-long class was devoted to presenting us with various ethical dilemmas and discussing how a good employee would go about resolving them. For instance: You go to use the Xerox machine and find a co-worker making copies of a flyer for the Girl Scout troop she leads. What do you do? Of course, any normal person would reply "Nothing," or "Good for her." But since this was an *unauthorized use of company equipment and cost the company money*, the correct answer was: *Report her to her supervisor and call Legal*. It was irrelevant that what she was doing was for a good cause—the sole crucial detail was that this was an *unauthorized use of company equipment and cost the company money* and was therefore unethical.

As we were presented with more of these examples, it quickly became clear (to me, at least) that there was only one guiding "ethical" principle involved—and it pissed me off no end that we were being subjected to this perverted interpretation of one of the most noble and indispensable concepts in all of human history: ethics. Once I figured out the single overarching answer, I made sure I was the first to raise my hand to address any of these examples. And my answer was always the same: "It cost the company money, so it's unethical. If you have any questions, call Legal." The instructor had no response to my answer. It was correct, so he couldn't discount it. But I'd called them on their shit, and he could never acknowledge that. I was able to voice my ultimate Correct Answer maybe three times before he stopped calling on me. But I made sure that mine was always the first hand in the air when the question was asked. By the end of that training session, most of my co-workers burst out laughing every time my hand went up, because they knew what I would say—and, hopefully, they realized the accuracy of my answer and the hypocrisy of the training. The classes were canceled soon after that. I could only hope that I'd played some role in that decision.

The other side of the coin was the mandatory Diversity Training, run by Bob Perri, a very low-key and laid-back Director. In addition to the expected stupid exercises, he also showed us an hour-long PBS *Frontline* documentary entitled "A Class Divided," about grade school teacher Jane Elliot's diversity training with her third-grade kids. The day after Martin Luther King, Jr., was shot in April 1968, Elliot embarked on a bold experiment: she informed her class that blue-eyed people were inherently superior to brown-eyed people, then began to discriminate against the brown-eyed kids, and encouraged the rest of the class to treat their brown-eyed classmates as inferior, stupid, and useless. A week later, she reversed the dictum, until eventually every child in the class had experienced discrimination firsthand. And every single one of the kids totally *got it*, as illustrated in follow-up footage of a class reunion almost twenty years later. I found this documentary (and Elliot's exercise itself) to be brilliant, bordering on genius. I was spellbound. I was touched. And I was angry that this exercise wasn't mandatory in every grade school in every state in the union—and I said so in the post-film discussion.

After the class let out, Bob Perri approached me with a wry smile. "I'm glad you got so much out of the class," he said. "I was warned you might make trouble." I figured he was referring to my response to the Ethics training. I got a kick out of his being wary of me as a loose cannon. But clearly he didn't understand why. "It's not the training I object to, Bob," I explained. "What I object to is *hypocrisy*, like the Ethics training. What you showed us is honest. It's important information, and it's just not taught in school. You did a great job here, and presented us with valuable material, not bullshit, so thank you."

In late 1993 I was given a new assignment (ironically, I have to think, since they still blamed me for "ruining" the Ethics seminars): write and produce an Ethics training video that would be mandatory viewing for all employees. I met with Supervisor

Fink to discuss the project. “Can you get me the training materials to base my script on?” I said.

“Oh, there are no materials,” he replied. “There’s no Ethics program. This is a first.”

“What about the material from those mandatory training sessions?” I suggested. “If I had that, at least I’d know what *not* to do.”

He shook his head. “No, that was an outside firm that supplied those materials. We can’t use any of that.” Not that I’d want to, but still...

“So, uh, if no Ethics program exists to base a script on, what am I supposed to do—just make it up?”

“Guess so,” he shrugged.

And that was the extent of my support from the company. It would be up to me to devise an Ethics training for every employee in LMSC—starting from scratch.

I did, as it turns out, deliver what I felt was a clear, easily understandable presentation that covered the key areas of ethics in the workplace, including such topics as honesty, personal integrity and accountability, and respect and tolerance for co-workers, among other simple, salient points. I illustrated each point with an example, scrupulously avoiding the bill of goods we were expected to swallow from the previous training.

The show was well received (and, like many of my shows, I discovered later, was shown to employees for years afterward). So when Supervisor Fink called me into his office one day in October of 1993, for once I didn’t expect a dressing down for some alleged infraction. I expected an “Attaboy,” at least... perhaps even a commendation.

I never expected it would be printed on pink paper.

THE END OF THE WORLD (AS I KNEW IT)

1993

It was the best of years; it was the worst of years. A quick list of the best: I was on TV every week—on PBS, yet. I spent August sitting in L.A.’s legendary Farmer’s Market several days a week, writing my third play (which was performed the following January) on my days off from co-starring in a feature film. I had a new sweetheart and was in love in love in *love.*

And, while all jobs suck, making videos for Lockheed sucked much less than any of the other jobs I'd ever had.

Clearly, that could not stand.

THE OTHER GOLDEN RULE

"Whoever has the gold makes the rules."
—Brant Parker and Johnny Hart, "The Wizard of Id"

October 1993

So it was, in fact, the best of years...until October, when it became the worst of years.

Like most corporations, Lockheed had a peculiar love/hate (or master/slave) relationship with its employees. (I think I've provided numerous examples of that by now.) When I joined the Company in 1981, the corporate culture was still rooted in the '50s—the hours, the equipment, the conservative attitudes—one aspect of which was that many people working for Lockheed had spent their entire careers there. Many expected to stay with the Company until retirement—or until they died at their desks.

But another part of LMSC's relationship to its workforce was rooted in the 1970s, when the aerospace industry in general suffered a sweeping downturn, forcing Lockheed to lay off hundreds, even thousands, of workers. Once the company recovered, the top management was determined to prepare for the clearly cyclical nature of aerospace work (not to mention government spending). They were determined that mass layoffs like those that occurred in the '70s would never happen again.

"Never" would later be redefined as "December 1993." Even a stable, ancient company like Lockheed was not immune to the '90s trend of "downsizing" (and corporations' attempts to subvert language by insisting it was actually "rightsizing," a ludicrous euphemism if there ever was one). Following months of minor layoffs, word came down From Above on October 1 that LMSC's headcount would be reduced by some 5,500 employees on December 10. Approximately one-quarter of the Sunnyvale workforce would be laid off in a mass purge. LMSC was planning to lay off so many people that a Federal regulation regarding "plant closure" was invoked, one aspect of which meant that the unfortunate quarter got 60 days notice of the layoff.

Department heads were required to hand pink slips to one of every four employees in virtually every department. Our Christmas bonus—our "peace dividend," following Bill Clinton's ascendency to the Presidency—would be a giant game of Musical Chairs, in which one of every four chairs was removed before the game even began.

I was Number Four. I didn't get a musical chair. Instead, I got a pink slip.

And I was pissed. When I was called into Supervisor Fink's office expecting a commendation but instead got my walking papers, I confronted him about this layoff, as he surely had a hand in deciding who got the ax...and I played my trump card. "You can't lay me off," I said. "I've been with LMSC thirteen years—longer than anyone else in this department. I have seniority." He looked genuinely perplexed. "You didn't hear?" he said. "Seniority has been discounted for this round of layoffs." My one advantage had been pulled out from underneath me like a throw rug. Seniority was *always* a factor—until it wasn't, thus once again proving the Other Golden Rule: "Whoever has the gold makes the rules." Yep, the rules are the rules —until they aren't. If policy gets in the way of your goal, just change the policy.

This is how you treat the employee who just delivered a mandatory training film on Ethics? And I thought *I* was a Master of Irony.

I tried to understand why I was getting the ax. I'd performed well: I'd won external awards and internal commendations; my annual performance reviews were excellent; my clients and co-workers enjoyed working with me (well, with one exception). I made a list of everyone in the department and attempted to recreate the managerial thought process about who to lay off, and why I lost the Layoff Lottery. My results came out something like this, in Management-think:

- We can't lay off more than one of our two African-American employees, or we might be open to a racism lawsuit. And we have to keep the one who is suing us, because it's illegal to lay off anyone with an active lawsuit against us. So: Good-bye, Donna!
- We can't lay off *both* the old-timers, or we might be open to an age discrimination lawsuit. But we can get rid of *one* of them, even though he's close to retirement. So: Good-bye, Tom!
- We can't lay off *either* of the gay employees, or we might be open to a sexual harassment lawsuit. Hello, turd burglars!
- We have only *one* videographer left, and he's already doing the work of three people, so we can't possibly lay him off. Davo gets a pass.
- So, given all these people we have absolutely *got* to retain, regardless of their value as employees, who *can* we lay off? Who can't possibly sue us if he's laid off? It can only be one of our two middle-aged, straight white men. And Biff has a wife and a mortgage and a new baby. So: Good-bye, Scott!

I suppose I could blame a shift in the corporate culture as well: I was hired for my sense of humor, but with a quarter of the workforce being laid off...nothing was funny anymore.

ONE MAN, BANNED

Lockheed, in its infinite corporate compassion, had left one loophole in the mass layoffs: If you could find another position in the company within 60 days, you could remain an employee.

But did I really want that? Did I really want to stay at a company that would cast me aside in such a cold, calculated, and shabby manner—one that would choose to ignore 13 years of service just to achieve its headcount reduction? Did I really want to continue to work in a place where any future complaints about work overload would be met with a response like "You're lucky you still have a job." And what other position could I possibly fill? After working in Video/Film, I was spoiled. I couldn't go back to filling out paperwork, writing status reports, being a pencil-pushing peon.

There were no positions like that available anyway—with a quarter of the company being given the boot, *no* unit had any open reqs. Every department was downsizing; no department was hiring. I sensed that the loophole of allowing us to scramble for a new job was little more than a cruel joke, or a sadistic implementation of Catch-22: *If you can find another position, you can stay...but we've eliminated all the other positions.* If there was, in fact, a position that needed to be filled, management would not have laid off whoever was currently doing that job. That's some catch, that Catch-22. The best there is.

What I wanted to do was continue making videos. And I got an inspiration about how I might exploit the employment loophole to make that possible...possibly. In my capacity as Video Columnist for the *Mercury News*, I kept up with trends in video equipment, and I realized there was a sea change occurring in the world of video production, namely the reduction in price and increase in quality of consumer electronics equipment. I did some research, crunched some numbers, and put together a proposal promoting myself as a one-man video production unit —a guy who could write, produce, shoot and edit digital videos with a quick turnaround and low cost.

I knew exactly who to pitch my proposal to: the VP in charge of Lockheed's Palo Alto Research Lab. We'd had several meetings with him when we were producing a video about his facility, so he knew me by sight—and knew we'd given him a world-class video about his world-class facility. He was a bit pompous, but that was a point in my favor: I knew I could take advantage of his ego.

I set up a meeting with him in his spacious executive office and presented my proposal. I pitched myself as a "one-man video unit" for the LPARL facility—an all-in-one video producer who could, for little overhead, be housed on-site and be his video bitch. He was clearly interested—rather than listen politely and dismiss me out of hand, he started asking questions —the right questions; questions I'd anticipated and answered definitively. How much would it cost to set up a digital video facility like the one I'd described? Only about $50,000 for the initial equipment (which could be amortized over the next few years), one spare room, and my salary. Who would you report to? I'd be on your staff and report directly to you. What exactly would you be doing? Documenting experiments, creating promotional videos... I could even shoot the visits of visiting dignitaries and hand them a tape of their tour as they left the facility. And so on. It was going swimmingly. I could tell he was intrigued—what a feather in his cap it would be to have his own personal video production unit! But ultimately, he shrunk back in his chair and sighed. "We're not immune to the mass layoff," he said. "I just don't have the headcount."

We were both crushed and disappointed. But he still had a job.

END OF DAYS

The next few weeks were odd, irritating...and surprisingly liberating. One example: Our departmental secretary (who had also received a pink slip, so was happy to subvert the Company any way she could) slipped me a copy of a company memo sent to all supervisors that prohibited any department from ordering any office supplies for the rest of the year—a clear accusation that we unfortunate victims would attempt to steal anything that wasn't nailed down before we left. The phrase "adding insult to injury" occurred to me...but I had to admit that they were, of course, correct. A quarter of a century later, I'm still using Scotch tape, Post-Its, and pads of lined green paper liberated from Lockheed as part of my self-awarded severance package. My goal was to stock enough office supplies to last a lifetime. I hope I live that long.

I experienced complications with the incipient layoff that rippled beyond the professional and into the personal as well. After years of bachelorhood, for instance, I had a new girlfriend at this time, and we spent a lot of late nights together. So I began ignoring my 7 AM start time and just showed up to work whenever I fucking felt like it—8 AM, 9 AM, 10 AM (just in time to start planning where to go for lunch), whatever. I discovered the brilliance of David Letterman on *The Late Late Show*, which I'd never before been able to stay up for. And naturally, I was using up my stock of sick days. When Supervisor Fink (the fink who laid me off) commented on my behavior, I had no problem growling at him, "What're ya gonna do about it—lay me off?" He mumbled something about how I was acting like Mike Weaver. He did not mean this as a compliment. But to me, it was one of the highest compliments I could be paid.

December 10, 1993: Black Friday

And on Friday, December 10, 1993—13 years less one month since I first walked into the Tech Pubs unit and entered the corporate workforce—I packed up all the shit I'd collected over the previous baker's dozen years and exited Lockheed Missiles and Space Company for the final time. Although my future was uncertain, I had one benefit: at least I knew I'd been spared the fate of dying at my desk at Lockheed.

Or, to put it another way… A decade later, in mid-2012, I attended a goodbye party for several old Video/Film co-workers who were being laid off, including Supervisor Fink. I held no grudge, even after a decade of struggle, especially since I had the last laugh. "You got laid off from Lockheed and now you work for Apple," he said to me at one point in the party. "All I got was laid off from Lockheed."

AND THEN...

A few months later, I discovered just why LMSC had laid off over 5,000 people—a quarter of its workforce—during that Black Christmas in 1993: Lockheed Corporation was gearing up for a merger with Martin Marietta, another of the country's largest aerospace companies, and wanted to enter negotiations (which began in March 1994) as a lean, mean aerospace machine. A few thousand fewer salaries would give them some negotiating leverage. ("Executives [Wikipedia reports] received large bonuses directly from the government as a result of the merger.") But even if they'd kept those unlucky 5K workers, most of us would have undoubtedly been let go soon after the deal was finalized in March 1995, since redundant functions would be eliminated.

LMSC may not have been great to me, but it was a good master to my extended family. By '93, Mom had already accepted an early retirement package but continued to operate in her function as a highly paid consultant for several years afterward, for instance. My younger brother, now (circa 2020) approaching retirement age himself, continued with Lockheed Martin as an electrician and worked his way up to a management position; he was able to purchase nice homes and raise three exceptional kids on his salary (including a Ph.D., a brilliant musician, and a beautiful daughter who currently works for…Lockheed Martin).

Over the next decade, virtually all my former co-workers from Video/Film left—by layoff, death, or retirement. I keep in touch with a few of them. Consensus about whether it was a good experience or a bad experience runs about 50/50.

Lockheed Martin remains one of the largest aerospace, defense, security and advanced tech companies in the world, as well as the world's largest defense contractor.

Hard to believe they did it without me.

PART II:

DIGITAL

"Sing to me of the man, Muse, the man of twists and turns,
driven time and time again off course."
—Homer, *The Odyssey*, Book 1

Chapter 15

1994: STRANGE INTERLUDE

"Sad disappointments in several plans
which I had sketched for my future life..."
—Herman Melville, *Redburn*

January 1994

I needed a job.

Or did I? I'd probably need a job sooner or later, I realized... but not at that precise moment. So I took 1994 off, partly because I figured I could live for quite some time on Unemployment Insurance, my severance package, and my cashed-in LMSC 401k (since there was nowhere to roll it over into). Additionally, I had nearly $100 a week coming in from my video column and VJ/host gig on KTEH. All I had to do was find a way to extend those resources long enough to revive Plan A—or, more likely, long enough to find a job.

I tried to cut back on expenses. But I had to pay rent and utilities. And eat. Could I spend less on groceries? Nope. I was eating for two now—not pregnant, but with a new bride (who was also unemployed). I offered my greedy-ass landlord a year's rent in advance *if* he'd give me a ten percent discount. His counter-proposal was that he'd allow my new wife to live there and not *raise* my rent. As a wedding present. What a guy!

SAD MATH

So I couldn't reduce my grocery bill. And the only way I could reduce my rent would be to move to a less expensive apartment. Consequently, I performed for the first time a calculation which would become all too familiar over the next decade: I could move to a cheaper place...but even if I could find a place that saved me a hundred dollars a month in rent, it would take nearly a year of living in that new place just to pay for the cost of the move. I had long ago exhausted the finite resource of friends to assist me in moving, so I had to rely on professionals. And I can tell you one thing for sure: at the amount they charged, the fucking Starving Students were *not* starving. At all.

Another factor in this calculation was the *where*: What if I moved to one end of the valley and eventually got hired by a company at the *other* end of the valley? I couldn't stomach the thought of an hour commute, twice a day, through stop-and-go traffic. But that kind of collateral damage was a distinct possibility. About the only thing I could save money on was gas, because I wasn't commuting anymore.

So I took 1994 off because I had resources. I took the year off for one other reason as well: I couldn't find a job. I thought I might have developed a skill set by producing videos at Lockheed for nearly five years, but I was disabused of that notion by interviewing at a professional video production company in San Jose. "Five years experience, huh?" the guy marveled. He picked up a pile of résumés stacked on his desk. "These guys, some of them have college degrees in video production. Some of them have been doing this for twenty years. And we should hire you with your *five years* of experience?" Then he laughed out loud. Literally. I had no idea. I should have been enraged. Instead, I was humiliated. But I learned that I'd never work at an indie production house, and dropped all plans to apply to others. My "résumé reel" would become just another videocassette on my shelf—a reminder of past glory days.

I had money. But instead of sleeping peacefully beside my new bride, I spent most nights lying in bed wide awake, shuddering with anxiety, haunted by the question: *What happens when the money runs out?*

I SAY PLAN A; THEY SAY PLAN *EH*

With an abundance of time and a modicum of cash, I did indeed make several attempts to revive Plan A in some variant version and create a profitable business. But of three major attempts, none came to fruition. Nobody wanted to play with me. Among the attempts that fizzled on the launch pad (I might not be working for Lockheed Missiles & Space Co. anymore, but I can still borrow their metaphors):

* I sent a proposal to the science fiction magazine *Locus* (which was produced right up the road in Oakland) to create an offshoot of their brand called *Locus Classicus* (defined as "an authoritative passage from a standard work that is often quoted as an illustration") that would desktop-publish a series of books featuring transcripts of the best of their hundreds of sci-fi author interviews. The publisher wrote back saying he was thinking of retiring and wanted less, not more, work.

* I contacted a woman who was seminal in the restoration of Impressionist artist Claude Monet's gardens in the south of France—and who herself had made a cottage industry of publishing annual datebooks featuring photos of the gardens—and suggested we collaborate on producing a video that would detail the restoration effort and dissolve between Monet's paintings of his gardens and their eventual reconstruction. (As good an excuse as any to revisit France.) She was interested, but passed.

* And I contacted a close friend—the man who'd introduced me to the scholar of mythology Joseph Campbell, and one of two people who'd ever co-authored a book with Campbell—about creating an instructional video detailing their creation of a new form of Tarot card reading, the "Jungian Spread." I knew there was a small but passionate market for New Age videos like this...and sincerely felt that Campbell's game-changing insights into Tarot divination deserved wider exposure and recognition. I told him we could shoot the video in a day. I'd do all the work, and he'd get half the profits. He decided: Nah.

Strike three. My best plans were met with nothing but shrugs.

Chapter 16

1995: SILICON GRAPHICS INTERNATIONAL (SGI)

The Adventures of a Carbon Unit at Silicon Graphics

D. Scott Apel
Consultant
Video Production

Mail Stop 105
2011 N. Shoreline Boulevard
Mountain View, California 94043-1389
Telephone (415) 390-2726
Fax (415) 390-6241
E-Mail: scotta@corp.sgi.com

SILICON GRAPHICS INTERNATIONAL (SGI)

January 1995

I needed a job. Where have I heard that before?

At length—a full year after being shown the door at Lockheed—an opportunity did present itself. One of my fellow VJs on KTEH informed me about an opening at the computer company where she worked: Silicon Graphics International. SGI had been founded in 1981 to design and manufacture 3D graphics workstations—high-end, visually-oriented computers. SGI was one of the hottest, highest-profile computer companies in the world at that time—and was rapidly becoming the tool of choice for Hollywood special effects. George Lucas' Industrial Light and Magic had been using Silicon Graphics workstations since 1987, for instance. The liquid metal T-1000 in *Terminator 2,* the dinosaurs in *Jurassic Park*, the special effects in *The Abyss,* and the ballroom scene in Disney's animated *Beauty and the Beast* were all created using Silicon Graphics computers.

(Once on board, I saw one reason why SGI was on the bleeding edge of tech: the graphics used in an experiment in cable video on demand in a few thousand homes in Orlando, Florida—referred to as "the Time-Warner trials"—included a rotating on-screen carousel of choices that did indeed almost appear to be 3D. A quarter of a century later, I've still never seen anything this advanced in any video menu—not iTunes or Netflix; certainly not the clunky Amazon VOD interface—all of which retain flat-surface, two-dimensional cover flows.)

The department my contact worked for was a sales unit dedicated to convincing the aircraft and automotive industries (among many other fields) that they could save time and money by doing their design work on SGI workstations as opposed to old school drafting boards. The head of the department wanted to establish his own one-man video production unit to produce short shows, using SGI computers, to promote this goal.

I was their guy. I'd even had a thorough, half-day training in creating digital video during my last days at Lockheed. In addition, I'd written a proposal for a similar one-man production unit that I'd pitched to Lockheed's Palo Alto Research Lab in my final days there, as a last-ditch effort to try to remain employed. I modified the proposal and met with the VP of SGI's Industrial Manufacturing department, "Joe DiTrolli." (Clearly not his name or the actual name of the department...which should give the astute reader some clue that this would not end well.)

Joe loved the idea, especially the budget: I'd done my research and convinced him that all the equipment necessary to form his own video production unit was off-the-shelf, "prosumer" stock, that he could set up the whole department for about $15,000—a drop in the bucket for him—and I would operate it, on a freelance basis, for $25 an hour.

I would have pitched myself as a candidate for permanent, full-time employment, but my contact (who was also Joe's Admin) cautioned me against that route; at that time, SGI was hiring almost as many temporary employees on a contract basis as they had full-time employees. They had plenty of money to pay freelancers cash wages, and by doing so they were freed from the "real headcount" burden of incidental costs like taxes, medical insurance, SDI, and so on. I was just happy to be working, doing something I thought I'd enjoy—and being paid a wage that was, for me, at that time, quite adequate.

SGI CULTURE (IN A PETRI DISH)

So one Monday early in January 1995, I reported to SGI, got badged and was escorted to my cubicle. I had a desk, a chair and a phone. The phone had a manual. The manual was nearly 200 pages long. I wondered what I'd missed being out of the corporate world for a year—did I now need a Ph.D. just to operate the telephone?

Only days earlier, SGI had moved into a brand new building in Mountain View, just off Highway 101. From the street, the building looked like nothing so much as an aircraft hanger with an ice cube tray wrapped around the front—one of those 1950s lever-operated ice cube trays that consisted of a grid of silver squares. The building's inner design was equally hideous, with exposed ductwork and wire trays running along the ceilings. My first thought was: *Might look nice once they finish it.* Later I discovered that this look was the new norm for high-end industrial spaces. Where was Frank Lloyd Wright when you needed him?

Although the workspace was appalling, on the brighter side, SGI was notorious for its perks. Once a month, for instance, a fleet of roach coaches would roll into the parking circle on a Friday afternoon, offering free food of many lands. One event even featured a "Margaritamobile." (I still can't figure out how that was legal.) And every Friday afternoon there was beer, beer, beer. *Good* beer, too! I love beer. And I found myself sitting at my desk late one Friday afternoon, sipping a Sam Adams, when it dawned on me: *They've broken the code*. They'd figured out how to keep me at work after hours: free beer.

Other free perks for employees prefigured those that Google, Facebook, and other major Silicon Valley companies would eventually institutionalize: foosball tables, free dry cleaning, a world-class cafeteria, and so on. Our building was shaped like a cross, and at the intersection there was a fully stocked, help-yourself coffee bar. When I wandered through our building I saw bicycles on cubicle walls and even spotted a sleeping bag under one programmer's desk. And it dawned on me that these perks were all just a cynical trap. Don't give the young, inexperienced employees any reason ever to leave the office, and they'll work far more than the standard 40 hours of traditional full-time employment. *Bwa-ha-haaaa!* SGI paved the way for this "frat house" culture that became the new normal in hi-tech startups. And when the company got into financial trouble, these perks were—of course—the first things to be eliminated.

Our core group was small—three or four sales reps, the boss, and his Admin. They all welcomed me aboard. They gave me a shirt with the SGI logo embroidered on it. They gave me a T-shirt with the SGI logo. They gave me a hat with the SGI logo. They gave me a satchel with the SGI logo. As one of my new co-workers informed me, "It's not just a job—it's a wardrobe!" They even all took me to lunch on Friday at the end of my first week. They decided on sushi. I hate fish. And *raw* fish was something I was never was going to put in my mouth. I knew, however, that the one way to alienate my hip, cutting edge co-workers was to say, "I hate sushi." Inconceivable! We hired some kind of freak! So I smiled and ordered a bowl of soup and hid the huge hole in my sock in this shoe-free restaurant so they wouldn't think I was poverty-stricken, even though I was. Somehow I suspected even then that this association with these smug Yuppies (Yuppies: still a thing then) would not end well.

Dramatis Personae

Let's meet our players! Even though our department had six or seven people, only a few are relevant to the story. And all of the names have been changed because...well, you'll see.

Joe DiTrolli—Joe was a little guy with a deep voice, and like so many little guys, he attempted to compensate for his small stature by acting tough and speaking in a loud, booming voice. Or maybe he would have been just as obnoxious even if he were seven feet tall. Sure, I have a degree in Psychology—but real people are a lot more difficult to analyze than the shit printed in textbooks. Joe was loudly extraverted, bald, and given to wild mood swings. Some days he was your best buddy; others, your worst nightmare. He was simply a tiny tyrant. I noticed that most of the guys tended to shrink a little when standing near Joe—slouching, perhaps, so they didn't rub his face in his midgetude. His arrogance would ultimately be his downfall—and, therefore, mine as well.

The Voice—The salesman in our department who was a ghost. Most of us never saw him. Many had never met him. He was on the road constantly. Maybe to make up for this lack of physical presence, he made his presence known verbally. He'd call our group voicemail and leave long, rambling messages about his philosophy of sales. We could hear freeway sounds in the background; it didn't take a brain surgeon to realize he was driving somewhere, alone and bored, and took it out on us.

Alain LeDouche—Joe was too busy to deal with small potatoes like me, so he assigned me to one of his salesmen,

Alain LeDouche. Alain was some piece of work, almost mind-bogglingly self-centered, arrogant and rude. And although the litany of Alain LeDouche rudeness stories could fill many pages, a single representative anecdote should suffice. Alain's favorite trick was to ask me to step into his cubicle, ask me a question, and as soon as I started to answer, pick up his phone and check his voicemail. On more than one occasion I wanted to grab his phone, rip the wires from the wall, throw it across the room, and scream, "I'M *TALKING* TO YOU, ASSHOLE!" But of course I never did. I needed the job. I have no doubt that Alain was a trendsetter—that twenty years later, he'd be one of those people who starts talking to you then checks his smart-phone when you reply, to check his texts or tweets or update his Facebook page…unless someone with even less impulse control than I have has already murdered this dick in his cubicle. No jury in the world would convict them.

MY JOB OF WORK

Once on board, I set about setting up my offline video suite. Not only did I have a cubicle, but I'd also been provided with an unused storage closet nearby for the suite. It was oddly shaped, long and narrow, but it was perfect for my purposes. And it had a door, like a real office. With a lock. Once I got the green light for my budget, I started ordering "pro-sumer" video equipment: a series of high-end VCRs in VHS, S-VHS and Hi-8 formats—as well as a Hi-8 camcorder, in case we ever needed to shoot any original video (and so I could, you know, test it out on week-ends). The centerpiece of the suite was a Silicon Graphics Indigo computer—not the top of the line SGI machine, but still worth several thousand dollars, and with plenty enough processing power to digitize and edit video.

In 1995, the gold standard for digital video editing software was manufactured by a company named AVID, so they were my first call. I almost dropped the phone when the sales rep scream-ed at me, *"Who told you we were working on a UNIX version?"* I assumed they already had one—but little did I suspect it hadn't been released yet. So I explained what I was doing for SGI and talked them into sending me a beta version of their software for

UNIX—a $10,000 program, mine for free...as long as I put their logo at the end of each of my shows. I was blown away by the fortuitous timing of my request: for once, I was ahead of the curve...if only slightly.

The only real technical problem I had was storage. Digitized video takes up a lot of memory, and I wanted to create a library of digitized clips I could mix and match with a few mouse clicks. So I purchased an external hard drive with the unimaginable capacity of *two gigabytes* of data. It was as big as a shoebox, and I marveled at its immense capacity. (By way of contrast, about 20 years later I picked up an external hard drive for home use that had a capacity to store three *terabytes* of data—about 1,500 times what my two-gig shoebox held. It was the size of a thick paperback book, and I purchased it with cash I had in my pocket—less than $100.)

ON WITH THE SHOW!

I never found out who thought up the task for which Joe and SGI had hired me, but it was actually one of the most brilliant ideas I'd ever come across in business (so it's doubtful it was Joe's idea). The plan was this: Rather than call or write the industry leaders to whom they wanted to pitch SGI computers, we'd send them a "video letter"—a video message created *specifically for them*. I'd write, produce, and edit a five-minute video for the target company's key people—a little show that was essentially an introduction to, and illustration of, SGI's product capabilities. We'd get an SGI exec—the highest exec we could convince to cooperate—to look directly into the camera and address the recipient by name. Our exec would introduce himself, show some eye candy clips of graphics that SGI computers could create, then propose a meeting between representatives of their company and ours.

A typical show would start out with an SGI exec in an office setting, casually perched on the edge of "his" desk. He'd look into the camera and say something like, "Hi, Orville. I'm Gary Lauer, Senior VP of Industrial Sales at SGI, and I'd like to take a minute to show you a few of the many ways Silicon Graphics computers can streamline and enhance your design and production efforts at Wright Stuff Aerospace." He'd add a couple of sentences praising Wright Stuff's products, then we'd cut to a series of clips pulled directly from SGI workstations—high-end graphics that illustrated the topics the SGI exec narrated off-screen. Each show would end returning to the SGI exec, who'd invite Orville (or Wilbur) to expect a call from one of our sales reps soon. Some versions would include explicitly specific closing lines like, "We're really looking forward to our meeting with you next month," or "I thought our meeting last month was very productive, and we're looking forward to taking the next step"—anything that would totally personalize the show, so the viewer *knew* this video was made *specifically for him.*

Well, specifically for him as far as he knew, anyway. While the one-minute intros and closes were, in fact, specific to the individual recipient, the center section of narrated clips was a plug-in that I used in virtually every video letter. This was my contribution, to streamline production: the only parts of each letter I'd need to write, produce and edit were the short intros and closes. Everything in between was boilerplate—"stock footage," in the Hollywood sense—but since it was narrated by the same guy the viewer had just seen on screen addressing him directly, it seemed as though *the entire show* had been created just for him. The transition between an SGI exec on screen and a clip show narrated by the same exec was seamless. This would save me countless hours of editing, and would save the exec on camera countless hours of shooting in the studio. We might have to shoot six or eight personalized intros and closes—that was the point—but we'd only need to have the exec record *one version* of the five-minute voice-over center section...a section in which he was not only unseen, but which was also not personalized—although I doubt any recipient ever realized this. I was very proud of myself for coming up with this time, cost, and labor-saving cheat.

HELL IS OTHER PEOPLE

"People. They're the worst."
—Jerry Seinfeld, *Seinfeld*

It wasn't until many years later that I realized a truth about working at SGI: Anything I had control over ran pretty smoothly—but anything I had little control over was often a total shit show. For example: researching and purchasing my equipment was easy. Connecting everything up to create an offline editing suite was simple. Digitizing and editing the shows? Piece of cake. But getting video clips of SGI work into my system? Hold it right there, bucko.

It's not like there were no existing SGI videos for me to cob clips from. Quite the contrary: SGI had a first-rate professional video production department, and was in the process of building a million-dollar editing suite. The company had a vast library of shows produced in-house. They just weren't keen on handing any of them over to me.

But I didn't know this when I dropped in on the Video Production Department's library one day early in my tenure. I met with them to discuss the procedure for obtaining copies of previously-produced videos from which I could pull clips, and to understand the process by which I could request copies of their high-end productions (originally produced on professional-grade Betacam SP) in S-VHS, the highest quality format I was set up to work with in my digital suite. I introduced myself and my position, but evidently my fame, or infamy, preceded me—and I discovered that the "real" Video Production Department was adamantly opposed to any small-time, independent video unit operating outside of their direct control. And I was, essentially, stonewalled.

The people in charge of SGI's video library were not just unhelpful, they were downright rude. And arrogant. They knew I was creating an offline mini-editing suite outside their realm, and they had nothing but contempt for the whole project. It was simply beneath their professional dignity to even acknowledge that any video production was occurring at SGI outside their bailiwick. It was as if my suite was an affront to their professionalism. Their resentment was palpable: I was not part of their professional endeavor but was, in their eyes, a competitor, and beneath their contempt. I was not part of their department. I was the idiot bastard little brother: an embarrassment; a wart on their professionalism. I was an *enemy*. One irate employee even told me, point blank, "We *do not approve* of Joe DiTrolli having his own personal video unit." Well! Fuck you very much!

I tried to convince them that my video letters were too minor for them to bother producing. I tried to convince them that I, too, was a video professional, having worked for years in Lockheed's Video/Film Department. I tried to convince them that we were all on the same team (Go Team SGI!). But I was beating my head against a silicon wall. They refused to acknowledge my legitimacy as an SGI video producer, and it took an executive decree to obtain even the most minor cooperation from them. Eventually, I was informed of the process for requesting the tapes I needed—the paperwork, the authorizations required, etc. Since this department was a service unit, and I was, technically, working for SGI, they couldn't refuse my requests outright (as long as—as one historical regime put it—*"your papers are in order"*). But they could make things as difficult for me as possible. And they did. Never once in my numerous dealings with this group did I ever receive anything beyond exactly what I requested—not even a smile.

After pulling those teeth, all I needed was a studio in which to shoot the personalized introductions. It was abundantly clear that the main SGI Video Department would be of no help at all. I was on the verge of requesting a small office somewhere in which to shoot these intros when I stumbled across an existing mini-studio in a building nearby. Like my offline editing suite, it was a one-man operation, small but professional—and another orphan outcast: no one in the main video production department took it seriously, either (or ever even bothered to volunteer its existence to me). But the guy in charge had everything I needed to shoot the short intros my video letters required, including an "executive office set" and a teleprompter. Best of all, he shot in S-VHS, so I could completely circumvent the main SGI Video Production Department and the need to transfer high-end video to S-VHS—a format I could use.

Once my suite was up and running, I hit the next problem in dealing with something I could not control: other people. Joe and Alain were not just sales guys, they were *industrial* sales guys. And they had what I discovered was an "assembly line" mentality. They assumed that if they gave me an assignment on Monday morning, I'd pull a lever, fire up the assembly line, and hand them a finished video on Friday afternoon. But production of these shows simply did not—*could* not—work like that. They were best done in batches. Although I wouldn't learn the phrase "managing expectations" for another decade, it's apt for describing the dilemma I faced with my bosses.

The sub-dilemma was this: *How do you explain a process to people who don't know the process and don't* want *to know the process?* Ultimately, I had to bite the bullet and explain to them that it would be an inexcusable waste of *their management's* time to ask a top executive to spend an hour or two *each week* shooting just *one single* personalized introduction for *one single* video. "It's much more efficient to ask that exec to spend *two* hours in the studio *once a month* and have him shoot five or six of these short introductions," I explained. "It's the studio set-up that takes time—getting the lighting right so the exec looks good, showing them how to read off a teleprompter and still sound spontaneous, and so on. Once we're set up and we start shooting, they'll be on a roll and can knock out several of these in a few minutes—and won't have to hang around wasting their time waiting while the studio, the set, the lighting, the teleprompter, and so on are set up. So," (I said to my brown-nosing bosses), "which is a more effective use of *your management's* time—one set-up once a week, for an hour, or one set-up once a month for ninety minutes?" Even they couldn't argue with that math and logic—although I did get the distinct impression they were sorry they'd ever agreed to discuss this with me.

There were a limited number of SGI execs we could call on to "host" the video letters. Some didn't understand the concept and declined. Some were too busy; others were just not interested. One confided that he'd never assist Joe DiTrolli in accomplishing *anything*—a refreshingly candid comment—and an attitude that was fairly widespread, I'd later discover. Our go-to guy became Gary Lauer, one of the Executive VPs, and one of the few truly decent people I met at SGI. He loved being on camera, and I took advantage of that, tapping him for our intros whenever we couldn't land anyone else. Fortunately, Gary was also good on camera: personable and professional. I reciprocated by making him look good and teaching him a few camera tricks. It was a symbiotic relationship, and I knew I could count on him in a pinch...

...like the time another Executive VP of SGI—let's call him "DJ"—failed to show up for a shoot. A quick call to Gary Lauer and we were back in business, able to use the studio time I'd booked, and able to meet my deadline for that batch of video letters. (Thank you, Gary!) I mention this incident only because of the aftermath. Landing DJ was a major coup—the second-in-command at SGI agreeing to introduce a batch of our little videos? Even Joe DiTrolli was impressed. And when DJ failed to appear—or even to call and cancel—nobody blamed me.

Exactly one week after DJ's no-show, however, I got a frantic phone call from the guy who ran the mini-studio. "You'd better get over here *right now*!" he whispered into his phone.

"Why?" I said. "What's happening?" We didn't have studio time booked for that day—or even for that week.

"DJ just showed up, He's ready to shoot his introductions."

I rushed over to the studio. Sure enough, there was DJ, resting his cowboy boots on a desk, cooling his heels and waiting to start his shoot. Question: How does a temp worker, at the bottom of the totem pole, politely inform the second-in-command of a major company that he'd shown up for his video shoot a fucking *week late?* But I had to try. I explained that the shoot was scheduled for a week ago, and I apologized that we had nothing for him to do at this juncture. He didn't want to look like an idiot, and I didn't want to get fired...so we agreed to blame his Admin for writing down the wrong date. I've kept an eye on DJ's career since then, and have scrupulously avoided investing in or working for any company with which he was involved. I mean, seriously—would *you* want to work for a guy who shows up for an appointment *a week late*?

MR. ED SPEAKS!

So we never got DJ on camera. But we did score the mother of all coups by getting the CEO of SGI, Ed McCracken, to agree to introduce a batch of video letters. Everyone in our group was excited. Except me. Joe DiTrolli insisted that our entire core group be present in the studio to watch Ed perform. I wasn't intimidated by this...but I did know it was in no way the optimal circumstance under which to direct the one guy who held all our fates in his hands. I'd have to be mindful not only of Ed, but also of Joe and Alain. And I'd have to try to keep my other co-workers under control so they didn't completely fuck up the shoot. Since their reactions indicated that they were only interested in Ed, my best performance would occur, I realized, simply by not drawing any attention to myself.

We had Ed McCracken scheduled for two hours, but he cut it back to one—and then showed up 40 minutes late (but, hey, he's the CEO, so who's counting?). When he arrived at the studio I was amused to notice that he looked so much like the actor Ed Begley, Jr., that they could have been twins—tall and gaunt, pale and bespectacled, with a shock of blonde hair falling over his forehead. Our entire group of six was present in the studio to greet him, and everyone took turns gushing over him as the guy in charge of the studio went to work lighting Ed in the "office set."

I introduced myself to Ed and explained what he'd be doing: delivering several personalized introductions and closes, just reading them off the teleprompter. He'd be out of here in an hour. We should all just relax, take a deep breath, and enjoy the process. And don't forget to smile! He did not smile. And when Ed McCracken, CEO, did not smile, Joe did not smile. I resigned myself to this being my last shoot for SGI.

I suggested to my co-workers—several times—that they'd be more comfortable out of the studio and in the control booth (and also out of the fucking way, although I could hardly say that). Joe made it clear that they were all gonna stay *right here* in the studio with their Glorious Leader. Fine, I agreed, but—in a dangerous display of my authority as the Person In Charge of this shoot—I insisted they stay in the shadows, "...so you don't disturb or distract Ed." Yep, make it all about Ed, and they quickly complied.

We did a take of the first intro. And it was nicely done—except for one fatal flaw: Ed McCracken, CEO of a multi-million dollar company, mispronounced a word. It was a common word; something you see around the house every day, as Groucho Marx used to say. But it was a vital word, and couldn't really be replaced with another word that was easier to pronounce (like, what's an alternate word for "February"—another word everyone mispronounces). And it sent up a Red Flag of Stupidity, like people who pronounce "et cetera" as "*ek* cetera," or say "based off" instead of "based on"—sure signs of incipient idiocy.

I approached Ed. "Nicely done," I enthused. "Let's do another one, just for safety."

"Let's move on," he said, deadpan.

"Well, I'd really like to get another take," I said, contritely. "It's standard practice. Oh, and by the way, you might want to pronounce the word *X* as *x*."

"That's the way we pronounce it in Iowa," he responded frostily.

Well OK, then! We weren't gonna get a second take. We for sure weren't gonna get a correction of the idiot "Iowa" mispronunciation. As a director, I knew that this set, this studio, this "talent," were all subject to my command. Unfortunately for me, Ed did *not* know this. Not to mention that he owned it all. So... we moved on.

And eventually (once we'd recorded the central voiceover narration), I called it a wrap. My co-workers took this as a starting gun to rush Ed and praise him for his Oscar-caliber performance. I breathed a private sigh of relief. I was mostly happy, convinced I could use what he gave us to create our next batch of video letters. As Pete Townsend put it, "This is no social crisis...just another tricky day for you." I'd successfully navigated a course between the rock of the CEO's mistakes and the hard place of my own management's high expectations. I didn't feel like a hero, but I did at least feel like I'd be working at SGI a while longer.

I FIDDLE AROUND WHILE ROME (OR SGI, AT LEAST) BURNS

And I did indeed work at SGI for a while longer—but not much. Late in 1995, I accepted a request to write, direct and edit a tour of the SiliconWorks Solutions Center—SGI's advanced research lab, which consisted of a single room full of SGI workstations. I had to bite my tongue to stop from laughing. They had the arrogance to call this a "lab"? After all, not two years earlier, I'd co-produced a show about Lockheed's Palo Alto Research Labs, which occupied an entire campus and worked with a host of truly advanced technology, including lasers, diamond films, satellite payloads and things so secret that if I revealed them here, more than half a century later, Lockheed Martin would have me assassinated.

Once I wrote the script, we settled on a date to shoot the video. And it was on that very day that the stock market hit the "flush" lever and SGI began to tank—to circle the toiletary drain. The stock was in freefall the entire day, which proved to be a major distraction for the employee-actors we had in the show, all of whom clearly had their futures and their fortunes tied to SGI stock. The day resembled nothing so much as the directions on a bottle of shampoo:

1) LATHER: Watch the employees work themselves up into a LATHER as they checked the stock price between takes;

2) RINSE their anxieties by insisting they focus on the task at hand, namely shooting the next scene;

3) REPEAT. All. Day. Long.

THE TALLY

Over the course of 1995 I produced something like 50 individual Video Letters targeted at companies like Kodak, Boeing, GM, Pratt & Whitney, Fisher-Price, John Deere, Maytag, The Gap, and dozens of others. How effective they were I'll never know. That metric would be difficult to quantify, for one thing—but even if it had been quantified, that kind of data was too far above my pay grade for any of the arrogant management to ever bother sharing with me.

IN WHICH I BECOME FURNITURE (or, ONE MAN, BANNED, *Part 2*)

October 1995

When the gods battle, the only indication we mere mortals have is the occasional blast of lightning that wipes us out like ants in a thunderstorm. Such was my fate at SGI: Victim of a War Between the Titans.

I mentioned the cold shoulder I'd received from SGI's Video Production Department. But I had no idea the deep level of resentment that Joe DiTrolli's little transgression against this department had incurred—nor the wrath and revenge of which the warring gods were capable. I would, however, find out.

The backstory: "Harry Hollywood," the director of SGI's Video Production Department—the *real* video production department at SGI—had always resented Joe DiTrolli's incursion into his domain. SGI video *belonged* to Harry Hollywood, goddamn it, and he *would not tolerate* any subversion of his bailiwick, such as Joe DiTrolli's one-man, homemade video unit. He *would* have his revenge against this impertinent upstart! Joe DiTrolli *would* learn that *You Do Not Fuck With Harry Hollywood!* And in a spectacularly arrogant and stunningly dumb move, Dopey Joe presented Horrible Harry with the perfect opportunity to exact his revenge in late 1995, when Joe spent $50,000 to produce his own SGI promotional video (which, BTW, was more than I made there in an entire *year*). Not only was Joe not authorized to do this, but he had the effrontery, the sheer *gall*, to have this show produced by an outside company—*not* SGI's Video Production Department. For Harry, this was the last straw: he could not condone any such insult to his fiefdom. And so he petitioned the Highest Management to censure Joe, and insisted that as punishment, Joe's little toy—i.e., my offline editing suite—should be wrenched from his grubby little troll hands and transferred to Harry's kingdom. As Pharaoh said (in the movie version of *The Ten Commandments*, anyway), "So it shall be written. So it shall it be done." And I found myself a pawn in The Pissing Contest of the Gods (or at least of the arrogant VPs).

I had no umbrella to protect me from this pissing contest. Although my six-month contract had been renewed in July, sometime in October I received word that Joe's entire video suite and all associated equipment would be transferred to Harry Hollywood's domain. The list of equipment included: all VCRs, the SGI Indigo workstation, the desk, the chair, the editor...

Wait. "The editor"? Me? Transferred to Harry's domain, like the desk and the chair? Apparently, I had become furniture.

And so I oversaw the packing and transfer of my offline editing suite to another building, where it would fall under the supervision of Harry Hollywood and the One True SGI Video Production Department. They stuck me in another closet, but I dutifully reorganized the suite and even canvassed for more work beyond Joe's video letters (which ceased production, for reasons that were never explained to me but should be pretty obvious given Harry's wresting of control away from Joe). I also repeatedly called and stopped by the office of my alleged new boss, one of Harry Hollywood's underlings. She was never in. For me. I never got an appointment to introduce myself or explain how I could benefit her. I left numerous messages on her voice-mail that went unreturned. I never met her.

I was having a strange feeling of déjà vu. This cold shoulder was reminiscent of the manner in which the Video Department Library personnel treated me in my early days at SGI: as though I was an annoyance and an enemy. A cancer. My homemade, offline editing suite was simply beneath their dignity—a wart on their Cindy Crawford; a hooptie parked next to their Ferrari—and beneath their contempt. Everyone I attempted to contact in this department simply ignored me.

My second six-month contract was set to expire at the end of the year. I informed my new boss of this, by phone and email—repeatedly—suggesting it be renewed. There was never any response. I was not being laid off...I was simply being allowed to expire, to fade away, to evaporate. Decades before social media crystallized the concept into a single word, I was being ghosted.

And so one afternoon, I packed up my few personal items and left SGI for the final time. If they wanted to know anything about my suite or my productions, they could renew my contract.

I never heard from anyone at Silicon Graphics again.

THE FATE OF THE HUBRISTIC, or WHEN SGI RULED THE EARTH

In February 1996, SGI purchased Cray Research, developers of the first supercomputer. Industry analysts were baffled by this move, since the two companies had little in common, either in their technology or their markets. The official story is that SGI planned to merge its high-end line with Cray to move into the supercomputer market.

I have a different perspective, however, to wit: SGI officials were so arrogant about their technology that the purchase of Cray was simply a way to signify SGI's status to the world and its dominance of the industry. *"Nyah, nyah;* you were the best, now we are, and we're gonna prove it by buying your sorry ass. *Now* who's Number One, bitch?"

During the years 1984-97, when Ed McCracken was CEO of SGI, the company's annual revenues grew from $5.4 million to $3.7 billion. But in 1998, following significant losses, CEO McCracken resigned. (According to Wikipedia, he was fired. Hey, Ed: You know how they pronounce "resigned" in Iowa? "Fired.") In 2003, Google leased the SGI buildings in Mountain View for their HQ, and purchased the buildings outright in 2006. (I assume they kept the coffee bars.) SGI continued its downward spiral and filed for bankruptcy in 2009.

Here's how hot SGI was when I came aboard in 1995: their terminals were featured in *Jurassic Park* as the computers that ran the entire park. Now SGI is the dinosaur and—unlike the dinosaurs in *Jurassic Park*—is unlikely ever to be resurrected.

THE MOUTH OF MADNESS

As closure, I present this representative story of my life at SGI. It might appear exaggerated, or it might appear as though I'd fallen down Alice's rabbit hole into some wacky Wonderland, but you have my word that this story is true, and that the conversation is recreated as accurately as memory allows. (Honestly, if I could write fiction this twisted, my Plan A probably would have succeeded.) But for a taste of the arrogance and illogic of this crazy place, try this on for size:

A few months after I started at SGI, when things were still going swimmingly, Alain LeDouche literally burst into my editing suite one morning, waving a sheaf of papers in my face. *"This is totally unacceptable!"* he yelled, and continued to harangue me about how *horrible* this was, how it *violated the culture* of SGI, how it was *indefensible*...and so on. He was beyond upset—he was livid. Apoplectic. I was afraid to interrupt him, so I just sat quietly and listened.

After ten minutes or so he wound down and asked me, "Do you understand that?" I shook my head and replied calmly, "Alain, I don't have the vaguest clue what you're talking about." He pushed the handful of papers toward me

"*This!* This is *totally unacceptable!*" I took the pages from him and flipped through them. It was a multi-page fax; a quick look indicated that it consisted of dozens of jokes, all "politically incorrect," to put it mildly—racist jokes, homophobic jokes, gender-bashing jokes.

"What does this have to do with me?" I asked. I hope I sounded genuinely perplexed, because I certainly was.

"This is *your fax*," he growled, stabbing the cover sheet with his index finger. Sure enough, the cover sheet had my name on it...as the recipient.

"Look here," I said, showing him the cover sheet. "*I* didn't send this. Somebody sent this *to* me. How could I possibly be responsible for something someone sends me?"

Alain's wrath would not be swayed by reason. "You *are* responsible for this!"

"*I'm* responsible for somebody sending *me* a fax?" I said. "This guy—the guy who actually sent it? He's an old co-worker. He said he wanted to fax me his résumé, which is why I gave him our fax number. Speaking of which, I never even *received* this fax. Where did you get it?"

He invoked the name of Joe DiTrolli's boss—three rungs up the management chain from Alain. "His Admin found this on the fax machine and she's *totally offended!"*

"OK, now just hold on for a second, Alain," I said, hoping he'd calm down and that reason would prevail. "What I hear you saying is that Mrs. Grundy *stole* a fax addressed to me, and it offended her. How does she play any part in this?"

"She found it on the fax machine and she's *totally offended.* She told her boss, he called Joe, and Joe told me to handle this."

"This fax has a cover sheet," I said, showing it to him. "It's addressed to *me.* Mrs. Grundy would have had to remove the cover sheet to see what was on the rest of the pages. So what I hear you saying is that she was snooping around and *eavesdropped* by reading it without my permission, then *stole* a fax addressed to me. And *she's* offended? *I'm* the one who should be offended!"

Alain insisted I apologize to Mrs. Grundy immediately. *Joe* insisted I apologize to Mrs. Grundy immediately—according to Alain, at any rate.

"If you want an apology," I said, "why don't you call the guy who *sent* the fax? Or *his* boss." The answer to this question was as logical as Alain's attitude was illogical: SGI didn't have any leverage over some guy who worked in another company. They couldn't threaten him with anything or demand an apology. Think about it: If somebody from another company ever called *me* demanding an apology—for *anything*—I'd tell them to go bugger themselves, and laugh while doing it. But Alain, and Joe, and Mrs. Grundy, and her boss—*Joe's* boss—did indeed have leverage…over *me.* A good offense might be the best defense... but not in this case, I realized. Not when I was being accused of the offense.

I could have gone straight to HR, perhaps, and pointed out the skewed, Alice in Wonderland logic with which I was being browbeaten. But I was just a contract worker—a consultant; a second-class citizen—so I could never win a fight against full-time employees. I could have told Alain he was out of his fucking mind, and to come back and talk to me when he was rational. But even if he ever realized how illogical this whole situation was (which in itself was doubtful), he was under orders from Joe—orders which he'd never contradict, no matter how irrational they were. He was a good Nazi, and would not question, or even think to question, his marching orders.

The bottom line was: I needed the job. So I swallowed my integrity and reason, turned on the charm, and apologized to Mrs. Grundy, the nosy, troublemaking, dried-up old cunt.

I dare you to try to get me to apologize for that, bitches.

Chapter 17

1996: STRANGE INTERLUDE 2.0

January 1996

I needed a job. Yes, again.

Silicon Graphics was never going to bring me back. I was beyond expendable. I was beyond furniture. I was actively exiled —a bad taste left in the mouth of the One True Video Department after their internal power struggle against my loose cannon of a boss, Joe DiTrolli.

I did have one ace in the hole, however. And so, in January of 1996, I drove up to San Francisco and met with my old friend and former roommate, Kevin C. Briggs, (aka "the roughest, toughest poet in the free world"), who was working for General Employment, a staffing and recruiting agency. I brought him a copy of my updated résumé (which now included a year at SGI) and bought him lunch. After the third or fourth beer, he agreed to take me on as a client.

Thus began 1996: The Gap Year—the one that simply drops off the résumé.

Before we dive into the dark inky waters of that *annus horribilus*, however, and just so I don't come across as a total depressive, I should mention that one good thing occurred in 1996: On February second, the movie I'd co-starred in way back in '93 aired on USA cable's "Up All Night" feature. I'd gone national.

MAGINET

March 1996

In late March, Briggs called with a lead. MagiNet, a hi-tech startup in Sunnyvale, was looking for someone to update their technical manual. It required very little tech writing, I was assured, but a high level of editing knowledge as well as proficiency with MSWord and desktop publishing. These were exactly my strengths. The Silicon Valley startup was offering four weeks' full-time work at $25 an hour—the same freelance wage I made at SGI. Maybe it was only temporary—but at least I wasn't taking a pay cut.

When I went to the interview, I was amused to discover that MagiNet occupied a building in Sunnyvale mere blocks from the building I worked in while in LMSC's Video/Film Dept. At least I knew the commute—and all the good lunch spots.

I met with G. Kelly Sides, an ironically small Texan with a round face, a squinty smile, and a soft drawl. When he asked if I had a background in editing and desktop publishing, I opened my briefcase and showed him some copies of the quarterly newsletter I'd been publishing for cult personality Robert Anton Wilson, and a copy of the book I'd desktop published a couple years earlier, consisting of a collection of material from the first ten issues of the newsletter.

He looked them over and furrowed his brow. Then he looked up at me with a curious, intense expression. "You know Robert Anton Wilson?" he whispered.

Oh, I was *in*.

"Sure do," I said enthusiastically. "Twenty years now. We've been business partners for the past decade." And I added the clincher: "I can introduce you if you'd like."

I hope I landed this job on the strength of my appropriate (albeit admittedly minimal) editorial skills. But if I got it because I was friends with a cult figure—and who'd ever guess that a middle manager and engineer in a tech firm would even be aware of Robert Anton Wilson—I had no complaints. Once again, my old Lockheed boss Bob Springer's fortune cookie aphorism was proving itself true: *The smart man knows everything; the wise man knows everyone.*

I applied myself, introduced myself around the small company, and turned in my assignment on time, under budget, and with minimal interference to Kelly or the operation of the company. And as an added bonus, I found a kindred soul in G. Kelly Sides, the soft-spoken, laid back boss with whom I would cross paths again—more than once.

May 1996

"That summer, like every summer,
was the worst summer of my life."
—HC, *MFU (Most Fucked-Up Man Alive Tells All)*

The MagiNet temp job was over. It was May and I'd worked exactly one month of the first four months of the year. And once again, I was unemployed.

But that was the least of my troubles—and my troubles were legion, and far outweighed that temporary problem. I had no job skills to get another job, for one. One of my two cats got into a fight and ended up dead. Worst of all, my wife had left me (not for my lack of employment, however). I was living in a Country and Western song. If I'd had a truck, it probably would have been stolen. (I don't mean to diminish the devastating effects of this suicide-adjacent tsunami of execrable events. But this is simply not that kind of book.)

I was buying groceries with credit cards—never a good sign, or a good idea. I was forced to sell a large chunk of my library as well as my ten-thousand-dollar comic book collection, just to pay rent and utilities for a few months.

All I had to look forward to was bankruptcy and vehicular residency...or another job.

I needed a goddamn job.

About once a month during that summer, Briggs sent me on a job interview. (The results of these abortions can be found in Part IV: "What I've Learned About: Interviews"; in short, let's just say that the results of those futile efforts did nothing to lessen my dark despair in the Summer of '96.)

By the end of May, I had resolved three things. The first was that, for various reasons, I was not going to kill myself. The second was that I would spend a minimum of one hour a day job hunting. There wasn't really all that much that could be done on a day-to-day basis, but I felt certain I could fill an hour a day.

I soon fell into a rhythm: Sundays I'd comb through the Classified Ads in the San Jose *Mercury News*, clipping anything that seemed like it had some potential. (Keep in mind this was 1996, in the early days of the Web. At that time I had a dial-up modem but was unfamiliar with any online job sites. Newspapers were still the main source of information about jobs, and whether or not a company posted a position online, they also still ran a newspaper ad.) That filled my hour for Sunday.

On Mondays, I'd tweak my résumé and write cover letters for the various Want Ad positions I'd discovered on Sunday. (Again, 1996: Most businesses, particularly older and established companies, still required a hard copy résumé sent by snail mail—the idea of an "email résumé" was considered radical, and often couldn't even be accommodated.)

Tuesdays I'd go to the Post Office, mail the résumé(s), and buy some groceries (with a credit card).

Wednesday was Phone-A-Friend day. Most of the job-hunting books or articles I'd ever read stated that networking was the best way to find a job. So I made a list of virtually everyone I knew who was employed and called a few each week, checking in and asking them to keep an eye out for any open positions. None ever panned out.

Thursday was Brainstorming Day. I'd spend a solid hour trying to think of something I simply hadn't thought of before. Sometimes I tried to calculate how far short of my monthly nut I would come if I just went out and got a minimum-wage job at a bookstore or in the fast-food service industry, until I realized that even a minimum-wage job wouldn't be of any use to my dire financial situation—it would only prolong the agony and take valuable time away from hunting for a professional position. Many Thursdays just I combed through the Yellow Pages for an hour to see if there was some forgotten skill I could leverage into a job, or some job function I could fulfill that required a skill that had simply slipped my mind. Since I never became an Aamco transmission specialist or a zookeeper, you can probably guess how that turned out.

And so on.

An hour a day, however, still left 23 hours a day to fill (or, say, 12 or 13 hours, after sleeping to excess). My third big decision, based on this luxury of time (and after I'd at least minimally recovered emotionally from the twin blows of the death of my cat and my marriage), was to research and write the movie guide for which I'd been keeping notes for years—a collection of excellent but overlooked films (aka "buried treasures") available on tape. I'd call it *Killer B's: The 237 Best Movies On Video You've (Probably) Never Seen.*

And so, after my hour a day of job hunting, I'd spend afternoons writing two or three reviews for the book, and evenings screening two or three movies while taking copious notes (and imbibing copious amounts of cheap brandy). It was a way to fill the hours, to keep the world at bay, and to forget my grim financial, marital and emotional situations for a moment.

And while even mentioning my film guide might seem outside the scope of this work history, writing *Killer B's* would eventually become the single best calling card for employment that I ever stumbled into...a side benefit that I wouldn't fully appreciate for nearly a decade.

As 1996 dragged on, however, I despaired of any future other than dying starving in a gutter somewhere. One simple phone call changed all that...

Chapter 18

1996: MAGINET

October 1996

"Hey, buddy," said the cheerful voice on my phone machine. (Before Caller ID, there was call screening, and I always screened my calls. If you could, why wouldn't you?) "It's Kelly Sides, from MagiNet. Pick up if you're there."

Aside from my single month at MagiNet six months earlier, I'd been out of work the entire year. It took me about a pico-second to decide to pick up. I liked Kelly. Maybe they wanted me back for a while. Hell, maybe they owed me money.

"Hey, Kelly," I replied. "What's up?"

"You still lookin' for work?"

"Uhh...yeah..."

"Why'ncha come in and we'll talk about a job?"

I didn't want to appear desperate. Even though I was. "Uhh... What *kind* of job?"

"Full time. Workin' for me."

So hell yes I went in. Probably the next day.

I don't recall the exact conversation we had, but the upshot was that I'd impressed Kelly and a few other key people at MagiNet, and they decided they wanted me to work with them. My lack of specific skills wasn't a consideration to them; it was my "fit" with the employees that dictated they find me some work. As it turned out, not only was my lack of specialization (i.e., no appreciable job skills) *not* a drawback, but my apparent flexibility in handling various unrelated tasks was actually, they'd decided, a benefit—a feature, not a bug.

"What I did," Kelly told me when we met in his office, "was ask five different managers what their least favorite task was. Then we agreed to toss those tasks into a big ol' bowl and hand 'em over to you."

Given the desperation of my current situation, the obvious and appropriate reaction would be grateful relief. Full-time work at a decent salary after nearly a year of unemployment? What's not to love? But clearly I'm not an appropriate kind of guy, and the obvious correct response was tempered by Kelly's description of the job. I'd be taking on the worst tasks of five different guys? At best, my job would be a big ol' bowl of leftovers. At worst, it would be a big ol' toilet bowl of yesterday's leftovers. Could it get any worse than that? I could hardly afford to turn down the offer. But I felt like I was in one of those movies where the guy is promised a big inheritance if he can just spend one night in a haunted house and survive. And you know how that usually turns out.

Clearly, there was no way I could say no way. But what sweetened the invitation considerably was Kelly's admission that he'd gone through General Employment to hire me...and that GE charged him an $8,200 finder's fee. I was worth paying an *eight thousand dollar* ransom for? That was twice as much as MagiNet had paid me for my entire month of temp work earlier that year. I suddenly realized how much Kelly really wanted me at MagiNet...and the idea of a Frankenjob didn't seem quite so unpalatable. I signed the offer letter on October 7, and we decided on a start date of October 16.

It amused me no end that the building MagiNet leased on Tasman Drive in Sunnyvale was only a few blocks from the Video/Film building I'd worked in at Lockheed—and that this building had previously been leased by Lockheed. Even more interesting to me was that the temporary fabric "MagiNet" sign in front of our building covered a sign, literally carved in stone, identifying the original occupants of this building: Pacific Data Images, one of the first computer graphics imagery (CGI) companies. They pioneered chyron graphic overlays and "flying logos" on broadcast television shows in the '80s, and contributed CGI effects to numerous movies in the '80s and '90s, including *Terminator 2*, from which I often pulled clips to illustrate the functionality of Silicon Graphics computers while working at SGI. PDI was using Silicon Graphics computers when I was at SGI, and would eventually create the world's second CGI feature film, *Antz*, which was released through DreamWorks SKG—a company that would eventually purchase PDI outright.

(*Side Note:* Although I could hardly know the intricate connections to my own eventual employment path at that time, the incestuous nature of work in Silicon Valley still boggles my mind. I would go on to interview at DreamWorks Animation while still at MagiNet, for instance, and PDI later moved to Redwood Shores, where I would work for a while in 2006 [see the chapter on Adchemy], in Redwood City, where I would live while working at Apple.)

A BIT OF HISTORY, OR BACKGROUND, AT LEAST

MagiNet was founded in 1991, and by 1996 the company was providing movies on demand to hotel guests in 13 countries worldwide, mostly in four- and five-star hotels like the Mandarin Oriental in Hong Kong, the Sheraton on the Park in Sydney, and the Imperial Inter-Continental Hotel in Taipei. In 1996, providing movies on demand to hotel rooms required a bank of VCRs housed in a room in the basement of each hotel. The local branch offices had personnel who'd make the rounds of the hotels in their territory, switching out videocassettes in the hundred-plus VCRs in each hotel once a month. It seems laughably archaic now, but in 1996, it was the state-of-the-art method for enabling hotel guests to order a movie through an on-screen menu in the privacy of their room using only the TV remote control.

And while MagiNet always offered a selection of new releases, classic cinema and kid's titles, what always rented best was—get ready for a real surprise—porn. Porn accounted for about 75 percent of our rentals, consistently, month after month, in every hotel in every country. I was baffled—not by the high percentage, but mostly because our "adult" films were essentially crap. The majority were cheesy, low budget Japanese imports ...and none of our porn rated above "Hard R" (as it's referred to in the industry). As an employee, I was allowed to borrow any, and as many, movies as I wanted...but even I gave up on our porn after a few disappointing screenings. And yet, foreign business travelers were evidently so starved for sex that they'd even rent our mediocre masturbatory movies. As a future president of the USA (who himself turned out to be no stranger to porn stars) might say, "Sad."

Despite the content—and despite the technological limitations—MagiNet was a mildly successful endeavor. By 1996, the company was providing movies on demand to more than 400 hotels. We had branch offices in Australia, New Zealand, Thailand, Japan, South Korea, Israel, South Africa, the Philippines, France, Singapore, Hong Kong, and Guam. I was not oblivious to the irony that even though I worked for a company that provided a service to these four- and five-star hotels, I could never afford to stay in one. (Wait—there's a four-star hotel on *Guam*?)

THE WORK

Even though my ostensible title was "Customer Service Coordinator," as might be expected given the eclectic (read "cobbled-together") nature of my position, my tasks were varied. I was expected—no surprise here—to keep the technical manuals updated, for example...the same job I'd performed during my apparent "audition" the previous April—and the core task that allowed me to claim the title Senior Editor. (The fact that I was the *only* editor did not affect the designation of *Senior* Editor.)

I was also tasked with the pixel-level responsibility of reviewing the statistics from each hotel faxed to us every day. (Faxed! How quaint!) This required manually thumbing through a stack of paper about an inch thick—one sheet for each hotel—and scanning the hundreds of bits of information on each page for anomalies. It seemed overwhelming, but once I became familiar with the "normal" values for each entry, the anomalies seemed to jump off the page as I flipped through them. At some point, I was able to see that VCR #32, say, in the Michelangelo in Johannesburg was underperforming for three days straight—at which point I'd drop an email to our office in South Africa suggesting that on the next switch-out of cassettes the operative check whether that particular machine was perhaps jammed, or turned off, or broken. I got no end of amusement knowing that I could sit at my desk in Sunnyvale and spot a jammed VCR in Thailand, or Israel, or South Korea. Or Guam. *Guam?*

The MagiNet system not only delivered movies on demand in hotel rooms but also included an option for the hotel to display an onscreen slideshow detailing the services available in that particular hotel. As Senior Editor, I coordinated with the hotels that requested this service, wrote all the onscreen text for these service screens, and worked with various software engineers—and a brilliant graphic artist named Gaird Schlesinger—to create and test this concierge function. Thus began my on-the-job education as to how to write clear and concise text for video screens—a skill I would struggle to refine and master over the next decade and a half (although the length of this book might indicate that I, in fact, never did learn the lesson).

Once I mastered the tasks I was assigned, I took on a new assignment, essentially that of internal Corporate Communications. I was to be the single point of contact between our Sunnyvale HQ and the 13 foreign offices—or, as Kelly defined the task, "you'll be the traffic cop." This proved to be a logistical nightmare in many respects, not the least of which was that the MagiNet foreign offices naturally operated on their own local time, and we in the Sunnyvale home office worked California time—weekdays, 10 AM to 6 PM. Queries from foreign offices usually took overnight for me to receive, and occasionally as long as 24 hours to be answered. Unless I worked 24/7, there was simply no way around this.

This time delay was one challenge. Another was that the staff in fewer than half of our client countries spoke English in any depth beyond rudimentary. I quickly realized that when I sent a message to all field offices, it had to be written in clear, simple English, with no ambiguities and no idioms. If I said, for instance, "Give me a ballpark figure," personnel in the Japanese office understood the reference, since we imported baseball to Japan after World War II. But the Thai employees were completely baffled by this colloquial phrase—baseball was simply not part of their cultural experience. This exercise proved quite illuminating to me as a writer, and reinforced the KISS principle as applied to communication: *Keep It Simple, Stupid.*

MAKING THE GRADE (IF THE GRADE IS "C+")

As the designated single point of contact for the field offices, I handled a lot of odd requests and even odder comments. After a few months, I began to detect a pattern of complaints from every one of our countries. In May, I took my evidence to Kelly and suggested that I write a questionnaire we could fax to the largest and most prominent of our 400-plus hotels, asking them to grade us on our service. He gave my plan a green light, and I developed a document with 20 questions in several categories, including the content we offered, the reliability of our service, customer complaints, and so on. Each question would rate our service on a scale of 1 to 5, with room for comments.

Out of the 150 hotels to which we sent the "Hotel Satisfaction Survey," 108 responded—a 72 percent the return rate. I carefully compiled the data, did the math, and transcribed the comments into a summary report. Overall, our average score was about 2.7 out of 5: a C+ grade. Wait, what? I was working for a C+ company? Reluctantly, I took my report to Kelly. He wasn't happy, but it didn't seem to surprise him (even though the ten hotels that expressed that they were "Extremely Dissatisfied" did sting a bit). For all our determination to make the MagiNet system "100 percent operational 99 percent of the time," we seemed to be falling far short of that goal.

AS AMERICAN AS A PICKET FENCE OR A PICKET LINE

Even though MagiNet was headquartered in Sunnyvale, the service had, ironically, no American presence. That space was dominated by SpectraVision, the brand name of OnCommand's movies on demand service for hotels and motels. But, as might befit an international concern, our home office crew was a real multi-culti mix, even though we had precious few employees in the Sunnyvale home office (somewhere between 35 and 50 as I recall). We had a couple of Chinese nationals on work visas, for instance, as well as several Australians, a Korean graphic artist, and even a Muslim woman in a hajib—not to mention a number of Texans, like Kelly. (The Texans might not have been foreigners, but they were certainly not locals.) It was a shock to me to discover that there were only two people in the office who came from Silicon Valley—and I was one. I cynically suspected that there was some kind of quota to fill, or that someone realized the black PR the company might get if anyone discovered that not a single employee in the Silicon Valley office was a local.

NOT THE YELLOW BRICK ROAD BUT THE SOCIO PATH

There always seemed to be tension between the Chinese and the Texans. And the single source of this was perhaps the most interesting employee at MagiNet—"interesting" in the same sense that that wiggly thing you discovered when you turned over that wet rock one time was "interesting." "Wah Wen Wong," as we'll call him, was the chief software engineer at the company; the guy responsible for creating, maintaining and upgrading the software that ran the entire MagiNet system. And he was a complete and utter sociopath. (Remember, I have a degree in Psychology and worked in two asylums. I can spot a sociopath from fifty paces.) Need evidence? At an All-Hands meeting, our CEO casually asked him what he was working on. Wah Wen Wong's response: "You're too stupid to understand what I do." Well. No one had any doubt about the accuracy of Wah's assessment. But what type of lunatic insults the boss's intelligence in front of the entire company?

Need more evidence? That, too, was provided. Since Wah Wen Wong was the original author of the MagiNet system software, and the single person who understood it, the executives were always urging to get him an assistant—a human "backup system" who could take over in case anything horrible happened to Wah (if only!). Wah unilaterally rejected this request until it became a demand—at which point he chose as his assistant Ricardo, a guy who embodied all the stereotypical attributes of a software engineer. Ricardo was smart, but so socially backward that many people thought he was retarded. In the politically correct language of today, we'd say that Ricardo was "somewhere on the spectrum" of autism.

But I liked Ricardo, if only because everyone else avoided or ignored him. And that's just not right. No one needs to dread going to work every day because none of his co-workers will talk to him, or even look at him. So I took him to lunch a couple of times and listened to his story. I attempted to make him feel comfortable and valued. And then one day Ricardo stopped by my desk. He looked upset. Our conversation, as best as I can reconstruct it, went something like this:

Me: Hey, Rick. What's up?

Ricardo: [long hesitation. Avoiding eye contact. Shuffling. I wait patiently.] You know that Wah Wen Wong picked me as his assistant.

Me: Yeah. Quite an honor.

Ricardo: Uhh... I've been looking at his code.

Me: And...?

Ricardo: You know what a "backdoor" is?

Me: Umm...it's secret code that allows somebody special access. I think.

Ricardo: Yeah.

Me: And...?

Ricardo: [long hesitation. Avoiding eye contact. Shuffling. I wait patiently.] I found a backdoor in Wah's code. More than one.

Me: OK. And that's a bad thing?

Ricardo: The way he's using it, yeah. You remember a couple months ago when the system crashed and Wah had to come in on the weekend and fix it?

Me: Yeah...

Ricardo: I think he did that himself. I think he crashed the system himself. So he could come in and fix it in a few minutes and look like a hero and a genius and get another raise.

Me: [long hesitation. Avoiding eye contact. Shuffling.]Fuck.

Ricardo: Yeah. So what do I do?

I was pleased that Ricardo trusted me enough to bring this information to me. But damned if I knew what he should do about it.

Me: Give me a minute to think about this...

I thought about it for a minute. Maybe two (which is about my limit).

Me: OK. First, are you *sure* about this?

Ricardo: Pretty sure. Yeah.

Me: Well, let's think this through... OK. You *know* that if the execs are given a choice between a subversive Wah Wen Wong who has total control over all the software that keeps this company running, and a minor programmer who people think is a bit...*off*...they'll choose Wah every time. You do realize that, right?

Ricardo: [sighing] Yeah.

Me: So here's what I'd suggest: If you're interested in keeping your job, don't do anything right now. But keep a record of these backdoors and of any "emergencies" that you-know-who might engineer in the future. Keep a paper trail. Then take the data to another programmer—somebody who understands what you're saying and can validate your data. I can't do that. Kelly can't. But another programmer can. Then we can take that data to the execs and see what they want to do about it. They might just fire all of us. But at least we will have tried.

Ricardo: Sigh...

Neither of us pursued this any further. But that was only, perhaps, due to circumstances.

THE DOG & PONY SHOW

Spring 1997

Sometime in early 1997, the execs decided it was high time to take the company public. MagiNet was privately owned, funded by investors who, like all speculators in tech startups, were looking to maximize their investments with a dynamite stock offering. Part of Silicon Valley's DNA—or of its legend, at any rate—is that one strong stock offering can make any number of people millionaires overnight.

I wouldn't be one of them. I knew that. I didn't have any stock options—I was just a worker drone. But so what? I never counted on that kind of windfall. If the stock offering was successful, the personal benefit was that the company would be around for a while...and I'd have a job for a while. Maybe even a better job, if we grew. (One of my running gags with Kelly, for instance, was to ask him frequently if there were any openings in the Paris office. We did not have a Paris office, but *oui*, I would have transferred *immédiatement*.)

We—the worker drones—were informed about the plan to go public when the President and the CEO of MagiNet held an All-Hands meeting. They explained that they'd be going to New York for the next few weeks, participating in the so-called "Dog & Pony Show" in which they'd pitch MagiNet to Wall Street firms whose geniuses would determine the valuation of the company and the price at which they should offer their stock. The execs showed us their "deck"—the slide presentation they'd be giving the financiers—and pumped us all up with their enthusiasm about conquering Wall Street.

When they returned a few weeks later, however, they sang a different tune—one that started downbeat and contained only minor chords. They held another All-Hands, where they explained—rather bitterly, it seemed—that those idiots on Wall Street had determined that our management had wildly overes-timated the valuation of the company...and that the initial stock price should be only about half of what they were shooting for.

This clearly came as a shock to the execs. I can only surmise they hadn't seen the report on my survey, in which our clients gave the company an overall grade of only C+. An A student might have commanded the valuation they believed was appropriate. But half that valuation seemed about right for a C+ company.

This Wall Street valuation was unacceptable to the founders, however. They expressed their disappointment and their bitter rejection of the whole rigged Wall Street valuation process. They felt they knew MagiNet's worth better than the so-called financial experts, and informed us that they'd be seeking "alternative avenues" to ensure the company got the valuation they believed it so richly deserved. (Emphasis on "rich.") My perception is that very few of us outside of the inner circle of top execs had any idea what those "alternative avenues" might consist of, or how they'd affect us.

NO DOG, NO PONY, NO SHOW

Here is an axiom I developed over the years:

In any company, there are no major changes that affect the workforce in a positive way.

Let's explore some evidence…

We found out soon enough what they meant by "alternative avenues." Sometime in mid-'97, the bosses held yet another All-Hands, and the 50 or so HQ employees dutifully filed into the one open space in the building large enough to fit us all at once. And they delivered their Breaking News: They'd sold MagiNet to an investor—an entrepreneur in the Philippines who wanted to take advantage of the company's existing hotel penetration to initiate in-room online gambling. Um...OK. If we'd drawn a giant cartoon thought balloon over the assembled workforce, it likely would have read: *What's in it for me?*

The answer was simple: Unemployment. The new owner wanted to relocate MagiNet's HQ to their own HQ in Manila. And the new owner chose to retain just three employees from the Home Office. Two of those three were the current President of MagiNet, and Bob Creager, the CEO and founder. And the third winner in the employment lottery? My boss, G. Kelly Sides, who'd be promoted from his current engineering position to Vice President of Business Development. He'd retain his employment with the company and get a promotion. I would receive the exact opposite: a demotion. To unemployment.

The old execs and the new owners were, I must admit, quite generous to the four dozen or so employees who'd be laid off in less than six months. On July 17th, we were presented with a "Retention Incentive Program": anyone who agreed to stay on through the end of the year would be given a $10,000 bonus.

I agreed, of course. Even if my position would soon be superfluous, the thought of job hunting once again was abhorrent. At least I was assured a steady paycheck for the next few months, plus the severance bonus. This paid respite would give me time to consider my options, which included taking stock of my alleged job skills and stockpiling enough cash that I could survive unemployment for several months while—*shudder*—searching for a new job.

EMPLOYMENT IS NOT IN THE (CREDIT) CARDS

I also discovered an additional, accidental benefit: Since I still had thousands of dollars of credit card debt, due to my unemployment in '96, I realized that if I were to take out credit card insurance in, say, February of '98, and pay the premiums for a couple of months (so it didn't appear as though I was attempting to scam them, which, of course, I was), then when I was laid off in April, I could get my minimum monthly payment on all four maxed-out cards made by the insurance for as long as I was unemployed. I was delighted that I'd found a way to beat the system. This gimmick, of course, would not work for everyone ever laid off from anywhere. The key was to know *in advance* that you were scheduled to be laid off. Sign up for the insurance, make a couple months' token payments, and then, Bingo! When you were laid off—right on schedule—let the insurance take over the payments. All that was required for that to happen was that you fill out and mail in a form once a month. The downside was that in those days, the "minimum payment" on a credit card didn't even cover the interest on the balance. The longer you made only a minimum payment, the deeper into debt you continued to sink—but far more slowly. The good news is that it bought me time, and at a fairly low cost. I wouldn't have to make monthly credit card payments, which would drain any precious cash resources—and I wouldn't have to file for bankruptcy. It was a tradeoff I was willing to make… if only to flip the bird at the mercenary credit card industry.

Within a few weeks, Kelly moved to Manila, and soon afterward he imported his family. He seemed very happy with the arrangement. He got a sweet deal: a promotion, a hefty raise, a family-sized apartment in Manila...and a car, complete with a driver/bodyguard who ferried his teenage daughters back and forth to the American school every day, as well as driving and escorting his lovely wife around town for errands and shopping.

I was sorry to see him go. But G. Kelly Sides had earned his place in my pantheon of Best Bosses, second only to Bob Springer at LMSC. Kelly became the model of how I desired and attempted to supervise people when that task fell upon me in later positions. And more than that, he was a friend.

Once the execs moved out of Sunnyvale...well, that's when the real fun began. After all, when the cat's away... I spent a couple of weeks of office time writing a manual covering the creation of onscreen information services our system provided to hotels. I answered the occasional email question from the new staff in Manila. But for the most part, I had virtually nothing to do. At all. For *months*. Workplace heaven.

I knew that to extend the time I could afford to be "between jobs" after I left MagiNet, I'd be smart to revive my freelance writing career, and to that end, I wrote several courses for Reel.com's new venture, Cinema U., the world's first online film school. And with abundant, paid free time, I went to the movies...sometimes three or four times a week. I saw *Contact* at a second run theater, for instance, and was so impressed that I went and saw it again the next day. I saw *Titanic*—and that runs nearly four hours. I'm fairly certain no one ever even noticed that I was rarely in the office—not that there were very many of us left in the office to notice.

A DREAM JOB AT DREAMWORKS, OR JUST A DREAM?

In November or December of '97, through some long-forgotten chain of events, I scored an interview at DreamWorks Animation. At that time, DreamWorks SKG had only been around about three years, and the Animation division was brand spanking new—their first film, *Antz*, wouldn't be released for nearly a year, and they were working simultaneously on their ambitious second feature, *The Prince of Egypt*, the epic story of Moses (which was released in December 1998, only a couple of months after *Antz*). The position I interviewed for was some kind of special effects librarian, tracking details of how certain effects (like fire, or rain, or ocean waves) were created, in order to assist future computer graphics animators in their efforts. Not the most thrilling or creative job, but...damn. *DreamWorks!* With a foot in the door, who knows where I could go? And it would be a hell of a step up from MagiNet.

DreamWorks flew me to Los Angeles, where I was met by a driver in a black Lincoln Town Car—Hollywood's "new limo."

I was delivered to the DreamWorks offices in the Universal City Plaza, where I was met by my contact—the guy who'd be my boss, God willin' and the creek don't rise. He was about 40 and dressed like a cowboy, from hand-tooled boots to a handlebar mustache. I'm not one for affectations—in other people, anyway—but I pretended this was totally normal. Shit, maybe it was, for Hollywood. He took me to the off-site building where I'd be stationed and introduced me to the other librarian, a young gay guy with a nasty attitude. But I could live with that. You don't have to actively *like* your co-workers, after all... you merely have to tolerate them. And once I was on board, I'd start looking for a better job and leave that jerk in my dust.

My cowboy escort took me to the cafeteria for lunch. I could see the Universal Studios theme park out the windows, and almost asked if we had time to go ride the "Back to the Future" ride before the next round of interviews. But I held my tongue. My heart sank, however, when I scanned the cafeteria and noticed that virtually every one of the employees I spotted was about half my age. I was 45, and even the supervisors I met that day were, at most, in their late 30s. For the first time, I felt the pressure of age. Both Silicon Valley and Hollywood were—and continue to be—devoted to Youth and simply have no use for older workers, despite the experience that might come with age. (Not in my case, but, you know, in general.)

After lunch, my escort parked me in a small theater and screened a 30-minute rough-cut excerpt from their work-in-progress, *The Prince of Egypt*. I was suitably impressed—not just with the unique style of animation, but I was actually touched by the musical number in this ultimate sneak preview. He walked me through a few areas where artists were making sketches and models for an upcoming production. I smiled and nodded and kept my mouth shut about how no movie about a smelly green ogre with a name like "Shrek" would ever be accepted by the moviegoing public. At length, we went to a conference room where I was grilled by a contingent of potential co-workers for a couple of hours, after which I was ushered back to my Town Car, taken to the airport, and flown home.

It was a whirlwind day, but I had no clue how well I did in the interviews. My one major concern was relocation. They'd let it slip that they had three candidates for the position, including one local; no matter what my personality or résumé did for them, the cost of relocation would certainly factor into their decision.

Since this is only the story of an interview, it seems fairly obvious that I did not get the position. My dreams were crushed by DreamWorks. So I continued the primary plan of staying at MagiNet until they shut the dump down, to qualify for the bonus. And I continued Plan A-Prime—ramping up my freelance writing career once again so I had a source of income during the next period of unemployment of unknown length.

MAGINOTHING

January-April 1998

The transition took far longer than the execs had expected, and with each postponement, those of us who agreed to remain under the "Retention Incentive Program" (could the acronym "R.I.P." be any more ironic?) were bribed with even more bonus money. Money for nothing and checks for free: not just song lyrics, by my preferred mode of employment.

Even with the extensions, attrition and other employment claimed those employees not willing to stick it out to the bitter end (and who were willing to forfeit a bonus of ten grand or more to find immediate employment). One by one, they quietly disappeared from the office, until our little building was a virtual ghost town. There were no goodbye parties; no closing ceremonies raising pints at the local brewpub; no teary farewells. The Sunnyvale headquarters just kind of...evaporated. And one day in late April, I packed up my personal items, walked away from my desk, and never returned.

I just hope the last one out turned out the lights.

Chapter 19

1998: INTERMISSION

PLAN A 3.0

May 1998

I didn't need a job. And, I thought, I might never need a job again, if I played my cards right. Clearly, I was not playing with a full deck. (One missing card, for instance, was my Queen of Hearts, who'd filed for divorce a few months earlier, after being MIA for a year and a half.)

I was, however, determined to take advantage of the enforced downtime, and was once again ready to attempt the leap from the corporate world into self-perpetuating self-employment. The advance notice that I'd be laid off (which I'd received more than six months earlier) freighted with it several benefits. And by May Day, 1998, I had all my ducks in a row to take full advantage of this propitious interlude. I had saved money. I had my layoff severance pay in the bank, as well as four weeks of payout for unused vacation time. (Since I'd never taken a single day of vacation, it was payment for every vacation day I'd accrued since Day 1 at MagiNet.) I had the ten grand the company paid me to stay through the transition, plus a few thousand in additional bonuses they granted us "R.I.P."ers as they repeatedly extended the transition. I qualified for unemployment benefits through California's EDD (Employment Development Department), at the max amount, and that was good for months. And I had cut my rent in half by moving into a new house with my new girlfriend, "Epiphany Jane" (aka "Piph," as she wishes to be (un)known).

I was, I figured, set financially for nine months to a year of unemployment without any strain and only minor conservative concessions to my lifestyle. And I vowed to spend that time diligently attempting to make enough money to attain "escape velocity" into a new career...yet another variation of Plan A.

A PROJECT OF KNOWLEDGE BECOMES A JOB OF WORK

I supplemented my nest egg by freelancing for an online company called The Knowledge Project. They were engaged in creating a database of movie reviews for essentially every movie ever produced, and I was one of their freelance writers. They'd fax me a 10- or 12-page list of titles they needed reviewed and I'd fax them back a list of those I was willing and able to write. (Even in 1998, we were still doing business by fax rather than email and attachments...or, I assume, by telepathy, if you're reading this anytime after The Singularity.)

These reviews were an exercise in concision. Each had an upper limit of 35 words, in which we were required to include a brief plot synopsis and some kind of recommendation (e.g., "For Jerry Lewis fans only; all others beware."). In addition, we were required to perform a kind of loose statistical analysis for each film, ranking about 20 different categories on a 1-to-10 scale. "Hollywood Style" was one, for example; "Family Friendly" another; others included the relative humor or intelligence or artistic style of each title. I had extensive viewing experience and a big stack of reference books, so I was always able to snag a full slate of reviews of minor flicks that no one else was able or willing to review. Payment was five dollars for each full analysis; I could do about four per hour without compromising quality. $20 an hour was, I decided, an adequate wage for a freelance job.

I came to think of these short exercises as haiku. And although I was not aware of it at the time, one benefit of learning to distill an enormous amount of information down to a few words would serve me well in later jobs where I'd be writing on-screen text for various video on demand services.

(As an aside, The Knowledge Project was ultimately purchased by Reel.com and integrated into Reel's film review website. Reel.com was purchased by Hollywood Video in July 1998 for *one hundred million dollars*. Hollywood Video was acquired by Movie Gallery in 2005. Movie Gallery filed for bankruptcy in 2010 and shut down the Reel.com website. Thus doth the old world passeth away.)

PUBLISH OR PERISH

Over the previous 20 years, my Plan A had proven a resounding success—in much the same way as the *Titanic*, the *Hindenburg*, and the *Challenger* had all been resounding successes. No publisher wanted to buy any of my (by now) six novels. Plan A 2.0—writing nonfiction—had been mildly successful, but hardly generated enough income to replace a corporate paycheck, and by 1998, after a decade of weekly video columns (at fifty bucks a pop), I was no longer writing for the San Jose *Mercury News* or appearing as a VJ on KTEH (at twenty-five dollars a pop). Magazine articles on movies and video paid a generous two hundred dollars each—but there were only two national magazines dedicated to home video. Even if I had an article in both magazines, every month, the total income for those would still only amount to four hundred dollars a month—less than a week's salary from my previous job at MagiNet.

So: freelance writing about film and video was a dead end—a month's work could at best only generate about the same amount of money as a week's work at any of my previous jobs, and that was—no surprise—far short of what it took to live in Silicon Valley at the time.

And so I launched Plan A 3.0: Publishing. One detail in my favor is that I was apparently in tune with the times; even though the phenomena of "desktop publishing" had been born more than a decade earlier, it was well established by '98, so tools and software were easy to come by. And I'd already desktop-published three books under my own publishing imprint, which, according to the Library of Congress, qualified me as a "small press publisher" (as opposed to being "self-published," or going to a "vanity press," where the author pays someone to print up copies of their unsold book—publishing paths roundly reviled by professionals as amateur alternatives). I was now focused on reinventing myself as a small press imprint. I'd attempt to make a living as a publisher, regardless of my friend Robert Anton Wilson's sage advice that "Every publisher should have a pimp as an older brother, so they'd have someone to look up to."

I did everything I could think of to succeed. I upgraded my computer. I purchased a good laser printer. I filed the requisite paperwork to become a legitimate company, registering "The Impermanent Press" as a DBA ("Doing Business As"), and opened a business checking account at Bank of America. I locked down the domain name "impermanentpress.com," and hired my brilliant former MagiNet co-worker, Gaird Schlesinger, to work his magic and build me a dynamite website. And I hooked up with an online credit card clearing service so I could sell books online for a nominal service charge.

And I started publishing. As my first project, I decided to reissue my 1986 book *Philip K. Dick: The Dream Connection,* a tribute volume to my dear old dead friend. The hardback version had sold well among Phil Dick fans, and Phil's legendary status had only grown in the fifteen years since his premature death. The original volume had been keyboarded onto five-and-a-half inch floppy disks, which even a dozen years later were woefully, even comically, obsolete, so the entire volume required re-keyboarding into MSWord onto 3.5-inch floppy disks (now woefully, even comically, obsolete). But I put in the work required and invested the cash required to print the book, and I was ultimately quite pleased that this quality paperback version ended up looking much better than the long-unavailable hard-back volume.

My next project was to publish a brilliant, outrageous comic sci-fi novel, *MFU (Most Fucked-Up Man Alive Tells All)* written by a reclusive tech genius who prefers to be identified only as "HC." He'd posted the book online for free, but I loved it so much that I convinced him he needed a trade paperback version.

And I promoted. I promoted the living shit out of these books and my website. For my film guide *Killer B's: The 237 Best Movies on Video You've (Probably) Never Seen,* I spoke to film groups around the Bay Area and sat on panels. I did radio interviews. I'd appear on any TV show in the Bay Area—broadcast, cable or public access—that would have me. I crossed paths with the local film community so often that at one point one member, Ken Karn, saw me show up and declared, "Here comes Scott, the total media whore!" He meant it as a joke (although clearly a passive-aggressive joke), but I proudly adopted it as my unofficial title: *Total Media Whore.*

I also continued my freelancing for Reel.com, writing capsule descriptions of old films for their ever-growing database, and writing courses for Cinema U., their online film school.

THOSE WHO CAN'T DO...

September 1998

Another gift fell into my lap during that period. Glenn Lovell, the primary film critic for (and my colleague from) the San Jose *Mercury News*, had been teaching a course in film history at a local college, but decided to take a sabbatical to write a book, and suggested to the college administrators that I would be an excellent replacement (or at least an adequate one, I guess, but I'm going to stick with excellent). And so I found work as an Adjunct Professor at Cogswell College in Sunnyvale—a small school located about a block away from the building in which I'd spent four years writing and producing videos for Lockheed. Silicon Valley is a small, small world.

Cogswell had been founded in San Francisco more than a hundred years earlier, but had continued to roll with the times; the Sunnyvale campus was a four-year institution devoted to awarding a single Bachelor's Degree, in Computer Graphics Imagery (CGI). (I used to joke that the school was producing the next generation of Pixar employees.) Since Cogswell was an accredited four-year college, however, in order to meet California state education requirements they needed to provide courses in the Humanities for their students—and that's where Film History fit in.

Although I was hesitant about teaching at any college that shared a name with "Cogswell Cogs," the competitor of George Jetson's futuristic workplace, Spacely Sprockets, all qualms evaporated when I discovered the propitious synchronicity that the school had been founded on a March 19th—my birthday.

And as it turned out, being a college professor—even an "adjunct" professor—was great fun. A captive audience was only one of the benefits. Another was screening a classic feature film each week...and getting paid to do it. In addition, this work would look great on my résumé when applying for any film-related job, along with my credentials of writing a video column for a major newspaper for over a decade, being a Contributing Editor to Reel.com and their online film school, and publishing a video guide.

Since Cogswell was devoted solely to a CGI degree, once I felt comfortable teaching (and once I'd proven myself to the administration), I pitched the Dean of Humanities the idea of a second course: The History of Animation. They approved it; I developed it; and it became one of the most popular courses in their curriculum. And two or three quarters a year, I got paid to talk about—and watch—cartoons. Over the next decade, I'd teach these courses more than a dozen times each.

I won't go into detail about my side stream teaching career here, since *No Plan B* is focused on my experiences in Silicon Valley hi-tech startups. I mention it only because all these film-related tributaries would in the long run flow together to put me in a unique position to work in the "movies on demand" industry ...although I could never have known this as I stumbled blindly into work that I found interesting, available...and borderline profitable.

I kept up all these activities for a year and a half—nearly twice as long as I'd originally predicted I could afford to be without a "paycheck job." But ultimately, I had to face the sad truth that no single freelance effort, and no combination of these efforts, could keep pace with the Big Bucks that a Silicon Valley job generated to meet the exigencies of making the monthly nut: rent, beer, utilities, beer, food, beer, and so on.

Thus, in late 1999 I found myself once again in the disappointing position where...

Chapter 20

1999: REPLAYTV

ReplayTV, Inc.

1945 Charleston Road
Mountain View
CA 94043-1201
Tel: 650.210.1143
Fax: 650.623.7143

D. Scott Apel *sapel@replaytv.com*
Zones Editor

www.replaytv.com

1999: REPLAYTV

"Don't just change the channel. Change the world."
—My suggested slogan for ReplayTV

I needed a job. Maybe not today. Maybe not tomorrow. But soon, and for the rest of my life. (Sorry; thought I was Bogart there for a moment.) Let's try again:

I needed a job. Not immediately. But soon. Yeah, soon would be good...

September 1999

Since being laid off from MagiNet 18 months earlier, I'd been living off the trifecta of Unemployment Insurance, my severance package, and all the freelance writing, publishing and teaching I could accomplish. But writing database reviews for The Knowledge Project couldn't go on forever, and Unemployment Insurance always comes with a hard cutoff date. And so, in September of the penultimate year of the millennium, I found myself on the shit end of the employment stick once again, forced back into the unenviable role of Jobseeker.

One major improvement over my previous job hunts was provided by the explosive growth of the internet during the previous four or five years. I now had access to numerous online job-posting sites such as DICE, Hotjobs.com, Craigslist and Monster.com.

But I already knew where I wanted to work: TiVo. They were new, they were local, and they had a product I thought was evolutionary, revolutionary, and totally cool: the Digital Video Recorder (DVR).

I hope someday someone with more ambition and journalistic experience than I have will research and write the definitive history of Digital Video Recorders...including an explanation as to why they never really caught on with consumers when they were first introduced. Maybe consumers needed more education about recording television on a hard drive—a device most commonly associated with a computer, which might have scared off the technophobes. Maybe consumer perception was that DVRs differed so slightly from the VCRs they'd been using for over twenty years that no one saw the need to invest in a new device just to perform a single function of a VCR, namely timeshifting their TV shows. Maybe the concurrent rise of DVDs abducted consumers' limited budgets for new video technology. After all, DVDs were so similar to VCRs (in terms of movie rentals, anyway) that precious little consumer education was necessary to understand how a DVD player could improve a viewer's life... but *way* too much education was necessary to teach consumers how greatly a DVR could enhance their television viewing.

We now return to the narrative, which is already in progress:

On one of the internet job sites, I ran across a listing from TiVo for a position I felt I was eminently qualified to fill: creating short promo videos. Hell, I'd spent more than four years at Lockheed writing and producing videos, and at Silicon Graphics I'd done essentially the job TiVo was advertising for: a one-man band creating and editing short digital videos. I tweaked my résumé and sent it in along with my video demo reel.

I never heard back from them. Let's call this Strike One for TiVo. They will reappear in this narrative...and not flatteringly.

I was rather baffled by TiVo's non-response. Did they receive so many applications for this position that they couldn't respond to them all? How was that even possible, since the position required a number of very specific and diverse skills? How many people could possibly possess all the required skills, as I did? Is it possible they could have found someone with more, or more pertinent, experience? Who was also local? How the hell could that be? The most depressing thought was this: Were there, in fact, *so many* candidates more qualified for this position than I was that I never even made the cut for an interview? Fuck me.

But all that *agita* lay in the future, at this point. And after I sent my submission package, while waiting for them to most assuredly respond, I called the people I'd listed as "Personal References" on my résumé, as a professional courtesy to alert them that they'd certainly be receiving a call from TiVo asking about me, as part of their HR background check. I appealed to my guys to be one hundred percent positive, and, when in doubt about my character or competence, to lie.

The first person I called was G. Kelly Sides, my most recent boss, at MagiNet. I told him to expect a call from TiVo.

"Oh, you don't wanna work for them," he said.

"I don't?"

"No, you should go to their competition."

"They have competition?"

"Yeah, place called ReplayTV, also in Mountain View. Our old buddy Matt from MagiNet hired in there and says he's very happy."

This was news to me. There were *two* DVR companies? Both located Mountain View? And I had a personal contact at the other one?

"Gimme his number! Gimme his email!" I requested. (OK, demanded.) But Kelly just chuckled and gave me his contact info.

WEEK ONE

I called Matt the next day and relayed my conversation with Kelly. He agreed to receive my résumé. "I'll make some copies and pass 'em around to the right people," he said. I tweaked the résumé—without the benefit of knowing what position I was applying for—and faxed it to Matt the next day.

The following day—I repeat, *the following day*—I received a call from the Director of HR at ReplayTV. "Your résumé has been circulating around the office and has generated some interest," he said. "We'd like to set up some interviews. Can you come in tomorrow?"

So that was the score: TiVo—no reply. ReplayTV—an invitation to interview *one day* after receiving my résumé. Guess which one had my attention.

Since I had no idea what position I'd be interviewing for, I stuffed my briefcase with everything I could think of: a videocassette of my demo reel from Lockheed and another with my work for SGI; a binder containing copies of several columns and articles I'd published in newspapers and magazines, along with printouts of the courses I wrote for Cinema U.; copies of the writing I'd done for MagiNet; copies of my résumé (on nice paper, not fax paper); and (of course) several copies of *Killer B's*. I was ready for anything.

I found the nondescript corporate headquarters building in a nondescript industrial park on Charleston Road in Mountain View —right around the corner from, and within walking distance of, the building I'd worked in during my stint at Silicon Graphics. (The last time I drove through that neighborhood, about 2012, this building and all those surrounding it had become assimilated into the Googleplex—the "sprawling" Google campus, as the media describes it.) And I did my interviews. I don't recall exactly who I interviewed with, but I remember that I told every one of them that: a) I was excited about the product; b) that the key idea for household electronics over the next few years would be "convergence" (whatever that meant in those days); and c) that we should position our product to "own the living room" and eventually become the proverbial Next Big Thing, the Holy Grail of the moment: the "home server." Oh, yeah, I'd studied the buzzwords, and I wasn't shy about trotting them out. And I got vehement agreement whenever I did.

The only disappointment was that the highest exec I was scheduled to interview with—"Lois Tantrum"—never showed up for our appointment. (Yeah, he was a guy named Lois, at least in this version. What, you never heard of a boy named Sue?) But as I was on my way out, I ran into him on his way in. I introduced myself, and we chatted informally on the sidewalk for a few minutes. He was enthusiastic about the product and seemed like a smart, pleasant guy. Foreshadowing: That was the last time he ever seemed either smart or pleasant—hence the name change for this book.

Apparently, I passed the gauntlet. The HR rep called the next day—I repeat: *the next day*—to offer me a position. "It doesn't matter that I didn't get to interview with Lois?" I asked. "Nah," the rep replied. "He approved you based on your other interviews." And on September 29, 1999, they made me an offer I couldn't refuse: employment. I was offered a choice: more stock options and a lower salary, or fewer stock options, a higher base salary, and an early review for a raise. I knew nothing about stock options at that time. I did, however, know what more cash would mean for me, so I chose what was behind Door #2. I signed the papers and officially became ReplayTV employee #52.

My new boss, Doug Shannon, a young, hip software engineer, was there with me when I signed. Doug was the guy who'd lobbied for me with Lois and the others. We adjourned to his office, a dark man-cave decorated like a tiki bar, where we talked about the next step. "Can you start tomorrow?" he asked. I wanted to say, "Nah, I need a couple of weeks off to get ready, since I probably won't have another vacation for years." But I refrained. *Of course* I could start tomorrow, I said. "We should get an early start," he said apologetically, and with a sheepish grin asked, "Is, uh, is ten o'clock too early for you?" "I think I can make that," I assured him. A decade earlier, my corporate masters at Lockheed thought 7:30 AM was late. But in this hi-tech startup, 10 AM was considered *early*? Man, I was *home*!

We started early the next morning—maybe 10:30, after Doug showed me where the coffee and the men's rooms were located. He fired up the ReplayTV in his office and walked me through the system.

ReplayTV (like TiVo) was both a set-top box and a service. The box itself was a jet-black rectangle about the same size and shape as a VCR or a DVD player. Customers purchased the box, plugged their TV cable into it, then plugged a second cable from the ReplayTV unit into their TV set (in 1999, still the old fashioned tube box). All video input ran through the Replay machine first and then onto the TV screen. This enabled the Replay to record programs, just like a VCR.

But these new DVRs boasted several additional functions that VCRs didn't have. One was an onscreen channel guide that contained ten days to two weeks worth of program data. This TV guide automatically updated daily: you plugged the DVR into your home phone line, and it auto-dialed a local number every night around 3 AM and downloaded updated program information. Other unique features that only digital recording could accomplish included the ability to pause live TV and later return to precisely where one left off watching—giving the viewer time to answer the phone (or pay the pizza man, or take a whiz) without missing a second of a broadcast show.

The most controversial function of the Replay DVR was the "commercial skip"—a button that jumped ahead in 30-second increments so the viewer could eliminate annoying commercials (if that isn't redundant). This feature was never widely promoted, for the simple reason that it was a huge thorn in the side of network TV, an industry that makes its revenue from commercials. There was always tension between ReplayTV and the networks over the inclusion of this consumer-friendly but network-antagonistic function...so much so that it led to a 2002 lawsuit against ReplayTV brought by the biggest TV networks and film studios, on the grounds that skipping advertisements violated copyright. (A judge disagreed.)

In 1999, the differences between the first models of TiVo and ReplayTV were minor. One was that only Replay had the commercial skip button. Another was their business models: TiVo operated on a subscription basis—users paid a ten dollar a month subscription fee to get the program guide—while the ReplayTV Service was free, with the intention of generating revenue the same way the TV networks did: advertising. And the primary outlet for advertising would be...Replay Zones.

Replay Zones: Doug Shannon's invention, and my new domain as Zones Editor. Once I was informed of this proposed business model, I felt a bit of pressure. Was the success or failure of this entire enterprise dependent on my ability to create compelling content? Fuck me.

IN A ZONE

Replay Zones are difficult to describe if you've never experienced them, as they were, in fact, something new and different. But just as the corporate business model depended on Zones to generate revenue, understanding them is vital to this chapter. So apologies in advance if I overexplain.

The ReplayTV units included a rudimentary search function that used the remote control. If you went to Search and spelled out "golf" on the onscreen alphanumeric keyboard, for instance, the unit would scan through the two weeks of upcoming programs available on your cable or satellite service, and would return results for any golf programs that were available for your viewing pleasure. But in addition to the golf you probably meant, and probably wanted to watch—tournaments, etc.—the simple search would also list returns for *Caddyshack, Tin Cup, Happy Gilmore*, and other movies *about* golf...as well as any TV program in which the word "golf" was mentioned in the description. (*Law and Order:* "A killer monkey uses a golf club to bludgeon his victim"; *Friends:* "Ross is bludgeoned to death by his golf club-wielding monkey.") Clearly, these movies and TV shows were not at all what a golf fan meant when searching for "golf" as a sporting event. Such returns tend to muddy the results and lead to viewer confusion—and frustration.

Replay Zones provided more refined, and more complicated, searches. (In 2020, we'd probably refer to them as "artisanal"). Zones were designed to provide fine-grained searches that we (i.e., I) believed most viewers would wish to perform if they had the ability to do so—in computer terms, true Boolean searches. Each "Zone" would be devoted to a top-level subject of television programming (Movies, Sci-Fi, NBC, etc.), and each would contain several "channels" of specific, highly refined searches. To expand the "golf" example, for instance, we might (and did) create a Sports Zone, with channels devoted to Football, Basketball, Baseball...and, of course, Golf. These high-level searches would be designed to filter outliers like *Caddyshack* and TV show episodes with the word "golf" in their description from the Replay Zones Golf channel. (Keep in mind this was years before "The Golf Channel" became a full-time cable channel.)

My job as Zones Editor was to determine—by research, experience, intuition and fiat—what it is that people actually want to watch on TV, and what they were most likely to search for...and then research and create those top-level Zones and their internal, subcategory Channels.

WEEK TWO: GIVE ME WOOD

They gave me an office—an actual office, and a nice one, too—on the second floor of the two-story building, in the same aisle as several of the top execs, including CEO Anthony Wood (who would much later become known as the father of the Roku streaming media players). And I was made welcome, particularly by an email from Anthony Wood addressed to All Personnel. He'd received the list of the week's new hires, and he responded simply: "Is that *the* Scott Apel?" Turns out he was a huge *Dr. Who* fan and had seen me many times on KTEH, introducing episodes of the show as the VJ for "Science Fiction Night." Once I'd emotionally processed this email, I walked down a few doors and introduced myself, and suggested we have lunch sometime, where we could talk about Dr. Who.

A few weeks later, we did, in fact, go to lunch. I offered to drive; when he saw my car he said, "Oh, you drive a Jaguar!"

"Yep," I replied. "And I love it, even though the electrical system is haunted and it leaks fluids I didn't even know cars had." I wanted to amuse my boss's boss's boss, so I attempted to turn this into a comic monolog. "There are three things the British are *not* noted for," I continued; "their engineering skills, their cuisine, and their dental hygiene."

"You know I'm British," he replied. Um...no, I did not. Not an auspicious start to what I hoped would become a friendly relationship. But he seemed more amused than insulted, and we had a lovely lunch—although he might have obtained his revenge when he didn't pick up the check. Guy's worth a billion damn dollars and he doesn't pick up the check for lunch with one of his loyal employees? Well, hell...maybe that's how he got to be a billionaire in the first place...

WEEK TWO: IN WHICH I ENDEAR MYSELF TO YET ANOTHER TOP EXECUTIVE

On Wednesday of Week Two, I attended the weekly new hire orientation. The conference room was full. Had they really hired something like 25 people the previous week? ReplayTV was founded in 1997, and when I interviewed, there were fewer than fifty employees. Judging by this spike in hiring and observation of the type of people being hired, it was clear to me that the company was positioning itself for a quantum leap in both production and marketing. Most of the new hires were either young, scruffy, relaxed guys—clearly hardware or software engineers—or young, well-dressed, hypertense women—clearly Marketing douches. I took a seat next to the one person who looked to be about my own age; a short guy, boyishly good-looking, wearing the rectangular glasses that were the fashion at that time.

"Hi," I said, offering him my hand. "I'm Scott."

"Kim," he responded, shaking my hand.

"I'm employee number fifty-two," I said, just to start a conversation.

"Fifty-*one*," he said, aiming a thumb at himself.

"No shit?" I said. "They go for two years with fifty employees, and the first two they hire are us?" He laughed, so I leaned in and said quietly, "I just hope these assholes know what they're doing. I got a lot riding on this."

"You and me both, brother," he sighed, shaking his head.

After we were welcomed by the person running the orientation, he suggested we go around the table and introduce ourselves—quickly, since there were so many of us. Name and job title, that'd do it. As I'd suspected, most of the homeless-looking guys were engineers...and most of the sharply dressed girls were Marketing douches. When it was my turn, I stood up and announced, "Hi, I'm Scott Apel. I'll be creating Replay Zones." And then my new friend, the guy sitting next to me, stood up and delivered his brief introduction: "Hi. I'm Kim LeMasters, the new CEO."

Say *what*?

I found out later that Kim LeMasters had had a very successful career in Hollywood, first as a programming exec at ABC (greenlighting *Kung Fu* and *Wonder Woman,* among many other shows), later as president of CBS Entertainment, and most recently as a writer (*Silk Stalkings*) and independent film producer (including 1999's *Wild Wild West*...but we forgive him for that).

IN A ZONE 2.0

Once Doug completed my tutorial on Zone creation, I was on my own to a great extent. I had only a handful of tools with which to perform my work, but *damn*, they were powerful tools.

First among them was unlimited access to the Tribune Media Services (TMS) database. The TMS maintained a complete guide for literally every television program available on every broadcast, cable and satellite channel throughout the U.S. TMS provided the data that updated ReplayTV's onscreen program guide, and would be the primary source of my research for Replay Zones—I could run search queries and determine whether or not there were enough programs available widely enough to warrant a Replay Zone Channel, for instance. (Golf, *si*. Equestrianism, *no*.)

The Tribune Media Services database provided what is referred to as "metadata," i.e., data about data. For every movie and TV show, for instance, metadata available from TMS included Title, Year of Production, Rating (MPAA rating for movies; TV rating for shows), Genre, Episode Title (for TV shows), a Description of the movie or episode, Cast, Director, Language...and so on.

In order to search these metadata fields, I coerced one of Replay's software engineers into teaching me some rudimentary PERL code, which allowed a Boolean search of the metadata fields. (Apologies for the tech jargon.) Although I considered myself a writer, and had never done any coding, PERL quickly became my second essential tool in creating Zones. Using PERL queries to the TMS, I could search for specifics—if I created the correct query, at any rate. I could create an entire Drama Movies Channel for the Movies Zone, for instance, with just a few lines of code that sorted all available movies into a Replay Channel restricted to those in which the metadata listed the genre as "Drama"—an automated channel that required no further effort or attention on the part of any human overseer (i.e., me).

Since I knew movies better than television, and was more comfortable with movies, I decided that the first Zone I would create would be the Movie Zone. This was a decision based not only on personal preference but on a calculated "return on investment" insight. A Movies Zone would be fucking *huge*. It would deliver massive results, no matter what broadcast, cable or satellite system a ReplayTV user subscribed to. And it would, I hoped, impress my new corporate masters: on my first attempt, I'd wrangled and herded a century's worth of films into Replay Zone Channels. The additional benefit to me was that a Movie Zone would be easy to create—movie genres were well established, and had their own field in the TMS metadata. Each genre would become a Replay Movies Zone Channel.

It quickly became apparent that creation of the Movie Zone I envisioned and desired would be a bit more difficult than I'd initially imagined. While it was easy to create Movie Zone Channels for the dozen or so top-level genres (Drama, Comedy, Sci-Fi, and so on)—I also wanted to add Channels for some popular subgenres. And while this was possible to accomplish technically, no metadata existed for the granular level subgenres I wanted to create. I really wanted to include a Cult Movies Channel, for instance—but there is no metadata field in the Tribune Media Service for "Genre: Cult." These granular Channels would require that I manually enter lists of specific titles rather than simply sorting metadata with a simple algorithm. I had to scour my numerous film books (and my memory) to create a hand-selected (and hopefully comprehensive) list of cult films, then manually keyboard the titles into the Channel's search parameters. So, while *Harold and Maude* would automatically show up in a Comedy Channel, for example, since the TMS tags it as "Genre: Comedy," I had to make sure that this exact *title* would be searched for in the TMS database and also routed into my Replay Movie Zone Cult Movies Channel. Ditto for the Film Noir Channel I created, and the Action Comedies Channel, and so on. (A "Classic Films" Channel was easy: I simply programmed the channel to sort anything before 1960 into that bucket.) I also decided to create *two* Movie Zone Comedy Channels: a Classic Comedy Channel that sorted anything before 1978 (the year *Animal House* was released) and a Contemporary Comedy Channel that included everything from 1978 to the present.

In addition to the actual technical labor of researching and creating these Zones, there was an artistic (and I use the term loosely) side as well. I had to write a short description of what the user would find in each Channel if they selected it. Due to technical limitations of the amount of text able to display legibly on a TV screen, these descriptions had to be concise. They also had to be accurate, compelling and—by my own standards—whenever possible, *amusing*. "They have to *pop*," Kim LeMasters counseled me on one occasion ("pop" being one of those Hollywood phrases like "over the top" that everyone seems to understand intuitively but which no one can define precisely—or can provide any clear direction as to how to accomplish it. "The weasel goes pop.")

THE GOOD

The good started almost immediately: Only a few days after I was hired by Replay, my girlfriend decided I needed a better car than the Toyota Celica I'd been driving for the previous 17 years, and (partially as a reward for landing this big-money employment, I suspect) bought me a classic old Jaguar—a dove-grey 1984 XJ6—at an auction for a fraction of its actual value. I'd been lusting after a Jag for years, and now I finally had one, complete with walnut-paneled dash and a "leaper"—the "springing jaguar" hood ornament. And that was just the beginning.

Holy shit, I thought at one point a few weeks into the job. *This is* fun*!* It was work, sure—but it was an intellectual challenge, one that drew on everything I'd been studying for the last fifteen years or more. Finally, my diligence in learning and writing about film and video was paying off in real work, real expertise...and real dollars.

It wasn't all work, however. The perks at ReplayTV included free vending machines, for instance, including one that stocked Frosted Chocolate Fudge Pop-Tarts. For free. I can resist anything except temptation, and free Frosted Chocolate Fudge Pop-Tarts was a perk beyond my ability to resist. I was never a breakfast guy, but, c'mon... Frosted Chocolate Fudge Pop-Tarts? For *free*? For the first time in my checkered career, I actually looked forward to going to work every day. Not just for free Frosted Chocolate Fudge Pop-Tarts, of course...but that didn't hurt. And like many startups that encouraged single workers to stay on-site long hours, ReplayTV shipped in catered dinners every weeknight. I rarely stayed for these, since I had a home and a girlfriend, but I did notice that there was a regular contingent of guys—always guys—who basically lived off the company's catered meals. And no wonder: there were any number of great restaurants in the general vicinity—Mountain View, Palo Alto and environs. I have to confess that even I stayed late a few times just for the free meal from some great place I couldn't afford to patronize even with my big-ass salary.

Pop-Tarts and free dinners were minor perks, admittedly. However, as the infomercials say, "But wait! There's more!" One major perk was that I was given a pair of ReplayTV units—one for my office and a second to use at home. I needed to familiarize myself with its functions, of course. And a unit in the office (where we were wired for cable) was absolutely mandatory in order to check my work and display it for my bosses and co-workers. (The fact that this was a "work machine," however, didn't stop me from locking myself in my office every afternoon at 4 PM to watch the daily rerun of *Moonlighting* on A&E.)

I was hanging with some fun guys as well. Doug Shannon ran with a "posse" that included a trio of software engineers, who I soon came to realize were not only the smartest guys in any room, and knew it, but also the funniest. A deeply dark sense of humor informed their worldview, and I was instantly on board. We went for coffee, we went for lunch, we hung out and talked work and science and science fiction and pop culture and trash. And at some point early in our group association—and for the first time I could remember—I realized that not only was I *not* the smartest guy in the room, I was the only guy in the room who didn't *think* he was the smartest guy in the room (unless that revelation of humility did, in fact, make me the smartest guy in the room. But that way madness lies.)

I greatly enjoyed just shooting the shit with Doug Shannon whenever we got the chance. The guy was truly brilliant, self-effacing, and viewed the world through gimlet eyes, as did I. We established that we had birthdays that were only a few days apart, and that we were perfect Pisceans. And we spent hours one afternoon locked in my office, diagramming the plot of *Back to the Future III* on my whiteboard and discussing the movie's temporal paradoxes and anomalies. Great, Scott!

Some months later, Doug came to me to tell me what a great job I'd done expanding his baby, Replay Zones. But there was something else on his mind as well. "You're gonna think this is bullshit," he began, smiling wryly, "but I used to watch you when you were hosting 'Science Fiction Night' on KTEH. And when I first decided I needed to hire someone to run Zones, I thought, 'Man, I wish I could get someone like Scott Apel.'" Still one of the most meaningful compliments I've ever gotten (assuming, of course, that it was *not* bullshit), although I assured him at the time that there was, in fact, *no one* like Scott Apel... including me.

BEATING ME TO THE PUNCH(LINE)

One of the social highlights of this period was my relationship with Kim LeMasters, our CEO—the guy who was hired the same day I was. He proved himself to be brilliant, gregarious... and hilarious. I thought it was worth a shot to try repeating my relationship with Don Jones, the V.P. at Lockheed with whom I established a personal connection by telling him jokes. But when I started to tell Kim LeMasters a joke one day, he dropped the punchline about two sentences into the set-up. *Impressive,* I thought, if somewhat rude. But he's the boss, and rank doth have its privileges. Even so, when he started to tell me a joke I knew by heart, I pulled the same shit on him: I blurted out the punchline as soon as I recognized the joke. I knew I was taking a chance—it's totally rude to step on someone's punchline...and you simply do *not* interrupt The Boss under *any* circumstances. But he got a kick out of it and we played another round, which ended with us both laughing maniacally. This soon became our signature interaction: Two or three times a week I'd drop by his office, and if he wasn't busy, he'd wave me in and close the door. And we'd trot out the jokes. The goal was to spit out the punchline as soon as you recognized the story. Whichever one of us managed to get all the way through a joke without interruption won that round, by knowing a joke the other guy had never heard before. I'd long prided myself on knowing every joke ever told, and the only person I've ever met who could make that same claim was Kim LeMasters. Far from being rude, we were competing in a game of our own devising, and the quicker one of us knew the punchline to the other's joke, the harder we laughed.

Not only would I stop by Kim's office, he'd occasionally drop by mine (which was located on the first floor, directly below his office, oddly enough). He'd close the door, grab a chair, and start joking. He always had his back to the window that looked out onto the hallway, but I could see people of every level of management sneaking peeks into my office, always with a curious look on their faces. What the hell was the CEO doing in the lowly Zones Editor's office? And what on earth were they laughing about like a couple of idiots?

Kim LeMasters lived in Los Angeles and was housed in a temporary suite in Palo Alto while he settled in at ReplayTV. A few weeks after we both started, his wife Donna came up for a visit. She was adorable: vivacious, verbal, energetic—a real firecracker. Kim, who was due in a meeting, asked me to introduce her around. She spent about thirty seconds talking to each of the people we met. She chose to spend two hours with me. The next day, I ran into Kim in the kitchen.

"Hey, man," I said. "That wife of yours is a real pistol."

"Ya want her?" he shot back.

"Um... Yes, please."

He shook his head. "You couldn't afford her."

"Sure I could, Kim," I countered. "After all, we'd have half of your money."

The other people in the kitchen were aghast. But my potential future wife's future ex-husband and I shared a huge laugh.

THE BAD

Yeah, I loved the work. And a couple of the employees. But—sooner rather than later—the bad began to outweigh the good.

Take, for instance, my closest co-worker. Creating Replay Zones was, for the most part, a "sorting puzzle," to figure out what people wanted to watch and how to get it to them as easily as possible...but since Zones were displayed on a TV screen, they needed artwork, a task far outside my skill set. Soon after I hired in, Doug Shannon introduced me to my new co-worker: "Craig or Greg Something." Doug explained that we'd be working closely together on Zones—I'd be responsible for the content and descriptive text; Craig or Greg would create appropriate onscreen art using Photoshop, applying the exacting requirements that the displays demanded.

Some people just rub you the wrong way the moment you meet them. There's no telling why—conflicting pheromones, maybe, or irritating body language. Whatever the reason, it was immediately clear that Craig or Greg and I took an immediate dislike to one another. I thought he was pretentious, arrogant and dismissive. I have no idea what he thought of me—I just noticed that he bristled and tensed up every time I came near him or talked to him.

The whole setup was irritating, honestly. Why didn't I get to interview him—or any other artists who might have applied for this position for that matter, since the Zones artist was the one person with whom I'd be working most closely on a day-to-day basis? *Well,* I told myself, *you can choose your friends, but you can't choose your co-workers.* Part of being a professional is leaving any personal animosities at the door when you arrive at work. I didn't need to be Craig or Greg's friend. I didn't even need to like him. All I needed was to know was that I could rely on him to do his job and make my intellectually brilliant Zones look good on a TV screen. And in that respect, Craig or Greg Something was entirely satisfactory. We'd never quite get along together or ever consider a social relationship outside the workplace, but we were both focused on making Zones an outstanding product in our own ways.

A few weeks after I hired in, when my training with Doug Shannon was complete, I was transferred from Doug's domain in Engineering to the ReplayTV Services department, reporting to Lois Tantrum. And I was moved out of "Mahogany Row" into an office in an area devoted to our department. Not a problem. It made total sense to gather all us Zones workers together in one location—and I still had a nice office. Greg or Craig had the office next to mine, and Lois had the big corner office, befitting his lofty stature as EVP of ReplayTV Services. There was another big corner office on the opposite end of the row from Lois's. I found out who was getting that space when Lois called me into his office one day and introduced me to a woman in her 30s with dark hair, an anorexic thinness, and a vapid expression. "This is Veronica," he grumbled. "She's in charge of Zones now. You'll be reporting to her."

I was gobsmacked. What the fuck? *I* was hired to be in charge of Zones! Lois had effectively *given my job away* to this stranger. Who the hell was she? Where did she come from? And why was Lois inserting a level of management in between us, effectively pushing me down the org chart?

A bit of investigation revealed the story. Veronica had originally hired into the Marketing Department, where her claim to fame was that she'd picked the colors for the box the ReplayTV units would ship in—which somehow made her a hero, a genius and Picasso all rolled into one to her boss. But she was not happy with her position, and wanted more authority. I'd met several women like her at Silicon Graphics—feral Marketing bitches who had no consideration for anything but their own rise to power. They'd throw anyone under a bus to gain an advantage and further their career. I avoided them like the plague. We had nothing in common, and they'd destroy you if you got in their way. They scared me, they were so focused and so fierce. It turns out that Veronica had gone to her boss, the head of Marketing, pouting about how unhappy she was with her few responsibilities; he talked with Lois, and together they decided she should run Zones. Hey, instant position! I can imagine a scenario in which the head of Marketing jumped at the chance to rid himself of this dimwitted dolly by pawning her off onto dimwitted Lois. It didn't seem to matter to any of them that I was already occupying this position and that they'd usurped my job, effectively demoting me to being the Zones Editor rather than the person in charge of Zones.

This new arrangement might not have meant anything to them, but I had to determine whether or not it meant something to me. On the plus side, I'd still be earning the same salary. I'd still have an office. I'd still be doing the same job. All I'd lose is my autonomy: the authority to create any Zones I deemed fit, on my own schedule. I'd have no final say in what art we'd use in the Zones. Sure, I'd have a voice, an opinion—but no decision-making authority. I'd now have to clear and justify all my ideas through Veronica and get her approval. And there was, of course, the bruised ego aspect: "We hired you for this job, but before you could do it, we're giving it to someone else."

On the other hand, I didn't particularly want to be management or to assume the responsibilities of supervising additional people as the department expanded. And Veronica would be the person who had to deal with Lois (a major point, as you'll soon discover). The only legitimate way to protest would be to quit—and there was no way that was going to happen. I enjoyed the work, and I was making more money than I ever had before—about the same salary I'd be making if I'd remained at Lockheed during the intervening six years, calculating in Lockheed's minimal annual raises. In the end, I swallowed my bruised pride, smiled, and welcomed her aboard.

It didn't take long to discover that if Veronica had ever been in the military, her name would have been Major Disaster. We were at odds from Day One, although she rarely seemed to acknowledge that I had strong opinions about my work—or that I even existed, for that matter. I offered to explain my job to her, to walk her through the steps required to create a Zone, for instance, but she declined. I explained that it would be to her benefit to understand how I spent my days and the unique challenges of Zone creation. But she had zero interest in understanding my job—the job she was ostensibly in charge of and responsible for. Instead, she spent hours locked in her office creating enormous, yards-long, multi-colored timeline spreadsheets that were supposed to guide our every Zone creation effort, but which were, in reality, impossible to conform to—or even decipher, for that matter.

We'd often have discussions like this:

Veronica: "What Zone are you working on now?"

Me: "I'm researching a Sports Zone."

Veronica: "Yuck. I don't like sports. I want you to work on a Fashion Zone."

Me: "Um... OK. Do you really think more users are interested in fashion than in sports?"

Veronica: "Oh, I'm sure they are. All *my* friends are."

Me: "Uh... OK. But golly, I don't know much about fashion. Can you suggest any fashion-oriented TV shows that we might put in a Zone channel devoted to fashion?"

Veronica: "Oh, I don't know if there are any. Just do some research. That's what you do, right?"

Me: "Uh, well, part of what I do, yeah. But we can't build a Zone that highlights fashion programs if there are no fashion programs on TV."

Veronica: "How long will it take you to make the Fashion Zone?"

Me: "Well, it depends on the amount of research and the number of programs, and the number of channels we want to put in the Zone. The Movie Zone took over a month. The Sci-Fi Zone took a week."

Veronica: "Can't you give me an estimate? Don't you budget your time?"

Me: "Budget my time? Yes, Veronica, I budget my time. I arrive at 10 AM and I leave at 7 PM. I take an hour for lunch. The rest of the time I work on creating Zones."

Veronica: "Well, that's not what I meant when I said you should budget your time. You should take a management course."

Me: "Well, what I'm saying to you is that it takes as long as it takes. I could give you a time budget estimate of, oh, let's say twenty hours to create a Zone. But twenty hours would just be a number I pulled out of my...hat."

Veronica: "Well, there, y'see? You just budgeted your time!"

Me: "What I'm saying is that there's no way to know how long it will take until I start the research. Some Zones might take twice that long to create. Or ten times as long."

Veronica: "Well, no, not if you've budgeted twenty hours. When you hit that limit, you just stop."

Me: "But the research might not be completed by then. We can't launch a half-researched Zone."

Veronica: "Well, I'm sure you'll work it out. Let's just say you have a budget of twenty hours for each Zone. Now I've got to get back to work."

Like talking to a fucking wall, or trying to talk sense to an algorithm—and not an algorithm designed for Artificial Intelligence. It was clear to me that structure was more important to Veronica than results—and that she had no interest in understanding how the process necessary to obtain those results worked. I started having flashbacks of the Marketing fucks at SGI.

I knew we were in trouble when Veronica took over attending some of the meetings I'd been attending, as a representative of the Replay Zones department. I was "uninvited" by her to attend these meetings now that she was in charge. But the engineers we met with would regularly stop by my office and ask that I attend instead of her. Their comments were always the same, and repeated frequently: *She's an idiot. She understands nothing. She asks stupid, off-topic questions*. In other words, she was not only slowing things down because she didn't understand how the technology worked, she was embarrassing our entire department with her lack of technical knowledge—and her lack of interest in learning anything technical—or anything at all, for that matter. But there was nothing I could do. My only strategy was to meet secretly with the people who tried to explain things to her but couldn't get her to understand…and to leave her alone, hoping that in the long run, she'd screw things up so badly that someone above her would notice her failure and relieve her of her responsibilities. Yeah, that'd happen...

She must, at some point, have realized that she lacked the skills to adequately perform the technical aspect of her job—or at least she got tired of wasting time on those dopey, boring engineers when she could be shopping online or creating a spreadsheet that would make Jackson Pollack proud—because she eventually hired an assistant to wrangle the engineers and supervise the worker drones (namely, me and Craig or Greg). So here was yet *another* level of management being inserted above me, pushing me even further down the corporate ladder. I had no intention of climbing the corporate ladder, but I certainly had no intention of turning work into a game of Chutes & Ladders, where I was regularly kicked to the chute.

(Veronica's hire—my new immediate boss—Jon Resnik, really belongs in a different section of this narrative, however, as he proved to be a very likable, intelligent and level-headed coworker. His claim to fame was that he'd been the line producer on the indie hit *Spanking the Monkey* in 1994, and had produced *The Pompatus of Love* in '95. I could have left him out of this story altogether, since he played a minor role in my time at Replay, but I liked him, and I believe that the good guys deserve a shoutout.)

...AND THE UGLY

If Craig or Greg was Painful Rectal Itch and Veronica was a case of hemorrhoids, Lois Tantrum was full-on Stage 4 colon cancer. He'd started his Hollywood career as a stuntman and still dressed like one—cowboy boots, blue jeans, embroidered work shirts. (I occasionally suspected that his mother had been traumatized by Gene Autrey when she was pregnant with him.) He'd most recently been a programming exec at the UPN (United Paramount Network), Paramount's ultimately doomed attempt to launch its own cable channel. (They tried again in 2018.) The high points of UPN programming were *Star Trek: Voyager* and wrestling (*WWE SmackDown*), and before he left to join ReplayTV, Lois was seemingly obsessed with finding a way to combine the two, to bolster the fledgling network's ratings. (A joke to this effect worked its way into the 1999 Fox TV sitcom, *Action*. As soon as I heard the joke I knew they were talking about Lois, and wondered how many other people would pick up on this insider reference.)

Lois was essentially an asshole who aspired to be a prick. He was the embodiment of the abrasive and abusive "New Hollywood" producer of the era, as satirized in movies like *The Big Picture*, *Swimming with Sharks* and *Tropic Thunder*. Their motto seemed to be, "Why talk when you can scream? Why compliment when you can demean? Why inspire loyalty among your staff when you can strike fear in their hearts and intimidate them into submission? *It is better to be feared than to be loved!"*

Lois once scheduled a meeting for 8 AM on a Sunday, for example. Yeah—he scheduled a meeting on a Sunday. *Early* on a Sunday. Craig or Greg and I dutifully showed up. Lois never did. We didn't mention it to him on Monday, to avoid being browbeaten. A few weeks later, however, when he scheduled another Sunday morning meeting, Craig or Greg and I discussed whether or not we should even bother to show up. But we did, and this time so did Lois. As we were waiting to get started, I casually mentioned that I'd been working in business for nearly twenty years, and this was the first time anyone had ever scheduled a meeting on a Sunday morning. His response was immediate and vehement: "Get used to it!"

Lois managed by intimidation, and a major component of his management style was that he never gave any constructive feedback. Craig or Greg and I would display our design for a new Replay Zone, for instance, and his initial comment was inevitably, "It looks like shit. And nobody will ever use it." The first couple of times this happened we asked him if he had any suggestions. "Yeah," he'd spit back. "Make it work. And make it not look like shit!" So we'd go back to the drawing board (literally, in Craig or Greg's case) and revise. We assumed that Lois's decree was some kind of "tough love," and that we'd see the error of our stupid, stupid ways and we'd dig deep and come up with something really, really brilliant. The problem with this approach was twofold: One, we'd already given the project our best shot—who wouldn't?—so anything else was a dilution, or slightly off-point, rather than an improvement. And second, even though Lois intimated that he knew what he wanted, he refused to give us any direction whatsoever. We had to guess what he wanted. And we quickly learned that our guesses were always wrong.

I think it was only after Lois got tired of playing this game that he'd approve our effort—and even then only in a disgruntled, defeated way. "So you idiots couldn't fix it," he'd say, sneering sarcastically. "It still looks like shit. But nobody's gonna use it anyway, so you might as well just launch the fucking thing." I often wanted to ask him if he had any confidence in ReplayTV at all, given that he never had a good word to say about the device or the service *that he was in charge of*. But by then I'd learned that the best way to deal with Lois was to recall the lesson my old Lockheed co-worker, Norman Leigh, passed on to me: KMS ("Keep Mouth Shut").

I caught a glimpse into Lois's management philosophy one afternoon while I was in the men's room. Lois walked in and accosted me at the urinal. He insisted I call an exec at NBC in Burbank and complain about how long it was taking to get some information. I zipped up and turned to face him, and, as he "explained" how "in his face" I should be when yelling at the guy, he kept getting more and more in *my* face, literally. I had to back up into a stall while he angrily "explained" that if I was furious and rabid with this NBC guy often enough, *"you'll have him eating the peanuts out of your shit!"* (At least Lois had chosen an appropriate venue for his graphic metaphor.)

My favorite Lois story is one that is representative of both his personality and his management style. About two months into my tenure, he stormed into my office around noon and announced "Leno's people will be here at four o'clock. They wanna see a functioning *Tonight Show* Zone." This was news to me—not that *Tonight Show* reps wanted a see a completed Zone that afternoon, but that a *Tonight Show* Zone was even on our agenda at all. This is the first I'd heard of it. But I didn't mention that to Lois. I didn't even bother to mention that even if we'd already created a *Tonight Show* Zone (and what would that consist of, anyway?), it would take at least two days to publish it to the system before anyone could see it on a TV screen. Instead, I mentioned the single obstacle to which I believed he could have no objection. "That requires art," I said, "and Craig or Greg is out sick today." "Well, *you* do it," he replied. "Lois," I said, "I'm a writer. I don't know Photoshop." His solution was to yell, "Well, *learn*!" and storm off. I guess he figured nothing is impossible if you shout loud enough. He could have had a great career as a political pundit on Fox News.

Over the following months, it became abundantly clear that if I accomplished anything in Replay Zones, it would not be because of Veronica and Lois—it would be in spite of them. And—in spite of them—our department continued to expand. I was given the title Senior Zones Editor when we added a second Zones Editor, who I trained. Then we added another, and another... Eventually, I was responsible for the activity of five additional Zones editors, who I also trained. They were my direct reports, and I was their supervisor—in everything but name. And salary. Veronica couldn't be bothered to actually supervise them—she had important charts to create.

We also hired a pair of additional artists. Among us, by the summer of 2000, we'd created some 50 Zones, covering everything from Movies to Music to Education to an "Extreme Zone" which featured cutting-edgy, counter-culture programs like *Family Guy*, edgy sporting events like the X-Games, and my Cult Movies Channel. The artwork featured Sean Penn vomiting up a guy on a skateboard while a monkey in a pink wig looked on. It was my single favorite piece of Zones artwork we'd ever created. (And to be clear, it was created by one of the new-hire artists, not by Craig or Greg.)

THE FUCUS GROUP

The ugliest aspect of my employment at ReplayTV was not a person or a process, but a Marketing strategy. Any company has numerous tools at their command to insult and demean their employees—demotion, censure, black marks on your record, termination. Most of these insults are the domain of HR. But perhaps not to be outdone in the competition for Most Evil Department, no one yet has devised a more devious form of corporate torture and insult than a Marketing department Focus Group.

A Focus Group is defined as "a demographically diverse group of people selected to participate in a guided discussion and provide feedback" about a product or political candidate—a form of "qualitative market research" based on the belief that the Average Joe or Jane will represent the opinions of, and react as a microcosm of, a larger population. In actual practice, a focus group essentially involves grabbing random people—people who have nothing better to do—off the street, showing them your product, and asking them what they think about it, in exchange for a few bucks and a few snacks. It's like a jury, but with pizza.

There are several major flaws in this approach. One is that the participants feel compelled to say *something*, even when they have no strong opinion. After all, they're getting paid for their opinion, so they'd better have one, even if they have to make one up. A more pronounced problem is that the more opinionated the participant (a trait highly valued by the people running a focus group), the closer the Marketing douches pay attention to that person, virtually ensuring that the alpha personality in the focus group dominates the group attitude—and the Marketing morons' attention. And it should come as no surprise that the Alpha Blowhard is rarely in favor of something, always against.

The single thing that chapped my ass most of all, however—the biggest, most flagrant insult—was that this company paid big bucks to hire people like me for our expertise...but they didn't trust it, and therefore relied on the opinion of random, pizza-swilling civilians, and considered the off-the-cuff opinions of these amateurs to be every bit as valuable as those of the experts. If this approach had any validity, we'd be teaching Intelligent Design in schools as an "alternate explanation" to Darwinian evolution. (Yeah, I know—that's already happening.) The point is that the majority of people are idiots. As J.R. "Bob" Dobbs is fond of saying, "You know how stupid the average person is? Well, statistically, half of them are even dumber than that!" And you're gonna trust the opinions of these marching morons to guide your Marketing efforts? Over the opinions of your highly-paid experts? Who's the moron now?

I only had to endure one of these pecking parties, watching from behind the two-way mirror, but it left me disgusted. When one woman opined, "The box it comes in is blue. I don't like blue. It should be green," for example, I watched the Marketing miscreants dutifully write that down as if it was Truth Revealed while the person who'd chosen blue as the corporate color groaned in agony. (Since it was Veronica, I was torn between the random idiocy of the participant and the sweet vengeance of her single contribution to ReplayTV being challenged by someone even dumber than she was.) The event also left me wanting to throttle the bloviating idiot who understood nothing of the technology or of the thousands of deeply discussed and debated decisions that went into crafting a product that *even he* could use, when he insisted, "I don't like it. I'd never use it. It's a piece of shit. Any pizza left?"

UHH... CAN YOU RUN THAT BY ME AGAIN?

So how are users supposed to trust a company that creates a function called "Guaranteed Record," but then whispers in the fine print of the User Agreement, "You acknowledge the term 'Guaranteed Record' ... does not guarantee that a program will be recorded." Logic like this does not guarantee that your head will not explode when attempting to understand logic like this.

IN THE YEAR 2000

April 2000

"April is the cruelest month…"
—T.S. Eliot, *The Wasteland*

April was the *coolest* month! (T.S., Eliot!) We were budding, blooming, blossoming! We'd won "Best of Show" in our category at the CES (Consumer Electronics Show) the previous January, as just one example. Investor funding (denoted in alphabetized "rounds") continued apace, and by April, ReplayTV had closed Round G, a $65 million investment. We were even running TV commercials—a series of odd, absurdist, non sequitur fever dreams that had literally nothing to do with the purpose or function of a DVR. (The fact that we were running commercials at all was ironic given that one of the main selling points of ReplayTV was the "commercial skip" button. It's possible, I suppose, that our commercials were designed to irritate people enough that they'd wish they had a commercial skip button…which they could obtain by purchasing a ReplayTV! My better sense dismisses this interpretation, however, as I firmly believe that "Marketing genius" is an oxymoron unless preceded by the word "evil.")

April (and beyond) also saw a number of media reviews that validated my approach to Zones. A blog post on HappyPuppy.com, for instance, said: "My particular favorite was the movie section, which then gets narrowed down to every particular genre you can think of, and more." And J. Takiff of *The Philadelphia Daily News Web* wrote that "Your kids will like the Gen X channel." One of our own chief engineers, Don Woodward, said in an interview, "I love the Movies Zone. That Zone kicks bootie."

Additionally, the Marketing Department had adopted most of my suggestions for "brand attributes," including words like: *Fun. Unexpected. Smart. Approachable. Inventive. Reliable. Entertaining. Cool.* After all, who was in a better position to define the characteristics we wanted the product to project than the guy who was defining the onscreen, "public-facing" persona of the service, through our Zones?

Meanwhile, back at the ranch… it wasn't all roses roses. The service was expanding so fast, for instance, that floor space was at a premium, and every hallway was stuffed with desks for new employees.

And even though Replay had begun making deals for advertising (like banner ads on Zones pages), the management insisted on experimenting with Zones devoted to nothing but advertising. This caused us all—including me, the alleged Zones expert —to scratch our heads: The whole point of Zones was to automatically sort TV programs into Replay-determined categories. But what the hell kind of programs would one put in a "Toyota Zone"? Car races? Shows about cars? (Even one of the first, *Top Gear,* wouldn't launch for nearly a decade.) *Knight Rider?* (No, that was a Pontiac Firebird Trans Am.) What kind of shows could we sort into a "Nike Zone"? And why would these companies sponsor a Zone when they're already advertising on TV?

Around this time I was privy to a couple of interesting studies. The first was a "user profile." Early adopters of ReplayTV were determined to be predominantly male, middle-aged professionals earning a salary of about $70,000 a year. I pointed out to my management that I was in all aspects that archetypal user—except for the fact that I was being underpaid.

I was also presented with a distressing study that indicated that fully 50 percent of ReplayTV owners had never used Replay Zones. That was the bad news. The good news was that among the 50 percent that *did* use Zones, the minimum number of Channels they'd selected was two. In discussions about this study, I gave my own spin to the figures, defending Zones in two ways. First of all, I argued, even though Zone Channels were designed so that selecting them automatically recorded any program sorted into it, it's unlikely that everyone would want to automatically record *every* show that is auto-sorted into a Channel. It was far more likely that most ReplayTV owners used the Zone Channel function as a more refined search tool, to discover what shows were available to them, which they then cherrypicked to record. (My claim was unsupported by evidence, however; there were no statistics on how many people used

Zone Channels as an advanced search feature like this.) The second defense was that even if half the users didn't know about Zones, once they discovered them, they selected *at least* two Channels to record the programs listed in them.

But maybe T.S. Eliot was right: also in April 2000—just one month after it reached an all-time high—the Nasdaq stock exchange took a nosedive and lost over a third of its value, which burst the overinflated "tech bubble" … just days before ReplayTV was scheduled to go public. Management wisely postponed the IPO. Little did they suspect at that time that they would never have one.

April 2000 was a milestone month for ReplayTV. But to understand the massive changes occurring within my own little sphere, it is necessary to perform a bit of retrograde motion.

DING DONG

For instance: One fine day in early 2000, Veronica announced that she was quitting. She was marrying her rich fiancé and he was sweeping her off to Italy, where she was going to live a life of leisure in a villa. Or some fucking thing. The important point is that she was leaving. I couldn't have been happier. Not for her, but for me. All she'd done for ReplayTV was slow things down and complicate every effort for her own narcissistic aggrandizement. All she'd done for me was steal my job and frustrate my efforts to do the part of my job that I'd retained. Oh, and she'd hired a guy to assume my supervisory duties when she couldn't be bothered. He'd take over for her after she left. I'd never get that job back.

MEET THE NEW BOSS, *Part 1 of Many*

> "Meet the new boss
> Same as the old boss."
> —The Who, "Won't Get Fooled Again"

March 2000

And then one day in March, Lois left us. (No, he didn't die. I didn't like the asshole, but I wouldn't wish him dead.) He just wasn't "with us" anymore. The only gossip I could ferret out was, "He was fired." About fucking time.

How awesome! Veronica was gone; Lois was history. These twin developments took a shit ton of pressure off me.

And then the new bosses arrived.

I was invited to a one-on-one with the new crew, who flew in from L.A. specifically to introduce themselves to the ReplayTV Services employees. I was greeted by a trio of people in a room barely large enough to hold four bodies and a table. Rob Kenneally was boyish and tanned, with a high forehead and wispy, sandy blond hair. He looked like he'd just stepped off a beach in Malibu with his longboard, dude. I later found out that he'd been an Executive Vice President at Fox Broadcasting between 1987 and 1991, where he was (according to a recent biographical sketch) "integral to the launching" of such shows as *The Simpsons, Married...With Children, Beverly Hills 90210, In Living Color,* and *Cops*. So far, so good—I liked three of those shows. It was only much later that I was introduced to the concept of someone being "hired for his Rolodex," but once I heard that term I immediately realized this described Rob to a T. He'd never worked in the tech industry before...but he had entertainment industry connections that could serve ReplayTV.

Kate Moulene came to ReplayTV from *InStyle* magazine, where she was the West Coast Bureau Chief. Since I'm using her real name here, it follows that I liked her. I can't really say anything bad about Kate aside from the observation that she seemed a bit shallow. I mean, *InStyle* magazine? Really? But you can't judge a magazine by its cover (except *Cosmo*, maybe). And since her ReplayTV days, she's redeemed herself (at least in my jaundiced eyes) as the organizer of an annual forum where key players in Hollywood meet with officials from the United Nations to discuss ways in which the media can support and serve major global issues. You go, girl!

As for the third member of this welcoming committee, I can't even give him a fake name, since I never saw him again. "He's not with us anymore," was all I was told in a later meeting. He looked like a shaved ape and passed through my career like a taco fart.

On this first meeting, however, this trio all sported wide, pearly-white smiles. They were *excited* about what we'd done! They looked *forward* to working with me! (Well, who wouldn't?) The best news of all, from my perspective, was that since they lived in Los Angeles, they'd only be around about once a week to check in with whatever we were doing.

Appearances can be deceiving, however, and new management is always suspect, but Rob and Kate proved to be exactly what they appeared to be: pleasant, intelligent people. Quite a relief from Veronica and Lois.

"GOOD NEWS, EVERYONE!"

Unfortunately, they were pleasant, intelligent people who lived in Los Angeles. And what originally seemed like a benefit —namely, that they wouldn't be around our Mtn. View offices much—quickly did a one-eighty. Sometime in June, once they'd settled into their new positions as the leaders of ReplayTV Services, Rob delivered unto us their Big Announcement. (If you're a fan of *Futurama*, this is the point at which Professor Farnsworth enters and exclaims, "Good news, everyone!"—meaning that he's about to send his crew on a suicide mission.) The Big Announcement? To launch the next phase of the ReplayTV Service, we'd all be moving to (dramatic pause) *Los Angeles!*

Hooray?

This was distressing to me on many levels. First and foremost is the fact that Silicon Valley was my *home*. I'd lived there for forty years—since long before the agricultural Santa Clara Valley morphed into hi-tech "Silicon Valley." All my friends and family lived there. My Credit Union and Post Office box—both of which I'd had for over a decade—were there. All my favorite venues were there: El Burro restaurant in Campbell, for example; the Tied House microbrewery and Harry's Hofbrau, both in Mountain View—not to mention our proximity to The City: San Francisco. (2020 aside: Sadly, all of the places mentioned are now closed. Except San Francisco.)

Additionally, all my *history* was in Silicon Valley—all my schools since fourth grade; all my previous employment; all my adventures and misadventures. And more—any claim I had to public recognition, however minor, was here as well: this is where I'd written the video column for the San Jose *Mercury News* for over a decade, and where I'd had a weekly presence as a VJ on Silicon Valley's PBS station for six years. (Even ReplayTV's founder recognized me from that gig.) This is where my plays had been produced and performed. Everything and everyone I knew and loved was within a fifty-mile radius of my adorable cottage on Peachtree Lane in lovely Santa Clara. And now, at age 49, I was supposed to kiss that all goodbye and start all over again in Los Angeles? Just to keep my job?

Of course it made perfect sense that the new management of the ReplayTV Service would want to move their department to L.A.: they lived there. Rob Kenneally was certainly not about to give up his home in Beverly Hills to move to some hick hamlet like *Mountain View*. Puh-*leease*! And, like Kim LeMasters, who was housed in temporary quarters in Palo Alto on ReplayTV's dime, Rob wasn't about to totally commit to a risky venture like ReplayTV by actually moving to where his job was located—not when he was high enough on the corporate totem pole that he could require that *everyone who worked for him* move instead. His team members were all hedging their bets, ready to retreat to their previous L.A. lives in case ReplayTV didn't pan out. They were, however, more than willing to upend the lives of some 35 minor grunts by uprooting them from *their* homes and transplanting them to L.A. rather than give up their Hollywood homes and lifestyle. I have no idea whether any of my co-workers made this same analysis and came to this same obvious conclusion; we simply did not discuss our reactions (or our personal responses). But this observation did not inspire confidence in me. (I must admit, however, that as it turned out, these execs proved extremely wise in covering their asses in this manner.)

The rationale Rob used to sell the idea of moving the "Creative Team" to L.A. to the ReplayTV Board of Directors was that the ReplayTV Service "needs to be near the client"—by which he meant near the Los Angeles-based television industry. He conveniently glossed over the fact that ReplayTV had *no connection to the TV industry whatsoever,* aside from the fact that the ReplayTV device—the actual DVR set-top box—was a delivery device for TV shows. But more importantly to the collective TV industry was the fact that the ReplayTV set-top box was a device that allowed users to skip over commercials at the touch of a button—hardly the greatest selling point for the advertising-based television industry.

Yeah, the L.A. move made perfect sense...but only on Opposite Day. In non-nonsensical terms, it was a blatantly transparent pretext for Rob and his staff to protect their own lifestyle. I never called them on this, however: you don't make any friends by pointing out that their cover story was a ruse, a ploy, completely illogical...and total bullshit. I realized that we were supposed to ignore the illogic and just swallow the Kool-Aid, smiling and without question. (As Tennyson put it, "Ours not to reason why..." You know the rest.) We were supposed to play stupid and buy into their scheme.

Rob tried to paint a picture of the L.A. ReplayTV Service to me one day, sensing my reluctance to sign on immediately. "Just think of it," he said, describing a vision that was equal parts Paradise, Valhalla and Disneyland. "You'll have a big office. You'll have an entire staff of editors reporting directly to you. And we'll be able to bring in prospective clients and show off the whole operation." Oh, I got the picture, all right...but I doubt if it was the picture he'd intended. What I pictured was a bullpen full of chimpanzees sitting at computers, as Ringmaster Rob led a group of Hollywood suits through our work area, exhorting in a carnival barker's voice, "Behold our dedicated keyboard monkeys, working 'round the clock, for *you*!"

FUCK ELIZABETH KUBLER-ROSS

My first line of defense against this move was this: *Denial.* I convinced myself it would never happen. The top-level execs would never approve a move like this. It would be far too disruptive, far too expensive, and would take an entire department 500 miles away from the yoke of the corporate HQ. *Nah, they'll never approve it,* I consoled myself. Until I discovered they already had. Strike One.

I skipped the next stage of grief, Anger, and moved on to my next line of defense: Bargaining. "Since the internet is ubiquitous," I explained to Kate, "geography is irrelevant. There's no need for me to be physically located in L.A. I can do my job just as well from Mountain View—and the bonus is I can act as a liaison between the L.A. and Mountain View offices." Sound logic, I thought. But Rob and Kate remained unswayed. "We need everyone in the same office," they explained. "We need that close-knit connection, so we can see each other every day and take spontaneous meetings, and bounce ideas off each other any time." Well, I'd tried to bounce an idea off them, and it bounced back and smacked me in the face. Strike Two.

I seriously did not want to move to Los Angeles. But nothing I said could convince my bosses otherwise. Ultimately, I realized I had only two remaining options to avoid the move. One was to politely decline and accept the layoff and severance package ReplayTV was offering to those unwilling to be relocated. The collateral damage is that I'd once again be out of work—after *voluntarily* giving up the best job I'd ever had. I simply could not do that. The next stage of grief—Depression—kicked in when I realized that the only other alternative—my third and final line of defense—was itself horrific: *Find a new job*. But I couldn't allow myself to sink into the final stage of grief: Acceptance. That was even more horrific. There was only one solution.

I needed a new job.

July 2000

IN WHICH I AM NETFUCKED BY NETFLIX

The L.A. move was definite, and scheduled for September. It was now July. But against all odds, I found a posting for a job that was right in my wheelhouse: Senior Editor at Netflix. Perfect! Maybe it was a lateral move, but I was fine with that: I could continue my new career without having to move to L.A.—without even moving from our lovely little house in Santa Clara. Working at Netflix would even cut five minutes off my commute.

So I applied...and, incredibly, got a quick callback to come in for interviews. I talked with several people, including Reed Hastings, Netflix's founder and CEO. I also sat for an hour with the six current Netflix writers and editors, being grilled about my résumé, my favorite recent movie (*Run Lola Run*—no objections there) and my management style (for which, see the chapter in Part IV, "What I've Learned About: Management"). I liberally handed out copies of *Killer B's* ("Hey! A walkaway!" exclaimed a delighted Tom). And I assured them I would not disrupt their process but would work with them and shield them from higher management issues.

But the L.A. countdown clock was ticking. When I didn't hear from Netflix for a couple of weeks, I called my recruiter/contact, just to inquire about the status of the position. (I'd read that this was acceptable behavior, as long as the candidate didn't bug the potential employer too often.) I was informed that a final decision had been postponed until later in the summer. The good news was I was still in the running for the position. The bad news was they were dragging their feet...and I was sitting on a ticking timebomb.

Sometime in August, Kate insisted that Replay needed my decision *tomorrow*. And the moment she left my office, I called my contact at Netflix to "check on the status of the job." I was informed that the selection was still unsettled. No final decision had been made. I was desperate, so I took a chance on pushing the point. "I know this might sound rather unorthodox," I explained, "but my current management at ReplayTV is planning to move our entire department to Los Angeles next month, and they insist that I give them my decision as to whether I'll be making the move by tomorrow. I'd much rather be working for Netflix than moving to L.A. for ReplayTV. So, while I know you can't give me a definitive answer about the position, it would be of enormous benefit to me if you could even hint whether or not I'm still in the running for this position... because if I am, I'll tell Replay I can't go, and I'll take my chances with you. But if I'm *not* still considered a viable candidate, I'd greatly appreciate it if you'd let me know now, so I can weigh my options with Replay."

There was dead silence on the line. I knew better than to interrupt her while she was clearly mulling over what I'd said. At length, she responded. "You might be better off considering your current employer's offer," she said, slowly and seriously.

"Thank you for your honesty," I replied. "I can't say I'm not disappointed. But you've simplified my decision-making process, and I thank you for that."

The new score: Netflix: Strike Two. And the score for my attempts to resist the ReplayTV move: Strike Three.

ALL ABOUT THE BENJAMINS

So I was going to Los Angeles.

Or was I? Previously, I had only myself to think of. But only months earlier my girlfriend and I had moved in together after enduring a long-distance relationship for several months. It was all well and good that I could decide to move if I was still on my own. But now I had to consider her needs and desires as well. (I was a sensitive '90s guy, after all.) Fortunately, the odds were on my side. She was flexible—after all, she'd moved three thousand miles from Pennsylvania to live with me, so another five hundred miles wouldn't be too much to ask. And she worked from home, so her employment was portable. (One of her guiding mantras is "Keep your sanity portable." Who wouldn't fall in love with a woman who said things like that, and "You can't cross a chasm in two big steps"?) We discussed the ramifications and complications of the move. And we decided that we'd go, and consider it a Big Adventure—more like Neil Armstrong's giant leap, I hoped, than Robert Scott's South Pole expedition.

On decision day, I stopped by Kate's office and gave her a thumbs-up: "I'm a go for L.A.," I said. She was all smiles. "As long as Replay can fulfill a few conditions," I added. Her smile faded quickly. "Um, what conditions?" she asked. And I handed her a two-page letter listing my...well, since I've always preferred the term "video on request" to "video on demand," I'd have to apply that preference of phrasing to my own...requests.

Oh, I had some conditions. You bet I did. And I had every reason to believe they'd be met, due to a single factor: attrition. With 35 people in the department, it was a virtual guarantee that not everyone would make the move. Early on, I determined to sit back and watch who chose to leave rather than commit to the move. Every defection put me in a slightly stronger position to negotiate. And the attrition started quickly. Only a few days after the announcement of our immanent departmental move, for instance, one of our new editors transferred to Marketing, and one of our new artists went back to his previous job (which, we discovered, he'd never actually left—he'd just taken leave of absence to give Replay a chance). And every week following, one or two or three people announced they'd found other work... or, like my co-worker who owned a small farm nearby, chose the layoff severance package over the relocation.

By the week before the execs insisted I make my decision, fully 33 of the 35 employees in ReplayTV Services had recused themselves from the move, one way or another. We were back down to two employees—Craig or Greg Something and me: Doug Shannon's two original hires. Since we were literally the only two people on the face of the earth able and willing to create new Replay Zones, we were in a position of enormous leverage. And we weren't the only people to realize this. As our default supervisor, Jon Resnik (who himself declined relocation), informed Rob and Kate, "If you don't find some way to get Scott to make the move, you are uniquely fucked." (One of the reasons I liked Jon was his no bullshit attitude. Another was his exquisite way with words.)

I realized that I was in the proverbial catbird seat—a once-in-a-lifetime position, perhaps. And I determined to take full advantage of my unique situation. I'd given Kate (and by association, whichever of her superiors had the authority to sign off on my requests) a list of what it would take to get me to make the move—and most of it was in terms they could easily understand: money.

Point One was an immediate $10,000 a year raise, my justification being that I had been low-balled on my entry salary due to Lois' mismanagement (an attitude supported by paycheck comparisons with my peers), and I wanted to catch up.

Point Two was a second $10,000 a year raise. My justification was that I'd hired in low, in exchange for an early review—but that my six-month early review, which was due to occur the previous April, fell between the cracks, as April was precisely when the shakeup in management occurred. Lois was gone and couldn't give me a review; Rob and Kate were too new to know my work and assess my performance. By my contractual agreement with ReplayTV's management, however, I was long overdue for a review and a raise. Again, I felt this was a pretty solid and fair request.

Point Three was to request yet another $10,000 a year added to my salary. I'd already been promoted to Senior Editor and had overseen a staff of up to seven junior editors (and would eventually again oversee several editors, they'd assured me). I wanted a raise commensurate with my new title, my new position, and my new responsibilities. And once again, I felt as justified as I did greedy.

Point Four was what I referred to as a "cost of living/ relocation raise" of another $10,000 a year. L.A. was a more expensive place to live in than Silicon Valley (at that time, anyway), I argued, so I'd need additional funds just to live there. Even though I knew my logic was weaker than their justification for moving to L.A. to be "close to the clients," I stuck this point in there for several reasons: first, to test just how badly they wanted to retain me; second, to have something to give up in a negotiation; and third, because adding in this final ten grand would push me up to the milestone of a six-figure salary: exactly $100,000.

Later that afternoon, Kate came down to my office carrying my letter. I could only assume she'd consulted with Rob and others—certainly with HR—and had an answer for me. She didn't appear angry at my requests, or anxious. But her brow was furrowed and she assumed a dead-serious tone. Without preamble, she sat down and said, "Well, first of all, I can tell you there's no way we're gonna give you $100,000," she said.

I laughed. "Thank you for your candor," I replied.

"But," she continued, "we did discuss it, and you've made some good points. So what we came up with as a counteroffer is this: we'll give you seventy-five at the move, and raise it to eighty in six months."

I'd asked for about twice what I thought I could realistically get. And she'd offered me half of what I'd asked for. So—

although she couldn't know it—we were on exactly the same page. I'd proven exactly how much they wanted me. I suppose I could have countered by asking for a one-time relocation fee (similar to a sign-on bonus, which was common in hi-tech companies in the '90s), just to push back a bit. But I'd gotten what I wanted, and I didn't want to get a reputation as being difficult.

"Deal," I said to Kate. "Let's go to L.A."

WELCOME TO L.A.

"The difference between L.A. and yogurt
is that yogurt is a living culture."
—D.S. Apel, President,
Silicon Valley Culture and Oxymoron Center

Like many Northern Californians, I've had a lifelong love/hate relationship with Los Angeles. Sure, I made frequent trips to Southern California throughout my life, sometimes as often as twice a year. But my destination was invariably the same: Disneyland (which is technically in Anaheim, not Los Angeles. But if you don't live there, most of SoCal is seen as one huge amorphous blob referred to as "L.A.") I rarely ventured into Los Angeles proper; most of what I knew (or thought I knew) about the city came from the same source that informed virtually everyone: movies. And even while I'd "lived" in L.A. proper—a few blocks behind Grauman's Chinese Theater, actually—for a month, seven years earlier, while co-starring in a low-budget feature (check IMDb), I had no real experience in finding my way around the urban sprawl, or in understanding its peculiar local culture (for lack of a better word). If I was going to live in L.A. I'd have to start from scratch in finding my way around, learning local traffic patterns, sussing out good grocery stores (not to mention a doctor, dentist, chiropractor, and so on). I'd spent four decades in Santa Clara Valley, and I prided myself on knowing where everything was. I could drive from any Point A to any Point B between Santa Cruz and San Francisco without the need of a map. (Maps. Ah, how quaint. Remember those colorful, poster-sized, impossible to fold navigational guides?)

Kate was generously helpful. She explained the SoCal freeway system to me, for instance—which roads to avoid, and when —and how most of L.A. was laid out as a grid, with major and minor streets, that made it easy to navigate. I was thankful, but I still hated being a newbie—requiring information rather than dispensing it.

My sweetheart Piph was enormously supportive, particularly since she was being uprooted a second time in less than two years. (We had no idea at that time that this nomadic habit would become a virtual lifestyle for us over the next decade.) She assumed the thankless task (even though I did thank her) of packing all my books (an entire garage full; some 200 boxes), as well as all our possessions, while I went to work in Mountain View every day. She even gave me a moving gift: copies of the Zagat Guides to Los Angeles restaurants and grocery stores.

Only one major detail remained. "I'm gonna have to find a place to live," I told Kate one day in August.

"Go find something," she volunteered. "We'll pay for your airfare, rental car, meals and lodging for a weekend. Just save your receipts."

Piph and I spent a few evenings researching rentals online, found six or eight likely prospects, then flew down one weekend and checked them out. Most of them were crap. Several were simply too far away for an acceptable commute. One was actually a mother-in-law unit underneath a swimming pool. ("You might want to be gone on the weekends," the cokehead owner advised. "We have a lot of all-night swim parties. They can get a little loud." Yeah, that'll work—um, not.) Eventually, we located a suitable place, an old Craftsman-style house on Wilton Ave., a few blocks south of Wilshire, wedged between a four-story brick apartment building and a Korean daycare center.

SO THEY LOADED UP THE TRUCK AND THEY MOVED TO BEVERLY...

And one day in early September 2000, a 24-foot moving van pulled up in front of our cozy abode in Santa Clara and loaded up everything we owned. The next morning Piph put the cat in the carrier, put the carrier in the car, and headed for our new home: Los Angeles. And forty years to the day from when my parents first drove into our new family home, the Santa Clara Valley, I climbed into my Jag and drove away, leaving my past behind me.

Replay had given me a paid week off to relocate and get settled. But at some point I had to quit unpacking and report back to work. The address I had for our new office suite was 9200 W. Sunset Blvd.—about six miles away, or a twenty-minute commute on surface streets. I could take Wilshire to North Doheny; a quick left on Phyllis would take me to the side entrance of our building. And on almost every mile of that commute I spotted something I'd seen in a movie, or recognized a street name from a movie or TV show. Wilshire Blvd. The Miracle Mile. The Four Seasons. When I saw construction underway for a new Bristol Farms—the ultimate high-end gourmet supermarket—on a corner of Doheny *right on my commute route,* I felt as though it was the city's way of saying "Welcome to L.A."

God*damn*! The film critic was actually *living* in LaLaLand!

The ReplayTV offices were located in the Luckman Plaza building, an iconic glass and steel high-rise on the corner of Sunset and Doheny—which, in larger geographic terms, was also the corner where Beverly Hills met West Hollywood. I parked in the underground garage, took the elevator to the fifth floor, and stepped into our offices. A new receptionist was stationed just inside the door. "May I help you?" she asked. "Yeah," I said. "I was wondering if you guys were hiring. I really need a job." Before I could tease her any further, Kate Moulene stepped out and welcomed me. She gave me a quick tour of our luxurious new digs...although someone clearly had forgotten to install the luxury. Most of the office was one big bullpen with a few workstation desks squeezed close together. Off to one side was a big room for Greg or Craig and his eventual crew of digital artists, and a small conference room. Rob Kenneally's office was in the corner (of course) at the end of a series of offices, including Kate's. At the other end of the space, beyond the office row, was a big conference room. I looked around and asked where my office was. Kate motioned to a desk wedged among several others in the bullpen area. I must have raised an eyebrow or something since she rushed to assure me this arrangement was "only temporary." She was excited about the fact that the entire sixth floor, just one floor above us, was being renovated and reconfigured to accommodate our expected exponential growth. We'd move in by the end of the year. (And we'd listen to construction noise until then.)

OK. I'd never bought into the corporate convention that one's office indicates one's status—although I was painfully aware that most "suits" had a shit-ton of emotional energy invested in that specific affectation. I squeezed myself into my little work-space and set up shop.

Only one thing made me feel better about this arrangement: a couple of weeks later, our CEO, Kim LeMasters, joined us for a few days. There was no office available for him, either...so he squeezed into the workspace next to mine. He didn't have to—he could simply have commandeered Rob's office, or set up in a conference room. But he chose to sit next to me—even though it was uncomfortably cramped for both of us. "Y'know," I said to him, "Rob and Kate assured me that if I came to L.A. I'd be rubbing shoulders with the Hollywood elite. I didn't realize they meant that literally."

Since exactly none of the Mountain View employees of the ReplayTV Service (except Greg or Craig and me) made the move to L.A., Rob and Kate busied themselves hiring new staff, especially Marketing people, so there were several new faces in the new office. We were all determined to be on friendly terms, and often lunched together at Hamburger Hamlet, the iconic burger joint just across the street. (HH opened in 1950, and was a prime late-night spot for trendy Sunset Blvd. club kids. It closed in 2011, but not before being immortalized by Ari Gold in the TV series *Entourage* as being a lame "power lunch" spot.)

Kate also brought in a woman she'd worked with previously to interview for a Zones Editor position. This woman had been a producer of rollercoaster documentaries that aired frequently on the Discovery Channel, and was looking for a new career...so she fit right in with Kate, Rob and Kim LeMasters, all of whom were pivoting from media to hi-tech media delivery. (I told her I was sorry she'd quit that job; if she still had it, I said, I would have been happy to simply swap jobs with her.) The new candidate was bright and pleasant, and Kate brought her aboard with my blessing. (I was fully aware, of course, that Kate would have brought her aboard even if I hadn't given my blessing. Such is the prerogative of the powerful.) I spent the next couple of weeks training her, as well as keeping up with my own Zone creation work.

Rob, however, virtually disappeared. He never seemed to be in the office. When I inquired about his absence, I was assured that while we toiled away in our Sunset Blvd. HQ, he was out every day, from sunup to sundown, meeting with movers and shakers to convince them that they should partner with Replay-TV—"the future of television." Breakfast meetings, power lunches, afternoon cocktails, dinners with decision-makers. I wondered how he didn't gain fifty pounds. And if I could maybe have his leftovers.

Unbelievably, the transition of ReplayTV Services from Mountain View to Los Angeles seemed to go fairly smoothly—both for the department and for my life-changing relocation. And I began to feel that the future held great promise for the career I wanted when I was asked to write and edit the first ReplayTV Studios original production: a half-hour show filled with trailers for upcoming movies. The plan was to broadcast this on numerous cable channels across the country at about 3 AM and "force" the operational ReplayTV units in homes to record the show. If it worked, we'd expand the production into a weekly "What's New on ReplayTV" show (which I would lobby heavily to write and produce. Yeah, and appear on, goddamn it.)

But that was The Future. What was needed immediately was a temporary narration to cut the video to (a "scratch track") which I was happy to provide to keep the two-person production on schedule. We'd hire a professional narrator later, when the show was finalized. Once I handed in the edited show, however, it was assumed to be complete...so it aired with my scratch narration, which promoted me to the status of having been broadcast nationally for the second time.

Not to put too fine a point on it, I was home. Every morning I drove my classic Jaguar to my office in a Beverly Hills high-rise, where I was playing a key role in disrupting and advancing the TV *and* tech industries—and making more money than I'd ever dreamed possible. I could shop at Bristol Farms and the

Farmer's Market. I could pick up dinner at Mulberry Street Pizza in Beverly Hills (and often did). And going to Disneyland was now a simple day trip, only an hour's drive away.

Another bonus of L.A. life is that you simply cannot live so close to Tinseltown without the frequent Brush With Celebrity. One day, for example, while walking across Sunset to go to lunch, I was almost run over by a red convertible Rolls Royce driven by The Handsomest Man Alive: Fabio. (I flashed on the blurb that would have run on *Entertainment Tonight* if he'd hit me: "Supermodel Fabio is reportedly in excellent condition after having run over a person of no apparent celebrity status.") Another day, coming back from lunch, I spotted Academy Award-free actor Pauly Shore leaving our building. "Loved your work in *Son-in-Law*, buuuuuudy," I hailed. He looked at me as though he was asking himself how anyone over the age of fifteen even knew who he was, much less how they could possibly like his work.) (*Special Note:* These stories, and 100 others like it, can be found in my book *Famedroppings: Close Encounters with 100+ Celebrities*, available in both ebook and print editions wherever fine literature is sold, and Amazon. Thus endeth the self-promotional commercial from the Total Media Whore.)

That Thanksgiving I had a lot to be thankful for—including the four-day holiday. But, as Joni Mitchell sang, "Just when you're thinking / You've finally got it made / Bad news comes knocking / At your garden gate." I hate that it doesn't rhyme. I hate even more that it's true.

BAD NEWS, BARE

Monday, November 27, 2000

It was the best of times, it was the worst of times...except for that "best" part...

Of *course* I was running late that Monday morning. After a four-day Thanksgiving holiday respite, I had to drag myself back to work. But when I arrived...the office was empty. Well, not exactly empty...I could hear vague sounds emanating from the big conference room at the rear of the office space. I walked in to find every single ReplayTV Service team member employed in the L.A. office, from Rob Kenneally and Kate Moulene to Craig or Greg to the receptionist—some twenty or more people—standing around the periphery of the room, silent, staring at their shoes. Whatever was going on, it certainly wasn't good.

"Holy shit," I exclaimed on entering the room. "Who died?"

Rob raised his head and repeated for my benefit the news he'd clearly just shared with the rest of the team. "The Board of Directors held an emergency meeting over the holiday break," he said with flat affect. "They've decided that the consumer DVR market can't support both us and TiVo. So they're getting out of the consumer market altogether, and are planning to license the Replay technology to cable and satellite companies."

"What does that mean for us?" I asked with trepidation.

"It means they're closing down our office and laying us all off. As well as the entire Marketing division."

My memory might be playing tricks on me, but here's what I remember saying, and rather loudly: "Mother*fuckers!*" Whatever it was I said, a lot of heads nodded in agreement.

"They're laying off two hundred and sixty people," Rob continued. "About a third of the company. They've agreed to keep our office open for four weeks so we can use the facilities—your computers, the fax machine, and so on—to do some job hunting. But we are done."

Eventually, there was nothing more to say; no more commiseration we could express to one another. We broke up and returned to our desks, like zombies. That's when I got a phone call from our landlady. She told me she'd just read an article in the Business section of the L.A. *Times* that said ReplayTV was laying off half its employees and closing its L.A. office. She wanted to assure we were going to honor the year's lease we'd signed. So: She found out about the layoffs in the newspaper, before any of the affected employees were ever informed?

Holy shit. Much earlier—and under different circumstances—I wrote a haiku that I think accurately expresses my feelings about this Black Monday development:

Just when you think you've
Hit rock bottom they come and
Take away the rock

Several of the staff just went home and we never saw them again. Six or eight of us, including Craig or Greg, and my new Zones Editor—out of work after something like three weeks on the job—went across the street to a little garden restaurant and got stinking drunk for lunch. And charged it to ReplayTV. That'll show 'em.

I was informed that I could exercise the stock options I'd been granted when I'd hired in. The amount it would cost to purchase these options was—ironically or by design—exactly the amount of my severance check. I respectfully declined. No one knew where the company was headed, and there was no fucking way I was going to invest in a company that treated me (and 260 others) as shabbily as this one had.

So: I was laid off. Again. And so were Kate and Rob. CEO Kim LeMasters was "allowed" to resign. The CEO got a golden parachute. I got a golden shower. As Max Klinger explained on *M*A*S*H*, "Rank does have its privileges." Kim and I had been hired on the same day...and now we were fired on the same day. It seems like that means something significant, but fuck me if I know what.

Very soon afterward I was called by someone in Mountain View—someone who still had a job—who explained that since Zones would *maybe* be an integral part of licensing the ReplayTV technology, they wanted to keep them alive and active. *Oh sweet Jesus,* I thought—*maybe they want to keep me on board and move me back to Silicon Valley*. Alas, this was simply wishful thinking on my part. I was asked instead to do two things: first, to train my replacement; and second, to stay on the payroll through January, at full salary (and on a Work From Home basis), as a consultant, to answer any questions my replacement might have. "If you're going to keep Zones alive," I countered, "why do you need a replacement for me? Why don't you just keep *me* on board as the Zones Editor?" Oh, no, that would be impossible: Zones were now the responsibility of Engineering, not Marketing—a department that no longer existed. The engineers (some of them, at least) were about the only employees ReplayTV was retaining. And, I was informed, Replay wasn't planning on launching any *new* Zones. I just had to train an engineer on how to update the existing Zones, if that ever became necessary. Fucked again. (Ironically, the engineer I was tasked to train had interviewed for a position as a Zones editor a few months earlier...and was rejected.)

...AND IT WAS AT THIS PRECISE MOMENT THAT MY SPIRIT WAS BROKEN

"Now I know I have a heart, because it's breaking."
—The Tin Man, *The Wizard of Oz*

Of course I accepted the deal. A month's pay for sitting around the house answering the occasional email or phone call? If I couldn't arrange a better deal, I would at least take that offer. A similar offer had worked for me when MagiNet moved offshore, after all. But my $75,000 a year salary? And the additional annual five grand I was promised after six months in L.A.? Gone with the flatulent wind.

Our work was over, so I didn't feel any obligation to show up in the office during December. ReplayTV had "generously" agreed to keep the facility open for a month, so we could use the office equipment to hunt for new jobs (not that anyone ever hires in December). But our 2000 holiday bonus was that the doors would close for good on Friday, December 22nd. Merry Christmas, everyone! Rob talked many of us into showing up on the 22nd, however, just to do the "idiot check" and make sure all our personal belongings were removed before they locked the doors and turned the keys over to the building manager.

At some point during that morning, the contractor who'd been in charge of the sixth-floor renovation showed up in our offices. He was out of work now, too—all reno of the new offices died with the Thanksgiving Massacre. But he offered to show us what they'd accomplished, even though the upgrade would never be completed.

There are times in life that one should (to quote Nancy Reagan) "just say no." Or, as *The Simpsons'* Ned Flanders put it, "There are things I don't *want* to know. *Important* things!" I should have just politely declined the contractor's offer and gone home. But the same curiosity that killed the cat got the better of me, and I agreed to follow him up to the sixth floor along with a couple of my (ex-) co-workers.

And as the contractor unlocked the double doors and swung them open, I got a glimpse into an alternate dimension—a parallel world in which the TV viewing public had grasped the concept of the DVR immediately and embraced it fully; a world in which ReplayTV had lived up to the dreams of its creators by becoming a powerful force in the television industry (or at least a viable household appliance).

The aborted ReplayTV offices covered fully half the entire sixth floor. The lobby contained a U-shaped receptionist's desk as large as many swimming pools. Glass partitions on either side of the lobby looked into massive bullpen spaces. The contractor led us through the lobby and into the workspace. "This here's the bullpen," he gestured. "Over there, that's where the Zones staff was gonna sit." There were spaces for as many as a dozen Zones editor's desks. He pointed to the corner office with floor to ceiling windows on both corner walls. "That's Rob Kenneal-ly's office" (of course). Next to that was Kate's office. And next to Kate's office was—the contractor checked his paperwork—"the Senior Editor's office. Guy named Scott Apple."

This was my office? One entire wall was a floor to ceiling window overlooking the entire Los Angeles basin—a sweeping vista from the hillside on which the Luckman Plaza building rose from Beverly Hills, past the single high rise on the Miracle Mile that I drove by every day, and on to the entire downtown district, rising like Oz from the vast, populated plain. The iconic, crowned L.A. library building was centered in my window.

This was my office? This was going to be my office? I could sit at my desk and see at a glance the entirety of L.A., from a nearly aerial viewpoint. I could sit here and watch my direct reports working away in the bullpen. I was third in the line of offices after Rob and Kate.

But I would now never live that dream. And it was at that precise moment that I felt my spirit break. So close... *So close...* But it was not to be. I could have been a person of some minor importance, with some little status, with a dream job in a dream office in a town in which dreams come true—but where, far more often, dreams are crushed.

And at that moment, all I could think of was a quote from Yoko Ono: "The dream is over."

AND THE BAND REPLAYED ON...

ReplayTV was founded in 1997. An email circulated by Anthony Wood a couple of years later proved that, oddly enough, both TiVo and Replay were founded, independently, during the same week, and from facilities less than a mile apart. As Henry Ford once said about technological progress, "When it's steam engine time, it steam engines." Too bad it wasn't DVR time.

The DVR never caught fire like the VCR and DVDs. I still have no idea why. All I know is that I was sitting in the galley of that wooden ship, rowing to the beat of a different drummer, when it sank. There were few survivors.

It wasn't until much later I discovered that ReplayTV had canceled its second attempt at an IPO in August (when there was still time to call off the move, the bastards) and were burning through venture capital cash at the rate of about $10 million a month, or that a year after launch we had only about 30,000 subscribers when the goal was millions. ("Although a specific figure is not available," *Variety* reported a day or so after the Thanksgiving Bloodbath, in a front-page article, "ReplayTV's sales have been in the tens of thousands. ... Ironically [the article continued], each sale means hundreds of dollars of additional losses for Replay, which has been selling the machines at a loss in hopes of reaching critical mass in order to generate ... advertising opportunities through the program service itself ... ReplayTV's production costs on each machine are about $600-700, but the consumer price is about $300." The article continued, mentioning that Replay had developed a business model that required half a billion dollars in cash flow.)

Other industry papers, including the *Wall Street Journal*, also carried articles about the demise of ReplayTV within a day or two. The San Jose *Business Journal* quoted a ReplayTV exec as claiming that "those laid off were being offered a very generous severance package." (It must be true—a VP said it! A VP who clearly still had a job!)

My feelings were perhaps best expressed in a good-bye email from the Director of Business Development: "I've enjoyed working with most of you some of the time." Aside from similar good-bye emails, I never saw or heard from any of my Replay-TV bosses or co-workers ever again...

...except once. In January 2001, I discovered that my ex-boss Kate had filed a suit against ReplayTV, claiming the company had "misled" her into accepting her position as VP of Content and Production. And she won! *Well,* I thought, *the company had misled me, too—as well as relocating me then abandoning me and stranding me in L.A. after only ten weeks. Maybe I have a lawsuit too!* I wrote a detailed letter to a lawyer I knew, whose eventual determination was discouraging: "I have not reached a conclusion that it would be wise for you to pursue any claim" against ReplayTV, he wrote. Well…it was worth a shot. But no.

And—due, no doubt, to some latent masochism or cat-killing curiosity—I did keep track of what the company was up to. The patents and technology changed hands several times. (SONICblue, for instance, the company that originally acquired ReplayTV, itself went bankrupt just two years later.) But the tech, and Zones, never resurfaced in any significant way.

Our first and only rival, TiVo, fared only slightly better. On August 17, 2018—nearly twenty years after the demise of ReplayTV—the tech website Gizmodo ran an article by Rhett Jones about Amazon's (alleged) plan to create its own DVR, and how that might have been responsible for TiVo's stock dropping six percent on the day the rumor broke. "You had a good run, TiVo," the article concluded. "Most people are surprised to hear you're still around..."

Chapter 21

2001-2003: STRANGE INTERLUDE 3.0

December 2000

The ReplayTV layoffs came as a shock to all of us in the L.A. office. But Rob Kenneally could (and did) return to his Beverly Hills home and to his previous life as an agent at CAA, and the other victims, being local, could go about their L.A. lives. I, however, was (to quote my ex-coworker Jon Resnik in a different context) "uniquely fucked." I'd been uprooted from my home of forty years in the Santa Clara Valley and relocated to Los Angeles. And ten weeks—*ten weeks*—later...I was once again unemployed. As if that wasn't bad enough, I was stranded in a city where I had no friends (aside from my girlfriend), no family, and no networking contacts for ferreting out a new job.

Piph and I discussed just packing up and moving back to the Valley. Points in favor of leaving were to regain what we'd given up: friends, family, familiarity. But even a return to Silicon Valley came with its own peculiar set of challenges. For one, the return move would be on our dime—and how were we supposed to afford that? And if we did return to Silicon Valley, where, exactly, would we move *to*? Anyplace we chose could conceivably result in an hour-long commute for me if we didn't luck out and pick a town close to any future employment I might find. Points in favor of staying in L.A. included our year's lease, and our landlady's litigious reluctance to let us out of it. Who needs a lawsuit when you're broke? Ultimately, I reasoned that in a city as big as L.A. there could be more employment opportunities—and a wider range of opportunities—than I'd find in the Bay Area. Maybe there were fewer hi-tech positions...but maybe that was a good thing. The last two hi-tech positions I'd had resulted in little more than a years' employment each, followed by a layoff. Maybe I'd find more opportunity in this vast L.A. region as a writer or editor. Or…something.

Once again I found myself living on the trifecta of severance pay (and several week's worth of accrued vacation pay), savings, and Unemployment Insurance. But I was determined not to just sit around and let the income run out before I started hunting for a new job. I decided I'd start stalking the elusive employment right after the holidays (because, let's face it, nobody hires in December—by December, even seasonal jobs were filled).

In the meantime, I'd take another stab at Plan A, resurrecting one of my novels and polishing and submitting it.

That Christmas and New Year's Eve celebrations were effectively the polar (or bipolar) opposite of our Thanksgiving festivities a mere month earlier. A year ago—hell, a *month* ago—we had everything to be thankful for. In the last month of the millennium...not so much.

NEW MILLENNIUM, SAME OLD SHIT

January 2001

Time to get busy. I began scouring the employment websites —Craigslist, DICE, Hotjobs, Monster.com, and many others— on a daily basis, running searches for any skill I could possibly leverage into a paying position (writer, editor, video producer) in any medium available (print, web, video). How hard could it be to find a job? After all, I'd hired into ReplayTV in just days. How difficult could it be to find a job in the entertainment capital of the country?

Fast forward to...

August 2001

Eight months and 200 résumés later, the responses I received could be counted on the fingers of one hand—a cartoon character's hand, even.

Editor of a city guide website for Portland, Oregon? (Sure, I'll relocate!) After one brief phone interview, I never heard from them again.

Editor of a science fiction magazine based in L.A.? What could be more up my alley? I emailed my résumé the moment the posting appeared, about midnight on a Sunday. A few minutes later, I got this email reply: “Wow. Impressive résumé. Call me tomorrow to discuss the position.” So of course I did. “She’s not in the office,” I was informed. I called twice on Tuesday, and each time received the same reply: She’s not in the office. By Wednesday, I pushed a little harder. When I was told once again that she wasn’t in the office, I mentioned that *she’d* asked *me* to call about the editorial position. “Oh, that was filled yesterday,” I was informed.

WTF? On Sunday night, she wanted to discuss this position with me. But by Tuesday she’d found, interviewed, and hired a more promising candidate? Seriously, dude, *WTF?*

It’s miserable enough to be ready and willing to sell out to Corporate America...but it’s both miserable *and* humiliating to have no takers.

N-O SPELLS TIVO

September 2001

I even took a chance and sent my résumé to the head of TiVo Studios. ReplayTV had bowed out of the consumer DVR business, leaving TiVo as the sole consumer DVR. And TiVo was beginning to produce the same kind of “What’s New” show we’d been planning for ReplayTV Studios. With my writing, video production and DVR service programming experience, I figured I was a perfect fit. To my surprise and delight, the head of TiVo Studios called me...and agreed. “You’re exactly the type we’d like to hire,” he enthused on the phone. “Unfortunately, we’re in a hiring freeze right now, so...”

So... TiVo: Round 2: Strike 2.

And so it went, to my bafflement. Evidently I’d overlooked a couple of salient points about employment in L.A. One is that talent of all sorts was a dime a dozen in this burg, so I was likely getting drowned in a sea of applicants for any position. The second salient point is that it was Silicon Valley, never L.A., that was home to hi-tech—and the one location where I’d be most likely able to leverage my meager experience into a job.

But even hi-tech employment was in a slump. The tech bubble had burst so explosively a year earlier that literally no one in hi-tech was doing anything that even remotely required the limited skills I'd developed over the previous few years at SGI, MagiNet and ReplayTV.

On a side note: I'm well aware that there are millions of people on this planet with issues far more important than my own little White Male Privilege/First World Problem of finding employment at a high enough level of pay to continue my upwardly mobile-attempting, middle-class American lifestyle. There are refugees, terminal illnesses, human trafficking, political oppression, and countless other horrors to which a significant portion of the human population are victims. But within the context of an early 21st-century American middle-class crap economy, *mein kampf* was just as real to me, and just as acute, as anyone else's. I couldn't end world hunger, or cure cancer, or find homes for refugees, or free all political prisoners. I couldn't even find a job to keep my own half-century-old self sheltered and fed. And the reality of being so close to so much conspicuous consumption in Los Angeles was both oppressive and depressing.

IN WHICH I MAKE A RUN FOR THE BORDER(S)

October 2001

I needed a job. Desperately. I realized I'd had that depressing revelation so frequently that my life was beginning to feel like *Groundhog Day*.

After months of trying, I couldn't find a single professional position, or even land an interview for one. It was clearly time to lower my standards, if only to be able to earn enough make rent. But what could I do? I was 50 and still had no marketable job skills. Very few companies hire unpublished novelists for the kind of salary my hi-tech jobs had commanded (or for any salary at all, for that matter.) But I'd worked in a couple of bookstores and enjoyed that...so that was my fallback, my "safety job." There was no money in it, but at least I might be able to make my monthly nut while extending my search for a "position" instead of just a "job."

First stop was a very posh, legendary bookstore on Hollywood Blvd., one noted for their celebrity clientele. No one wanted to wait on me or even talk to me. Friendly place. I finally corralled an assistant manager who grudgingly handed me a sheaf of application papers when I told him I was looking for a job. I went down the street to a coffee shop to do my homework and discovered that the application form was *ten pages long*. There were, of course, the standard, expected questions (name, address, work history, etc.) followed by some unexpected but understandable personal info. (What's your favorite book? Why? Who's your favorite author? Rank his/her works in order of literary quality.) Then came the really odd personal shit—essay questions about *Ulysses* and *Moby-Dick* and William Burroughs, for instance. WTF? It seemed more like a college entrance exam than an application for a job shelving books. I got the impression they were looking more for a soulmate than for an employee or co-worker...except that even dating sites didn't ask this many personal questions or require this much depth. I gamely filled in all the pages, attempting to craft answers that were brilliant, insightful, impossible to argue with, and, whenever possible, witty. I'd learned to fake all that pretty well. Clearly, what I had not learned to fake was the requisite pretentiousness, since once I handed in my application essay I never heard back from them. I also never shopped there again.

Next stop was a Borders Bookstore branch in West Hollywood. I'd driven past the store many times and had always meant to stop in. Now I had a reason. I don't recall the details, since everything went so smoothly. I asked if they were hiring for the holidays; John, the HR Manager, said they were and gave me an application. I filled it out and quite possibly interviewed with him right then and was hired right there. "Can you start tomorrow?" he asked. You bet!

Hallelujah! I had a job. At age 50, I would be a minimum wage clerk in a chain bookstore. But at least I wouldn't starve to death in the gutter. Maybe.

The West Hollywood Borders was located at 330 N. La Cienega, on the corner of Blackburn, just a block north of San Vicente Blvd., and a couple of blocks south of the imposing Beverly Center shopping complex. The Borders store was a massive, stand-alone, two-story building (a former carpet warehouse and showroom, and—20 years later—a PetSmart) with its own large parking lot. The place was huge and featured a wide, sweeping, curved staircase as its centerpiece. The first floor was dedicated to books and magazines; the second floor was half books and half media—CDs and DVDs—as well as the Borders Café, a standard appliance in every Borders store.

My first night there, John put me to work in the backroom. This was where shipments were received, where boxes were opened and emptied and the contents sorted, and where overstock and books awaiting shelving were stored. John explained that shipments doubled in the months leading up to the holidays, and the single current backroom employee simply could not keep up with the influx. I would work nights, continuing his daytime work: opening boxes and sorting books into shelves lining the walls, where the early-morning shelving crew would move them out to the floor to their appropriate locations.

I stayed in the backroom for weeks, rarely interacting with my alleged co-workers. But I had no complaints. I was left almost entirely alone. There was only ever a single assistant manager on duty at night, for instance, and he was busy enough with the store that he never bothered to check up on the backroom. And it was quiet. Often, when my work was done—when I'd caught up with the day's deliveries; when I'd opened the final boxes and sorted the books they contained—I would sit in the backroom reading every book the store stocked on job hunting, résumé writing, and employment interview techniques. (In the chapter "What I've Learned About: Résumés" in Part IV of this narrative, I claim to have read more than 50 books on the subject. This was how that occurred. Unbeknownst to Borders, they were paying me to learn how to get a better job.)

I AM NOT HAPPY, ALTHOUGH MANY OTHERS ARE GAY

One night, a few days before Halloween, John the HR Manager—a big hairy bear of a guy—burst into the backroom looking for a book. John worked days, so his showing up at night was a bit of a shock—but not as big a shock as the way he was dressed: leopard print dress, fur stole, a '50s style lady's hat. "Going to a Halloween party?" I greeted him. "No," he replied. That's when it hit me: *This was him* in his off-hours. Not only was he enormously gay, he was a transvestite as well. His being gay was no surprise—this was West Hollywood, after all, the gayest town in the USA. I quickly discovered that fully half of my male co-workers were gay. I didn't care—but it was quite amusing to realize this, like twenty years earlier, when I learned that most of my co-workers at Monolithic Memories were gay.

One day a few months later, John showed up to work dejected and depressed. "What's the trouble?" I asked him. He told me his boyfriend had left him, and he was devastated. I knew what it was like to have a lover leave you. I tried to comfort him. And I had an epiphany: gay or straight, we're all looking for the same thing—someone to love who will love us in return. If I ever had any aversion to gays before that revelation, it ended for all time in that emotional moment. I don't care what anyone does behind closed doors. But we're all human beings with hearts that can be nurtured or broken, and we can all only be connected by compassion. Thus endeth the sermon.

NEW YEAR, SAME OLD SHIT

January 1, 2002

My three-month trial period at Borders was over on January first. I had to work New Year's Day, but that was a small price to pay for being employed. I showed up for work and approached John, smiling. "Happy New Year," I greeted him. "Of course we're keeping you!" he replied, seemingly reading my mind. "And you're getting a raise. Two, actually." He explained that the California minimum wage had risen to $6.75 on that very day, and that Borders gave a twenty-five cent per hour raise for every three months you stayed with the company. So in just one day, I'd increased my pay by fifty cents per hour! Happy New Year indeed! At this rate, I'd re-attain my ReplayTV salary in only...26 years! Sure, I'd be 76 years old by then, and long retired, or dead (at that point, either alternative was acceptable) —but I was back on the track to employment success!

Even though I knew I was working far beneath my station or potential and trapped in a low-rent limbo, Borders wasn't pure hell. There were, it turns out, some benefits, however minor. There was no specific dress code, for instance (unlike Barnes and Noble), which allowed for the comfort of working in jeans and a T-shirt. Every three months of employment generated an automatic twenty-five cent per hour raise. Managers could reward you for extra effort by filling out a little folded brown card that read "You've been caught..." and on the inside, "...doing something good," with a space for the manager to fill in what you were being congratulated for. These commendation cards could be turned in for a free drink in the in-store café. We also got a 15 percent discount on purchases and were given a $20 gift card every month (the equivalent of an additional $5 a week pay, or a $240/year bonus). These little perks might not have been much... but they were tiny bright spots in an otherwise bottom feeder existence.

Full disclosure: The guilty truth is I actually began to enjoy the job. I had the backroom all to myself at nights, for one thing. I didn't have to run a register or deal with customers at the Information Desk (and Beverly Hills customers were an *enormous* anal pain to deal with. They were the Privileged Class and *you* were a nothing more than a *clerk*—one step above their servant; two steps above their slave.) Alone and unmolested in the backroom, I could set the radio to L.A.'s classical music station and work at my own pace. In addition, I was the first person to see every book that would be sold in the store. My only moments of grief came when I happened to unpack a book by one of my friends. A new edition of a Philip K. Dick novel, for instance, forced me to realize that even though my friend Phil Dick had been dead for nearly twenty years, he was still more successful than I was.

I rarely interacted with my co-workers who worked the floor; usually the only reason they came to the backroom was to check for a book a customer had requested but which was not (yet) on the store shelf. I went out of my way to be helpful, assisting them in finding a title among the new releases or tucked away on the overstock shelves. When I did have a chance to talk with them, I was surprised to find such an intelligent crew. And when I mentioned this to one assistant manager, he told me, "It's a buyer's market. The job scene is so bad we can pick up some really good, overeducated people and pay them shit wages." I'm not sure if he was just being blunt or if he simply didn't include me in his description because in his mind I didn't fit it.

I also greatly enjoyed the company of Brad, the main backroom guy. He worked 10 to 6 and I worked 4 to 11, so our hours overlapped every day. He'd show me what he'd accomplished during the day and what I needed to finish. And I discovered that he was not only exceedingly intelligent, but that our interests aligned on many subjects, including cosmology, physics, astronomy, and other areas of science. During those overlap hours we often engaged in philosophical discussions about futurism and the implications of the latest discoveries in astronomy and physics while we sliced open boxes and unpacked the day's deliveries.

I mention this not to rub my exceptional intelligence in your face (if I'm so smart, why was I so underemployed?) but because of the place our intellectual flights of fancy took us. One day in March I said to Brad, "You know, you're an intelligent, informed guy. You know as much as I do on a layman level about these advanced areas of science, for instance. So if we're so smart, what are we doing schlepping boxes in the backroom of a chain bookstore for minimum wage?" He had no answer...but a couple of weeks later he announced that he'd be leaving this job. "What you said struck a chord," he told me. "And when I saw that the position of Café Manager was opening up, I applied, and John hired me. So I'm going to learn some management skills I can use to get me out of Borders and into a better job eventually."

I was flabbergasted. Something I'd said had actually changed someone's life? And for the better? I told him I was overjoyed... but that I'd miss him. "Take your own advice," he counseled me. "Apply for my job." And with that suggestion, he'd returned the favor. I went to John the HR manager and told him I'd be applying for Brad's backroom position. We went through the motions of an interview, laughing at every corporate-mandated question. "Do you have any experience?" he asked. "A little," I said. "I've been doing this same exact job at night for nearly six months now."

"Yes," he replied gravely. "But can you do it in the *daytime*?"

Of course I got the position. How could I not? For once, there were no other, better-qualified candidates who got their résumé in ahead of me. OK, so it wasn't much—but it did get me another two-bit raise (in both senses of the phrase), and stable hours, as well: I didn't have to show up at 9 AM and prep the store for opening like most of the clerks; I could saunter in at 10 AM, wave hello to my co-workers, and sequester myself in the back-room for the day. I could take a break, or my lunch hour, any fucking time I wanted. And I didn't have to work until 11 PM, cleaning up the store and returning stray books and magazines to their appropriate locations, which the losers—pardon me, the *closers*—had to do: I could clock out and stroll out at 6 PM and have my evenings (and weekends) free. At some point, I realized that if the job paid twice what it did, I'd be happy...and if it paid three times what I was making, I might never leave.

NOW APPEARING AT YOUR LOCAL BORDERS...

Another mixed blessing of working in the West Hollywood Borders was the frequent appearance of celebrities in the store. I was off the days that the "berries" (Halle Berry and Dave Barry) dropped in, unfortunately. And I wouldn't (and didn't) go out of my way to meet that fat walrus, David Crosby. But I had a delightful conversation with *SNL*'s Kevin Nealon—"Mr. Subliminal" himself—as well as with the actress Amy Irving, whose movie *Voices* I'd included in *Killer B's*. ("So you're the one who saw it," she joked.) I was tempted to approach Sharon Stone, but I couldn't think of anything to say to her other than, "I liked seeing your pussy in *Basic Instinct*. You should do more movies where you show your pussy." Two decades later, I'd realize that this would have been a very Presidential comment. But at the time, I thought she might not appreciate that kind of in-depth career guidance.

One afternoon, a limo pulled up in front of the store and an enormous man in an expensive-looking suit entered and asked to speak with the manager. He introduced himself as Michael Jackson's bodyguard and explained that Mr. Jackson was in the limo and would like to do some browsing in the store...but he requested that all video surveillance be turned off while he was shopping. The manager politely declined, and the bodyguard got back in the limo and drove away. Every one of us congratulated her for not capitulating to the demands of privilege.

(Special Note: These stories—and many other similar stories —can be found in my book *Famedroppings: Close Encounters with 100+ Celebrities*. Remember: Total Media Whore!)

And that, pretty much, is how I spent most of 2002—working for an RCH above minimum wage, enjoying everything about the job except the pay, continuing to comb the web for better employment possibilities and…

TIVO: TAKE 3

…jumping at unexpected opportunities. One night in March, for instance, I picked up a consumer electronics magazine and opened it to a review of TiVo. The reviewer listed the DVR's pros and cons, but one criticism practically jumped off the page and smacked me in the face: *Suggestions*. TiVo's "Suggestions" function consisted of automated algorithms that recommended and recorded other shows it thought you might like based on your TiVo viewing history and your "thumbs up/thumbs down" voting. And it never worked. It was one of the most mocked and disliked features of the TiVo—a function which, to this day (2020), is still regarded as "invasive" and "overkill."

But I knew how to fix it. Maybe not the precise algorithm, but certainly by applying the categorization technique—the taxonomy—I'd developed for Replay Zones. Upgrading TiVo's Suggestions function might require human eyes, attention and intuition to guide and temper the automation, but I was confident that adding logical, intuitive, human oversight to the algorithms could turn a reviled bug into a useful feature. I made five xerox copies of the review page. I circled the negative writeup of the Suggestions feature with a red marker and wrote across the page "I CAN FIX THIS." And I sent those copies along with a cover letter and my résumé —prominently listing my tenure and job description at ReplayTV—to the five top executives at TiVo: the CEO, the head of Engineering, and the heads of Operations, Programming and HR.

The net net: I never heard a word back from any of them.

Is it possible that every one the five people who (hopefully) received this bold claim (backed by experience earned at their first and only rival) just shitcanned my letter without a second thought? Is it even conceivable that *none* of these five ever mentioned it, even casually, to one of their peers? ("Hey, did you get that insane letter from that asshole who claims he can fix Suggestions? I saw you cc'd on the cover letter." "Yeah. Fuck him.") Are we to believe that *none* of these recipients had any interest at all in making Suggestions work? I'll never know what actually happened to my quintet of communications. All I know is my shotgun approach missed the side of the barn. By a country mile.

My score with TiVo was now: Attempts: 3; Successes: 0. Or, to continue the earlier metaphor: TiVo: Strike Three.

ESCAPE FROM L.A. *(not starring Kurt Russell)*

November 2002

Piph and I had now spent over two years in the City of (Fallen) Angels, our hell away from home. Some people are seduced by L.A. We were basically raped.

We took advantage of some time off from Borders to drive up to San Jose in November and spend Thanksgiving with my mom and my siblings and their kids. While dinner was being prepared, the two of us snuck away and took a drive down to Los Gatos, just a few miles away. It was a nearly perfect fall day, cool and crisp, with a hint of golden sunlight. The autumn leaves of Los Gatos were as colorful as any New England hamlet, and the streets were clean and slick from a recent shower. I was reminded how much I'd always liked this little village—so much so, in fact, that years earlier, in my first comic mystery novel, I'd located my fictional detective's office on a key downtown corner.

Apparently, Piph was reading my mind, which was not uncommon. "Why are we still living in L.A.?" she asked.

"Well," I said weakly, "my job is there."

"But doesn't Borders have stores everywhere?" she asked. "Can't you transfer to another store?"

"I can," I said. "And goddamn it, I *will*. Where do you want to live?"

Once back in L.A., we spent the next week investigating places we'd like to live. The primary requirement, of course, was that the town had a Borders Bookstore to which I could transfer. We settled on Santa Cruz, a small, laid back college town only half an hour's drive south of Los Gatos. For a hundred years, Santa Cruz had been the oceanside vacation spot and day trip beach getaway for Santa Clara Valley residents. It was close to Silicon Valley, in case I ever found gainful employ in the hi-tech industry again; it was very common for Silicon Valley workers—including several of my former co-workers at Lockheed, for instance—to live in the Santa Cruz mountains and commute to Sunnyvale. Santa Cruz was close to my extended family, as well—but not *too* close, if you catch where I'm drifting. We could visit for major holidays, but skip many of the lesser family functions (cousins' birthday parties, for instance). An added enticement was that we had an old friend—a recently widowed writer in his 70s suffering from Post-Polio Syndrome—who lived in Capitola, just one town over. We could visit frequently, make sure he was fed and in decent health, and keep him company.

IN WHICH I GIVE NETFLIX *ONE MORE CHANCE*

So Santa Cruz it was. But before I called the manager of the Santa Cruz Borders store to inquire about a transfer, I took one last shot at real employment. I called the resident movie critic at Netflix—with whom I'd interviewed a couple of years earlier when I'd applied for an editorial position—to see if he could endorse a writing position I'd applied for at Netflix. I called several times a day for several days, but he never answered—and apparently didn't believe in voicemail. And then one day, I lucked out: he answered the phone, live and in person. I reminded him of who I was and where we'd met, and asked if he'd object to my putting his name on my résumé for Netflix as a professional reference, since that would clearly pull some weight. The line was quiet for a moment, then he replied, "I have to go. I'm doing a phone interview in a few minutes. I only picked up because I thought it might be them calling early." And he hung up.

Netflix: Strike Two. Netflix movie critic: Eat shit and die.

I didn't waste any more time. I called the manager of the Borders store in Santa Cruz and explained my situation—namely that I wanted to escape L.A. and transfer to his store, if he had an opening. He said that he did indeed have a position opening up mid-January—about a month later—and that it was mine if I wanted it. (I assume the advantage to him was that he could free himself of the burden of advertising and interviewing for the position—not to mention that there would be far less paperwork in hiring an existing employee than some jerk off the street—or, more precisely, some *other* jerk off the street.) Having been burned in this type of situation before, however (see the entry for B. Dalton, Bookseller)—namely, relocating on a verbal agreement only to arrive and discover there was, in reality, no job waiting for me—I suggested we exchange whatever paperwork was necessary to effect the transfer, and that I'd see him in January.

With only a month to prepare, Piph (as always) took point in organizing the move. She informed our landlady that we'd be vacating, for instance. (We'd fulfilled our one-year lease over a year earlier, so she couldn't sue us.) She located a mover at an acceptable price. And she started packing. She also drove up to Santa Cruz and located a suitable house—during one of the worst rainstorms that area had seen in decades. She was (and is) a talented and tireless organizer, as well as totally game about how often we had to move just to follow my work. (Foreshadow alert: This pattern would continue for another decade—but ultimately it would be worth the effort for both of us.)

And, early in January 2003, we attained escape velocity and escaped from L.A. (This was not accomplished without a Snake Plissken-level of effort, however: I was stuck in Buellton for several days when my car overheated and required a new radiator before I could complete my exodus, for instance. And sadly, Piph did not have to transport the cat this time—my beloved Eros had passed away a few months earlier, after a full twenty years of constant companionship.)

SANTA CRUZIN'

January 2003

The Borders Bookstore in Santa Cruz was located downtown, on the corner of Pacific and Soquel. This was the heart of the Pacific Street Mall, which had been all but destroyed by the 1989 Loma Prieta earthquake and had been rebuilt as the dynamic shopping district of this sleepy little town. This Borders store was maybe half the size of the West Hollywood branch; it occupied a two-story building, but the only things on the second level were the café, the restrooms, and the offices. The store was under the domination—I mean supervision—of manager "James Brown." (I use this pseudonym for two reasons. One is that this Borders manager was the very antithesis of the famous musician James Brown; where the original James Brown was black, tirelessly energetic, and known as the "Godfather of Soul," Borders Manager "James Brown" was enervated, so white as to be almost albino—and had no soul whatsoever. The second reason is that his real name, if I revealed it, proves every bit as ironic.)

"James Brown" (not the hardest working man in show business) put me to work in the Music department, shelving CDs. Well, OK. I knew I'd have to accept any position that would make the transfer possible. I would have preferred books, or DVDs—either of which I knew far more about than music. And if I was exiled to Music, I would have preferred music I knew something about, like Rock, or Classical, or Soundtracks. But since I was the "new kid," I got the dregs of the music department—the sections that no one else wanted, like Jazz, World Music, and Spoken Word. I knew virtually nothing about these genres—but I learned quickly. To this day I know far more about jazz than I ever cared to know.

Much of the daily work involved "policing your section": adding newly-arrived CDs to the bins, straightening out the section, returning to their proper locations discs that idiot customers had just stuck anywhere...and so on. And I was finally trained to be a cashier—a task I'd avoided like the plague in the L.A. store.

I quickly discovered that nearly half of my female co-workers were lesbians. This came as no surprise; just as West Hollywood is the Gayest Town in America, Santa Cruz was well known as the Capital of the Lesbian Nation. And again, I feel compelled to add this disclaimer: recognizing (and mentioning) that many of my co-workers were lesbian is in no way a judgment, just an empirical observation. The fact is that (with one notable exception), the Santa Cruz lesbians loved me, and I adored them. There was no sexual tension between us—there *couldn't* be, by definition. And that was, truth be told, kind of a relief, after experiencing nearly half a century of sexual tension with women. We were all just human beings, relating on an intellectual and emotional and professional level, sexuality be damned...and what is done behind closed doors in the name of love is nobody's goddamn business except the participants'. (Thus endeth the rant. Death to all fanatics!)

WITH A LITTLE HELP FROM MY FRIENDS

Yes, we'd escaped L.A. But I was still only one small step above unemployment—and, as I was over fifty, I was perhaps the world's oldest bookstore clerk. It was, I realized, retrograde motion: after twenty-plus years of corporate work, I'd landed in the same job I'd had a quarter of a century earlier.

My depression must have been manifest, at least occasionally. One afternoon, for instance, while I stood behind the counter feeling the weight of my bottom-feeder fate, the lovely lesbian Kirsten eyed me critically and said, "You look sad. Do you need a hug?" And when she said that, I realized that *Yes*, goddamn it, I *did* need a hug! Never before in my work life had anyone ever had the acute observational powers to recognize this, much less the guileless innocence to mention it and the selfless fortitude to suggest such an intimate solution...and this to a straight old guy she barely knew. I opened my arms and we embraced, warmly and completely. It's difficult to explain how significant that simple friendly gesture was to me. Perhaps the idea that I spent an entire paragraph describing a hug might be some indication.

From that day on, Kirsten was my work friend and confidant. We got along so well, in fact, that she organized an unofficial "Scott Apel Day" in the store that July—a day in which everyone dressed up in my typical outfit of blue jeans, T-shirt and red suspenders. A couple of my co-workers even taped on fake beards and sported wireframe glasses. Customers were baffled. I was touched and amused.

But not everything was supercalifragilisticexpialidocious. Occasionally, for instance, while manning the register, I was accosted by some customer who recognized me from my Bay Area television presence a decade earlier. Their most common question was, "What are *you* doing here?" And I gave them my stock answer: a wide smile and the response, "Livin' the dream."

WHAT KIND OF COMPANY WAS BORDERS TO WORK FOR?

We had the freedom of informality—the casual dress code, for instance—but there were limits. As an excerpt from the Borders employee manual put it, "The goal is to...formalize the informal nature of Borders stores." Oxymoron much?

I found another example in a corporate memo, which informed us that "We have changed the wording on our discount coupons. The wording now reads: 'This offer cannot be combined with any other offer.' We have to do this for legal reasons. In reality, this offer *can* be combined with any other offer."

BOOK SHELF LIFE

It was bad enough that I was the world's oldest bookstore clerk—me, a white-collar salaryman, a nationally-acknowledged film and video expert, a college professor—a goddamn *novelist*, goddamn it!—now relegated to shelving CDs while hovering slightly above minimum wage. But Manager James Brown (not Soul Brother No. 1), like Massa himself, was determined to make life under his Iron Hand as difficult as he possibly could for all of us. When an employee accidentally spilled a coffee drink (and cleaned it up), for instance, JB banned all liquids from the floor. What? We were supposed to work our shifts without coffee? Or even *water*? Yep. (Naturally, that decree was universally ignored the moment anti-Elvis left the building. Nobody was willing to put up with that kind of oppressive shit, nor should they have to.)

Many of us found subversive ways to fight back. The timeclocks we used to clock in and out of our shifts, for instance, provided one such opportunity. They divided each hour into ten segments of six minutes each. So if you were scheduled for 4 PM, you could clock in anytime during the six-minute period from 4:00 to 4:06 and still be on record as being "on time." The disaffected among the staff (which included about half of us) never clocked in before :06. That way we got an additional tenth of an hour's pay without actually having to perform that six minutes of work. Sure, it sounds miniscule...but do this every day of a five-day workweek and you've actually gained half an hour's pay without doing half an hour's work.

The timeclocks provided a similar opportunity at the end of the shift as well: clock out at 11:01 instead of 11:00, and you'd get an additional tenth-of-an-hour pay for that six-minute period which ended at 11:06. Do *this* five times a week and it adds up to an *additional* half hour's pay *for which you did no work.* If you could keep up this discipline all week, you'd end up with an additional hour's pay every week without doing an additional hour's work. It's minor; it's petty; it's almost too complicated to arrange for the meager benefit it provided. But it was a fine "fuck you" to a management that had no problem exploiting us worker bees for their own advantage and profit. And it might serve as an illustration of just how disaffected many of the employees were that we'd go to these lengths to squeeze an extra hour's pay out of our minimum-wage job.

Why did we need this extra hour of pay? To put this microrebellion in perspective, I should mention that Borders was absolutely, completely and thoroughly paranoid about paying overtime—to the point that a "full-time" job was defined as 37.5 hours, not a full 40...because they'd be forced to pay overtime for anything over 40. So not only were we being paid near minimum wage, we couldn't even get actual full-time hours. Who could fault anyone for responding by figuring out a way to get an extra hour's pay every week? It seemed only fair: if they're going to remove two and a half hours from our "full-time" job, we'll remove an hour of work from the remaining 37.5 hours.

At some point, the wrath of Manager James Brown (not Mr. Please Please Please) became focused on yours truly. Why, I will never know. It might be because I naturally polarize people. (If you've read this far, that should be obvious.) It might be because so many of his staff liked me (see "Scott Apel Day," above) and hated him (see his drink prohibition above as one example). Whatever the reason, he seemed determined to make my life a living hell. He scheduled me for the evening shift (4-11 PM) and for weekends, for instance. What he didn't realize was that these were exactly the hours I preferred (and only partly because these were hours he was not in the store). And when I got an offer from Cogswell College to continue teaching my film courses on Wednesdays, I made it clear to James Brown (not the James Brown who said, "Say it loud: I'm black and I'm proud") that the one day of the week I would *most like to work* was Wednesday. So he scheduled me for every Wednesday off. Oh, please don't throw me in the briar patch! What a tool.

IN WHICH I BECOME A MASTER THIEF (ALLEGEDLY)

I didn't realize the full extent of James Brown's (not Mr. Dynamite's) animus toward me until that fall—even though I was regularly "called to the Principal's office" and dressed down by this detail-stickler for such felonies as "reading on the job" and "giving out too many bathroom tokens" to customers. (It was JB's policy to force us to intentionally embarrass customers who requested to use our locked bathroom by making us ask them, "Is it an emergency?" before we could give them an entry token.) And although I could make a list of trivial details that might convey the flavor of being the wage slave of an oppressive and petty tyrant, I believe this single story can serve as a prime example of the atmosphere...but a bit of background is necessary to put JB's management style (and his campaign against me) in perspective:

The Santa Cruz Borders store, unlike the West Hollywood store, had a Daily Report—a page or two of pertinent information printed out and attached to a clipboard and left at the registers. It was our own little small-town newspaper—an effective way to quickly inform the staff of what was happening in the store: new policies; what promotional or discount coupons we might encounter when ringing up customers; upcoming events (like the midnight release of a new Harry Potter novel); who'd left and who'd been hired; and so on. All employees were required to read the Daily Report at the beginning of their shifts.

One day's Daily Report contained the results of a recent inventory—specifically the "loss" statistics, or an account of how much merchandise had gone missing from the store during the previous twelve months. The figure was nearly $165,000, which seemed to me to be shockingly excessive. How could $165,000 worth of merchandise go unaccounted for, even over a year? I did some quick math, dividing that figure by 363—the number of days each Borders store was open annually (closed Thanksgiving and Christmas)—and came up with a figure of slightly more than $450 in merchandise missing *per day.*

How the fuck could that much merch disappear, I wondered? The obvious answer is theft. But we already had a world-class theft prevention system; one that involved magnetized metal strips in small plastic rectangles stuck inside every CD and DVD and inserted into most books. The strips were demagnetized by clerks when a purchase was made (manually, by running the merchandise over a magnetic plate next to the register, activated by a foot pedal). If someone attempted to leave the store without getting their purchase demagnetized, gates installed at each door would sound an alarm. The alarm went off maybe once a week—and more often than not it was either a false alarm or a mistake on the part of the clerk who botched the demagnetizing process rather than someone attempting to walk away with unpaid items. When the alarm sounded, staff were supposed to drop whatever we were doing and approach the customer (aka "the potential thief"), detain them, ask to see their receipt, and rummage through their bags to check the contents against the receipt. This made us many friends among customers who would never shop there again. The whole process was so intru-sive, confrontational and embarrassing that many of us simply ignored the alarm. Why bother to respond? We couldn't physically restrain anyone actually attempting to rip us off—that was illegal. The best we could do was to *ask* them to stay in the store while we called the cops—who rarely showed up on the rare occasions anyone did call them. Clearly, the anti-theft system was working (as well as working against good customer relations), and there was no possible way that $450 worth of merchandise was leaving the store every day through customer theft.

Not that customer theft could be eliminated entirely. Maybe once a week, some skateboard punk would snatch a DVD or two, run out of the store (setting off the alarm) and wheel away. We all saw this happen occasionally—and usually just shrugged and went about our work. Not only was it clearly futile to try to chase down a skateboarder on foot, even if we caught up with the pissant, there was nothing we could do, legally speaking. If you even touched the little nosepicker, that's an assault charge just begging to be filed. Besides, the store had a Loss Prevention floorwalker whose full-time job it was was to haunt the store for his entire shift to "keep an eye" on any suspicious activity or "person of interest." Fuck it—let him do the running. And face the legal blowback.

So I was curious about the euphemistic "loss," but I never really give it much thought. After all, it wasn't my problem.

Until it was. Until the Loss Prevention guy from Corporate HQ came around to investigate our "high loss" store—and by "investigate," I mean, "interrogate the employees." One by one, he "met" with each of us in James Brown's (not...you know) office, often for an hour. We were all aware that something was going on—but those who left these meetings would only whisper that they'd been ordered not to discuss what was going on.

Finally, it was my turn in the barrel. Oh boy! I'd finally find out what was going on! Larry The Loss Prevention Guy was a real piece of work—middle-aged, walrus mustache, aggressive attitude, very full of himself. He seemed like one of those wimpy guys who always dreamed of being a cop but couldn't pass the physical (or the psychological) exam and became mall security guards instead, with an enormously overinflated sense of self-importance to compensate for his failure to become a real cop. He was the last line of defense against rampant criminality among the employee class—and his attitude reeked of his prejudice that we were all guilty. Of something.

He had a lot of questions, but never any answers. He wanted to know if I'd ever seen theft occurring in the store. Sure, I said, and described the skateboard punk scenario. He wanted to know if I thought my co-workers were honest. Of course, I replied. They never gave me any reason to think otherwise. He leaned back in his chair. "That's interesting," he sneered. "Every one of your co-workers said the exact opposite." It seems that trusting my peers were honest was the wrong answer—an answer that only a guilty person would give. I just shook my head. "And I thought *I* was cynical," I chuckled. He was not amused.

He never made any direct accusations against me. He couldn't. Unless he had some evidence, I could sue him for slander or defamation, or for wrongful termination, if they decided to fire me *just to be sure*. He simply attempted to make me (and, I assume, everyone he interrogated) feel guilty and uncomfortable, implying that we were worthless thieving scum and that *he was onto us*. "I understand you drive a Jaguar," he drawled, for instance—the implication being: *How can you afford to drive a high-end luxury import on the shit wages we pay you without supplementing your pay by stealing from us?* But I wasn't going to acknowledge any of that.

"Yep," I replied. "A seventeen-year-old Jag I picked up for two grand at an auction a few years ago. Like my girlfriend says, 'You don't have to have money to have style.'"

He was not amused.

"You came here from the West Hollywood Borders," he continued, consulting his notes. "Are you aware that that's considered a High Loss store as well?" The implication, of course, being: *You've worked at two stores considered High Loss, which can't be a coincidence.*

"As well as what?" I said. That seemed to throw him off.

"As well as this one."

"I didn't know this was considered a High Loss store," I said. "Being informed of things like that is above my paygrade."

"Well, it is. And so was West Hollywood."

"I can't say I'm surprised," I said, laughing. "Your notes will probably inform you that the West Hollywood store was horribly mismanaged. The guy who was manager when I started there was demoted and transferred to another store."

He glared at me. My sidetrack was irrelevant and non-incriminatory, so he had no response...or any interest in hearing it.

"Borders has more than 1,200 stores," I said after a few moments of enduring his seething silence. "How many are considered High Loss?" The implication being: *It's not likely that these are the* only *two stores considered High Loss...so it's a coincidence, you fucking moron.*

The glaring continued.

Eventually, after a bit more cat and mouse like this (in which we each thought that we were the cat and the other guy the mouse), he let me go back to work. I wished him well and thanked him for the information and for taking into consideration what we employees think. I knew that would piss him off.

End of story? Hardly. Larry The Loss Prevention Guy was back a few weeks later, once again to subject the employees to an "interview." No one on staff went missing following his earlier round of chats, so clearly, no one was fired. No one had broken down and confessed to...well, anything, apparently, no matter how guilty he tried to make them feel about...well, nothing, apparently. So now it was time for him to become No More Mr. Nice Loss Prevention Guy. He'd have to dig deeper and browbeat with extra effort to discover...well, nothing, apparently.

This time I was ready for him when I was summoned to James Brown's (not Mr. Living in America's) office for his follow-up phishing expedition. He tried the same tricks to get me to confess to...something. And then he dropped his bombshell: "We caught you on the security cameras."

"Doing what?" I asked, aghast-like.

"Appropriating CDs," he gloated.

"Boy, I'd like to see *that*!" I enthused.

He was more than happy to oblige. He had the tape cued up and played it for me on a monitor. Sure enough, there I was, walking along the upstairs hall with a basket of CDs. I unlocked the storeroom and a minute later, walked out without the CDs (or the basket).

I knew exactly what he'd "caught on tape." So I decided to fuck with him. Heck, he'd earned it.

"Well, ya got me," I said. "I did indeed drop a basket of CDs in the backroom. I suppose you caught my accomplice as well?"

"Your— What?"

"My *accomplice*. I move the CDs into the backroom; she retrieves them and gets them out of the store. Just scan the security tape ahead to the next morning."

Of course he did. He was *onto* something now—maybe a huge ring of thieves; a network of corruption responsible for the store's $160,000+ annual loss. He'd be praised by his corporate masters as a Loss Prevention Hero. Maybe he'd get a raise—and a promotion. He couldn't fast-forward that tape fast enough.

Eventually, he hit the spot, and right there on the security cam footage, in living black and white, was the image of a co-worker entering the backroom and exiting with the basket of CDs. The biggest shock of all (to him, anyway): it was the Assistant Manager! Cue the "Dramatic Hamster" footage from YouTube. (OK, that wouldn't be posted for a few years. But you can do it now.)

Larry's brain went into something like vapor lock. He could not believe what he was seeing—an *executive* (albeit the lowest management-level position available) conspiring in this gigantic rip-off ring? From the look on his face, I assumed he was thinking, "Inconceivable!" But I do not think that word means what he thinks it means. (OK, *The Princess Bride* had been released by then...not that Larry probably knew about it.)

So I let him off the hook. "You see, Larry, this is called *procedure*. Once a month I swap out the CDs in our listening stations and return the used CDs to the backroom, where we shrinkwrap them and sell them as *new* CDs—not that there's anything unethical about *that*. But yesterday I didn't have time to shrinkwrap them and add the price labels. And this morning, the Assistant Manager told me she didn't want me leaving those listening station CDs in the backroom anymore—so she'd put them by her desk in the bullpen next door."

Curses! Foiled again!

Round Three came soon after that. This time, Loss Prevention Larry was determined to get me for...something. But since I had never done anything even remotely suspicious, he had no evidence of any wrongdoing. He *couldn't* have had any evidence—it didn't exist. Even when he *thought* he'd had evidence, it was only evidence of his own ignorance of store procedure.

But I'd about had it with his intrusive and frankly insulting implications of illegality. When I mentioned that I knew the exact figure of Loss at the store, for instance, he jumped on that. How did I know that? I told him that the figure had been posted in the Daily Report, months ago. It was no secret—every employee was required to read the Daily Report, so we all knew the figures. I told him that $160,000 in loss for the previous year — a year which began *six months* before I even transferred to the Santa Cruz store, I also mentioned—seemed high to me, especially when parsed out into a daily loss figure of $450, and that the enormity of the figure made me curious as to how it could be possible.

"So I did think this through, and I'd like to help you out here," I said. "You might be able to benefit from my curiosity. I mean, just think about it. Four hundred and fifty dollars translates to *thirty* CDs or DVDs at fifteen dollars apiece. That's a stack over a foot high." I illustrated by hovering my palm a foot above the desk. "Hardbacks go for an average of twenty-five bucks apiece, so four hundred fifty dollars equals eighteen hardbacks. That's nearly a full box. So how is it possible that any one employee—or even any group of employees—could remove that much merchandise? We're talking thirty CDs every day the store is open, seven days a week...and employees only work five days a week. To anyone with a lick of logic, it's clearly impossible for any employee to be responsible for this loss."

He just glared at me. But he didn't stop me. He'd probably learned in one of his Junior G-Man classes that the longer a perp talks, the more likely he is to implicate himself. But I knew that too...and I had nothing to hide, so I continued.

"Have you ever worked the floor in a Borders?" I asked. "Worked the shipping and receiving function in the backroom?" He just glared. "Well, let's assume you haven't. But I have, for a year in West Hollywood. We receive merchandise in boxes, on shrink-wrapped pallets—about forty or forty-two boxes per pallet. Those boxes have a bar code, and when we receive them, we scan the bar code into the computer system to acknowledge that we've received the box. The key here is that we acknowledge that we've received a *box* of merchandise, not that we've received the individual items in each box. If we had to scan every single item in every single box to prove that we've actually received it...well, that would require a full-time employee just to do that scanning. In every store. So *that* ain't gonna happen. In other words, we operate on good faith—we assume that we've received every item on the manifest in every box we accept.

"But what if we don't?" I continued. "What if someone in the warehouse, someone who packs these items into the boxes, leaves out just *one* CD from every box? Or just *one* DVD? Or just *one* hardback book? Maybe it's incompetence. Or maybe he squirrels them away in the warehouse and sneaks them out later. Either way, missing *just one item* from every box in a pallet of forty boxes would easily add up to more than the missing thirty CDs or DVDs, or the eighteen hardbacks. So why aren't you investigating the warehouse packers?"

No answer. Just the glare. Still, he hadn't stopped me, so I continued my fuckery.

"Or consider another scenario," I said. "Maybe it's *not* the warehouse crew. Maybe every single piece of merch that they say they added to the boxes was actually added to the boxes, and the store actually received every single item. Then ask yourself this: *Under what circumstances could someone remove that much merchandise from the store?* And that leads to several other questions: Who has keys to the store? Who has 24/7 access? Who knows all the security precautions and procedures, and how to work around them?" His brow was beginning to furrow, so I closed in for the kill. "Yeah," I stated emphatically. "That's right. I'm talking about *management*. But you will *never* investigate the possibility that *management* might be responsible for this Loss, because it would reflect poorly on *all* Borders management. You can't tell your bosses that Borders might have hired some *scofflaw* for a position of authority—it would cast doubt on the entire vetting process, and make too many people look like fools and idiots. And you'll *never* investigate the warehouse scenario either, because that would be too much like *work*. So you'll settle for harassing the only people you have any authority over—the minimum wage floor staff—even though you know, logically, that they can't *possibly* be responsible for what you've been tasked with investigating."

He dismissed me. I waited to be fired for insubordination. Not like that never happened before. But maybe, I thought, just maybe, I got through to Loss Prevention Larry, and he'll stop harassing the powerless employees and do some real research. That dream went up in a puff of smoke when soon afterward, Manager James Brown (not the singer with the cape) announced a new policy: No employee who didn't work in the backroom was allowed in the backroom. They were clearly committed to their original "the employees are ripping us off" scenario and doubling down on attempts to keep the staff away from the stock. Naturally, this made life much easier for the floor staff—instead of pulling our new stock from the backroom ourselves, we now had to wait for a member of the backroom crew to be available to assemble it for us and bring it out to us. Oh, well. Take your time, guys. I'm hourly. I can wait.

I never heard from Loss Prevention Larry again. But I did hear *something*. Sometime in December, as I was lying on the floor of the store, swapping out CDs in the listening stations under the CD bins, Kirsten approached me with a wry smile. "Oh, you are in *so* much trouble," she smirked.

"Now what did I do?" I sighed. "Or not do?"

"I was in the manager's meeting this morning. James Brown came in, and I've never seen him happier."

"Like you've ever seen him happy at all."

"He announced that they'd found the Master Thief," she said; "the guy responsible for $160,000 worth of merchandise loss over the last year...and that it was *you*." She could barely contain her laughter.

I was only half as amused as she was. I was also baffled and on the verge of being pissed. "If I stole $160,000 worth of merchandise in the last year," I asked her, "including the six months before I even *worked* here—then why am I lying on the floor, swapping out CDs in the listening stations, instead of lounging around in the Caribbean? Or in handcuffs being hauled away by the boys in blue?"

She just shrugged. "He didn't go into that."

"I'll tell you why. Because he's an idiot. Because he has zero evidence. He couldn't have any, because there *isn't* any."

She looked down at me lying on the floor and pointed to the CDs. "So you gonna stuff those down your pants and steal 'em?"

"Well, I am *now*," I said.

We both had a good laugh over that.

The day wore on, but no cops appeared to cuff me and haul me away. The next day was police-free as well. I just kept showing up for work, waiting for the hammer to fall, anxious for the opportunity to confront...*somebody*, and argue these idiotic charges. And if they came right out and openly accused me, I wouldn't waste a moment calling my lawyer. (OK, I didn't actually *have* a lawyer...but I *knew* one. He was an actor who I'd cast in a couple of my plays, so I figured he owed me.)

But no one ever did anything. I wasn't arrested. I wasn't fired —which James Brown (not, you know) could have done by fiat, without any necessity to explain. Maybe I was being closely watched. I hoped I was, so they'd learn something about what it means to be a hardworking, *honest* employee.

No, no one said anything. But a few days later I received a snail mail letter from Borders Corporate. The first line read:

You have experienced a COBRA-qualifying event: Termination.

Oh, really. Did it just slip someone's mind to inform me that I'd been terminated? Clearly, the termination paperwork had been filed, kicking off the (probably automated) process of offering me a COBRA follow-on health insurance policy. But I was still scheduled for my shift and my days. Were they trying to get some free work out of me? "Let him work this week, *then* we'll let him know he'd been fired last week and *won't be paid. BWA-hahaha*!"

I didn't take the "COBRA-qualifying event" letter to the albino James Brown and ask for an explanation. What I heard through the grapevine was that he was all set to fire me, and even filed the paperwork—then had a change of mind (or of heart, although it's a matter of debate as to whether he actually possessed either). Maybe he talked with the Legal Dept. and was informed he was an idiot and had nothing against me but his own unfounded prejudices and bile...and that if he fired me after announcing I was the Master Thief *to witnesses*, I could sue for wrongful termination...whereas if he'd just kept his stupid mouth shut, he could have laid me off without any reason, and with no fear of legal retaliation. (It's called "At-Will Employment.") Who the fuck knows? I just kept my head down and checked the next week's schedule.

Yep, I was employed.
Goddamn it.

POSTSCRIPT:
READERS (NOT DOCTORS) WITHOUT BORDERS

In 2003—the year I spent working at the Santa Cruz store—Borders had 1,249 stores (including their Waldenbooks outlets) and employed about 19,500 people. But they made a number of missteps and outright blunders entering the digital age—mainly ignoring the rapid growth of online bookstores like Amazon, and the rise of ebooks—and had their last profitable year in 2006. The company staggered along for a while, struggling, but the last Borders Bookstore closed on December 31, 2010, and the corporation filed for Chapter 11 bankruptcy protection in February 2011.

When I checked in 2017, the former location of the Santa Cruz Borders Bookstore was a Forever 21 clothing store.

Chapter 22

2003: AKIMBO PART I

THE WORLD'S OLDEST LIVING BOOKSTORE CLERK

December 2003

I needed a job.

OK, technically, I had a job. But even after two years, I was still making less than ten dollars an hour working at Borders. And the only things working at Borders had gotten me recently were harassed, persecuted, and fired. Or not fired. Who knew? I was Schrödinger's employee.

What I needed was a *better* job: a job where I could put to use my (admittedly minimal) tech skills, my growing knowledge of film and video, and my niche experience in video on demand in service of making a decent living. I needed, in short, a professional job that paid a professional wage.

I needed a *real* job.

It's not like I didn't spend hours every week combing the Silicon Valley job sites for something—*anything*—for which I might qualify, because I did. On a good week, I would find maybe two open positions, one or both of which I could justify emailing a résumé to apply for. On a bad week—which included most weeks—zero opportunities presented themselves. It seemed that the tech sector—where I stood my best chance of employment—had not yet recovered from its bubble bursting a couple years earlier. No one seemed to be hiring for any position my specialized skills could fulfill. And absolutely nobody was doing anything with video on demand, where I had most of my hi-tech experience.

I had one hope—and it was a long shot. But, as they say, desperate times call for desperate measures. In February 2001, two months after my former employer, ReplayTV, quit the consumer DVR market and laid off half their staff, they sold their assets (patents, copyrights, etc.) to a company named SONICblue. And SONICblue seemed committed to keeping the ReplayTV Service alive. This meant that maybe—just *maybe*—they were committed to keeping Replay Zones alive. And Zones, my former domain, probably hadn't been updated since I left, two years earlier. After all, when I was given the boot, I trained an engineer on Zone creation and maintenance...not a TV or movie buff; not a writer or editor; not a "customer-facing" person. An *engineer*. Most of the Zones were automated, so the engineer didn't need to do anything to keep them updated. But what would an engineer know (or care) about keeping the various handcrafted Zones like the Cult Movie Zone up to date—Zones that required regular manual updating, editing, and tweaking? I determined to contact someone at SONICblue and offer my freelance services to give Zones a thorough update (and, if possible, to parlay the temp work into a full-time job).

First, I wanted to clear this idea with Doug Shannon, the genius who'd invented Zones. Maybe he'd had the same idea; if so, I didn't want to step on his toes. If not, I could certainly use his blessing—as well as anything he might have heard through the tech grapevine concerning SONICblue and their plans for the ReplayTV Service. I dug out his contact information and gave him a call. We caught up on the last couple of years, but before I could delineate my plan, he hit me with a surprise.

"Weird that you should call now," he said. "Just a few days ago I got a call from Steve Shannon. He's been looking for you."

"Who's Steve Shannon?" I said.

"You know," he replied. "*Steve Shannon*. From ReplayTV. He was one of the founders, with Anthony Wood. He was CFO or something."

I'd never met him, even when ReplayTV had only 50 employees. Or if I had, he'd left no lasting impression. But if he was looking for me, I wanted to talk to him. Maybe he had a job opening. "Gimme his contact info!" I told Doug, coolly and calmly. "Right fucking now!"

I dropped Steve Shannon an email, like we were old buddies: "Hiya, Steve! Doug Shannon says you've been looking for me. Here I am! What's up?"

He wrote back to let me know he'd founded a new startup and might be able to use me to do some freelance writing. Once again, the old "good news, bad news" answer. On the upside: more work —and writing work at that. The downside: just another freelance assignment, not a job. Ah, well. When you're hovering just above minimum wage—and just above the abyss of bankruptcy—every penny counts.

A BRIEF PHILOSOPHICAL ASIDE

Calling Doug Shannon was a lesson in hope, or optimism, or perspective. For years I'd felt totally isolated in a bubble of underemployment and low wages, without recourse or options. But unbeknownst to me, behind the scenes—outside of my bubble—there was a guy with a job looking for me. None of us have the Big Picture, I realized, and good things might be secretly headed our way even in the worst of times.

Yeah, it's unlikely. But it is possible.

AKIMBO

Steve invited me to see his new startup, Akimbo, in San Mateo—about an hour's drive north of Santa Cruz. (Just a side note on Northern California culture: Distances are always given in time, never in miles. Who cares how far away a destination is geographically? All we want to know is how far away it is temporally; i.e., how long it will take to get there...which varies widely by the hour of the day. San Jose to San Francisco is only about 50 miles, for instance. At noon, using freeways, the drive can be made in an hour. During rush hours, even though the distance remained unchanged, the travel time for those same 50 miles could easily double. Einstein would probably turn over in his grave if he knew that in NorCal, space was fixed but time was malleable.)

I made the trip on one of my days off from Borders, and found Akimbo in an eight-story office building on Bovet Rd., a block or so from the intersection of El Camino Real and Highway 92. The building was old (or "classic," depending on your appreciation of age and architecture). Akimbo had offices on the sixth floor and an engineering lab on the seventh.

Standing at the door to the Akimbo office, I realized I was in trouble. Although in the email I'd pretended that we were old compadres, I didn't know Steve Shannon from Adam (of the proverbial "Adam and Steve"). I'd never recognize him. I had to hope a receptionist would call him and he'd come out to greet me, at which point I could smile and shake his hand and enthuse about how great it was to see him again. But if he was standing in the lobby with other people, I'd never be able to identify him. And if he sent someone else out to greet me, I wouldn't recognize that this guy wasn't my "old buddy" Steve. And I'd look like an idiot claiming how great it was to see someone "again" who I'd never met before. I'd have to play it by ear.

Luckily for me, when I walked through the door, Steve Shannon was standing in the little lobby. Alone. And *he* recognized *me*. The odds of a guy in this office who recognized me being someone other than Steve Shannon were slim, so I took a chance. "Steve! Great to see you again!" Social crisis averted!

He showed me around the small office space, introduced me to the CEO, Josh Goldman (even though Steve was the founder, he'd handed the lead role to someone he considered more qualified), and then unveiled his product: the Akimbo player. It was a black set-top box, about the same size as (and virtually indistinguishable from) the ReplayTV device or a good VCR. He explained that it was, in fact, similar to ReplayTV in that it was a hard drive video recorder. But the similarities ended there. The difference between the two DVRs was that while the ReplayTV hooked up to a cable or satellite TV service and recorded broadcast television, the Akimbo player plugged into the internet and recorded video sent through the web.

We talked a bit about the device and his business plan. What Steve wanted from me was a short writeup to use for advertising and marketing purposes, touting Akimbo's revolutionary operation, ease of use, and so on—the typical new hi-tech product happy horseshit ("Revolutionary new product." "It will change your life." "It will make the world a better place." You know—all the same clichés and catchphrases they mocked on HBO's *Silicon Valley*.) I was happy to take the assignment, and handed him a short essay within a few days—and got paid as much as any magazine article I'd ever sold, for about a tenth of the work. Yeah, maybe I *did* belong in the hi-tech world...

I suspect this assignment was some kind of test, because Steve soon called me back to alert me he might have a position for me, once they had enough work to keep me busy. If it was indeed a test, however, I'm not sure how I passed it, as I soon realized that I had completely misunderstood the purpose of the Akimbo service. I thought it was a great idea to create a box that would seek out and download some of the ever-growing wealth of video on the web (think YouTube, although this was a year or more before YouTube was even founded). But what Steve actually had in mind was the creation of a new end-to-end video service, where TV shows and movies could be purchased through the Akimbo player using onscreen menus, then sent from our servers through the internet and downloaded directly into the player.

In 2020, delivering video content through the web, by downloading or streaming, is an everyday fact of life. But in 2004, it was a radical concept—and only barely accomplishable due to recent advances in internet speed, video compression, and hard drive storage capacity. (To put this in a historical perspective, iTunes wouldn't start offering movie downloads through the web until late 2006—three years later—and in 2004, Netflix was a company that still sent DVDs through the snail mail; they wouldn't start a streaming service until 2007.)

Steve's vision of an online video service was radical in another way as well. The general viewing public was growing increasingly frustrated with cable TV (and, by extension, satellite services) with their business model of paying a set fee and getting all the basic channels. There were clearly many channels that a viewer never watched, and was tired of paying for. Why should I pay for several shopping channels, for instance, when I never use them? Why should I pay for a Korean language channel, and two Chinese language channels, and three Spanish language channels, when all I speak is English? (And that not all that goodly.) The real question consumers wanted to ask the cable and satellite services was this: *Can't I just buy the channels I want and pay less?* Answer: No. But the Akimbo service would allow the user/viewer to step away from the "buffet" approach of the cable companies to an "a la carte" model where you paid only for what you watched. In that respect, Akimbo was another set-top box, but not *just* another set-top box—it would be the beginning of a new era of television viewing; a liberation from the dictatorial dictates of cable and satellite's repressive restrictions, business model and pricing policies. Yay!

But Akimbo would only work if it had content worth yanking your cable—hence one of the buzz phrases from that era: "Content is king." Steve was dedicated to creating a video service that included TV, video, and (if possible) movies, from a variety of sources including movie studios, indie film producers, TV and cable networks, and imported TV shows (hey, it works for PBS!). If Akimbo could offer enough content, enough *good* content, and enough *unique* content—content unavailable on TV or cable outlets—then the venture stood a chance of success. Most start-ups aim for the stars. A very few—Netflix, Google, Amazon, Facebook Twitter, Instagram—catch fire and become institutions. ReplayTV had crashed and burned. But maybe Akimbo had a shot.

ESCAPE FROM TURD ISLAND

"I had a whole new attitude. I woke up fresh and alert each morning, and began each day with the absolute certainty that *tomorrow* would *definitely* be the first day of the rest of my life. But meanwhile, *today* could, like, go blow itself."
—"HC," *MFU (Most Fucked-Up Man Alive Tells All)*

First, however, I had to get in. Meanwhile, I was stuck at Borders. Piph and I spent another Cratchit-under-Scrooge Christmas in 2003, and while 2004 held a dim glimmer of hope, I still had to work on New Year's Day, sorting CDs and ringing up purchases on customers' stocking-stuffer Borders gift cards.

Every day at Borders was torture. But after my meeting with Steve, every day at Borders was *pure* torture. The manager hated me. I hated the job. Maybe Steve would call. But not today—today was eight hours of horrorshow. One of my favorite *Killer B's* movies is a comedy entitled *Clockwise*, starring John Cleese. As his world comically unravels around him while he tries to hold it together, he confesses at one point what devastates him most: "It's not the despair," he sighs. "I can handle the despair. It's the *hope*." Hope was all I had, but every day the hope did not come to fruition, I was more devastated.

February 2004

And then one day in late February, I got The Call. "Why don't you come on in and interview?" Steve said. "I think we're ready for you now."

When I went in to interview, I was introduced to Akimbo's Content King, Kevin Donohue. Kevin was in his late 30s, all smiles... and the big brother of one of my old co-workers in the Lockheed Video/Film Department. I asked how Tim was doing since we'd both been laid off a decade ago. I shared my favorite Tim Donohue story with him, and we both had a laugh. We talked movies. I think at some point I dropped a Monty Python line, and he continued the skit's dialog without missing a beat. And at that moment I knew we could work together.

I also interviewed with Morgan, one of Akimbo's key engineers. (That story is significant enough to make it into the Part IV chapter "What I've Learned About: Interviews"). And I sat for a few minutes with the CEO, a genial little guy who made such a deep impression on me that, nearly 20 years later, I had to look up his name in my old files to remember him.

Finally, Steve came into the conference room where I'd met with the others. "What do you need?" he asked. "I'm good," I said. "Maybe a water." "No," he said. "What do you need as a salary? What do you need to get by?" The question stymied me. It wasn't a question in any of the books I'd read about interviewing. I was used to being *told* what I'd be making. Sometimes you could negotiate, like at ReplayTV. Sometimes you're just informed, like at Lockheed, where entry-level salaries for various positions were carved in stone. I might have been prepared to answer a question like, "What do you *want*?" But what did I *need*? What did I need *to get by*? What the fuck was that even supposed to mean? With Piph and I both working, we were able to make our monthly nut and "get by." Did I "need" more than that? Or was he talking about what I thought my experience and ego required to be satisfied? All I knew for sure was that I needed a hell of a lot more than minimum wage, or the less than ten dollars an hour I was raking in at Borders.

Steve waited patiently while I tried to untangle what he meant—and what I needed. I figured the best way to move forward was to put things in a perspective he could relate to.

"Well," I said at length, "I was making seventy-five when Replay relocated me to L.A., with a promise of eighty in six months."

He nodded. "I can give you sixty," he stated.

"I can do sixty," I said. It was still four times what I was making at Borders.

Welcome aboard.

I knew it would take a few days for Akimbo to get the paperwork together. And I showed up to work at Borders every one of those days. I was—like so many underpaid people—living paycheck to paycheck, and since it would be at least two weeks from my start date before I got my first check from Akimbo, I needed the money—and there was no telling what disasters might befall this new position before the Akimbo execs signed the contract. It had happened before and made me wary of burning bridges—before I crossed them, at least. So I showed up at fucking Borders and I filed fucking CDs and I ran the fucking cash register and after the store closed every night I replaced the pile of fucking magazines that thoughtless fucking customers had left lying around the fucking café and I smiled and kept my mouth shut about the idea that one day soon I might just *not show up*—just in case I *did* have to keep fucking showing up.

That week seemed like a month. The months before that, waiting for Akimbo to be "ready" for me, seemed like years. Then one afternoon—February 25th, precisely—I received an offer letter from Steve. Two days later, he faxed me a contract. I signed it and faxed it back immediately. I'd start in a week.

I had a new job. Hallelujah.

So, Steve Shannon, if you ever happen to stumble across this narrative and read this chapter, please accept my heartfelt thanks for definitely saving my career, certainly saving my sanity, and possibly even saving my life. You are a hero.

IN WHICH I MAKE A RUN FOR THE BORDER(S EXIT DOOR)

February 28, 2004

The day after I received the Akimbo contract, I was scheduled to work—at Borders, not at Akimbo. A few minutes before I was due to arrive, I called the store and asked for the manager. And I experienced one of the most satisfying and gratifying moments of my entire working life.

"Hey, James," I enthused once the pasty-faced schlub answered the line. "It's Scott. Good news for both of us, buddy: *I quit*. I got a job that pays per day what you pay per week. My keys are in my cup in my cubbyhole. So...buh-bye!"

He started to say something. "Are you—"

"Hey, James," I interrupted, hitting him with a line he'd been known to use to insult his team, "what part of 'I quit' don't you understand?"

And I hung up. God*damn*, that was fun!

I never saw or heard from him again. Bonus!

Chapter 23

2004-05: AKIMBO PART II

"We're pioneers, so we take the arrows."
—Steve Shannon

March 2004

My start time at Akimbo was 9 AM. As a biological "night owl," I'd vowed years earlier that once I was out of Lockheed, with its 7 AM start time, I would never again take a job that began earlier than 10 AM. I managed to live up to my vow for a decade (although I was unemployed through much of that period, and there's no start time for unemployment. Or freelance work). But at Akimbo, this 9 AM start time was a contractual obligation. Steve Shannon told me he didn't want to run the kind of loosey-goosey startup where people came and went whenever they felt like it, so start times were written into everyone's contract. When the engineers united in protest, they got their start time bumped back to 10 AM. I asked if my job could be transferred to Engineering, but Steve just looked at me sourly. So. 9 AM it is, then.

Any new job starts with a new commute, and my drive from Santa Cruz to San Mateo was a doozy. The Bay Area might have a relatively small geographical footprint, but that doesn't mean that every point is within commuting distance. The greater Bay Area covers nine counties and stretches from Santa Clara County in the south to Sonoma County in the north—nearly 200 miles. Santa Cruz, where we were living, isn't even part of the San Francisco Bay Area, technically. It's part of the *Monterey* Bay area, and the distance between our house in Santa Cruz and the Akimbo office in San Mateo was about 60 miles—well over an hour's drive, even at freeway speeds and when the roads were clear. During rush hours—which in Silicon Valley ran from 6 AM to 9 AM and 3 PM to 7 PM—it could easily mean a two-hour commute. Each way. Five days a week. Driving to the full-time job was the equivalent of a part-time job.

I left home that first day at 7:30 AM, figuring that would give me sufficient time to navigate the four freeways I'd need to use to get to San Mateo: Highway 1 in Santa Cruz would take me to Highway 17, which would take me over the Santa Cruz mountains to Highway 280 in San Jose, which would take me to San Mateo, where I'd transfer to Highway 92, drive six miles across the Peninsula, and exit on El Camino Real, a couple of blocks from Akimbo HQ. What I didn't count on is that every of those freeway exchanges was so congested during rush hour that just to get off one freeway and onto another added an additional ten minutes of drive time to the commute, ultimately snowballing an hour drive into a 90-minute commute. Jesus Christ.

When I showed up five minutes late, Steve greeted me in the lobby. "First day, and you're late," he said, shaking his head. "I just spent ninety minutes commuting here," I protested. He laughed. "I'm just pulling your chain," he said. Disaster averted!

A BRIEF DETOUR CONCERNING THE BANE OF SILICON VALLEY EXISTENCE: COMMUTING

"The Commute" is an important part of life in Silicon Valley, albeit one rarely discussed—but one that warrants discussing in some depth. For the working class, commuting is like coffee or bathroom breaks—experiences so common that they're taken for granted, and rarely mentioned in polite conversation. What could be more boring than someone else's commute? (Answer: their dreams). And yet people in Silicon Valley (and possibly elsewhere) often decide where to live based on the location of their workplace and the degree of difficulty it takes to travel between those two points. Or, if they wanted to purchase an affordable home outside The Valley, they resigned themselves to a long daily commute.

Oddly, although it took 90 minutes to drive north from Santa Cruz to San Mateo during rush hour, the return trip took only an hour—possibly because it was "downhill," I joked to myself, but more likely because I'd wait until 6:30 or 7 PM to leave, at which point even Silicon Valley's rush hour had essentially tapered off. Even so, I quickly realized that spending two and a half hours in the car every day was not a viable lifestyle. My first thought to change this was: find a different route.

There was really only one alternative: California Route 1, which runs over 650 miles from Orange County to Mendocino County, mostly following the coastline. In 2002, the National Scenic Byways Program, administered by the Federal Highway Administration, declared Highway 1 an "All-American Road," due in large part to its scenic grandeur. And I discovered that the stretch of road from Santa Cruz to San Mateo was one of the most beautiful drives anyone could ever hope to take. The downside was that it was still a 90-minute commute—but an hour of that drive was traffic-free, and wound through simply spectacular scenery: rocky coastline, crashing ocean waves, numerous picturesque beaches, gentle pine forests, the Pigeon Point Lighthouse, and additional highlights too numerous to mention. Some mornings, sections of the coast were thick with fog; on others, the glare from the ocean was so bright I had to put on sunglasses at 8 AM. As an added bonus, just as the Santa Cruz classical station faded out on the radio, the San Francisco classical station kicked in. I'd arrive at work calm and happy. That 90-minute commute was not only the longest of my career but also the best—and the only commute I miss.

But still...90 minutes was a bit much, so I developed a strategy for driving Highway 1 at speeds above the legal limit. For the most part, I rarely saw another car on the road. But if anyone came up behind me and wanted to pass...I let them. I'd let them pull far ahead of me but still within my visual range, then match their speed. If any local cops or Highway Patrol were laying in wait to catch a speeder, it would be *them* who'd be caught, not me. I'd get the benefit of their speed with none of the risk. To quote J. Montgomery Burns, "Excellent!"

AKIMBO: DAY ONE

Steve set me up at a desk in a long, narrow room with two co-workers, Morgan, an engineer, and Mark, a handsome, young, ambitious (and brilliant) fellow who did "partner relations." We were the trio of "customer-facing guys," so it made sense to cluster us together in one room. We also turned out to be three wild 'n crazy guys, so it made sense to isolate us from the more serious-minded staff. One example: A couple of months after I started, Morgan discovered a primitive online "Arnold Schwarzenegger soundboard," where the click of a mouse played an audio clip of *Ah-nold* saying various words and phrases ("Yes," "No," "What do you want?"), as well as many of the most quotable lines from his films ("I'll be back," "It's *not* a tumor," "Who is your daddy and what does he do?," "Fuck you, asshole," "Shut the fuck up" and so on). There were probably 50 different audio clips, and Mark, Morgan and I spent nearly a week mixing and matching them to hold virtually all our conversations—always punctuated by gales of laughter.

Despite the fun, work came first, of course—and we had our work cut out for us. Once I familiarized myself with the content that had already been contracted for, I had two major tasks. The first was to work with Mark to come up with a pricing scheme. If we were selling content "a la carte," what would be a fair and reasonable price for content? What was the lowest we could charge for a piece of content and still make a profit? 29 cents might be the right price for a short film or cartoon, for instance, but due to the cost of the infrastructure and partner percentages, we'd lose money selling anything for less than 49 cents—so that set our lower limit. Mark and I drew up a chart that divided content into increments of 50 cents: we would sell content for 49 cents, 99 cents, $1.49 and $1.99. Maybe super-premium content could go for higher. My motto at this time was "Anything under a dollar is essentially free"—an insight into consumer habits that would later become widely adopted by internet retail in general. (Case in point: iTunes, with its 99 cent songs.)

The next decision was how to price each video. I suggested we use a time-based metric, and tie price to length. We quickly abandoned a "pay-per-minute" approach, since this would result in every piece of content carrying a different price, which would definitely be confusing for a user/viewer. But we could use a more chunky metric; a stairstep approach that defined a few price tiers tied to larger units of content length, like 15-minute segments. This way, anything under 30 minutes—a 7-minute cartoon, for instance, or a 12-minute episode of Adult Swim's *Aqua*

Teen Hunger Force—would fall into the lowest price tier of 49 cents. Half-hour TV shows would be priced at 99 cents; hour-long shows at $1.49, and full-length feature films (if we ever got any) would sell for $1.99. This became the basis of our sales model.

Company executives considered our pricing schema and approved it, with one major revision: every piece of content would be bumped up one price tier. That 12-minute episode of *Aqua Teen Hunger Force* would sell for 99, rather than 49, cents, for example. (When iTunes launched their TV store a few years later, they set the lowest price for any content at $1.99—so we were still rationally and reasonably priced. Relatively.)

Further complicating our price scheme was that the content acquisition team had free rein to cut deals that allowed the content providers to set their own prices—which, according to the Wikipedia entry for Akimbo (as of August 2017), "resulted in erratic pricing and exorbitant costs for users, as content owners would often set prices of 5-9 dollars for a 30-minute show, and load the show with commercials." (If this had happened during my tenure, I would have remembered it—and protested. So I assume it happened a year or two later, when Akimbo was struggling to survive and willing to make any deal for any content.)

My next task was taxonomy—a fancy word for categorizing content. As Senior (and only) Editor for the Akimbo System, it was up to me to assign content to various categories...categories that would be logical and user-friendly (a phrase we still used back in 2004). My goal was to connect the user/viewer with the content they wanted in as few steps as possible. To that end, I classified each individual video into at least two genre pigeonholes. My reasoning was that wherever a person *thinks* they should find a particular piece of content, that's where they *will* find it. (When I proposed this overlapping tagging, the lead software engineer objected on the grounds that "it's not good computer science." My defense was that our viewers were not computers. I won that round.)

My taxonomilogical task was aided in two ways. First was a wealth of well-established genre classifications that had been around for decades, or longer: comedy, drama, action, romance, documentary, and so on—as well as numerous descriptive sub-genre labels developed for television. The second was my previous experience in taxonomy at ReplayTV, classifying all TV programs and movies into subcategories that were both logical and intuitive. The Akimbo taxonomy had to be robust enough to incorporate any potential content, yet simple enough that a user/viewer could find any show with the fewest clicks of their remote control.

I was thrilled. This was my wheelhouse. My dharma. My *métier*. This was what I'd wanted at ReplayTV but had never attained: personal control of an entire network of programming. Whenever the question arose as to what people will watch, my answer was both arrogant and accurate: "They'll watch what I tell them to watch." (It wasn't until many years later that I ran across this quote from Steve Jobs: "People don't know what they want until you show it to them.")

I'd suggested early on that any Akimbo provider agree to make at least ten percent of their content available free of charge. I pitched this to Steve as a "win-win-win" situation: user/viewers could check out new and unknown content at no cost; providers would benefit by contributing free samples that might lead to sales; and Akimbo would earn a reputation as a generous, customer-focused service. Steve liked the idea and approved it. He gave this new direction to the content acquisition team and tasked me with coming up with a name for this new collection of free samples.

That might sound like a simple task—but what would *you* come up with? I made a list of about 20 possible channel titles, but the one I really liked was this: *Lagniappe*. The dictionary definition of *lagniappe* is "a small gift given with a purchase to a customer, by way of compliment; a bonus." Steve nixed the idea, on the grounds that no one would know what it meant. But I kept pitching it. Sure, this was a regional word, mostly used in Cajun country, but it fit exactly—and might even inspire some curiosity on the part of our user/viewers to look up the definition. Standing in the doorway of Steve's office one afternoon, once again attempting to sell him on the idea, out of the corner of my eye I spotted one of my co-workers walking down the hall—a Matthew McConaughey look-alike who'd grown up in New Orleans. "I'll make you a deal," I said to Steve, without looking down the hall. "Next guy who walks by the door, we'll ask him if he knows what the word means—and if he does, we'll use it." As if on cue, Luke walked by. "Hey, Luke," I greeted him. "Do you know the definition of the word *lagniappe*?" "Sure do," he replied, with his buttery Cajun accent. "It's a little somethin' extra you get from a storekeeper. Like the thirteenth donut in a baker's dozen." I turned to Steve, triumphant and justified. "See? *He* knows what it means!" Steve just shook his head. "Nice try," he said, and went back to work.

Well, goddamn it, I tried. Nicely. In the end, Steve approved my second choice: *Free For All.* Evidently it mattered little to him that this colloquial phrase meant "a fight or argument open to everyone and usually without rules." Other descriptive adjectives defining a free-for-all include *disordered, impulsive,* and *out of control*. But at least it was literally accurate: the content *was* free. And it *was* free for all Akimbo owners.

Dramatis Personae

STEVE *(Shannon, not Jobs)*

It occurs to me that the picture of Steve Shannon I've painted so far is of a rather sour, negative guy. Nothing could be further from the truth. These mini-conflicts make for good stories. But overall, Steve was the very soul of calmness and rationality, and was very often very funny. At our Halloween party, for instance, he told Piph that I was "the worst negotiator" he'd ever seen. (Maybe so…but I'd learn—and I did, in fact, manage to quadruple the salary I was making at Borders just by taking Steve up on his salary offer.)

Steve Shannon was also a shrewd and practical businessman. Early on, for instance, I asked him why he located the startup in San Mateo rather than Silicon Valley. "You kidding me?" he replied. "Floorspace in the Valley goes for about two dollars per square foot. *This*," he said, gesturing around to our office space, "is *fifty-eight cents* per square foot."

He had a good answer for why he named the company Akimbo as well. "I know what 'akimbo' means," I said one day. "It's like the classic Superman pose; fists on hips and elbows angled out. But why did you name the company 'Akimbo'? What's that got to do with video on demand?"

"I learned that from ReplayTV," he replied. " 'Replay' is a common word, and a good description of what the product did. But it's not *sticky*—it didn't make an impression on people. It was that nonsense word 'TiVo' that caught peoples' attention. So I went through the dictionary and decided that 'akimbo' sounds so meaningless and nonsensical that maybe it would stick in peoples' minds."

Made sense to me (even though he clearly didn't go very far through the dictionary to come up with the word).

KEVIN DONOHUE

There were only maybe 40 people at Akimbo when I started, most of them hardware or software engineers. I was pleased to be able to work closely with Steve to implement his vision, and I enjoyed the company of my closest co-workers, Mark and Morgan—enough so that I even socialized with them outside the office, something that hadn't happened since my days in Lockheed's Video/Film Department more than a decade earlier.

I also found a kindred spirit in Kevin Donohue, one of two content acquisition people. Kevin was a wild man—not only good at his job, but energetic and wacky in every setting. I actually looked forward to our content meetings, where Kevin, Steve, Mary—Kevin's fellow content acquirer—and I met weekly to discuss status, upcoming content, and the "state of the service." Dress at Akimbo was already casual, so Kevin thought we should go one step beyond "Casual Fridays," for instance, and pioneer "Pantsless Fridays." ("We could even have a pants-off dance-off!" he enthused at one point.) He was so quick-witted, and so funny, that I found myself being the audience more often than the instigator—and I felt a touch of relief that after twenty years of attempting to be the Hawkeye Pierce of any department I worked in, the burden of being the local Joker had now been assumed by Kevin.

We talked one day about science fiction, which led to time travel, which led to a routine we used a couple of times a week: Kevin would appear in my cubicle, declaring, "Scott! I'm *you* from twenty minutes in the future! No time to explain, but you absolutely *must* go into Steve's office and pour a pitcher of water over his head! *The fate of the universe depends on it!*" Or I'd burst into his office and declare fervently, "Kevin! I'm *you* from twenty minutes in the future! No time to explain, but you absolutely *must* go into the CEO's office and drop trou! *The fate of the universe depends on it!*" With each round, we'd grow more vehement, and make an even more outrageous request, which *must be done immediately*, because *the fate of the universe depends on it!*

Our gleeful goofiness was not without its practical applications, however. Over lunch one day, for example, we discussed what we'd like to see as TV ads for Akimbo, if we ever reached that stage. For some reason, he was fixated on creating a scene from the '60s sitcom *I Dream of Jeannie*, where Jeannie's routine response to a request was, "Your wish is my command."

"Yes, master," I said, crossing my arms like Jeannie the Genie. "Your wish is *on demand*."

His jaw dropped and his eyes popped. "That's our slogan," he whispered.

My jaw dropped as well, as his insight sunk in. "Yeah! *That's our slogan*!"

We accosted Steve as soon as we returned from lunch and pitched this as our catchphrase for marketing and advertising. He loved it. Even better, he trademarked it. Best of all, our slogan was printed on every Akimbo packing box and much of our marketing materials.

I can't claim sole authorship of this slogan—I thought it up, but Kevin recognized its potential. I can, however, claim the distinction of being TM'd.

DIGITAL EXAM

In 2012, I went online and purchased, for a couple hundred bucks, a little machine that takes VHS videocassettes and digitizes them onto a DVD. Easy-peasy. But in 2004, digitization of video was not a refined technology. It was barely a science, and mostly an art—an art of trial and error. Digitizing video took massive amounts of computing power, constant tweaking of the hardware and software involved, a clear, sharp eye, and infinite patience. Each piece of video to be digitized was essentially (as a 2020 hipster might say) an *artisanal product*—handcrafted, and often viable only after multiple attempts.

To put Akimbo's video digitization difficulties in some perspective, when I started at iTunes Movies two years later (2007), the entire digitization team, using all the most advanced digitization machinery and techniques on the planet (not to mention the most experienced and knowledgeable people in this industry), were able to digitize *at best* six or seven movies per week with high enough quality to add to our weekly releases.

But in 2005, the question was this: How was a little startup like Akimbo—a video on demand service that was gearing up to digitize, store and download hundreds of hours of video—ever going to attain that goal?

The Akimbo execs knew that this was a weak point in their model. So they solved the problem in much the same manner that a much larger company would attempt to solve the problem: by throwing massive amounts of money at it. They found a guy in Wisconsin or Michigan or somewhere who was ahead of the curve; a guy who'd started his own video digitization business; who'd invested thousands of dollars in equipment; who'd become a self-created expert in the field...and they bought him. They bought his entire company, including all his equipment, and paid to have it all shipped out to San Mateo and reassembled in his own lab at Akimbo HQ. They also hired him for his expertise, paid for his relocation, and even hired his wife as a program manager.

"Herbert" was a big guy, rather laconic, with a flat, affectless Midwestern accent. He was a bit standoffish, and viewed California (as many Midwesterners do) as a land of rampant insanity and liberal degeneracy...like that was a bad thing. (This opinion was entirely correct, and we California natives wouldn't have it any other way.) By contrast, his wife was a raving psycho bitch who did her best to make everyone's life a living hell.

KEEP MOVIN'

April 2005

As much as I enjoyed the 90-minute commute from Santa Cruz to San Mateo on Highway 1, I knew it was not sustainable. So I began looking for a place to live in San Mateo. One day while I was out driving the nearby backstreets, looking for a gas station, I drove past a For Rent sign on a triplex. It was on a quiet street only three blocks from Akimbo. I called the owner and asked to see the unit. The apartment was small but cozy: two bedrooms, one bath, a small living room and a huge kitchen. What impressed me most was that it was easily the cleanest apartment I'd ever seen—the counters, floors and appliances simply sparkled. The owner and landlord, Milt, was a retired schoolteacher and one hell of a nice, smart guy. I realized that if he was that conscientious about his property, he'd probably make a good landlord—both responsive and responsible. I put a deposit on the place to buy me time to show it to Piph on the weekend. She had the same reaction I did: This place is great. It was settled: we'd move to San Mateo. And—for the first time in my life—I'd be walking distance from work.

(*A Note About San Mateo:* Although it's totally peripheral to this narrative, I must admit I had no idea what San Mateo was all about. Even though I'd lived most of my adult life less than 40 miles from the town, I'd never had any reason to go there. As a matter of fact, most of the Peninsula—the region between Palo Alto and San Francisco—was usually considered a "No Man's Land" to people from Silicon Valley or The City. The entire Peninsula was something that swept by the car windows on the way from San Fran to San Jose, or vice versa. But I must also admit that once I got to know San Mateo, it became my favorite place I've ever lived.)

It's almost impossible to overestimate the relief I felt being once again employed at a decent rate of pay. Virtually all the stress and depression I'd felt daily since the ReplayTV layoff—the unemployment; the underemployment at Borders—was at heart financial. And suddenly that weight was lifted. No longer would I have to obsess over pennies—as I found myself doing one day a few months earlier in the Ralph's supermarket in Santa Cruz while mentally calculating whether buying a jar of mustard for my hot dog dinner would mean that we wouldn't have enough money left in the bank account to cover rent. Now I could shop (cautiously) at Draeger's, for instance—San Mateo's gourmet grocery store, and the proverbial Center of the Foodie Universe. Now we could go out to one of San Mateo's many good but inexpensive restaurants on a Friday night, or ride the train down to Mountain View and have beers at Tied House on a Sunday afternoon. We'd even have enough disposable income to attend a Beethoven program at the San Francisco Symphony once or twice a year. We'd endured. We'd survived. And we could finally relax...for a bit.

DO YOU WALK TO WORK OR CARRY YOUR LUNCH?

Being walking distance from work was a mixed blessing. On the plus side, it would provide me with a bit of exercise and save a lot of gas money. But it also meant that I had to *walk*—and my pedestrian commute took 15 minutes. In the Olden Days, my commute to Lockheed only took 20 minutes; ditto SGI and ReplayTV, in both Mountain View and in L.A. So there was no appreciable time saved. The good news: there was a Starbucks on the corner of El Camino and our street, so I figured I could stroll through, grab my morning coffee, and drink it on the walk. The bad news: there was always a line in the friggin' Starbucks, and waiting in line would double my commute time. Sure, I could get up early...but get up early to stand in line? Fornicate that feces. And more: if it was raining in the morning, I'd drive—but if I'd walked to work and it was raining in the evening, I had to call Piph to come pick me up. Worst of all, by crossing busy El Camino during rush hour, I discovered that I was literally taking my life in my hands. In a slow, driving commute, you might get in a fender bender and be inconvenienced. But attempting to cross a major thoroughfare during rush hour—even with the lights and crosswalk signs in your favor—you could conceivably die. I was, in reality, nearly run down...*twice*. (The good news is that I discovered the face of the New Enemy: oblivious obese women in SUVs.)

But mostly it was a good thing. There was a Safeway supermarket less than a block from our apartment, for instance (which made my weekly grocery shopping very easy—I could almost have left the car in the driveway and just wheeled the shopping cart home), and Piph and I would occasionally rendezvous there for lunch from their deli. Perhaps the most amusing aspect of this move was that from my sixth-floor office I could literally "see my house from up here." Piph would get me on the phone, go out into the backyard, and we could wave and gesture at each other. (Yeah, often that gesture.)

QUOTH THE RAVEN

But my house and my sweetheart weren't the only things I could see from there. A couple of months after I started, a raven took up residence in one of the big pine trees just outside our sixth-floor window. If the window could have been opened, I could have reached out and grabbed him, he was that close. And I wanted to—if only to throttle him, after he invited his friends and family to move into the trees nearby. Every afternoon about 4 PM, half a dozen or more of these giant black crows swooped in and performed a symphony for us—a symphony of cacophony. I couldn't decide whether they were mocking us or just mocking our work.

EVEN THE BAD NEWS ISN'T SO BAD

And then one day Steve announced that Akimbo had grown too large for our current offices, and we'd be moving. My heart sank. No more walking to work. The good news, however, was that we were moving only a block away. So I could continue to walk to work, even if the move added a couple more minutes to my pedestrian commute. (I might be an optimist, but I'm not naïve enough to ignore that there is *always* a downside.)

Akimbo's new offices encompassed the entire first floor of a large building with an L-shaped footprint. Engineering took over one wing, and the rest of us—sales, marketing, editorial, content acquisition, and executives—were located in the other wing. Weeks earlier, when our one HR guy was drawing up the floor plan, he showed it to virtually everyone. I politely requested that I have an office, like Steve, and both Content Acquisition team members, and the head of Sales, and the head of Marketing, and all the execs were getting. I was a department head, too, I reminded him—Senior Editor—and I assured him that I needed to concentrate so deeply on my work that the quiet and lack of distraction an office would provide was a virtual necessity. I thought this would at least put me back to the level I'd attained at ReplayTV...even if my new office wouldn't overlook the entire Los Angeles basin. He assured me that I was absolutely going to have my own office.

But (as they say about politicians) you can tell when an HR rep is lying: his lips are moving. When we moved into our new building, I had...a cubicle. I went to Mr.HR and gently reminded him that he had promised me an office. He shrugged. "We couldn't work it out," was his explanation. I pointed out to him that there were several unoccupied offices in this new space right now. Another shrug. "We have to reserve those for new executives," he "HR-splained." So that was my status at Akimbo: I was outranked by people who hadn't even been hired yet.

For once, I was pissed. Hell, I'd worked in cubicles before—and bullpens, and even (when I was at SGI) a fucking *closet*, for fuck's sake. And I never bought into the whole "location is status" mythology of corporate culture. But the fact was that *everyone else did*, so it meant something to other people whether you were in a corner office, or an office at all, or a cubicle. Or a closet. And goddamn it, *I'd been promised an office!*

Worst of all was the cubicle itself: one of several standard pre-fab units with built-in desks that were—by structural necessity—on the opposite side of the space from the entryway. This virtually guaranteed that the cubicle dweller had absolutely no privacy whatsoever: not only was your back always to the "door," so you couldn't see who was sneaking up behind you, or watching you behind your back, but your computer monitor was pointed toward the "door," and visible to anyone who walked past the cubicle. That weekend I went to Cost Plus and bought a lovely, inexpensive three-panel shoji screen and set it up behind my chair. This effectively blocked anyone's view of my monitor or of the "keyboard monkey" at work, as well as creating a mini-hallway through which visitors had to walk so they couldn't sneak up behind me. I thought this was a bold move—clearly a "fuck you" to HR—and fully expected Mr. HR to demand that I remove the screen for some obscure, illogical reason—a building code violation, or an insurance issue, or some such happy horseshit. Instead, to his credit, when he saw it, Mr. HR laughed and complimented me on the clever solution. I had no hesitation in informing him that the only reason I had to be clever was because he didn't deliver on his promise of an office.

These new cubicles were the fairly standard corporate cubicles—segmented walls covered in beige fabric—with one exception: our walls were six feet high, which I thought was unusual. The guys I worked with closely, like Mark and his partner, were on the other side of my wall, but I couldn't just stand up and look over the cubicle wall to talk to them. I solved this problem by bringing in a set of finger puppets of famous artistic figures—Monet and Beethoven, for instance—and giving some to my far-side-of-the-wall co-workers. When I saw Edgar Allen Poe or Dostoyevsky pop up over the cubicle wall, I knew they had a question, or information to share, and replied with my Einstein finger puppet. We carried out any number of conversations using this "Punch 'n Judy" network.

THE WORK

It's possible that the differences between a job and a career are this: a job is something you endure; a career is something you enjoy. A job is something you leave at work when you leave work; a career is something that occupies much of your time and mental effort 24/7—by choice, because it's interesting.

If this binary analysis is accurate, working at startups was, for me, some bastard hybrid of job and career. My career was in the VOD (video on demand) industry, for instance—but it had included numerous individual and separate jobs, working for various companies. So even if Akimbo wasn't a career, I was at least enjoying my job. And I had no problem taking work home with me. Most employees were issued a pair of Akimbo units, for instance—one for the office and a second to use at home. I used both units literally every day—if not to check out the new content, then to test, as a consumer, the navigation I'd created, to make sure we were delivering content in the quickest, cleanest manner possible (computer science be damned). I was, in effect, beta testing the equipment and the service, reporting on any mistakes, glitches, or anomalies (and often fixing them.)

It's difficult to believe that, less than two decades later, I can't recall how I spent eight or ten hours a day, five days a week...and yet that's the position I find myself in with Akimbo. We all know that staring at a computer screen for hours on end is a timesuck. Maybe it's also a memorysuck—or worse, a total brainsuck. I know I spent long hours with spreadsheets, working on the taxonomy of new programs, and on crafting short, hopefully clever descriptions of these shows, as I'd done at ReplayTV. If I'd saved my Activity Reports, I could probably go into deep (and deeply boring) detail about how I spent my hours at my terminal. Thank whatever you think is holy that that paperwork is lost forever. The takeaway for you, the reader, is to recognize that every time you read a description on a VOD service, understand that some writer agonized over that sentence or paragraph or punctuation, which undoubtedly went through several rounds of approval or revision before it was ever allowed to violate your eyes.

THE MOST IMPORTANT PERSON IN ANY MEDIA COMPANY

One lesson I learned working in various media companies is that everyone involved in these endeavors—especially the engineers—truly believed *their job* was *the* most critical part of the company. Of course, this is entirely self-aggrandizing and arrogant bullshit. To these engineers, I ask: What good is a box that records video without offering video content compelling enough that consumers want to buy the box? To the Content Acquisition teams, I ask: What good is compelling content if you don't have a working box to download it into? To the Sales Team, I ask: How the hell are you going to sell these boxes if they don't work, and if you can't deliver programs that are both unique and worth a consumer's hard-earned dollars? And, of course, I ask myself (just to keep myself humble): What good is a simple, intuitive interface if you don't have any compelling content, or a working box to download it into—or any sales? In my alleged mind, it's very clear that every department's effort was a contribution—but that each of these contributions was only one piece of the overall jigsaw puzzle.

THESE ARE NOT THE BOXTOPS YOU CAN SAVE AND REDEEM FOR A PRIZE

When customers browsed through the videos available on the Akimbo system, each piece of content displayed on their TV screen along with a description, price, and a 30-second clip from the show. (This same "free sample" video clip or Preview approach would be adopted by iTunes Movies a couple of years later.) These clips had their own window on the purchase screen; a rectangle in the upper right corner that we dubbed a "boxtop." (I have no idea why. Some things are simply unknowable.) Our main problem with these clips was that there was no way to automate them—they had to be selected and edited manually. Technically, I could have assumed this function myself, given my background in digital editing at Lockheed and SGI—and, I must admit, I enjoyed the process so much that I considered assuming this task. But, as Senior Editor, I had higher-level functions and responsibilities, and cutting preview clips was nearly a full-time job. So I began looking for someone skilled in desktop video, aka digital editing.

I don't remember how we found Nic Hill, but it was a blessing for me (and I hope for him). Nic was an aspiring filmmaker, a graduate of the University of San Francisco's Media/Film Studies program (like my good and great friend Danny McGuire, who went on to become Executive Producer at PBS stations KTEH-TV in Silicon Valley and KQED in San Francisco). Nic had recently completed a documentary, *Piece by Piece*, about the history of San Francisco's controversial graffiti art movement. He was young, dynamic, the epitome of cool and as smart as they come. I liked him immediately (if only because he was everything I wasn't but aspired to be). Once I described what his role at Akimbo would be and offered him carte blanche to create a digital editing suite for Akimbo, he signed on. We agreed that he'd work freelance rather than as a fulltime employee, since he regularly took off for days at a time to screen his doc at various film festivals in the U.S. and abroad.

Nic proved brilliant at his task. Once he was up to speed, I never once had to reject or revise his work. Granted, it was pretty simple work; it was actually *so* simple that I felt like I had to challenge him to keep him on board and interested. He was so close to a successful career in film that I was worried he'd "quit his day job"—namely, cutting boring video clips for Akimbo.

So I came up with a couple of challenges. The Akimbo previews started with a still frame; clicking on it launched the clip. I saw one clip he'd created of two people talking in a car, and challenged him to end it on the same frame he'd started it with, so it would look like a loop. And he did. Then I gave him a larger challenge. TCM (Turner Classic Movies, our only movie provider at the time) had given us *North by Northwest*, Alfred Hitchcock's classic thriller, and I challenged Nic to take the iconic five-minute scene with Cary Grant being chased through a cornfield by a biplane and edit it down to 30 seconds for an Akimbo boxtop—but without eliminating anything vital. And *goddamn* if he didn't do exactly that! The clip worked perfectly, digesting the scene down to its essence without losing any of its integrity or suspense. I was both slack-jawed and impressed. "Nic," I told him, "you've done the impossible. You've actually *improved* a Hitchcock scene!"

IN WHICH I EXPAND MY DOMAIN

At some point, I had enough "on my plate," as they say, that I was given the OK to hire an assistant, someone who would handle my more mundane tasks. Chief among these was manually assigning and keyboarding the 17-digit alphanumeric strings that identified each unique piece of content—a task that had to be performed precisely, since computers are entirely unforgiving about even the most minor error, and a single digit error in these content IDs could have disastrous consequences—like losing the content in the system forever. An error of a single digit could tank the entire event, like asking a lover to 68.

Being allowed to have an assistant turned out to be a two-edged sword—at first. I was already so overworked that even management acknowledged my need for additional fulltime help—and yet, before I would get any relief, I had to deal with résumés, interviews and training—all further impositions on my already overburdened schedule. Out of some 250 résumés that were submitted (see the Part IV chapter "What I've Learned About: Résumés" for the full story), I interviewed a handful of people and ultimately selected Jana, a middle-aged Indian woman with an engineer husband and a son in high school. She had little experience, but was whip-smart, detail-oriented and very pleasant. I took an immediate liking to her and had every confidence that we could work together without any problems. For once, my intuition was accurate. There will be only one more Jana story in this chapter, since we never had a single moment of drama, a cross word, or a problem. I believe she was, in fact, the perfect co-worker and the perfect assistant.

MEET THE NEW BOSS, *Part 2 of Many*

Sometime after we moved into our new digs, Steve called me into his office to meet "Scooby"—my new boss.

My new...what?

Turns out that Steve and Scooby were old buds, and Scooby was looking to get out of the internet radio startup he'd been working at. So Steve hired him as a Program Manager to direct the Content Team. This did not sit well with me, although I didn't express my distaste. I didn't want to be labeled "difficult" or "uncooperative," and I certainly didn't want to be labeled "not a team player."

But in my mind, Scooby started out with three strikes against him. First, the Content crew was doing just fine, thanks—we didn't need a replay of ReplayTV's Veronica, who did nothing but obstruct the people who did the real work, who assumed decision-making authority with no understanding, experience, background or even any interest in the areas in which she was granted control, and who contributed nothing but incomprehensible schedule spreadsheets. No thanks. And God knew what bizarre ideas Scooby would attempt to inject into an already smoothly functioning process.

Second, I resented the insertion of another level of management between me and my boss, Steve. Now I would have to go through Scooby to get to Steve—not to mention that the company org chart just gained another level...a level above me, pushing me further down the org chart. While I had no interest in "climbing the corporate ladder," I still felt disrespected by having another rung in the ladder inserted above me.

The third strike I had against Scooby was that he was so darn *likable*. He was a big, shambling, gawky guy whose deferential body language indicated that he was enormously eager to please. It was clear that he was sincere; however ingratiating he might come across, it seemed to spring from a genuine desire to please people. He wasn't charming, but he wasn't smarmy; he wasn't obsequious or unctuous or sycophantic—but the very idea that I have to invoke those words to define what he *wasn't* might indicate how he came across to me. He reminded me of nothing so much as a big puppy (hence his pseudonym), wiggling around, wagging his tail and bobbing his head, begging for love or attention...or at very least for a Scooby treat.

Worst of all, he was even deferential to his direct reports (like me), which is a horrible management technique. I could have run roughshod over him, I'm sure, beating him over the head verbally to let me continue to do what I was doing without interference. But in deference to Steve, and for the good of Akimbo, I swallowed those feelings and determined to give him a chance—and to get along with him.

I quickly discovered that the puppy analogy was totally appropriate. Several of us regularly invited him to lunch, for instance, to make him feel like part of the crew and to get to know him, but he always declined. After several such refused invitations, he confessed that he spent every lunch hour (and often another hour later in the afternoon) driving home to Mountain View *to walk his fucking dog*.

I began to suspect he was more enamored of that dog than of anything else in his life—a theory that was verified a few months later when he invited his six direct reports to his house for a pizza party. I met his wife—a vivacious, attractive, witty nurse; a woman most men would kill for or die for. And while we watched Scooby play with his dog, I broached the subject gently.

"I get the impression," I said, "that he loves that dog more than anything."

Her face darkened. "He loves it more than me," she growled through gritted teeth. "That's for sure."

COUNTDOWN TO LAUNCH

October 2004

Akimbo's official launch was set for the end of October, and throughout the summer of 2004, everyone's every effort was focused on that goal. Kevin and Mary, our Content Acquisition team, were signing up content providers at a record clip. Akimbo signed deals with A&E, Adult Swim, the BBC, Cartoon Network, CNBC, the DIY Network, the Food Network, HGTV, The History Channel, NatGeo, and, in a real coup, Turner Classic Movies (TCM).

I was delighted that we were going to offer movies from TCM—until I found out the TCM deal was for *one title per week*. Ah, well. Even that was better than nothing. Ultimately, TCM did provide us with numerous classic films from their vault, including *Dr. Jekyll and Mr. Hyde* (1941), starring Spencer Tracy, *The Three Musketeers* (1948), starring Gene Kelly, *Seven Brides for Seven Brothers* (1954), and even *Forbidden Planet* (1956), starring Walter Pidgeon, Leslie Nielsen and Anne Francis —my own favorite film for 30 years. Our TCM lineup might have been skimpy, but it was first-rate... including the first title they sent us to offer on the Akimbo system: *Citizen Kane* (1941), widely regarded as the finest film ever made (says the film history professor).

Citizen Kane represented several things for Akimbo. Not only were we finally including movies in our lineup, for instance, but we were offering *great* movies. It represented a challenge to our technical team as well: a great film demands a great image. Our digitization had to be perfect—any glitches, or a muddy image, or anything that was lesser quality than a rentable DVD could easily brand us as a second-rate service—or worse. Once Herbert the digitization magician had cast his best spell on the conversion, six or seven of us (including Steve, Morgan, Scooby, and me) gathered around a large monitor to watch several scenes, solely for the purpose of determining whether the quality of the digitization was good enough to approve releasing the movie to the Akimbo System. It passed, unanimously.

Akimbo was in the movie business.

"THE PINK WILL KEEP US IN THE BLACK"

Akimbo was also quietly moving into another business: pornography. And while it might sound difficult to believe, there were actually several executive decisions made at Akimbo in which I was not involved or even consulted—like, all of them. But this one I approved of, whole-heartedly.

Trigger Warning: If you are morally opposed to pornography, or to a frank, explicit discussion of sexually-oriented material, you should skip this section so you don't burn your eyes out or burn in hell, you prudish fuck. You've been warned.

It was common knowledge that pornography had driven the rise of the VCR a generation earlier. Who wouldn't want to rent a triple-X rated movie and watch it in the comfort of their own home rather than slink into a sleazy theater to see it (except maybe Paul Reubens, and look how that turned out for him)? The only downside is that renting porno tapes involved handing a stack of kinky titles to a video store clerk, who was, of course, not judging you at all as some kind of degenerate pervert. The opportunity to eliminate even this minor embarrassment led many of the top porn production companies to investigate distributing their films on Akimbo.

I was excited about our entry into the Adult video space. I knew this single feature could be the content that drove sales—after all, I'd discovered at MagiNet that nearly three-quarters of our rentals were Adult content. I knew the history of video on demand; I knew the potential of Adult content; and—since I'd spent many years as a video columnist—I knew the history and trends of the Adult video industry. In addition, since I'd been a bachelor for many years, it's entirely possible that I'd even actually rented and viewed a triple X-rated Adult video or two... thousand. (All in the name of research, you understand.)

Let's not say I volunteered to become the Porn King of Akimbo—that sounds so...unprofessional. Let's say instead that I agreed to assume the additional responsibilities of overseeing Adult content on the Akimbo service—even if that meant that, to assure they met our high standards, I had to actually watch some of these titles. Or most of them. Or all of them. Whatever. The point is, I was willing to make the selfless sacrifice of being paid to watch pornography in order to ensure a superior customer experience. Yes, working for a living is indeed Hell.

Kevin (in his role as the King of Content Acquisition) and I poured over title lists from Adult content providers eager to cut a deal, choosing which to add to the service. (This was hardly unusual—we did this with virtually every content provider or potential provider.) And we cobbled together a loose set of guidelines for Adult content on Akimbo, subject to Steve's approval. We would refuse anything that involved sexual violence, for instance—choking, bondage, maybe spanking. (Or maybe not.) We would reject the more fringe areas of the industry —golden showers, bestiality, dwarf porn, and so on. (To our surprise—and often horror—the more deeply we researched Adult content, the more of these kinky offshoots we discovered.) And, to dip our company's toe in the water, we oxymoronically chose a conservative approach to X-rated content, concentrating on straight sex. (Mostly.)

One of my tasks was to devise a clear but euphemistic name for the Akimbo Channel in which these films would be found. I presented about a dozen alternatives, including "Behind the Green Door," "The Champagne Room" and (my personal favorite) "Member Fulfillment" before Steve finally approved "Akimbo After Dark."

The inclusion of Adult content might have been a boon for Akimbo, but it created a mini-nightmare for HR. Our single HR guy had ensure, for instance, that no one was watching porn—excuse me, "Adult content"—in their cubicle, on the off chance that a random employee or guest might be walking through the building and accidentally be exposed to material they might consider personally offensive—and (to use an apt phrase) sue our pants off. (I was quite pleased that HR Guy's cubicle layout, which I'd protested from day one, was coming back to haunt him—or, in a metaphor more appropriate to this topic, to bite him on the ass.) In addition, HR Guy had to add a disclaimer to the standard employment contract that warned potential employees that they could potentially be exposed to this content, and absolved Akimbo from any liability if they took offense.

The major headache for HR Guy, however, was our content checkers. Since digitization was such a new technology, Engineering had created a backroom bullpen where as many as eight low-paid workers did nothing during their 40 hour work week but watch *every minute* of content we'd prepared for the service, to check its digitization. This Quality Control crew had a detailed checklist of problems to look for—glitches, pixelization, and so on—which, if observed, would send the content back for another attempt at digitization. They now had to be vetted for their attitude toward X-rated content. No one was actually *required* to watch any Adult content—but if any one of them chose not to be exposed to this degenerate filth, they'd have to be moved from the bullpen into their own closed-off workspace—and barred from entering the bullpen, since they'd almost certainly be exposed to Adult content the other QC viewers were vetting. Fortunately, and to their credit, every one of these kids was game, and no one ever chose to opt out.

HR's follow-up headache was that the QC crew would now have to be trained as to what Adult content Akimbo deemed aceptable (and un-), following the guidelines I'd developed. We'd also have to tutor the crew as to what precisely constituted an R rating, or a "Hard R," or an X (that is, XXX) rating: the specifics of anatomy and exposure of various organs. Since I'd been teaching college courses, I knew how to run a classroom, and since I'd written up the guidelines, it was decided that I'd deliver a brief training course in Porn Appraisal to the video checkers. I found this eminently amusing: I'd be getting paid to stand in front of half a dozen employees and talk dirty.

My one objection to adding Adult content to Akimbo was that there was so little of it. The execs had decided to limit the amount of X-rated content to just ten percent of our total content. (I made them clarify whether that meant ten percent of titles, or ten percent of the total hours of content offered on our service. Wisely, they chose the higher figure.) When they saw the initial rental figures, however, they raised the limit to 15 percent, which inspired me to lobby for even more Adult content with the slogan, “The pink will keep us in the black.” And when it became clear that they were going to continue to cap the content that could conceivably skyrocket us to success, I discussed with Kevin the idea of proposing a separate spin-off company that would rebrand the Akimbo players as a different set-top box and create an entirely new VOD service which would be solely devoted to X-rated, Adult content. (I suggested calling it the “XXXbox,” or “Triple Xbox”—but jokingly, since that would clearly have set us up for a lawsuit by Sony.) I had no doubt which of the two media companies would be more successful. But the execs nixed the idea, and stuck to the 15 percent upper limit. When I asked why they were so adamant about this, the answer was, “We don’t want to embarrass...

WILLIAM RANDOLPH HEARST III

Like virtually all hi-tech startups, Akimbo depended on venture capitalists, or VCs, to raise investment money. And there was no more respected VC firm in the industry than Kleiner Perkins Caufield & Byers—usually truncated to “Kleiner Perkins,” or simply “K-P.” By 2004, they’d invested in Google and Amazon and later would invest in Twitter and Snapchat, among more than 850 other companies. Nearly a decade earlier, in 1995, Kleiner Perkins had welcomed a new partner: William Randolph Hearst III.

“Will,” as he is known, is the grandson of the legendary newspaper publishing magnate William Randolph Hearst. Will Hearst grew up spending summers at La Cuesta Encantada (“The Enchanted Hill”), which we peasants know as The Hearst Castle in central California, before it was ceded to the state as a historical landmark. He’d spent his career in and out of the newspaper industry, and later served on the board of directors of several companies in which K-P had investments. He had a net worth of somewhere in the neighborhood of two billion dollars... which is not a bad neighborhood.

Apropos to this story, Will Hearst liked Steve Shannon and Akimbo so much that he not only invested K-P VC money in the company—some $12 million in 2004 alone—and not only took a position on the board of directors (a common step for VCs), but he further decided he wanted to be CEO, so he could take an active, hands-on role in shaping the future of VOD in general and of Akimbo in particular.

Great. We were now the plaything of a billionaire. Our jobs, our careers, our futures, were in the capricious hands of someone who thought nothing of showing up late to a meeting, apologizing that he "just flew in from Tahiti," where he was looking at real estate. The rich, they are a different breed than you and I. If nothing else, they have more money.

Or so my prejudiced and jaundiced attitude dictated. But then I met him, and discovered he was a complete sweetheart—smart, composed, funny, interested, and simply one of the damned *nicest* people I'd ever met. He was heavyset, balding, mustachioed, soft-spoken, and quick to chuckle at anything even mildly amusing (like most of my alleged jokes and *bon mots*). He thought nothing of dropping into our offices in San Mateo every few weeks just to check in and see how things were going, for instance. And he never failed to stop by my miniscule cubicle to chat for a few minutes—to drop some gossip he'd overheard at a film festival, or ask a question about some obscure movie, or invite me to meet his friend, the director Peter Bogdanovich.

Goddamn it, I *liked* the guy.

I had to question my own instincts, however. I liked Kim LeMasters, CEO of ReplayTV during my tenure there, as well. Was I simply being seduced by the wealth and power of these Alpha Males? I decided no—after all, I was nothing but disgusted when I'd first heard that Hearst had assumed the role of *capo di tutti capi*. It wasn't until I spent some time with him that I overcame my initial prejudice and had to admit to myself I was wrong about my reaction. He was, in fact, a "regular guy."

And just what kind of guy is Will Hearst? I can offer a couple of illustrative anecdotes. On one of his visits to the Akimbo offices, for instance, we were showing him clips from some of the newest content we were launching on the service, including the A&E show "America's Castles." The opening montage of mansions included a shot of La Cuesta Encantada, and as it flashed by, Will pointed to the screen, and exclaimed excitedly, "Hey, that's my house!"

Sometime in the fall of 2005, I finally managed to talk Steve into moving Akimbo into original production. My idea for a premiere show was that we'd shoot an hour-long interview with Will Hearst and offer it as a free download to all Akimbo service subscribers. Steve loved the idea, and apparently so did Will, since he signed off on it as well. I tapped my good friends and former Lockheed Video/Film co-workers, Curt Brown and Dave Lee, to borrow the necessary video equipment, and on the appointed morning we all schlepped up to Will Hearst's little *pied a terre* in San Francisco—an apartment in The Fairmont Towers, a highrise across the street from the Museum of Modern Art. His condo was on such an altitudinous floor that we could, in fact, gaze down upon the top of the iconic zebra circle of the SF MOMA roof from the massive picture windows lining the living room. Once again our differences were put into grand perspective: his living room alone was larger than most apartments I'd ever lived in. And some of the houses. A grand piano was angled aesthetically in one corner; couches and easy chairs lined an inner wall. I have no idea how big the place was (I thought it might be rude to ask for specifics, or a tour, or the cost) so we settled into the massive living room and prepared for the shoot.

Will Hearst and I spent over an hour discussing topics of mutual interest (and hopefully of interest to Akimbo viewers), including his biography, his involvement in San Francisco film festivals, the future of digital media, and (of course) Akimbo. Naturally, we talked about his famous grandfather, and Orson Welles' scathing take on him in the film masterpiece, *Citizen Kane* (now available on Akimbo!). I was able to present Will Hearst with my theory that their feud was a complete mistake.

(*Side note, for film lovers only:* Welles' original concept was to film a veiled biography of Howard Hughes, but his writing partner, Herman Mankiewicz, convinced Orson that William Randolph Hearst would make a more dramatic subject. Welles insisted on adding details and anecdotes from the lives of other millionaires of the period—like the opera house incident, which was appropriated from the life of Chicago utilities magnate Samuel Insull, as well as an eerily similar incident involving industrialist Harold McCormick. And it was Mankiewicz, not Welles, who had been a member of Hearst's "inner circle" and who spent many weekends at La Cuesta Encantada—but who ultimately became, for reasons unknown, *persona non grata* at Hearst's Castle. The feud between Welles and Hearst was in reality more a grudge match between Mankiewicz and Hearst, with Orson stuck in the middle and taking the blame.)

Will Hearst was a natural on camera—pleasant, well-spoken, both interested and interesting. (Years earlier he'd performed in several commercials promoting the *Examiner*. And now I was appearing in a video with the guy who'd appeared in videos with Dr. Hunter S. Thompson, one of my college cult heroes.) Will Hearst even—although reluctantly, and only at my urging—agreed to a closing gag I'd thought of to wrap up the hour. I thanked him and addressed the viewers, assuring them that I'd "see them next time." At which point Will chimed in, "Yeah, about that... Hasn't your boss talked to you yet?"

The ultimate revelation of William Randolph Hearst III's true personality occurred just minutes later, however. While my friends were packing the video gear, I joined Will in his home office for a "post-game analysis," and, of course, to thank him for his participation. I noticed that his desk was situated so that his back was to the picture window. I had a panoramic, bird's-eye view of The City, while all he saw from his chair was the office wall. "Will, " I said, "why on earth would you sit with your back to the window when you have that spectacular view?" He cocked his head and replied, "I want my guests to have the best view." I felt ashamed for not realizing this myself. And I knew that not only was his answer sincere, but it was also the expression of a considerateness to which I could only aspire.

To William Randolph Hearst III, I can only quote Jack Nicholson from the film *As Good as It Gets*: "You make me want to be a better man." And a billionaire. That wouldn't hurt either.

PLAN A REDUX

I'd rarely mentioned Plan A to co-workers during my corporate career, aside from those few who became friends outside the workplace. I didn't want to deal with the inevitable questions ("You write novels? What are they about? What have you published?"), or be forced to make the admission that I couldn't get my fiction published to save my life. If I wanted to flaunt my creative credentials (and I was certainly not above that), I was building a reservoir of visible activity that I could trot out to avoid the whole "failed novelist" indignity. Depending on the year and the job, I could point to my ten years of newspaper columns, for instance, or to the hundreds of newspaper and magazine articles I'd published, or to my six-year stint as a weekly presence on the local PBS station, or to my video guide, *Killer B's*, or to my plays, produced by a local theater company —and so on. But the novels were my idiot children, the fruit of my loins and the creations closest to my bitter, broken heart. I wasn't willing to talk about them to just *anybody*.

So it was rather galling when Scooby revealed to me that he was working on a book of his own—a comic tale of his engagement and wedding, and how he managed to successfully stumble through these major events while being a complete doofus. He even had a title for it, some dopey pun like *Wife Sentence*—which, even then, I thought sounded a bit demeaning to his delightful wife. (Researching this narrative in 2017, I discovered that his ebook is available on Amazon, although his bio clearly hasn't been updated since the Akimbo days.) I smiled and wished him well, looking forward to hearing his tales of publisher rejection while I snickered in secret.

A few weeks later, he came to work bouncing around like a puppy with a new chew toy. "My book's gonna be published!" he told me. "I was at a party last weekend and struck up a conversation with a guy who said he's an agent, and he loved the idea for my book. So he called a publisher, and they're gonna buy it!" My reaction? I felt much like the Nic Cage character in the movie *Adaptation*—the serious screenwriter who suffered to make his work good enough but who was trounced by his own twin, an idiot who'd written a dumbass, clichéd action flick and sold it immediately. But I smiled and congratulated him. "Man," Scooby continued, shaking his head, "if I'd known how easy it is to get published, I woulda written more books!" I smiled. I thought about the hundreds of rejections I'd gotten from agents and publishers alike during the previous two decades. I thought about the thousands of hours I'd devoted attempting to craft intelligent, entertaining fiction. And then I smiled some more. *He's my boss,* I told myself. *Just smile. Do not attempt to educate him. Do not superglue his door shut and trap him in his office. Do not tip him over in his chair and push a Scooby treat up his snout.*

There was, however, one upside to this distressing turn of events: I decided that I would—once again—revive my Plan A, and attempt to get published. To that end, I combed through my stack of seven (count 'em, *seven*) unpublished novels, and settled on the first of my trio of mystery novels, *The Coincidence Caper*. I'd written the first draft in 1979—more than a quarter of a century earlier—and the second draft in 1981, while at Lockheed, at the beginning of my corporate career. And every five years or so I'd take the manuscript off the shelf (actually, the cliché is "pulled it out of a drawer," but I do attempt to avoid clichés—and I did keep it in a box on a shelf), dust it off, and edit and polish it to whatever higher standards I might have developed from writing non-fiction through the previous five-year period.

In this new attack, I scoured the note file I'd kept over the previous 25 years, in which I collected all my follow-on ideas about the book. And I began the painful and painstaking process of integrating these newer elements into the older manuscript. I added new characters, new incidents, new dialog. I added new foreshadowing and new themes, subthemes and undercurrents. To make a long story short, I made this short novel longer: the early drafts of about 60,000 words ballooned into a major, 160,000-word novel. By this time it bore so little similarity to the first drafts that I even retitled it, as *The Uncertainty Principle?* (adding the question mark to the title as an illustration of uncertainty). I think it's one of the best things I've ever written (but what do I know). It's currently available in both ebook and print editions, and I'm very proud of it—even though I doubt whether anyone has ever read it. But if nothing else, it's published, and waiting to be discovered—a literary time bomb. I have to think of Scooby and his goofy little wedding book and his sheer dumb luck in publishing it as the grain of sand irritating my oyster enough to produce this pearl.

OUT TO LAUNCH

October 31, 2004

Eventually, Akimbo had all its ducks in a row. We had certified a manufacturer (Motorola) for the set-top box; we had a deal with Amazon to be the official retailer; we had a critical mass of video—thousands of hours from nearly 200 content partners (see above for a partial list)—all nicely organized for ease of discovery (you're welcome); and there were no major technical hiccups to address. (I had also come up with a number of slogans that were never used, including: "Think outside the idiot box," "Show your TV who's the boss," "Just watch it," and—given the literal definition of "akimbo"—"Hands-on Hip." They never used any of them—which, I must believe, contributed to their eventual downfall.)

I quietly harbored reservations about whether consumers would be willing to shell out 300 bucks for the privilege of purchasing content. And it occasionally crossed my mind that, given our content offerings, we were in effect the world's worst cable TV channel. But I kept my doubts and negative opinions to myself and maintained a public face of total confidence, since a sociopathically positive attitude is mandatory in startups, where never is heard a discouraging word, and the skies are not cloudy all day—even in a hurricane.

And so, on Halloween 2004, the Akimbo system was launched, to great fanfare...if we redefine "great" to mean "no." According to the Wikipedia entry (circa 2017) on Akimbo, "Initial reactions were mixed, with criticisms of high prices of unknown content being leveled at it, although the user interface was regarded as intuitive and responsive." So I was on the right track with the interface, at least. The Wikipedia entry further described Akimbo's onscreen guide as "TiVo-like," which is ironic, since I was the guy who created Akimbo's onscreen guide but who couldn't get TiVo to hire me—and who'd never seen any more than a brief glimpse of TiVo's onscreen guide.

"About a month after launching the Akimbo service," the Wikipedia entry continues, "the company had about 120 active set-top boxes, about 60 of which were being used by employees and/or investors." I accounted for two of those 120 boxes—so I alone accounted for about 1.7 percent of "users."

The number of set-top boxes sold or in use wasn't information that was shared with those of us in the trenches, however. I never knew those figures until researching this book in 2017. And I'm glad I didn't—it would have been just too disheartening. Even worse: "On average," Wikidepressingpedia continues, "only about 20 of those 120 players downloaded any content during a month." I downloaded content to both my players virtually daily—which means that *I alone* represented about 12 percent of all Akimbo download activity. And I often downloaded 20 or more hours of content per week, to test the navigation, check the quality of the video, and familiarize myself with new content (not to mention, of course, to watch the porn). I have to guesstimate that my personal activity probably accounted for about *half* the content accessed in any given week. In some sense, then, Akimbo *really was* my own personal TV network!

My policy at Akimbo—one which I proselytized evangelically among my co-workers—was to perform our work in the most professional manner possible; to make decisions and act *as though* we had a million users/viewers, so *if and when* we actually attained a million subscribers, we'd already be up to speed and wouldn't have to raise our standards or modify our procedures. I had no idea that we were using our million-viewer professionalism on fewer than a hundred users (many of whom were me).

"The initial content was a bit eccentric," the Wikipedia entry continues; "Turkish-language shows, independent films, British dramas from Granada TV, a lot of skin flicks..." Oddly, the very day I found this entry in 2017, Wired.com had a list of Netflix's latest initiatives, including their first original Turkish language series. Maybe we were indeed pioneers, a decade ahead of our time. Unfortunately, we were also a decade ahead of our potential audience. ("Who knows why Constantinople got the works? It's nobody's business but the Turks'.")

2005: IN ONE YEAR AND OUT THE OTHER

2005 was the year of Business As Usual: Weekly Wednesday meetings with Scooby, Mark, Morgan, and the Ops team to review incoming content and determine digitization priorities; weekly Friday meetings with Steve and the Content Acquisition Team (Kevin and Mary) about upcoming providers and content (when we weren't laughing at Kevin's sharp wit and antics); writing weekly reviews of some of our new programming. The job. The work. The smoothly-operating machine routine.

One day Kevin got a call from a content aggregator who asked him whether Akimbo videos could be watched on a cellphone. Kevin related this bizarre question to me and we both had a good laugh. Watch video on a *phone*? As Bugs Bunny used to say, "What an aquamaroon." It wasn't until a couple of years later, when smartphones hit the market, that I realized that while we at Akimbo thought of ourselves as pioneers in the VOD industry, this unknown content provider with his ridiculous question was clearly years ahead of the curve—a real visionary, and far beyond the current cutting edge.

The Akimbo Service was growing—maybe not exponentially, maybe not even geometrically, but incrementally, and steadily. We were adding, on average, one or two new content providers and over one hundred new pieces of content every week. My weekly Activity Reports for late 2005, like one for the week ending October 28 (which completed our first full year since launch) detailed that we'd published 110 titles from 19 providers that week alone. Later Activity Reports included similar entries:

November 4: 138 titles from 31 providers.

November 11: 83 titles from 19 providers.

December 2: 144 titles from 21 providers.

There was no Activity Report for the period of November 12-25; this entry on my November 11 report explains why:

SCOTT OUT OF OFFICE: I will be taking my first vacation in over 20 months (since joining Akimbo) beginning Monday, November 14. I will return to work on Monday, November 28.

Jana and [Scooby] have been fully briefed and are prepared to cover my absence without any impact to the Service, with the possible exception of the absence of some panache.

Yes, things were going so well for so long that I felt comfortable enough to violate my own rule about startup employment, "Never take a vacation."

And then came the best news of all.

December 2, 2005

During our Friday afternoon content meeting, Mary broke the Big News: She'd landed a deal with a major film studio, allowing us to sell not just content from their library but also their recent releases. We were all ecstatic. We'd finally have movies on the Akimbo service! Big movies! *Recent* movies! I'd always been convinced that films would be the magnet that would attract home video viewers to Akimbo. Instead of having to go to Blockbuster and hope that a copy of the DVD they wanted was available, they could download a film from the comfort of their living room couch. And we all knew (because, as a Film History professor, I had educated them) that the studios were copycats—if even one was willing to break the digital logjam and allow digitized downloads of their content, the others would quickly follow suit so they didn't fall behind the curve and miss out on the potential profits.

I went home that afternoon and announced to Epiphany Jane that our worries were over: Akimbo was getting movies, and we had a bright, long term future.

ADIOS, AKIMBO!

December 5, 2005

"When life looks like easy street
There is danger at your door."
—The Grateful Dead, "Uncle John's Band"

Except no.

When I arrived at the office the following Monday, before I could even sit down, Mr. HR asked if I could step into the company president's office. Mr. President was seated at his table. Mr. HR sat down and invited me to sit.

There was a folder on the table. In my experience, that meant only one thing.

"Am I being laid off?" I asked. They said I was. To their credit, they both looked a bit embarrassed and uncomfortable. "Is it because of something I did? Or failed to do?" They both almost fell over themselves assuring me that this was in no way a performance issue—they acknowledged that I was a perfectionist ("*Painfully* perfect," Mr. HR volunteered. I'm still not entirely sure whether that was a compliment).

They explained that over the last couple of weeks, the Board of Directors had met several times to assess the status of Akimbo after a year of being live. And they'd decided to make some major revisions to the business model—revisions which didn't require or include a Senior Editor. The company was going to get out of the consumer business and retool itself to be ...something else.

I started having ReplayTV flashbacks. Wasn't it just four years ago—almost to the *day*—that this happened before? It was déjà vu all over again. ReplayTV 2.0. A Replay replay.

Even while sitting there in shock, taken by surprise, a plan to save my ass occurred to me. The number one priority of layoffs like this was always to reduce headcount and all the costs associated with full-time employees. I could make the case that they should keep me and lay off my assistant and the young engineer who published our content to the web every week. The benefits to Akimbo would be that the combined salaries of these two entry-level employees would about equal what I was making, and that they could reduce headcount by two instead of just one. I'd trained both these junior employees, so clearly I could do their jobs (since I had done their jobs)—but neither of them, or anyone else in the company, for that matter, could do mine. And they'd be honoring my seniority. But I kept my mouth shut. I didn't suggest that alternate course of action. I simply could not stoop low enough to be the kind of guy who'd throw other people under the bus to ensure my own survival. I was almost ashamed to even have conceived a plan like that.

They walked me through the severance package, wished me well, and cut me loose.

I wasn't about to stick around. I would return after hours to pack up my minimal cubicle garnish. The one stop I made on my way out was to explain the current state of affairs to my assistant, Jana. I told her in a few sentences that: a) I'd just been laid off; b) they'd probably rely on her to keep the system operating; and c) if they do, she should ask for a big raise, or threaten to quit. If we were both gone, they'd lose the ability to update the service at all. She'd be in the catbird seat.

And then I walked home.

Piph was surprised to see me at 10 AM.

"Are you sick?" she asked.

"Nope," I replied. "Under what other circumstances would you expect to see me home this early?"

"You've been laid off?" Yep, it was that predictable.

"Again," I sighed.

AKIMBO: THE AFTERMATH

"At the time when the company began its first round of layoffs," reads the Wikipedia entry on Akimbo (circa 2017), "about a year and a half after the initial launch, the number of users had grown to only about 140." At launch, we had 120 active units, all belonging by employees and investors. So more than a year after launch, we'd sold a grand total of...20 units.

Holy shit.

Akimbo, which, at its peak, employed some 80 people, reinvented itself as a "turnkey, end-to-end video solution"—whatever the hell that meant. All I knew was that this new incarnation didn't require an Editor.

Whatever it meant, Akimbo hung in there for a while, albeit with all new management for its all-new function. On August 1, 2007, Akimbo ended its VOD service. And on June 2, 2008, Akimbo formally went out of business.

If only they'd listened to me about the porn...

Chapter 24

2006: STRANGE INTERLUDE 4.0

December 2005

I needed... Well, if you've read this far, it ought to be clear what I needed. Besides an editor.

Oddly, the Akimbo layoff, while totally unexpected, did not leave me gobsmacked. Maybe it was because I was freed from the daily and weekly schedule and deadlines—freed from the emotionally draining business of attending to every detail under my dominion, and simply so burned out that the "end of work" came as something of a relief, like a Giant Friday. Maybe, as happened when ReplayTV laid me off, I was just too numb to register what this action implied for my immediate future...even though I knew full well what to expect. Or maybe I was just getting used to the startup lifestyle of 18 months on, 12 months off.

I hoped I was just numb.

I sensed another sinister pattern at work as well: Given the fits-and-starts nature of startup employment, I began to suspect that at this rate I'd have to work until the day I died; that any retirement I might have was going to be piecemeal, taken in disjointed chunks of time between jobs: a year here, a year there.

And once again—for the fourth time in a dozen years—a December layoff put a damper on the holidays. I thought of Father Guido Sarducci's proposal to reduce the materialism of the holidays by alternating "Big Christmas" with "Little Christmas." And I realized that his satirical proposal was becoming a literal lifestyle for me: a December layoff ensured that we'd have a "Little Christmas," at least in terms of gifts.

But since nobody hires in December, I tried to enjoy the "free month," to detox from the stress of the startup activity over the previous couple of years.

And despite (yet another) depressing holiday season, I frequently found myself thinking of the title of a 1933 Al Jolson movie: *Hallelujah I'm a Bum.*

YO-HO, YO-HO, A STARTUP LIFE FOR ME…

January 2006

Here's a question you'll never catch an employed person asking him- or herself: "Is this Sunday or Monday?" When you're unemployed, every day is a weekend.

Once again I began combing the employment websites, looking for some position that fit my increasing, but increasingly niche, skills. Since Akimbo was a pioneer in the VOD industry, however, I was alone on a melting iceberg. I read an article that estimated that unemployed hi-tech personnel should count on being out of work one month for every $10,000 in salary they wanted to command. That kind of made sense—I could probably go to some bookstore and get a $10,000 a year job within a month, for instance. (But not Borders—they'd certainly look up my file and show me the door.) But did I really have six months or more of unemployment to look forward to before I could find a position that paid me as much as Akimbo? Jesus Christ. What the fuck was I supposed to do for money during those six months except comb the employment websites every day while watching my savings circle the drain?

I did take solace once again in the safety net of the Unemployment Trifecta: California State Unemployment Insurance, my savings, and Akimbo's severance package and vacation time payout (less a week's pay, since I made the rookie error of actually taking a vacation while working at a startup instead of insuring that my accrued vacation pay would be there for me at a potential layoff). It wasn't like we were going to starve, or couldn't make rent—for a few months, anyway.

Up until this time, I always felt a little guilty collecting Unemployment—like I was a burden on society, or a painful pimple on the body politic. But then I discovered that the funds for Unemployment Insurance are raised by a tax *on employers*. That's when I began to truly enjoy the "free money." They refused to keep me employed? Well, "Play or Pay" is the freakin' *law*, motherfuckers...and if they weren't willing to play me, then (to quote Kurt Russell in *Big Trouble in Little China*): *"Son of a bitch must pay!"*

I had what I thought might be an ace up my sleeve in the form of Steve Shannon. As the founder of Akimbo, he was just as upset about its demise as I was (although, as a ranking officer, he retained his position and salary). He felt genuinely bad about my being laid off and offered to help me find employment any way he could. "Where do you want to work?" he asked me over lunch a week or so after the layoff. "I have a lot of contacts and I can give them a call."

I had no hesitation in answering: "Google," I said. "Specifically, Google Video." At that time, Google Video was a tiny department of the biggest, best, most popular internet company of the era, and Google Video appeared to me to be undervalued, underused, and (hopefully) understaffed. "They aggregate video clips," I continued, "but Google doesn't seem to be doing much with Google Video. I think I could apply the skills I learned at ReplayTV and Akimbo and help organize the site and build it up into something special."

He agreed to call his contacts at Google. In the meanwhile, I sent the manager of Google Video my résumé and a video sample reel. I never heard back from them.

IN WHICH I AM REJECTED BY YOUTUBE WITHOUT EVEN APPLYING

When the layoffs started at Akimbo in December 2005, Kevin Donohue, one of my favorite co-workers, saw the writing on the wall and knew it wasn't just graffiti. Within a couple of months, he left Akimbo for a position as VP of Content at a little startup also located in San Mateo—a repository of user-created video clips called "YouTube." The startup had been founded on Valentine's Day the previous year (2005)—just days before I hired into Akimbo—by a trio of ex-PayPal employees, and launched on December 15, 2005—just days after I'd been laid off from Akimbo. I'd never heard of it. And neither one of us could figure out their business model. How did they expect to make any money as a video aggregation site, where clips were shared for free? Kevin's guess was advertising or sponsorship. He was hired to help figure out how to "monetize" the site.

In March or April, Kevin invited me to visit YouTube's HQ, located in the second story of an old building in downtown San Mateo, over a Japanese restaurant and a pizza parlor. The place was just a big brick-walled, open-space bullpen, full of rows of tables rather than desks or cubicles. A spaghetti of cables dangled from the rafters down to the table-top computers, where maybe 30 people hunched over their keyboards and stared at their monitors. Kevin introduced me to his new boss: Chad Hurley, the CEO and one of the founders—a casual, laid back young guy. The three of us chatted for a few minutes. I gave him a copy of *Killer B's*. He flipped through it, nodded seriously, then addressed me.

"You're exactly the kind of guy we'd never hire," Chad said.

Excuse me? I wasn't there to apply. I wasn't there to interview. I was only there to see where Kevin had landed.

"And why is that?" I asked, genuinely perplexed.

"You're editorial," Hurley explained. "We're peer-to-peer. We don't want any gatekeepers telling people what to watch."

Oddly, this was not the first time I'd been gratuitously rebuffed. Years earlier, while attempting to sell a comic science fiction novel, among the 30-plus rejections I received was one from a publisher to whom I'd never even submitted the book. "We understand you're circulating a novel entitled *A Night at the Space Opera*," the letter read. "Please do not send it here."

Well. Thank you all for saving me the time and effort!

2006 was the year that YouTube exploded on the internet. By July, the site was receiving 65,000 video uploads and getting 100 million views every day. And in November, Google purchased YouTube for 1.65 *billion* dollars. By the end of the year, *everyone* knew what YouTube was. Kevin got to go along for the Big Ride. But I didn't. (It occurred to me that had I been able, with Steve Shannon's assistance, to land a spot at Google Video months earlier, I probably would have been folded into YouTube once Google purchased it. Yet another alternate future cut off at the knees.)

REEL LIFE…BUT NOT REAL LIFE

So this was my life now: teaching a couple of film courses, working on the novel I'd been inspired to update given Scooby's irritating, lucky success...and searching for work.

Teaching, I thought, might be the ace up my sleeve. For several years I'd been teaching "Film History" and "History of Animation" at Cogswell College, and they'd recently commissioned me to develop and deliver another course, "The Great Directors." So I had a small paycheck coming in to augment my meager Unemployment and savings.

And—to my amazement—I found a couple of film-related freelance writing jobs. One was for Jaman, an online video on demand service launched by some prominent Bay Area art house film folk. Jaman specialized in "world cinema" (a snooty term for foreign language films) that played on computers along with a scrolling, side stream text commentary filled with analysis, questions for the viewer (to inspire deeper thinking about the movie), and trivia—all written by people like me. The movies were mostly crap. (I hope I never have to sit through another Bollywood musical or "comedy," for instance.) But Jaman paid well, and on time, and I could work while lying on the couch with my laptop right where (as its name implies) it belonged: in my lap. (Jaman ceased operation in April 2017, but kudos for a run of over a dozen years. They were VOD pioneers, but lasted a hell of a lot longer than Akimbo.)

I also got an offer from Reel.com—now owned and operated by the Hollywood Video video store chain—to write reviews of new release movies. New releases! I was going to be a film critic? Now we're talking! I got some brilliant, insightful and eminently practical advice from another Bay Area freelance film critic, Pam Grady, who was kind enough to walk me through the process end-to-end, including who to contact to get on the sneak preview and critics preview invitation lists.

Watching free movies, expressing my opinion, and getting paid for it? How could being a film critic not be the greatest job in the world? Well...let me count the ways:

1) First off, freelance movie critics are often informed of a sneak preview on a last-minute basis—usually just a day before

the preview. Since the "work schedule" is random, it's impossible to make personal plans, as they might have to be scrapped at the last minute in order to "go to work" (i.e., attend the preview). This plays havoc with a personal life—and I like to think that I had one (although I would not have been surprised to have a Game Warden insist I throw it back because it was too small).

2) Previews are held in major cities. I lived in San Mateo. Virtually every one of the previews I attended was held in San Francisco, which meant a 30-minute drive *and* paying for parking. I dreaded getting the call that a preview would be held in the Sony Metreon complex, for instance, since parking there cost *ten fucking dollars*. In 2006, I could see the same movie in a local theater the following day for seven dollars—and park for free. (To be overly detailed and precise, I could actually have *walked* to the theater in downtown San Mateo and avoided driving and parking altogether.) But to attend the sneak preview and make fifty bucks for writing a review cost me more than the price of a ticket—and cost *twenty percent* of my earnings—just to get into the damn movie.

3) Many previews are held on Thursday nights, before the film opens wide on Friday. And Reel.com had a Thursday midnight deadline so the review would be live on Friday morning. I'd get out of the preview at maybe 10:00 PM, drive half an hour home, and then have less than an hour to analyze the flick and write and file the review. The scramble to submit was deadly, and allowed no time for subtlety or research.

4) The venues (like the films) were a total crapshoot, and often a total shitshow. On the one hand, one preview I attended was in an ornate little theater built into an office building on Market Street. I had no doubt that the public was rarely, if ever, invited into this plush, private venue. This preview had an audience of: me. Awesome—but a total exception to the norm. Most previews I attended were held in large public movie theaters, and many were stuffed to the gills with radio contest winners. One memorable screening was slammed with contest winners from a heavy metal radio station—a rowdy crew of headbangers, tattooed bikers and loud speed freaks. And me, a Moody Blues fan. I was seated next to a tweaker, who squirmed around in his seat through the entire film while narrating it and

providing his own critical commentary to his girlfriend. ("Oh man he's got a knife. Look out, man, he's got a knife! Oh man he better get the fuck out of there before— Oh shit, he *stabbed him* with the fuckin' *knife!* Oh *shit* man he's bleedin' *everywhere*, man!" And so on.) I couldn't change seats since the theater was full. I could have informed an usher, but they'd all wisely left the theater after the audience started throwing things—about five minutes into the flick. I could have told the tweaker to shut the fuck up, but oh man he might have a knife, man, oh shit, fuckin' tweaker might *stab* me with the fuckin' *knife* man... As a total professional, however, I did not let my theatrical experience influence my objective review of the piece of shit movie.

Film critic: Altogether one of the worst jobs I ever had. Prior to this film critic gig, anytime work got tough, I could always content myself by remembering my first job and thinking, "Well, it could be worse. I could be shoveling shit in a dog kennel." But there were moments during the film critic phase where I nostalgically actually missed the smell of fresh dog shit.

Oh man I needed a fuckin' *job* man...

Chapter 25

2006: ADCHEMY

August 2006

I needed a job. If ever I'd needed a job before, I needed one now. Right fucking now.

By August 2006, my resources were tapped. Unemployment had run out, and teaching and freelance film reviewing weren't going to keep us above water. I had literally no idea how we were going to make September rent, and started rehearsing speeches to our landlord ("If you can just stake us a month's rent…") Worst of all, Piph couldn't work since she was virtually bedridden, nursing a benign tumor the size of a grapefruit that required an expensive operation to remove—and we had no medical insurance. Of course.

It was a soap opera, and I was bending over to pick up the soap.

A BRIEF ASIDE: FUCK WELLS FARGO

To add insult (and additional injury) to injury, about this time Wells Fargo pulled one of the sleazy tricks that has made them so beloved to their customers over the years. I'd used my debit card several times one Saturday, as I did most Saturdays, to do our grocery shopping. And on the following Thursday I got several overdraft notices in the mail—the snail mail. If they had notified me by email, I might have received the notifications on Sunday or Monday—or even that same Saturday, if the process was automated. My first thought was: What? Why the hell did they approve the debit card purchases when they knew there was no money in the account? Worse, they charged $25 for the first three overdrafts, and $35 for every one after that. I owed them over $100 in overdraft charges alone—not to mention payment for the purchases they'd approved once the dregs of my account were drained. Even though they knew full well that my account was empty, they'd still approved the purchases. I scrambled around the house, gathering all the cash I could collect—literally, all the money we had on hand, down to the spare change jar and the week's laundry quarters—and walked half a block to the nearest Wells Fargo branch to pay off the charges in person. Problem solved!

Um...not quite. I continued to receive overdraft charge letters, which I found distressing, since I'd paid off the purchases. Once again I walked down to the end of the block and took this up with the branch manager. He informed me that it was a Wells Fargo policy to pay their own overdraft charges first, which is where my recent deposit had been applied. Anything left over went to paying off the purchases that had generated the overdraft charges. WTF? They paid *themselves* first? Yep. And the longer I went without paying off the purchases, the more delinquency charges I accrued since, technically, I hadn't paid off the purchases that caused the overdrafts in the first place.

This was not banking—this was extortion, pure and simple. And it came at the worst possible time. As the comic Gallagher said, "Why do the banks insist you give them more of what they know you don't have any of?" The difference between Gallagher's joke and my situation was that my situation was not funny. Even if I borrowed enough to pay off the extortionists, this would demote food, rent and utilities to a lower priority than paying the motherfuckers who'd kidnapped my bank account and were holding it hostage, with the collateral damage of fucking up my credit rating, which was always in a precarious condition anyway. I only had one bank account, so I couldn't even use a debit card for food, or write a check for rent or utilities without first depositing money in that account—money which Wells Fargo would first use to pay themselves before honoring my payments for food, rent, utilities, etc.

I wanted some kind of revenge, but I didn't want to stoop to their unethical level. So I first made sure that I paid my bills—the legitimate debts—so that every penny of the money I owed Wells Fargo was nothing but their own overdraft charges. Then I took every dollar I had, walked across the street, and opened a new account at Washington Mutual. I cut up my Wells Fargo debit card, ripped up the remaining checks, and never dealt with them again—although, well over a decade later, I still occasionally receive mail from a collection agency offering me special deals to pay off my "debt" to Wells Fargo for pennies on the dollar (usually 100 pennies on the dollar). These form letters provide me comic relief and an occasional reminder that *I won.*

A couple of years later I discovered additional details concerning this scam. The first revelation was that when a Wells Fargo customer used a debit card on, say, five charges (actually, withdrawals, since it's a debit card) of varying amounts without realizing that the account was overdrawn, Wells Fargo would not necessarily post these withdrawals in the order in which they were made or received. They would instead post them in descending order of the amount that was charged, with the largest withdrawals paid first. So if a customer had, say, $100 in his or her account and made four charges of $10 on Saturday morning (which would still leave $60 in the account) and one charge of $100 on Saturday afternoon (which would empty the account), Wells Fargo would post the $100 charge first, and pay it—ensuring the account had a zero balance, and enabling them to post the four earlier charges as overdrafts, on which they then charged *four separate overdraft fees*...three at $25 and the fourth at $35. Had they posted the withdrawals in the order in which they were made, the account holder would have had just one overdraft, and one overdraft fee. But simply by choosing the order in which to post these withdrawals so that they led to an overdraft, the Wells Fargo rigged the system to ensure they could charge several overdraft fees instead of just one. In this example, the bank would require $110 in overdraft fees from the account holder, rather than a single $25 overdraft fee.

I also discovered that I was not alone as a victim of this authorized Wells Fargo scam—it was so well-known, so prevalent, and occurred so frequently that it even had a name: the "order of posting" scam. Since that time (2006), Wells Fargo has regularly been caught running other illegal and unethical scams on their customers—like signing 3.5 million of them up for accounts without their knowledge to boost the company's stats, or signing up small businesses for unnecessary insurance, or signing up 800,000 people for auto insurance they didn't want or need and never requested—and has been fined millions of dollars in civil penalties.

Why anyone would ever do business with Wells Fargo is a mystery to me. And why the US government doesn't just disband the entire company for its history of fraudulent practices is a further mystery. If, as the Supreme Court insists, corporations are people too, this is one corporation that deserves jail time for being an unrepentant serial con artist.

Thus endeth the rant.

BACK TO THE FUTURE
Or at least to the narrative...

This was the low point of my work life, my personal life... and my life. (I even considered changing my name to "Ralph Nadir.") I had no work, no money, no health care for my sick sweetheart. Vehicular residency was only a few weeks away. Homelessness and dying of starvation in the gutter loomed on the horizon. Would we be forced to live in our storage locker? Or even worse—would I, at age 55, be forced to move back into my 75-year-old mom's house? (And how would we pay for *that* move?)

Is this how it ends? I wondered.

But then I got a nibble. On August 23rd, I found a Craigslist job listing and applied for a writing position at a company called Adchemy—a local startup that did internet advertising—and they wanted me to come in for an interview. They had nothing to do with movies, video on demand, or any entertainment-oriented content. Good. And they were proud of the fact that although they were a startup, they were a *profitable* startup. Double damn good!

The job posting on Craigslist included, among other things, this description and list of requirements:

Content Editor/Search Relevance Analyst/Taxonomist

We are looking for a world class, fun-loving Content and Search Editor/ Taxonomist/ Quality Analyst to join our small team and work on a wide variety of projects. The person should be detail-oriented and a creative individual who enjoys creating order out of semi-structured and unstructured data. This role includes managing, measuring, and growing various knowledge bases. In particular, the individual will create, expand, and maintain multiple taxonomies. Excellent written and verbal communication skills and good analytical skills are mandatory. Previous experience working with ontologies [sic] *is a plus.*

Other required qualifications:

- *Bachelors degree in a relevant area*
- *Previous information and knowledge management and classification experience*
- *Experience working on ontology* creation and taxonomy design on the Internet*
- *Ability to work well in a team environment*

The following are other plusses:

- *Previous experience managing a Web directory or a large-scale Web sites' content into categories*
- *Experience working in start-ups*

(* If this book had footnotes, this would be one: I'm not sure they really understood the meaning of "ontology," which is defined as "that branch of metaphysics that studies the nature of existence or being." Or maybe they understood it better than I realized, given what I discovered later about the company's precarious life-or-death relationship with Google.)

Well, hey! Boy howdy! I met every one of these requirements. *Every single one!* I'd managed, classified, ontologized and taxonimized the shit out of TV, movie and video content at both ReplayTV and Akimbo. And I sure as shit had "experience working in start-ups," goddamn it. Maybe my expertise was in media, but a move to more mainstream, proven content might be a way to stay employed for longer than 18 months...even if it was in advertising and marketing. I could do Satan's work if the wages were high enough (and I don't mean the wages of sin). And so I submitted my résumé…and was almost immediately invited to interview.

I did my due diligence, using the web to study the company, its personnel, and all the buzzwords used in their press releases and on their website. I might not know how to perform SEO, or even what it was, but I did discover it meant "Search Engine Optimization." I could fake familiarity.

And on Thursday, August 31, I drove to Adchemy's HQ in full "smart and charming" mode. I made sure everyone took away a copy of *Killer B's* as well as the obligatory résumé copy. And I ended up having the most grueling interview experience of my life. Each of six different execs spent a full hour with me, grilling me about my background and their own specialties. Much later I realized they were all just getting a feel for whether or not I was smart enough and imaginative enough and flexible enough to do the job...and pleasant enough to be invited into their tight-knit little company community.

It was the most thorough vetting I'd ever received, and also the oddest. One exec, for instance, grilled me about cars. Cars? The fuck did *cars* have to do with internet advertising?

One of the exchanges during these interviews went like this (and stuck in my mind in detail because it was so odd):

Interviewer: "Name something irrelevant about a car."

Me (riffing off the top of my head, stalling while I thought of a better answer): "Well, just to put my answer in perspective, it's always been my contention that the engine is the most important part of a car—until you get a flat tire. So any answer is relative to the situation. I think most people would say the *color* of a car is irrelevant—but we both know that people have a psychological investment in the color of their car. It's a reflection of their personality...like a boring woman I dated once who bought a new car that was gray with a gray interior. So while the color of a car might not have any relevance to its *technical* performance, it has a *psychological* significance to the owner. And car color is definitely relevant to some people—we all know that red cars are more likely to get pulled over for speeding, for instance. Tire size is not terribly relevant—even though car manufacturers recommend a specific size, in a pinch you can use a different size—case in point is those tiny emergency tires that some cars include instead of a full-sized spare. Tire *brand* has limited relevance, except, perhaps, for a perception of quality. A cheap, off-brand tire will get you where you want to go just as well as a Michelin or a Firestone...it just might not last as long. But if I had to isolate a single aspect of a car that I think is totally irrelevant, it would be the shape of the taillights." (I didn't tell him that 25 years earlier, I'd bought my wedge-shaped Toyota Celica specifically because I fell in love with its cat's-eye-like taillights.)

And so it went, for nearly a full working day.

I went home feeling like a squeezed sponge. But I must have passed the tests, because they called and offered me the position. Maybe I only *barely* passed the tests, however, because they offered the position tentatively, and with a major caveat. I'd work on a freelance basis for a three-month trial period, being paid a weekly rate based on the salary I'd earn if they decided to add me to the headcount after the trial period. The offer for the eventual salary was $70,000. On a freelance basis, that was $1,350 a week. But even if I only lasted a couple of weeks, we'd be out of our financial black hole, I calculated, and I'd have enough left over to give me another couple months to hunt for yet another job. I agreed without negotiation.(Clearly I'd learned nothing from Steve Shannon or my experience at Akimbo.) But it was ten grand a year more than I'd been making at Akimbo—and I wasn't about to do anything to queer the deal, like demand more money. It was good money—and I desperately needed it.

Piph had her surgery a couple of days before I started work on Tuesday, September 12. The good news was that the County picked up her hospital tab, since technically we were both unemployed and living below the poverty line on that day. The better news was that we were finally out of the financial woods—as long as I made it through my three-month trial period.

HELL IS A COMMUTE (EVEN IF YOU DRIVE A CLASSIC JAG)

Adchemy was located in a business park in Redwood Shores, sharing a landscape with the futuristic cylindrical towers of Larry Ellison's Oracle, just a few blocks away. This was perfect! My new job was only *five miles away* from our current home in San Mateo. We wouldn't even have to move!

Google Maps gave me three possible routes to get to work, none of them taking more than ten minutes...except during Rush Hour. I was due in at 9:00 AM—the very heart of rush hour—and I discovered to my dismay that driving that five miles took half an hour. Do the math (OK, I'll do it for you): that's an average speed of *ten miles per hour*. I could bike there faster, if there had been bike lanes on El Camino or 101. But instead, I had to crawl onto 101 south and spend a total of nearly 20 minutes of stop-and-go traffic to travel a mere two freeway exits to Holly Street and then to our building.

The only good part about the commute came compliments of Piph, who saw how depressed I was at the new job. "I know what will cheer you up," she said one day a couple of months after I started. "A Jaguar." (I had, months earlier, discovered that my '84 XJ6 would never pass the semi-annual California emissions test, and repairs to bring it up to spec would be more than the car was worth. I donated it to a local charity and used it as a tax write-off.) She'd located a guy in Marin who specialized in refurbishing and selling, Jaguars and BMWs. We drove up to his lot one Saturday in December and I fell in love with a '94 Jaguar XJS—a car I'd always considered one of the ten most beautiful automobiles ever designed. It was British Racing Green with a tan interior. It was spotless and perfect. I later discovered that this model was released a year or two after Jaguar was purchased by Ford, who had by then fixed the brand's perennial internal problems—multiple fluid leaks, for instance, and a haunted electrical system—without fucking with the classic body design. The best of both worlds. And it was well within our (new) budget. She purchased the car with a credit card and I drove it home. And loved it for the next seven years.

TO MARKET, TO MARKET…

"If anyone here is in advertising or marketing...kill yourself. You are Satan's spawn, filling the world with bile and garbage. You are fucked and you are fucking us. *Kill yourself.*"
—Bill Hicks

Adchemy had a suite on the ground floor of a high-rise office park building right next door to Electronic Arts, the premier video game company. The layout of our little company was (as they say on HGTV) "open concept"—one big room with a conference room on the side wall (the wall with windows) and a few small offices for private conversations and one-on-one meetings. It was a decidedly egalitarian layout: we all sat in the bullpen, even the CEO. I was rather taken aback to discover that we had no cubicles, no desks, and no telephones. But we had no business-oriented reason to need a phone—and in 2006, it was taken for granted that you'd have your own cell phone, duh. Our "desks" consisted of large folding tables arranged four in a square, often surrounding a building pillar. When I asked about this bare-bones, minimalist workspace, I was told, "Which would you rather have—a desk and a phone or a large salary?" To quote *Jerry McGuire*, "Show me the money."

Adchemy had been founded just two years earlier, in 2004, and was backed at that time by about $8 million in outside funding. The website described the company as "a next-generation online marketing company...deploying proprietary technology that embodies highly scientific, algorithmic approaches... including statistical machine learning, combinatorial optimization, information retrieval, and experimental design." Or, more succinctly, "Computational Performance Marketing."

Like you, I have no idea what any of that means—didn't then; don't now. What I do know is that Adchemy employees were very proud of the fact that the company was one of the few profitable startups in Silicon Valley, and even more proud of the fact that it had been co-founded by Rajeev Motwani, professor of computer science at Stanford University and former professor and advisor to the founders of Google, as well as one of the original developers of Google's PageRank search algorithm.

I soon discovered that Adchemy was intimately and incestuously intertwined with Google, and not just in the shared parenthood relationship with Motwani. Adchemy at that time specialized in "lead generation," or placing banner ads that paid a bounty for every form filled out by a potential customer for the services advertised. In 2006, that meant the University of Phoenix, the online college that was Adchemy's largest (and perhaps only) client.

Adchemy's cutting edge advantage in internet marketing was using "A/B testing." They'd create two versions of a banner ad with minor differences, run them in different geographical locations and track them for a few days to see which of the two generated more clicks, then replace the runner-up with the winning ad in all locations. The differences between the two ads were usually minute: green background instead of blue, for instance, or a photo of two men and a woman vying for supremacy against a picture of two women and a man. About three-quarters of Adchemy's revenue depended on Google—not just Google's AdWords function (essentially an online auction for the most-searched words and terms), but also by placing ads on websites highly ranked by Google, for maximum exposure.

What I discovered was that Google had essentially kicked Adchemy off its search engine recently, because Adchemy was not "giving enough back to the community," whatever that meant in Google-speak. Google felt that Adchemy was too greedy, and punished them through sanctions or by withholding data, or whatever insanely technical sadism Google used at the time to keep advertisers in line. Adchemy needed to heal this rift and solve this problem...ASAP. In order to survive, Adchemy needed to get back on Google...so they needed to give something significant "back to the community."

This virtual blacklisting caused no end of headaches among the Adchemy execs—in part because Google had two sets of requirements for approval: the steps they were willing to demand from an internet marketing company like Adchemy... and a second, secret set of requirements that could only be guessed at, and which the Adchemy execs attempted to fulfill by trial and error. Even though I was the lowest-level employee at Adchemy, the tension and anxiety were palpable—and gossip, like shit, trickles downhill. It didn't have far to travel in a company with fewer than three dozen employees. Along with continuing its core activity, internet marketing, Adchemy added an additional objective, focusing on an initiative known in-house as "Get Back On Google." To accomplish this, they had to find some Google-approved way to "give back to the community." And their solution, at least in part, was: me.

I didn't discover this until near the end of my tenure, (spoiler alert!) six months later, but it seems that a lot was riding on my work (along with that of others, of course), to prove to Google that Adchemy was, in fact, "contributing to the community," so we could return to Google's good graces. All I knew was that my first assignment was to create content for a website (not associated with Adchemy) that encouraged young people to seek careers in occupations that required college degrees in areas offered by Adchemy's primary client: The University of Phoenix.

At that time Adchemy employed about 35 people, approximately half of whom were Vice Presidents. Top dog among them was Scott Johnston, VP of Business Development. I quickly realized that when people referred to "Scott," they meant Johnston, not me. I was the lesser Scott; the emergency backup Scott. This name identity never caused any confusion among the staff, but it did set me on edge several times a day, as people would walk past my table-desk saying things like, "Scott says we should do this," or "We should check with Scott," or "Scott's out on a business call." (No I'm not, I'm right here—oops; sorry ...wrong Scott.) I often felt like a "pretender to my own name."

HIRE EDUCATION

My immediate superior was a sharp, well-groomed guy in his 30s, Tai Thumasathit, the Vice President of Product Management. He looked like he could have been a Thai warrior in a past life: blunt, driven, intense, and confident to just this side of cocky. I appreciate people who have qualities I don't possess, so we got along nicely—and everyone in the company seemed to like and admire him, which I found out when small groups of co-workers went to lunch together once or twice a week.

(Just as a side note, I discovered Tai had come to Adchemy from an online price comparison shopping site called NexTag, and that the NexTag office was literally right across the street from our home in San Mateo—closer even to our house than the Akimbo offices. Had I known this a few months earlier, I might have walked across El Camino Real one day, résumé in hand, knocked on the door and inquired whether they needed a top-tier taxonomist. Tai and I could conceivably have been working together months earlier—and I might have avoided months of depressing poverty. I might even have followed Tai to Adchemy when he made the move. Was my presence at Adchemy somehow fated? Who the hell knows. NexTag later moved to Redwood Shores, home of Oracle, Electronic Arts, and, of course, Adchemy—thus illustrating once again the intricate, overlapping crosscurrents of life, employment and coincidence—or synchronicity—in greater Silicon Valley.)

THE WORK

Tai and I sat for many hours over many days creating a flowchart for a website devoted to higher education, focusing (of course) on those concentrations and degrees offered by the University of Phoenix. We settled on eight top-level categories: Law Enforcement & Criminal Justice, Healthcare & Medical, Nursing, Engineering, Education, Art & Design, Business, and Technology. Each would have its own landing page, in which we would provide an overview of the field and the general requirements for employment (usually a BS, BA or at very least an AA degree, of course, since we were subtly pitching a college). But while we were promoting higher education in general, no mention would be made of *where* a degree could be obtained—this website had to remain objective, ad-free, and above all, accurate. So when I wrote for the website:

"Most positions in this field require a minimum of a bachelor's degree in the appropriate subject to qualify for employment... [In] general, the more advanced the degree, and the more specific to the task that degree is, the greater the range of career and employment options that become available."

...that statement was honest, unbiased and factual, encouraging the reader to pursue higher education wherever they could obtain it. Ditto with this website advice:

"Choice of schools is critically important when pursuing a degree... Be certain to investigate and compare the curricula of several schools that offer degrees in [this field] before deciding which one is best for your specific needs. Make sure you choose a school that offers the course of study and the degree which will further your career goals."

...yeah, like the University of Phoenix, bitches! But no. No mention could be made of the University of Phoenix, even though a Google search of the degree or field under consideration would return UP as one of the top search results, and a cursory investigation of the field or degree would bring up one of Adchemy's banner ads promoting degrees and study in this field at...guess where.

So I found myself in the ironic, outsider position of working for a marketing company but being barred absolutely from doing any marketing. I loved the idea that the only way Adchemy could continue their marketing efforts was if they proved they were adept at *not marketing*. And that they were a marketing company paying me to *not market*. I had no qualms about working for an evil marketing company to create an objective, honest, accurate site about higher education—even if the only subjects we covered were the core curriculum of...well, you know. For everyone who Googled a degree or field and encountered an ad for the University of Phoenix along with their search results, there would be plenty of others who would discover that their local Junior College or state college could provide the same educational opportunities.

Once we had an outline for the website, I drew up a schedule based on how much research and writing I could actually accomplish. And there was plenty I'd need to do. The Education field, as a typical example, encompassed 11 different potential careers and degrees, from Administration and Adult Education to K-12 instruction, Special Ed, and Distance Education. Nursing encompassed 13 subcategories, from the expected (RN, LVN) to Forensic Nursing, Geriatric Nursing and even Midwife. And so on. Altogether, we identified more than 80 specific degree areas

—each one of which would require its own unique web page on the site. Add the text that needed to be created for the eight category landing pages, as well as the text explaining the mission of the site for a top-level landing page, and I had nearly 90 web pages to research and write.

After a couple of trial runs, gauging how long it took to actually do this work (and getting approval of the finished content from Tai), I crunched the numbers and calculated that I could potentially handle three topics per week. This would require 30 weeks of effort. I pitched the time budget to Tai and justified it with my first experiments. We could launch the website within a couple of months, I explained, with two or three completed categories, and expand it as I finished new "verticals." The whole process would take about six months. Tai, to his credit, listened to my justifications and explanations, and approved this new estimate and plan. And I set about doing the actual work.

Given the approval of the layout and schedule of the website, and my proof-of-concept first drafts of the information each page/profession should contain, my job became much more independent. I didn't meet with Tai daily, for instance; we met only once a week, so I could report my progress. But the task also became infinitely more complicated. What I would do for the next six months is this: research and write, often simultaneously...and seemingly endlessly.

IF I HAD MY PICK, I'D BE A DATA MINER

Each topic went through a three-phase process. Phase I was researching a specific profession or vocation in deep detail. I combed the web and quickly discovered a handful of sites that proved to be invaluable sources for high-quality information about each of the 80 occupations that would populate our website. The U.S. Department of Labor's Bureau of Labor Statistics, for instance, includes a "Career Outlook Handbook," a huge online vocational database that contained much of the core information I required—and it was copyright-free, since it's taxpayer-funded. Additionally, virtually every vocation we wanted to include in our higher education website had one or more professional organizations associated with it, which provided even more online information.

Just pulling information from a couple sites like this and throwing it into a web page probably would have been enough to create a lazy higher education website. A quick and dirty hack job like that might very well have satisfied my corporate masters. But I took my mandate seriously. If Google wanted us to contribute something of value to the community, I was dedicated to doing that in spades. I'd give them a unique site full of in-depth information that no other single site would contain. I'd give them a profession-education-information site that would knock their fucking socks off.

Whenever possible, for instance, I wanted to include information on typical (and regional) wages, handy tips, what to expect in a typical day on the job, in what geographical areas one was most likely to find employment, and an outlook for the future of the field. Dental Hygienist, for instance, was a growing field at that time, with a good outlook for employment, and required only an AA degree—but other professions were on the wane, or overstaffed and therefore underpaid. So each vocation required extensive research and often included scanning occupational blogs devoted to a specific occupation to uncover this kind of granular information.

Phase II was to organize the raw data and write the web page for each researched topic/vocation. This "wordsmithing" was my wheelhouse, and is so boring that it barely deserves mention (unless you care deeply about such grammatical trivia as when to use "that" instead of "which," for example), except for…

Phase III: Quality Control. Not only did I have to research each individual occupation and digest the requirements into clear and concise text, but I was also tasked with an additional requirement: to write these descriptions in such a way that *no single phrase* on our site could be Googled and yield any of the research sites I used in the first two pages of Google results. So this was the very opposite of a cut-and-paste project, which might have been completed within a few weeks. I discovered that, to their credit, Adchemy's execs were as deeply dedicated as I was to making this a unique website. The company had its own agenda with this restriction, certainly (it's all to impress Google and get back in their favor)—but it dovetailed nicely with my own perspective, which was to create an informational site that was both unique and comprehensive.

And so, for every vocation I'd researched and written about, before it could be approved, I also had to take every phrase of three or more words and Google it. If any of my research sources appeared among the first two pages (or 20 links) of results, I had to go back and rewrite the phrase until it was unique. No wonder they needed someone with flexible writing skills! (And a big...what's the word? Oh, right—*vocabulary*!) I had to be a walking thesaurus—although I'll admit I did keep on online thesaurus open on my laptop as a backup to my own gray matter. (Here's one I never solved: What's another word for "thesaurus"?)

GROUNDHOG DAYS

On a typical day, I'd arrive at 9:00 AM on the dot. Tai would already be at his desk scowling at his monitor. I'd nod hello (we had no time for social amenities beyond that), then plug in, boot up, get a cup of tea, don my Skullcandy headphones and start the day by opening an internet radio site and selecting the "All Beethoven" channel. Then I'd check my email. And then, at 9:01, I'd start working. (Joke. Usually it was more like 9:04.)

Since we worked in a big open bullpen, earphones were as much a mandatory piece of work equipment as a chair or a laptop (but not a phone). At any given time during a typical day, half the employees were staring at their laptops while sporting headphones. It helped. On a good day, my "All Beethoven" channel would play one of the nine symphonies. And I'd get a chance to close my eyes and listen to the final movement, transported to another, more beautiful, empathic and transcendent world than the current real-world reality of sitting at a table in a big room as a keyboard monkey for an internet marketing firm. Beat the hell out of a coffee break.

And five minutes after Tai left for the evening—usually around 6:30 or 7 PM—I'd pack up and go home. At first, I locked my Adchemy-provided laptop in Tai's desk. But about a month into my employment, he saw me doing this and said, "There are people here who are worried that you're not taking your laptop home with you and working from home in the evening." I assumed that those "people" were Tai. I could hardly tell him that once I walked out the door in the evening I never gave this place a second thought, much less went home and continued working. So I said, "I've never worked at a company that allowed freelancers to take equipment home before. But if you give the OK, I'll be happy to do so." He approved, and I began taking my laptop home with me each evening. Sadly, however, I never did get around to continuing my work at home…

SOCIALISM FOR CAPITALISTS

Maybe as a result of everyone's work being so insular, we found ways to bond as a company community. About once a week, for instance, a small group of us would go to lunch together. This was a fun group; talkative, joking, laughing. But far more often, lunch was a solitary, rather than a social, affair. A couple of times a week I'd go across the street to Togo's, bring back a meatball sub, and eat at my desk—so it looked like I was so dedicated that I'd work through lunch.

And occasionally—far too infrequently, in hindsight—I'd go to Togo's with one of my co-workers, a tall, brilliant, Rebecca Romijn-level attractive blonde. She was the very image of one of those '40s *femmes* that Cary Grant would approach, remove her glasses, untie the ribbon in her hair and let it tumble down around her shoulders, and proclaim, "Why, Miss Jones...without your glasses, you're be-*you*-ti-ful!" I admired her protective camouflage, which made her look gawky and mousy, like Chris Reeves' Clark Kent in the 1978 *Superman* movie. But once I discovered her secret, I realized she was less Clark Kent/Superman than Diana Prince in the office and Wonder Woman in a more accepting setting. During our lunches, we'd talk about how we didn't feel like we fit in at Adchemy, and mock the people we didn't like, from co-workers to celebrities. We talked about many things, actually—our histories, our backgrounds, our favorite books and movies, our hopes and dreams, our past relationships. One thing we never talked about was our future. There could be no "our" in our futures. I was old enough to be her father (well, technically, anyway), and I had a fabulous woman at home, so I never acted on my instincts and followed up on this effortless connection to get closer to her. The most likely outcome of such a bold move, I knew, would have been embarrassment—for me. But when she made a point of sitting next to me at my good-bye party, actually pushing people out of her way so she could sit there, and squeezed my leg under the table—repeatedly—I can't help but regret that I didn't risk that embarrassment and take the next step. I'll leave her name out of this narrative, but you know who you are, blondie. "Of all sad words of tongue or pen..."

Another way the employees "bonded" was Beer Fridays. Sometime around five o'clock every Friday afternoon, a buzz would start running around the office: "When is Scott [the other Scott] gonna announce?" And about half-past, Scott would at last announce: "It's beer-thirty!" And we'd all head for the fridge. Adchemy was generous enough to stock the fridge with cases of beer—decent beer, too: Stella Artois, Sierra Nevada Pale Ale, Corona. We'd all grab a bottle and schmooze, or go back to work. As I'd discovered at Silicon Graphics, the key to getting me to stay late and work late was simple: free beer.

Once a month, one department would be chosen, on a rotating basis, to plan and host a Friday afternoon theme party, with plenty of liquor flowing. When it was Tai's department's turn, we decided on a Hawaiian theme, with pineapple and coconut treats, tiki torches and—of course—plenty of rum drinks. I had no clue at that time that I'd end up retired in Hawaii less than a decade later. I didn't even own an Aloha shirt in those days—I had to dress up in a flower print shirt, a Disneyland Jungle Cruise hat, and wraparound sunglasses. I have a photo from that party. I look like an old retired general still wearing his camo.

The parties stopped a few months later, after one of our co-workers got into a fender bender on the way home, and the execs realized that if anyone got hurt or killed or arrested for a DUI, they'd be liable. Pity. But the parties were mandatory fun while they lasted.

ON THE WAY UP, OR OUT

December 2006

In some ways, I dreaded the holiday season. I'd been given the boot by Lockheed, Silicon Graphics, ReplayTV and Akimbo in previous Decembers. But this year I got more than a lump of coal in my stocking for Christmas: once my three-month trial period was up, Adchemy decided to hire me for reals.

Despite the approval of being hired as a full-time employee, and despite the attempts at bonding with my co-workers, I still felt like an outsider. I often wondered if anyone at the company besides Tai actually knew what I was even doing there. No one ever asked. In addition, I never took my work home with me, and never discussed it at home. Not only was it too boring, I just didn't want to dwell on it. The job was a paycheck; the work was acceptable.

February 2007

But it wouldn't always be that way. The previous October, I'd estimated that creating an "education for professions" website would take about six months. And by early February of 2007, I could see the end of my website work on the horizon. Tai had hired a former co-worker from NexTag to be my immediate superior on the next initiative: SEO. Search Engine Optimization. My strengths lay in my writing and taxonomy skills. I didn't know shit about SEO—and frankly, didn't particularly want to learn. It sounded dull and technical. But I smiled and kept up a façade of enthusiasm. In one meeting with Tai and the CEO, they announced that the next "vertical" we'd be attacking was...*cars*. (Ah, so now his crazy questions in my interview months earlier made sense!) I wanted to show what a dedicated team player I was, and responded with an enthusiastic, "I'm ready to hit the deck running!" Tai leaned over and whispered in my ear, *"It's expected."*

Some time later, I finished work on the Higher Education Information website. In the six months I spent researching and writing the site, I generated more than 500,000 words of text. To put that in context, half a million words is about twice the length of *No Plan B*, and exceeds Stephen King's longest novel, *The Stand*, (472,376) by almost ten percent (or by as much as Stephen King's *The Colorado Kid*, a shorty that clocks in at 36,346 words).

I dreaded the day when I'd get a new assignment—one which I probably wouldn't understand, and certainly didn't want to learn. ("I'm a taxonomy monkey, dammit, Jim, not an SEO monkey!") That's when I found a Craigslist posting for a job at Apple—and immediately applied. And got a response. (The full story is in the first Apple chapter.) A week later, I found an even more appropriate position at Apple and called my recruiter, urging her to consider me for that one.

I was scheduled to interview at Apple on Monday, February 19. I worried that my pitiful résumé would be mocked at a world-class company like Apple. But on Friday, February 16, I got one of the greatest gifts a person can ever receive: confidence. That Friday, representatives from Google spent most of the day in our conference room in in-depth, wide-ranging discussion with all of Adchemy's top execs. I wasn't invited, of course, but Tai was. And when the Googlers finally left, I asked him what it was all about. "We're back on Google," he announced, both happy and relieved. "They told us they'd never seen a company make such a rapid recovery in so short a time and get back in their good graces so quickly."

"Did they tell you why?" I asked.

"Yeah," he replied. "We actually asked them that specific question. And they gave us a very emphatic, one-word answer: '*Content*.'"

Content? *Content?* That was *me*! I'd fulfilled my mandate, and did it in under six months—faster than anyone had ever counted on. Due to my efforts, apparently, Adchemy was back on Google. Adchemy was back in business.

That objective validation was *precisely* what I needed to bolster my confidence enough to walk into my Apple interviews the following Monday morning fearlessly. I knew for a fact—a fact verified by both Adchemy and Google—that I was a highly effective employee. Apple would be lucky to have me.

I was hired by Apple on Friday, March 2. On the following Monday, when I arrived at Adchemy at 9 AM, the first thing I did was ask Tai if I could talk with him privately for a minute. We went into one of the phone booth-sized meeting rooms and I gave him my prepared and polished speech (annotated here with my delivery tactics):

"Tai," I began, "there's no way to say this easily, so I'm just gonna come right out and say it: I've been offered a position at Apple, running the new iTunes Movies store, and I've accepted.

"But I want you to know two things," I continued, switching from Blunt Honesty mode to Soothing White Lie mode, and taking into consideration the pride that Adchemy employees exhibited. "First is that I wasn't looking for another job. They came to me. The video on demand world is very small and incestuous, and apparently, word got around about the work I'd done at ReplayTV and Akimbo in that field. It's very flattering, but I wasn't looking for it. I'm quite happy here." I checked my nose to see if it was growing.

"Second is this: The fact that I've accepted a position at Apple should in no way be taken as a reflection on Adchemy, or on you or the management here. Adchemy is an exceptional company, and I'm proud to have been chosen to be a part of it. But Apple has offered me something that speaks to my core skills—which I never thought would happen." I checked my pants to see if they were on fire.

"Finally," I continued, returning to Honesty mode to bracket my little speech, "I can tell you that writing is my core strength. I don't know anything about SEO. So Adchemy got the best of me over the last six months, and I'm certain I could never contribute as much to an SEO effort. So in some way, this is a good opportunity for you—I've done what I do best, and now I'll get out of your way, which will allow you to hire someone who's much more knowledgeable and skilled at SEO than I am."

"How much did they offer you?" Tai asked.

"One-ten," I said. A slight rounding up, but I had to make sure I was out of his price range in case he wanted to make a counteroffer.

He shrugged. "No way we could match that," he said. Bingo.

"Well, it means a lot to me that you'd even consider it," I said. Honesty mode. "But, yeah—they made me an offer I can't refuse...one-ten, and addressing my core skills."

"When do they want you there?"

"Well," I chuckled, "you know Apple. They want me there yesterday. I told them I was honor-bound to give you two weeks' notice, but I'd see if we could cut it down to one week." I wasn't about to start at Apple any sooner than two weeks. But if I could leave Adchemy after one week's notice, I could have a week's vacation between jobs—a vacation that I could, for once, afford and enjoy.

"We've got a lot to accomplish in the next two weeks," Tai said. Bye-bye R&R.

He kept me very busy during those two weeks, mostly writing additional material for the website, including something I suggested—one of my freelance specialties, a "roundup" piece discussing the Top Ten movies about inspirational teachers. I didn't finish my final assignments until the last day of those two weeks.

As I was getting coffee that afternoon, one of my co-workers, a cute young Asian woman, joined me in the kitchen. "I'm really happy for you that you escaped this place and got in at Apple," she said. "But I'm gonna miss you."

"Really?" I said, and, to return her sweet gesture, I admitted that I never felt like I fit in at Adchemy.

"Are you *kidding* me?" she exclaimed, wide-eyed. "You should have seen them the day after your interview! They were all running around, all excited, yelling, 'He wrote a book! He wrote a book!' "

I laughed at the image of these reserved business types actually doing that. But it didn't sound like the kind of thing someone would make up on the spot. "I wish you woulda told me that six months ago," I chuckled.

My takeaway from that one casual conversation was that after a decade, *Killer B's* had supplanted my Bachelor's degree as a "calling card" to qualify me for a professional position.

THEY GOT ALONG WITHOUT ME, APPARENTLY

In the following years, Adchemy changed its mission and its core product several times. By late 2013, Adchemy employed over 100 people. It was acquired by Walmart Labs on May 6, 2014, which seemed somehow fitting—an evil marketing company acquired by the Evil Empire.

THE COINCIDENCE OF OPPOSITES

In one of those strange coincidences that happen only in cheap novels and real life, *No Plan B* is not the first memoir about employment in Silicon Valley in which Adchemy plays a role. As I was doing my "due diligence," researching other books similar to what I had in mind for this one, I ran across a memoir of work life in hi-tech in which the author was hired by Adchemy precisely a year after I left. I'm not about to mention the title—partly because it's competition, and partly because the author had nothing but bitterness and bile for the company and its founder, Murthy Nukala.

For the record, I never found Murthy to be anything other than intelligent, committed and intensely involved in his company. I might have (and do have) little but bile for Marketing in general, but Adchemy never really seemed to me (regardless of my previous jokes) to be part of the "evil empire" of Marketing—no more so than my co-workers at Lockheed a couple of decades earlier seemed like warmongers devoted to the nuclear decimation of our enemies. And Murthy in particular recognized my skills and provided me with excellent employment, even though I never had a dark Marketing heart.

But, according to the author of this other memoir, Murthy was a "weasel"; a "sycophant" with investors and a "tyrant" to his employees. Maybe Murthy had changed in the year between when this guy and I knew him, but this kind of behavior never happened on my watch. I never once heard him raise his voice in a "rant," or insult an employee in public, as the other author claimed occurred frequently.

But, hey—maybe this other guy is right. No one I'd worked with at Adchemy only a year earlier was mentioned in his book

—not Tai, nor Tim, the head of engineering, or The Main Scott. It appears that they'd all left. I'll never know their reasons, of course, but a complete change of high-level personnel in under a year is not a sign of a stable company or a less than volatile management.

On the other hand, to put this other author's comments about Murthy and Adchemy in some context, what would you expect from a self-proclaimed asshole who claims he never hated any man more than he hated Murthy...except his own father. That comment alone, I think, puts our different perceptions in perspective—and the context of his book, where he goes out of his way to paint himself as an anti-social, blunt and angry asshole (and the only truly honest man!), probably puts most of his perceptions in perspective.

Finally, this author claims that the only chapter in Silicon Valley history Murthy Nukala will ever have is the one in his screed. He was wrong about that, too.

PART III:

A BITE OF THE APPLE

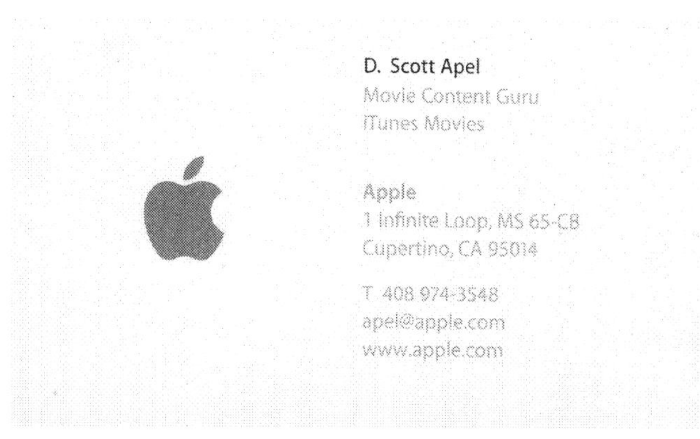

"The journey is the reward."
—Steve Jobs

Chapter 26

2007: THE APPLE OF MY EYE

February 2007

I was at an unusual point in my career: I was employed.

Writing internet content for the online advertising firm Adchemy was...a job. But it wasn't a career. It wasn't fun. And it certainly wasn't a future—so even after hiring into Adchemy, I continued to comb online job sites for an upgrade. Early in February 2007, I found a posting for a position at Apple, writing a weekly email newsletter for iTunes customers about the latest releases. It required minimal web skills (and my skills were nothing if not minimal) and a heavy concentration on writing.

Writing? About media? That was my specialty! I tweaked my résumé and submitted it immediately. And—miracle of miracles—within a few days I was contacted by an Apple recruiter. Given this encouragement, I purchased my first cell phone, so she could reach me anytime (which was difficult to do during business hours at a company where I had no desk phone) and so I could call her without using one of our few work phones.

And then the Mother Of All Miracles occurred: While waiting for the Apple recruiter to set up a round of interviews, I continued checking Craigslist, simply because...you never know. And late one Sunday night—still in early February—I found yet another job posting from Apple: *iTunes Movie Guru.* As I read through the list of qualifications, I was simultaneously encouraged, distressed and confused. Encouraged, because the list of required skills was essentially...my résumé. Distressed, because any list of job requirements that aligned so closely with my own experience must be a cruel practical joke of some sort. My experience was a hodgepodge of unrelated activities—how could it possibly integrate into the exact constellation of some larger, singular endeavor? And confused, because...how could iTunes post my résumé as a job description?

WTF was going on here? Was someone sending me a coded message, trying to contact me indirectly? How likely—or unlikely—was it that someone could create a job description that virtually mirrored my own job experience—my own résumé? And even if they had, how many other applicants were there out there with a similar background, skillset and résumé? I'd always assumed my work history was so quirky as to be unique. But who really knew?

The worst thought of all was this: *What if someone beats me to this position?*

At 9:00 AM the following morning—figuring that was the earliest I could catch someone at work—I called my Apple recruiter and made the most important phone call of my life. "June," I said, after identifying myself, "I know we're discussing a position as a newsletter writer in iTunes. But I want you to do something that will benefit both of us. I want you to look at Apple's latest job posting." I read her the ID number of the Craigslist post. "I want you to look at the list of job requirements side by side with my résumé. What you're going to see is a one-to-one correspondence between my experience and the job requirements—except in those areas where I *exceed* the requirements." I tried to sound assured and confident rather than anxious and desperate. And I bet the farm: "The newsletter position is *not* my job," I told her. "My job is iTunes Movie Guru." She said she'd look into it.

I'd done what I could. If June ignored me, maybe I hadn't completely screwed myself out of a chance at the email newsletter position and could still get into Apple. But if I'd been convincing and she was willing to invest five minutes fulfilling my request, there was simply no way she could ignore me. I hoped.

An hour later my cell phone rang. *June.* I dashed from my desk out to the lobby to answer. "I'm setting up a series of interviews for you with the iTunes Movies group," she said. She mentioned that a couple of the people I'd be talking to were "new" to Apple—"they've only been with us two or three years." After enduring the startup lifestyle where 18 months was akin to an infinite stint, the idea that Apple employees were still considered "new" after even three years was a breath of fresh spring air.

"Is Monday the 19th good for you?" *Absolutely*, I replied. I could take a day off from Adchemy to do the interviews, even though I could never reveal that I was taking the day off to interview for another position. As it turned out, I wouldn't even need to take the day off: Monday, February 19, 2007, was President's Day—a holiday that Adchemy honored, but one on which Apple employees worked.

Monday, February 19, 2007

In 2007, Apple's Cupertino HQ was just off Interstate 280, one of two major north-south arteries (like the so-called "digital highway," 101) that bisect Silicon Valley and run from San Jose to San Francisco. The six buildings of the Apple campus—including the main building, which housed its own Apple Store (and was nicknamed "The Mother Ship")—were built inside an oval road jokingly named Infinite Loop. But just as iTunes was not a central part of Apple (the company had only recently changed its name from "Apple Computers" to simply "Apple, Inc."), the iTunes offices were not part of the main campus. Instead, they occupied several single-story buildings lining Valley Green Drive, across De Anza Blvd. from the main campus. It was clear that iTunes was the redheaded stepchild of this technology company.

I was met in the lobby of Valley Green 5 (VG5) by my iTunes contact, Crystal, a fashionable and fashionably thin woman of about 30. She signed me in and ushered me to a small conference room off the main hallway. And we began the interviews. I came prepared with a briefcase full of résumé copies and my signature calling card, copies of my film guide, *Killer B's: The 237 Best Movies on Video You've (Probably) Never Seen*. Crystal and I talked. When we were finished, she took me to another small conference room and I talked with Jean, a woman close to my own age—which was a pleasant surprise, given that most of the crew I saw wandering the hallways were about half my age. We talked. No big whoop. Crystal showed up half an hour later and took me to another small room in a building across the street. Even she couldn't figure out why every interview was being held in a different room in a different building—often not even the building the interviewer worked in.

We broke for lunch, but it was a working lunch: I'd be meeting, greeting and eating with Gary Stewart, an iTunes consultant. We walked across De Anza Blvd. to the main Apple campus, through the spacious lobby of the main building, then out the back door and across the quad and to Caffè Macs. A lot of ink has been spilled (and a lot of pixels marshaled) describing the cafeterias of various Silicon Valley tech giants—about the gourmet food available, for instance, or the three meals a day offered (often free, as an enticement to employees to work late). Caffè Macs wasn't free, and it wasn't gourmet, but it was big. And crowded. And cheap. And accommodating, too: if you forgot your wallet, you could flash your badge to the cashiers and the cost of your meal would be subtracted from your next paycheck. There was a station for the usual grill fare—hamburgers, hot dogs, chicken sandwiches; there was a Specialty of the Day station; there was a sushi station (by order of Steve); there was a do-it-yourself sandwich bar, for PB&Js and the like. There was a pasta bar, which I would discover was excellent. I queued up behind Crystal at the pizza station. Three chefs created per-request thin crust pizzas and baked them in a wood-fired oven while you watched. (And they were delicious!) Caffè Macs was mobbed, but we got our pizzas and drinks and found Gary. We ate and we talked.

THE SOUL OF iTUNES

A few words about Gary Stewart. He's a big shambling bear of a man, dresses exclusively in Cuban *Guayabera* shirts, and is one of the smartest, most informed and most goddamned *pleasant* people on the planet. He was a VP of A&R at Rhino Records for 25 years, and in September 2004 (two and a half years earlier than this point in my narrative), he was tapped by iTunes as a consultant for music content. During his nearly ten-year tenure as a consultant at Apple, he built the iTunes Music service into something far more than just an online record store, and something far beyond simply a new way to purchase music. He and his team turned iTunes Music into the digital equivalent of legendary local record stores, where the community of audiophiles would gather to comb the stacks and spend long hours debating the relative merits of various obscure bands. (See the movie *High Fidelity* to get a taste of this milieu.) To iTunes' music selections, Gary's team added in-depth essays about artists, bands and styles of music, provided guidance about what to listen to, and penned insightful analyses and reviews of songs, albums, artists and bands...and much, much more. From a purely business standpoint, this was an attempt to ensure return visits and build customer loyalty. From an audiophile perspective, this supplementary information was a source of reliable and in-depth information, education and deeply informed opinion.

As we sat and chatted and munched our pizzas, I realized that Gary Stewart was a walking encyclopedia—and not just of modern music but of movies as well. Had I met my match? Why would iTunes need me if they had Gary Stewart? I gave Gary a copy of *Killer B's*, and he flipped through it, frequently exclaiming, "I know that movie! I *love* that movie!" He forced himself to put the book down so we could talk. And laugh. And express our enthusiasm about movies. If Gary's opinion could sway things with Crystal and the Movies team, then I was in.

On the walk back with Crystal, I casually inquired, "Did you ever return *Maria Full of Grace* to Netflix?" She stopped dead in her tracks and pointed a finger at me. "You *Googled* me!" she accused. "*Of course* I did!" I replied, and we both laughed. *Of course* I'd Googled her. I'd done my due diligence on everyone I was scheduled to interview with. And Crystal had come up in an old *Newsweek* article about people torn between watching a Netflix DVD they'd held onto for months or returning it unwatched to free up their queue for new titles. She'd held on to this particular DVD for *20 months.* Her illustrative example resulted in a new diagnosis of psychology: Severe Netflix Disorder. The irony is that at the time of her interview with *Newsweek*, Crystal was actually working for Netflix—and her fiancé was still employed there as an engineer. (It always intrigued me that no one ever considered the conflict of interest between Crystal's involvement on the iTunes Movies team and her fiancé's employment at our main and only competitor, Netflix.)

MEET THE NEW BOSS (WE HOPE), *Part 3 of Many*

It was time to meet The Boss: "Marshall Dylan," the man in charge of iTunes Movies, and the one guy whose thumbs-down could put me back out on the street instead of installing me in a cubicle doing the job I'd inadvertently educated myself for during the previous twenty-plus years. (*Special Note:* In respect for his wishes for privacy, the name of this Hero has been changed.) Marshall Dylan reported directly to Eddy Cue, the head of iTunes, and Eddy reported directly to "SJ" (as Steve Jobs was always referred to in-house).

Marshall Dylan had a small, glass-fronted office in a row of similar offices inhabited mostly by iTunes Music middle managers. These micro offices (often referred to as "fishbowls") were just about big enough for a wraparound desk and a pair of chairs in addition to the occupant's Aeron chair. Dylan himself was tall, dark and lanky; loose and relaxed. If he'd had a buffer physique, I might have thought he was a bantamweight pugilist. Crystal had clearly told him about the web research I'd done on her, and Marshall mentioned it with amusement. "Sure," I said. "I Googled everyone on my interview list. But I couldn't come up with anything on you."

He chuckled and grinned, looked down at the tabletop between us and shook his head. "I like to keep a low profile," he said. (Hopefully, this should explain why, among the Heroes, he was one of the few whose name I changed.) And we chatted. Turns out he knew Steve Shannon, my old boss at Akimbo. I wondered if they'd been ski bums together. I took a chance. "I hope you liked him," I said, "because I love the guy." Dylan assured me he thought Steve was a hell of a guy.

Near the end of our half-hour together, Marshall asked, "You have any questions for me?"

"I do," I said. I probably should have asked something like, "What are our projected sales for 2007?" or "What percentage growth rate do you expect to see over the next four quarters?" But I'm Creative, not Business—and I'd been burned before. So I asked the one question that was actually—and seriously—on my mind.

"We mentioned Steve Shannon and ReplayTV," I said. "Replay relocated me to Los Angeles and then laid off the entire office ten weeks later. I don't want that to happen again. Since we're working with movies, do you have any plans to move this department to L.A.?"

"Over my dead body," he said. "I'm a San Francisco guy. If we ever moved anywhere, it would be there. But SJ likes to keep things close to home. We're not moving."

IN WHICH I BECOME AN APPLE POLISHER

And we were done. Crystal escorted me to my car, stopping only once to show off her new engagement ring to Lindsay, a tall blonde artist given to wearing tight sweaters—and who was totally able to pull off that look.

At the car, I congratulated Crystal on her engagement and thanked her for shepherding me around through the interviews. "I want you to know," I wrapped up, "that even if this process never moves forward, it's been an honor just to interview with Apple." I had officially become an apple polisher.

She said she'd be in touch. Yeah, I'd heard that one before. But still, I hoped for the best.

Now all there was to do was...wait. Well, not quite. June still had me down as a candidate for the newsletter position. When she asked if I wanted to move forward with that, I said absolutely. If the Movie Guru spot fell through, I still might have a shot at being employed by Apple.

For the first time ever, I had a Plan B.

A week or so later, I jumped back into the meat grinder once again with a round of interviews for this backup position—the "safety school" of employment. I talked with Jennifer, an Editor, and perhaps the most attractive woman I would ever encounter at iTunes. And I talked with Keith, who ran the email division. Things went well, as far as I could tell. Maybe the round of interviews with the Movies Team gave me some familiarity with the Apple interview process—a process that was much looser and more relaxed than any other interview experience I'd endured in the previous decade. (See the chapter in Part IV: "What I've Learned About: Interviews.") No one I talked to at Apple seemed to have an agenda, for example—they seemed much more interested in whether I was a good fit for the "culture." As evidence, no one I interviewed with ever asked key questions, like "Do you know Excel?" I felt that my résumé spoke for itself when it came to a background in film writing—and handing everyone I interviewed with a copy of *Killer B's* was, I assumed, rock-solid evidence that I was deeply involved in film and film writing.

My short round of interviews for this position lasted only until about noon. When we were finished, Keith escorted me out of the building. And as I was crossing the small lobby, who should come streaking toward me but...Crystal. She'd clearly been lurking in the shadows—literally—until Keith left. She grabbed my arm and led me back into the building, to a nearby conference room.

"We'd like to make you an offer," she said. Only hearing one or two women in my life say "I love you" even came close to the music of those simple, life-changing words.

It seemed pretty clear, even at that moment, what was going on: Movies didn't want to lose me to Newsletters. I was being fought over. *I was being fought over.* By *Apple.* Of course, as I'd told June, the Movies position was essentially created specifically for me, however inadvertently. So in my mind, there was no question which job I'd accept. But Crystal didn't know that. If I had to—if I wanted to—I could pit the positions against one another.

"We'd like to make you an offer," Crystal said.

"I'd like to hear it," I chuckled.

Her offer was immediate employment as the iTunes Movie Guru, with a salary of $100,000 a year.

I'd done it: I'd broken the six-figure barrier.

I told her I'd let her know within twenty-four hours...even though every fiber of my being was screaming, "Say YES! Right now! Sign the papers before they change their minds!"

We shook hands and parted. Once home, I immediately called my advisor on matters of employment, Piph's sister Lucille. Lucille had herself worked as a recruiter, and therefore knew the process, the rituals—and the tricks. It was Lucille who'd advised me not to accept an offer immediately, and not to give any excuses about why it would take me 24 hours to make up my mind. ("You do *not* say you have to discuss it with your spouse," she'd advised. "That makes you seem weak. You should be capable of making a decision on your own.")

Furthermore, in earlier informal tutorials, she'd prompted me to always ask for more money than was offered. "You *never* accept the first offer," she advised. "It makes you look like you're desperate." I thought back to my salary "negotiations" with Steve Shannon at Akimbo, and realized I already had proof of that concept.)

"But what if I ask for more and they say take a hike?"

Her response was a worklife revelation: "No one ever lost a job offer by asking for more money," she said. Whoa! Who knew? (Except, of course, a recruiter.)

"OK, so how much more should I ask for?"

"At your level, a fifteen percent raise is standard." I did some quick mental calculations, starting with the inflated salary I'd told Apple I was making at Adchemy. "Ask for another five grand," Lucille advised. "That'll put you at fifteen percent. If they offered you 100, they're probably authorized to go to one-ten. Maybe higher. So they can't object to another five. And they'll think you know what you're doing."

Done deal. The following day I called Crystal, asked for the 105—"which would put me at the industry average of fifteen percent"—and her response was: "Sure." I was privately gobsmacked—in a good way for once. I got five grand just by *asking?* I got the equivalent of a *car* just by asking? OK, a used car...but five grand is five grand. And (as Lucille educated me) annual raises—a percentage of salary—would result in more cash annually the higher my starting salary. Money would snowball.

I went in. I signed the papers. I drove home and walked into our tiny apartment in San Mateo. And I said to Piphy, "OK, baby. I'm in. After a decade of uncertainty, we can finally start planning for the future."

Monday, March 5, 2007

All that was left was to break the news to Adchemy. And so, on Monday morning, I approached my boss and told him I'd accepted a position with Apple to run the iTunes Movies store.

A bit of a stretch, there—I'd hardly be "running" the place—but I wanted to emphasize the kind of opportunity I'd been offered —as well as the salary that Adchemy could never match. (The full story can be found in the Part II chapter on Adchemy.)

OK, so I lied. But I lied on the side of politeness. It seemed like harmless white lies to assuage the feelings of my Adchemy management. I'd have to be a real asshole to just march in and declare, "I'm outta here, guys. Don't like the work. Never did. I'm going to a real company to do work I've trained for, for decades, while enjoying a salary you could never match. *Adios*!" The first lesson I ever learned about corporate life was: *Don't burn your bridges behind you.* And the good folk at Adchemy certainly didn't deserve to have their feelings hurt. They'd hired me; they'd paid me well; they liked my work. What more could one ask from a job? Except work that engages one's core skills... and provides a quantum leap in salary.

But Adchemy wasn't done with me, not quite yet. Shit. I was hoping my boss Tai would shake my hand and escort me out the door once I'd made the "I've accepted another position" announcement. Or at least agree to one week's notice instead of the standard two. That way I could tell Apple that Adchemy requested two-weeks' notice, and I could take a week off to relax before I reported to Apple. Who knows how long it would be before I could take a vacation from Apple? But such was not to be: I'd leave Adchemy on the afternoon of Friday, March 16, and start at Apple on Monday, March 19. I'd get no more rest between jobs than a weekend. Maybe this was karma—the payment for my lies catching up with me. But I tried to put a positive spin it: my last several "between jobs" periods were counted in months, not hours.

DON'T SIT UNDER THE APPLE TREE WITH ANYONE ELSE BUT ME

Monday, March 19, 2007, 9:10 AM

My first day at Apple, and I was already late.

I'd lived in Silicon Valley on and off for nearly half a century, yet I still took a wrong turn off the freeway on my way to the Apple campus. When I spotted Netflix's pseudo-Spanish style buildings in Los Gatos, I realized my error and rushed to correct it. Within a few minutes, I'd backtracked and found One Infinite Loop, where our orientation was to be held. I also found a packed parking lot. I drove every lane, searched every nook and cranny, only to find every single parking space filled. When I spotted an employee walking through the lot I stalked him with my car until he pulled out and drove away, then slipped into his spot. Let him worry about where to park when he returns.

WELCOME TO THE CULT

Once in the main building, I got my temp badge and was escorted into the orientation room on the first floor. I was half an hour late, but luckily the orientation group was running even later and hadn't started yet.

Were these signs good or bad? I know the Valley, but I take a wrong turn. I end up at Netflix—iTunes' rival, and a company that had refused to hire me. Repeatedly. There's no parking—then suddenly there's one space. I'm late; they're later—and no one even seems to have noticed that I'd arrived late. Trivial details take on a greater significance when under the hyperaware stress of Day One. As if I needed the extra *tsuris*.

There were maybe 20 new hires sitting at a series of long folding tables lining the walls of our conference room, all facing the center of the room. I'd only been gone from Adchemy for a weekend, but I was already getting flashbacks about the workspace decor. We each had a laptop in front of us. Were they going to put us to work immediately? I had no time to ponder this: it was Showtime.

You'd expect a Trainer to open with something like, "Good morning!" or even a more arrogant, "Congratulations on joining Apple!" But no. The first words out of his mouth were: "All those rumors you've heard are true: Apple *is* a cult!"

He got his laugh, then launched into the training schedule. Turns out that as well as signing our papers, checking our new hire packages, getting our phone book-sized insurance packets and being outfitted for our badges, we'd also be spending a couple of hours *learning how to use an Apple computer*. Was this irony or brilliance? We were Apple employees now, but since PCs running Windows were the default tool of most businesses, even Apple couldn't guarantee that any of us newbies knew how to use one of their machines.

Ha! I had an advantage here. I'd been using Macs at home for desktop publishing for years. But in tech terms, my Apple knowledge was outdated to the point of being virtually obsolete. Advantage: Apple. I relinquished any claim on being ahead of the curve and performed all the exercises presented by the Trainers. I was a newbie. I even took notes…including one that read: "There is no IT. If you have a question, ask a co-worker." I was in uncharted territory now.

The orientation finished at noon, and when we filed out of the room, we were all met by our teams—another Apple tradition, I discovered, was to take new hires to lunch on their first day. Marshall, Ross (more on him later) and Crystal all congratulated me (for surviving the orientation, I guess), and we went off to a buffet lunch set up for the new cult members and their teams. I looked around to make sure there was no Kool-Aid.

Eventually it was time to go back to the office—even though I had no idea where our office was. Turns out it was in one of the first buildings in which I'd interviewed: Valley Green 2 (VG2, as it was known internally). iTunes occupied several buildings along Valley Green Drive; ours was wedged between the Apple Fitness Center and the mysterious VG3, a server farm to which access was forbidden for...well, almost everyone. In nearly six years in this location, I never saw anyone enter or leave this mysterious tech temple.

Our building was a repurposed warehouse space built in the "open architecture" style popular in the '90s, with exposed ducts and pipes hanging overhead. These spaces always looked to me like they weren't quite finished; like someone had forgotten to install a ceiling. The three wings of the building had been turned into a maze of cubicles and small, glass-fronted offices around the inner perimeter, like the one in which I'd interviewed with Marshall Dylan—my new boss. The Movies team was confined to a single aisle next to the Old Vets—the Music Store employees, many of who had been around for years. iTunes launched as a music service on January 9, 2001, but I never met anyone who claimed to be there from Day One. And despite the fact that they all sat just a few feet away, the "Music guys," as we referred to them, might as well have been on (and from) another planet, as contact between Them (Music) and Us (Movies) was less than minimal. I'd try to change that, and I'd befriend a number of different Music guys during my time there, if only because they were fun to hang around with.

Floor space was tight even then, and until they could find a separate cubicle for me, I was wedged into Crystal's long, narrow workspace. There was barely room enough for her, but she was a good sport about sharing her tiny domain. Given our literal shoulder-to-shoulder proximity, I brought in a tin of Altoids and did my best not to eat anything for lunch that might later foul the air. Crystal is the only one who can say whether or not I succeeded.

The iTunes Movies Store had launched in September 2006—just six months earlier—and Crystal, due to her incipient nerdiness (not slander—she'd be the first to admit it, and it's something to be proud of), had been designated the store's Programmer. In iTunes, the job description "Programmer" had an entirely different meaning from the typical computer-oriented definition of "a software engineer who writes code." An iTunes Programmer was more like a television network or radio station programmer—the person who determined what titles were prominently featured on the store. In our case, the Programmer also arranged the iTunes Movies home page display for maximum effect. This was my job now.

WHAT A TOOL

Crystal introduced me to the programming tool used by all of iTunes: an internal web app called "DJ." No one I ever met at iTunes knew why this tool was called DJ, although rumor had it that the top-secret beta version created in 2001 had the code name "Jingle," which accounts for the J, at least. Others insisted that since iTunes started by selling music, the programmers were not unlike club DJs, hence the moniker. Regardless of the origin of its name, by using DJ, Music and Movies store programmers could request artwork from the Design department, arrange images on the iTunes pages for their media type, and add links to collections, among other functions. It quickly became clear to me that while Steve had decreed that his devices must be user-friendly, this attitude did not necessarily apply to our internal tools, which were minimal, ugly and buggy.

I also learned that (much like at Akimbo), most of my time would not be spent with movies per se, but with spreadsheets. I worked with an increasing number of spreadsheets over the years, eventually necessitating the construction of a meta-spreadsheet to track where information was located on the numerous other spreadsheets. Even more ironically, virtually all iTunes employees used Excel, the spreadsheet program created by our mortal enemy, Microsoft, but which had become the industry standard. Even after Apple developed its own suite of similar business tools, any co-worker using Apple's "Numbers" alternative was roundly chastised by everyone else for not using Excel like everyone else. (Sorry, Steve.)

The real challenge for the iTunes Movies Store Programmer in 2007 (first Crystal; now me), however, was the dearth of movies. When I hired in, there were only about 700 titles on the service, and they were available only for purchase—rentals were just a pipe dream at that point. We had three of the top ten Hollywood studios signed up to allow the purchase of downloads (two and a half, really, since Lionsgate was a minor player in those days). The Big Two were Disney and Paramount—and Disney was only on board because of Steve Job's influence.

A statement like that could easily lead to an entire chapter on the history of digital movie downloads—or to an entire book. For our purposes, let's just say that Steve was the hero here. Years earlier he'd financed Pixar, which he sold to the Walt Disney Company in 2006—a sale that resulted in his becoming the single largest shareholder in Disney, as well as member of its Board of Directors. I can just imagine the meeting where he informed the Disney Board that he was going to launch iTunes Movies, and despite the major studios' reluctance to go digital, Disney was *going* to permit digital downloading of their films. As Pharaoh said (in *The Ten Commandments*, at any rate), "So it shall be written. So it shall it be done." In a very real sense, Steve Jobs singlehandedly broke the logjam that had prevented the major studios from allowing digital sales of their titles, due to their fear of accepting this new technology, which they pretended was a fear of digital piracy. The iTunes Movies Store featured new releases every week, but plans for upgrading the store included adding themed collections of films to promote catalog (i.e., older) titles...which, given my background in doing that very thing, is one of the key reasons I was hired (I assume).

Themed collections were my specialty as a freelance movie writer—but they proved to be a challenge at iTunes. When writing about film for newspapers, magazines and websites, for instance, I had the entire history of movies at my command. If I wanted to write an article about horror comedies (which I did, "Die Laughing"), all I needed was a quick search and a good memory. But with only 700 titles from three studios available on iTunes, I was forced to be clever enough to find enough titles to constitute a theme. Further complicating matters was the limited space available on iTunes to define the theme of a collection. In an article, I could write a paragraph or two describing the idea and the ground rules for the choices. But since my iTunes work would be seen only on a computer screen, any text description was limited to a few words—a very few words. As an example, the first week we worked together, Crystal and I came up with a dozen titles in which the film's setting was a major element of its appeal (*Forget Paris*, for instance). I suggested we steal a motto from the real estate trade and title the movie swoosh "Location, Location, Location." We congratulated ourselves on our cleverness, and the feature ran the following week.

Now all I'd have to do is find a way to parse out a handful of movies into a different and compelling theme *every single week*.

MEETINGS, *Part 1 of Many*

Digital processing of films was still in its infancy in those days (see the Part II chapter on Akimbo for more details). Once a week Crystal and I met with Ernest, the leader of the digitization team, to set our priorities for the next week's releases. I'd list ten titles we wanted to release, derived from the list that the studios had delivered to us. Ernest's team was able to complete maybe six—seven, on a good week. After several months, his team hit all ten for the first time—then continued to meet this goal every subsequent week. We considered this a major breakthrough. I never asked what kind of upgrades to equipment, personnel and experience they'd struggled through to reach this milestone. I was just happy to get my ten titles a week—at which point we raised the bar to 20, and when they consistently hit that, to 50. Eventually, the team would digitize hundreds of films per week, keeping a staff of engineers and quality control checkers busy 24/7, and we abandoned the concept of a prioritized list altogether. After a couple of years, our weekly meetings changed from an agonizing account of the handful of films they were able to process to a discussion of the few problem titles out of hundreds that had been recently digitized and would be added to the service on a daily basis.

Meetings weren't all business, however. Not when I attended, anyway. In one weekly status meeting a couple of years later, for instance, with about 20 people in attendance, we were all psyched that we were finally getting *GoodFellas* for the store. But the Engineering team had encountered a problem digitizing the film. "It looks...funny," the engineer told me. I realized immediately that I'd just been handed a dream straight line. "Funny *how*," I whined, in a Joe Pesci accent. "Funny like it's a clown; it amuses you?" The room burst out in laughter (except for a couple of attendees who were completely out of the loop and didn't get the reference). Thank you; I'll be here all week.

This was one of the side benefits of working at iTunes: most of my co-workers, were very pop culture savvy. They had to be —we were supposed to be experts in our fields, after all. I could drop a movie line, and as long as even one other person in the room laughed, everyone else knew it was a reference they'd missed, not just some random nonsense.

Sitting in a conference room with a dozen other people, for instance, waiting for the boss to arrive and start the meeting, I was staring through the glass walls when a random worker headed for the coffee pot in the lobby. "Put down that coffee," I growled out loud. "Coffee is for *closers*!" Only one person responded, but he was the guy who'd later take over iTunes...and he nearly fell out of his chair laughing. "Best drop *ever*!" he congratulated me later.

YEAR ONE

Marshall Dylan, Crystal and Ross proved to be excellent co-workers—smart, friendly, and dedicated without being complete corporate knobs. The team took me under its wing and made me feel welcome. For months, for instance, the four of us went to lunch together literally every day. We'd talk movies, promotional possibilities, our weekends, food, company gossip—whatever. I learned quickly that these were quality people, and we got along swimmingly, even when we didn't see eye-to-eye about some detail—like the urgency of doing something new or different. At least once a week, for instance, Marshall would exit his office and muster us for an impromptu motivational session, which always started with the phrase, "Guys, here's something we gotta do right away..." We never got to the point where we dreaded hearing the phrase, but at some point there was a bit of eye-rolling.

We'd meet as a group formally once a week to determine which movies (of those that had satisfactorily completed digitization) should be promoted at what level, and what we might do to upgrade the Movies service in general. And once a week, Crystal, Ross and I would endure a call from the head of Disney's digital division, who often went ballistic over the most miniscule detail. Case in point: He once complained that, in the store artwork for *Finding Nemo*, Nemo's eyes were *one pixel too far apart.* Ross and Crystal showed what I believe was remarkable restraint in responding to this insanity by not hopping the first flight to L.A. and stabbing him in the heart with a pencil, but simply pointing out that *we'd gotten that artwork from him.*

SPRECHEN SIE iTUNES?

As new personnel joined us over the years, I always took the earliest possible opportunity to pass along whatever hard-won wisdom about the job I'd managed to intuit. My first bit of Revealed Truth was always this: *iTunes is a language.* Like many professions, iTunes had its own vocabulary, and the quicker one learned the language, the easier the job (and communication about the job) became.

I meant to spare you, the reader, any technical jargon in this book, but a quick definition of certain specific terms frequently referenced in this section is unavoidable. Most of these are items that customers see when they visit iTunes—the visible tip of the iTunes iceberg that most people knew as "the store."

All iTunes stores were designed visually in horizontal levels, and these are a few of our internal technical terms for those various images and levels:

Showcase: The rotating images at the top of each store's home page/main page, and the place where the biggest releases of the week are promoted. Many customers seemed to consider these "banner ads," but no attempt was ever made to educate users that they were not really ads, but instead, clickable links to the content promoted in the image. (I guess we figured people would figure this out for themselves eventually.) Showcase technology evolved over the years as Engineering upgraded the store. By 2020, in the revamped iTunes in which music, podcasts and video (movies and TV) have been broken out into separate apps, many of these Showcases feature editorial comments, which were strictly *verboten* in my day.

Swoosh: A horizontal line (or "shelf") of product cover images (in my case, box art from a movie's video release). A "slider" underneath the shelf allows users to scroll through the entire shelf of covers (which would "swoosh" by). The number of images allowed enlarged as Engineering upgraded the stores.

Brick: A smaller, non-moving, rectangular piece of art (shaped like a brick, hence the origin of its name) promoting some particular piece of content, like "Prison Movies."

Uber/Duber: An uber is the artwork at the top of the page of a specific piece of content ("über" being German for "above"). If you click on a Movie store Showcase and are taken to an information page and see a picture at the top of the page, that's an uber. In 2007, we were restricted as to the number of ubers we could ask Design to create for us weekly. By 2012, we'd allowed the studios to create and upload their own ubers, so very few film pages were without one. A "duber" was a subcategory of ubers—the "death uber." When some notable croaked, we'd rush a duber into production to capitalize on the publicity and interest their passing generated. (My first duber: Paul Newman.)

Finally, in the wack language of iTunes, there was only one way to request that someone contact you: "Ping me." And there was only one acceptable word to express agreement: "Cool."

HOW iTUNES WORKED *(circa 2007-2013)*

In a company and culture in which change happens with a fast and furious certainty, there were very few things that were obstinately resistant to change. One of these was the iTunes production schedule, which varied by not a minute during the entire six years I was there—and which gives no sign of variation to this day (2020).

The "iTunes week" technically begins on Tuesday at 12:01 AM EST, when the newly updated weekly store is released. (We always referred to it as "the new store," which is clearly a misnomer. The store remained the same; only the content promoted on the media pages changed.) All efforts of all iTunes media departments—Music, Movies, and later, Television, Podcasts and Books—were focused on this weekly debut of new product.

I can sum up the iTunes production schedule in one word: *juggernaut*—a massive, inexorable force, both merciless and unstoppable, that crushes whatever does not move out of its path. Employees had to stay ahead of the relentless forward motion of the production schedule or be crushed by it. Fail to meet a deadline and the juggernaut will roll over you and leave you behind, ruined: your work will not be displayed, and heads will roll. (An alternate dictionary definition of "juggernaut" is "anything requiring blind devotion or cruel sacrifice," which is also both accurate and appropriate, but which will be addressed elsewhere in this narrative.)

A day-by-day accounting might provide some insight into the intricacies of the process. Although I'm using my Movies store experience here, the schedule was essentially the same for all Programmers of all media types.

Tuesday

On Tuesdays, we began programming the store that would launch the following Tuesday ("Tuesday" being defined by iTunes as "Monday night"). Yep, mere hours after the new weekly store was released, it was already obsolete—live, but yesterday's news; background static that had a life of its own and didn't need to be addressed (except in an emergency). Using the online DJ tool, I'd request artwork for movies that would be prominently promoted in Showcases and Bricks. (There was no need to request art for each individual movie that would be featured on Movies Main; this "box art," derived from the video or DVD box cover art, was provided by the studios as part of their metadata package for each title—a package that also included information such as the title, year of release, MPAA rating, run time, cast, director, and so on, all automated to appear on the store without much human intervention).

Each request we made to the Design department would also include any text to be added to the art, such as "$4.99 Movie—Limited Time" or "99¢ Rental." Every one of these tags had to be approved by Editorial—not just to be sure they were grammatically correct, but also to retain a "house style" of text messaging across all media types. It was mind-boggling to me witness how many hours were spent debating miniscule details, such as whether, and when, an ampersand (&) was acceptable.

There were several pieces of information necessary to program each "shelf," or line of movie covers, on the Movies Main page; so much so that I developed a spreadsheet that I dubbed the Programming Worksheet (I am nothing if not literal), on which I collected, in advance, all the pertinent information I'd need to quickly perform the actual online programming. This Programming Worksheet was designed to accomplish multiple goals, including: a) being a single document from which I could program the entire Movies store without the need to stop and look things up; b) acting as a checklist for the finished work I needed to double-check during the store turn, when we launched the week's new store; and c.) serving as a history of precisely what we'd featured during any given week. I had one additional goal in mind for the Worksheet as well: to allow me to spend as little time as possible in DJ, since that tool was such a pain in the ass. My first Programming Worksheet consisted of two pages. Six years later, each week's Worksheet ran more than 20 pages and included six tabs.

Wednesday

Wednesday was Meeting Day, yay! While the Design department was busy fulfilling the requests I'd made on Tuesday, I'd meet with my supervisor—whoever that was at the time—and we'd flesh out the store that would launch in two weeks. The supervisor had already met with his boss and they'd determined the relative importance of the upcoming titles, so our meeting was mostly to pass this information along to me. They decided; I implemented. We'd also choose a theme for the Theme Swoosh and discuss what new movie collections we'd launch. We'd determine specific wording for any text tags—subject to Editorial's approval, of course...which we got pretty good at second-guessing.

Wednesday was also the meeting of representatives of the various media departments to determine the layout of "Main Main," the first page iTunes visitors encountered before they selected a specific media type. Music was virtually always the Big Dog in this forum; Music had seniority, and even when iTunes had launched Movies, Television, and Podcast stores (and later, Apps and iBooks), Music was the Most Favored Nation, or the first-born older brother. Occasionally, however, Movies got top billing on Main Main, when we had a film release that was undeniably higher profile than any of the week's music drops. (*Twilight* beat a new album from John Mayer, for instance—but not without debate.) We counted any Movies-prominent Main Main positions as major victories, and as Movies grew, we fought for more and more of them. "Fought" gives the wrong impression, however, as these weekly meetings were always exceptionally civilized and good-natured—attitudes that can be directly attributed to the attendants. I looked forward to seeing these people—some of whom I interacted with only in this weekly meeting—and sharing gossip and ideas, debating the relative pop culture importance of various new media releases, and defining a storefront that literally millions of iTunes users would see a few days later.

Wednesday was also the day of our big Movie Status meeting, where reps from Engineering and Quality Control would deliver updates to a representative from Movies (i.e., me) about films in the hopper, problems in digitizing, and so on. Reps from Design and Editorial would also attend to deliver status updates about our requests, and we'd discuss and resolve any problems. During the first couple of years I was there, attendance at this meeting grew from two people (me and Ernest) to more than 20 at one juncture. This meeting was one of my favorites...but we developed such a freewheeling style that, as the crowd grew, not everyone appreciated our high-spirited, joking camaraderie, which would ultimately result in Big Trouble for me. (See the Part IV chapter "You Can't Spell 'WHORE' without 'HR.'")

Thursday

Thursday was review day. I'd receive an email from the Design department that included all the artwork for next week's store—the material I'd requested Tuesday—and I'd comb over it for any errors or typos. The iTunes Design crew was superb—total professionals with a keen eye for aesthetics. I rarely needed to return anything for correction or adjustment. Our assigned artist in the early days was Sean Harold, a sharp and efficient young guy. He was promoted after a couple of years, and his direct reports continued his exceptional work. I took him to lunch occasionally—not only to thank him for supporting Movies so diligently, but also because I liked him and enjoyed his company. Over the years we developed a relationship that put him in a very special and very limited category: a co-worker who I considered a friend.

In the off-hours between deadlines and meetings during the week, my efforts were concentrated on maintenance, research for future sales and theme rooms, and writing. With Editorial's blessing, I did what no other programmer in any other iTunes medium did, namely write all the text that appeared on Movies, including short introductions for each of our theme collections as well as the Movies entry in the weekly all-media New Releases email newsletter blast (the newsletter I'd interviewed to compile). (Oddly enough, the woman who was hired to fulfill that position had attended the same college as I had.)

Friday

Friday was the best day of the week for an iTunes Programmer. The deadline for all programming was close of business Thursday, in order to provide the Builders—the next step on this assembly line—enough time to stitch together all the elements from Programming, Design, Featured Content, UI, and other departments, and translate it into something that could go live as a new store the following Tuesday.

Marshall Dylan early on declared Friday as "Work From Home" day. None of us had any meetings or other responsibilities that would necessitate our physical presence on the Cupertino campus. As long as we could be reached in an emergency, we were freed from the commute (and the office environment).

Of course, there was always work to be done—it just didn't need to be done from a desk in Cupertino. I spent many Fridays doing research, prepping for the next store turn, creating spreadsheets of available films for future themes, and so on. "WFH Fridays" would remain a staple of iTunes Movies, surviving numerous changes in management—until just after I left.

Monday

Monday mornings were devoted to our departmental Staff Meeting. We'd review the previous week's sales and statistics for "click-throughs" on various featured content and promotional offers. And since the "new store" that would be launched that night was hands-off to Programmers once the Builders had worked their magic, there was little for a Programmer like me to do in terms of working on the store.

After I'd been on the job about a month, I suggested to Marshall Dylan and to the Editorial lead, Jennifer, that I spend these downtime Mondays writing short reviews for some of our films—text that could be incorporated into the artwork at the top of an individual movie's store page (the uber). Writing was my long suit, after all, and was what I was hired for. They readily agreed. It took me about 90 minutes to research and write a 150-200 word review, emphasizing why a potential viewer should be enthusiastic about watching (and owning) a particular title. It was no stretch for me to emphasize the positive; my movie guide, *Killer B's,* consisted entirely of recommended movies, for example. The trick with iTunes titles was to choose to write reviews of only those flicks I could honestly recommend. The bestselling movies on iTunes in early 2007, for instance, were Mark Wahlberg's action flick, *Shooter*, and Ben Stiller's comedy, *Zoolander*. I chose to write about the latter.

By the end of 2007, I'd written reviews for over 200 movies. And about a year later, the engineers upgraded the store in some way that necessitated removing all the artwork from movie pages, and all 200 of my reviews were unceremoniously shit-canned overnight. I never considered my writing as deathless prose. But I was a bit miffed that it became expendable prose.

TO EVERY STORE, TURN, TURN, TURN

Monday, 9:00 PM

All efforts of all iTunes employees were dedicated toward a single focal point each week: 9:00 PM (Cupertino time) on Mondays, when we'd launch the new store. This weekly "Store Turn" was the front line of the battle; the field where one would prove themselves a warrior or become a corpse. The Store Turn accepts no excuses. The Store Turn takes no prisoners.

Following the precedent of a couple of decades of video releases, no new media could be released to the public for sale until a precisely specified time—in this case, Tuesday. Somehow iTunes managed to negotiate the definition of "Tuesday" as beginning at 12:01 AM East Coast time, which translated to 9:01 PM West Coast time. Californians thus had a three-hour leg up on all other legal sales of "home video" releases, including DVDs. (Other digital movie sales were not only irrelevant but virtually non-existent, as there were virtually no other digital film sites in 2007—legal sites, anyway.) This meant that the most ardent fans of a flick like *Twilight* who lived on the West coast could technically purchase, download and even watch the movie hours before anyone else in America could even purchase the DVD. In more personal terms, this three-hour early definition of "Tuesday" gave us Cupertino iTunes workers a major break, since we could perform the store turn at 9:01 PM and not have to sit up every Monday night waiting until midnight before we could even start the process.

Precisely at 9:00 PM Cupertino time, about 35 iTunes employees—Programmers representing all media types, plus Designers, Builders, Editors, UI and Featured Content overseers, most of us working from home—would open iTunes on our laptops, log into a Chat Room, and start the vetting process. Minutes after 9:00 we'd see the store morph from the current version to the brand new, updated version. That was the starting gun, and the signal to hit the deck running. Every Programmer was expected to check every change on every page for which he or she was responsible. We'd observe the Showcase art at the top of our media's main page and check to ensure it was the correct art, with the correct text tags, rotating in the correct order—and that the link to its media page worked. We'd check Swooshes to ensure they were displaying the titles as intended. We'd check any new features (like, in my case, a new theme movie room) to make sure the link worked and the contents of the new room were complete. And we'd check prices, especially on discount merchandise. (It just wouldn't do have the promotional art for a discounted movie link to the movie available only at full price.)

And so on. We checked literally every element on the home page of our media types. I was always glad that I'd been clever enough to create a Programming Worksheet to use as a checklist to review the new content, so no detail was overlooked (and less memory was required. I've never had a great memory. As far as I can recall.) And if we found a mistake, we'd Chat with someone who could fix it: creating new art; changing a text tag; fixing a broken link, and so on.

One reason to aim for perfection was, of course, that we all took pride in our work. But the practical reason was simply to finish the goddamn Store Turn as quickly as possible. If a Movies home page fix was necessary, it seemed to take forever to correct: a Designer had to fix incorrect art; I had to program it; the

Builder had to build it and push the change to the store... and then we all had to wait ten or fifteen minutes until the change "propagated through the system" before it displayed in the live iTunes store, where we could check it again and move on (or go through another round of correction).

In the early days, this process often dragged on until midnight or beyond...but it got easier year after year. By 2012, I could often check the entire store in half an hour, and the results were frequently perfect—no changes or corrections necessary.

Tuesday Redux

"And when the morning light comes streaming in,
I'll get up and do it again. Amen."
—Jackson Browne, "Pretender"

And then on Tuesday, we'd get up and do it again. The schedule cycle would repeat itself: same efforts, same deadlines, same meetings, same goal. Amen.

The first thing that occurred on any given Tuesday, however, would be to fix any errors that crept through on the store turn the previous night and could not be resolved during the turn. Most errors could indeed be fixed during the turn. But occasionally something went awry that could not be addressed by the store turn crew, such as incorrect pricing. Very rarely was there anyone available on a Monday night who could take the numerous steps necessary to change the price of an item, which often also required consulting with a studio representative—and you *know* those guys weren't gonna sit around on a Monday night waiting for a frantic call from an iTunes worker drone.

THE PRISONER OF iTUNES

As the months wore on, a curious and very personal thought crossed my mind: *Why did no one at Apple recognize me?* After all, I'd hosted "Science Fiction Night" on the Silicon Valley PBS station for six years in the early '90s. Weren't high I.Q., hi-tech Apple employees and iTunes media experts the core audience for shows like *Doctor Who, Red Dwarf* and *The Outer Limits*—

not to mention *The Prisoner*? And yet no one had ever approached me and said, "Hey, didn't you used to be on TV?" It wasn't a matter of ego, really—I'd left that life behind a decade earlier. It just seemed odd. Maybe they were all just too young to remember something that occurred in the '90s, I thought. Or too new to the Valley. Whatever. So I shrugged and got on with my work.

Then one morning when I was in our building's kitchen getting my tea, the Lead Engineer for iTunes approached me. We ran into one another often enough while getting our morning caffeine that we'd developed a "Hi, harya?" relationship. But this morning was different. He smiled a kind of chagrined smile and said, "Y'know, I've been meaning to thank you." "For what?" I asked. "Well, back in the day when you were introducing *The Prisoner* on KTEH, I got invited to a '*Prisoner* viewing party.' And that's where I met my wife."

My takeaways from that conversation: 1) How sweet is that, me being matchmaker for one of the world's finest engineers? And 2) *I'm still famous, goddamn it! Woot!*

A CASTLE IN THE SKY

This is a book about Work, but it's unavoidable that Life sometimes overlaps that narrow topic—in this case: my residence. When I hired into Apple, Piph and I were living in the small triplex in San Mateo that we'd moved to a couple of years earlier so I could be closer to work (at Akimbo) and avoid a 90-minute commute. My life-long preference was never to have a commute longer than 20 minutes, but San Mateo to Cupertino was about a 35-minute drive. Given that I wanted to be closer to Apple—not to mention that we now had the Big Apple Bucks—we resolved to move back to Silicon Valley, and began looking up rentals and vetting them out on the weekend.

And we came away disgusted. The Valley was thick with traffic and pollution, and rentals were outrageously high for outrageously miserable lodgings. Then one day Piph called to me from her computer. "Hey, Honeyman!" she said. "You wanna live in a castle?" I was intrigued. The pictures of the building in Redwood City did indeed resemble a French Normandy chateau, a four-story building complete with a pair of cone-capped turrets that flanked the awning-covered entry. Even more intriguing to me were the pictures of the unit itself—I simply could not figure out what the floorplan was from the photos. It was as though M.C. Escher had designed the apartment.

"Let's call 'em up," I suggested, "and pretend we're interested in renting it and want a tour. Then we can solve the mystery of that wack floor plan." And so we did. And I was sold the minute we entered the building, what with its wood paneling, its thick red carpeting, its central stairwell, and its elevator. An elevator?! The building appeared to me like an elegant grand hotel from the '20s, old and faded in its grandeur, but still lush and comforting. It reminded me of nothing so much as Disneyland's Tower of Terror ride—only benign.

The apartment itself was simply incredible: hardwood floors, a huge bedroom, two full baths, and a living room so large that furniture could easily be used to split it into two still sizeable living areas. The dining room was one of the turret rooms; a semi-circle bump-out of round wall. Best of all were the French windows stretching across the living room and up to the high ceiling—windows that overlooked a quartet of mature redwood trees. And on top of all that, the rent was several hundred dollars lower than we were prepared to spend in Silicon Valley.

"OK," I told the landlord at the end of the tour. "This is the part of the process where we'd usually go off and discuss whether we want to submit an application. But I'm ready to say right now that we'll take it. I have to live in this place." We filled out the paperwork and moved in a couple of weeks later. And loved it.

IN WHICH I AM ALMOST APPLE SAUCED

Once we moved, my commute from Redwood City to Apple was only about 25 minutes—mostly down Highway 280. And, as good fortune would have it, I was always commuting against the flow: as I drove south every morning, there was no traffic. And as I drove north in the evening, ditto. (This, as opposed to anywhere we looked in the Valley, where rush hour traffic created a commute of half an hour even to nearby lodgings. I could live cheaper, faster and better by staying on the Peninsula.)

Highway 280 is, oxymoronically, a rather lovely freeway once it leaves the Valley and winds through the Peninsula: four lanes; graceful curves; pastoral vistas while passing by Stanford in Palo Alto and the nature preserves to the north. But it's still a freeway, and one on which a driver dare not let down his guard.

One summer morning in 2007, for instance, I was driving to work in the next-to-fast lane when I came upon the only other vehicle on the wide road, an open-backed utility company truck in the slow lane. The truck hit a bump, and a pair of wheel chocks came flying off the back. (Wheel chocks are wedges, in this case wooden, connected by a rope, that drivers wedge behind truck tires to prevent the vehicle from rolling.) The chocks bounced erratically at 60 miles per hour. I didn't want to slam on the brakes—I had no time to check if there was a car behind me—and I feared I might run into the chocks if I sped up and tried to speed past them. They bounced again, into the lane next to me. The chocks appeared to be bouncing across the freeway, and I intuited that if they followed that trajectory, they'd bounce right in front of me then off the road entirely, into the scrub along the shoulder. But a piece of equipment as erratically-shaped as two trapezoids connected by a length of rope also bounced erratically…and when they bounced again, they made a 90-degree twist and shot directly toward me. They hit my windshield and it shattered. Pebbled safety glass shot through the car, covering my lap and leaving a huge, gaping hole.

I wasn't scared. Actually, I was rather irritated that that chocks had smashed into my beautiful, beloved Jaguar…so I sped up, determined to pull the truck driver over and accost him. Which I did. He was apologetic and got on his cab radio to call the Highway Patrol, who took down the details (so I could get PG&E to pay for a replacement windshield. Which they did.) And I proceeded to Cupertino.

It wasn't until later I realized that if those wheel chocks had hit even a couple of inches lower, they could easily have decapitated me. And I had one other revelatory insight as well: I realized that if I ever died in a similar accident, I knew exactly what my final thought will be: *Aww, shit…*

WHY RENT WHEN YOU CAN BUY?

Sometime in late 2007, I was informed that iTunes Movies had a new charter: rentals. Following Steve Jobs' dictate, iTunes lawyers had been negotiating in secret with several major Hollywood studios to allow rentals of digitally downloaded movies. The new service would launch on January 15, 2008, and would include rental titles from all ten of the top Hollywood studios.

Disney, Paramount and Lionsgate were already represented on iTunes, selling movies as digital downloads. But soon we'd be offering both sales *and* rentals from *all* the major studios, including 20th Century Fox, Warner Bros., Universal, Sony, MGM, Touchstone, Miramax and New Line Cinema. An Apple press release distributed at the debut of the service in January promised "over 1,000 titles by the end of February."

The ability to rent movies online was, without hyperbole, a milestone in the history of digital media. In 2007, online movie rentals simply did not exist. Even my old company, Akimbo—the company that pioneered online video and movie rentals—had by this time changed its mission and was no longer offering online rentals. Steve Jobs—bless his spiky little heart—had once again changed the world, using his clout and reputation to persuade the entirety of Hollywood to forego their fear of digital piracy and hop on board his Next Big Thing. No longer would "home video" include two trips to the video store to rent and return a DVD. We'd be able to rent movies from the comfort of our couches, offices, dorm rooms—wherever. Movie rentals would be available on computers and laptops, on the iPhone, and through an AppleTV set-top device connected to a big screen TV in our living rooms.

Every department involved in iTunes Movies—those involved in digitization, pricing and contracts, engineering (since rentals required an entirely new type of store functionality), and many more shifted into high gear. Our four-person Movies team clearly had our work cut out for us as well. Even though the technical details of digitizing the films and paying for the rentals were being worked out by the Engineering staff, our little Gang of Four had to determine how to promote the new service, which movies to promote, and how to entice our customers into trying this new-fangled idea of renting movies online.

IN A (MAC)WORLD OF HURT

January 15, 2008

About twenty minutes into his Macworld Presentation at the Moscone Center in San Francisco, Steve Jobs noted that in the previous nine months (coincidentally, exactly when I came aboard), iTunes had sold seven million movies. "But," he sighed, "it did not meet our expectations... We think there's a better way." And he introduced iTunes Movie Rentals. He showed a slide of Movies Main (well, a mockup of Movies Main, anyway) then scanned through a number of big, recent titles that would be among those available to rent: *The Simpsons Movie. Ratatouille. Harry Potter and the Order of the Phoenix. Pirates of the Caribbean: At World's End. Spider-Man 3*. Initially, iTunes would make new titles available for rental thirty days after their release on DVD. (This window of availability would be continually renegotiated to the point where digital releases became available to rent day-and-date with their DVD/ Blu-ray release...with many available for purchase a full two weeks *before* their physical media release.)

And about 30 minutes into his presentation, Steve was done with iTunes Movie Rentals. "I think we've got it all together," he concluded.

Wait, what? He was *done*? And he still had another 45 minutes to go? I sat in the audience feeling proud but confused. He'd said he had four things to talk about in this presentation. Movie rentals was number three of four—the penultimate announcement. But what could possibly be more important than being able to rent digital movies from every Hollywood studio? Digital rentals was groundbreaking. Unprecedented. A game-changer in the home video and entertainment industries. *What the hell could possibly be more important?*

We found out when SJ introduced (drum roll, please)...*the MacBook Air*: "The world's thinnest notebook." WTF? Movies on demand was what I'd dedicated my career to, for a decade.

But this historic breakthrough was trumped by...*an anorexic computer?* Content might be king, I realized glumly, but Apple was, first and foremost (and despite its recent name change from Apple Computers to Apple, Inc.), a *computer* company, and apparently more interested in a new version of an old product than in potential revenue from digital movie rentals—or in claiming yet another place in media history. Steve had plenty of those wins already. What a disappointment.

99 CENTS IS THE NEW FREE

For most consumers, "digital rental" was a brand new world, and our team had to find ways to convince them to try it. In order to promote movie rentals, one of our first tasks was what we'd referred to at ReplayTV oh so many years ago as "customer education" (even though it failed miserably there). I suggested we choose one movie each week and negotiate with the studio to allow us to offer it as a 99-cent rental. Maybe potential customers reluctant to risk three or four dollars on a movie rental in an untried medium would be willing to risk less than a dollar to try the service. That was my rationale, and Marshall jumped on the idea and made it happen. I suggested *Breakfast at Tiffany's* as our trial title, since Valentine's Day was only a couple of weeks away, and we could piggyback on that romantic holiday by offering a classic romantic film. The stats we received the week following the offer showed an enormous uptick in rentals—nearly three times the number of rentals of that title than during any previous week. Ladies and gentlemen, we have a winner! Starting with that first title, not a week has gone by without at least one "Movie of the Week" being offered as a 99-cent rental.

Years later, I'd wonder if perhaps the "99-Cent Movie of the Week" concept would be retired, since it was originally designed only to encourage new users to try digital rentals. I was prepared at all times to defend the program, but it was never necessary to do so—the 99-cent Movie of the Week persists even to this day (2020). *Maybe,* I thought, *that's my legacy at iTunes Movies*. So if you've ever rented a 99-cent movie on iTunes... you're welcome.

CHANGE IS GOOD...CAN YOU SPARE ANY?

I've always said, "In bad times, comfort yourself by knowing 'This, too, will pass.' And in good times, remind yourself, 'This, too, will pass.'"

Our little four-person Movies Store team was a well-oiled cog in the Big Machine that was iTunes. But that Big Machine was growing, expanding, and changing, and our tight little team was forced to change with it.

Crystal, for instance, was always more interested in engineering than in the marketing that was her role in iTunes Movies, and she left us for a new position in advanced features development. Now our department really was an "old boys' club"—just me and Marshall and Ross.

When I was reassigned to report to Ross, he informed me that this type of musical chairs was standard for Apple. He should know, I figured; he'd been here for over a decade. I assured him I had no problem with the reassignment—we'd been working together for over a year, and I both liked and respected him. From that point, and for the following year, we'd sit together once a week and design the upcoming store. I can't recall us ever having a disagreement, much less an argument.

"ROSS"

(*Note:* "Ross" is a Hero, but since he's still at Apple as of 2020, I felt it was in his best interests to protect his identity.)

During my Apple years, Ross would prove to be a model coworker: pleasant, friendly, and enthusiastically helpful. At first, I was slightly suspicious of his attitude—who goes out of their way to be that helpful? Ultimately, I realized there was no hidden agenda with Ross: both his warm personality and his eagerness to assist were genuine and sincere. While we never became friends in the sense that we socialized outside the office, I came to realize that I could go to Ross at any time with any problem and he would drop everything to help me, even long after we were working together.

Ross was not the most handsome guy in the world, but his smile was infectious and stretched from ear to ear. He managed to marry an absolutely beautiful blonde and father two incredibly lovely girls. He'd been around Apple long enough that he was full of Apple lore, as well; when I joked about how someone with a high-powered rifle in the apartment building next to the main campus could hold the whole company hostage, he told me the secret story about how that had actually happened years earlier, for instance. He was to me the epitome of the Apple employee: smart, flexible, dedicated but not jingoistic, and always available. Over the years, and for long after he was my immediate superior, he became and remained my "Apple culture" counselor, as well as my financial advisor and confidante. (And, as of 2020, we still talk occasionally.)

Just so this doesn't come across as a total bromance, I'm willing to point out a couple of Ross's endearing quirks, like how he signed virtually all his emails with the phrase "Please advise?" And if Ross had a single pretension, it was to feign ignorance of pop culture from the '60s and '70s, reminding us that he'd "grown up in Europe and missed that." Those of us who heard him trot out that excuse numerous times took great pleasure in needling him about it whenever possible. ("McDonald's hamburgers? No, Ross wouldn't know anything about those... He grew up in Europe, you know.")

Ross was also a master of psychology. I sat in on any number of his phone calls with studio reps, for instance, many of whom would often suggest some idiotic scheme to increase sales or enhance the position of their titles on the store. Ross would listen patiently, then begin to ask seemingly guileless questions about the mechanics of their idea that gently guided them to realize for themselves the unworkable nature of their brainstorm. It was the Jedi mind trick, or mental jiu-jitsu, gracefully turning an opponent's momentum against them...and it worked. In virtually every case, the studio rep would sooner or later admit, "Yeah, let's not do that. It's a dumb idea." And Ross would smile, his opponent having defeated himself, and without the necessity of argument or insult. This is a diplomatic skill that I lack entirely, but which I admire greatly—and I've never known anyone who could perform it with more panache than Ross.

What I didn't realize when I was reassigned to Ross was what a burden Crystal's exit was to him—a burden that existed solely due to the assignment of job functions unique to iTunes Movies, which included dealing with the film studios. This was a division of labor specific to our group. When iTunes was a music-only service, the burden of communicating with (and dealing with) the various music labels was the province of the Programmers. Andy, who programmed classical music, for instance, dealt directly with reps from Deutsche Grammophon, EMI, London/Decca and many other music labels, to determine what was new and what was worth promoting; to negotiate price reductions and sale pricing; and so on. The TV team followed suit, each Programmer dealing directly with several broadcast and cable networks. Fortunately, I was spared that duty. Films were concentrated in the hands of so few studios, and were such big money business, that iTunes Movies had staff specifically dedicated to dealing with them—namely, Crystal and Ross.

But without Crystal to share his responsibilities, Ross's plate was getting full. He alone had to deal not just with me as his direct report, but also with representatives of all ten major studios represented on iTunes (as well as several content aggregators who bundled independent movies from various sources).

We needed another Ross. Marshall set up some interviews.

NEW CHARACTER ENTERS!

March 2008

Among the candidates we interviewed was a guy named, let's say, "Richard Zucker." Zucker was tall, lanky, and late 30s, with a deep, booming voice. (If I were casting for the movie, I'd choose either Drew or Jonathan Scott from HGTV's *Property Brothers*. With a deeper voice.) He wore a long-sleeved dress shirt buttoned to the top button to the interview, but no tie. Odd, I thought—but who was I to question his fashion choice? After all, in those days, I wore suspenders. It wasn't until he started working with us that I realized why he'd dressed that way: he had a full set of tattoos running the length of both arms and right up to his neck. Clearly, he was hiding his sleeves, in case one of his interviewers had some problem with them, or whatever lifestyle they implied. Frankly, I could care less. I never even inquired how committed an Illustrated Man he was—whether he'd inked his chest, back, lower body, whatever. I did not want to know.

We chatted. It was an interview filled with sharp intelligence and punctuated by laughter. He'd been with Apple for a decade; I later discovered that at that time he was working on some doomed product and looking for a change—a promotion, if he could swing one, I suppose, or simply abandoning a sinking ship. I tried to explain what I did, what he'd be doing, and how our job functions would correlate. I explained that my time was limited, and the technology of iTunes was even more limited—so any requests from the studios that were too time-consuming, self-serving, or impossible to implement technically would complicate both our lives and set us both up for failure. "The one thing I'd ask of you," I said, "is that when you're dealing with the studios, don't write any checks that I can't cash." He seemed to understand and agree.

At some point, I had to ask. "So," I said, tentatively, "your name is Richard Zucker? Dick Zucker?" He rolled his eyes and laughed. "Yeah, I know," he said, "I've been getting that all my life." "Well," I declared, "I'll make you a promise: If you get this position, as long as we're working together, I will never refer to you as 'Dick Zucker.' I'll call you Richard, or Rich, or even Mr. Zucker, if you'd prefer the fake formality. But I won't embarrass you by calling you 'Dick Zucker.'" He thanked me and said he appreciated it. (I lived up to that promise. But we're not working together anymore, Dick.)

And he was hired. He was "the new Crystal," assigned to work closely with Ross, who would tutor him in how to deal with the studios—from their everyday concerns to their frequent outrageous demands. For weeks I sat in my cubicle doing my work, listening to them perform their Studio Relations vaudeville act on the phone, often chuckling at their diametrically opposed methods of communicating—Ross, gentle and, when required, subversive; Zucker, up-front and confrontational.

Richard Zucker and I worked together to implement the agreements he and Ross had cobbled out with the studios, and to design each weeks' new iTunes Store. We had a great time, often debating the pros and cons of a title's placement, the weekly themes, what was worth promoting at what level of the store's main page—Showcase, Brick or Swoosh—always defining and defending our opinions, debating until the other guy agreed. Eventually, we always agreed on the arrangements, even if it took a few rounds of "Shut up," "*You* shut up!," "No, *you* shut up!" to break the tension. I liked this guy. He was smart, he worked hard, and he seemed to be open to having fun with our jobs. And, against all odds, his aggressive extraversion was a comfortable counterpart to my introverted, film scholar attitude.

So...things were back to (relatively) normal—even though I was still putting in 50 to 60 hours a week attempting to keep on top of everything that needed to be done to keep the iTunes Movies Store operational 24/7.

2008: EXECUTIVE REVIEW

2008 was a banner year for iTunes. In January, for instance, Steve Jobs announced that we'd sold over seven million movies, and over four *billion* songs—"surpassing Wal-Mart," the *Wall Street Journal* noted, "to become the biggest retailer of music in the nation."

It was a banner year for iTunes Movies as well. We'd added all ten of the top Hollywood studios. We'd launched movie rentals. We'd begun offering movie pre-orders, HD quality downloads and digital copies (buy a DVD, get a free download of the title). In April, I added a dozen genre-specific pages to the Movies store; in May, we added the ability to rent and purchase movies through the AppleTV set-top box—and on the same "day and date" as their release on DVD. (Articles in the *Wall Street Journal*, L.A. *Times,* Washington *Post* and other media outlets hailed this as "a game changer.") In September, iTunes launched the "Genius" automated recommendation function. In addition, during this same year we launched iTunes Movies stores in Canada, Australia and New Zealand, and the UK (the "Axis of English," as I called it)—and I was tasked not only with training the new store Programmers but also with being their single point of contact with the Big Dog, the US iTunes Movies store. (As our boss at that time informed them in an email, "Scott will be your Obi-Wan Kenobi.")

All these developments were great news for the store...but bad news for me. Each of these upgrades virtually doubled my workload. The AppleTV and iPhone versions of the Movies store, for instance, not only had to be updated weekly, they had to be programmed individually, separately from the programming done on the store that displayed on computer screens—and often required device-specific artwork as well. Ditto the dozen new genre pages. By the end of 2008, I estimated I was doing *eight times* as much work as I'd been doing only six months earlier. I did my best to keep up, continuing to put in 60 or more hours a week (while also teaching college courses in film in the evenings). It was a hump, but things were moving along smoothly.

That's when the feces intersected the air circulation system.

MEET THE NEW BOSS, *Part 4 of Many*

October 2008

It seems that Ross and I weren't the only guys overwhelmed with work. Ross got some relief in the form of Zucker, but I was at the bottom of the totem pole, and only those above me were able to hire relief...people like Eddy Cue, the Apple VP in charge of iTunes. His job responsibilities were growing exponentially—from iTunes Music to Movies, TV, and the new App store, which was just fucking *exploding*. Eddy needed assistance, and his solution was to hire someone to run iTunes. Sometime around Halloween (appropriately enough, as it would turn out), we were introduced to his successor, the new Vice President and General Manager of iTunes, "Gerald Fitzpatrick," at an SRO meeting in our building's main conference room.

Fitzpatrick came with some heavy credentials: He'd been the Acting Chief Operating Officer for Disney's home entertainment division for the previous several years, with "global responsibilities" (and most likely was the Disney exec tasked with implementing that studio's digital involvement with iTunes Movies a couple of years earlier); before that, he held a top management position in sales and marketing at a high-profile food conglomerate. He was in his 50s, maybe; pale, and with a full mane of white hair; a Tony Robbins clone, physically towering over everyone else in the room.

OK, a new boss. My boss's boss had a new boss. So what? Eddy Cue had already created a mean, lean, well-oiled machine in iTunes. The new guy would have to be a complete idiot to mess with success.

You can probably guess what happened next: Gerald Fitzpatrick messed with success.

My first indication that we were in trouble came when he walked the aisles of our cubicle farm in a glad-handing tour, introducing himself to the worker bees and the drones. I was returning from a meeting when I saw a small crowd—Ross, Marshall, a couple of other people, and Gerald Fitzpatrick—all casually chatting and laughing. (It was only the fact that they were gathered outside my cubicle that prevented me from turning around and skulking away from this funfest.) Marshall introduced me, then said to Gerald, "Scott's our resident Disney fanatic." Gerald responded by enthusiastically offering "If there's anything I can ever do for you with Disney, you just let me know!" I wasn't sure what that meant, or what he had in mind. Disneyland tickets? Memorabilia? Get one of my screenplays to Disney's movie division? But I did have one idea.

"Well," I said, "it was my dear old, gray-haired, 80-year-old mother who turned our entire family into Disneyphiles. The one thing I've always wanted to do to thank her is to take her to dinner at Club 33"—the legendary invitation-only private restaurant on the second story of New Orleans Square in Disneyland. "You think you could arrange that?" Gerald's Fitzpatrick's smile froze and turned into a glare. His eyes narrowed and I could almost read his thoughts from his facial expression: "You son of a bitch. You're not actually supposed to *ask* me for anything...and certainly not for something *I can't provide*." Oops! My bad!

The next telling detail occurred a few days later, when Gerald Fitzpatrick called an All Hands meeting to introduce his changes. When he projected an org chart on the big screen, I knew he had no clue about "Apple culture." Rule One of Apple: *We don't do org charts.*

But clearly Gerald Fitzpatrick *did* do org charts, and his was a shakeup of magnitude 8.0. His reorganization of iTunes juggled several levels of management...but (like the projected org chart) didn't stretch far enough down into the sub-basement to include me. As usual, I was so low on the totem pole that I was literally off the chart. Less than zero.

The changes above me, however, were distressing. Gone were Marshall and Ross—their invaluable work in creating and launching the iTunes Movie store was *so* last year's news. Apple, like most sociopathically soulless corporations, seemed to operate on the principle "What have you done for me lately?" Marshall and Ross had created iTunes Movies, but now that the store was up and running, a new set of management skills was (allegedly) required to expand the store, both domestically and globally. Evidently, Gerald Fitzpatrick assumed that Marshall and Ross did not possess those skills...in which case, they simply weren't needed anymore, and were cast aside.

But not cast out. Both were reassigned to nebulous assignments that I couldn't help but suspect were designed to ease them out of Apple or provide them with an incentive to quit before they could be dumped. Ross, for instance, was bumped to another position in iTunes Movies marketing, in charge of organizing "special projects." Even that position seemed to evaporate after a year or so, but Ross remained in some other nebulous marketing position. I was never quite sure what that position entailed, but Ross had been around for many a year and was flexible enough to retain a position in Apple.

His new assignment seemed to be a compromise: "Get him out of the way, but don't get rid of him completely." This new position also seemed to distress him somewhat, although he was too savvy to ever express his discontent publicly. He seemed to accept it philosophically; I got the impression that he followed the advice he'd given to me, understanding that positions and management changed virtually annually, and he should just settle in, endure the blow he'd been handed, and wait for an opportunity to upgrade his job or position. In the meanwhile, he would perform any task he was assigned with the utmost professionalism, if only to stay on board at Apple, so he could continue to live in pricey Willow Glen and raise his lovely family. Good for him. Marshall, too, was shunted aside, given a nebulous assignment designed, it seemed, to convince him that if he wanted to advance his career, it wasn't going to happen here.

MEET THE NEW BOSS, *Part 5 of Many*

Crystal had transferred; Ross and Marshall were ousted. I was now the only remaining member of the original iTunes Movies team. Worst of all, according to Gerald Fitzpatrick's org chart, my new boss was a guy named "Buford Squack." Wait a minute... I knew this guy. He was one of the lawyers who negotiated the contracts with the Hollywood studios that made iTunes digital rentals possible. The fuck did he know about movies, except as a saleable commodity, like potatoes? And yet, there he was, prominently featured on Gerald Fitzpatrick's New, Improved Apple iTunes Org Chart, as the new boss of both Richard Zucker and me.

I knew Squack slightly. He had a cubicle across the aisle from me, and we had a cordial if distant relationship. Our paths rarely crossed; when they did, our interactions essentially ended at "How ya doin'?" My primary impression of Squack was that he was an Okie—a skinny, goofy-looking, unsophisticated hick, complete with an annoying drawl that made him sound even dumber than he looked. This was my new boss? Fuck me.

Squack lost no time in taking over. And we hit it off right from the start, except...no. In a meeting with Squack and Zucker to discuss our various roles, for instance, I ended up saying, "You guys make the deals. I'll run the store." It didn't take me long to realize that I had completely put my foot in my mouth with that statement. What I meant was, "You make the deals; I'll implement them," or, "You give me direction; I'll take care of the details of getting your decisions on the store." But what I'd said came out completely differently—arrogant, dismissive, disrespectful. Squack visibly bristled at what he thought I meant. Clearly, he wanted complete control over the store, and resented that I'd postured myself—his employee; his *subordinate!*—to lock him out of any decisions about the weekly storefront.

In short, Squack and I rubbed each other the wrong way from Day One. I can't claim complete innocence here: I resented the change in management, and I thought he was a rube who had no clue about either movies or of the everyday workings of the store (which would prove accurate soon enough). I did my best to keep these opinions to myself, however, and act like a professional. But I've never been good at hiding my true feelings, and I'm sure my sub-surface resentment could be detected beneath my attempt to maintain a "friendly professional" veneer.

BOBBING FOR FRENCH FRIES

My relationship with Squack only deteriorated from there. On the first Monday night store turn of his new reign, for instance, he was online watching the process—and interfering with it to the point of annoying everyone else involved (something like 35 people trying to do their job). The following morning, I dropped by his office as soon as he arrived, and attempted to give him an explanation and a gentle course correction, as diplomatically as I could. "Mark Twain said something like anyone who likes sausages or laws should never watch either of them being made," I began. "The same holds true of the iTunes store. The point here is that every Monday night at nine o'clock, thirty-five iTunes employees gather in a chat room to perform the store turn. We've all been doing this for years, and we're there to spot problems and fix them. That's our job. Last night, I saw your numerous emails about discrepancies, and I need to inform you that every one of the problems you pointed out had already been spotted and was already in the process of being fixed. Your emails just complicated and slowed down the normal procedure, and it's a measure of the respect we all hold you in that the people you emailed treated your requests so politely. But since I'm your direct report, I want you to look good to our co-workers, so I feel it's my duty to tell you what's really going on, even if you don't like it. The key point here is that participating in the store turn is *way* beneath your level of concern. You really don't need to be involved in it. You need to trust us. And if there's a problem we can't solve during the store turn, I guarantee you, you'll be the first to know."

I have no idea how he took my admittedly awkward attempt at diplomacy. But I do know that he never again interfered in a store turn.

Our relationship continued to deteriorate, even as I tried to repair it. A few weeks into Squack's new administration, for instance, I realized that, as a "legacy employee"—someone he'd inherited rather than chosen—he probably had no idea why I'd been hired in the first place. This was an opportunity! A chance for a fresh start! If I could explain to him that I was originally hired to create features for the Movies store rather than just program it on a weekly basis, I might be able to begin doing the job I'd trained and studied for, for over 20 years...the job I was hired to do.

I sent Squack a formal meeting request, for the sole purpose of re-introducing myself, my background, and my mandate at iTunes Movies.

"I'm currently programming the Movies store," I began, once we'd settled into the table that served as a meeting area in his office, "but I'm only doing that because there's no one else to do it. The job I was hired for is quite different. You're familiar, I take it, with the Music store's features—biographies of artists and bands; detailed criticism and reviews; themed features centered on various genres, and so on—all those features spearheaded by Gary Stewart?" Yes, he was. "Well," I continued, "I was hired to do the same thing for Movies. I was brought on board to be the Gary Stewart of iTunes Movies. I've already written over two hundred reviews for movies on the store, for instance, and I should be creating features like themed collections, to promote catalog titles."

I showed him a copy of my résumé and walked him through it on a line-item basis. First, I established my "movie guru" cred: More than 200 published articles on film. Ten years as the Video Columnist for the San Jose *Mercury News*. Teaching film courses at the college level. *Killer B's*. Then I focused on my work history over the past decade: Senior Editor at three different media companies, responsible for all taxonomy and onscreen descriptions and text. "In all my previous positions," I continued, "my job function was about ninety percent creative and ten percent technical. But if all I'm doing here is programming the Movies store, that ratio has been reversed. Sure, I can program the store as well as anyone—but anyone could be trained to program the store. It doesn't require any in-depth knowledge of movies. So, as long as I'm not performing the creative tasks I was hired for, iTunes is ignoring and, frankly, squandering my core strengths—the detailed knowledge of movies for which I was hired."

Squack listened attentively, without interruption. And when I was done, he shared his own perspective. "We don't need editorial features," he stated bluntly. "I hate that shit. The iTunes Movies store exists for one reason and one reason only: to sell movies." These are verbatim quotes...and the end of the meeting.

Thus endeth my career...

DOWN IN THE VALLEY

...but not my job. I went back to my cubicle in a daze. My plan for nearly two years had been to wait patiently, programming the store until I could pass that job function on to a more technically oriented person, and then assume my mandated role as a featured content creator. But this unexpected disruption in management had rendered that goal impossible. My temporary job, Movies Store Programmer, was now my main job description. And it was a job that played to my weaknesses (tech) rather than to my strengths (writing, and knowledge of movies).

So now I was just another Programmer. I had no creative assignments. I had no decision-making ability. I was nothing more than an implementer of other peoples' decisions. A lackey. A gopher. A keyboard peon. Any hope of claiming my original mandate had vanished in the bad attitude of a guy who was the trifecta of assholiness—lawyer, middle-management moron, and marketing douche—a guy who saw what I had to offer after twenty years of work, study and effort, and then stated to my face that he hated "that shit." What I'd hit was not a glass ceiling, but an ass ceiling.

Well, fuck me. My future dream job had turned into a nightmare. I was no longer a movie expert. I was no longer a contributor to iTunes Movies. I was little more than a console jockey.

What the hell was I supposed to do now? Leaving was out of the question. There was literally nowhere I could go with my VOD skills, except maybe Netflix, and I'd already been rejected by them three times in less than ten years. I could tweak my résumé to emphasize my writer/editor skills, as I'd done to get into Adchemy, and seek employment outside the VOD field—Marketing, maybe. But I'd hated that work—and if I went that direction, I'd have to admit to myself that my years studying film had been a waste. A dead end. Worst of all, Apple had become for me the same kind of money trap/honey trap that Lockheed had been a couple of decades earlier: There was nowhere I could go with my VOD and film-specific skill set to command the kind of six-figure salary I was getting at Apple.

In every job I've ever had, no matter how stoked I was to be doing it at the beginning, at some point some event occurred that made me say to myself, "*Well, the honeymoon's over.*" My iTunes honeymoon was definitely over. So I sat at my desk and programmed the store. I just did my job. I stopped making creative suggestions—neither Zucker nor Squack wanted them. They just wanted to sell movies, and refused to believe that features and theme collections in any way "moved the needle" on sales and rentals. My job was simply to implement the decisions they made about which titles to promote at what level, in the order they'd determined would sell the most movies. My job was simply to place the right video box covers on the right shelves.

I was, I realized, little more than the world's highest-paid video store clerk.

I was reminded of Joseph Campbell's story about businessmen who spent their lives climbing the corporate ladder only to discover that it was placed against the wrong wall. Maybe all I had was a corporate stepstool...but even that had been yanked out from underneath me.

SQUACK ATTACK!

Squack's approach to managing the store seemed to be "Do the exact opposite of whatever you were doing before." We had weekly differences of opinion about details as minor as, say, how many titles to include in the coverflow. He wanted fewer, so the user wasn't overwhelmed. He wrote in one email "...we need to get away from the mentality that the more shit we cram into our page the better... this great company I know of named apple [sic] has proven that with their marketing and product lines. diversification [sic] works in investing, but not in retailing." (The lack of caps in this email is all Squack.) Both Zucker and I wanted as many titles as possible on the Movies Main page, since illustrating breadth of content was a major weak point of the store, and the coverflow could be reprogrammed daily if we so desired, with no need to involve any Production department other than the Builder...who took direction from me. When I suggested that viewers liked lots of titles in the cover-flow, Squack's response was: "Prove it with data!"

Squack also began objecting to my approach to the weekly "theme swooshes" on the Movies Main page: "...our merchandising efforts should be around customer segments" (i.e., demographics.) Collections I'd created such as "The Big House" (prison films) and "Military Madness" (war movies), "don't have a common appeal," he emailed me. I responded that my approach was to create "themes [that] cut across genres and demographics. No one is going to buy all 8 sci-fi or date movie flicks, but a larger cross-section of customers can find one movie...from a theme that includes solid titles drawn from a number of genres." He acknowledged the logic but insisted on his approach: "...something meant to be a little for everyone ends up not being much for anyone." I disagreed—but not to Squack. His mind was made up, and the fact that I'd sold a couple of hundred newspaper and magazine articles based on my approach made zero difference to him—it wasn't selling movies. And so I was constrained by demographics to create theme swoosh collections for, say, "teenage girls"... collections which would be ignored by anyone *but* teenage girls browsing Movies Main, thus sacrificing two-thirds of our users who had no fucking interest whatsoever in what movies teenage girls wanted to watch. (This was all complicated by the fact that Apple's privacy policies prevented us from sorting film sales and rentals by demographic; on more than one occasion I had to ask one of my young nieces or nephews "what movies you kids are watching these days" to get an idea of what to include in a swoosh.)

When I lobbied for a great little film, *The Life Before Her Eyes,* to be in our "Best of 2008" feature, Squack offered to buy me lunch "if it [sold or rented] more than 50 copies per week." When I responded that sales were irrelevant as a criterion for choosing the *best* movies of the year ("...we should have at least one of them actually *be* one of the best movies of the year"), he countered with this (the lack of caps is all him): "ha! sales are never irrelevant. title of this should be 'best movies of 2008 that we think you'll buy once we show them to you.' we exist to sell and rent movies...nothing else. if there's some mystery in that then we have a problem." That "nothing else" apparently included quality, critical opinion, informed guidance, and any of my other core contributions. This was mercenary merchandising at its finest, I realized. (As if that wasn't bad enough, in an email a few days later, Squack requested that this title be removed from the "Best of 2008" feature altogether, since a customer review made comments "about anti-abortion christian [sic] stuff... I don't want any more controversy." It made no impression on him when I pointed out that the customer's comments were mistaken—there was no "anti-abortion christian stuff" in the film.)

And it only got better—if we define "better" as "far worse." When I showed up at Squack's office one day with data that indicated that: a) my workload had increased eight-fold in the previous year, and b) that I was putting in more than 60 hours a week (which was illegal), his response was this: "Why don't you write me up a list of all your job functions and the time expended on them." Although my Vulcan brain understood that he wanted this information to justify hiring another programmer, my Klingon brain spoke first: "I come to you and tell you how overworked I am and your response is to give me *more work*?" I assumed I'd expressed that more as a Vulcan than as a Klingon, however, since when I left his office, the walls weren't all covered in blood.

Oh, Squack and I were definitely off to a flying start...if I could just avoid crashing and burning...

HAVE YOURSELF A BRUTAL LITTLE CHRISTMAS

The management shakeup continued to create aftershocks from the top down. As the end of 2008 approached, Gerald Fitzpatrick decided that we'd all been lazy lima beans and that we had to make a balls-to-the-wall effort to *sell, sell, sell* iTunes media over the upcoming Christmas season. He decreed that throughout December, representatives of each media type would meet every morning at 8 AM to discuss what they were doing to hype their merchandise. I could almost feel the collective groan among the working class—my people. My own start time was 10 AM. But since that was often earlier than either Zucker or Squack arrived in the office (or were willing to), naturally I was tasked with attending these daily 8 AM meetings and reporting on whatever ideas they were promoting and the sales promotions they were planning. Oh happy day. The hours were long and the tempers were short. Often these early touch-base meetings would be attended by grouchy grunts like myself, resentful of having to arrive hours early to report that *not a goddamn thing had changed since yesterday*.

Marching orders came thick and fast in those days, as Gerald Fitzpatrick attempted to turn the world's biggest ship on a dime, when any good captain knows it takes miles to modify the course of so large a vehicle.

Gerald Fitzpatrick's mandates were complicated by his ignorance…or, to be a bit kinder and gentler, by his newness. He had no idea of the standard procedure or process of creating a feature on iTunes, or of the timing and resources involved in implementing many of his mandates. And neither did lawyer-turned-media-expert Squack. But, as we all know, shit flows downhill, so it often fell upon me to take their outrageous demands to the Production teams—Design, Features, UI, Engineering, Build, Editorial—and bear the wrath of those departments...and then have to attempt to explain to my own superiors why what they wanted was, according to Production (the umbrella department encompasssing all the aforementioned units) *absolutely impossible*...and to bear *their* wrath. Translating between the uneducated and the unwilling was not part of my charter. No one wanted to hear what I had to tell them...and that disconnect would come back to bite me on the ass in a few months.

INTO THE WEEDS!

Further complicating our new management's lack of knowledge of the iTunes process—particularly of the technical limitations—was their insistence on hands-on interference in the most trivial details. Without stooping to that level here, I will mention a single example: an email chain involving some *seventeen people* (including some I'd never even heard of before), all determined to chime in on the appropriate wording of a single tag on a single piece of artwork. Should it read "Great Movies Under $10"? One voice objected to the use of the adjective "Great," claiming it sounded "too editorial"...in other words, it was an unsupported opinion. Another objected to "Under $10," when he spotted a $14.99 title that somehow snuck through the price filter. A third insisted we must include a time limit, like "Limited Time Only," prompting another to insist that "Limited-Time" must include a hyphen, and a third to point out that this was too much text for a tiny piece of artwork. And so on. At least this idiocy didn't go unnoticed or unchallenged; even Squack sent an email to everyone but Gerald reading, "For Christ's sake, can't we keep [Gerald] out of the weeds on this?"

Him, we could keep out of the weeds. The rest of us…not so much.

HAPPY HOLIDAY SCHEDULE!

Possibly because Steve Jobs' father had worked for Lockheed, SJ adopted the same holiday schedule for Apple as Lockheed had used for years. Throughout the year, employees would work a few holidays that most other businesses had off, like Martin Luther King Day and President's Day. Those days off "owed" to employees would then be clustered at the end of December, so the entire company (with certain exceptions) could enjoy a full week off between the day before Christmas Eve and the first Monday after New Year's Day. Although Apple store employees and many engineers had to work those days, the rest of us got anywhere from a week to ten days off, depending on what day of the week Christmas fell in any given year.

This schedule was a gift, but it made perfect sense for iTunes. In order to clear internet bandwidth for those millions of users who wanted to spend the iTunes gift cards they'd received as stocking stuffers, virtually all iTunes employees were locked out of the system for that time period. We couldn't make any updates or changes even if we wanted to, outside of the most dire of emergencies—and even that would require approval at the highest levels. Like all holidays at iTunes, however, this lockout necessitated enormous additional effort in the weeks leading up to the holiday break. If every single detail on the store wasn't perfect on December 23rd, when the lockout began, heads would roll, since the store as it appeared on December 23rd would be what millions of iTunes users would see for over a week.

December 26, 2008

At last, some relief! I settled into the break period—until the day after Christmas, when I received a frantic phone call from an Apple employee I didn't know, waking me at 8 AM. He needed a paragraph of description for a movie that Steve Jobs was going to mention in a presentation, and he needed it *in an hour!*

"What?" I said, groggy from being awakened far too early. "Steve's giving a presentation *today*? The day after Christmas?"

"Oh, no," he explained. "This is for a presentation in February. But we're putting it together now so he can rehearse."

I was too flabbergasted to be angry. But it did give me some insight into Steve Jobs, and the kind of insane loyalty he could command—and of the 24-hour dedication to the job (and to The Jobs) that Apple demanded.

Bottom line about the Christmas sprint: we survived. And iTunes posted record sales for that holiday season...even though we most likely would have had record sales even without the annoying early musters and meaningless meetings.

Chapter 27

2009: THE GOLDEN APPLE OF DISCORD

"Hail Eris! All Hail Discordia!"
—Robert Shea & Robert Anton Wilson, *Illuminatus!*

MEET THE NEW BOSS, *Part 6 of Many*

January 2009

At heart, I am—against all evidence and despite my better judgment—an optimist. Given a week off, and a Christmas in which for the first time in a decade I actually had a bit of expendable cash to invest in presents for my sweetheart—I was feeling pretty good when we all returned to work in January. True, I knew I'd never have my dream job. But I also knew that if Ross's concept of frequent management shifts was correct, I might someday get newer management that might be more accepting of my original mandate.

Turns out that Ross was correct, albeit ironically. On January 29, Squack emailed everyone involved in iTunes Movies, from his boss to the entire Production team, announcing that Richard Zucker would be taking over the day-to-day operation of the Movies store, "tasked with responsibility for all movies programming, content planning and merchandising," in addition to studio relations. "Of course," his email continued, "considering the above, Scott Apel will now report to [Richard]. This will give Scott the support he needs in terms of day to day direction ...so he can focus more effectively on merchandising."

WTF? My co-worker was now my boss? Promoted to a position that did not exist until Squack created it? My immediate impression was that Squack was simply tired of dealing with me and my "editorial" focus (versus his "merchandising" attitude), so he promoted Zucker and made me Zucker's problem. The collateral damage to me was immediately apparent. Could Zucker and I ever again debate the layout of the store, now that he was my putative boss? For sure we'd never again play "No, *you* shut up." His word would be law. My argumentative co-worker was now my boss, which put an end to any debate about how the store was going to be run. It was going to be run exactly as he decided it was going to be run, following the direction of *his* boss, Squack...a guy who had no use—or even any respect—for my core skills.

Additional collateral damage: Once again, a level of management had been inserted between me and my boss, pushing me down the org chart. I'd been with Apple less than two years and I was already being demoted. (Technically, I wasn't being pushed down; they were building up new layers on top of my foundation, heaping more misery on my already overburdened shoulders.) I had flashbacks to both ReplayTV and Akimbo, where new levels of management were inserted above me, effectively pushing me down the management ladder and putting a barrier between me and the decision makers.

Oh, and just in passing, thanks, Mr. Squack, for informing me face to face about this change in management structure instead of simply taking the coward's way out and forcing me to discover this change along with everybody else, in a general email. How insulting *that* would have been! Oh, wait...

I sat with Zucker to discuss our new roles. I explained that I thought of myself as his "First Officer"—Commander Riker to his Capt. Picard. I was there to remind him of the regulations, to protect him from error by questioning iffy decisions, and to offer alternatives and bounce ideas off of him, but ultimately to implement his orders. His response: "I never watched that show."

It was about this time that I made a list of people who had the power of authority over me. If any of them said, "You have to change this," I had to change it. Only Squack, Zucker and Gerald Fitzpatrick were my immediate superiors up the Movies totem pole. But I also had to conform to the will of Editorial, Featured Content, and four additional people in other departments. I felt like Peter Gibbons in *Office Space* when he tells the consultants, "I have eight different bosses right now. So that means when I make a mistake, I have eight different people coming by to tell me about it." I also realized that while my management had no problem branding me with the demeaning term "wordsmith" instead of "writer," I thought they might object if I returned the favor and referred to them in their various prestigious levels of management as "salesmen."

And still—*because I am a goddamned optimist, goddamn it* —I counted my blessings: the paycheck, the steady employment, the esteem of working at one of the world's great companies. Livin' the dream!

SUNDANCE LIKE NOBODY'S WATCHING

One additional blessing revealed itself in January 2009: I didn't have to go to Sundance. While that might sound counter-intuitive—why would a Movie Gury *not* want to go to the world's premier indie film festival?—the whole scenario sounded like a horror show to me. Strike One was the weather. The annual Sundance Film Festival is held in the little mountain town of Park City, Utah...a quaint, snowy mountain town with January temperatures averaging between 37 snowy degrees in the daytime and 20 frigid, snowy degrees at night. And did I mention the snow? As a Californian, I didn't even own a coat, much less the kind of foul weather gear and footwear necessary to endure ridonkulous weather like that.

Strike Two: The movies start screening at 8 AM, and every single screening is a crapshoot. Sometimes you'll luck out and see a random flick that will be buzzed about by critics for months. More often, however, you just get the non-shoot part of the crapshoot. I should be at a movie theater at 8 AM to buy a pig in a poke? I think not.

Strike Three: Even if I attended the festival, the Movies store would still require programming for the following week on its typical schedule...and since, I was informed, the Apple cabin outside of Park City had no Wi-Fi, I'd have to: a) find a way into town every morning; b) find an internet café from which to program the store; and c) miss all the screenings because I was *doing my fucking job*. And in the evenings, the full extent of my participation at any party—if I was even allowed into any party

—would be that I'd be part of the audience for the celebrities, the investors, and the studio douches. I'd be the background for their celebrity fuckfest—an extra in the movie that was their fabulous, high-profile lives. What fun!

Squack and Zucker urged me to accompany them and a couple of others who were eager to attend. I suggested I should stay in Cupertino, attend our weekly meetings, and generally "hold down the fort." They bought it...and I had a week's breather while they schmoozed and glad-handed C-list celebs and froze their testicles off (I hoped).

THIS LITTLE PIGGY WENT TO MARKET

By January 1, 2009, the iTunes Movies store had nearly 4,500 titles available for purchase or rent (or both)—a far cry from the 700 titles on the store when I'd come aboard in March 2007 (like 6.5 times more titles in less than two years).

My education—in both Marketing and executive insanity—kicked into high gear under the new regime. As Squack wrote in an email to me on January 9, following a review of my 90-day goals, "In my view, the biggest opportunity you have is to develop and demonstrate a greater commercial/marketing sensibility for the mass market and effectiveness in merchandising for and speaking to our largest customer segments." I could hardly point out to him—not if I wanted to keep my job, at any rate—that this was never my mandate. Or my background experience. Or of any interest to me whatsoever.

He wasn't finished with me, either, as this email grew increasingly more strident (all the lower case words, missing punctuation, and typos are verbatim): "flexibility: were changing things fast. speak your mind, lets have the discussion, but lets move on once a decision has been made," for instance; and "none of us works on an island. you can't operate like you autonomously merchandise the store and the rest of us are there to 'run the business'. if that used to be the case, it clearly is not [sic] longer."

SILLY RABBIT…METRICS ARE FOR KIDS

"Your methodology sucks!
—*Cannibal Women in the Avocado Jungle of Death*

So how was I supposed to prove my efficacy, my "effectiveness in merchandising"? I ran into this same difficulty in every one of my media company editorial positions: there was simply no way to quantify my efforts. There was no way to indicate their merit or success; no way to measure the effectiveness of my writing to determine whether or not it influenced a purchase. Did my writing encourage sales? Did it have any effect or impact whatsoever? While I'd dodged the bullet of a statistical evaluation (and judgment) of my work, I could also never point out that my work was of any monetary value. Even so, I determined to try.

In January, I attempted to illustrate to Squack (and by extension, his boss, Gerald) that I could indeed merchandise to our "customer segments," by coming up with two new collections: a selection of movies that appealed mostly to "tweenage" girls (*Mean Girls, Twilight*) entitled "OMG!," and one full of outrageous, scatological comedies targeted at teenage boys (*Superbad, Step Brothers, Pineapple Express*) entitled "LOL!" Design produced a pair of minimalist bricks to promote these features—just the text against a pink or blue background—and they received immediate feedback. "Freaking brilliant!" Marshall Dylan wrote in a general email. But Gerald hated, hated, *hated* them, calling the artwork "cheesy," "sophomoric" and "off-brand." (I had to assume that this guy, who'd obtained his position a full two months earlier, had in that time completely mastered what the "iTunes brand" was, more so than those of us who had worked there for years.) The wider the debate raged, the more polarizing the entire concept became. But bosses are like Highlanders—there can be only one—and Gerald doubled down, deciding that not only did the artwork suck, but the entire *concept* sucked. Within a few days, OMG! and LOL! were DOA. I pulled them from the store, once again wishing Marshall Dylan was still my boss—and despairing of ever mastering this "merchandising" thing, at the altar of which Squack and Gerald Fitzpatrick worshipped.

That altar must have been pagan, because it clearly included human sacrifices. Not only was my blood shed regularly (if symbolically), but Squack had no love for movie studios that did not fall into line either. He regularly requested that some individual title, or occasionally *any* of that studio's releases, not be featured as prominently as we'd planned, because the studio had failed to agree to whatever deal he was attempting to negotiate with them. It always seemed to me a bit misguided to "punish" a studio this way when the real effect would be to reduce *our* sales and inconvenience *our* customers. When Disney was recalcitrant about some point concerning the digital release of their animated flick, *Bolt*, for instance, Squack ordered that the title be placed low in our Movies Main cover flow. "*That'll teach those Mauswitz guys to f*** with iTunes!*" Squack wrote in an email to Zucker and me on March 20. (Pretty bold talk for a guy who in 2019 would end up as middle management at Disney+. Not to mention that the term Disney employees came up with to express their discontent was spelled *Mauschwitz*.)

My favorite example, however, came from Squack through Zucker in a November 2008 email in which I was instructed to ignore a set of titles from MGM in a feature I was planning because "WE THINK MGM ARE A BUNCH OF BITCHES." (Yeah, all caps.)

APPLE FRITTERS (OUR TIME AWAY)

Life under Gerald Fitzpatrick's leadership was...odd. Early on, for instance, he insisted that the Movies team do "store visits" to check out the competition. These grade-school style "field trips" were supposed to occur weekly. I think we made one. We piled six or eight people into an SUV and headed for the Hollywood Video store in Santana Row, a new, upscale mall in San Jose, just a few miles down 280 from Apple's HQ.

We cased the store for an hour or so, like a wolf pack, as Gerald and Buford pointed out displays, discounts, genres, and whatever else captured their short attention span as something our store was doing wrong, or something smart that we could steal and repurpose for iTunes. I refrained from pointing out displays like "Staff Picks," which would clearly be "too editorial" for their merchandising minds. (As Squack reminded me in an email on January 13, Gerald "already thinks we do way too much editorializing.") I didn't mention that I was a Contributing Editor to Hollywood Video's website. And I certainly didn't mention that I planned to return to this store later—alone—to purchase a couple of DVDs that were selling at a price far below iTunes' price.

Gerald also took on the role of arbiter of taste. On January 26, Squack wrote Zucker and me that Gerald was "not super happy with all of our programming these days and honestly, he's justified most of the time... His criticisms are fare [sic]." My subsequent email exchange with Zucker went like this: *Me:* "If he [Gerald] is 'justified most of the time' in his displeasure, why did he OK all the programming? Clearly, it's all our fault for agreeing with [Squack]." Zucker's reply: "no shit. i am not happy about this."

THE LIGHT AT THE END OF THE TUNNEL (IS AN ONCOMING TRAIN)

In March, I actually received some good news: After repeatedly assuring me over the previous six months that he was "seriously considering" hiring a second Programmer to provide me with some relief, Squack actually began setting up interviews for candidates. (An email from him some five months earlier, for instance, included the line "We are working urgently to get you some help, btw." If five months is what Squack considered "urgent," I'm glad I never had a heart attack in his presence.)

I was prepared to give Squack a list of requirements for a Junior Programmer position—the distillation of my knowledge of two years on the job—but he had only one question for me: "Do we need another movie expert, or can we just hire a keyboard monkey?" And once again I obtained some insight into the workings of his alleged mind: Since I was a movie expert who he'd effectively blocked from implementing any movie expertise, in his view I was clearly little more than a "keyboard monkey."

I brought my former Akimbo assistant, Jana, in for an interview. I knew how well we worked together, and I knew she could handle anything Apple threw at her. I also thought it might be nice to extend to her the same kind of major career break I'd gotten when Apple tapped me. But even though I would be the person working most closely with a junior Programmer, mine was only one voice among many in the hiring process, and no one seemed to care that Jana and I were a proven team. On April first—a date which should have sent up a red flag—Squack announced his choice: the position would go to "Andrew Merry," an internal candidate who was currently working on the Quality Assurance team for movies. For Andrew Merry, this was a major promotion. For me, it was a major headache.

MERRY, ANDREW (GOOGLE, IT)

"Andrew Merry" was a Millennial and a hipster wannabe (although "hipster wannabe" might be redundant). Anything more I could say about him would be even more derogatory. So I will, of course, say it. He was thin, sprouted a hipster goatee, and wore hipster glasses with thick black rectangular frames. He was 30ish but acted about 13. During his one-on-one interview with Zucker, for instance, Andy asked, "How metal are you?" Zucker, with his tattoo sleeves and annual Coachella pilgrimages, could claim some legitimate metal cred. But how "metal" one was was hardly a basis for employment (except, perhaps, in iTunes Music). When I found this out, I was curious why he didn't ask me how "metal" I was, the ageist whippersnapper. His loss, since I actually had an answer, even though I'd cribbed it from the cartoon series *Metalocalypse*: "I'm so metal that I buy live lobsters and throw them into pots of boiling water because that's *the most metal food ever!"*

Even though he wasn't my first choice, Andy was smart and pleasant and eager to prove himself. But we ran in problems from Day One. Literally. We'd agreed to share a double-sized cubicle during his training period, so I would always be close at hand to assist him and answer questions. After he settled into his new work area, we began his training...during those periods when he wasn't checking his iPhone for messages, which was literally every five minutes. (Yes, literally.) As a college professor, I'd had young students before—mostly people in their late teens and early 20s, so I understood that they were easily distracted when listening to a lecture (which is why I always repeated the key points twice, since half the time half the class was thinking about sex), but I'd never experienced this ADD-level of distraction before. I tried to be cool about it, but after a couple of days of his frequent distractions, I had to ask him, "Are you waiting for test results from your doctor or something?" He seemed confused. "No, just lunch plans," he replied. "Well, I'd think you'd be more interested in learning your new job," I said, "...the job that pays for your lunches." He took the sledgehammer hint from the Old Fart and cut back checking his phone messages to only three or four times an hour—or anytime I turned my back. (Yes, literally.)

Ultimately, Andy proved reliable (enough), capable (enough) and pleasant (enough) to tolerate. It was an effort to train him, but I was committed to making that effort. If he fucked up, no one would blame him—they'd simply conclude, "Scott didn't train him well enough." So ensuring that his performance was at least adequate was a win-win situation—and a virtual necessity.

I occasionally wondered if I had appeared to my elders at Lockheed as the kind of goofball Andy appeared to me...so I cut him some slack at times when I wanted to just smack him silly. (I hardly needed to do that—he was silly enough already.) One exchange gave me some insight into his attitude toward me, however. We were talking about *Star Wars* and the briefing given to the fighter pilots before their final run on the Death Star. I suggested that when the Rebel leader running the briefing asked if there were any questions, I'd love to see some random guy in the back row raise his hand and ask about the Rebellion's health plan. "We don't *have* a fucking *health plan*," the Trainer would shoot back. "We're the fucking *Rebellion*, for fuck's sake!" "Well, what about overtime policy, then?" the pilot would ask, sending the Trainer into an apoplectic fit. I riffed on this idea of a member of the rebel forces treating his position like a corporate job ("Will my performance in this Death Star attack be on my annual review, if my Supervisor lives?"), and Andy was in stitches, doubled over with laughter.

After a few minutes of this, he asked, "Where'd you hear this?" So I told him. "I didn't hear it anywhere. I'm making it up as I go along!" And as quickly as if someone had hit his OFF switch, Andy immediately stopped laughing. "Oh," he replied, and turned back to his keyboard. So if it was someone else's routine I was reciting, it was brilliant and hilarious. But if *I* was creating it, how could it possibly be funny?

Even so, by September, when annual Performance Review time rolled around, Andy's comments after his six-month training period stated that "Scott has been a champ. He never hesitates to offer help nor does he complain with the kinds of nit-picky questions that come up when you first learn a job. My experience with him has been almost one-hundred percent positive."

EPISODE V: THE EMPIRE STRIKES BACK

June 11, 2009

"...can someone without a sense of humor
be taught to have one, or must it be beaten into him?"
—Jack Handey, "The Mysteries of Humor,"
The New Yorker, January 15, 2018

When I walked into our weekly Wednesday afternoon meeting to discuss Main Main content placement, I was surprised to see my immediate superior, Richard Zucker, in attendance. He'd never come to one of these meetings before. Maybe he was actually interested in learning something, I thought. Oh dopey me.

Immediately following the meeting, he led me to another conference room, where a third person was waiting. I recognized him as a member of Apple's HR staff. This should have sent up a red flag...but what did I have to be concerned about? I was a model employee.

Turns out I was wrong. HR Guy had a two-page document that he slid across the table to me—a document that turned out to be a catalog of my "offenses" against Apple and its employees, compiled by my peers.

The infuriating (and humiliating) details can be found in the Part IV chapter "You Can't Spell 'WHORE' Without 'HR.'" For the purposes of this portion of the narrative, however, suffice it to say that a number of people had each contributed a miniscule detail to a catalog of "corporate culture" crimes that included such transgressions as "he missed a deadline," "he doesn't always answer his phone," and "he sometimes makes sarcastic comments." HR chipped in their own indictment, that I was "argumentative" —a Catch-22 characterization specifically designed to undercut any explanation or defense.

My favorite allegation, however, was this: "He tells jokes that not everyone understands." That one bothered me. "I tell 'jokes some people don't understand'?" I replied to that ludicrous "transgression." "Why is that my problem? What am I supposed to do, not say anything? Not join in while others around me are joking around and enjoying themselves?"

HR Guy shrugged. "Maybe that's a good idea," he said. "Maybe you should restrict your communication to only work-related information."

I was gobsmacked. How was this possible? I was always on my best behavior at work, and I seriously believed I was upholding the Apple culture in every way possible, like injecting a little levity to brighten up my peers' days. But, it seems, not everyone —one humorless agitator in particular, I realized—saw me that way. And now I was in deep, deep Applesauce. I was assigned to a program entitled "Documented Training"—a kind of probation, where my immediate superior, Richard Zucker, would be required to accompany me to *any meeting I attended,* to monitor my behavior and ensure I didn't offend anyone. Zucker didn't defend me in this meeting, and sided with HR at every turn, even though once the HR rep was gone he admitted that this entire action was "bullshit." It was at that precise moment that Richard Zucker stopped being a "Richard" in my mind and became a "Dick."

It took me far too long to realize that virtually every alleged transgression on this HR document was the direct result of the Christmas crunch a few months earlier (with the possible exception of making jokes that someone born without a humor gland had failed to understand). I'd been caught between the rock of our new management, who made impossible demands that I was required to pass along to Production, and the hard place of a Production department that was inflexible and overtaxed.

I say they were "overtaxed," but we were *all* overtaxed during that period, and I'm not willing to let them off the hook that easily—not after their sneak attack on me. *No Plan B* isn't journalism, so I have no need to be "fair and balanced" any more than Fox News does. The fact is that those in charge of one or more of the Production departments at that time were rigid, inflexible, and procedure-driven. They would insist that I follow their procedures while never actually spelling out their procedures...and the only answer I ever got to my questions about their procedures was, "You should know that by now." It was fucking frustrating, not to mention stupid and downright rude. And yet, here they were now, the stupid and rude, abusing the company's harassment policies by filing a formal objection against me for attempting to do my job—that is, for attempting to implement my management's ridiculous requests—and for trying to alleviate the situation with humor which some (or more likely, one) among them clearly did not understand.

If I'd figured all this out quickly enough, I might have appealed to my management to intervene in the HR process—to step up and take responsibility for "my" transgressions, like missed deadlines that were, in reality, the direct result of their demands and their ignorance of iTunes production procedures. I could point to things like the email Squack had written in November 2008, early in his tenure, asking me to handle some Design problem because "I'm already in enough trouble with Production." I could point to an email chain among Squack, Zucker, and myself in which they identified the guy responsible for spearheading my HR censure as "that prick," because of his attitude and inflexibility, or to the chain that named "that prick" again a few days later, when we received some substandard work from his department and Zucker wrote, "This is exactly the kind of thing Scott was trying to resolve last week and got beat down by [that prick]."

If I'd figured out the genesis of these complaints quickly enough, maybe I could have even counted on my management for intervention—to address HR directly and explain that I was not at fault for attempting to implement their requests. But I didn't figure it out until far too late, and had to settle instead for the, ahem, "support" of my management. Zucker himself admitted the charges were "bullshit"; as for Squack, I had to settle for an email that read in part "I know that was hard to hear. Thanks for being receptive to the feedback. You have my full support as you go through the process."

Yeah, thanks for making your support necessary, you egregious anus. And even bigger props for telling, me a year later, once all the burned bridges were rebuilt through my dedicated effort and I had redeemed myself by all accounts from all my peers as an exemplary employee, that you "didn't think you could do it." Now, that's support!

Once HR Guy left the meeting room, Zucker and I sat there.

"This is bullshit," I said.

"Yeah," he agreed. "It's total bullshit. But ya still gotta do it. Just play the game."

Yeah, OK. I'd play the game. If my sense of humor wasn't appreciated by Apple, then Apple wasn't going to get the benefit of my sense of humor. I would follow HR Guy's suggestion and simply never engage in conversation of anything other than work-related matters, even if it meant my co-workers wrote me off as that humorless old guy with no personality. It wasn't like they'd care; I was twice as old as most of them anyway, so it's not likely we'd become friends, or that they'd want me to hang out with them. But the majority of my co-workers, who *did* appreciate my personality, would be sacrificed to the minority that did not. I would become the invisible antiquarian who had no personality—a sure-fire way to connect with my hip young co-workers. As with my run-in with HR at Lockheed a decade and a half earlier, the lowest common denominator would once again define the acceptable behavior of the entire group.

Well, if that's what Apple wanted, that's exactly what they'd get. But they'd be suppressing—and would be deprived of—the best of me...much as my own management had done in eliminating the main reason I'd been hired as Movie Guru, leaving me stranded as a Programmer with no creative capacity.

This decision was a mixed blessing. On the plus side, I didn't have to work so hard to be amusing and to lighten up the workplace. My co-workers would have to do that for themselves. On the negative side, I would have to adopt an entirely new persona to display in the workplace—not the happy, jovial comrade, but the quiet, serious, all-business old man who never added anything to meetings or discussions. I would have to build an internal censor that prevented me from participating in any joviality. If I had a quick comeback to someone's comment, I would have to train myself to bite my tongue.

Ironies abound. Here I was, for one, always the "A" student, now being given low marks in "plays well with others." And what a difference a decade makes! Ten years earlier, I was swapping jokes with my CEO; now I was prohibited from being funny. And another: During all the years at Lockheed when I actively attempted to be subversive, I was pretty much ignored and left alone—encouraged, even, since I was hired into the Video/Film department to inject humor into industrial videos. But now that I had taken a sip of the Apple-flavored Kool-Aid and was actively attempting to be a Good Employee, I was slapped down, castigated, chastised and censured for subverting the "culture."

The ultimate irony, of course, was that in a company that claims to worship individuality, I was being instructed to *not* "think different," and to *not* be myself. I was being ordered to be someone else. It was a sad realization that I had more freedom to express my personality and felt more comfortable being myself at Lockheed, the old school, conservative dinosaur, than I did now at hip, bleeding-edge Apple.

Speaking of Lockheed, it occurred to me that, like some rampant cancer, HR was evolving since the days of my first run-in with them, becoming more and more powerful. In 1993, HR had the authority to demand the removal of a non-work-related item in my cubicle (or anyone's workspace, for that matter) if someone claimed it was offensive. In 2009, HR "suggested" that I not engage in any non-work-related *communication* in case someone might find it offensive. I cannot express how delighted I am that I will not be employed in 2025, when HR will conceivably continue this trajectory and escalate this intrusion to prohibit any non-work-related *thoughts*…just in case someone might find one offensive. I hope this is one.

So, only two years into the job, I found myself in a peculiar —and precarious—position. My management didn't want my skills and knowledge, and didn't want me to do the job I was hired to do. And my co-workers (or at least one vocal, humorless, self-proclaimed definer of Apple culture with some power of persuasion over his employees) didn't want me to be…me. As I mentioned earlier, in every job I'd ever had there came a moment when I'd realize that "the honeymoon's over"—but I'd never had a job where I'd had to invoke that phrase of defeat so frequently.

I TROUBLE

In light of this appalling development, I made a difficult decision: I wouldn't get mad. But I would get even. First, however, I'd have to dig my way out of this grave that had been dug a teaspoon at a time by my "peers."

Well, I'd known since the outset that I'd joined a cult. Maybe I hadn't taken as big a drink of the Kool-Aid as I'd assumed. Now it was time to drink from a Big Gulp cup. If I wanted to remain at Apple, I decided, "I" would have to become...someone else. I would have to craft a persona that I would put on like a mask every time I entered the office or dealt with an Apple co-worker. I could not be myself. I had to be somebody else. I would have to become a person who no one could possibly complain about, even if that meant they had to strain to remember who I was because I was so forgettable. I would have to reinvent myself as the ultimate "friendly professional"—smiling, bland and hollow, but helpful, error-free...and Politically Correct.

This was not an easy task, but I did have a couple of advantages. First, I stopped caring. My original mandate—to create an iTunes Movies store that mirrored the depth of knowledge and passion of iTunes Music—was dead in the water. My position was no longer a mandate to create a world-class film site; it was now simply to do what I was told. My professional position was no longer a calling, a labor of love…it was just a job. I'd get the same paycheck whether I beat my head against a wall to create features that enhanced the store or simply placed movies on digital shelves as ordered. And the only reason to beat your head against the wall is because it feels so good when you stop.

Second, I actually had some training in being "someone else." I'd taken acting classes for several years, for instance, and in the '90s had hosted the weekly "Science Fiction Night" programming on Silicon Valley's PBS station, performing as the goofball "King of the Nerds" (a persona that was described by one correspondent as "relentlessly cheerful"). And I performed that character every week for six years, through depressing employment, even more depressing unemployment, and even through the heartbreak of both romantic breakups and divorce. No one ever suspected the true emotions I was feeling when I was on camera. I was *good.* Oscar-caliber good, I thought on occasion. So I could certainly pull this new character off.

I developed several ground rules. One was that I would never, *ever* miss a deadline again, no matter how short or trivial or stupid. (I should be online on a Sunday at 6 AM for the launch of a shit title like *Kung Fu Panda* because the studio was releasing the DVD at Walmart at that precise moment and had granted iTunes the honor of a simultaneous release? No problem, boss! You just go ahead and sleep in while my entire weekend schedule is shot to sh— *Oops!* Can't say that, ha ha!)

I borrowed a second rule from my old Lockheed co-worker Norman Leigh, and his necklace with the "KMS" ("Keep Mouth Shut") ornament: I'd go to meetings and smile and listen while other folks joked and regaled us with stories of their weekends or escapades or whatever. I would laugh and nod and agree at the appropriate times. But I would not join in. If you never say anything, you never say anything allegedly offensive—and therefore, you never get in trouble. It was abundantly clear that there were a few fucks—I mean, *folks*—who didn't want to hear what I had to say anyway. The rest—the people who might actually enjoy something I had to say—would have to go without. Their loss. Apple's loss—and Apple's choice.

Ground Rule #3: Be sincere. Be sympathetic and empathetic. Who can find fault with someone who's always on your side? So I swallowed my native cynicism for the benefit of people who—although I barely knew them—I liked.

And thus I set about attempting to repair relationships that needed no repairing, and rebuilding bridges that someone else had torched.

Over the next couple of months, few people noticed this drastic change in my personality—that I'd undergone a humorectomy. When the rare, insightful co-worker asked why I wasn't amusing anymore, I told them the truth: "I've been prohibited by HR from being funny." Maybe the job-blocking analysis related to me in confidence following a job interview years earlier was, in fact, an accurate assessment: *"Too funny to work in an office environment."*

EPISODE IV: A NEW HOPE

June 2009

I don't know how it happened. Maybe my boss Zucker lobbied his boss, Buford Squack, on the idea of including new editorial features for the Movies Store. Maybe Squack finally came to his senses and realized the store did indeed need "that shit" (i.e., editorial features). Maybe his boss, Gerald Fitzpatrick, observed that iTunes Movies had nothing similar to the features Netflix was creating, and sent a directive to Squack to create some features. Maybe they all got busy, or comfortable in their jobs, and just ignored us. I don't know. All I know is that we began to sneak themed features onto the store—features that promoted merchandising and sales, of course...but themed features nonetheless.

In January, for instance, I suggested we gather all our standup comedy films into a room entitled "Standup Guys." (Sorry, emancipated ladies, if the phrase is sexist—but that's the phrase.) In February, we launched a room full of "buddy" movies (*Lethal Weapon, Rush Hour, Dumb and Dumber*, etc.) under the title "Bromance." And in March, I made a case for a room that gathered together iTunes' best Australian movies, like *Strictly Ballroom, Gallipoli* and *Crocodile Dundee.* (I also included *Babe,* although, technically, that's a New Zealand film). (A couple of years later, I used this room as a wedge to expand into an umbrella feature entitled "Destination Movies," with separate collections devoted to films from numerous countries including France, the UK, Ireland and Japan.)

And by late June, Zucker had received the green light to create a new editorial (i.e., non-sale-oriented) feature on the store. In an email sent just before our 4th of July holiday, he announced that we were going ahead with a series of "thematically grouped collections editorially chosen by us as the best of breed." After more than two years, there was finally a chink in the armor, with a ray of light shining through. Maybe I'd finally get to do the job I was hired for.

Hold it right there, Mr. Optimism. When I went to Zucker, volunteering to start pulling together title lists, he cooled my jets: "Save it for the big meeting next week." Why would I do that? I can get started on this immediately. "But that would put everyone else at a disadvantage," he replied. Everyone else? Everyone else *who*? "Oh, I've invited a *bunch* of people," he replied. "Dan from Editorial. Lydia from Production. Andy. Our summer intern. And Gary Stewart. Among others."

Oh. I got it. My job—the job I'd hired into iTunes Movies to perform; my mandate to be the Gary Stewart of iTunes Movies—was now the dominion of a committee. A committee that included our summer intern, whose input would be considered the equal of mine. The opinion of the Movie Guru would be reduced to merely one vote in a democracy...a democracy of people who had no background in film (except Andy, of course. He'd worked in a video store). In a democracy, all voices are equal, so the voice of the loudmouthed Producer who'd once worked as a birthday party clown—just like the voice of the guy who did studio relations, and the voice of the unpaid, temporary summer intern—was clearly the equal of that dumbass keyboard monkey who'd published over 200 film articles and a book, taught college film courses, and had a video column in a major newspaper for over a decade.

At least Gary Stewart was invited, I sighed. He knew movies. He had taste and knowledge and a brilliant brain—and he knew the difference between personal indulgences and objective criticism. And he had a mastery of dealing with office politics that I lacked. Maybe he and I could team up against the amateurs invited into the selection process and—against all odds

—create something that would actually display some critical insight. Maybe.

In our initial meeting, we defined what this feature should be. I suggested we *not* call it "Essentials" echoing the similar iTunes Music feature, since we didn't yet have all the movies in any genre that would constitute a bulletproof critical list of "essentials," and that we should save that specific word for a later feature. We finally landed on "iTunes Picks" as the overarching title for the feature. We pooled our knowledge of the limitations of the iTunes technology and decided that each genre-based page would contain six "lockers," each containing six titles. This would give us the opportunity to critically select 36 films, which we would then group into half a dozen subcategories—if we could. Zucker insisted that this feature must be a "catalog" promotion, eliminating newer titles to promote sales and rentals of older titles. No one, including me, had a problem with that: it would be presumptuous to include a recent title in a selection of films we were trying to promote as among the all-time best.

I wrote a blurb for the feature, which doubled as a kind of Mission Statement to guide the selection committee: *What is an "iTunes Pick"? It's a must-see movie. An iconic film. A generally recognized "best of breed." Our iTunes Picks are also a handy way to discover the cream of the crop of a theme or genre. The choices—often the result of spirited debate among the iTunes Movies team—constitute a collection of culturally significant films that are also great entertainment. Click a theme and start exploring...and enjoying.*

We established a schedule: We'd meet every week, and release a new iTunes Picks every two weeks. We discussed and debated the categories we thought would work for our customer base, and decided to kick it off with one of the most popular (i.e. best-selling) subgenres: romantic comedies. "iTunes Pics: Rom-Coms" would launch later in July, followed by iTunes Picks features devoted to Sci-Fi, Romantic Dramas, and "Films of the '90s." We all began combing through spreadsheets of titles currently available on the store (as well as "wish list" titles we would keep an eye out for, if and when they became available, to add to the feature).

I never openly protested the idea of a bunch of amateurs choosing the "best of breed" titles, even though the very idea seemed to undermine the concept of critical analysis. (It's not elitism or splitting hairs to point out that there is, in fact, a difference between "an opinion" and "an *informed* opinion.") But I did go into each meeting prepared for mortal combat (but subversively, with a smile and polite arguments). It turned out to be unnecessary. I liked everyone who attended these intellectual free-for-alls, and I actually missed our intern when she left—if only because her absence changed the group dynamic. The amateurs had some solid opinions, and, as I saw it, represented the point of view of our customers—the viewers, rather than the critics. And Gary Stewart always had solid reasons for including (or excluding) a particular film. He and I were nearly always in agreement—and that consolidation of knowledge seemed to outweigh any objections by the undecided amateurs. I looked forward to these meetings and the debates and discussions they included. It was a hell of a lot more fun than sitting alone at my desk, programming the store. The group-mind selection process wasn't as simple and efficient as it would have been had the selection and definition of the *crème de la film* been solely my responsibility. But I rarely came away from a final title list disappointed.

Zucker apparently felt that the committee approach was working, and he continued to use that format for the next several years for various features, like our annual year-end review, "Rewind," and our aborted attempt in late 2011 to create a weekly feature, "iTunes Buzz," imitating the back page "Bullseye" feature in *Entertainment Weekly*. While our excitable group was gung ho over the idea of a "Buzz" feature, they soured considerably when I began asking simple questions like "Does iTunes have the technology to support this? And who's going to make the selections and do the writing and programming?" These were key production questions. I thought I was the voice of reason... but all I got in return was a reputation as a foot-dragger.

One more representative story about my role in the group meetings: We all loved Wes Anderson's movies. Zucker and Andy and I would quote *Fantastic Mr. Fox* dialog at length for each other's amusement, for example. ("Cuss me? Cuss *you*!")

And so I suggested that we should create an "iTunes Movies Award" and give the first one to Wes Anderson. Not only would it be great publicity, but it would give us a chance to invite him to The Cupe and hang out with him. Every time I brought this idea up, however, it was greeted with the same response—individual variations on: "That's stupid." And then in one of these group funfests, Richard Zucker announced some exciting news: "Eddy Cue has decided we should create an iTunes Movies Award and give the first one to Wes Anderson." The responses ranged from "Cool!" to "That's awesome!" And when the cheering was over, I asked the crowd a simple question: "Where have we heard this idea before?" OK, so I didn't make any friends rubbing their brown noses in their hypocrisy. But it had to be done. (The upshot: We never did create an iTunes Movies Award and never gave it to anyone, including Wes Anderson.)

Over the next couple of years, we created something like two dozen iTunes Picks pages. A quick check in 2017 couldn't find a single one still on the store.

PERFORMANCE REVIEW ANXIETY

Many years ago I suggested to a friend that when people attend high school and college reunions, they ought to be issued an old yearbook to pass around so former classmates could write down what they recalled about you from that time. His response: "Man, you *are* a masochist, aren't you?"

Well…no. But if it took a masochist to think up this idea, it took a sadist to implement it. Which, of course, brings us to HR.

Although this might be common practice in companies in Silicon Valley (or around the world, for all I know), Apple's annual Performance Reviews included solicitation of comments from one's peers about the subject's performance. Each employee was allowed to submit to their management a list of co-workers from whom to request these remarks; the responses were purely voluntary on the part of the peers and anonymous on the Review. (I declined to comment on the performance of anyone who I considered less than stellar, although if I'd been granted the opportunity to express my opinion of the knob who organized the HR action against me a few months earlier, I would have had no hesitation in flaming that flaming asshole.)

EGOMANIA vs. CYA

Before delving into Performance Reviews, let me make a few points very clear.

First, while I'm including only a sampling of comments, they are a *representative* sampling. I am not cherry-picking just the best remarks to make myself look good. When there are unfavorable comments, I've included those as well, if only to provide some illustration as to the confusing nature of contradictory perceptions.

Second, while I've gone into some detail (and will again in future chapters), these details are not included just to toot my own horn. In 2013, these reviews would become very important in establishing my efficacy as a "Solid Performer" at Apple.

And the final reason is, of course, because I'm awesome and want to toot my own horn. If the above seems contradictory, all I can do is quote Walt Whitman from *Song of Myself:*

> "Do I contradict myself?
> Very well then I contradict myself.
> (I am large, I contain multitudes.)"

PERFORMANCE IS CONFORMANCE

By the time my annual Performance Review rolled around in late September 2009, every one of my teammates and colleagues seemed to notice a difference in my attitude—although the various peer comments were at best multi-faceted. "Scott has had a year of ups and downs," Zucker wrote in his summary. Well, yeah. In the Ups column, he noted that "Without Scott there would be no new iTunes movie store each Tuesday." But in the Downs column, it was confusing to compare side-by-side peer comments like, "Scott could be more pleasant and less sarcastic" with "Scott's definitely toned down the snark." (It appears that there is a sliding scale of snark.)

As for being "argumentative," I apparently argued at least a couple of co-workers out of that opinion. "I've noticed that some of his best ideas have come from his desire to push back or offer alternative suggestions to a problem," said one, for instance; another wrote that "When he pushes back, he gives good reasons or raises good questions." No argument there!

Evidently, I was making progress in rebuilding a relationship with peers with whom I'd never had any real problem in the first place…and that this progress was not just in being more congenial with my colleagues. Maybe I was getting a handle on that elusive Marketing thing as well. "Scott's strengths, besides his knowledge of film, are his writing and, honestly, his marketing ideas," one peer wrote. "Despite his anti-business demeanor he often comes up with some really good ideas." (Another co-worker mentioned "I've seen some major shifting of attitude with him regarding his keeping his '60s era anti-corporate dogma in check." Yes, in check—but still a core belief.) And Zucker's analysis was that "He consistently has good merchandising ideas."

Only one peer contributed a comment that I thought was deeply insightful and one hundred percent accurate: "I'm guessing that many of the problems of the past were mostly due to his being spread too thin." Thank you, nameless colleague, for your understanding.

Chapter 28

2010: AN APPLE A DAY

"The rest of the ... year is a jumble in my recollection
of the daily strife and struggle of our new lives..."
—Charles Dickens, *David Copperfield*

By 2010, we had pretty much sanded down the rough spots in our weekly procedures and were on our way to becoming a well-oiled, smoothly-operating machine. As one example, I performed my third perfect store turn in a row on January 5th. What could possibly go wrong?

APPLE 2010: PROFESSIONAL MILESTONES

March 2010

We were hit with several tragedies in late March. Squack got in a car accident, for instance; although he was fine, we were all a bit shaken. (I didn't like the guy, but I didn't want him dead. What kind of monster do you think I am, for Christ's sake?)

Far worse was that a member of the Build team, a vivacious and enormously personable young woman whom everybody adored, was swept out to sea and drowned while attempting to save her dog from the same fate. All of iTunes was dumbfounded. A little memorial held in our lobby a few days later resulted in both prayers and tears.

Simultaneously with these events, we stopped hearing from Gerald Fitzpatrick. *No news is good news*, I figured. And then one day we were called into an All Hands meeting and who should show up but...Gerald Fitzpatrick, with his arm in a sling (which went unexplained). He announced he was leaving Apple, and this was our opportunity to thank him and say goodbye. (I chose goodbye.) He gave no reason for his departure. No one I talked to had any clue about why he was out as quickly as he'd been in. Given his early-morning holiday meetings dictum, I speculated that he'd proven himself a "Rotten Apple" and was summarily dismissed, although the cast and sling suggested that maybe he was dying of cancer or some rare, bone-destroying disease, and was physically incapable of fulfilling his duties. I struggled to hope I was wrong about that diagnosis (which I was: a Google search in 2017 revealed he was working as a media expert for a state government. So he ain't dead yet.) Anyone who knew why he was out wasn't talking—not unusual, given Apple's culture of secrecy.

All we knew for sure was that after a year and a half, Gerald Fitzpatrick was gone—and that the damage he'd done in reorganizing iTunes lived on as his legacy. If he was fired, no one stepped in and reversed his reorganization (perhaps because that would be tantamount to admitting that hiring him was a mistake in the first place); if he'd left voluntarily, no one stepped in to perform a second reorganization that might correct or undo some of his more ridiculous decisions. Squack's momentary boss might be gone, for instance, but Squack retained his Fitzgerald-granted position as head of iTunes Movies... so his appointment of Richard Zucker as store manager remained intact as well.

To Gerald Fitzpatrick, all I can say is: So long, you meddling motherfucker. Thanks for fucking up iTunes, my job, and my career and then fucking off, leaving little behind you but a wake of destruction.

April 2010

On April 10, the iPad was released—and we had a whole new Movies store to program, with its own specific restrictions on art and functionality.

A far more interesting Apple event occurred in April 2010, however, when an Apple engineer accidentally left a prototype iPhone 4 in a beer garden. This unreleased model iPhone was quickly obtained by the tech website Gizmodo, where it was dissected and publicly discussed. The story—and Apple's outrageous machinations to recover the lost device—is a matter of public record.

My connection to the affair, however, is lesser-known. The engineer left the phone behind at the Gourmet Haus Staudt, a

Redwood City taproom, the day before my birthday—a birthday that I celebrated at this same location, since I lived in RC, loved beer, and had discovered this local treasure only days earlier. (My friends and I would soon afterward make this delightful beer garden our Friday night hangout…and Piph and I would tie the knot there a couple years later.)

May 2010

By the end of May, Production reached a new milestone by successfully digitizing 300 movies in one week—a far cry from just three years earlier, when we had to prioritize ten movies each week and considered ourselves lucky if we got even half of them ready for release on the store.

June 2010

In June, Russian President Dmitri Medvedev visited our campus. Nobody I knew at Apple ever saw him; we only knew about it because SJ sent an email informing us. I hope they at least gifted him with an iPad, even though even I didn't have one yet to check my work on.

July 2010

Closer to home, in late July, Alex joined the iTunes Movies team. He'd previously worked for Gary Stewart, and before that had produced and directed a feature-length documentary about (according to its IMDb description) "the world of queer hip-hop." We were all so impressed by his knowledge, intelligence and easygoing manner that we simply had to bring him on board. He proved his worth a thousand times over during the next couple of years.

November 2010

On November 15, 2010, iTunes attained yet another milestone: the Beatles' catalog would now be available on iTunes for digital downloading.

This was a major coup: Eddy Cue and other upper management had been trying to get The Beatles on iTunes for a full decade, since the store launched in January 2001. Apparently, the guy who held the rights to the Beatles' catalog (and who refused to allow digital access) died, and the new rights holder was eager to cash in on the digital music market. While the poet John Donne (in his poem in which the most recognized line is "Do not ask for whom the bell tolls; it tolls for thee") may have claimed that "any man's death diminishes me," the croaking of that regressive obstacle enhanced the world of digital music immeasurably.

ME 2010: PERSONAL MILLSTONES

July 31, 2010

One Saturday in late July I arrived home from my weekly grocery shopping expedition ("Home is the hunter; home from the hill") to report to Piph that I felt a little weird—not sick, not nauseous, not in pain...just a little...*weird.* She entered my symptoms into WebMD and asked me, "Do you have a loss of appetite?" And I realized that I hadn't eaten anything in the last 36 hours—and didn't even realize that I hadn't eaten anything in the last 36 hours. "That's not like you," she said. And she was right. I hadn't eaten but I wasn't hungry. Among all my other minor symptoms, that seemed significant. "Might be appendicitis," she determined. I agreed. "Let's go to the Emergency Room at Sequoia," I suggested. The hospital was right up the street from our apartment in Redwood City—walking distance, if I wasn't dying.

They admitted me, inspected me and did an MRI. A few minutes later the nurse informed me that "the on-call surgeon is on his way." The what now? Turns out it was indeed appendicitis, and they were intent on removing the vestigial organ before it burst and I died—which, she informed me, could happen *any minute.* If I didn't feel bad before, I certainly did now. I won't go into detail about the procedure, although I consider going under anesthesia one of the most intriguing altered states of consciousness in a life full of voluntary experimentation with various altered states of consciousness.

They sent me home the next day, Sunday, and I sent Richard Zucker an email explaining the situation. “The good news is the doctor says I can sit and work while I recuperate for a few days,” I wrote, “but the bad news is I can't commute while taking the painkillers. I should have no problem—physically or psychologically—with performing my normal job functions during the upcoming week as long as, with your permission, I can work from home.” With Andy out on vacation and me on sick leave, there was literally no one to program the next week’s store, which would have spelled disaster for Zucker and Squack, and would have left iTunes Movies with a big black eye—the only store that ever missed a weekly update. I figured that while I could legitimately have claimed medical leave, this was a rare opportunity to prove to my superiors that I was a loyal and dedicated employee, one who’d crawl out of his deathbed (groan, cough) to ensure the smooth continuity of our Sacred Mission. Zucker not only agreed to let me work from home, but also sent a gift tray topped with a basket full of cookies and other edible goodies. (I still use the tray on a daily basis.) I dropped him a note thanking him for his “gesture of caring and compassion.”

So here is yet one more way this book and I are alike: neither of us has an appendix.

HOW CAN I HAVE A WORK WIFE WHEN I’M MARRIED TO THE JOB?

September 2010

Zucker needed an Analyst for Movies and actually had the budget to hire one. He consulted with both Andy and me about whether he should hire “Melody,” who had been performing Movies Store analysis for us, on loan from another department. (*Note:* “Melody” is a Hero, but since she’s still at Apple as of 2020, I felt it was in her best interest to protect her identity.)

We both enthusiastically endorsed Melody as a team member. She was smart, attractive, composed and reserved—plus, we suggested, this all-male team could use a feminine touch and a female point of view to counteract our testosterone poisoning. Zucker hired her immediately.

Melody was petite, demure, and the very image of a "Good Girl"—a devoted Christian who went to church every Sunday and led a simple, upstanding life with her beloved golden retriever and her "very Chinese" husband (her words). But beneath that sweet, innocent exterior, she proved to have a scalpel-sharp, lacerating sense of humor. (She once described herself to me as "little but lethal.") Once I realized that she was, among my iTunes compatriots, perhaps the only one who had her head screwed on straight, we became fast friends. We spent as much time together as was appropriate, and exchanged numerous personal emails over the years. She and her husband lived in Redwood City, not far from the castle in which Piph and I were living, and we occasionally ran into one another in "the RC's" small downtown area during its frequent public events.

Melody, I realized at some point, had become my "work wife"—the co-worker with whom I spent more time than I spent with my actual significant other at home, and with whom I shared an attitude (cynical) and point of view about our office environment (skeptical). Our relationship was of course entirely platonic—that is, after all, a key element of the definition of "work wife." There was never a whiff of impropriety—our personal lives both included a dedicated spouse—but in the office, on the job, we were able to whisper our reservations about Apple and iTunes policies and insanities (and Zucker's irrationality) to one another without fear of offense or reprisals…or of being reported to HR. She was a confidante, and our minds meshed without friction in our attitude towards our work environment. (And in 2020, she's one of only two former Apple co-workers with whom I maintain contact.)

BACK IN THE SADDLE AGAIN

October 2010

My annual Performance Review took place in early October, just days before I was scheduled for two unusual events: oral surgery on Friday, followed by a two-week vacation (in part to recover from the oral surgery).

The review contained little out of the ordinary, aside from proving without any doubt that the unpleasantness of the HR-mandated Documented Coaching of a couple of years earlier was ancient history. In 2010, my peers all gave me glowing endorsements, and even Zucker agreed that whatever Apple-aberrant behaviors I'd been accused of had long since been "corrected." The scorecard:

Missed deadlines? Solved: "He demonstrates a strong ability to plan work assignments to meet deadlines," wrote one peer in the comments solicited for this review. Or, as another wrote, more succinctly: "Scott is always on time."

Snarky humor? Solved. He "finishes work in a smooth, systematic and often humorous manner." Exhibit B: "his wit and humor are delightful in this often fast-paced work environment."

Personal relationships? Solved. "He is now very easy to work with," one comment read, continuing, "It's really awesome to be able to leverage his amazing knowledge of cinema into more and more editorial based features." And: "Scott is one-of-a-kind and a joy to work with." And: "Scott always maintains a positive attitude in his daily job and shows tact, courtesy and effectiveness in dealing with others and never hesitates to recognize others for their contributions." And: "Scott is a natural leader due simply to his long time experience and knowledge of movies. People trust his opinion and value his point of view." And my favorite peer comment: "He knows every single movie ever made."

Regardless of whatever bullshit I'd been accused of before, I'd proven to every one of my peers that I was meeting or exceeding their expectations. (And was happy to do it: I liked these people, and had zero interest in offending them.) Any burned bridges had been rebuilt. I was the very model of the modern iTunes employee.

Of course, there's always one sour apple. Even though not a single one of my peers mentioned this, Zucker somehow felt obligated to include this note: "The number one thing Scott can do…is understand he has a contrarian streak and try to stifle his initial response which is often negative," even though later in the same comment he admitted, "he is sometimes correct." Apparently he overlooked how often we were in agreement—and, apparently, mindless agreement was expected, and only my questioning a decision made any impression on him.

IF I WERE A RICH MAN...

There was, however, one surprise in this discussion of my Performance Review, although it wasn't part of the actual Review itself. "Are you following your stock?" Zucker asked me when we'd finished going over the paperwork. I couldn't give him the real, in-depth answer, that I'd never purchased any Apple stock. My prior experience with stock options indicated that they were a joke. At ReplayTV, for instance, if I had exercised my stock options when I was laid off, it would have cost me my entire severance package. Considering that ReplayTV was collapsing, and changed owners something like three times in the following few years, I felt I'd been justified (not to mention spared bankruptcy) by not investing in the place. And if Apple pressured employees to purchase stock to prove their loyalty, as Lockheed had done to get employees to purchase U.S. Savings Bonds, I didn't want to reveal to my boss that I was a renegade—a traitor to the cause. So I just shrugged and said, "Nah, I never pay any attention to that stuff."

"Well, you should," he replied. "It's worth nearly a million dollars."

And I thought: *This man has clearly lost his mind.* But I just smiled.

I did, however, check into this ludicrous claim, and discovered what I'd long forgotten (and, given my attitude toward stock options, had never paid any attention to in the first place): that I had been granted 3,000 RSUs ("Reserved Stock Units") by Marshall Dylan when I initially hired in. During the intervening three and a half years, Apple stock had skyrocketed, from about \$90 a share to nearly \$300 a share—more than tripling in value. At the price I was allowed to purchase my 3,000 shares once they fully vested in about six months, Zucker was correct: my RSU options were worth nearly a million damn dollars.

Holy shit. Once again, I was gobsmacked—but, as a rarity, this time in a good way.

Piph and I spent our two-week vacation returning to the Big Island of Hawaii, discussing what we would do with a million dollars. And for once in my life, the speculation was not just an idle daydream.

Chapter 29

2011: WHO WANTS TO BE A MILLIONAIRE?

January 2011

Naturally, all I could think of following the revelation about my stock options was the stock price. I realized why that was the first thing many of my co-workers checked when they logged on every morning. I became one of those guys.

Now, I'm a huge believer in synchronicity—"meaningful coincidence"—and I discovered yet another reason to validate my belief: On Piph's birthday, January 6, 2011, Apple stock hit $334 per share, making my options worth a million dollars (and change). It was her birthday, and my present to her was that I became a millionaire. A *one* millionaire, to be sure, but a millionaire all the same, goddamn it! As early as age 18 I'd realized that my fantasies about having a million dollars were limited; that a mill wouldn't buy all that much even in those days. I also realized that I'd probably never have "that kind of money." I have never been happier to be proven wrong.

I sought out Marshall Dylan, the man who was singlehandedly responsible for giving me that stock grant, and thanked him. He told me Apple was giving out a lot of money in those days and I was lucky to have come aboard at that specific time. I could not disagree.

That was the penultimate time I ever saw Marshall Dylan. The last time was about a month later, at his going away party. The man who launched iTunes Movies, the man who built a team that ultimately got all ten of the major Hollywood studios to sign on for digital movie downloads and rentals, the man whose avowed goal was to make iTunes Movies a billion-dollar business—not to mention the guy responsible for making me a millionaire—had been kicked to the sidelines when Gerald Fitzpatrick came on board. And he'd continued to be kicked aside ("Special Projects," my ass) until he was forced out altogether. He made me rich; they made him vanish.

HOME AWAY FROM HOME, or WE INTERRUPT THIS NARRATIVE

Regardless of the money, I kept up with my work, of course. After all, I had to last at least through the end of April before my stock was fully vested. This gave me a renewed commitment to my tasks…although I secretly debated whether I should put up a little sign in my cubicle in April, imitating numerous Google employees who became millionaires overnight when that company went public: "Don't fuck with me—I'm fully vested."

Clearly, my head wasn't entirely in the game. During our stay in Hawaii a few months earlier, Piph and I decided we loved the Big Island enough that we wanted to live there when I retired in a few years. Now I pointed out that we were currently in a unique position, and for once it was to our advantage: the stock price was high, and since the bottom had fallen out of the housing market nationwide a few months earlier, housing prices were tumbling. Many lovely houses in the area in which we wanted to live, for instance, were going on the market at thirty percent below the asking price of just a few months earlier. A lot of second homes and vacation homes in Hawaii were being divested at rock-bottom prices. I suggested we take full advantage of this leverage and strike while the iron was hot. As soon as the stock was fully vested, we should cash in enough to purchase a retirement home—one we could use as a vacation rental until I retired and we moved in full time.

Piph began scanning real estate listings for homes in our area of choice, with our requirements, in our price range. She'd check daily and select candidates, then on Saturday night we'd hook her laptop up to the big screen TV and indulge in what was referred to at that time as "real estate porn." We found an agent we liked, Nika, who lived in the area; we knew she was good because at the end of every day she'd send us links to the same places Piph had found doing her own daily search. And at some point, Nika informed us that we'd better get out there and look at some real estate soon, since no one could predict how long the market would be so depressed, or how long any of these properties was going to stay on the market. She suggested we send her our "Top 10 Candidates" list and a date when we could visit and she'd make arrangements to tour the properties.

And so, on April 11, I walked into Richard Zucker's office unannounced, sat down, and without preamble uttered a sentence that has perhaps never been spoken before: "I have to go to Hawaii."

"I'm so sorry for you," he said.

I explained the situation. We checked the calendar and blocked out a good vacation time. And in early May the lovely Epiphany Jane and I went. We looked. We found a house. And we made an offer.

Of course, it was hardly that easy. We looked at every one of our Top 10 candidate properties that were still available and were not at all satisfied with any of them. I was discouraged and was ready to call it quits and return in a few months to try again, when late in the afternoon we took a break in one of the rejected properties. I spotted a binder on a coffee table in the living room titled "LIVE IN HAWAII." *Well, that's what we came here for*, I shrugged, and opened the binder. It was full of real estate listings, and the very first listing caught my attention immediately —and the more I read of the description, the more perfect the place sounded. I showed the page to Nika. "They took it off the market," she said. "But what the heck—I'll call them. Maybe they've changed their minds." They'd tried to sell the house, they told her—but they'd lowered the price by 10 percent three times and still got no interest, so they decided to take it off the market and use it as a vacation rental until the market recovered. Even more perfect! Using the house as a vacation rental was what we wanted to do until I retired, and this place was a turnkey operation.

We toured the house—a round house built on a round pedestal, so the entire living quarters were on the second floor...at the top of a wide spiral staircase. It took my breath away. The living room had an entire wall of French doors that looked out on the Pacific Ocean, and a covered lanai the size of three extra rooms. It had three bedrooms and two baths (and an additional half-bath, we discovered later). It had palm trees. It had Wi-Fi and cable TV. I was sold.

"I want this house," I said to Piph.

"I want that garden," she replied. I supposed I could let her live in the house.

"Shall I make an offer, then?" Nika asked quietly. Oh hell yes!

The upshot: In early June, we cashed in enough stock to purchase the house, with enough left over for a modest retirement in a few years, even after enduring the outrageous extortion of…

('CAUSE I'M) THE TAXMAN

"What a revoltin' development *this* is!"
—William Bendix, *The Life of Riley*
(also Ben Grimm/The Thing, *The Fantastic Four*)

A million damn dollars! Is that great or what? Well…what. Technically, it was only half-great, because I ended up with only about half the grant. Who got the other half? The motherfucking IRS, of course. Turns out that a stock grant of the type I received is considered "income," not a bonus or a reward or any kind of gift at all. *Income.* And since I cashed in about a third of the grant to purchase the house, the IRS insisted that my "wages" for 2011 were, in fact, my annual Apple salary *plus* the cash value of the stock I cashed in.

WTF? For one year, I was a One-Percenter. But unlike the *real* One Percent, I had no finance managers or accountants to protect my money in tax dodges or offshore accounts, so my once-in-a-lifetime windfall was taxed as though I were a common peasant. A year later, I was enraged to discover that while I paid income taxes at about a 50 percent rate, multi-millionaire presidential candidate Mitt Romney paid only *15 percent* of his earnings in taxes in this same year. Son of a *bitch!* No wonder it's so difficult to get ahead in America, if Uncle Sugar extorts half of your "income." I'm a huge proponent of higher taxes for the rich…but logic demands that there be some kind of differentiation between the actual wealthy, who are rich every year, and the lucky few like me who receive a one-time bump in "salary." I felt like I was being divorced by Uncle Sam and he took half of everything I owned, the bitch.

As if to add insult to injury (or one more obstacle to actually getting ahead in the world), the company that administers Apple's stock plans—let's call them iTrade—informed me that I had to pay the tax on that "income" as soon as I cashed in the stock. They would selflessly take it upon themselves to transfer the amount of taxes owed on my cashed-in stock directly to the IRS. "But this is June," I objected, "and income tax isn't due until April 15 next year—a full ten months from now." If I had that cash, I could have invested it for *ten months* until my 2011 income tax payment was due, and maybe recoup a few thousand of the hundreds of thousands of dollars the IRS was commandeering nearly a year before they had any claim to it.

You can guess how that line of reasoning worked out. So that was several hundred thousand dollars that would never even pass through my hands. From iTrade to IRS, with no meddling middleman (i.e., me) to foul up the works. What's the problem, Uncle Sammy? Doncha trust me?

I was, however, able to strike one blow against the Empire. Since Piph had no income in 2011 (she was launching her own startup), we realized we could save a few thousand dollars in income tax by filing jointly…and so we decided to do something neither one of us had had any interest in doing previously: tie the knot. Our mutual friend Mary McGuire was thrilled to get a one-day pass from the County to legally officiate our marriage, and we picked as a venue our usual Friday night hangout: Gourmet Haus Staudt, a convivial taproom in Redwood City. The owners were delighted that we'd chosen to hold our impromptu ceremony on their premises (we asked their permission in advance), and even brought out a bottle of champagne for toasting. And on December 30, 2011, the fourteenth anniversary of our moving in together, we invited a few friends and neighbors to the bar and, as they used to say, she made an honest woman of me. Or something.

My second act of vengeance is this: now that I'm over 67, I can make as much money as I want and never pay another penny in income tax. So all I have to do now is make a few hundred thousand dollars to get even. I hope to hell you paid full price for this book.

But this is a book about work life, not about *life* life. So as much as I'd love to continue to wax rhapsodic about my beloved round house and cast shade on the IRS, we must return to the drudge of The Job of Work, which is already in progress...

A GOD AMONG MEN (AND WOMEN)

October 2011

By 2011, we had pretty much sanded down the rough spots in our weekly procedures and were well on our way to becoming a well-oiled, smoothly-operating machine. Exhibit A: my 2011 Performance Review.

By this point, even Zucker mentioned the "persistent praise from his peers," for example. (Apparently, my love of alliteration, which he hated, was infectious.)

A sample of that persistent praise…I mean, of the comments submitted by my peers…would include:

"Excellent at hitting deadlines."

"…always on time and a gifted writer."

"…consistently the model for Programmers."

"I can count on him to meet deadlines (and often exceed them, by completing tasks early)."

"Week to week Scott comes up with interesting editorial ideas…"

"I'm a huge admirer of Scott's organizational skills."

"…really proven to be a leader in sharing his knowledge and experience."

"Scott excels at communicating … no matter how complicated the requests or subject matter. [His] communication …. is always courteous and responsive."

"Scott is great (& funny!)"

"I'm very happy to be working with Scott, who is always cooperative, friendly and maintains good relationships with everyone on the Production team. I particularly enjoy Scott's wit and humor (aside from his vast movie knowledge). Our weekly meetings never fail to provide me with a laugh or two, making the...dry and technical subject matter a bit more interesting."

"…[a] tremendously positive attitude and display of tact, courtesy and effectiveness in dealing with others."

"His communicative, collaborative and flexible nature is a breath of fresh air."

"His passion for film shines through his writing… I wish that other folks were as knowledgeable and passionate about their media types as Scott is to movies."

So: *I'm back, baby! Woo-hoo!*

I was even winning over the skeptics, it seems: "He has a pronounced anti-authoritarian streak though sometimes this can be a good thing because he doesn't accept 'common wisdom' and sometimes common wisdom is just lazy thinking, so he [is] right."

Thank you, thank you—I'll be here all week!

And yet, there's occasionally a worm hiding in even the juiciest apple—one contrarian with a bad attitude determined to ignore his peers' praise and contradict their glowing comments. "Scott has a harder time with disagreement than most folks and it can be disruptive to the group when it devolves to nastiness." I honestly cannot think of a single time when a disagreement "devolved into nastiness," so this comment is itself suspect—particularly when contrasted against the sterling comments from a dozen other peers.

How could one person out of a dozen be so completely out of step with his (or her) colleagues? Which one of my peers—all of whom I believed I had excellent relationships with—was so thin-skinned that he (or she) would overlook our superb rapport and mention an incident that clearly made no lasting impression on anyone else…and possibly never even happened? To put it another way: Who pooped in the punchbowl of our little interdepartmental lovefest?

I can think of only two possibilities. The first is that one of my co-workers was only faking a warm, friendly relationship—hypocritically smiling while stabbing a knife in my back. ("One may smile, and smile, and be a villain," as Shakespeare put it in "Hamlet.") A second possibility is that Zucker went off my list of suggested peers from whom to request feedback, specifically to include someone who still held a grudge against me—but because my list was comprehensive concerning other co-workers with whom I interacted regularly and frequently, this would by definition be a person with whom my contact was minimal and infrequent. If so, how could he or she make a statement like this, and based on what incident?

FIGHTING DIRTY

There was one additional work-related incident in late 2011 that I mention only because of its later repercussions. In early November, Warner informed us they were about to send us a huge list of titles—nearly 2,000 movies—and wanted us to come up with a promotional plan that would split them up into different categories and price tiers featuring a different set of movies every week for seven weeks. Naturally, that work fell on me. I came up with a plan that Zucker decided was "confusing" but refused to discuss. With the deadline looming, I informed him via email that if he would answer just one simple question I could refine the plan, but he repeatedly ignored my requests.

"You asked me to analyze this data and come up with a plan," I wrote eventually, hoping to goad him into action by pressing the issue in some other way than constantly bugging him about providing me with the information I required—and so I wouldn't be the one pointed to as being responsible if we missed the deadline. Since repeated requests were apparently ineffective, I'd have to take a different tack. "If you are too busy to take the time to understand the analysis, or to answer one simple but key question," I wrote him, "I have to assume this is not very important and that you're willing to live with whatever plan I come up with."

The following morning, Zucker summoned me into his office. *Great,* I thought. *He's finally come to his senses and wants to discuss this promotion and provide me with the information I need to initiate it.* I thought this because it's logical, and because I'm an optimist. But Zucker proved himself neither, as he spent our time together dressing me down for "undermining his authority" by including a third person on the email—the one other person on our team who'd been assigned to this promotion.

I left his office chastened but confused. He could have spent the time discussing the promotion, but he didn't, so I was still in the same precarious position. He could have assured me that he was working to get the information I required, and I'd get it as soon as he did. But he didn't. Instead, I was lambasted for "undermining his authority." On reflection, that made no sense at all. How was I "undermining his authority" by cc'ing the other member of this project on my email?

Eventually, it dawned on me that he'd simply deflected my criticism by accusing me of something entirely different—that he'd taken a minor detail (i.e., including another person on the email) and inflated it into his major complaint…not that I accused him of not caring, or that he was delinquent in providing vital data, but that I was *undermining his authority*. That didn't solve the problem. He'd merely created an entirely different problem—spinning the event to make it *my* failure, not his.

While I can't say I'm happy this incident occurred, analyzing and understanding it did, in fact, prove invaluable in future confrontations with Zucker. I'd stumbled upon his primary strategy and fundamental tactic for dealing with conflict: *The best defense is a good offense*. Deflection was his defense. He'd spare no brain cells to find some way, however ludicrous, to make a dispute the other guy's fault—and I was often the "other guy."

And this was the guy I reported to…

Chapter 30

2012: FALLING FAR FROM THE TREE

January 2012

WFH. WTF?

We all returned from our holiday break refreshed and ready for yet another year of madness and insanity. And we hit the deck running: On Tuesday, January 3, our first day back, we performed the first store turn of the new year at 10 AM. I barely had time to get tea before diving once again headfirst into the deep end of the cesspool.

Back to business as usual.

One day later, however, on January 4, Richard Zucker, my immediate superior (and I use the word solely in the bureaucratic definition), appeared outside my cubicle. "Can I see you in my office for a minute please?" he said.

A request like that, no matter how polite (or maybe *especially* when so polite) was, in my experience, never a good sign. I might not be such a pessimistic employee but for the fact that my worst fears were so often validated.

"Close the door," Zucker said as I entered. Never, never a good sign.

We sat. He slid a piece of paper across the table to me. "Sign this," he said.

"Um...," I replied, "do you mind if I read it first?" What am I, new? For all I knew, he could be soliciting a kidney transplant. For his dog.

"All it says is that I've arranged for you to work from home from now on. Your coughing is driving everyone crazy."

His explanation was debatable, but I wouldn't know that until later. It was also complete bullshit—but I wouldn't know that until later, either. Right now, I read the paper, an HR-approved medical request to allow me to work from home.

"Well, OK," I said. God forbid that after all my hard work during the last three years rebuilding relationships I should appear argumentative. "But I'll still need to attend some meetings. Like the Wednesday morning two-hour powwow where you and I design the next week's store. And the iTunes Picks collection meetings. It just won't work to phone in to that, since there's so much discussion. And Hitlist. That's my meeting—I have to attend. But the good news is that all three of those meetings are on Wednesday. So why don't I work from home four days a week and come into the office on Wednesdays. That'll give us a chance to touch base in person."

"Great idea," he agreed. "Do that."

INDUSTRIAL DISEASE

As for the coughing... One of the things that has always irritated me about the corporate environment is the lack of privacy about one's physical ailments. When you call in sick, you're expected to provide details. But maybe I don't want my boss intimately involved in my health problems. Maybe I don't want to have to explain that (as my co-worker Andy once wrote in an email to our group) "I was up all night squirting from both ends." TMI, dude. (Also, yuck.) Or maybe I didn't want to have to confess that I wrenched my back (a dead giveaway that I was an old man in the domain of the young and healthy) and that I've got to go the chiropractor and down a few Vicoprofen instead of commuting 20 miles and sitting at my desk in agony all day. Why the hell does my boss—who is not a doctor—need to be privy to my unique physical sufferings? Can't he just take my word for it that I'm sick? (When I started at Lockheed, we had a sick-day code to avoid just such oversharing. You'd call in with "eye problems," explaining, "I just can't see coming in today.")

But the sad fact in this particular case was that I did indeed have a coughing problem—kind of. It wasn't anything life threatening, like TB or emphysema or black lung or pneumonoultramicrospicsilicovolcaniosis. It wasn't communicable. But I had a condition where I felt a need to clear my throat every minute or so. I tried to do it quietly; it wasn't even loud enough that I couldn't go to a movie theater for fear of being yelled at or ejected, for instance. Eventually, it would take seven doctors nearly three years just to figure out what it was—and when they did, none had any clue about its origin, or a cure, or even a treatment. I spent a year with the allergist who treated Steve Jobs' kids (figuring if he took his own kids there, she must be the best), but it wasn't allergies. I tried an Ear, Nose & Throat guy, who couldn't find anything wrong. I tried a heart specialist, figuring I'll work my way down the tract until somebody finds something. But he didn't. Two gastroenterologists were stumped as well. I told the Stanford GI doctor that I felt like I had continual low-level aspiration. After a full day of tests at Stanford, her diagnosis was: *microaspiration.* And I thought to myself, *Now do I know more than I did?*

Zucker's claim that my coughing was "driving everyone crazy" sounded like bullshit. Standard casual operating procedure in iTunes was to have headphones on while working. My co-workers couldn't have heard me clearing my throat through their headphones—and they certainly weren't wearing headphones just to block out the sound of my throat-clearing. For the record, I did inquire about Zucker's point quietly among my peers. The consensus of opinion was: "What coughing?"

So I sat in this meeting, baffled by this new development. My first reaction was something like...*shame.* What had I done wrong that my boss would exile me from the office and my peers? My second reaction was, *There goes lunch at Whole Foods every day, goddamn it.*

So the next day, I did not rise at 9 AM, make my tea, dress, drink my tea, and commute 25 minutes down 280 from Redwood City to Cupertino to be at my desk at 10 AM. I rose at 9:50 AM, put on my robe, made my tea, sat down at the huge rolltop desk that was my home office, and got to work. At 10 AM. I'd arranged with Zucker that I'd log onto iChat when I was "in the office" so he could see I was online and hard at work at home.

WFH? AOK!

"We get up at twelve and start to work at one
Take an hour for lunch and then at two we're done.
Jolly good fun!"
—*The Wizard of Oz,* "The Merry Old Land of Oz"

The next day I did the same thing. And I did that for a couple of weeks, until I realized that no one ever called, and no one ever tried to iChat me until after lunch, if at all. And so I began my new WFH routine: I would rise at 9:55 AM and log into iChat precisely at 10:00, to prove I was "at work." I'd skim my email and would always answer one or two, to leave a digital paper trail proving that I was indeed hard at work answering emails at 10:05. And then I'd go back to bed. Until noon. I'd rise, make my tea, and while everyone in Cupertino was at lunch, I'd double-check to make sure no one had tried to iChat me while I was out of the office in Dreamland. If they ever had, I could always explain that I was in a meeting, or away from my desk, or whatever excuse would explain that missing hour or so of time before I responded.

I detailed my plan to Piph, and she agreed to cover for me if, in the case of some extreme emergency, Zucker ever called the house with a fire drill. We had a list of acceptable excuses, including: "He just went downstairs to get the mail"; "He's in the bathroom"; "He stepped out to stretch his legs; he's down in the rose garden"; and so on. Each would be followed by: "Can I have him call you back in five minutes?" And then she'd wake me up and I'd phone in. Guess what? In more than a year of working from home, no one ever called with an emergency. (And, to be clear, I never missed a meeting or a deadline, even with the sleep-till-noon six-days-a-week schedule.)

I was also saddened to think that I'd have to forego my Monday lunches at the AMC Theater in Cupertino. Monday was a "hands-off" day for iTunes Programmers while the Builders cobbled together the week's new store that we'd launch Monday night, so there was very little for me to do on Mondays, aside from remaining at my desk to prove what a loyal wage slave I was. But my good friend Danny McGuire, who'd been a Producer for various PBS stations until his recent retirement, lived only a couple of miles away—and Danny was, like me, a huge movie buff. We arranged to hit the movie theater in downtown Redwood City virtually every Monday afternoon that year. I always took my iPhone (set to vibrate, because I didn't want to be rude) in case Zucker called with an emergency. I'd tell him I was at the chiropractor but that I could be home in 15 minutes. Even if I couldn't roust Danny out of the theater to accommodate my emergency, I could stroll home in 15 minutes. But guess what? During that entire year, no one ever called with an emergency. (And, again, to be clear, I never missed a meeting or a deadline. Or a new release movie.)

It quickly became apparent to me what a boon it was to be exiled and forced—*forced*, I say!—to WFH. I had to make the best of an uncomfortable situation, and I did. Oh yes, I certainly did. (Was I a "bad employee"? I prefer to believe I was instead a *smart* employee. And given the fact that for a solid year, no one at Apple ever knew my self-determined schedule, my reputation as a good employee was never sullied.)

And so it went through 2012: sleep till noon every day but Wednesday; hit the movie theater every Monday; make a token appearance in The Cupe on Wednesdays to attend my meetings—and, of course, to have lunch and shop for beer at the enormous Cupertino Whole Foods.

THE IRONICAL AND/OR IRRATIONAL MR. ZUCKER

By late 2012, the WFH directive instigated by my Dr. Jekyll boss, Richard Zucker, seems to have been completely forgotten by my Mr. Hyde boss, Richard Zucker. Numerous emails bear out his schizophrenic attitude toward his own decision to make me work from home.

When our modem failed in September 2012, for instance, I sent him an email (via my iPad) alerting him that I would be without wi-fi and therefore offline for a few hours until Comcast replaced their failed modem. His reply: "why [sic] don't you just come into the office?" If I did that, I responded, there'd be no one at home to let the cable guy in to replace the modem. (Duh.) His response was a masterpiece of ignoring reality: "Let me clarify that I am not OK with you not being online today because your modem is out. Working from home is a privilege not a right and if you can't get the job done from there you need to be in the office."

Well… Is working from home a "privilege" if it's mandatory? Perhaps he overlooked the fact that *he himself* initiated the WFH order.

Apparently, he did *not* remember, as future emails would indicate: On October 22, for example, he wrote (about some minor delay), "This is part of the problem with you working from home." And on December 6, he groused that "These are the kinds of things that make you working from home problematic."

WTF? Don't blame me for minor glitches that you believe were caused by my working from home, asshole, since *you are the guy who demanded that I work from home in the first place.* Jesus.

APPLE, PEELED

Mid-year, Melody and I engaged in an email conversation I could entitle "Why We Will Not Get Raises This Year." We were both skeptical of the reward to come, and amused each other by listing all the possible excuses Apple would trot out to justify cutting back on our raises.

Stock options, for instance, were off the table. They used to give us stock as part of our annual bonus. In 2010 I was given 40 RSUs, for instance. But a year later—and just after Steve's passing—when Zucker tried to give me almost four times that much, he was informed that he was using an outdated request form, and that "employees would no longer be given stock as part of their annual compensation." Nice to know he thought that highly of me, but…damn. At the stock price at that time, that was half a year's salary he tried to give me but was denied.

A couple of months later, I read a short piece in the Business section of the San Francisco *Chronicle* entitled "Apple rewards executive team" which said that in order to keep the current top management from leaving after SJ's death, six top people were each given 150,000 RSUs. Eddy Cue alone got 100,000. So *that's* where my RSUs went, along with everybody else's! I contributed one percent of one exec's RSU grant. No wonder they call them the "One Percent."

I enumerated several anti-raise excuses I'd experienced in the past and thought Apple could easily trot out, including:

- "Well, we've added two new people this year, but the compensation pool hasn't increased, so we have to share the same amount of real dollars among more people."

- "Well, TV had a smaller compensation pool, so with the restructuring of the Video Dept. to combine both Movies and TV, the combined compensation pool to draw from is smaller, but we have just as many/even more people eligible for annual compensation, so…"

- "Well, with the increase in competition of other companies like Netflix, Amazon and Hulu moving into this space that we used to dominate, we have a smaller piece of the overall VOD pie and slower growth in overall YOY (Year Over Year) revenue, so we have to tighten our belts to stay competitive." (Gotta love that one. They fail as business decision makers and *we* get less money?)

"You'd think if I could come up with all those 'logical' excuses," I wrote Melody, "that I'd be good management material! But that will never happen, because even though I can spot the BS easily, as management I'd also have to refrain from disclosing the (likely) truths that they *won't* tell us, like:

- "You make so much already that if we give you the same percentage as a person who's paid less than you it draws more money from the compensation pool and means less for everyone else." (This one was the winner, and would prove both accurate and prescient in a couple of months.)

- "We want to give bigger raises to the new people, so they'll want to stay. We don't need to give you a big raise, because you ain't goin' *nowhere*."

- "Now that *real* business people are running this company, and not some visionary genius, the days of overpaying employees are over."

- "In this economy, with 14 percent unemployment, you're lucky you have a job at all. And now you want more money for doing it? I think not."

- "Now that we're *the most valuable private company that ever existed*, we want MORE...and if we can't get it through traditional (and difficult) routes like higher sales, groundbreaking new products, and opening new markets, we'll get it by cutting costs...like your compensation."

Melody replied: "hahaha! so true!! I've heard them all. the bad thing for us, is that we're now going to have our salaries compared to the 20 year old TV guys. Its gonna be like...TV only makes $1/per hour and you make $5/hr... We need to get them more in line. I say.. um, I'm 40, and have more experience to make decisions and be efficient, blah, blah, blah. Bet you a buck us oldie moldies will get hosed b/c of taking on TV. They're young and cheap. Have low expectations so we won't be let down."

And I responded: "Wow, you're good—you came up with BS I didn't even remember, like 'we need to get them more in line...' Good one! We should write all these down and start a pool—$10 bet on which excuse each of us will be given. Except gambling is illegal, and wrong! (Hear that, HR?) Or we could play 'BS Bingo'—create a card with each of these excuses and see who gets told the most.

"I used to amuse myself in all-hands meetings at ReplayTV [I continued] by keeping a running tally of business clichés, like "At the end of the day" and "Moving forward..." But BS Bingo would be much more fun, if only because the stakes are higher.

"Don't count on experience to be a factor in compensation, or respect, or, really, for anything [I ranted on]. I got this job on the strength of my knowledge of movies, and 25 years of writing about movies, and for working in electronic delivery of movies at 3 previous media companies. And yet I spend all my time punching buttons on a console to organize art for movies that other people have decided we should promote. On a good week, I'll get to write maybe 3 sentences. So while my skill set is 90% featured content creation and 10% understanding of electronic delivery of video, my actual job reverses that, so I spend 90% of my time dealing with [programming] and less than 10% on content or content collections. The skills and talent I was initially hired for are virtually ignored. At this point, I know I'll never have the 'dream job' that I hired into iTunes for (to do for Movies what Gary Stewart did for Music), but I'm so tired of the BS and so close to retirement that I don't even care anymore. After more than 5 years of NOT being able to do what I came here to do, I don't even WANT to do it anymore.

"And as far as respect for one's talent goes, keep this in mind: I've published 200 articles on movies, and a book, and teach college courses on film. [Andy] worked in a video store. And our opinions [on content] are considered equal by our management."

IS IT EVEN *POSSIBLE* TO MAKE TOO MUCH MONEY?

October 2012

Since I was convinced that monetary compensation would not likely be forthcoming, I was inspired to come up with an alternative. Things were going so well in iTunes Movies that I determined to ask for an additional favor during my annual performance review. And sometime in early October, I sat with Zucker going over the multi-page review, which was virtually a xerox copy of the previous year's review—and of the year before that. Same function; same high-level of functioning; same glowing comments from my peers (see below). In my position, there was never an opportunity to be a "hero" and rescue the department or create something that "moved the needle" of sales or rentals. I'd been barred from attempting the latter anyway. The best I could do was be as perfect as possible in my assigned tasks, and not fuck anything up. Clearly, I fulfilled both those goals.

To cement the idea that I was a solid performer, given what would occur a few months down the line, I present a small sampling of the peer comments submitted for my review, including:

"...super responsive and helpful ... either early or right on time with his input every week.

"...extremely timely in response time."

"...always knowledgeable and has a positive attitude."

"...a great guy to work with..."

"Always super pleasant, and fun to work with..."

...and my favorite peer comment from 2012:

"Scott Apel remains the heart of iTunes."

These comments went far beyond simply fixing what was perceived as broken years earlier. Editorial, for instance, praised me for writing all the copy for the Movies store, relieving them of the burden "while we're very strapped for resources." ("I REALLY [sic] appreciate this," my Editorial contact continued, "since no doubt his plate is full"). Our UI contact wrote, "Best of all: I can always count on Scott to check my links"; and our Builder, Wolfgang, stated "He continues to be a model Programmer," and that he held my work up as an example to Programmers worldwide. (He's German—he knows from efficiency.)

There was, however, one aspect of this review that was slightly different than the previous years: I usually received the maximum allowed raise, which was four percent. But this year, even with a review virtually identical to the previous two years, my raise was only three percent.

"Why is my review identical to the last several," I asked Zucker, "but my raise is only three percent instead of four?"

"You make too much money!" he responded. I'd describe his delivery as vehement.

OK, he cleared that up. I had no idea at that time that I'd later identify this as a major revelation, and one that would change the course of both of our lives and careers.

At this time, however, everything was copacetic—so much so that as my review drew to a close, Zucker asked me a question that no boss had ever asked me before in the entire history of my working life:

"How can I make your life easier?" he said. I knew him well enough to spot sarcasm—and this wasn't it. He was sincere. And he'd handed me the exact opening I needed to launch into my special request.

"Well," I said, "it would be of enormous benefit to me if I could work remotely."

He looked confused. "You're already working from home," he said.

"Right," I agreed. "But I'm working from a home in Redwood City that costs me nearly two grand a month in rent. The 'H' in 'WFH' I'm talking about is the home that I *own*—my house in Hawaii."

To his credit, Zucker didn't dismiss my idea out of hand and toss me out of his office. He leaned back in his chair and cocked his head. I took this as a green light to continue.

"You know iTunes allows people to work remotely regularly. Sarah—one of the Builders I work with—lives in Kentucky, for instance. And Rob"—who ran the fledgling iBooks store—"moved his entire family to Oregon. I've been working from home for nearly a year, and it hasn't impacted my performance," I continued, gesturing to the printout of my review. "We could easily FaceTime our weekly store creation meeting. You could even fly me back here a couple of times a year for a week or two, at your discretion, like we do with our foreign store programmers…for the annual Engineering training for Programmers, for instance, or for the annual All Hands meeting. I'd even be willing to forego a raise at all," I added on the fly, given his earlier concern about my salary, "since I'd be saving over twenty grand a year by not paying rent to live in the Bay Area."

He nodded at each of these points. And at length he said, "Let me roll this around for a while and see if I can work it out."

"Yeah, sure," I agreed enthusiastically. "Take your time. I'm more than willing to discuss this again later and hash out the details."

I was in. Until…

THE FINAL SQUACK ATTACK

On October 11, just days after my review, Buford Squack sent an email to all the people he worked with in iTunes:

"Hey guys," he wrote, "at the culmination of some conversations I've had with Eddy over the past several months, Apple and I have decided to part ways."

"Part ways"? Was there ever a more PC euphemism for "I've been canned"?

He attempted to explain: "It's been clear to me for some time now that given what the current structure allows for me, and what I want to be doing professionally, that I need to find another role either with Apple or elsewhere. And for the foreseeable future there's simply not such a role for me at Apple. So, the best decision overall is for me to move on and I'm doing so effective immediately. I'm looking forward to a bit of time off for the first time in my adult life, and then to finding my next professional opportunity."

You leave without another job to go to? Yep. You've been canned.

"I wish this didn't have to come as a surprise to you guys," he ended. *If only all surprises were this pleasant,* I thought…

Pleasant, yes—but the end of Squack's career at iTunes freighted with it an unintended consequence: the death of my plan to relocate to Paradise. Even leaving, Squack fucked me up.

"Let's hold our chat about Hawaii for a couple of weeks until the dust settles," Zucker wrote me on October 17—less than a week after his boss's exit. "Who knows what kind of re-org we're in store for and it might change things."

Even as late as November, we were still discussing the move, however. (On the 20th, for example, I sent an email to a friend about "trying to talk my corporate masters into allowing me to work remotely from our house in Hawaii" but that "they've deferred any decision until after the holidays.")

Little did I realize that I was perched on the razor's edge of (as Buckminster Fuller put it) "utopia or oblivion."

To Be Continued…

Chapter 31

2012: HOW DO YOU LIKE THEM APPLES?

In 2012, sent to Work From Home, freed from the drudgery of office politics and given a bit of perspective due to my "out of the cubicle" experience, I had time to make some larger observations about my five years at Apple; insights not necessarily shackled to any specific date or incident, like:

By early 2012, we had pretty much sanded down the rough spots in our weekly procedures and were well on our way to becoming a well-oiled, smoothly-operating machine. Yeah, I know I said that about 2010—and about 2011—but we were still sanding two years later. And yet (to change metaphors) this smoothly paved road still had a lot of gravel on it, and even the paved parts had some unexpected speed bumps. We dealt with so many moving parts, and with so many other departments, that occasional friction was unavoidable and inevitable.

So, just to indicate that "t'was ever thus," we'll start with…

THE WAR WITH DESIGN

The Design department, part of the Production division of iTunes, consisted of graphic artists, and they can be a touchy and sensitive breed. (I lived with a graphic artist for five years during my tenure at Lockheed in the early '80s, so I know whereof I speak.) In my early days at iTunes, there were a couple of prima donnas in supervisory positions who were such sticklers for procedure that they made my life a living hell.

Speaking of Lockheed, in my early days there I'd observed a strange phenomenon among some of the hourly workers: they were not allowed to say "No" to a request, at the risk of being fired...but they could become real pains in the ass if they didn't want to do the job, quoting procedure and policy and generally dragging their feet and being obnoxious, to express their discontent. This was what I was experiencing from these iTunes department heads, "CW" and "SD." CW was a prime candidate for Anger Management therapy, going ballistic at even the smallest deviation from "policy," and SD was a smug, self-righteous prig; a self-proclaimed arbiter of taste and guardian of "Apple culture." Aptly enough, they couldn't even get along with each other. On one memorable occasion, I watched them snipe at one another for several minutes, and after SD left, CW growled to me, "I just can't work with him when he's like that!" It didn't help that SD was tall, skeletal, bald and covered neck to foot with tattoos. He looked like the bastard offspring you'd get if a biker fucked a spider.

The Movies group, like all iTunes media groups, was provided with an "allowance" of "design points" every week, used as internal payment for the creation of the various art elements that made up our store pages—particularly our Main pages. These points were strictly adhered to by Design and were sacrosanct—an off-schedule request, or a request requiring an extra artwork point would only be honored if it was deemed "business-critical" by top iTunes management. Otherwise, if I (or any iTunes programmer for any iTunes media store) exceeded their allotted points, the Design Nazis would punt any excess ...and we (and our bosses) would receive a scathing email about adhering to our points allotment. It's understandable, given Design's limited resources, that they would negotiate a maximum amount of work that could be requested each week, to protect their artists from being inundated with requests and overworked. No argument there. But there was plenty of room for argument in their treatment of those of us requesting artwork for our stores (usually at the command of our own management).

My friction with Design—by which I mean specifically these two managers (who, a couple of decades earlier, would have had no more elevated title than "lead")—began early and quickly developed into a full-fledged war. The crux of the matter seemed to me to be their insistence that I follow established procedures ...without ever detailing what those procedures were.

"It's very frustrating to ask for information about the procedure for something and then get slapped down just for asking," I wrote in an email to my immediate superior, Ross, in January 2008. "I *want* to follow their procedures—they just won't tell me what those procedures are! When they eventually do get around to explaining them, the instructions are often vague or contradictory—I've been told at different times to 'contact a producer first' and 'a producer will be assigned to you.' So, uh, which is it?"

Nothing much changed in the next six months, during which my occasional requests or questions were met with responses like "You should know that by now." Everyone else I dealt with in every other department was more than happy—eager, in some cases—to answer my questions and explain their procedures. But not the Design Nazis. On the occasions when I just wanted a quick conversation with a graphic artist to determine whether an idea was even possible, much less being planned or requested, I was stonewalled by the Stonewall Twins. "Too often my requests for information are misinterpreted as requests for action," I wrote to SD, with no response. Of course. (In this case, his frequent answer would have been entirely appropriate: I should have known that by now.)

I also sent an email rant to Randy in the Featured Content department, to get his take on my friction with the Design Demons, since he was usually involved in any discussion between the Movies team and other teams like Design and might, I hoped, use his authority to intervene and muzzle the monsters. There were numerous reasons I chose Randy: he always seemed calm and rational, for one; because he'd chimed in on the most recent misunderstanding; and because, I wrote, "at least one other person should be aware of how thoroughly off-base [SD's] email was. And you'll notice that I've sent this *only* to you," I continued, "as one of the things that most irritated me about his email is that he distributed it widely. That's kindergarten-style tattling—and that's a polite way of describing how I feel about it." I detailed the recent incident in an attempt to indicate that SD was "180 degrees off base" about his objections. "I'm growing very tired of trying to educate myself about the Design process and having my questions misinterpreted as requests or demands... I rarely get a straight answer to a question; instead I get a lecture about procedure that misses the point and doesn't even answer the question. The flow of communication among co-workers and departments is vital, and not every question is a call to action or an attempt to bypass procedure or usurp somebody's authority. How is anyone supposed to know precisely which questions are off-limits to which personnel? Just last Friday I received an email from [my UI contact] in which she stated, 'You can ask me questions any time. No worries, at all.' So I can ask her questions but I can't ask [a Design department artist] questions without his boss jumping down my throat? Does not compute. Curiously, among the people I question the most in Design and UI, the one answer I have *never* received is 'Ask a producer.' That answer has been forced on me by a couple of middle managers, who insinuated themselves into a conversation between me and another person. If the answer to any question of Design and UI is 'Ask a producer,' then why don't their own direct reports seem to know that, and answer questions that way?"

It felt good to rant, and even better to explain. But, of course, it had zero results.

I also forwarded the Design Dipshits' less-than-helpful replies to Ross, reminding him that I was "looking for a solution [from them], not a lecture." But poor Ross was getting it from both sides. "With all due respect to how awesome Scott is," CW wrote him in June '09, "Design and Production have asked him a million times to please always always go thru a producer and to never never go straight to design. This just happened like 3 weeks ago, as I recall. Seriously, it's not funny anymore. What about this extremely simple process does he not understand? As his manager, can you please help." (I suspected that her reply contained just a bit of exaggeration. Except the part about how awesome I am.)

"It drives me more than a little crazy," Ross wrote to me, privately, "but I have yet to find the magic keys. Will keep sluggin'—don't let them get you down."

Our relationship with these conjoined jerks only continued to degenerate, to the point where one of them took active steps to slap me down and force me to conform to their vague, unexplained and contradictory policies. (For the full story, see the Part IV chapter "You Can't Spell 'WHORE' Without 'HR.'") As late as November '09, I wrote my new manager, Richard Zucker, saying, "This is the kind of thing that irritates me about

[them]—they tell you you've done something wrong before they tell you how to do it right, or that they've changed the rules."

Thank God (or Allah or The Flying Spaghetti Monster) the Anger Twins were later reassigned, after which they were rarely involved in our day-to-day operations. Following their departure, our relationship with the Design department only grew closer and friendlier, to the point where every few months I took graphic artist Sean to lunch on my own dime to thank him for his exceptional efforts. Our department also treated the entire team to lunch once a year for the same reason.

And yet the more self-righteous half of the Ballistic Twins still managed to make trouble at the slightest provocation. As late in the game as January 2012, SD took issue with a piece of artwork his team had created and our team had approved for a movie collection called "Young Love." The illustration showed two pair of feet, clad in tennis shoes, on tiptoe, almost floating on air above a sidewalk. But the clenched bunghole, Miss Grundy mindset of SD was worried that this innocent picture might be interpreted as depicting a double suicide in which a teen Romeo and Juliet were hanging themselves.

Of course, to any normal, sane person, this interpretation was virtually incomprehensible. Andy (who had even less of an internal censor than I did) responded, writing, "I hadn't seen it that way myself but assuming that is the case for some people, might not the Date Night [movie collection artwork] also appear to be the image of a woman being lifted off the ground while being strangled (Darth Vader style)? Honestly I think they are both fine: the promotion itself is called Young Love so anyone who sees it as two children hanging is reading way too much Edward Gorey... Either way, if you're going to change one for looking like a double suicide you might as well be consistent and change the other for looking like a date rape strangling."

To state the obvious, we all know that sarcasm does not work well in email—or under any circumstances with people like SD who tragically lack a humor gland. His response to Andy: "Can we assume you're kidding?" Uh, no doi.

Having suffered the consequences of SD's aggressive humorlessness before, and with Andy's continued employment in mind, I replied to Andy (and *only* to Andy):

"My advice," I wrote, "seriously—is to send an apology to [SD], and quickly. It was an email much like yours that prompted some unknown but highly motivated, dedicated, and open-minded gentleman much like [SD] (who I admire and respect greatly for his skills and orientation) to request that HR pay me a visit and perform an intervention to assist me in reforming my wrong-headed, politically incorrect ways as long as I was an employee of Apple. To spare you a similar fate, it would be a point in your favor to recant your message." My sign-off line read, "Trying to be a friend to a wayward soul who has stumbled into a den of wrong-headedness, I remain, your co-worker (and still an employee at Apple), Mr. Apel."

Of course, idiot Andy ignored my warning and attempted to explain to SD that his objections were ridiculous. Unbelievably, SD ignored his response. Perhaps it was enough for him to be informed that, yes, Andy was "just kidding." And, of course, our Fearless Leader, Mr. Zucker, had to have the last word with Andy (via email): "Please stop these slightly condescending/ extremely sarcastic emails to anyone outside our immediate team." (As a side note, his wording does make it sound like he was OK with our sending "slightly condescending/extremely sarcastic emails" to one another.) Nothing further was said on the subject, even while I expected the HR Nazis to descend on Andy any minute at SD's demand and haul him in for a mandatory "attitude adjustment." But no—Andy successfully dodged a bullet I had taken in the gut a couple of years earlier, damn him anyway.

BORDER SKIRMISHES WITH EDITORIAL

I always felt a kinship with the iTunes Editorial Department —I am, after all, at heart a writer myself. One of the first warm interdepartmental relationships I established in iTunes was with Jen, the lead editor. I spent a lot of time with Jen during my first few months in iTunes, if only because she edited the more than 200 movie reviews I wrote for the Movies store.

As a writer, I appreciated Editorial's dedication to precision in language. Even so, the intersection of the English language and "iTunes style" occasionally resulted in dialogs and debates that would make the Marx Brothers proud for their absurdity.

One example is an email chain that circulated among half a dozen people to determine when, and under what specific circumstances, it was appropriate to use the word "and" on a piece of store artwork, versus an ampersand (&) or the "plus" symbol (+). (That one was resolved, and you can still see art on Movies Main with tags that read "Movies + More.")

So there was never a "war" with Editorial, as there was with the irritating middle management in Design—but there were frequent hiccups, debates and differences of opinion. It occasionally seemed to me that these debates about wording—and what constituted "iTunes style"—occasionally dug so deep as to become parodies of any rational discussion. When describing a selection of sale movies, for instance, we were informed that we couldn't say "best," since that's a value judgment and might offend someone or spark debate. But we could say "great," since that's so vague as to be meaningless. And at some point during his brief tenure, Gerald Fitzpatrick barred us from using the word "sale"—so the ultimate title for a discount promotion would be "Great Movies, Great Prices." (I still see that wording on iTunes in 2020.)

But the only real friction between our team and Editorial revolved around two points. The first was their highly conservative—almost cowardly—insistence on avoiding controversy at any cost.

CASE STUDY: "BROMANCE"

In February 2009, I assembled a movie collection about men who became buddies while bonding in crisis situations. I suggested the current colloquial title "Bromance" for the collection, and requested art from Design. I sent them an email that read, "The idea is Great Buddy Movies, which we are defining mostly as action flicks and comedy action flicks that involve two guys teaming up and bonding in crisis situations (or comic crisis situations)." The email included a list of sample titles to illustrate the concept and give them some inspiration about how to illustrate the feature, including *48 HRS, Bad Boys, Men in Black, Lethal Weapon, Pineapple Express* and *Starsky & Hutch*. Our graphic artist asked if the title was approved; Jen informed them that is was, and Buford Squack agreed.

Pretty clear and straightforward, yeah? But SD, the Snidely Whiplash of Design, the tight-assed Arbiter of Taste, had some reservations. "After further consideration," he wrote to the group, "Design would like to push back on this promotion. It should also be noted this is the name of a current TV Show."

His reservations encouraged Editorial to escalate the debate to Eddy Cue's No. 2 man, the purported Czar of iTunes, if only because (per the opinion of Jen's boss in Production) "we've had problems with past editorial promotions sharing the name of a currently airing TV Show or recent Movie."

Squack, for once, came to our defense. "Bromance is a pretty common term," he wrote to the group, "and I don't think anyone has ever heard of this series. Doubt they have it trademarked. What sort of issues do we have? Legal or internal policy?" He even offered to call Gerald Fitzpatrick for a determination, "just to get this done."

Later that day, we heard from Jen, who reported: "Heard back from [#2]. Bromance is not an option—we should go w/ Buddy Movies." Squack, to his credit, was unconvinced. "Whats [sic] the problem with it?" he wrote. "Is it the tv show? Or deemed off brand?" Jen replied, "He didn't elaborate." So we went with "Great Buddy Movies." And that was the end of that. But it seemed to me to be overkill that a simple collection of movies required the combined efforts of four levels of management to agree on a title...and a less expressive title, at that.

This type of escalation was common in 2009, but grew increasingly rare. Far more intrusive was Editorial's insistence on being involved with our promotions and how we described them. I have an email chain from December 2009, for instance, in which Editorial questions our choice of names of a couple of sub-categories of Kids Movies. "This is a waste of time," I wrote Zucker. "The four of us [and you] went through several potential choices and settled on these. I recall a spirited discussion ... and we were all satisfied with the results. I don't see how there's anything inappropriate about the … titles, [and] I also don't understand why Editorial and Design have any say in this. I vote to tell them we're fine with this exactly the way the five professionals put it together, and to please just move forward."

"I agree," Zucker wrote back, "and started to write a terse response, but in the interest of playing nice did not." Editorial insisted on renaming the collection; Zucker informed us "this is not better but I'm done fighting it." I agreed with his idea to "play nice," but cautioned about setting a bad precedent: "...if they think we'll cave anytime they make a suggestion (even a bad one), they're more likely to do it more often and think that *we're* the ones being arbitrary if and when we decide to reject a change."

We played another round in January 2010, when I attempted to name a collection of contemporary leading men "Modern Men of the Movies." This time, however, I had no support. "Let's go with Modern Leading Men," Zucker responded. "It's better anyway... I am happy to fight editorial when they are screwing things up but Modern Men of the Movies is a crap title (what is it with you and Alliterations?)." Thanks for the support, you nattering nabob of negativism.

And we played yet another round in April, when Editorial requested changes to subcategories ("lockers") within a movie collection room. "We debated those locker titles at length," I wrote to Zucker, "and we were all happy with them. Since you're the ringleader of this team, you should pronounce the final judgment." His reply: "I am really over them." And so Editorial insisted on the changes, prompting me to ask Zucker, "Is there realistically a way to push back on things like this, or can Editorial override us all at their whim and make decisions by fiat that we are constrained to conform to?" Zucker sent Editorial a nasty email questioning their intrusion into our decisions—but the same day, he sent me an email informing me that I have got to "get over this territorialism." I was confused. I was right; he agreed with me…but *I* got spanked?

It seemed like about every six months we butted heads with Editorial over some wording. In 2011, for instance, we engaged in a debate about whether the genre is "Western" or "Westerns" ("Westerns," duh) and whether the term "Biopix" for biographical movies was generally understood. "I haven't ever encountered that term before," the senior editor wrote. (Apparently she'd never seen an issue of *Variety*.) Her boss chimed in that it made her think about "movies about biology." Ohhhhh-kay... The upshot: we used "Biopics" rather than the standard, *Variety*-style contraction. (I guess it was the "pix" that made the big boss think about biology, rather than the "bio.") The same editor objected soon afterward to a selection of documentaries about food I'd titled "Food for Thought." ("Our voice here at iTunes has to be in line w/ overall Apple voice and style. That means that we need to be straightforward and clear—'food for thought' stray[s] too far over into cliché territory.") What could possibly be a clearer name for food documentaries than "Food for Thought"? And even though I, too, dislike clichés, what could be more generally understood than a cliché—especially in this case, when it clearly and precisely defines the contents?

In June 2012, we engaged in yet another protracted battle of words. I'd put together a collection of movies about policemen and named it "Good Cop, Bad Cop." Editorial objected (for some unstated reason) and suggested renaming it "Buddy Cops."

"Well, that's the problem," I wrote Zucker. "About half of these titles are cops who are buddies, but the other half [are] cop partners who are *not* buddies, or who bicker but have each other's backs. I'll be happy to change it to Buddy Cops, however, if everyone will overlook the inaccuracy." His response did not address the central point, but rather my attitude about it: "please [sic] don't say things like 'if everyone will overlook the inaccuracy' in a group email with editorial. It wastes everybody's time. Just say OK and no one would be the wiser." Well, being none the wiser did not sound to me like a viable attitude. It would, if nothing else, mean that they were right and we were mistaken (which I'd attempted to prove was precisely *not* the case), or worse, that we were willing to settle for less accuracy for no apparent reason. But given this executive direction, I replied, "OK, got it. My point of view is that I spent considerable time finding a phrase that *was* accurate and succinct, and it's rather irritating to have Editorial prefer a phrase that is easily understandable but inaccurate."

But these are minor irritations. My point is not that every word I ever wrote for iTunes was carved in stone, merely that the Editorial department's alternatives often appeared arbitrary —and often involved a dozen or more emails and as many people chiming in on a debate. Nothing good ever gets written by committee.

Perhaps the more important point is that we were more often than not on the same page as the Editorial team—they approved the Movies Team's (i.e., my) wording 99.9 percent of the time. Even when we disagreed, we won maybe half the battles we fought with Editorial—but we would have lost 100 percent of those battles if we'd adopted Zucker's frequent final pronouncement ("I'm done fighting/I'm over them") with every disagreement; if we'd just caved without engaging. What kind of noncommittal wimp would I be if I didn't defend my best efforts; if I allowed someone—or anyone—to question my contributions with no debate? I did not want to become a Dick Zucker—the backbone of a spineless enterprise.

So the real story is not our petty squabbles—even in the best relationship an occasional tiff is inevitable—but is instead the close and warm relationship we developed with various editors over those years. Zucker regularly invited members of the Editorial staff into our creative brainstorming meetings, and they were always welcome and always valuable contributors. As much as I would have liked to have been the sole developer of our film features, second best was to work with a team of bright, happy, informed and passionate individuals.

(The secondary story is that of yet another failure of management to support our efforts. But that's a continuing theme.)

My relationship with Editorial developed well enough that not only did I write all the copy for the Movies store, but they often asked me if I had the bandwidth to handle some of their overflow. Of course I always agreed. I was happy to help; happy to be writing; pleased with my unique relationship with their team...and figured that being tapped to contribute more widely to iTunes than just Movies store programming could not look bad on my annual Performance Review. (Not to mention that my iTunes blurbs were probably being read by more people than anything else I'd ever written or published.)

Senior Editor Jen was even willing to put her money where her mouth was, bless her heart. On November 11, 2011 (11/11/11!), Jen send an email to Squack informing him that "We really appreciate the great writing that Scott did for [the]

Rewind [feature]. It really helped ease the load on my team. If it's cool w/ you, I'd like to give him a $250 spot bonus to say thank you." For once, even Squack seemed impressed, writing to me that "I wanted to add my thanks and appreciation. I've heard nothing but great things about your contributions to the team and your great work with [the Production teams] over the past year or so. The way you've raised your game and learned to be a strong team player vs. past years is impressive and very much valued. Keep up the great work!" I was willing to accept the compliment, even as left-handed as it seemed. And I was more than willing to accept the money, although after years of reflection, I realized I probably should have used it to take the Editorial team to Tied House for a beer bash. Ah, well…they can't miss what they were never offered.

EQUAL RIGHTS FOR ZOMBIES!

Every job has its irritations. To me, one of the biggest irritations at Apple was a few peoples' insistence on Political Correctness, often elevating PC to absurd lengths.

In August 2010, for instance, I wrote this blurb for a collection of zombie movies: "If we take zombie movies seriously, one implication is that there is new hope for the living dead. These gruesome voodoo victims have evolved from ambling, shambling mindless brain munchers with no will of their own to mentally clever afterlifers with lightning-fast reflexes and a culture and society all their own. (They'll probably want the vote next.) Track their progress and learn their secrets with this collection of movies, some of which have been resurrected for digital consumption and all of which have taken on an afterlife of their own."

When I submitted this blurb to the Editorial staff, I received this email in response: "Just wanted to follow up to let you know the Zombie line about getting voting rights was cut—we received a couple internal comments (about it being potentially construed as drawing parallels to the struggles of women and blacks to earn voting rights). Just a heads-up that we'll want to please be mindful of people's potential sensitivities going forward as we inject some lively personality into these blurbs."

So Politically Correct sensitivity must now include *zombies*? Will you please just shoot me now? (Might as well; even if I come back as a zombie, these PC Police will look out for me.) (I know; I'm missing their point. But their point seems a bit overly sensitive. *My* point—which *they* missed—was that it goes without saying that some people of course deserve the vote...but do we really want to give it to undead monsters whose sole goal in life is to *kill us and eat us?* Fucking Millennials.)

A year later, in August 2011, I was forced to deal with yet another member of the PC Police (aka the Korporate Kulture Kops) going overboard (the italics in the key phrase are mine): "I wanted to catch up with you," he wrote, "because in the beginning of the meeting, we'd casually talked about [a co-worker's] demeanor. *I couldn't quite tell how serious you were being* but if [she] really is being rude and yelling, please let me know immediately. It's important that everyone feels respected at the workplace and I'm happy to have a chat with [her] if you feel uncomfortable or if the situation is less than professional."

After four years at Apple and enduring an HR spanking, I'd learned one lesson at least: *Don't poke the bear*. I knew that any response to a humorless PC Nazi had to be clear, unambiguous, and lacking in even a whiff of sarcasm or irony. "Please be assured that whatever was said about [the co-worker in question] was said in the best good-natured way" I responded. "All I was trying to get across was that she is a force of nature—very dynamic and awesome. Our entire team's feeling about [her] is that we adore her and consider her a valuable—nearly indispensable—addition to our team. Her contributions can't be underestimated, from her knowledge of movies to her take-charge attitude to her excellent organizational skills. I have never, ever seen or heard [her] acting in anything other than a professional manner and would vehemently defend her against anyone who made such a claim. (Including you! Neither [Andy] nor I remember using words like "rude" or "yelling" when we chatted.) Sorry if our conversation was misunderstood or misinterpreted in any way. [She] is a blessing as a co-worker, both professionally and personally, and I would feel terrible if anything I said about her was misinterpreted in a negative manner, which was certainly never my intention." Clear and emphatic, if maybe overkill. But to emphasize the point to a person whose head was clearly up his own ass—and to indicate that I was 110 percent in his corner—I added the following: "Thanks for keeping an eye on the corporate culture!" Even if this was sarcasm, he would never suspect (or recognize) it as such.

The proof lay in his reply: "Great to hear, thanks for the reply Scott. I take interpersonal conduct very seriously here and while I love all of my teammates, sometimes there are always bound to be personality clashes (as there are at any company). Just want to make sure you're being treated fairly, and very glad to hear that you are." I refrained from pointing out that: a) he was not involved in any way; b) that he was being a Politically Correct busybody; and c) that it was, in fact, *none of his fucking business*.

Not everyone in the Korporate Kulture was such a tight-ass stickler for Political Correctness—only a very few, it turns out—but (as I'd learned at Lockheed with the nutless knob who objected to my Marilyn Monroe calendar) those humorless few, intent on inserting themselves into any interaction and policing the behavior of the majority, ironically shaped the workplace into the very thing they were attempting to prevent: a watch-your-back, walk-on-eggshells environment where nobody felt comfortable enough to relax and be themselves without the ever-present threat of HR retaliation.

A FULL-TIME JOB

One thing I was not prepared for at iTunes was that many of my co-workers—and most of our management—considered iTunes a full-time job...but less in the standard 40-hour work-week sense than in the startup company sense of continual, clock-agnostic effort. Everyone seemed to feel free to contact anyone at any hour, including late nights, or any day, including weekends and holidays. And we were expected to perform store functions at any hour of any day, including late nights, week-ends and holidays. The prime example of this is our Monday night store turns, in which 35 or more people logged into a chat room at 9 PM for up to three hours to proofread the week's new store. The unstated message was that we should expect to be on call and available to do iTunes' bidding 24/7. This was not just a job—this was a *lifestyle*. A *life*. No startup I'd worked for before ever demanded that kind of round-the-clock, calendar-ignoring commitment.

Another example: Richard Zucker at one point offered that Apple would pay my monthly iPhone bill—a generous gesture, I thought...until he revealed his caveat: I must keep the phone turned on 24/7 and carry it with me at all times. I respectfully declined this short leash.

But it hardly ended there. At least once a year, we store turn participants were expected to pull an all-nighter, waiting endlessly for Engineering to approve and release a technological upgrade to enable iTunes store functionality on a new device like the iPhone or iPad...to sit up all night waiting to have the baton passed to us, and *then* do our work.

The problem of off-hours effort was uniquely worse for the Movies team. The movie studios occasionally insisted on a specific date and time for the release of a high profile movie on iTunes, and these off-cycle releases often occurred on Sundays, or at midnight on Saturday night. But we complied, even though I brought this up with Randy, the manager of Featured Content and my simpatico confidante, pointing out that employees were working "banker's hours" (i.e., 9 to 5) on a store that was open 24/7—and that regardless of our scheduled hours, we had to conform our hours to the store, no matter what those hours were. "You can't sprint a marathon," I told him. Not only did my clever analysis fall on deaf ears, but I was shocked to discover how few of my co-workers shared this objection—they were devoted enough that they just shrugged off the abuse. They were young, however, and probably had no other corporate experience, so they considered this normal. But after a lifetime of corporate exploitation, I had to point out that this impact on our lives outside the company was an imposition, and that this "new normal" was just wrong.

In February 2009, I sent Buford Squack an email objecting to this trend. I knew Squack wouldn't give two shits about inconveniencing me, so I attempted to focus on the others involved. "[T]hese Saturday night releases...are now occurring at least once a month," I wrote. "Example: Someone (probably Sara) will have to push the *Twilight* FC [Featured Content] at 9 pm Fri. March 20, and then push the *Bolt* FC at 9 pm the next night. Sara & others are already giving up every Monday night to do the store turn, and it seems a bit much to ask them to also give up *both* weekend evenings just to release two titles. We should work on a better system that doesn't require inconveniencing employees so frequently. Once a month, those involved are happy to help. But when we start asking for them to work two weekend evenings in a row, we're getting close to abuse, and will certainly get some pushback from Production [the department that Sara and others involved worked for] if we continue these frequent off-cycle requests."

My objections were read by a blind eye. I realized that 24/7 was in reality the "new normal," and that I'd better just swallow the blue pill, Neo, and get used to the abuse in The Matrix.

Even worse, however, was...

THE HORROR OF HOLIDAYS

"Every day is a holiday
Another motherfuckin' dollar day."
—Witchdoctor, "Holiday"

To most corporate clones, a holiday is a reason to rejoice—a day off from the grind. To iTunes employees, however, holidays complicated everything. Just as "the show must go on," the store must be updated. In order to prepare for a holiday, every aspect of the typical weekly production schedule had to be condensed to the point that often even a single day off, like Memorial Day, required that two weeks' worth of effort be accomplished during the preceding week. Deadlines were truncated; Design points were reduced; features and changes and updates were limited. A two-day holiday, like the 4th of July, doubled the complications. Often by the time the schedules and deadlines were condensed and the increased workload was complete, we actually *needed* a day or two off, just to recover.

Thanksgiving always had a slightly ironic element to it. Steve regularly announced that if the company met its goals, he'd give all of Apple the entire Thanksgiving week off...so we never knew until the last minute whether we'd be working that week or not. Given that uncertainty, there was no way to make plans in advance. And whether we were granted the week off or not, the store still needed to be updated. So even though SJ decreed that we should "take the week off," all that meant to iTunes employees was: "Work from home that week." (This should not be construed as a complaint; it's still better to work from home than to have to commute to the office.)

Christmas break was particularly dreaded. In order to clear server space to make room for all the iTunes customers using their new stocking-stuffer gift cards, iTunes employees were literally locked out of the store for a week between Christmas and New Year's Day. We could make no changes or updates, except in the most dire of emergencies. The Store as it appeared on Christmas Eve (or earlier) would be what the world would see until the next store turn—after the New Year. The façade was locked in; we were locked out. Complicating this even further was the emphasis on sales, sales, sales. While very few new titles are released by studios during the last couple of weeks of the year, the holiday features and sales that took precedence had to be programmed to operate perfectly and without intervention for as long as two weeks.

ALL HANDS ON DECK

Of all the meetings I attended at iTunes (and there were thousands), some of the most memorable were the All Hands meetings, where all iTunes employees were gathered together so management could tell us how we'd been doing during the past year and validate (or deny) rumors we'd read in the *Wall Street Journal, Forbes,* Gizmodo, and other journalistic sources. These mandatory meetings were almost always held off-site and always demanded an afternoon of attention. We could finish our day's work later, at home, after the meeting. The good news is that there was free food. The bad news is there was never any alcohol. This was a *work* function, goddamn it, not a friggin' *party*.

In one All Hands, they proudly announced that iTunes Movies was going to start adding "Extras" to many movies—the kind of peripheral "Bonus Feature" videos that were standard on

DVDs. Management had high hopes that the inclusion of these features would encourage more purchases of movie downloads, since these side stream videos would not be available on movie rentals. I had mixed feelings about this. If I bought a movie, it was because I knew I'd watch it several times. And while I did, in fact, watch most DVD bonus features, I watched them exactly once. I couldn't believe that adding these features to movie purchases would possibly inspire more sales (while increasing our cost of processing and storing a film). I thought it might make more sense financially to *rent* the bonus features at a separate, lesser charge than a movie rental, if a viewer only wanted to watch them once. But no one asked my opinion. I did feel justified, however, when the presenter asked the 500 or so audience members how many of us watched the DVD bonus features and exactly two hands went up: Gary Stewart's and mine. Clearly, bonus features were not something 99.6 percent of viewing audiences were interested in. Nevertheless, the initiative went forward, despite the overwhelming lack of interest.

Another All Hands took place in a punk nightclub in downtown San Jose. It was a space designed for urban raves, and looked awful with the lights on—cheesy, dirty and sad. When the presenters were finished, we were informed that we should stay in our seats, since we would now be the audience for a punk band filming a music video that would debut on iTunes. I made a stealthy beeline for the exit as an alternative to being forced to endure the music as a conscripted audience member. I hadn't hired into iTunes to be a mandatory music video audience member. It seemed a bit shifty (not to mention duplicitous) to bus in a fake audience for a music video, and I felt a bit abused that the management would even arrange this without informing us in advance—and without obtaining our consent.

The 2012 All Hands was held on January 25th in the Fox Theater in Redwood City—the town where I lived. *How convenient,* I thought; I don't even have to commute—I can *walk* to the meeting. Which I did. And when it was over, when everyone was milling about the lobby eating appetizers, when I couldn't find anyone to talk to, since they were all clustered in small groups talking about their kids, or their ski weekends, or their San Francisco hipster hangouts, and I was 61 years old and had none of that in common with them, I just walked a couple of blocks to Gourmet Haus Staudt, my Redwood City taproom hangout, got drunk, and called Piphy to drive over and join me (so I didn't have to drink alone. Or walk home.)

In some unconscious way, I think I was reprioritizing my enjoyable personal life over the grind of iTunes...or of any corporate employment. But I didn't realize that yet.

MEET MARKET

The Meeting Is In "Sanity"

The conference rooms at iTunes were named informally, after TV shows and movie characters; "Lost," for example. We'd be told to meet in "Itchy," not "Scratchy," for instance, or in "Howdy," not "Doody." (I have since discovered that this quirky and humorous naming of conference rooms is typical in hi-tech companies.)

A typical meeting during my final years at Apple followed the same entry format: choose a seat at the conference table, open your iPad (or your MacBook laptop if you were still lugging that around) and place your phone on the table. Only then were you ready to engage.

The Dilbert Index

I was always proud that Apple scored almost zero on the "Dilbert Index"—the informal measure of a company's illogic and insanity as indicated by how many "Dilbert" comic strips were visible on cubicle walls. I can only recall ever seeing one, actually—and that was in the window of a conference room, and was about naming conference rooms with funny names.

"FU"

Every benign authority figure needs a soulless executioner to do his dirty work so he can keep his hands (and his image) clean. For Eddy Cue, his right-hand hitman was the mysterious figure known as, we'll say, "FU." FU's very presence inspired fear among us drones. He looked like a skull on a stick, and his full name had far too few vowels for any human to pronounce. If FU had walked onto the set of *Star Trek: The Next Generation*, no one would ever have questioned his authenticity as an evil, emotionless alien (with a name that had far too few vowels for any human to pronounce). Anytime I saw FU walking down the street, the images that came to mind included Jack Skellington and Jack Pumpkinhead from the Oz novels—minus their smiles.

Luckily, I didn't know Jack. In six years, I had to endure only three encounters with this sinister specter. In November 2007, when I'd been on the job only half a year, he materialized before me and handed me a DVD. "Watch this tonight," he ordered without preamble, "and let me know if there's anything that will embarrass us. I'll be back tomorrow for your critique." I guess I knew what *I'd* be doing tonight! I took the disk and nodded, thankful that I had not been struck down by his scythe.

The DVD contained a movie entitled *Purple Violets*, written and directed by Edward Burns. I knew who Ed Burns was, and had almost admired a couple of his previous films, *The Brothers McMullen* and *She's the One*. So I anticipated no problems in reviewing his latest effort, a drama about a couple of struggling writers. I quickly discovered that it wasn't a very good movie, and, as a writer myself, I took issue with his vision of "the writer's life," which was almost ludicrously false in every detail. Aside from that, however, it was competent filmmaking. I found out from Marshall Dylan (still my boss at that time) that this movie was a really BFD for iTunes—it was to be the first feature film released on iTunes instead of in theaters. I was also informed that Ed Burns was a scheduled guest on Oprah Winfrey's show the next afternoon, where he would promote his flick and praise iTunes for releasing it. I realized then that my mandate to review the movie was a minimal and expendable part of this process; even if I'd given it a thumbs down, the PR steam-roller built around "the first feature film released exclusively on iTunes!" would trump any objections.

FU did indeed return the following day. "Well?" he said. I was at least savvy enough to know that he didn't want a full film critic review, so I gave him my quickest critique: "It's not very good, but it won't embarrass us." He walked away without thanking me—but also without turning me into a pile of cinders with his laser vision. I breathed a sigh of relief. And he disappeared back into the shadows.

I didn't see FU for nearly a year after that. Miracles happen. Sometime in September 2008, however, I was summoned to a conference room in our building—but denied entrance. The room was packed, and FU exited and hovered over me. "There's a Michael Moore movie we've just released," he said. "*Slacker Uprising*. We just discovered we don't have the rights. You need to get rid of it immediately."

"You want it pulled," I asked, "or hidden?"—two completely different processes.

His reply: "Why are you still standing here?"

I could have responded, "Because you haven't answered my question yet." But I didn't; by now, the fear of FU—through numerous horror stories from my co-workers—had been seared on my soul. There's a cliché that always seemed ludicrous to me: "When he says 'Jump' you ask 'How high?'" No no no... If an authority figure says "Jump," you *jump*—you don't ask "How high?"—at least not until you're already in the air. So I remained true to my own insight, and turned around and left. I'd let the head of Production determine whether the movie should be pulled or hidden. Let her decide how high to jump.

In late June 2009, FU returned to me once again, like a bad clam belch. This time he had a DVD of another iTunes exclusive: *World's Greatest Dad*, starring Robin Williams, written and directed by Bobcat Goldthwait. Everyone loves Robin, and I was a huge fan of the dark, edgy insanity of the Bobcat. But this time I did, in truth, have some objections. I spared FU my full analysis, but sent a detailed email to both Squack and Zucker, along with my "three strikes" against it being promoted as a major iTunes release:

1. *Pervasive obscene language.*

2. *Not of interest to our core demo, i.e., adolescents.* The teens are all portrayed as easily-duped idiots and stereotypes (Goth girl, gay guy, dumb jock, etc.) which could actually offend our core demos. The movie is about a middle-aged man's crisis of conscience and spiritual renewal caused by the suicide of his son—topics all miles away from the majority of our best-sellers, especially among our core demographics.

3. *It's unclear whether this is a very edgy adult drama or a very dark black comedy.* (Given that it was written and directed Bobcat Goldthwait, I'd guess the latter.) "Either way," I wrote, "it's very disturbing."

I didn't even bother to mention the nudity (Robin Williams naked—what a concept!) or the film's clichéd ending. But of course, despite my objections, we launched the movie. It was a coup and it would sell, so content and quality and potential offensiveness be damned.

APPLE IS PERKY

Apple offered many perks beyond the salary. In June 2007, for instance, SJ announced that all employees who'd been with the company for at least three months would soon receive a free iPhone... "and not just the base model, either," he emphasized. "You're all getting the top of the line model." I checked the calendar. I'd been there three months and a week...so I qualified. A few months later (after all the initial pre-orders for actual retail sales shipped), we all received our iPhones. I still had a working cell phone, so I kept my iPhone in the box for a year or two before I activated it. (Like a fine wine, it's best to let the Kool-Aid age before you drink it.) But I still have that original gift; even though it long ago outlived its functionality, it's a reminder of Steve Jobs' generosity...not to mention his managerial savvy (i.e., getting everyone in the company on the same phone) or his marketing genius, as every Apple employee became a walking, talking, living advertisement for the iPhone every time we used it in public. (Not to mention that most of us became iPhone evangelists.)

Other perks included free 15-minute chair massages about once a month, as well as frequent mixers. Most Friday afternoons there was a beer bash on the main campus, for instance—a chance to socialize with co-workers and Apple staff from other departments. (Not to mention free beer.) And maybe once a month, caterers would descend on our building and turn a couple of conference rooms into cornucopias of beer and wine and appetizers and desserts—yet another opportunity to ignore work and socialize and eat and drink.

And then there were the occasional free movie screenings in local theaters for features like *Scott Pilgrim vs. the World, The Black Swan* and *True Grit*, among others. At some point, Richard Zucker held in-house screenings of pre-release DVDs, too, which is where I first saw a couple of films that became favorites, *Black Dynamite* and *Tropic Thunder*.

In my specific position, I enjoyed a perk that only a few others in the company could claim: free DVDs. Not a week went by that I didn't receive a box or mailer containing pre-release DVDs from one of the studios represented on iTunes. I'd keep the ones I wanted and trade the others with the guys in the fledgling iTunes TV store for boxed sets of shows they'd received. It always struck me that this gifting was just a bit ironic: iTunes was attempting to move the media world away from physical media like DVD and Blu-ray, and toward digital downloads. In other words, we were getting gifts from the very people we were trying to put out of business. Suckers!

AM I A CLOWN TO YOU?

My favorite perk, however, was the circus. Once a year, Steve would purchase an entire performance of Cirque du Soliel just for Apple. (In 2010 our day at the circus was March 18—a day before my birthday and my third anniversary at Apple). We'd all drive (or take buses that were provided) to San Jose for the afternoon, where we'd not only enjoy the performance but also the open snack bar. Hot dogs, ice cream, candy, popcorn—as much as you wanted, and all free. When other people would tell me their work horror stories, I'd smile and say, "My boss said, 'Let's all blow off work and go to the circus!' "

"SJ"

Steve Jobs was a visionary and a genius. On this point, I am adamant and will brook no argument. He was also, however, many other things to many other people, including difficult, arrogant, obnoxious, and prickly. His own daughter, Lisa Jobs-Brennan, in her brilliant, extraordinary 2018 memoir *Small Fry*, described numerous incidences of his emotional distance and "cold" personality. A good friend of mine who interviewed him several times labeled him frankly "a sociopath." Oh, well. Picasso was an inveterate horndog; William Faulkner (and about a zillion other writers) were raging alkies; an aging Gandhi slept with teenage girls in the belief that their physical proximity would keep him young. Clearly, people who are both geniuses and visionaries are also complicated and multifaceted. (Don't even get me started on my Scottish kinsman Andrew Carnegie.)

Working for "SJ" (as he was always referred to around The Cupe), however, was very different than just interviewing him, or even just meeting him. While I had every excuse to seek him out and present him with a copy of my film guide, *Killer B's* as his Movie Guru, I could not predict how he might respond. He might be gracious, and pleased that his people had hired such a knowledgeable and intelligent film writer for the iTunes Movies Store—or he might think that one of his slaves was getting too uppity and should be fired. So I sacrificed any potential personal contact with Apple's *capo di tutti capi* out of fear. I liked my job. I *needed* my job. I couldn't gamble that SJ might take an irrational dislike to me and show me the door.

I only ever encountered Steve on one occasion, and only in passing. Early in November 2008, SJ announced that if Apple "met our numbers" for iPhone sales, he'd give the entire company the entire Thanksgiving week off with pay as a thank you. We did indeed hit that corporate goal...so the vacation was on. I'd been at Apple for a year and a half, and was still in the habit of walking from our iTunes building to the Mother Ship to have lunch at Caffè Macs. As I was walking across the grassy, sidewalk-lined quad in the center of the six main buildings, I saw Steve saying goodbye to a couple of people and begin walking along the sidewalk behind me. We were far enough apart that I would have had to run to rendezvous with him. Not cool. But as he passed in front of me, maybe 20 yards away, I called out, "Thanks for Thanksgiving week, Steve." At first, I thought he didn't hear me, or was ignoring me. But then he stopped, turned in my direction, and replied, "Yeah. It's gonna be great, isn't it?"

"Yes, sir, it is," I said. And we each continued walking, in opposite directions.

I know my "I met Steve Jobs" story could have been better. But then again, it could have ended in tragedy. I mean, how good is a story that ends, "And I lost my high-paying job at Apple because Steve Jobs thought I was a pain in the ass"?

That story isn't even unique.

SJ's PRESENTATIONS

There was always a hierarchy for attending SJ's presentations. The top level, reserved for the upper management, was to be present at the event site itself—San Francisco's Moscone Center, for instance, or Cupertino's Flint Center (only a mile and a half from our corporate HQ), or wherever the event was held. Those key execs and middle management employees who didn't make the cut were invited to the Town Hall on the main campus, where the event would be streamed on a movie screen. The rest of us could go to one of several campus locations where the live video stream was projected onto large screens.

The first presentation I attended occurred only a few weeks after I'd started in 2007. I got to work surprised to find our building empty, only to discover that everyone had migrated to the most prominent location they could attain. All work stopped on these mornings. I found the nearest mass screening in an iTunes building across the street. The large lobby had been outfitted with row after row of folding chairs—hundreds of chairs—and I took a random seat since I was too new to know anyone to sit with.

And SJ presented. For hours. Polished and professional, sure—but I had work to do...and those damn folding chairs were never meant to be sat in for hours on end. It seems I was not the only employee in the audience with similar thoughts, because the moment Steve ended the presentation and introduced a bonus—a special performance by Randy Newman—virtually the entire congregation watching in our campus building stood up as one and walked out. Either they had vital work to do, I guessed, or they were not big Randy Newman fans.

I sat through many of these meetings, cheering on cue when SJ announced some radical new lifechanging breakthrough in... whatever. The one moment from any of these presentations that entered my long-term memory occurred when Steve was discussing some recent friction with Eric Schmidt, then CEO of Google and a member of Apple's Board of Directors. SJ was getting more and more visibly agitated until he finally broke script. "You know their motto, 'Don't be evil?' " he growled, almost sputtering. "That's just *bullshit!*"

THE DAY THE MUSIC DIED

I'd often marveled at the unusual celebrity status Steve Jobs held in American culture. Few people could name the CEO of GM or AT&T or Walmart, for instance, but "Steve Jobs" (like Bill Gates) was a household word. Even more intriguing was the public association between the stability of Apple and Steve Jobs' health. (I used to say, "Steve sneezes and the stock falls ten points.") His health issues were even mentioned on the San Fran evening news. What other CEO gets that kind of attention?

On January 12, 2009, all employees received an email from SJ, informing us that his "health crisis" was more severe than he'd originally believed, and that he'd be taking a leave of absence until June, leaving Tim Cook in charge. We all wished him well.

Almost exactly two years later, on January 17, 2011, all employees received an email from SJ informing us that the Board of Directors had approved his request for a medical leave of absence to focus on his health, and appointing Tim Cook to take over his day-to-day responsibilities. "I love Apple so much," he closed, "and I hope to be back as soon as I can."

Steve never returned. He died at his home in Palo Alto on the fifth of October, 2011. We were informed via email. I could report that there was sobbing and wailing and gnashing of teeth in the office that day, but no... His passing was inevitable; the only question for months had been *when.* Around the iTunes offices, the day's work went on precisely as scheduled, although the building seemed a bit quieter and my co-workers a little more subdued.

A memorial service was held on the Cupertino campus a couple of weeks later. "It was nice," I wrote to a friend outside the company. (I wasn't about to waste time finding a more descriptive adjective than 'nice' in an email.) "More people than I've ever seen here before. Tim Cook, the new CEO (that Steve had been grooming to take over for years) spoke, Norah Jones sang a few songs, Johnny Ive, who designs all the Apple products so they look cool, spoke and added some humor to the gathering, then Al Gore gave a little speech, and Coldplay played a few songs. It was half memorial, half free concert, since Apple and the iPod have totally dominated the music industry for years now. Then it was back to work, even tho the mood around here has been pretty somber for the past week. Not much more to say except we're all pretty sad."

Steve Jobs was, I feel, directly responsible for providing me with a career and a retirement. One measure of my respect is that I thank "SJ" almost daily—far more often than I thank God for anything.

THE DISAPPEARED

> "My! People come and go here so quickly!"
> —Dorothy Gale, *The Wizard of Oz* (1939)

Indeed. At Apple, people came and went very quickly—and not always of their own accord. Some left Apple voluntarily: Crystal, for instance—frustrated that she could not push through the advanced engineering projects she'd left the Movies team to pursue—quit Apple late in 2009 to return to Netflix and join her engineer husband. She sent a nice email saying goodbye to the friends she'd made during her short tenure. Marshall Dylan bowed out as well a year or so later, after being kicked to the sidelines as his reward for successfully launching the Movies Store. We threw a lovely luncheon for him, attended by a roomful of well-wishers, myself among them. It should be noted that, although people frequently left for another job, in the six years I spent at Apple, I never once encountered a retirement party.

It's not unusual for co-workers to leave; Silicon Valley is notorious for its turnover rate. But then there were those co-workers who simply...disappeared. One day you'd see them in the hall; they'd be sending emails, working hard...and then all communication from them would simply cease. Usually, it took a week or two to notice—everyone was busy doing their job, for one thing, and the MIA employee might be on vacation or whatever. But at some point, their absence would be noticed. Often, when I enquired about them, the standard response from management was: "Oh, he/she isn't with us anymore." Any further questioning was often met with just a shrug.

I saw this virtual vanishing occur numerous times. Take Alison, for instance—one of the original iTunes TV Store programmers; a tall, extraverted ginger who appeared to be a gawky scatterbrain. Her cubicle was right across the hall from mine for several months, so we got to know each other a bit. In addition to her effervescent personality, one of the many things I admired about her was that she was committed to personal growth, always taking courses to improve her education and management skills—a determined course which paid off when she transferred to a position of more responsibility. When I saw her a few months later, she'd blossomed into a calm, confident, competent individual. And then she disappeared. When I realized I hadn't heard from her for a while and shot her an email, it was returned as "undeliverable." When I asked around, I got the standard stonewall answer: "Oh. Alison. She isn't with us anymore."

Her cubicle was filled by a new hire, one JC, a jolly little guy who'd been hired to improve the quality of our digital encodes. We struck up a friendship and often lunched together, our corny senses of humor meshing well enough that we kept each other quite amused. When he showed me around his lab a few months after he'd come on board, I realized he'd been given an equipment budget that amounted to a small fortune...and I got a sinking feeling in the pit of my stomach.

"Y'know," I said casually, "it seems like you're spending an awful lot of money. You should really be careful." But he was undeterred: quality is not cheap. Then one day he failed to show up for work. *Sick day,* I thought. He didn't show up the next day, either, or the day after that. *Vacation,* I figured, although he hadn't mentioned a vacation when we'd last had lunch. When another week rolled around and JC still had not returned, I asked Marshall Dylan what happened to him. His answer: "Oh. JC isn't with us anymore."

Shit, I thought. *Maybe that cubicle is cursed.*

But perhaps this kind of quiet firing was preferable to the fate of Gary Stewart. Gary had been named "Chief Musical Officer" for iTunes in August 2004, reporting directly to Eddy Cue and charged with overseeing and curating all iTunes Music content. Under his direction, the Music store added features like the "Essentials" collections; they also created playlists and developed a taxonomy that organized the wide world of music into intuitive, intelligent categories. Sometime in late 2011, Gary's management decided he'd served his purpose and was superfluous, and he was summarily let go—apparently a victim of the "What have you done for us lately?" syndrome. I never ever got the full story, of course—only Gary (or Eddy Cue, or Eddy's hitman, FU) knew that story. But Gary Stewart's banishment came as a shock to everyone else in iTunes.

TEAM MOVIES GO!

Is there anything worse in any job than Team Building exercises? Can't we all just get along at work? But no…many of the (bad) bosses who plagued my existence also demanded that we co-workers bond as a team. Joe DiTrolli at SGI, for instance, used to hold regular offsites, and during every one he included an agenda item entitled "What I Hate About You" (comparable, I suppose, to Kramer's Festivus activity "The Airing of the Grievances"). And although I was spared from ever having to participate in idiot shit like "Trust Falls," Buford Squack did attempt to launch his own team building exercise, disguised as a "reward" for all our efforts: an evening at the Go-Kart track.

How did I hate this? Let me count the ways. First of all, I want to be the one to choose my off-hours activities and playmates. I'm forced to spent all day with these people—paid to do it—so let's not push it by requiring that I also spend an evening playing with them. Second, as an introvert, and at that point over 60, I should be required to engage in a loud, stinky, dangerous competitive activity with a bunch of Type A's half my age? I think not. And finally… Go-Karts? Seriously? If you look up "fun" in the dictionary, you do *not* find a picture of a Go-Kart. Even though I was pressured by my peers to "join in the fun," I respectfully declined.

DOES HUMOR BELONG IN THE WORKPLACE?
(Part 4 of a Nearly Infinite Series)

The Ultimate iTunes Joke:
Q: How many iTunes engineers does it take
to change a lightbulb?
A: We don't track that data.

Regardless of the stress—or perhaps because of it—we could still have fun. Occasionally. Conflict, like bad decisions, makes for good stories, but the fun stuff is far more important and memorable.

Our original team—Crystal, Ross, Marshall and me—knew that behind closed doors we were free to say anything, about anyone or any policy, in any fucking language we felt appropriate, and we often let our hair down in the safe space of a locked room—to the point that Marshall frequently admonished us, "Guys, it all stays in this room, or we're all fired."

In our later team, Zucker, Andy and I shared a Venn diagram of humor that overlapped mostly in the "Loud and Outrageous" category. We often spouted or shouted lines to one another from crazy-ass flicks we loved, like *Anchorman* ("Why don't you go back to Whore Island where you came from!") and *The Fantastic Mr. Fox* ("Don't you point and cuss at me!"), or from TV's *Archer* ("Danger Zone!" "*Laaaaaaa-naaaaaaa!*") And every time the price "99" came up in store planning, we'd spend a few seconds all just repeating "Nine nine nine nine nine!" like spastic parrots, and break up laughing. (Why was this funny? I have no explanation. No idea. Guess you just had to be there.)

Zucker once (June 6, 2010, precisely) sent me an email about Warner not updating the sale price of some movie, which caused iTunes endless headaches; his list of action items concluded with: "Kill everyone at Warner, leave no survivors."

A few months later, when he reversed his decision about not making some "stupid" change on the store and I inquired as to why the about-face, he wrote, "Apparently Steve made this call…" When I replied that "we're all counting on you to storm right up to [Steve's] office and tell him how dead wrong and dumb this is. And it was nice working with you," his response was, “You kidding? I think this is dead on. GENIUS!” All I could do was reply, “That’s what I meant. I’m totally signed up. Where’s my Kool-Aid?”

An email exchange in June 2011 that began with Zucker announcing he was thrilled that we’d be adding *Citizen Kane* to the store for its 70th anniversary led to this exchange:

Me: Rosebud was his sled, y’know *(I replied).*

RZ: ahhhhhh damn. thanks a lot!!!!

Me: And that chick in *The Crying Game*? A dude.

RZ: uuuuuggggghhhhhhh

Me: Old Yeller? They shoot him.

RZ: SHUUUUUTTTTTT UPPPPPPPP

Me: The Wizard? A humbug. Rhett? Leaves Scarlett; doesn’t give a damn. Batman? Turns out he’s billionaire industrialist Bruce Wayne. *Rashomon*? He said, she said. Nobody knows for sure.

Not all attempts at humor worked out exactly as expected, however.

Example 1: In mid-2010, I alerted Andy via email that he’d spelled “radar” backwards. And then had to explain it to him.

Example 2: On February 2nd of one year I wanted to create a swoosh on Movies Main that had nothing in it but the movie *Groundhog Day*, repeated about 20 times. I was informed that the technology could not support such a request.

Example 3: Labor Day, 2011. In mid-August, while planning the store for the first week of September, I said to Zucker, “I’m tired of promoting the same old list of movies every year for these holidays. Why don’t we do something different this year? Instead of movies about work for Labor Day, why don’t we display a selection of movies about pregnancy and childbirth—*Juno, Knocked Up, Baby Mama*, and so on. You know…the *other* ‘labor day.’”

“Love it,” Zucker replied. “Just to make sure, let me check with Squack.” Squack loved the idea as well and I was given the green light.

On August 30, the day we released the swoosh, some random blog ran a short piece entitled “iTunes Celebrates the Wrong Kind of Labor Day.” “There are 24 movies in the Labor Day section of iTunes right now [it read], all of which are about making babies or having babies... No sign of celebrating the working man…" the author noticed, completely missing the point. A post on another blog also failed to get the joke, speculating that perhaps iTunes was outsourcing its selection of themed movies to India.

So the idea wasn't gold. It was more like something you'd find in a diaper, it seems—and upper iTunes management was the fan it hit. Since diaper contents flow downhill, I was forwarded an email from the head of Production to Squack, Zucker, and one of her own direct reports, the head of Editorial, in which the relevant sections read: "I am very concerned about the editorial selections in movies… we need to discuss why we did not catch this and why it was allowed to go live. It's off brand, in poor taste, and insulting to vets… No idea why we did this, it's silly and gratuitous."

I can't be sure she misunderstood the meaning of "gratuitous." But her comment about being "insulting to vets" is evidence that she for sure didn't understand the meaning of Labor Day, clearly confusing it with Memorial Day. (I can only imagine how these bloggers would have responded if they were informed about her decision to "honor our vets" on Labor Day.)

It took me years to realize that if we'd simply named (or renamed) this feature "The Other Labor Day" or "Going Into Labor Day," we might have been able to avoid all the brouhaha and ended up instead with just the ha-ha. But probably not.

WHAT KIND OF COMPANY WAS APPLE TO WORK FOR? (HR EDITION)

Like most companies, Apple requires an annual refresher course in HR topics like diversity, harassment and my favorite oxymoron, corporate ethics. Ours was a self-paced online course, in which one was only allowed to move to the next topic once successfully answering questions about the topic at hand. Even if you always answered every question wrong, you were given enough do-overs that sooner or later you'd pick the right answer, even if by chance rather than knowledge, and could move on. I dutifully engaged.

It quickly became apparent that diversity was the key: "employees" pictured and featured in the examples included workers of virtually every ethnic persuasion, from IT guys in Thailand to Marketing women in China to African American Apple store employees to... Well, you get the picture.

About midway through the course, however, I noticed a curious lack of one ethnic group: middle-aged Caucasian males. I was one, but I wasn't represented in the rainbow of diversity in this HR training. I looked around the office and discovered I was pretty much *surrounded* by middle-aged Caucasian males. Why weren't we in the mix?

At length, I did find one topic that was illustrated with a picture of a middle-aged Caucasian male. The topic? "Violence in the Workplace." I thought of contacting HR and objecting to this insulting stereotype, but decided against it. I'd had enough trouble with HR already, and figured my objection would only get me into more...or might revive the "argumentative" label they'd branded me with years earlier. Or even worse, it would reinforce their sorry-ass stereotype that middle-aged Caucasian males are all angry assholes, and thus become a self-fulfilling prophecy. I wouldn't give them the satisfaction.

JUST A MOMENT...

Tolstoy famously observed, "Happy families are all alike; every unhappy family is unhappy in its own way." The same can be said of jobs, I believe: every unhappy worker is unhappy in his or her own way...and, like happy families, there are damn few happy jobs. I've spent an inordinate amount of time in this narrative detailing the indignities, the unpleasantries, and the ironies of bad jobs (including the worst job of all: job hunting). But—if only to prove I'm not a complete curmudgeon—I want to relate this little incident.

Sometime in 2011 or '12, I found myself on a Saturday morning (OK, noon) engaged in my usual "slow wake up" routine. I was settled in my big, comfy leather easy chair. My tea (Earl Grey, hot) was just the proper temperature. I was reading a book by the Dalai Lama (I've read them all). My precious black cat, Skitten, was curled up in my lap, asleep. Beethoven was playing on the San Francisco classical music station. I was gazing out the four enormous French windows of our top floor apartment at the quartet of giant redwood trees that fronted our faux Normandy castle building.

And I found myself counting my blessings: I owned a house in Hawaii. I had enough money in the bank for a modest retirement. I drove a breathtakingly beautiful classic Jaguar. I was working for the most valuable company in the world. The smartest and most evolved woman I'd ever known and I had been together for well over a decade, so, hey, maybe that would work out, too. And best of all, I knew enough by now to realize that a perfect moment like this was both precious and evanescent, and that I should appreciate the fleeting.

Life was good.

Chapter 32

2013: UPSETTING THE APPLE CART

January 2013

We now return to the chronological narrative:

Several essential members of our smooth-running, long-term team (like Sean in Design and Wolfgang in Build) got promotions in the new year. I was happy for these young, ambitious, talented and hardworking guys, even while realizing that I'd never see a promotion, since I was already doing the only job for my skill set. But that was OK—they were at the beginning of their careers, and I was near the end of mine…even though that end would come earlier than I ever expected.

At any rate, we had a new team to break in. We'd lost our boss, Buford Squack, a couple of months earlier, and there was no indication of any replacement to assume his duties. If that wasn't enough of a shakeup, now Apple was physically moving us—along with every other iTunes department from every other building lining Valley Green Drive—out of our buildings and into a new location a couple of miles away—a building on the motivationally-named "Results Way."

The move made some kind of sense, I suppose. We grunts were never privy to the economic reasons for the move, but we were informed that gathering all branches of iTunes under one roof would unquestionably lead to enhanced productivity. Rather than forcing members of the iTunes Music, Movies, TV and other stores to walk to a different building to meet with Production departments like Design, Build, UI, Editorial, and others "across the street," we'd all now be housed in the same single edifice. As it turns out, we were all so spread out in this enormous new building that very few minutes (or steps) were saved in walking over to a different department. But at least we wouldn't get rained on, or run over in the road.

Our new home was located at the rear of a series of warehouse-like buildings on the industrial outskirts of Cupertino

—so far around the back, in fact, that it took nearly five minutes just to drive through the corridor of this new campus (it was hardly a street) to our parking lot. Worse, the frequent speed bumps threatened to ruin my low-slung Jaguar. The only good news about the location was that the Cupertino Whole Foods was exactly one mile away—the same distance as from our old building. (Clearly, Whole Foods—or as we all referred to it, "Whole Paycheck"—was the center of the iTunes Universe. SJ always talked about the serendipitous benefit of running into co-workers in the hallways for impromptu meetings; he could have accomplished the same thing by setting up a dedicated lunch-room table at the Cupertino Whole Foods. I ran into far more of my co-workers there than I ever did "wandering the halls" at work, where everyone was always in a hurry to get somewhere and had no time to waste on an "impromptu meeting.")

The new building was big. Sprawling. And it was austere. The enormous lobby, stark and unfurnished, had a floor of polished stone that made footsteps echo and was completely empty save for a single receptionist desk wedged into an alcove. It was, in a word, soulless. After a decade of occupancy, our old building at least had some character, and housed some history: old iTunes posters on the walls; framed gold records from artists made famous by the revolutionary music service (like Flo Rida and Sarah Bareilles); stained rugs and dented ducts and messy, messy offices and cubicles. It was lived in, and looked it. The new building was sterile: white walls, stanky new carpet, beige in every direction unto the horizon, and the same tiny wall-lining offices for everyone above the foot soldier level. (The only upgrade for middle management was that their wall of windows was frosted, so no one could see in. They no longer inhabited what in the previous buildings were referred to as "fishbowls.") Worst of all: it was quiet. There were none of the comforting sounds of distant music, clunky, clunking ducts, and murmured conversation that we'd all grown accustomed to ignoring. The silence was scary. Downright creepy.

I still had no office. But that was never gonna happen. I'd reconciled myself to that. The good news, if you could call it that, was that my cubicle was twice the size of everyone else's. Why they gave me a double-wide cubicle—especially considering I was still working from home four days a week—I'll never know. The really good news is I'll never care whether I know.

One afternoon after we moved in, I said to Richard Zucker, "You think they're trying to tell us something with this move, this building? Like now that we're the world's biggest music retailer, we can't act all loosey-goosey as though we were still a crazy-ass startup? That we gotta grow up and stop having fun and take this all *seriously*?"

"Yeah," he said with a sigh.

He was the only one who knew how really serious things would get—although I doubt he realized it would start with him.

MEET THE NEW BOSS (AGAIN, SIGH)
Part 7 of Far Too Many

In early January, Keith, who'd been filling in for the ousted Buford Squack during the previous few months, called a general meeting for all Music, Movies and TV personnel. It wasn't on a Wednesday (my one day in The Cupe during my WFH quarantine), but I decided to show up anyway—it sounded important.

And it was. Keith announced that Josh, one of the Music managers, would be taking over Squack's role, among other duties. Yesterday, Josh was Richard Zucker's peer. Today, he was Zucker's boss.

I knew this would not sit well with Zuck. I suspected (or assumed) that Zucker had lobbied and campaigned for this position, since he was ambitious and an empire builder. And since the last major management change in iTunes was nearly five years earlier, I couldn't see Zucker patiently waiting for years for his next chance to grab the brass ring. So there was bound to be friction between these two guys, if only because Zucker had been passed over for the position—not to mention that he had no respect for Josh whatsoever. I immediately went to Josh's office and congratulated him, hoping if nothing else to distance myself from Zucker in case there was trouble.

THE END,
OR AT LEAST THE BEGINNING OF THE END

New boss, new building, new team. Could it get any better? (As Homer Simpson said, "That was sarcasm in case you didn't notice.") On January 9, I would find out just how much, um, "better" it could get when Richard Zucker announced our new team assignments, yay! The gist of his reorganization was that Andrew Merry and I would be trading job functions: Andy would assume my duties as lead Programmer, taking over ownership of Movies Main, and I would perform his central task, curating and expanding the movie genre pages.

This made no sense to me at all. Programming Movies Main had been my *one job* at iTunes, and I'd been doing it for nearly six years. I knew the ins and outs of the schedules and processes (not to mention the quirks) and the entire history of Movies Main—where the bodies were buried. Andy had programmed Movies Main less than a dozen times in four years—only when I was on vacation, and always with the handhold of a detailed document of instructions I left for him. And not three months earlier, Zucker and I had had a private conversation in which we agreed that Andy was not temperamentally suited to perform my job function. So why was I being demoted?

Zucker had an answer. More than one, actually. It didn't impress me that he wanted "fresh eyes" on Movies Main to "get us out of a rut." He was the one who designed the store every week, after all. He was the one who determined the placement of every element on the page. His were the only "eyes" on the store—no one but Richard Zucker could put "fresh eyes" on it. It wasn't like Andy was in any position to start changing things around; as I had done for the previous six years, Andy would merely implement the decisions made by people above his pay grade. He would just do as he was told. *Maybe,* I thought, *Zucker just wants to prove to his new boss Josh that he's not stagnating in his position—that he's willing to try new things; to shake things up.*

There was, however, one reason this job swap would be highly beneficial to me, Zucker explained: "This will free up your time to expand our movie collections and concentrate on special features." Now *that* I could get behind! After nearly six years of being undervalued, underused and literally prohibited from fulfilling the mandate I'd been hired to accomplish, my core talents were finally being recognized and rewarded. Zucker had always lobbied for editorial features with his boss, Buford Squack, who hated "that shit." But with Squack out of the picture, I would finally have the chance to turn iTunes Movies into the kind of in-depth movie site that Gary Stewart and his team had created with iTunes Music. I could create features based on directors, actors, and subgenres like Film Noir and Rom-Coms. I could build layered features like Music had done—dividing Hitchcock movies, for example, into categories like "Essential," "Entertaining" and "Deep Catalog." I could finally put to use everything I'd learned in order to teach college courses in Film History. This could be the single best thing that ever happened to me at Apple—maybe in my entire career!

Here are a couple of things I learned soon afterward:

1) People lie; and

2) Hope is not your friend.

THE MIDDLE OF THE END

But in February 2013, before I was reminded of those depressing lessons, things were going great. I developed a plan of action for my new assignment that covered most of the year, starting small with the low-hanging fruit—a list of new Movie Collections I wanted to assemble—and moving on to more complicated features I would tackle once the ball was rolling.

The first clue I had that something was rotten in Denmark was when I suggested to Zucker that we hold a luncheon for our old and new teammates in Design and Build—the people who'd worked closely supporting our efforts for three, four, even as long as five years, and to whom we owed a great deal of our success. This could serve as a way to introduce ourselves to the new faces and welcome them aboard, and to say thanks and good-bye to our long-term collaborators like Sean and Wolfgang.

Zucker thought that was a great idea. Too bad he invited everyone but me. OK, I could shrug that off—he claimed I was using a new version of our shared calendar that didn't integrate with the old version he was still using, and that's why I never got the invite. (We were all supposed to upgrade to the new version—was I the only one who did? Not to mention, I discovered later, that the two versions were *not* incompatible.)

And then the unthinkable happened: I missed a meeting.

(Sidebar note: If it seems as though I'm subjecting this seemingly minor incident to microscopic scrutiny, or spending an inordinate amount of time on apparently inconsequential details, I beg your indulgence. Perhaps this incident is the kind of thing that happens a thousand times a day in offices around the world ...but since Zuck's angry insistence on making a mountain out of this molehill would become a career-ending event for at least one of us, it seems only appropriate to present the incident in all its gory details.)

So I missed a meeting. So what? It wasn't a particularly important meeting. And I hardly needed to be there. A few days earlier, I'd met one-on-one with Wolfgang's replacement, our new Movies Store Builder. We'd compared notes and devised a way to streamline the process we'd been using for...well, forever. I suggested we set up a meeting for the Movies & TV Programmers to explain this new procedure. I further suggested that our team would pay much more attention to this information if it came from her—an "outsider"—than they would if it came from me. She could verify that we'd discussed this and that she'd approved it, and we could all begin doing our business this new way. So it was settled. I asked Zucker to set up the meeting, and it went on everyone's calendar (including, suspiciously, mine!) for the following Wednesday at 1:30.

Wednesday was my day in the office, so it was also my day to get lunch from Whole Foods. Melody and I went to lunch together and spent the time talking about how sullen and out of sorts Richard Zucker had become over the past few weeks.

"You know he's having his kitchen remodeled," she said.

"Yeah, I suppose that's plenty stressful," I agreed.

"Not only that," she dished, "but while his kitchen is torn up, he's staying with his ex-wife. And her new husband."

"Oh, ouch!" I said. "No wonder he's gone nuts."

"That," she agreed, "and losing the job to Josh."

"Maybe," I suggested, "we should just keep a low profile for a while until he calms down."

We arrived back at the office about 1:20. But when I checked the calendar to find out the location of the meeting, I realized I was in trouble. A new building meant new conference rooms, and I had no idea where this one was located. I hit the intranet and searched Apple's building maps but still could not locate the room. I decided to ask around—but oddly, aside from Melody, no one was in their cubicle. *Still at lunch?* I wondered. *Or did they know where the meeting room was and were already headed there?* Melody didn't know the location of the conference room either, but suggested asking the receptionist. "If she doesn't know, she'll have a map of the building." When I walked up to the receptionist's desk, however, she was involved in a protracted argument with a phone company installer. I stood there for several minutes before I could politely interrupt and ask for the location of the room. She showed me a map, and traced a path that led through the building and down a staircase to a sublevel. "We have a basement?" I asked, then headed for the stairs.

By now it was about 1:40—ten minutes after the scheduled start of the meeting. I wasn't worried, however, since no one ever showed up to meetings on time, particularly Zucker. He was so consistently ten minutes late to every meeting that it was a running joke among the people who most frequently met with him. Given that I didn't need to be there in the first place, showing up late should pose no problem.

I found the conference room, and, lucky me, no one else had shown up yet. So I sat and waited. And waited. And waited. And not a single other participant showed up. After ten minutes, I gave up and went back to my desk. Everyone might show up to meetings a few minutes late, but 20 minutes late? Something was wrong.

Part of my WFH agreement with Zucker was to contact him or someone if I was unable to phone in to a meeting, so I applied that same procedure and started iChatting the three co-workers I knew would be in that meeting, including Zucker. *Where are you? Where's the meeting?* I received no reply from anyone. So I whipped out my iPhone and started calling the same trio only to get diverted to everyone's voice mail. I even sent emails to all three: *Where are you? Where's the meeting?* And eventually, about two o'clock, I just gave up. As W.C. Fields put it, "If at first you don't succeed, try, try again. Then give up. No sense being a damn fool about it." I was out of communication options anyway. I'd left my bullhorn and carrier pigeons at home.

A few minutes later, the door to Zucker's office opened and my co-workers and our new Builder exited. They'd been in Zucker's office this whole time? A few feet from my cubicle? How could I know? The calendar listed the distant conference room, and the window-walls of all the managers' offices were frosted glass. I couldn't see them inside; they couldn't see me walk by in my numerous attempts to solve the mystery of the missing meeting.

To my shock and dismay, Zucker was livid. "Why weren't you there?" he demanded, in front of the entire team. I tried the simple, rational explanation: that I didn't need to be there; that I'd developed the procedure with the Builder who related it to the team, so I was superfluous. "Nobody's superfluous," he bellowed. "It started at one o'clock," he insisted. "You should have been there."

OK, I decided; if he wanted more detail, I'd give it to him—even though I knew he wasn't going to like it. "It was scheduled to start at one-*thirty*," I explained. "You should know. You set it up. But apparently the time *and the location* were changed—and no one informed me." I took care to phrase this so that it was not an accusation, even though we both knew he was the only person who could have changed the time and location. But I did go on to enumerate my numerous attempts to contact anyone who could tell me where the meeting had moved to, and how I'd received no responses.

"Why didn't you just knock on my office door?" he demanded

"Because you weren't supposed to *be* in your office," I replied. He clearly wanted to get into this, so I was determined to present him with the facts—unvarnished. "You were *supposed* to be in the meeting—the meeting that was scheduled to start at one-thirty. In the conference room listed on the calendar. The meeting where *you* changed the time and location and failed to inform me." His response was to go into his office and slam the door. (I feared for the frosted glass.) It was clear that he was unwilling to discuss the issue any further—not because we were both getting a bit hot under the collar, but because he knew he was wrong and couldn't come up with a deflection explanation quickly enough to bounce the blame back onto me. I'd learned months earlier that he would never admit to being wrong, no matter how easy it was to prove that he was solely responsible for my missing the meeting, and despite everything that I'd done to find it. It's not like this hadn't happened before. It had.

I went back to my desk and went back to work, figuring that was the end of it. He'd never admit culpability, so he'd drop the entire affair. It's not like that, too, hadn't happened before, because it had.

But this time I was mistaken. A while later, he sent me a blistering iChat demanding that I account for my every action for every minute of the meeting I'd missed. His outrage proved contagious: I realized I'd been working in corporate America since 1981—over thirty years; since the time he was still smoking in the Boy's Room in high school—and I had never before had such an outrageous and insulting demand made of me, or had my professionalism so impugned and disrespected.

Now I was pissed.

I was not about to succumb to my own ire, however, no matter the extent of the indignity. I began, then trashed, several responses, including one that detailed, minute by minute, the odyssey I'd been forced to take to even *locate* the damn meeting —much of which is written above. (That version ended with me pointing out that I'd just lost a full hour of productive time in order to comply with his demeaning request of detailing where I was during that time.) But I didn't send that one either.

At length, I sent a simple response: *Why did you change the time and location of the meeting and fail to inform me?* I'd learned the hard way that Zucker attacked by deflection, but since this was clearly his cock-up, I was not about to engage in *his* argument. Instead, I determined to use his argument techniques against him—to use "email aikido" to turn his own ire against him. My own form of deflection was to insist on returning to the one key question: Not what I was doing that made me miss the meeting, but why *his action* resulted in my missing the meeting. I received no reply.

It occurred to me that what I should do is forward his demand to HR and query them as to whether this type of communication constituted "creating a hostile work environment," which qualified as harassment—and whether they approved of this as a management technique. But it made me sick to my stomach to think I might be turning into "that guy"—the same kind of self-righteous prick who turned me in to HR years earlier, choosing to hide behind HR's skirts rather than confront an interpersonal problem directly.

No, my being a sleazy weasel or a good little Nazi and reporting Zucker to HR was not an option. For me, anyway. But, I would discover, it clearly was for him.

Chapter 33

2013: ONE BAD APPLE

"No, no!" said the Queen. "Sentence first—verdict afterwards."
—Lewis Carroll, *Alice in Wonderland*

"I know enough of the world now, to have almost lost the capacity of being much surprised by anything, but it is a matter of some surprise to me, even now, that I can have been so easily thrown away at such an age."
—Charles Dickens, *David Copperfield*

SPOILING THE BARREL

(*Note:* A fuller account of these events can be found in the chapter "You Can't Spell 'WHORE' Without 'HR'" in Part IV.)

And then I was fired?
The question mark is not a typo. I *was* fired. Sort of.

Tuesday, April 2

When I went into The Cupe on Tuesday, April second, and walked into Zucker's office at 2 PM for our weekly touch-base, I was surprised to find him talking to an attractive young woman who I did not know. He introduced his visitor as a person I'll refer to as "HR Girl," and informed me that he'd asked her to join us "to facilitate."

"Facilitate what?" I asked.

Zucker brought out a document and announced, "We're concerned that some of your behavior from the past is resurfacing. I've listed several incidents here, and I'd be happy to go through them paragraph by paragraph if you'd like." I knew we'd had a couple of miscommunications lately that Zucker was upset about (as well as being responsible for), but two pages? Single-spaced? I had no idea what the purpose of this meeting was, so I preferred to find that out first of all.

"No no no," I said, "I don't think we need to go through everything." I suspected I knew at least a couple of the incidents he'd written up, like that recent missed meeting, and I knew that his perspective was incomplete and inaccurate, since he'd refused to even listen to my side of the stories. It's not like this, too, hadn't happened before, because it had—repeatedly.

"I don't know what he's got on that document," I said to HR Girl, "but I can assure you it's only one side of the story. I guarantee you that whatever incidents he has listed on those sheets, there are alternative points of view, good explanations, different perspectives, other opinions that you're not getting."

That's when Richard Zucker made Big Mistake Number One. "Since I'm the boss," he replied, "my opinion is the only one that matters."

I was almost literally jaw-dropped. How could someone in authority make such an arrogant, inflammatory, self-incriminating statement like that at all—much less in the presence of an HR rep? But HR Girl ignored him and informed me that I was not fulfilling my job responsibilities—that my productivity was lower than expected

"If that's the case—" I replied, "and I'm not admitting it *is* the case; I'm just saying that *if* that's what I'm being accused of, then there is only one person responsible for that: Richard Zucker. For six years, I did *one job* here in iTunes: program the Movie Store. But in January, Richard Zucker decided that from now on, our junior Programmer should do that job, and I should do his job. So if my productivity is less than expected, it's solely because Richard Zucker *gave my job away* to a junior co-worker and assigned me to do his task."

This seemed to make no impression on her. She and Zucker apparently decided to just "move forward," and took turns recounting incidences of my alleged disobedience (patently false) and other vague charges. And then HR Girl informed me that I was being "involuntarily terminated."

"Am I being fired?" I asked, point blank.

HR Girl was undeterred by my blunt question and suggested we take our meeting to another room so we could discuss my future. I learned later that she was there to offer me a second Documented Coaching "opportunity," although—Big Mistake Number Two—she failed to ever mention this. I can only figure that since I waived the "reading of transgressions," she took this as an indication that I was not interested in Documented Coaching—even though it had never been offered, much less declined—and she skipped right to termination.

TURNING THE CONFERENCE TABLES

HR Girl and I found an empty conference room, where she outlined the terms of my euphemistic "involuntary termination." I would receive eight weeks' pay, two months of COBRA (follow-on medical insurance), and I would be allowed to keep my equipment, including my laptop and iPad.

I knew from past experience with HR that there was nothing I could do to dissuade her or even reason with her, so I just sat there and listened…until she made Big Mistake Number Three:

"How do you feel about this?" she asked.

How do I *feel* about this? *How do I feel about this?* How the hell was I *supposed* to feel about this? Happy?

"How the hell do you *think* I feel?" I growled. "It's total bullshit! Everything Richard Zucker told you is a lie, and you won't even investigate it. This is a career-ending decision, and I deserve better. I've been a model employee for years but once my boss decides he doesn't like me, I'm out? I'm arguably the oldest person in iTunes—is this how you treat your older employees?"

If this had been a cartoon, I could have seen red flags popping up in HR Girl's eyes. Was I claiming age discrimination? Was I threatening a lawsuit? And it was at that precise moment she decided that since I felt that way perhaps it would be a good idea to discuss my termination with her superior. "Let's just say for now that you're suspended until we can clear this up," she backpedaled.

Fine by me. She promised to set something up ASAP and send me the details. But she also suggested that I pack up my desk and take a few minutes to say good-bye to my co-workers.

Once home, I had to try to explain the situation to Piph...a difficult task, since I didn't understand the situation myself. Was I fired? Laid off? Suspended? Who knew?

HR AIKIDO

Given a day to think through this incident, I realized several things. The first was that Dick Zucker clearly never had any intention of allowing me to concentrate on creating features for iTunes Movies. He flat-out lied to my face a few weeks earlier when he reorganized our department and gave our junior guy my job while stroking me with the rationale that it would "free up your time" to concentrate on my original mandate in iTunes Movies. Demoting me then claiming I was underperforming was a great Catch-22.

It also became clear that I'd been bushwhacked—a standard HR trick. The initial plan—either Zucker's, or his and HR Girl's—seemed to be to offer me Documented Coaching and discuss the incidents that led up the offer. But as soon as I corrected or contradicted Zucker's version of the incidents, or made any attempt to defend myself, they'd cry "Argumentative!," withdraw the offer of Documented Coaching, and can my ass. I'm quite certain this was the plan because that's exactly what happened—more quickly than either of them had expected, perhaps, but without a word of discussion between them once HR Girl perceived that I was becoming "confrontational" with my manager (a claim he'd undoubtedly poisoned her mind with in advance, and which she would soon confirm).

I also discovered later—once I had a chance to actually read the document Zucker was holding but didn't let me see in that meeting—that the list of alleged offenses was, in reality, little more than a pile of horse manure—twisted perspectives if not outright lies. "You are often difficult to reach via iChat and/or phone"? Never happened. "Failure to meet deadlines"? The only deadlines I had were mid-April, and this HR intervention was held in early April. "You have not demonstrated the initiative I expect … I am seeing significantly higher levels of productivity …from employees well junior of your position"? You think maybe that's because you *gave my job away* to a junior-level employee, then weeks before I had my first deadline claimed I'd missed "deadlines" (plural)?

I also noted that the list of conditions of this unoffered second Documented Coaching "opportunity" were so restrictive as to be ludicrous. "Hourly check-ins with your Manager" is just one example, and there were a dozen more stipulations that were equally odious—and equally impossible to fulfill, if only because they were based on misconceptions. (How was I supposed to ensure, for instance, that I was "available" on iChat or by phone or email, when I was *already* always available on iChat, phone and email?)

I felt sure that this list had been carefully crafted to give the appearance of a fair chance for me to rehabilitate my alleged bad behavior—and I was equally certain that this second Documented Coaching opportunity, with its prison-like constraints, was crafted to set me up for failure.

So, I realized, even if I had sat quietly and listened to Zucker's charges and not contradicted or corrected them, and the offer of Documented Coaching had been presented, and I agreed to it, the restrictions were so impossible to adhere to that if I committed a single violation (which was virtually inevitable, given the number and nature of the restrictions), Zucker would go back to HR and say, "Well, I tried, but he violated the terms, so we have to fire him." I'd be skating on thin ice for the remainder of my days at Apple—which Dick Zucker would attempt to ensure were few. He and HR Girl clearly screwed up by not offering me Documented Coaching, but in this scenario, it was never meant to be a legitimate offer in the first place. Another clue that my termination was a foregone conclusion: When I checked a request for vacation days at the end of May that I'd made weeks earlier...my request had mysteriously disappeared from the schedule. One way or another, Zucker knew in advance that I would not be an employee by then.

A further realization was that—partly by accident and partly by design—I'd been able to short-circuit HR's Standard Operating Procedure of the Surprise Attack. (If you flail around enough you're bound to hit something.) Although HR Girl was unmoved by my assertions that Zucker's data was all bullshit, by simply mentioning that this action might be age-related, I had bought myself some time to recover from the initial shock of this ambush —and I could use that time to my advantage, devising a strategy to deal with the upcoming interview. This was, in fact, (as I informed HR Girl) a career-ending moment for me, so I had nothing to lose by pushing back. If I was going to meet with her superior, I could spend the intervening time crafting a case against this unwarranted HR action, supported by documentation that I'd have time to research. And if I was being given an audience at a higher level, I would clearly outline what my perspective was, whether my defense was considered argumentative or not.

I had an additional insight as well: My previous run-ins with HR over the years had in some perverse way prepared me for this career Armageddon, this professional Ragnarök. I knew some of their tricks: the Surprise Attack; the Catch-22, Chinese Finger Puzzle charges made against their targets (like labeling the victim "argumentative" so they could dismiss any objections, defense, or discussion); the adamant attitude of "guilt by accusation." And I knew some of HR's vulnerabilities, like overreacting to employee complaints, no matter how ludicrous. I'd been on the shit end of that stick before. But now, if I played my cards right, I could take advantage of this hard-won knowledge and turn HR's own playbook against them.

As a further benefit, I could prove to myself that I hadn't been paranoid in keeping a paper trail and obsessing over the techniques of the injustices visited upon me over the years by HR—that I was, in fact, operating under the twin principles of "Know Thy Enemy" and "forewarned is forearmed." I'd have no hesitation in using their own underhanded machinations against them; I'd put them on the defensive when they perhaps had no defense against their own strategies. And I would feel great about it—"Revenge is a dish best served cold," the old Klingon aphorism goes.

But HR Girl wasn't through with me yet.

Thursday, April 4

We connected by phone on Thursday afternoon. (I had the presence of mind to take notes, so the quotes below are verbatim.) She informed me that after she'd discussed our Tuesday conversation with her colleagues, the "performance-based involuntary termination" would now "revert to a voluntary termination," with two paid months of COBRA coverage. Friday, April 12 would now be my last day with Apple. I asked her if I would still be receiving eight weeks' pay. Her response: "My colleagues weren't comfortable with that."

"We had a deal," I replied. "Do you not have the authority to make that deal?"

Her response was vehement: "Of course not!"

"But we agreed to the terms," I said. "We even shook on it."

Her response: "Oh, I was just shaking your hand to say goodbye!"

I ended this call feeling…betrayed. (Betrayed by HR? How shocking!) She'd offered me a deal on Tuesday, but once I agreed to the deal, it was rescinded. This seemed to me to be something far beyond miscommunication—possibly even purposeful misrepresentation. I had a strong suspicion that HR was simply toying with me, and that the good faith compromise I had made—that I will allow myself to be laid off in exchange for the agreed-upon items—was being taken advantage of by HR by their reneging on the agreement.

ENDGAME: AVENGER

Friday, April 5, 2013

I did finally hear from the person HR Girl turned this action over to on Friday, and we agreed to meet on Monday, April 8, at 2 PM, in her office.

I spent the weekend preparing my defense, as focused as a trial lawyer. If I was being granted an audience with a senior member of HR, maybe they would listen to me, which is more than Zucker and HR Girl were willing to do. This time, the Spanish Inquisition would not catch me unaware. In this meeting, I would be adamant about clearly outlining what my perspective was, what the facts were (and how Dick Zucker had misrepresented or invented them), and would delineate Zucker's long-term agenda to get rid of me.

I also spent time that weekend debating and deciding what I actually wanted from this encounter beyond an opportunity to be heard and to tell my side of Zucker's fabricated and warped story. It was depressingly obvious to me that my time at Apple was over—and, at 62, with skills that could only be used at iTunes, my work life was over as well.

I entertained a spectrum of approaches and possible demands, weighing each as to the verification I had to support them and their chances of success—or pushback. At the hard-ass end of the spectrum, I could go in swinging and threaten to bring an age discrimination lawsuit against Apple. I'd recognized years earlier that Silicon Valley was the Valley of Youth—"no country for old men," as Yeats put it—and that older workers found it increasingly difficult to find gainful employ. I'd kept up with the horror stories of age discrimination legal cases, and I knew—as I'm certain any HR rep knew far better than I did—that such claims were notoriously difficult to prove. Even so, I might have attempted to make a case; after all, I was arguably the oldest employee in iTunes, for one, and the timing of the initial HR contact—less than two weeks after my 62nd birthday, the age at which I became eligible to collect Social Security—was suspect (in my mind, at least). But I knew I was on shaky ground without any verbal or written insults about my age.

I thought I could make a much stronger case that my dismissal was "wrongful termination," and threaten a lawsuit over that if push came to shove. I was on solid negotiating ground with that approach, I felt, as long as I could convince... *someone*... that a termination based on Zucker's misinformation, missing information, skewed recounting of past incidents, and occasional downright lie was unfounded. I could reveal that during my most recent two performance reviews, when I was 60 and 61, I had informed Zucker that I was planning to work until I was 65, and that, if we were still working together then, I could spend my final months seeking out and training a suitable replacement (since we'd agreed that Andy was temperamentally unsuited for my position). I could then claim that I was being wrongfully terminated three years in advance of the date I had defined, and that Zucker was aware of that. I could claim that through Zucker's insidious machinations, I was being wrongfully deprived of the following: three years' salary, bonuses and raises; loss of full vestment of the RSUs I'd been granted in the years before Steve Jobs' death; loss of three years of investment in the Employee Stock Purchase Plan (which allowed employees to purchase stock at 15 percent below market price) as well as loss of three years' contributions to my 401(k)—a six percent payroll contribution matched by Apple. All this lost revenue added up to an amount of money technically defined as "a shitload" that I would be deprived of by this wrongful termination. I'd be willing (I could say) to settle for half that estimated total—or, if they balked, for half of three years' salary.

But I knew that the more money I demanded the harder they'd fight back. And frankly, I was exhausted. I realized that perhaps age did (in this instance, at any rate) make a difference—not in terms of performance, or of a "fit" with the company culture, but simply because I was sick and tired of dealing with the bullshit I'd endured over the years from people like Zucker and HR reps, and too old to have the energy to even want to fight it anymore. If my work life was over, I just wanted to get the hell out of Dodge, move into my dream home in paradise, and start enjoying my retirement. The thought of engaging in a protracted legal action of any sort, with all the time, effort, stress, and money involved in fighting one of the world's largest companies (a fight which, I had to admit, I might not win) was simply so repellant to me that I was content with merely using the veiled threat of such an action as leverage to perhaps extract me from this "involuntary termination" situation. If this was the end of my working life, I didn't want to spend my retirement money on revenge (that I might not obtain); on proving I was "right" but dying of starvation in the gutter.

As a bottom line, I was prepared to accept Apple's terms of "voluntary termination" with the severance package I'd originally been offered, and walk away satisfied. The one thing I would make a stand against, however, was "involuntary termination." I'd begun my work life with termination from my first real job, and I was goddamned if I was going to bookend my career with a termination at my last job. Termination was the one charge I would fight.

And I came up with a plan to do exactly that.

THERE'S A REASON "ER" ALSO STANDS FOR "EMERGENCY ROOM"

"Outwit, outplay, outlast"
—Motto of the TV show *Survivor*

Monday, April 8

I drove back to Cupertino Monday afternoon to an address in a business park far away from both the Mothership and the new iTunes building—an Apple complex I had no idea even existed. And I met with a middle-aged Asian woman I'll call "Doc Brown" for reasons that will become clear later.

A brief aside: It always intrigued me that Apple had included a digital audio recording function in the iPhone, but no one ever seemed to use it—at work, at any rate. Of course, it would be thoroughly unethical to visit the Men's Room before a meeting and activate the "Record" function, then slip the cell phone into the breast pocket of one's dress shirt and surreptitiously record an entire private conversation, no matter how important that meeting might be. What good would that do, anyway? Such an undisclosed audio recording could never be used in a court of law; at best it would serve as a reminder of precisely what was said during such a meeting. (If I had thought of this before my surprise meeting with Zucker and HR Girl, for instance, it would have been very easy to prove that their offer of Documented Coaching had never been made.) If, however, this unconscionable action had, in fact, taken place, excerpts from a transcript of a meeting might read something exactly like the verbatim quotes included below.

Once we settled into Doc Brown's office, she introduced herself as an "Employee Relations consultant." *Employee Relations?* Wasn't that the old-timey (i.e., pre-1980s) designation for Human Resources, before HR was subverted into being a bludgeon for management? *Maybe, just maybe*, I thought, *there is some hope of intervention, or at very least of being listened to.*

She explained that ER was a support function for HR, and that the ER team looked into sensitive employee matters—"things like what recently came up with you in your meeting with your manager." If HR calls ER and says, "Hey, we've got an allegation of a claim that came forward that we really need a third objective party to take a look at," then ER investigates.

She wanted first to cover a couple of "housekeeping" items so I was clear on her role. "I'm actually investigating this matter, so I want to make sure that you understand that my expectation is that you'll be honest and forthcoming, which I'm sure that you will be."

"Cross my heart," I said. "I was a Boy Scout." And we both laughed.

"The whole idea is I have no connection with your business," she said. "I don't know you, I don't know your manager. I don't have any bias one way or the other. I don't understand your business, I don't know the players. And so when I look into these sensitive employee issues it's helpful because I don't have any kind of predisposed notions."

I pointed out that since many of the incidents with Zucker revolved around the way iTunes worked, and since iTunes had its own internal language, she should feel free to ask for clarifications of anything I might say that was not clear. (My favorite quote is from Voltaire: "If you wish to converse with me, define your terms.")

Once we'd defined our terms, we talked. And we talked. And we talked. Man, did we *ever*! We talked for nearly three solid hours. And it's a good thing we *did* define our terms, given that the first incident of miscommunication occurred only a few sentences into our discussion.

"You probably know more than I do," she began, referring to my meeting a week earlier with Richard Zucker and HR Girl, "but what was the meeting about? I thought the meeting was your manager talking to you about concerns he had about your performance and then actions that he would take to help you improve your performance. But you make it sound like it was about age discrimination."

"Oh my gosh!" I laughed. "OK, this is a surprise to me. I was under the impression that we were here to discuss the terms of my termination..."

"So in that meeting, were you being terminated?"

"Yeah, I *was* terminated."

"OK," she said. "I was not clear on that."

I pulled out my notes and explained that I'd made these notes immediately after each conversation with HR Girl while the events were fresh in my mind, and that I'd be happy to go into detail. We began by walking through my initial meeting with Zucker and HR Girl on an almost line-item basis. She explained what she'd been told by HR Girl, and I verified or corrected her, often adding details she was not aware of.

I read through my notes about that first meeting (which are digested above and spelled out in detail in the chapter "You Can't Spell 'WHORE' Without 'HR'" in Part IV). She listened attentively, interrupting only once by asking me to repeat Zucker's assertion that "Since I'm the boss, my opinion is the only one that matters." I assured her that was a direct quote. "It made quite an impression on me," I pointed out.

We went over every detail two, three, even four times. The idea, I assume, was that she wanted to be clear and unambiguous about every detail; to go over them as often as necessary for her to get The Big Picture. (In a different context, this is similar to how police interrogate suspects, to make sure they tell the same story repeatedly in an attempt to catch the perp in a lie or a contradiction. What I had working in my favor was that the entire story was very clear in my mind—and that I'd taken voluminous notes while the incidents were fresh. Also, of course, that my version hewed much more closely to the truth than Richard Zucker's pack of lies ever did.)

I'll include one example of this repetitious and reiterative redundancy in which we tried to establish the sequence of events of that first meeting—and the key point that never occurred.

"You had no idea what this meeting was about?" she repeated. "You hadn't had any indication prior to this that there were any concerns or that any of your behaviors had 'resurfaced'?"

"That's exactly right," I agreed. "I couldn't have stated it better myself. This was really out of the blue—a complete surprise to me. I had no indication. Quite the contrary...for the past few months, I'd been assured that everything was going along very well. I meet with Richard Zucker every Wednesday afternoon and we discuss store concerns and he never brought up anything that was out of the ordinary."

"This is news for me," she said, "that that meeting was a termination, and the terms of the termination. You weren't in the meeting saying 'This isn't fair,' or 'This isn't right' —"

"No. It was a done deal, as far as I could see. I was being involuntarily terminated."

"In that first meeting with Richard, didn't he deliver you a Documented Coaching?"

"He did not," I replied. "This is a key point and I'm glad you brought it up."

"That's what's confusing me."

"That's what confused me, too," I said. "And that's why I made notes, so I could be very clear in my own mind about what actually happened in that meeting. What Richard said to me was, 'We're concerned that some of your behavior from the past is resurfacing. I've listed several incidents here and I'd be happy to go through them paragraph by paragraph if you like.' That's not an exact quote, but it is I think a very close paraphrase of what he said. No mention of Documented Coaching. As soon as I said, 'No, I don't think we need to go through this paragraph by paragraph,' the next step was HR Girl telling me I had been involuntarily terminated. Documented Coaching was never offered to me." Strike Two against HR Girl: she clearly had screwed up this meeting.

"OK," Doc Brown said. "And is it at this point—I'm trying to step into your mind—"

"Careful," I cautioned, and we both laughed. She'd passed my personal Turing test.

"The reason you don't want to go through this point by point is because you believe that Richard isn't really gonna listen to you based on your recent experience with him, that although there are other explanations, you're not really prepared nor willing to go through that kind of back and forth with him—"

"Well," I corrected her, "I *would* be willing to go through it with him. I didn't really see that that was an option. It seemed to me as though this wasn't really a discussion and that he wouldn't listen to any other explanations. And frankly, the main reason I said, 'No no no no no, I don't think we need to go through this point by point' is that I didn't know what this meeting was about. I wanted to find out what our meeting was about before I started responding to individual incidents, point by point. No one ever told me what the meeting was about."

"And it's not until afterward, or later on in the meeting, that you find out your employment has been involuntarily terminated."

"Quickly after that. Almost immediately after that. So the sequence of events was: Richard says, 'I've got these performance issues; I'd be happy to go through them paragraph by paragraph if you like'; I say, 'Nah, I don't think we have to go through them point by point'; I turn to HR Girl and say, 'I can guarantee you that whatever it is he's got listed on there, there are alternative points of view, explanations, different opinions,' and Zucker replies, 'Since I'm the boss, my opinion is the only one that matters.' At that point, HR Girl told me that I was fired. The offer of Documented Coaching was never made. If—and I can't emphasize this strongly enough—*if* Richard Zucker had said, 'We're going to give you a second opportunity at Documented Coaching, and here's why,' it would have been a completely different meeting—a completely different conversation. That was never done. ...I hate to be suspicious and think I was set up, that they purposefully misrepresented this second opportunity at Documented Coaching by not offering it, but I can't help feeling somehow that that's a possibility. No one mentioned Documented Coaching; immediately after I was involuntarily terminated I was informed *twice* that *no one* gets a second opportunity at Documented Coaching...so why would I think they were going to offer one to me?"

"They gave you the document?"

"Yeah, as I left. I didn't even read it until the next day. That's when I discovered it was a very detailed Documented Coaching plan—and had been an option that was never offered to me. My experience of that meeting was I went in there, I was being involuntarily terminated, and they were willing to explain why I was being involuntarily terminated. I can't emphasize this enough, that the Documented Coaching was never an option. It was never offered to me. Quite the contrary—HR Girl said twice in that short meeting that Apple employees only get *one* opportunity at Documented Coaching. So why would I even suspect this was a second offer?"

"Why do you think that happened?"

"I don't know," I replied. "I don't want to have a suspicious mind and think I was being set up, that I was always gonna be involuntarily terminated, that Documented Coaching was never an option. But if it *was* an option, it was never presented to me. That may have just been a failure of communication. On Richard Zucker's part, perhaps? By not saying it? HR Girl never mentioned it. She told me, 'You get *one* opportunity at that,' which confused me. Why would she be telling me that? And why would they offer me a second chance if she's adamant that you [only] get *one* Documented Coaching opportunity? It's very confusing. Like I say, I don't want to be suspicious and think it was a purposeful misrepresentation, but that is a possible answer. The answer I would prefer is that it was just miscommunication, mishandled by the other participants. All I know for sure is that I never knew that Documented Coaching was an option. I was never informed about it and never knew about it until I went home and looked at the Documented Coaching document. Then I had to ask myself, 'Why did they write this all up and not offer it to me? Why did I go into that meeting and immediately get terminated?' Very confusing."

"So when you read that [document]," she said, "when you realize what it was, you're like, 'Oh. This explains it.' "

"No," I replied, "it was *more* of a mystery! I assumed the meeting was for my termination, and that the behavioral incidents that Richard Zucker wanted to discuss were the reasons for my termination. Kind of the inverse of what they might have thought. Maybe they thought they were going to offer me Documented Coaching, and if I didn't accept it, they'd go to involuntary termination. But they got it in the wrong sequence—they terminated me first. I only found out about the Documented Coaching later."

"So you're pretty sure that early on in that conversation—and I'm not questioning—but is it possible that somewhere in the first part of that conversation, you missed— 'We're here to offer you Documented Coaching and we're here to discuss that with you?' "

"Absolutely not possible that I missed that," I replied. "I was very clear in my notes and in my memory. Not being informed about that explains a lot of my confusion about why I was being told twice that you only get one opportunity."

"Yeah. I'm trying to make sense of how that could have evolved from 'I'm having concerns about your performance, Scott, that have resurfaced from the past' and 'I've got this Documented Coaching in hand'—

"No," I said, correcting her. "What he said was, 'I have some incidents of your behavior that I'm willing to go through them with you, paragraph by paragraph.' Never was the phrase 'Documented Coaching' used; never was the offer of Documented Coaching made."

"Do you think," she continued, "based on the level of interaction you were having with Richard at the time and the tone of the interaction, that when you said, 'We're not gonna discuss those items,' do you think he could have inferred from that, or perceived that to be 'he didn't even want to talk about it.' Like, 'There was no use going through it because he doesn't even want to entertain—' "

"Given his attitude over the past six months, I would say that's a possibility," I agreed, "that he would say, 'This is a useless attempt—just fire him.' But without him consulting in any way with HR Girl, she jumped right into involuntary termination. If this was an actual offer, I would think that they might have connected somehow to say, 'Well, Option A doesn't work, so we're gonna go to Option B.' But they weren't even looking at each other. She went right to involuntary termination. On a phone call with her a couple days later, I asked her why I was never offered the DC, and she said, 'Well, that option was removed when you became confrontational with your manager.' What? When did I become confrontational?

"This is the crux of the problem here," I continued. "Zucker will not listen to any other point of view. 'I'm the boss, so my opinion is the only one that matters.' My intention was in saying to HR Girl, 'I guarantee you that whatever incidents he's got in there, there are alternate explanations, different points of view, different opinions' was to point this out. And that's when she terminated me. So yes, I can see how he might have thought, 'Well, this is useless,' but from my point of view, I was thinking the same thing: 'This is useless. What's the point of talking about these things when he's not listening to reason, when he won't listen to explanations, when his opinion is the only one that matters because he's the boss? It's a hopeless case.' "

(I could also have mentioned to Doc Brown that it didn't occur to me that Zucker would even be willing to listen to my side of his stories; that if he had been, it would have been the first time he was willing to discuss these incidents, having rejected all my earlier attempts to discuss or explain them, so her explanation didn't fit the facts as I experienced them. And I refrained from mentioning that I'd been through this before with my first Documented Coaching, when the HR rep was willing to sit patiently and listen to my explanations of the charges against me, but unwilling to change a single thing, or even investigate my version of the incidents. So why, in this case, should I even bother to discuss these incidents, when as far as I could deduce, Zucker and HR had clearly already made up their minds?)

"This is becoming clearer to me," Doc Brown stated.

"That's what we want," I replied.

"So, this is news for me," she admitted, "that that meeting that you had with Zucker and the meeting you had with HR Girl were termination, and the terms of the termination."

It seemed as though the redundant recounting had finally sunk in, so we moved on to my follow-on meeting (also detailed previously), in which HR Girl offered me a "soft-landing" termination package. "She said that?" Doc Brown asked. It appeared to me that Doc had never heard that terminology before; either way, it seemed another strike against HR Girl and another point in my favor, since she'd mishandled my termination.

This second meeting was the encounter in which I'd expressed my anger about age discrimination, which was clearly the pry bar that earned me this current parley with Employee Relations. But by now (and to her credit), Doc Brown had moved beyond her original reason for being in this meeting—to investigate possible age discrimination—and had moved her concerns to my termination and the reasons behind it. My territory.

"You were trying to convey to HR Girl at that point that Richard Zucker is a difficult guy to work for, and here's why," she realized. "Can you articulate those reasons?"

Could I ever! "I think the main point is that his philosophy seems to be that the best defense is a good offense, and he was never willing to listen to explanations. He was settled in his own opinion… All I was trying to convey to HR Girl in that first meeting was, 'Listen, all of this is a big misunderstanding; these events have simple explanations, but Zucker is unwilling to listen to them, possibly because he was the cause of the some of the problems to begin with.'"

"So you felt like he was not open to hearing your side of the story. Not willing to entertain that there might have been other factors."

"Exactly. Other factors or other *facts*. Once his mind was made up, any attempt to explain something to him was countered by 'You're argumentative.' Argumentative is the last thing I want to be—he's my *boss*, y'know? If I had a concern that we were going in a wrong direction on something, I could talk to him about it. If something went wrong, I could explain it to him. But in the last six months, that has not been an option. He has been completely unwilling to listen to reason or alternate explanations. And I think that all crystallized with him saying, 'Since I'm the boss, my opinion is the only one that matters.'"

"It sounds like to me," she said, that "it didn't really surface for you until recently... It was like, 'Oh, yeah, I've been observing or experiencing that for the last six months but couldn't really put my finger on it.' "

"Exactly. A series of small things that when you combine them builds a clear pattern of a change in attitude and a clear pattern of not being willing to listen to explanations. I've been trying to be independent enough to not have to involve him in the trivial things. But then when *he* brings up the trivial things, he won't listen to an explanation. Any explanation I give sounds to him like it's argumentative, because he's already made up his mind and his opinion is the only one that matters. You don't go firing your employees because you're unwilling to listen to an explanation of why some detail went wrong."

"You've brought up twice now during our talk things that went wrong that Richard Zucker caused," she said. "I think there's something there that you want to share. And that I want to hear about. Can you give me an example, over the past six months, of where you experienced that the collaborative relationship changed, and the 'I'm the boss' kind of behavior took over?"

"I could give you several," I chuckled.

"Give me one."

I told her about how I'd suggested we hold a luncheon to say good-bye to our long-time collaborators and to welcome the new ones, and how he invited everyone but me. I told her the story of the "Dial-In Only" meeting—a form of meeting in which the participants did not gather in person in a conference room but instead simply phoned in to a conference call. Zucker had put it on the schedule, then changed the time as well as changing it to an "in-person" meeting, and failed to inform me about either change, causing me to miss the meeting—and then blamed me for not trying hard enough to find the meeting. And since she didn't interrupt me to point out that she asked for one incident and I'd given her two, I went on to relate the story of the recent meeting where Zucker changed the time and location and failed to inform me…then once again took me to task for not looking hard enough to find him—and then demanded a minute-by-minute account of my activities during the time of the meeting I'd missed.

"It's really not my responsibility as a participant to track down where a meeting's been moved to," I said. "It's his responsibility as organizer to inform the participants that there's been a change in the time or place. He didn't do that—instead, he blamed me for 'not looking for him hard enough.' Now, I didn't make a big thing out of this, because as soon as he mentioned the magic word, 'argumentative,' I immediately dropped it. I don't want to be argumentative. I can't win anyway. Anything I come up with I figured he'd come back at me with something else, whether on topic or not, since to him, 'the best defense is a good offense.' It was a no-win situation. Anything I did was incorrect; any explanation I could give was considered argumentative. And those are pretty representative incidents."

I was on a roll, so I continued, bringing up a couple of downright fabrications in the document Zucker and HR Girl gave me in our first meeting—his self-serving, warped spin on actual events. While he claimed that he changed the format of our weekly departmental meeting because our verbal sparring was upsetting the other two participants, for instance, I pointed out to Doc Brown several inconsistencies in this analysis: First, that it was *me* who discovered our banter was making them uncomfortable and suggested to Zucker that we tone it down, which we did immediately; second, that he changed the format of that meeting to exclude Andy because the information was totally irrelevant to Andy and a waste of his time—which is something I brought to his attention and he agreed with; and finally, if our banter was making *anyone* uncomfortable, it would have been our one female co-worker, not Andy (who chimed in as often as either Zucker or I did)—and yet it was Andy who was uninvited to this weekly meeting, not her. Zucker's story and his logic simply did not make sense. "But when Richard Zucker writes this incident up," I said, "it sounds like he's taking full authority for changing the format of this meeting because I was being argumentative. The main reason he changed the format was *not* what he wrote down here. None of the details are accurate. He's manipulating the facts to make me look bad."

"So," she summarized, "the items in there you believe have been kind of molded to fit a situation."

"Yep," I agreed. "Distorted and incomplete."

"Why do you think that happened?" she asked.

This was the opening I'd been waiting for—and I hadn't even needed to guide the conversation around to it.

"Well," I said, "up until now I've tried to present nothing but facts—exactly what was said, as precisely as I could—as well as my reactions to these facts and my thoughts at the time. But since you ask, I'm more than willing to share a bit of speculation. I believe Richard Zucker has been engaged in a systematic effort to remove me from iTunes and Apple—a plan that stretches back maybe even six months. And I can give you three data points to support that theory. The first was six months ago, when he told me point blank during my annual performance review, 'You make too much money.' The second was in January, when he reassigned the job I've been doing at iTunes for six years to the junior member of our team. And the third is that a couple of months later, he conspired with HR to accuse me of 'underperforming,' as well as for a few trivial miscommunications, many of which he was responsible for, but for which he refused to allow me to attempt to clarify for him—possibly because he knew he was responsible for them but refused to take responsibility.

"Maybe the attempt to provide me with a second Documented Coaching opportunity is part of that plan as well," I continued, "since they never offered it but skipped right to 'involuntary termination.' That's what made me suspicious, what made me think, 'There's something going on here beneath the surface. I'm being pushed out.' And connecting the dots of these three events indicated to me with abundant clarity that Zucker had been engaged in a long-term campaign to discredit me and eject me from Apple."

She queried the details; I repeated them. Twice. She was still interested in whether I considered any of these items age-related. Of course she was; she thought we were there to discuss possible age discrimination. That was the original point of this meeting—the whole point of this meeting—in her mind.

I'd recognized years earlier that even while older workers in Silicon Valley found it increasingly difficult to find (and retain) gainful employment, it was virtually impossible to prove age discrimination. Per my plan, I assured her age played no part in any of this.

This was part of the endgame. I'd learned long ago that in any negotiation, you always add an item or two you were willing to sacrifice, or even counted on sacrificing, so it gives the appearance that you are giving something up, when, in fact, you were not, and that you were a reasonable, rational person, and willing to compromise—which, in this case, I most assuredly was not. So I was willing to give her this—a clear statement that there was no age discrimination occurring here and that she needn't be concerned about a potential lawsuit. I was willing to sacrifice a powerless pawn to protect my larger chess game.

I intuited there might even be positive aspects of this move beyond setting her mind at ease about a potential age discrimenation lawsuit. With that settled, it might clear her mind so she would listen more closely to my other points, for one. If my "confession" bought me some trust as well, so much the better. And I could perhaps even subtly imply that HR Girl had mishandled this entire affair, if she'd mistaken my objections about being fired for a complaint about age discrimination, which might lend some credence to my credibility…and that might lend some verification to Doc Brown's own insight that much of what had occurred in this affair was mainly the result of miscommunication.

"Frankly," I continued, "I'm proud of the fact that I've been able to keep up with people half my age. I'm a very active, dynamic, solid performer. All my reviews reflect that. I'm sure you have access to them, and you should definitely read through them. I have a core competency in programming the iTunes Movies store that is unmatched by any other person in the world, literally. But when Zucker takes that job away from me then accuses me of being an underperformer, it gets a little suspicious. Age may have nothing to do with it. But it gets a little suspicious."

"Do you have other concerns other than what you've said to me today?" she asked.

"Well, my central concern is being terminated."

"Obviously."

"And wrongly, I think. What I'd like to do is take this whole mess, this whole situation, the whole termination thing and step back and look at it from a larger perspective. It's clear that Richard Zucker does not want to work with me. That's his right, as a manager. I have no problem leaving under the terms HR and I agreed to, because I clearly cannot go back and work for him. Apparently, we just can't work together, and if we can't work together, I don't want to work together. I don't want to work with him if he wants me out. So I'm perfectly willing to step back, if I were given the agreement I made with HR. But since they rescinded their offer, I have nothing to agree to. I just don't know the status of my employment at the moment."

"You view this situation as untenable at this point," she stated. "You don't feel that situation is recoverable? That if you were to go on this Documented Coaching plan...?"

"Well," I said, "my suspicion is that since the Documented Coaching plan was never offered to me, even if I went on it, Richard Zucker would find some other excuse to get rid of me in a few months. For whatever reason. The inaccuracy of incidents that he's listed here, and the fact that he's willing to ignore the truth, spin the truth, and occasionally even reverse the truth just to prove that *I'm* the problem employee—the fact that he's willing to compromise his professional ethics, manipulate HR policies, and put his own career in jeopardy just to get rid of me, tells me how determined he is to get rid of me. I can see that I'm just not wanted anymore. And why should I stay somewhere that I'm not wanted? I have no hard feelings about that. We just need to come to some agreement about how I'm going to leave. I thought we had, but then that agreement was rescinded. HR Girl told me later that she wasn't authorized to make a deal like that. Why did they send her, then? Why were we even discussing this stuff at that point? What kind of outcome did they expect? So just taking this whole situation, I'm fine with calling this 'voluntary termination.' Give me the deal and I'll walk away happy. I will always speak glowingly of my time at Apple and the people at Apple. That's acceptable to me. That was acceptable to HR, originally. I don't know who it's not acceptable to after we already agreed to it."

"Yeah," she agreed. "Like you said, I think there's been a series of miscommunications along the line, including by me, in thinking that today's conversation was definitely to learn about your concerns and keeping an open mind about that, but what I thought we were gonna talk about was a Documented Coaching plan [she laughs; I laugh uproariously] that you were about to go on and commenting on that Documented Coaching because I understood that you had some concerns about or comments about your age."

"I think you've been given a... miscommunication."

"Yes. It definitely sounds like that."

"And I thought we were here to discuss the terms of my termination," I said. "It's kind of a surprise to me that what you want to talk about is age discrimination and Richard Zucker. The age discrimination is not there; it's not an issue. The Zucker issue, however, we've gone into some detail...more than I ever expected or intended."

"Well," she said, "I got a lot of good, detailed explanation, and some really solid examples as to why you feel like this situation is not tenable anymore."

"Untenable, yes. So I'm willing to call it quits. I'm willing to say, 'Look, you made me an offer; I accepted it; let's part friends.' Zucker will be happy; I'll be happy; HR will be happy —everything will be resolved. No problems. But the offer was rescinded; it changed; it was this, now it's that. I'm confused as to why I'm being jacked around like that, frankly. I'm willing to come to some agreement that will be acceptable to everyone. As a matter of fact, if you are willing to listen to another option, I think I've come up with a solution to this dilemma that will benefit everyone. In iTunes, we're encouraged to think outside the box—"

"OK, so you're talking to me about a creative, out-of-the-box solution to this situation?"

"Yeah. I think I've come up with a solution that would benefit everyone—a real win-win situation that would allow all of us to walk away feeling good about ourselves and our jobs and about Apple, and you are interested in hearing this, correct?"

She nodded.

"The solution is simply this: I retire. Let me retire. Give me a severance package and allow me to retire. This is a great solution, I think—a win-win, with some distinct benefits. Zucker doesn't have to work with me anymore, for one. For my team, they won't have to work under the burden of knowing that they can be fired on a whim, or on trumped-up charges. For me, this wrongful termination is a career-ender. I'm 62, and nobody is gonna hire me anymore, particularly with the specific skillset I have that can only be applied at Apple. This would allow me to walk away from my career with some dignity, knowing that Apple really lived up to the high ethical standards we're always promoting and that we all believe in, and that Apple is the world leader in creative solutions to difficult problems. So for me, this is a benefit because I could go away and say, 'My career is over; it ended beautifully; Apple treated me like a real human being instead of just discarding me like waste paper and firing me on fabricated reasons.' And we can just dump this entire wrongful HR action of any kind of termination.

"You can go to your manager and tell her you've solved a sticky situation using a creative solution that makes Apple look good, cost us a pittance, prevented a potential lawsuit. We all win—everybody's happy. [Whispering] And if you want to take credit for this solution, you can take credit for it. I'd be more than happy for you to take credit for this. [End of whispering.] You'd be able to go home tonight and look in the mirror and say, 'I did something good today. I upheld Apple's high ethical standards and did a good thing for a valued employee who's contributed to the success of iTunes and the growth of Apple,' because after talking to you for a couple of hours, you really don't strike me as the kind of person who'd go home and look in the mirror and say, 'Today I ended an old man's career and kicked him to the curb.'"

"Yeah. We don't want to be doing that."

"No, you don't want to be doing that." I mentioned my lost income and what I felt was a dollar figure that would be an acceptable severance or retirement package. "I don't know if you are authorized to make that kind of agreement, but if not, I really need to talk to someone who can—a decision-maker—because I'm convinced this is the solution to this sticky situation, untenable situation."

"It's a very creative solution," she said, "and I appreciate all of the time you took and the thought that you put into … this type of an arrangement. I think what it boils down to on that solution is consistency and fairness across the board."

"How so?"

"Why would you receive a package like that when another person didn't?"

"Who's the other person?" I chuckled.

"I'm sure there's other folks in similar situations," she said.

"What HR Girl told me was that I was, this was, a special case from the start."

"It is," she replied.

"I'm trying to give you a special solution to a special case," I continued. "I don't really think it's appropriate to bring in other people's agreements with Apple. This is between me and the company. Fairness and consistency? This I think is a fair solution. I was offered what I thought was a fair solution, which is very similar to what I'm asking for, but it was withdrawn."

"I see what you're getting at. I think that we can probably make arrangements for that."

"That's acceptable to me."

"I know. I know, and I appreciate your open-mindedness. I just wanted to acknowledge your creativity... I mean, I think it's absolutely worth... I mean, I mean...you don't get what you don't ask for."

"Exactly," I said. "On the other hand, I didn't ask to be fired, but I got that."

"I would like some time to noodle on what we talked about today," she stated. Good sign—my solution wasn't being dismissed out of hand. "Like you said before, I myself don't have the authority to negotiate a settlement or a resolution but I can talk with the right people. So what I'd like to do is be able to go back to my superiors to talk about what 'resolution' means to them, or what they're agreeable to, and then I'd like to circle back to you."

"That's always a bad sign," I chuckled. "After all, consulting with her colleagues was what led to HR Girl rescinding her original offer."

"No no no!" she protested. "It's not a bad thing. I myself can't... I don't want to speak and not be able to fulfill any commitment I make."

"OK," I said. "That's fine. I trust you. Another of the benefits to this agreed 'parting of the ways' is that it will probably send a very clear message to Richard Zucker that he can't 'manage by termination.' That he's got to take responsibility to listen to his employees and not just fire them.

"Yeah. Exactly," she agreed. "And regardless of how your situation turns out, I have some work to do in looking into in more depth. The concerns that you raised, while I originally thought I was going to be investigating an age discrimination termination case, there are still concerns—the things that you raised are still things that I want to look into further, but those are separate and apart from what you want to happen."

I overlooked her comment at the time. I wasn't at all interested in what "other concerns" she might want to look into; I was focused on my problem—my exit, and whether Apple would agree to my retirement plan and shitcan the whole HR termination action. Several months later, however, I would receive some inkling as to what those "other concerns" might have been.

She continued: "So you said, 'This is what I want. I understand and I get that the manager/subordinate arrangement between me and Richard cannot continue, for a variety of different reasons.' You don't see it moving forward; you don't believe that he sees it moving forward, otherwise he would have offered you the Documented Coaching."

"Exactly."

"Yeah, and that's what I gathered from you. So I think based on that, we can begin talks about..."

"How I will leave."

"And you're saying that you're in a position today where that would be an acceptable, desirable solution."

"Correct. What is *not* an acceptable or desirable solution is voluntary termination and nothing else, like the deal that I was originally offered. That is not an acceptable situation. I've put in a lot of time and effort in building this store, outlived three separate sets of management... I think I deserve to be treated less shabbily than Richard Zucker wants to treat me."

"And you just don't believe that going on the Documented Coaching is going to end well—that there's already a kind of pre-determined idea about your status."

"Exactly. And that is based on what is written in the Documented Coaching. The incidents of behavior in which the facts are distorted and incomplete, not to mention occasionally completely fabricated. Since the recovery program is based on distorted and incomplete information, how can the correction program be undistorted and correct? I feel it's kind of a lost cause. I feel like there's a consistent pattern in Richard Zucker's behavior, at least over the last six months, that all points towards getting me out of iTunes. And I say, 'Fine. Let's just end it. Let's end it amicably; let's have a happy divorce.' "

"Based on the circumstances, you're ready to leave."

"I'm ready to leave under the right circumstances. I was offered the right circumstances, then they were withdrawn. As for going back to work for Zucker, well, he just doesn't seem like the same person he was six months ago. I think he wants to clean house and start over, but I don't think it's really ethical or appropriate to manage by termination. If he'd ever expressed a problem to me about my performance—which he never did—I would have listened to him. If he'd ever listened to my explanations about things—trivial things—that he thought were a problem, we probably wouldn't be having this conversation. But at this point, it's just simply untenable. However, there are solutions on the table."

"Yep yep yep," she agreed. "I'm just asking for a little bit of time while I talk with the appropriate folks."

We wrapped it up. I'd wait at home; she'd consult with her management and would be in touch. I had guarded good feelings about this. Even so, I drove home that afternoon—as I'd done nearly a week earlier—in a state of uncertainty. Was I fired? Or was I still an Apple employee? Would they accept my proposed retirement plan? Or would HR find some new, improved way to screw me? Once again, I was Schrödinger's Employee.

YOU GOT NO CHOICE BUT TO (LIVE IN) LIMBO, JIMBO!

The fun was hardly over, however. When I arrived home, I found an email from Zucker in my inbox—his first communication with me since the "involuntary termination" meeting a week earlier. It was a list of what I should be working on.

Now I was more confused than ever. As far as Zucker knew, I'd been fired. So why was he telling me what I should be working on? I forwarded his email to Doc Brown. "Given our discussion," I wrote, "that neither you nor I knew what my job responsibilities should be while the termination situation is being resolved, and given your and HR Girl's council to 'stay home and do nothing,' how would you suggest I reply? I want to respond in a manner that will not be taken as argumentative or confrontational, but clearly some of these deadlines cannot be met as long as the termination question is unresolved. I hope you can provide some guidance."

"I advise that you should perform your job until I can pursue what we discussed today," Doc Brown quickly replied. "You are continuing as an active Apple employee receiving a paycheck, so I do believe it's reasonable for Richard to ask you to perform work. You should continue to perform work as if your employment is not affected."

"As if"? As Wayne of *Wayne's World* would say, "As if!" She further asked for "a bit of patience" while she attempted to resolve the situation. Hey, as long as I was still on the payroll, she could take as long as she wanted.

While Doc Brown was busy determining my future with her consultants, I spent the weekend in Workman's Limbo. I had no idea whether or not I was even still employed, or would be next week, or whether I was fired or retired. Was I as American as Apple pie or was I a road apple? I didn't know Applejack.

On the positive side, it is to Doc Brown's credit that she was willing to listen to me present my evidence, even though the topic I presented to her was in no way related to the topic she believed we were meeting to discuss. My irritated mention to HR Girl of my age were the magic words that got me this follow-on meeting, but it was only my persistence, I believe, that led Doc Brown to understand my points, eventually—that, and my learning enough of HR's sleazy tricks to use those same tricks against them. And it was Zucker's arrogance and HR Girl's incompetence, I believe, that provided me with the leverage I needed to turn this situation to my advantage.

THE FULL RELEASE HAPPY ENDING

Monday, April 8, 2013

Doc Brown called—with good news. My request for retirement—complete with a severance package—had been approved. "Based on complex circumstances and a unique situation, as well as the concerns I had [she said], Apple wants to move forward with an offer." Could I come back to her office tomorrow to sign the paperwork?

Hell yes, I could! And did. The entire retirement "ceremony" didn't take more than half an hour (most of that spent reading the paperwork before I signed it). (I still didn't trust HR. What am I, new?) It didn't even bother me that after 20 years of dedicated effort to ensure I never had a start time before 10 AM at any job, on the final day of my working life I was supposed to show up at 8 AM. I'd give them that.

And now I can reveal the reason I referred to my ER contact as "Doc Brown"—a reason encapsulated in this exchange of dialog between Jennifer and Doc Brown at the end of *Back to the Future Part III*, when she shows Doc the blank page of paper that previously informed Marty "YOU'RE FIRED":

Jennifer: "Doctor Brown, I brought this note back from the future, and now it's erased... What does that mean?"

Doc Brown: "It means your future hasn't been written yet. No one's has. Your future is whatever you make it. So make it a good one."

I'd walked into my meeting with ER as a schmuck who'd been fired. She changed that so I was retired. She erased the page. She changed the past and helped me write a new future, as well as an uplifting and triumphant end to the saga of my roller-coaster career (namely that I won my final battle with HR). I can guarantee you that had this situation not worked out this way, I would have spent the remainder of my life bitter and angry about my work life—and would never have written this book (for better or worse). "Doc Brown" had joined my Pantheon of Heroes.

I drove home and showed the paperwork to the woman who'd endured the ups and downs of that rollercoaster with me for the previous decade and a half. And we literally danced around the house, chanting, "Not fired—Retired! Not fired—Retired!"

And so it was over. After a lifetime of labor, after more than three decades of sporadic employment at companies both large and small, my alleged career was finally over, and I'd emerged the victor.

I'd done it: I'd won work.

THE AFTERMATH

"What I have purposed to record is nearly finished; but there is yet an incident conspicuous in my memory…without which one thread in the web I have spun, would have a raveled end."
—Charles Dickens, *David Copperfield*

So: Retired, not fired. My last day with Apple would be the end of that week: Friday, April 12, 2013. I had nothing to do until then. So not only did I get my retirement package, but I'd be getting an additional week's pay simply by showing up Tuesday and signing the termination papers. (The terms were confidential, so I can't reveal them. But I was satisfied that ultimately Apple had treated me fairly and compensated me adequately.)

The work itself wasn't entirely finished, however. While I could have simply remained incommunicado and let Dick Zucker deal with the lack of six years worth of history, spreadsheets and paperwork that clogged my MacBook, I took the time that Tuesday afternoon to email him virtually every relevant file concerning my time in iTunes Movies, for future reference. "This is incredibly helpful and very much appreciated," he wrote —and all he wrote—in an email to me on the 11th. Not an apology. Not even a *buh-bye*. Asshole. Dick Zucker.

And because I was not being "disappeared" ("Scott? Oh. He's not with us anymore"), I did get the opportunity to say good-bye via a mass email—after clearing the text with Doc Brown. "I think this is a lovely message," she wrote; "very sincere, appropriate and a really, really nice way to leave." And so on Friday, April 12, I sent a farewell email to about 50 people in my address book:

Dear Team iTunes—

Today will be my last day with iTunes and Apple. It's time to move on to challenges as yet unknown; until they arise, I finally have the time to concentrate on the Three B's: Beethoven, Books (reading and writing), and Beer.

My first day at Apple in 2007 was also my birthday, and it was the best birthday present I ever received. After 25 years of freelance writing and teaching about movies, and more than a dozen years at startups pushing the envelope of "video on demand," I was able to apply all my specialized skills in the service of iTunes Movies as your Movie Guru. Now I am ready to push away from the banquet table that is iTunes and leave an open seat for another lucky soul to enjoy the festive feast.

In my 32 years of laboring in nearly a dozen companies, both large and startup-small, I can honestly say that the people in iTunes are the smartest, most dedicated, and, yes, the nicest band of peers I've ever had the honor of working with. Over the past six years, many of you have offered me advice, guidance, training, and mentoring, and always with great patience and good humor. My respect and affection for you (as Spinal Tap put it) "goes up to 11."

Thank you, and I wish you all great success in your careers and unbridled happiness in your personal lives.

—Scott

And I did keep in touch with a couple of (now ex-) co-workers. Two weeks after my exit, I asked one if Zucker had said anything about my mysterious vanishment. "He hasn't said anything at all that I've heard," she replied. "I've been surprised it hasn't come up at all since you were here forever, then gone."

THE FATE OF THE FURIOUS

"Best intentions get misunderstood
But *that* motherfucker is up to no good."
—Rancid, "Up to No Good"
(on the CD *Let the Dominoes Fall*,
ironically given to me by Dick Zucker)

"A man who makes trouble for others
is also making trouble for himself."
—Chinua Achebe, *Things Fall Apart*

"Payback's a bitch, ain't it?"
—Randy Quaid, *Independence Day*

About six months later, in late October 2013, I received an email from the same ex-coworker. She informed me that Richard Zucker had left Apple to join his old iTunes Movies Store boss Buford Squack at an Apple competitor. She'd seen him carrying out his personal effects from his office earlier that day, and he informed his boss and his team about his departure that afternoon. "Guess I thought it may happen back when Josh took over and I sensed [Zucker] wasn't loving it anymore," she wrote. "But then nothing happened so I figured I was wrong. Guess he was just waiting for another stock vest," (which occurred on October 15). "They walked him out since he was going to a competitor."

"Not loving it anymore" was the same suspicion I'd had about Zucker the previous January, since it appears that he'd been passed over for a promotion and might not have another shot for years. But I also can't help but hope that one of the key reasons for his leaving after 13 years was Doc Brown's cryptic comment to me at the end of our first meeting, in which she stated, "I have some work to do, looking into in more depth. The concerns that you raise are still concerns that I want to look into further."

It seems entirely possible, given that the only other concerns I raised with her were about the unethical and conspiratorial treatment I received at the hands of Zucker, that she'd want to look into that further. Maybe HR put the screws to Zucker and pressured him into leaving like he pressured me into leaving.

It was never my intention to throw Dick Zucker under the bus. My sole intention was to save my job—and my ass. On the other hand, I have no problem with poetic justice. He engineered a career-ending situation for me, so I have no problem thinking that the blowback might have created a career-limiting situation for him. (As of 2019, one of my ex-workers informed me that Zucker was making calls to her about circulating his résumé…so maybe that initial move didn't work for him either. And I recalled one of my favorite lines from the 1983 film *Scarface* …no, not "Say hello to my little friend," but Tony Montana's response when Hector is berating him and Tony simply shoots him in the head: "I told you, man, I told you! Don't fuck with me! But you wouldn't listen, [and] look at you now.") But as of 2020, Zucker apparently followed his old boss Buford Squack to Disney+. Be afraid for your children…

WELCOME TO PARADISE

"Bali Ha'i may call you
Any night, any day
In your heart you'll hear it call you
'Come away, come away.'
Bali Ha'i will whisper on the wind of the sea
'Here am I, your special island
Come to me, come to me.' "
—Rogers & Hammerstein, "Bali Ha'i"

April 2013

Sometime during the previous December, Epiphany Jane and I had determined to move to our house in Hawaii later in 2013. She'd move there in June to do some maintenance and upgrades while I'd rent a room from friends and continue working at Apple, spending my evenings and weekends combing through the massive amount of stuff in our storage locker (mostly mine, I admit), divesting and digesting it and eventually shipping out the remainder then retiring around the end of the year. So, one final irony in an irony-rich career: If Dick Zucker had just been patient, he would have been rid of me within a year. There was no reason for him to go through the byzantine and underhanded machinations of conspiring to get me fired. But fuck him.

Given this major change of conditions (i.e., retirement)—and the fact that our landlord had just raised the rent again—we decided it was simply too expensive to remain in the Bay Area. As much as the area was my home, as much as I loved it, life in NorCal was simply too expensive for a retiree who wasn't making the big Silicon Valley bucks anymore. We set a new date for our escape: May 31. This left us six weeks to accomplish six months of work.

The upshot is: we did. We sold our furniture (since the house we'd purchased was fully furnished) with the exception of our desks, my bookcases, and a few of Piphy's inherited antiques. Throughout April and May, we spent our evenings sorting through storage locker boxes, shredding old documents, tossing out crap (99 percent mine) and packing the few items closest to our heart, divesting so much stuff that we made Marie Kondo look like a hoarder. We held a giant yard sale, where I stocked three used bookstores—literally—by selling off my forty-year collection of books (except for the cream of the crop, which I took along as a comfort in my old age).

As the late May date approached and the final countdown began, we (technically, our hired movers) loaded everything we owned into an enormous shipping container that would travel by sea for a few weeks while we settled into our new home. With tears in my eyes, I donated my beloved classic Jaguar to a non-profit (it would not have survived the rugged roads and rust-promoting climate of the Big Island). And with tears pouring from my eyes I put my beloved but freaked-out cat Skitten in her carrier and delivered her to an airport facility that would ship her to Honolulu for quarantine (don't ask). And on May 31st, Epiphany Jane and I handed over the keys to our Castle apartment to the landlord and handed our tickets to the Big Island—one-way tickets—to the flight attendant. We boarded the plane and left the old life behind—the life of startups and layoffs, of stress and exhaustion, of outrageous wages and long-term unemployment, of Bay Area culture and Silicon Valley insanity—and shifted gears into the next phase of life, and one we were lucky to have attained: the Fool's Golden Years.

We were free.

PART IV:

2020 HINDSIGHT

"ARBEIT MACHT FREI"
("Work sets you free")
—Sign over the entrance to the Auschwitz concentration camp

Chapter 34

WHAT I'VE LEARNED

"You learn something wrong every day."
—D. Scott Apel, *No Plan B*

Unless one is a complete idiot, one can't spend over forty years working without picking up a few insights into (or at least opinions about) the culture of work. And even while I very well may qualify for the idiot position (I'm not the dumbest guy on the planet, but I can see him in line from here) I will nonetheless attempt to summarize here my hard-won wisdom from nearly half a century of toiling in the orchard of fruitless trees.

WHAT I'VE LEARNED ABOUT: RÉSUMÉS

The first step in attaining a job of work is: a résumé. And crafting a winning résumé is both an art and a science.

There are literally hundreds of books and websites that will tell you how to compose a winning résumé. I've read many of them, and herewith digest the few real rules—the first two of which you will never read in a book on résumés, but which are the most important rules of all...and which were only learned by experience.

First and foremost: There is one thing you must *never* do on your résumé: Lie.

Second (but no less crucial): There is one thing you must *always* do on your résumé: Exaggerate.

You don't want to lie because you might get caught. At the very least, this would be embarrassing. At the very most, you could lose your job.

Optimizing your experience, however, is mandatory.

This is how I learned how to accomplish this delicate task.

DUE DILIGENCE OR DOO-DOO DILIGENCE?

During my first few days of underemployment as the Backroom Boy at the West Hollywood Borders Bookstore in late 2001, I knew I needed help breaking out of this minimum wage jail. It didn't take long to realize that I was in an excellent position to find out how to do that. I worked in a friggin' *bookstore*, after all, and we stocked literally dozens of books on résumés. And I was alone in the backroom at night, so, during the slow hours, I could do what the floor clerks were expressly prohibited from doing: I could read. (Workplace Irony Alert: You work in a bookstore but it is forbidden to read on the job.)

I ended up reading something like 50 books on résumés, interviews and jobhunting in general. I might not be the sharpest rocket doctor in the tool shed, but eventually, it dawned on me that where résumés were concerned, there were essentially two camps, giving contradictory advice—all of which was presented as gospel truth. If a hiring manager subscribed to Camp A, God forbid you should send them a résumé in the Camp B format, and vice versa. So right from the start, your chances of being considered for a job were a toss-up, with a 50 percent chance that your résumé would be tossed out for completely arbitrary format violations of which you were unaware.

One key point of contention between these camps was *length*. Camp A insisted that a résumé should never be longer than a single page. Camp B allowed two pages, especially for older candidates with a wide range of experience. But other aspects were equally contentious, right down to acceptable fonts (and font sizes), format (there are a variety), and even the type of paper on which the document was printed (clearly a remnant of Back In The Day, before electronic submissions).

Some of these conflicting "requirements" made some sense ...sometimes. Others seemed completely arbitrary—advice both decisive and divisive. Examples:

- Camp A: *Be sure* to include a statement of the type of position you're looking for.

- Camp B: *Never* include a statement of the type of position you're looking for. Why would you be applying for the position if it wasn't the type of position you were looking for?
- Camp A: *Certainly* work from a list of buzzwords ("achieved," "trained," "managed").
- Camp B: *Never* work from a list of buzzwords, since you never know which are considered clichés ("dynamic," "team player," "results driven") that will get your application immediately deleted.

Often these competing philosophies couldn't even agree on what they were talking about: is it a résumé, for instance, or is it a CV (*curriculum vitae*)?

This is not to say that the wording on your résumé isn't important. Quite the contrary: it's vital to use as few words as possible to convey your accomplishments. And they must be the right words. Like haiku, this restriction presents enormous opportunity, especially if you own a thesaurus. If I had to explain what I did at Borders, for instance, I might say, "I unpacked boxes of books and sorted them into piles by category." But my résumé entry might read: "Processed and categorized over 2,000 print volumes daily." Sounds pretty impressive, right? Not bad for one guy whose only tools were a box cutter and a table. (Although to be fair, after 9/11, a boxcutter was considered a totally effective tool.)

THE FUTURE OF RÉSUMÉS, OR WORSE

By 1999, most companies were accepting résumé submissions by email. This saved us job seekers some money, certainly, as we no longer had to buy high quality paper, or make a Kinko's run, or pay for postage. But there was a tradeoff: We lost the ability to design an attractive layout for a hardcopy résumé...not to mention losing the personal touch of some (alleged) human in HR opening our envelope and actually (allegedly) reading the cover letter and résumé. Even as early as 1999 many companies just scanned snail mail résumés into their databases rather than reading them. (Whether the résumé emails went directly into the database or an HR rep actually read them, one thing is certain: they were untouched by human hands.)

Also by 1999, most hiring managers spent less than two minutes reading a résumé. And it only got worse. By 2018, much human intervention seems to have been replaced by complicated algorithms that screen out unworthy candidates before any live person is ever exposed to them.

The future looks even worse than that. *Wired* magazine reported in 2017, for instance, on the rise of "AI recruiters"—intelligent chatbots that interview and evaluate job candidates; a move designed to reduce the influence of human moods and biases from the interview process, as well as to ignore "gender, ethnicity, age, employment gaps, or college attended." And Intel is reportedly using software called HireVue that claims to be able to extract 25,000 data points from a video interview. These assessments are "based on everything from facial expressions to vocabulary" and "can even measure such abstract qualities as... empathy." (Sounds like the Voight-Kampff test from *Blade Runner*: "If you saw a turtle on its back...") Such software seems tailor-made for leveling the playing field among applicants—unless (as *Wired* also reports on regularly) it's designed, consciously or un-, to enhance biases and prejudices and to limit diversity (as in the early 20th-century employment listings, which informed potential applicants that "No Irish Need Apply").

This new development raises yet another Workplace Irony Alert: What kind of idiot HR employee would hire someone to build a program that would make their own job obsolete?

I'VE LOOKED AT RÉSUMÉS FROM BOTH SIDES NOW

I had, one time, the opportunity to be on the other side of the résumé: the hiring side. When I got the thumbs-up to hire an assistant at Akimbo in 2005, I posted the position on Craigslist ...and received over 250 résumés within the first week. I was shocked by the response...and overwhelmed. I had *work* to do, goddammit—I couldn't sit around all day pondering the finer points of 250 random résumés. I had to print them out and take them home with me each evening and skim through them on my personal time.

I quickly realized that I needed a strategy—some set of ground rules or criteria that would allow me to reject a résumé without the need for a line-by-line study (and interpretation) of each candidate's qualifications. One such criterion was location: this struggling startup simply could not afford to relocate a person to fill an entry-level position. If the applicant couldn't commute to San Mateo, it was an immediate *adios*. The second helpful indication was this: any résumé that had even *a single typo* or spelling error was automatically shitcanned. Sure, the position I was hiring for required great attention to detail, but this criterion for expulsion is generally applicable to any résumé for any position. Your résumé is your best presentation of your best self...so any errors are inexcusable.

RÉSUMÉ HACKS

Additional insights I've gleaned from special circumstances:

1) If your résumé has gaps, list only the *years* of your previous jobs. Unless you're out of work for over two years, a year-by-year accounting can cover most gaps. SGI stopped returning my calls in February 1996, and I wasn't employed again until November of that year. But my résumé reads: SGI (1995-1996); MagiNet (1996-1999). Nobody needs to know there was a ten-month gap between jobs. For all they know, it could have been ten days, or ten minutes.

Caveat: Even this trick can fail if you're out of work for over two years. Or, in my case, by 2004 I simply did not want to clutter a sterling hi-tech résumé filled with Senior Editor positions and extensive experience in the video on demand industry with the two-year interruption of this apparent career spent as a clerk at Borders, during which time no one was advancing VOD (and certainly not hiring for it). When asked about the gap, I was fortunate enough to have a provable backup story: "I was concentrating on my freelance writing career until something opened up in my field." I indicated the 200 articles I'd written, and hoped I'd score some points for being a dynamic self-employed writer whose deep skills kept him afloat rather than an aging schlub with no discernable workplace skills who couldn't get hired anywhere decent to save his fucking life. Worked for me.

2) If you're over "a certain age" (usually 50, although that continues to drop), especially if you're jobhunting in the youth-oriented hi-tech world or the baby-oriented Millennial social media circles, leave any trace of your age off your résumé. By all means, include your college and degree—but not your graduation year. (I'm not alone in this advice: "Almost everyone I know over 40 tends to omit their graduation year from their résumés and eliminate or streamline their past experiences," wrote Karen Wickre on the Wired Backchannel site on June 2, 2017.)

3) Speaking of "streamlining" past experience, by middle age what you did at the beginning of your career probably has no connection with the position you're applying for, so sacrifice the early jobs. Just slice them off, and make sure your résumé only goes back 20 years or so. (If the recruiters or hiring managers give it any thought, they can figure out that you're at least forty...but they might not suspect you're a Baby Boomer or a rapidly-aging Gen-X old fart. If they're that curious, let them bring you in for an interview. Then die your hair and beard. And refer to people as "brah" or "bro" instead of "dude" or, God forbid, "man.")

AN EXEMPLARY EXAMPLE

To illustrate some of the above points, below is my own résumé. The "Résumé Version" is followed by the *Real Life interpretation* in italics. I fooled them then and I'm retired now, so I don't give a shit who knows what egregious exaggerations I conjured up to inflate my work experience.

APPLE, INC.

Cupertino, CA - 2007-2013

TITLE: iTUNES MOVIE GURU

Job Description:
Hands-on management of the iTunes Movies store on a day-to-day basis.
AKA "the world's highest-paid video store clerk." The computer world equivalent of manual labor.

Responsibilities:
Keep iTunes Movies store updated and accurate on a daily basis.
Fix mistakes—mostly my own.
* Program art and content for an entirely new storefront weekly.
Request and move thumbnail images around the intranet app.
* Create theme-based movie collections on a frequent basis.
"Create" defined as "sift through a list of thousands of titles to find a few that fit a theme, then cut and paste them into an Excel spreadsheet." "Frequent" in this case is defined as "whenever your management will let you."
* Provide copywriting for special features and weekly iTunes newsletter.
If it's a good movie, write a few words that will compel users to buy it. If it's a shit movie, write a few words that will compel users to buy it. Write a few words no one will read that introduce the theme of a collection. Don't ever *be clever.*
* Contribute in-depth media knowledge and extensive guidance to content acquisition team.
Lobby ineffectually with groups of salespeople about "quality." Give them a benchmark of movie analysis and film history that they can ignore.

ADCHEMY, INC.

Redwood City, CA - 2006-2007
"2006-2007"? Sounds like two years, don't it? Actual dates were September '06 thru mid-March '07, or about six months. But since those six months straddled two years, time appears magnified fourfold!

TITLE: SENIOR EDITOR

Job Description:
Research, write, edit and manage all content for Internet-based lead generation company's Search Engine Optimization (SEO) websites. Edit all company documents.
Create a website associated with the company's client businesses that will appear to be objective so that Google will allow the company's clients to be listed in user searches.

AKIMBO SYSTEMS, INC.

San Mateo, CA - 2004-2005

Again, what sounds like two years was only about 18 months, from March '04 through early December '05.

TITLE: SENIOR EDITOR

Job Description:
Write and edit all metadata and descriptive text for the first video-on-demand (VOD) service delivered through the Internet to TV sets. Develop categorization scheme to simplify content searches.

Responsibilities:
* Write and edit all descriptive text for web and on-screen user guides; prepare metadata.
* Create, expand and maintain categorization scheme; categorize all content.
* Provide compelling copywriting and flawless editorial support to Marketing department.
* Train and supervise editorial team, including metadata and video editors.
* Contribute in-depth media knowledge and extensive guidance to content acquisition team.

Key Accomplishments:
* Wrote or edited program descriptions for 5,000 titles.
* Created logical and intuitive categorization schema to simplify viewer searches.
* Wrote more than 100 full-length program reviews and 25 weekly newsletter issues.
* Developed in-depth rating protocol for Adult content and trained personnel in its application.
Oddly, this is all fairly precise and accurate. I worked so hard I didn't to have to exaggerate.

REPLAYTV, INC.

Mountain View, CA - 1999-2000

Once again, a little date sleight of hand magically transforms 14 months of employment (September '99 through November '00) into two years.

TITLE: SENIOR EDITOR, RTVS (Replay Television Service)

Job Description:
Write descriptions for user-searchable guide in consumer hard drive Digital Video recorder (DVR) product. Establish, expand and maintain categorization scheme; oversee editorial staff.

Responsibilities:
* Execute ninety percent of writing and all categorization and copyediting of on-screen text.
* Supervise four junior editors.
* Perform technical and creative training of all incoming departmental personnel.

Key Accomplishments:
* Designed and developed categorization scheme that sorted all broadcast and cable television programming into 50 unique, user-friendly genre categories.
* Wrote daily column of television's "best bets" for user guide.
* Wrote script for nationally broadcast TV program, "ReplayTV Presents."
* Wrote technical and creative manuals for category creation procedure.
Again, this is all fairly accurate. Not that it ever did me any good.

MAGINET, INC.

Sunnyvale, CA - 1996-1998
Abracadabra! 18 months (October '96 through March '98) becomes 3 years with mathemagic!

TITLE: SENIOR EDITOR

Job Description:
Write text for, and supervise production of, all on-screen content for supplier of on-demand video in more than 400 five-star hotels worldwide. Coordinate among management, software developers, digital artists, freelance writers, and branch offices in thirteen countries.

Key Accomplishments:
* Developed categorization scheme and wrote all text for on-screen viewer guides.
* Wrote all non-technical print material, including user surveys and end-user guides.

COGSWELL POLYTECHNICAL COLLEGE

Sunnyvale, CA - 1999-2007

TITLE: ADJUNCT PROFESSOR

Position Description:
Develop and teach film history courses for General Education Dept. of four-year college.

Responsibilities:
* Research, write and present course material.
* Create, administer and score all course tests, term papers and examinations.

SGI (Silicon Graphics International)

Mountain View, CA - 1995-1996
Sure, it sounds like two years. It was actually about 12 months, but since I kept showing up in month 13, I listed January 1996 as "1996." That month only seemed like a year.

TITLE: VIDEO PRODUCER

Key Accomplishments:
* Established SGI's first digital (non-linear) editing facility to produce quick turnaround, low cost, customized sales and marketing videos.
* Wrote, produced, directed and edited more than 100 personalized CEO-to-CEO "video letters" for numerous SGI departments.

LOCKHEED MARTIN

(formerly Lockheed Missiles & Space Co., Inc.)
Sunnyvale, CA - 1989-1993

TITLE: WRITER/PRODUCER/DIRECTOR,
VIDEO/FILM DEPT.

* Project management of all phases of video production, including concept development, research, scriptwriting, and schedule and budget management; directed crews and talent during studio and location shoots; supervised all post-production, including editing.
At some point, I sliced off all previous positions at Lockheed, since a.) they bore no relevance to any position I was applying for in the New Millennium, and b.) including my initial hire date of 1981 immediately pegged me as an Old Fart.

FREELANCE WRITER/EDITOR (1985-present)

* Video Columnist for the San Jose (Calif.) *Mercury News* (1985-1995); wrote 534 consecutive weekly video columns and more than 50 feature articles on film and video.
* Published four non-fiction books, including the video guide, *Killer B's: The 237 Best Movies On Video You've (Probably) Never Seen.*

* Published more than 200 articles in newspapers and magazines throughout the U.S., including the San Diego *Union-Tribune*, San Francisco *Examiner*, Philadelphia *Inquirer*, and the L.A. *Times* Syndicate.
* Contributing Editor at Reel.com since 1996, writing over 1,000 movie synopses for its film database and more than two dozen articles for its online editorial content. Developed numerous film courses for Reel U., the world's first online film school.

EDUCATION
* B.S., University of Santa Clara
(Notice that no year is included to give a clue as to my age, nor any specific discipline, because what good would a degree in Psychology do you when you're applying for a position in a hi-tech startup...or anywhere, really, for that matter?)

To sum up: Don't sell yourself short...sell yourself out. And keep in mind that souls are evidently recyclable: once you've sold yours to a corporation, you can sell it over and over again to other corporations. It could even prove profitable.

WHAT I'VE LEARNED ABOUT: INTERVIEWS

The second hurdle a jobseeker encounters is, of course, The Interview. Your résumé apparently having passed muster, the HR monkeys now want to sniff your butt in person.

Your prospective employers want to see you in person for several reasons: to discover how you dress, if you smell, and whether you'll grate on their nerves in ways a résumé can never capture (an annoying laugh; you're fugly, etc.). In the current tech market (circa 2020) it's called "culture fit." In high school, it was called "cliques." If they like you, you're in. If not...buh-*byeee*!

The rules for interviewing are actually quite simple and obvious: Dress nicely, or at least appropriately. Show up on time. Do some research on the company and have a few intelligent questions ready to ask if and when an interviewer asks if you have any questions. Be polite. Don't be humble—you are, after all, attempting to sell yourself to them—but on the other hand, don't be arrogant.

In short, just keep in mind that all a job interview really requires is "first date behavior."

VARIETIES OF INTERVIEW EXPERIENCE

Interviews can be divided up into any number of categories, "good or bad" being the obvious first pigeonholes (as in "good" = landed the job; "bad" = buh-*byeee*). But we can also sort them in another way: Formal or Informal. And while a Formal interview might seem the more difficult to pass, the Informal interviews are often an even trickier minefield to maneuver.

Below are a few examples of various types of interviews I've encountered and endured (although sometimes barely).

THE HONEST INTERVIEW

The best, most succinct, most honest job interview I ever had occurred in March 2005, courtesy of Morgan, a software engineer at Akimbo. He entered the conference room where I was waiting, sat down, and without introduction or preamble said, "I guess they're gonna lock us in a room long enough to figure out if we can work together without killing each other."

I'd worked with enough codeheads to understand and appreciate the dark, warped sense of humor they all seemed to share.

"I dunno, man," I said, shaking my head. "It's been *hours* since I killed anyone, and I'm gettin' antsy."

We both laughed. I'd passed the Turing test.

At heart, interviews are that simple.

THE INFORMAL INTERVIEW

August 1999

The most formal interview I ever experienced was performed by a woman at Fatbrain.com—but not before an informal interview with one of her direct reports. Fatbrain started life as the Computer Literacy bookstore in Sunnyvale in 1983, ultimately expanding to four brick and mortar stores. In 1998 it went public as an online store for technical books. The company's mission, I was informed, was to become "the Amazon.com of technical books."

I'd applied for an editorial position, editing the synopses of tech books written by their staff of young writers. It's a measure of my desperation that I even considered applying for such a dreadfully boring position—basically a Grammar Cop; the person assigned to do little more than point out to your co-workers what they've done wrong. But I figured it was a job I could do with one eye closed while keeping the other eye on Monster.com until a better position became available.

I met first with a young woman whose last name was Kenedy —with one "n," a detail that would prove significant. We walked through my résumé, and I presented my credentials; i.e., the several books I'd edited (and desktop published).

"What about the other job requirement," she asked. "We're looking for someone with excellent Internet research skills."

I knew that. It was in the posted job description. And I'd done my homework.

"OK," I said, suppressing a smile. "How's this? You graduated from Sarah Lawrence in '91, where you were on the soccer team and on the staff of the college newspaper. You have an older brother who's been in and out of trouble with the law but seems to have found a stable position with a marketing firm in Boston. Your father passed away about ten years ago, and your mother has since remarried." (*Note:* The details have been changed to protect Ms. Kenedy, given her reaction below.) In 2020, all this and far more could easily have been gleaned from a glance at her LinkedIn entry or her Facebook page. But keep in mind this was 1999, five years before Facebook launched and years before it was even a gleam in Zuck's larcenous heart.

Ms. Kenedy's jaw dropped following my data dump. "Where did you—" she started, interrupting herself to growl, "My stepfather. He posted his genealogical research online, didn't he? I'm gonna *kill* him!"

She was right—it was, in fact, her stepfather's site that gave me my clues to deeper research on her life history. What I didn't tell her is that researching her was a piece of cake since she had a relatively unusual last name. If she'd been a two-n "Kennedy," I no doubt would have been in deep trouble finding out anything about her, aside from the fact that she had a distant relative in politics who'd lost his head over his job.

THE FORMAL INTERVIEW

August 1999

Apparently, my "mad research skillz" impressed Ms. one-n Kenedy, since she arranged a follow-up interview with her boss, an ex-Navy woman about 40 with a stiff, no-nonsense attitude and a generic interviewing playbook. She barked out a series of textbook behavioral interview questions:

"Tell me about a project you led to success."

"Tell me about a time when your work was criticized, and how you handled it."

"Tell me about a challenge you faced."

"Tell me about a time when you thought you went above and beyond the call of duty at work."

"Tell me about a problem you had with a co-worker and how you resolved it."

It seemed pretty obvious that she was drawing from a workbook—simply going down a checklist borrowed from some management manual. Our "conversation" seemed less like an interview than a military interrogation, or Scientology auditing.

These "behavioral questions" are designed to put you on the spot. I fucking hate them. I'd been in the workforce for over 20 years—how the hell was I supposed to immediately recall an example of each of these situations, *and* spin them in a positive manner? Was this a test of memory and quick-wittedness? But since this procedure was rigidly Formal, there were clearly some rules to responding that could be applied—interview hacks, if you will.

"Give me an example of a time when you did something wrong, and how you handled it." Claim you'd never done anything wrong? Flunk. Admit that you thought you were right and were disgruntled when a superior decided you were wrong? Flunk. Did the "wrong thing" you did involve lying to your superiors? Might as well just pick up and leave—no way in hell they'll hire a subordinate guilty of insubordination (and stupid enough to admit it). So what's left? The primary goal is to make yourself look good: to spin a question about your weakness into a strength. For example, when they ask, "What is your major weakness?" you give the Pavlovian response: "I care too much about my work," or "I put in way too much time at work." You know it's bullshit. *They* know it's bullshit. But they also know you've done your research and have learned the appropriate Call-and-Response.

Another method is to search your memory (beforehand, if at all possible) for a minor transgression—one for which you are chagrined and apologetic, and which you can assure them will never, ever happen again. Then maybe you've got a shot. Barring that, you can just lie. "I took the last piece of cake at a birthday party at work, and the birthday girl didn't get any. I bought her a cake the next day to make up for my boorish behavior." Yes, the worst thing wrong I ever did on the job was a trivial incident that haunts me to this day. I'm your guy. *And* I'll buy you a cake!

The Informal interview process might never ask these tough questions, but it does address the Morgan test: Can I work with this person without killing him, her, or (as of 2020) them? And while the Formal interview process is more difficult, the advantages are all to the candidate. What job seeker hasn't researched these typical questions and prepped some answers? Or would, to prepare for his next interview, once he caught on that this brand of interrogation might happen again? The other candidate advantage is an enormous disadvantage to the interviewer: They'll never know if you're lying.

One question I didn't expect in this Formal interview, however, was this: "Who's your hero?" Oh dopey me—I tried to give her an honest answer: "I outgrew the need for heroes long ago. My goal now is to live the kind of life that will allow me to be my own hero." The answer seemed to baffle her. "Well, then, who do you most admire?" she tried. Again, I made the mistake of telling her the truth. "The Dalai Lama," I said. Not only was this answer true, but it had an additional advantage: Who would possibly have the audacity to argue with it?

A day passed after the interview, with no response from Fatbrain. Well, that's OK, I thought—they probably have other candidates to interview, or at least to discuss. Then two days passed, then three. I called Ms. Kenedy.

"I'm just checking in on the progress of filling the editorial position," I said.

"We've decided to go with another candidate," she said quietly.

I'd studied and knew the accepted responses to this bad news. "Well, I can't say I'm not disappointed," I said. "But if you could give me some feedback that might help me in my next interview, I'd appreciate it. Is there some technical skill I lack that I can learn to be a better candidate for a similar position, for instance?"

"Well..." she said hesitantly, "it's not that. My boss won't hire you."

"Why not?"

"I'm really not supposed to reveal the reasons for decisions like that," she literally whispered into the phone. "But she said you were too funny to work in an office environment."

Too funny to work in an office environment?

I mentally scanned our interview. I'd smiled and had been polite and charming; I'd been relaxed and subdued but focused and interested. I knew she had a military mindset and background, and did everything I could to mirror her body language, speaking style and no-nonsense attitude. And I was *still "too funny to work in an office environment"? WTF?*

There's a scene in the original *Terminator* movie where The Terminator is sitting in a hotel room cleaning his gun when the manager knocks on his door and asks him, "Hey, buddy, you got a dead cat in there, or what?" We see through the Terminator's eyes a computer-generated list of "Possible Responses" (including "Yes/No; or What?," "Go away," and "Please come back later.") He chooses Number Four: *"Fuck you, asshole!"* I had a Terminator moment on the phone at that juncture. My choices of response included the following:

1) " 'Too funny to work in an office environment'? *Well, I'm not laughing now!"*

2) "Why would I want to work in an office where humor is prohibited?"

3) "Thank you for telling me that."

4) *"Fuck you, asshole!"*

If I'd been talking directly with the manager, I probably would have gone with Number 4. But since I was talking with a person who: a) took a chance on telling me the truth, and b) was probably a victim of this attitude herself, I went with 3. And I never heard from any of the fatheads at Fatbrain ever again.

Fatbrain was acquired and devoured by Barnes & Noble in late 2000. Who knows what became of any of the employees, or what would have become of me? All I know for certain is that it would not have been funny.

THE NON-STARTER, or ANTI-INTERVIEW

July 1996

I'd been out of work since Silicon Graphics had declared me *persona non grata* (or worse, a "non-person") months earlier. But even as I was being ghosted by SGI, I resorted to an alternative to solipsistic job hunting: an employment agency. My old college friend and ex-roommate Kevin Briggs was working for General Employment, a San Francisco staffing company, so I handed him my résumé and signed up as a client. If I landed a position they'd referred me to, the company that hired me would pay General Employment a bonus for their expert assistance in locating the right candidate. But as much as I appreciated Briggs' efforts to find me a job, our association got off to a rocky start.

One day in August 1996, for instance, he sent me to interview at a company that designed "medical imaging equipment"—whatever that was. The interview was that very afternoon. Great. No time to tweak my résumé to match their req, or even to research the company. In 1996, I didn't even have email at home, much less web access—if this company even had a website.

Complicating the situation was the fact that Silicon Valley was in the midst of its annual heatwave. The temperature was over 100 degrees that afternoon. Regardless of the weather, I put on a suit and tie and drove my (non-air conditioned) car to the address in San Jose. Once there, however, I simply could not bring myself to put on the suit coat. I didn't want to arrive looking like last week's flowers. I'd spin this to my advantage—I'd mention in passing that I was exhibiting intelligence and flexibility by flaunting the custom of dressing up for an interview. Damn, I was good!

The building was refreshingly cool. My interviewer, a stiff, solemn, middle-aged guy who reminded me of nothing so much as a mortician, met me in the lobby and introduced himself. The first words out of his mouth after that were these: "You know, it's traditional to show up for a job interview in a suit." Oh, we were off to a flying start! "Yes, sir," I replied. "I'm fully aware of that. It was a conscious decision to leave the coat in the car, since it's over a hundred degrees outside. I took a chance that you'd respect intelligence and personal initiative over tradition, because how dumb would you think I was to show up in a suit coat in hundred-degree weather, just to conform to some convention, and not exhibit some flexibility based on extenuating circumstances?"

"*I'm* wearing a suit coat," he said quietly. He'd spun my spin. Oh, yeah, I was definitely gonna get this job. We went to a small conference room and began.

His first question was: "Do you know FrameMaker?" I knew that FrameMaker was a professional document-processing program, widely used by technical writers. But I'd never used it.

"No, I don't," I said.

"Then why are you applying for this job?" he responded—actually sounding irritated.

Here was another Terminator-in-the-motel-room moment. Among the possible responses that flashed through my mind:

"Because you invited me to interview."

"I've learned a lot of software programs in the past ten years, and my brain's not full yet."

"Fuck you, asshole."

The response I chose was this: "Because your job description says you're looking for a *writer*. I'm a writer. I can learn whatever software you want me to use."

He asked a few more questions, but I could tell his heart wasn't in it. Mine wasn't either. We were just going through the motions. There was no way I was getting hired by this company. That insight, at least, exhibited some intelligence. And the longer I could string out this air-conditioned interview, the longer the respite from the triple-digit heat outside.

My takeaway from that experience: Silicon Valley wanted "plug-and-play" employees. "Snap-to-grid" employees. They'll hire you to do what you were already doing—but not what you aspired to do. Horizontal movement was the standard. A promotion was the anomaly. And advancement? Virtually impossible.

THE CONSULTANCY

August 1996

General Employment sent me out on another interview a few weeks later—but only after I'd ragged on Briggs about the previous fiasco. I was clearly unqualified for the position, and he'd wasted my time sending me there. He assured me that I was eminently qualified for this next position. I was skeptical. But I was also using credit cards to pay for food and rent, so I went.

The company was located in an industrial park outside downtown San Jose and was a spin-off of a Xerox product that had earned enough status (and profits) to become its own separate business. The product was something like a video conference call, where participants at a distance could view, discuss, and modify images on a large video screen—essentially, the equivalent of a group whiteboard, as I understood it. The position was editorial: creating a GUI manual for users. ("GUI" is tech-talk for "Graphical User Interface"—using icons instead of text, like the desktop of a Mac or a PC. It's a nasty acronym that's pronounced like it looks: "gooey.") A video whiteboard was not the sexiest product in the tech world, but its parent company was Xerox, which implied that there was at least some stability, some money...and some hope for success. After all, Apple stole many of its key ideas, like the mouse (not to mention GUI) from Xerox PARC years earlier.

I was greeted by the man who'd be my immediate superior if I got the job. He was middle-aged and non-descript, but smart, soft-spoken and pleasant (always a good combination). He took me into a huge auditorium-like room filled with row after row of tables. I assumed it was some sort of classroom or training facility. We went through my résumé. I showed him the books I'd desktop published. And we talked about the specific requirements of the position.

"Have you ever worked on a GUI manual before?" he asked.

"No," I admitted. But before we could do a replay of the medical imaging company abortion of an interview, I was prepared with an answer. "*But*," I continued, "as I understand it, the production of a GUI manual would parse out into several distinct individual functions, all of which I have, in fact, performed. I proceeded to list the steps and the skills required to perform these sub-functions, while he nodded and agreed with my dissection and analysis. (I won't bore you with the details. I don't remember them anyway.) When I was through, I pointed to my résumé. "If you look at this with a pieces-and-parts approach," I said, "you can see that I have, in various previous positions, performed *every single one* of these tasks and mastered every single skill necessary to create a GUI manual. I did X here," I continued, pointing out the job functions; "I did Y here; I did Z here.

"So what I'm saying," I concluded, "is that while I might never have created a GUI manual end-to-end, I'm familiar with every phase of effort necessary for this kind of production, and I've performed every essential task required for this kind of production. All the tools are in my toolbox, and all of them have been proven. All we have to do is collect them in a new toolbox and arrange them to apply to your task."

He smiled. He nodded. "You make a very compelling argument," he chuckled. Hopeful...but where was the inevitable *but*? Wait for it... wait for it... "But..." *aaaaand* there it was. "But the thing is, you've never worked on a GUI manual."

Time for the closer. "Look at it this way," I said, in an attempt to turn a bug into a feature. "That's to your advantage. I won't come in here with a head full of preconceived notions about how things *should* be done. You won't have to put up with listening to me say things like, 'Oh, that's not how we did it at SGI!' You actually have the opportunity to mold me into an editor who does things the way *you* want them done, because I *don't* have prior experience getting in the way."

He chuckled some more. I could tell the radical concept appealed to him. *But:* "I'm still not sure my boss would buy it," he said, shaking his head.

"I'd be happy to talk with him," I said. "This is an exciting product, and I'd love the opportunity to be part of it." OK, so it wasn't exactly an exciting product. It was a pretty lame product, actually. What *were* exciting prospects to me at that time, however, included: a.) receiving a regular paycheck; and b.) not starving to death in the gutter.

"Well," he confided, "we do have our problems. Let me tell you our biggest technical challenge. Maybe you'll have some insight into it."

"Sure," I said. "What's the prob— Uh, what's the challenge?"

There's no need to go into technical details. Hell, they might be proprietary anyway—although I suspect that this company has long been moldering away in the graveyard of fallen start-ups. Oddly enough, however, once he finished outlining the problem, I felt like I could actually offer some insight. "What you're describing to me seems less like a technical problem than a lack of user knowledge," I said. His ears perked up. I took this as a signal to continue. And I did.

Once I'd redefined the problem—the *challenge*—he asked me the critical question: "How would you go about solving that?" But he didn't ask this like it was a question from a Formal Interview. *("Ve haff vays of making you tell me about a time you solved a problem.")* Somehow, we were way beyond interviewing at this point. We were two guys on the same wavelength; a couple of fellow employees (fingers crossed) brain-storming on how to solve the biggest technical problem this startup suffered.

Life is full of moments tagged "If I knew then..." This would prove to be one of mine. If I knew then what I know now, I would have closed my briefcase, thanked him for his time, smiled and walked away. But who knew then?

So instead of leaving, we talked. We talked and talked and talked some more. We designed a user questionnaire, crafting specific questions. We developed a distribution and analysis protocol. We talked psychology and technology and the interface between them. We didn't stop for coffee or bathroom breaks. We didn't need them. We were on a roll. The summer sun set, and people started sticking their heads into the room to yell good night to my interviewer. And sometime around 7 PM, after a full six hours of non-stop discussion, he led me to the front door.

"This was great," he said. "Amazing. I truly believe you've solved the problem we've been just *agonizing* over for *months*. I'm gonna demand that my boss sit down with me tomorrow morning and I'm gonna tell him what we've accomplished here. I'll definitely be in touch."

I drove home elated. I wanted to land the job, and I'd stuck the landing. My disastrous financial days were over. I was going to work for a Xerox company. I was going to work for a guy with whom I got along famously—and who thought I was brilliant! Turns out, as Voltaire said when informed that a peer of whom he had always spoken highly did not reciprocate his high regard, that "perhaps both of us are wrong."

I don't recall if I literally sat by the phone the next day awaiting his call. But I know I didn't go out, in case I missed it.

But there was no call that day. And there was no call the next day. Or the next. When Friday rolled around, I was baffled. I violated protocol and phoned him.

"Did you get a chance to talk to your boss about all the things we discussed?" I asked, skirting around the real questions of my start date, salary, and the number of vacation days I'd be getting. Once again he was profuse in his thanks. Yes, he'd talked with his boss. Yes, he'd outlined our plan to save the startup. Yes, he'd gotten the green light to institute virtually everything we'd discussed, determined and designed.

"And the editorial position?" I asked.

"Oh, he won't let me hire you," he said.

"Uh... Why not?"

"Because you've never worked on a GUI manual."

D'oh! Back to square one. Worse—square zero. Maybe even square *negative* one. It was like living in a horrid version of Abbott and Costello's classic routine, "Who's On First?" I'd given away a day of my time and volunteered an expertise for which I could probably have charged them a thousand dollars as a consultant. And what did I get in return? Squat. No, worse: *diddly*-squat.

I determined that if this situation ever reoccurred, I'd tell the interviewer this story and then offer him or her a choice: They could hire me and I'd solve the problem. Or they could hire me as a consultant and I'd solve the problem for a fee. But I would never again give away another free lunch when I could barely afford to buy my own.

POST-INTERVIEW

No matter how the interview went, be sure to immediately send a "Thank You" email to everyone with whom you interviewed. Even if they were assholes, you don't have to be.

WHAT I'VE LEARNED ABOUT: MANAGEMENT

"Bosses. They're like gnats on a camping trip."
—Bill Hicks

MANAGER'S EXPECTATIONS AND MANAGING EXPECTATIONS

You know your boss is an idiot. Most of us have felt this way at some time. I've felt this way about half the time.

Work is supposed to be an alignment of effort between management and employees toward the same general goal. Far too often, however, work is a war between employees and management—or, more gently, work is a *game* between employees and management. And it's a game with specific rules:

1) *The Prime Directive of Management:* Get as much work as possible out of your employees while giving back as little as possible. Dick Zucker, my boss at Apple for several years, for instance, objected to my suggestion that we take a team that worked closely with us out to lunch to thank them for their exceptional effort; his rationale was that we should not be rewarding them "for doing their job."

2) *The Prime Directive of Employees:* Get as much as possible from your employer while giving as little as possible in return. As Nietzsche's aphorism states, "Only give seventy-five percent."

The game can be condensed into this old Hungarian proverb: "They pretend to pay us an honest wage and we pretend to do an honest day's work."

Of course, the rule for employees does not apply to those workers who believe they are on a management track, or to those of us who take some pride in our work. But even we can sense when we're being taken advantage of. As an editor at various hi-tech companies, for instance, I learned that in a financial crunch, Editorial is the first department to go. And, speaking as a writer, management knows I'd be writing something, whether I was paid or not...so they get as close to "not" as possible. The Management rule, however, is virtually universal and inviolable.

During the years I worked at Lockheed, they had a Management Trainee program in which candidates for promotion were schooled in management techniques while rotating through a series of temporary supervisory assignments to practice their skills. (Think of it as on-the-job management training—or think of it as I did, like having a substitute teacher. "Our regular boss said we could work outside today.") One part of the program was to spend a couple of weeks in what was referred to internally as "Charm School," although no one I ever knew who'd gone through the course ever displayed any charm...or revealed any of the school's secrets. They all returned a bit sobered and distant, however, as though the Big Secret revealed to them was that their underlings will slit their throats if they turn their backs. (Shit! They're onto us!)

MANAGEMENTATION
or, How Managers are Trained to "Think"

I've had the best of bosses, I've had the worst of bosses. I believe, however, after decades of dealing with bosses both good and bad, that the covert training they received must have included a few fundamental points, including:

1) there is no caps key.

2) Always be a few minutes late to meetings. Make your subordinates wait *because you can*. Don't think of it as "lost productive time"; think of it as an investment in asserting your authority—and as taming the wild beasts; i.e., the bottom-feeders on the Org chart.

I also believe that middle management is entirely concerned with *asses*. The Three Rules of Ass Management:

1) Kiss those above you.

2) Kick those below you.

3) Cover your own.

Before you buy me a ticket to Cynicism City (where I already have a timeshare), please be aware that, unlike unicorns or honest politicians, there is, in fact, such a thing as The Good Boss. As I see it, the characteristics of The Good Boss are also three-fold:

1) Give clear direction about goals and deadlines.
2) Be available to answer questions.
3) Leave me the hell alone.

Examples:

1) *Give clear direction about goals and deadlines*

At ReplayTV, our departmental *führer* "Lois Tantrum" only ever gave us vague, general goals. "You know what to do," he'd say, and then disappear. He knew we did indeed know what to do—but we came to realize that whatever we thought we "knew to do" would be summarily rejected by him. He reveled in performing live dissections of work we were proud of... eviscerating his underlings by proxy. All we ever knew is what he *didn't* want—namely, anything we presented to him. Not only was this not "clear goals," it was in effect *anti*-goals, and an enormous waste of work-hours (in addition to the sadistic attempts to beat us down).

2) *Be available to answer questions*

No matter how clear the goal, at some point in any project a question is going to arise that is above your paygrade to answer —often a question that stops all forward progress until it gets answered. The Good Boss makes himself available to answer the inevitable questions. But if you attempt to reach The Boss and he's incommunicado, your choices are limited: wait to reach him, or attempt to answer it yourself, usually without access to key details. If you're right—good guess! But if you're wrong, you might have to scrap everything you'd done and start over... not to mention that you might be castigated for exceeding your authority.

A prime example of The Bad Boss in this respect would again be Lois at ReplayTV, who was rarely even in the office, and when he was, refused to provide constructive criticism—just criticism. Even though Lois intimated that he knew what he wanted, he refused to give any direction whatsoever. We were left to guess what he wanted—which was, perhaps, *precisely* what he wanted: to keep his underlings off-balance and anxious.

3) *Leave me the hell alone*

Leave me the hell alone translates in biz lingo as "Don't Micromanage." One Lockheed manager informed me not only of what my goal was, but the steps I should take to achieve it. I knew from experience that my own method was more effective. So I just did things my way and never informed him that I didn't do it his way. The projects were completed more quickly...and he never knew.

This point builds on points 1 and 2: If the method for achieving the goals isn't clear, I'll ask—or I'll figure it out. But don't tell me how to do my job—especially if I've been doing it for months or years and you've never done it. Trust my experience, goddamn it. It's what you hired me for.

One final thing I've learned about Management: *It's easier to get forgiveness than permission.* But forgiveness isn't always all that easy to obtain, either.

THE INCREDIBLE SHRINKING ORG CHART, *Part 1*

When I joined the Corporate Cabal in 1981 by hiring into Lockheed, there was a hierarchy that was instituted at virtually every major company and corporation in America. It looked like this, generally, from the top down:

- CEO
- President
- Vice-President(s)
- Directors
- Managers
- Supervisors
- Leads
- You

Sometime in the early 1990s, however, along with the rise of the dotcom culture, this traditional org chart began to morph like a kaleidoscope on acid. New designations and new titles sprouted like mushrooms on cow patties. Now, in addition to the CEO, other senior positions were created—CFO (Chief Financial Officer), Chief Operating Officer (COO), CTO (Chief Technology Officer), and so on. These newly-created positions might have reached the point of ludicrous (or perhaps parodic) absurdity when John Lassiter was dubbed CCO (Chief Creative Officer) at Disney.

The Vice Presidential level suffered no worse a fate, rapidly devolving into a title that encompassed everyone from people who were previously Directors down to Supervisors, conferring upon them increasingly ludicrous titles like VP, Senior VP and even Senior Executive VP. (I had to bite my tongue at Apple to stop from laughing when a Disney "SEVP" handed me his card and I first encountered this phony-baloney title.)

A currency exchange might look something like this:

NEW TITLE / OLD TITLE

- CEO = CEO
- All the other C*Os = VPs
- Senior Executive VP = Director
- Senior VP = Manager
- VP = Supervisor
- You

Well, what the hell. I suppose the upper management rationale is that if you won't pay the underlings more, or provide them a corner office with a window, the least you can do is inflate their status through their title.

YOUR TITLE: A CASE STUDY

That's the theory, at least. In reality, it doesn't always work out that way. When new middle management took over ReplayTV in 2000 and decided to move our entire department to Los Angeles, for instance, I requested a raise and a promotion as one of my requirements for making the move.

"Absolutely," said my immediate superior (a Vice President of something). "Any title you want."

"I like Executive Editor," I said. "Like on a newspaper, since I oversee all the other editors."

She wrinkled her brow, as though pondering the request. “Mmm,” she balked at length. “I’m concerned about the ‘Executive’ part. It might make it sound like you were an executive.”

“OK,” I shrugged, playing along. “How about ‘Editor-in-Chief,’ like on a newspaper, since I oversee all the other editors?”

She furrowed her brow even deeper. “Mmm,” she demurred. “I’m concerned about the ‘Chief’ part. That might make it sound like you were in charge of the entire department, like a Chief Executive Officer.”

“OK,” I conceded—not that I believed her logic, even for a second. I simply didn’t care what title I had...but I needed to test the waters with my new bosses to see just how flexible (or insane) they were.

“Hey!” she said, in an allegedly brilliant insight. “How about ‘Senior Editor’?”

“Well, I’m *already* the Senior Editor,” I sighed. “I *hired in* as Senior Editor. And I was Senior Editor at my last job. I thought I was getting a promotion.”

“OK, then,” she said brightly. “Senior Editor it is!”

I wasn’t going to fight the “promotion.” (I did end up fighting for the raise, however.)

THE INCREDIBLE SHRINKING ORG CHART, *Part 2*

Another development in Orgchartville occurred in the early 2000s when various startup managements began insisting on a “flat” org chart, for whatever reason. Naturally, the CEO and VP positions remained at the top of the hierarchy. But the bottom rungs of the corporate ladder were supposed to be collapsed in some way, making all middle management and low-level employees relative equals…on paper, at least. We at the bottom still reported to someone who had the authority to hand out assignments and hire and fire us...even though, according to the company documents, we were technically all peers on the same level. The illogical ambiguity was something we simply had to learn to live with.

SPEAKING WELL OR SPEAKING ORWELL

Buzzwords are one thing. They're euphemisms; stupid but clear. (I've always been amused, for instance, when management declares we need a "Come to Jesus" moment, or when someone points to a corporate tool and sighs, "He drank the Kool-Aid.") Often, however, we are presented with the buzzword's more sinister and Orwellian cousin, Corporate Doublespeak.

I first became aware of this in the early '90s, when a new management philosophy sweeping business and industry dictated that employees should be "empowered" to make decisions. I empowered myself to make a few decisions above my paygrade when circumstances dictated the necessity. And what I discovered was that the phrase was a dual-edged sword that essentially translated as: "If you do something on your own initiative that your management likes, you were empowered. But if you empower yourself to do something on your own initiative that management does *not* like…you fucked up."

A few key management phrases have repeated like a cheap burrito during my career. Eventually, I interpreted them. Below, the fruits of my efforts. These are, of course, just a cherry-picked sample including examples I have personally experienced; the reader can no doubt provide numerous additional examples.

Orwellian Phrase: "Choose your battles."

Actual English Interpretation: "You can't win this, so don't fight it." (At one such junction, when my boss "wisely" advised me to "choose your battles," I replied, "OK. I choose this one." He had no response. He'd run out of clichés.)

Orwellian Phrase: "Be creative."

Actual English Interpretation: "Be creative in a way your management likes, and not in any other way."

Alternate: "Be creative in a really familiar way."

(iTunes-specific interpretation: "Never, *ever* be clever.")

Orwellian Phrase: "We're gonna have to work extra hard on this one."

Actual English Interpretation: "You're gonna have to work extra hard on this one."

Orwellian Phrase: "Let's circle back on this."

Actual English Interpretation: "We are never going to discus this again."

Orwellian Phrase: "Let's take this offline."

Actual English Interpretation: "You're an idiot and you're irritating me. Don't make me look like an asshole by smacking you down in public. I'll do it later, in private."

Orwellian Phrase: "May I see you in my office for a moment please?"

Actual English Interpretations:

a) Best Case Scenario: "You fucked up."

b) Worst Case Scenario: "You fucked up and you're fired."

Orwellian Phrase: "Your services are no longer required."

Actual English Interpretation: "We're laying you off."

Orwellian Phrase: "We're rightsizing."

Actual English Interpretation: "We're downsizing."

Orwellian Phrase: "He/she isn't with us anymore."

Actual English Interpretation: "He/she has been fired."

Orwellian Phrase: "He/she moved on to new challenges."

Actual English Interpretation: "He/she has been fired."

Orwellian Phrase: "He/she has graduated."

Actual English Interpretation: "He/she has been fired."

Orwellian Phrase: "It is what it is."

Actual English Interpretation: "I'm an idiot."

WHAT I'VE LEARNED ABOUT:
THE STARTUP LIFE

"Fail first, fail often."
–Familiar Silicon Valley mantra

"Move fast and break things"
–Familiar Silicon Valley mantra

IT'S A HARD-KNOCKS…
I MEAN *"A STARTUP"* LIFE FOR US

My parents had Depression-era consciousness ("Clean your plate—children are starving in China," and so on). In the late 20th century, to be employed in Silicon Valley required that one develop "Dot-Consciousness": living in a state of constant uncertainty as to whether you'll have a job next year, next month, or even tomorrow. Stories of startup employees arriving at work only to find the doors locked are legion.

After a decade of living The Startup Life, I recalled a story my friend Dr. Timothy Leary related in his brilliant 1973 essay, "Starseed." In this parable, there was once "a great castle that was separated from shore by a swamp. Pilgrims, searchers, warriors seeking the castle disappeared into the marsh because each rock they stepped on sank from view. The Hero and his mate sat on the bank and watched for days. Then He rose and held his hand to Her. He whispered [these] instructions: 'Leap from rock to rock more swiftly than they sink. The trick is simple. Have courage and keep moving.'" This story seems to prefigure and encapsulate one of the Prime Directives of Silicon Valley: "Move fast and break things."

Here are a few of the rules I discovered about working in a startup and living a startup lifestyle:

1) *Never take time off:* You'll need the vacation pay you've accumulated to tide you over between jobs, for one thing. And if they find out they can do without you for a couple of weeks, they'll realize they can do without you, period. As Kafka put it

in *The Trial*, "…he did not want to be removed from his workplace for even one day, as the fear of not being allowed back in was too great."

2) *Never consider yourself indispensable*: As Charles de Gaulle said, "The graveyards are full of indispensable men."

3) *Never is heard a discouraging word:* If you're not 1000% convinced that your product or service will be a runaway success (and change the world), what the hell are you doing there? If you ever express any doubts out loud, you will be ostracized, even if the people with whom you share your skepticism are thinking exactly the same things. The first rule of Doubt Club: *You do not talk about Doubt Club.*

4) *If you're not looking at your computer, you're not working.*

5) *It's easier to get a job if you already have a job.*

6) *Be nice to your co-workers.* You never know if one day you'll be reporting to them, for one thing. And if they move on and remember you fondly at their next job, they might help you get employed there after the startup you're both currently working at implodes.

(Besides these specific benefits, "be nice"—aka "don't be a dick"—is good advice for anyone anywhere, goddamn it.)

7) *Don't bring your dog to work.* Just don't. They're smelly, they're distracting, and not everyone loves dogs.

And here are a few of the myths about startups (in the Piph sense that "Myth = Lie"):

1) *Startups are fun!* Startups are places where the fun never stops…because it never started. No matter how many beanbag chairs, foosball tables, nerf gun fights and free snacks they provide, a startup is *not* a fun place to work. They are lying to you and trying to fool you with surface diversions. They are trying to glue your ass to your chair so you have no reason ever to leave—or ever to stop working. Ever. You might read about such "fun" workplaces, but you'll never read about them attaining huge success *because they went out of business*. Startups are not fun. They are work.

2) *"People come first."* Totally true, if you use the alternative spelling for "people," which is "profits." The only time people come first is when a company hits a rough patch. Then the first

cuts are to people: initially, their perks; and then, personnel. If your company cancels its weekly beer bash...update your résumé immediately.

3) *"We're trying to make the world a better place."* All start-up founders claim this. And it's true: they're trying to make the world a better place for themselves by making a bajillion dollars.

STARTUP JOB POSTINGS

Startups use a peculiarly Orwellian doublespeak to advertise for open positions. A few of the euphemisms I've noticed, along with a translation to "honest English" include:

When they say: "Committed"
It actually means: 80+ hour work weeks

When they say: "Team Player"
It actually means: Takes orders without question

When they say: "Exciting new"
It actually means: "We'll tank in 12-18 months"

When they say: "We're seeking a dynamic employee"
It actually means: "We're seeking a workaholic"

When they say: "Creative"
It actually means: "Come up with ideas we like but which we are too dumb to come up with ourselves."

When they say: "Work/life balance"
It actually means: There's a reason "work" comes first in in the phrase "work/life."

There are, of course, far more similar phrases—and they are always evolving. These are a few I've encountered. The rest are left as a painful exercise for the reader.

WHAT I'VE LEARNED ABOUT:
AGEISM

"I grow old… I grow old…"
—T.S. Eliot, *The Lovesong of J. Alfred Prufrock*

While *No Plan B* is a document of personal experience, much of my personal experience has been subject to the whims and demands of the zeitgeist—the breaking winds of fate—especially where age is concerned.

While I can't honestly say I was ever subject to overt age discrimination, for instance, my age does seem to fit into larger observations about a corporate culture that values youth. A few examples:

- According to the *AARP Bulletin* (May 2014), "Between 2007 and 2013, the number of unemployed who are 55 and older increased more than any other age group. In 2013, it was 70 percent higher than it had been in 2007." (I was 56 when I hired into Apple in 2007, and when I was shown the door in 2013, I became part of that 70 percent.)
- According to an article entitled "Getting On" by Tad Friend in the November 20, 2015, edition of *The New Yorker*, "A recent AARP study revealed that sixty-four percent of Americans between forty-five and sixty had seen or experienced age discrimination at work."
- According to a 2019 *Harper's Index* entry, "56% of U.S. workers over 50 lose longtime jobs before they are prepared to retire, and 90% never recover their earning power." Not to mention those who were offered—or forced into—early retirement.
- A column by Michelle Quinn in the January 15, 2019, San Jose *Mercury News*, quotes PayScale, an online salary information company, that "the median age of an Apple worker is 31." By 2013, when I left Apple, I was exactly twice that age.

As opposed to overt ageism, what I experienced was a more subtle, more social, form of age discrimination. Since most of my Apple co-workers were literally half my age, for instance, many of them had no clue about the participants in several of my favorite stories about myself. They didn't recognize the names of many of the seminal cultural figures I'd interviewed and even befriended during the previous forty years: Martha Mitchell, Joseph Campbell, Shari Lewis, Philip K. Dick, Marilyn Chambers. And when I mentioned Timothy Leary, who I'd visited with about once a year since 1976, one puzzled co-worker said, "He was that drug guy, right?" Fuck me.

In a larger sense, aside from the widely-recognized observation that Silicon Valley prizes youth (and therefore low salaries) over experience (and high salaries), there's probably a good reason why many companies, both within and outside of the hi-tech arena, don't hire or retain older workers: we've heard all the lies and suffered all the hypocrisies—and if we're observant enough, we've wised up enough not to swallow them anymore. (I am reminded of an early '90s Lockheed co-worker, who was in his late 50s when I was in my late 30s, who used to regularly yell "Bullshit!" during management meetings.)

Fool me once, shame on you...but try to fool me repeatedly throughout a career... well, still shame on you.

WHAT I'VE LEARNED ABOUT: THE MYTH OF HALLWAY MEETINGS

"The idea is to make sure they [Apple's thousands of employees] get in each other's way … bump into each other and be inspired to think in new ways."
—*Smithsonian* magazine, December 2017

One pervasive Silicon Valley myth is that people from various different departments and disciplines can be inspired by spontaneous, random encounters—running into one another in the kitchen, for instance, or at the coffee station, or in the hallways. This thesis is patently false.

I believe it was middle management at Hewlett-Packard who originated the concept of MBWA ("Management By Wandering Around"). Apple took that concept seriously, at least at the highest levels. The idea of "the hallway meeting," however, where you run into a co-worker and informally develop some earthshaking idea, is little more than a myth. It has never, ever happened—or it's happened so close to zero times that it's statistically indistinguishable from zero.

At my low level—and at any level of employment or management I was privy to witness—if we were away from our desks, we were all always too busy rushing to a meeting to stop and discuss strategy or some blue-sky idea. During my Apple years, if we were walking to a meeting with someone in tow, or sitting in a conference room waiting for Richard Zucker to show up—I mean, waiting for the meeting to start—we'd schmooze about our weekends, our families, our latest apps or gadgets or whatever—but we rarely if ever talked about work, except to commiserate about how overworked we were.

In my experience, there is simply no such thing as an informal hallway brainstorming session—and Apple's entire new UFO campus was designed based on this faulty logic. It still looks cool, though.

WHAT I'VE LEARNED ABOUT: APPLE'S CULTURE OF SECRECY

I could tell you, but then I'd have to… (*Shhh!* You know...)

WHAT I'VE LEARNED ABOUT: APPLE'S PRIVACY POLICY

My views on privacy are nobody's business.

Chapter 35

YOU CAN'T SPELL "WHORE" WITHOUT "HR"

"I now approach an event in my life, so indelible, so awful,
so bound by an infinite variety of ties to all that has preceded it,
in these pages, that, from the beginning of my narrative, I have
seen it growing larger and larger as I advanced, like a great
tower in a plain … As plainly as I behold what happened,
I will try to write it down."
—Charles Dickens, *David Copperfield*

"Fury said to the mouse,
That he met in the house,
'Let us both go to law:
I will prosecute you.—
Come, I'll take no denial;
We must have a trial:
For really this morning
I've nothing to do.'
Said the mouse to the cur,
'Such a trial, dear sir,
With no jury or judge would be wasting our breath.'
'I'll be judge, I'll be jury,'
Said cunning old Fury;
'I'll try the whole cause and condemn you to death.' "
—Lewis Carrol, *Alice's Adventures in Wonderland*

A BIT OF BACKSTORY TO PUT THINGS IN SOME CONTEXT

Nobody's perfect. Even Mary Poppins was only "*practically* perfect in every way." And since you're not perfect, chances are that at some point in your career you've been (or will be) in trouble. I am so far from perfect that I was in trouble frequently.

The trouble could be as simple as being asked politely to step into the boss's office... "and close the door." That phrase alone is enough to strike terror into the heart of anyone who wishes to remain employed. In my experience, that phrase preceded every form of punishment from dressing-downs to layoffs to firings.

Far worse than the Angry Boss experience, however, is the HR experience—a form of oppression so sneaky and overwhelming that it transcends any simple hand-slap from an alleged superior by several orders of magnitude.

It wasn't always this way. In the dim dark days of the business world, circa the 1950s, every corporation and large company had a department called "Personnel" or "Employee Relations." Personnel managers performed numerous functions, not the least of which was to advocate on behalf of an employee who believed he or she was being treated unfairly by their management. While an individual employee might have little power in the workplace to stand up against their superiors (if they didn't belong to a union), ER would intervene for them and investigate claims of harassment or other unethical treatment or conduct, thus using the clout of an entire internal department to provide the individual working person with a voice in the workplace without fear of management reprisal.

Sometime in the '80s, however—the "Greed Decade"—the ER department was turned inside out and became its own evil, goatee-clad twin, and the kindly Dr. Jekyll of Employee Relations morphed into the sinister Mr. Hyde of "Human Resources." ER and Personnel departments, once a helpful tool to level the playing field for employees, were subverted into becoming yet another tool for Management control.

This is common knowledge—anyone who reads Scott Adams' comic strip "Dilbert," for example, is familiar with his character Catbert, the evil Director of Human Resources, whose various HR policies include requiring employees to schedule sick time in advance and insisting that bathroom breaks be counted as vacation time. The fact that Catbert first appeared in 1994 validates my timeline, I believe.

Verbal association (in my writer's mind, at any rate) places the phrase "Human Resources" right next to the phrase "Natural Resources." The association is both natural and human, I suppose: natural resources include forests of tall trees and a countryside rich in minerals, clean water and fertile land that can be purposed for economic gain. The difference is that Human Resources treats employees in the same manner as the worst abusers of natural resources: clear-cutting, strip mining, fracking and piling on the fertilizer. The only part of the definition that remains intact is, of course, the economic gain. Employees were now not seen as individual human beings, but as one more asset to be managed like any other piece of capital equipment.

And Lord protect the poor peasant who incurs the wrath of Human Resources.

HR people want you to believe they are the voice of reason, compassion and integrity. So why is it that two separate 2018 polls indicate that between 70 and 80 percent of tech company employees don't trust HR? (72 percent at Apple.) Let's find out!

Although several HR encounters are touched upon in the main narrative of *No Plan B*, I believe these three specific incidents warrant detailed accounts (including some unavoidable repetition of information from the earlier, truncated versions) as they so acutely illustrate my completely justified acrimony, animosity, antipathy, bitterness, contempt, disgust, enmity, hostility, ill will, loathing, rancor, repugnance, repulsion and revulsion against Human Resources (so much so that I had to exhaust a thesaurus just to introduce them). In short, I believe that all HR employees should have a sociopath as an older sibling so they'd have someone to look up to—and to use as a role model.

If you have been unfortunate enough to be subject to an HR interrogation or disciplinary action, perhaps these incidents will strike a note of familiarity. And if you have been lucky enough to have avoided being victimized by HR, consider these stories a public service, presented as both cautionary tales and as preparation for any potential future confrontation you might be forced to endure. Some good might yet come from my suffering.

Special Note: After decades, I can't in good conscience vouch that the conversations below are reproduced verbatim. But they made a deep impression on me at the time, so not only did I pay close attention but I also made copious notes immediately afterward—and these traumatic experiences were replayed so many times in memory that I can state they are perhaps 80 percent accurate, both in what was said to me and in my replies, and 100 percent accurate in the descriptions of my mental processes and emotional turmoil. If the dialogs aren't 100 percent verbatim, only the details have suffered (or have been edited): the intentions behind the reconstructed dialogs, I assert, are exactly as recounted.

ROUND ONE:
I LOVE I LOVE I LOVE THE CALENDAR GIRL

"...this really can't be all that important. That follows from the fact that I've been indicted, but can't think of the slightest offence for which I could be indicted."
—Franz Kafka, *The Trial*

March 31, 1993

My first taste of the awesome power of Human Relations came in 1993, while working in Lockheed Missiles and Space Company's Video/Film Department—and the sheer illogic of the incident left me feeling like I'd run into a brick wall of insanity at 80 mph.

It started with the obligatory red flag, when my supervisor Lorin "asked" if I could please step into his office "and close the door" so he might have "a short word with me." DANGER, WILL ROBINSON! WARNING! WARNING! He came right to the point. "I have to ask you to take down that Marilyn Monroe calendar you have up in your cubicle."

"And why would I do that?"

"Merdle objects to it. He says it creates an offensive and hostile work environment for him."

Of course, if anyone would object to something as innocuous as a Marilyn Monroe calendar, it would be our co-worker "Merdle." He was notoriously conservative, to the point of writing letters to the local newspaper complaining about the "risqué" Macy's lingerie ads.

"Yeah," I replied. "So what? Tell him to mind his own business," I suggested. "Tell him he's gone overboard and to drop his request. Better yet, tell him to go fuck himself. What the fuck business of it is his *what* I have on my cubicle walls?"

"You gotta take it down," Lorin repeated, ignoring my objections. Clearly a direct attack wasn't going to work. My best defense was not a good offense—I'd have to resort to calm logic.

"Are you familiar with our policy against sexual harassment?" he continued. I told him that I was, in fact, familiar with LMSC's policy concerning harassment, and that it hardly applied in this case. In a case like this, I continued, the policy was ambiguous—subject to more than one interpretation—and that it was, in this case, arbitrarily applied. He said he thought the policy was very clear. I replied that if we can't even agree on whether the policy is clear or ambiguous, it must be ambiguous. I repeated my position that this was an ambiguous policy being arbitrarily enforced, and an abuse of the harassment complaint system. I also tried explaining how ridiculous this request was.

"I've had a Marilyn Monroe calendar on my wall every year for twelve years," I continued, "—ever since I started at Lockheed. There is absolutely nothing offensive about that calendar. It's glamour photography—Marilyn Monroe in one-piece swimsuits, in peignoirs; that kind of thing. There's no nudity. It barely qualifies as cheesecake, even. I could send my ten-year-old nephew to any bookstore and they'd sell him a copy."

Lorin admitted that he knew that sexual harassment was never my intention. He also informed me that he had the power to physically confiscate the calendar, but he wasn't going to do that—yet. But he was adamant about one thing: "Merdle finds it offensive, so you have to take it down."

I tried a different tack. "You know where that calendar is located," I said. "It's on the inner wall of my cubicle. No one can even see it unless they're sitting at my desk. And Merdle has no excuse for even going into my cubicle, much less for sitting at my desk."

"Well, he does IT, so he has to sit at your desk to upgrade your software."

"Well, there you go." I smiled. "Let him schedule those updates. I'll remove the calendar when he's scheduled to be in my cube and replace it after he leaves. Problem solved."

Lorin shook his head. "No, he objects to it being there at all. Says it's not appropriate in the workplace."

"*Of course* it's appropriate," I argued. "We work in Video/Film, and Marilyn Monroe is an icon of film. Not to mention that she was once a Lockheed employee." It's true: in 1941, young Norma Jean Baker was briefly employed as a riveter by Lockheed Aircraft in Van Nuys. Lorin just shrugged. "Can't you just go talk to him?" I asked.

"No," he said. "I can't talk to him about this. You can't talk to him about it, either."

"Why the hell not?" I demanded. We were both getting frustrated—Lorin because I refused to simply agree to his "request"; me, because he would not listen to reason. And at length, he revealed why he wouldn't listen to reason. "It's not up to me," he said. "Merdle filed a harassment charge with HR and they ordered me to order you to take down the calendar."

I was gobsmacked. I'd never heard of anything like this. They can't just come along and order you to do something non-work related.

"So that's it?" I said. I might catch on slowly, but I do catch on eventually. "I have no say in this? It's a *fait accompli*?" When he looked confused, I modified my analysis. "It's a done deal? Merdle whines to HR, and gets what he wants with no debate? No one will listen to reason?"

"That's the policy," he said.

"Well, can I talk to HR, then? I might be able to convince them that this is an unreasonable demand, and they can talk Merdle out of it."

He shrugged. "Sure. You can talk to HR. But in the meantime, you have to take the calendar down."

I took the calendar down as a gesture of good faith—and also because I didn't want to test whether I could lose my job over this. But I did insist on meeting with an HR representative to discuss this unfair application of the harassment policy. At that point, I didn't know I couldn't win—that the deck had been stacked against me from the get-go, and that reason played no part in the process. But I'd be educated, as well as schooled.

"Well if you're innocent it's all very simple."
"My being innocent does not make things simple," said K.
—Franz Kafka, *The Trial*

So Lorin and I met with an HR rep; a guy who reminded me of no one more than *The Simpsons'* jovial and chuckling Dr. Hibbert—but a guy who was adamant in his stance. And he verified what I'd suspected: there was no avenue of recourse for me. If Merdle says the calendar creates a hostile and intimidating workplace for him, then he's right. Period. The claim itself is judge and jury, and HR is his tool, the executioner. There could be no contest, no debate, no trial, no appeal to reason. No recourse. End of story.

I believed that some form of retaliation was not only appropriate but virtually required, if only to protest this unreasonable policy or to stand up for my own rights. But if I refused to remove the calendar? I wouldn't be fighting an irrational HR decision...instead, I'd be guilty of insubordination, a firing offense (which I knew first-hand from my final day at Frontier Village, more than 20 years earlier).

The HR rep informed me that literally *any* non-work-related material on display in the workplace was subject to removal if someone complained. So at Lockheed Missiles and Space Co., a photo on your wall of a missile holding nuclear warheads was OK. That was our product. But a photo of your nuclear family on your wall? Not work-related, so if anyone complained, it would have to go.

I turned to Lorin. "You understand the implications of all this. don't you?" I asked. His confused look indicated that he did not, so I spelled them out for him. "It means that anyone can claim that any non-work-related item creates a hostile work environment for them, and it would have to be removed, no questions asked." He nodded, tentatively. "So," I continued, "I could say that the family photo you have on your desk is oppressive to me because I don't have a family and you're rubbing my nose in that fact, and I'm offended, and that creates a hostile work environment for me. Although according to what our HR guy here is saying, I wouldn't even *need* to you give a reason. All I'd have to do is walk Mr. HR rep here through our building and point to every non-work-related item in every room, every office, and every cubicle, and demand they be removed. And you'd have to take them down."

Lorin looked genuinely alarmed. "But you wouldn't do that, would you?"

"*Of course I wouldn't do that*," I growled. "I wouldn't do that because I'm a *reasonable person*! It's *Merdle* who's being unreasonable!"

Of course I wouldn't do that. But it quickly occurred to me that I did indeed have other options. In fact, I had precisely three other options: 1) Submit. 2) Quit. Or 3) Resist. And be fired. HR had raised the stakes to the point where if you did not agree to follow their orders, you would lose your job, one way or another. No matter how well you performed the tasks you were hired to perform, if someone decided a photo on your desk was in some way "offensive"...out it goes, or out you go. I couldn't pressure them with the threat of quitting—they'd be happy to let me go, if only so I didn't set a dangerous precedent that *HR could be negotiated with*. And, like every other employee, I was, of course, considered expendable.

I was defeated, and I knew it. I'd been sucker punched—knocked out without even being invited to the fight. But I still wanted to drive my point home, if only to make them uncomfortable with their blind, robotic acceptance and application of rules and regulations without any conscious consideration. This brought to mind a phrase written by my good and great friend Robert Anton Wilson, about institutions designed to "enforce the morality of the most narrow-minded hypocrites among us."

"Lorin," I said, "Are you seriously saying that you're going to force thirty-five people in a locked building to conform to the moral standards of the most conservative person in the department? That one tight-ass's vote outweighs all thirty-four other people's opinions?"

Lorin's response was a deer in the headlights look—confusion verging on panic. Moral dilemmas were clearly above his paygrade. So I continued.

"Are you guys at all aware of the irony of this situation?" I asked. Given their quizzical looks, I felt like I was trying to explain quantum physics to a dog. But I attempted to clarify.

"Merdle claims my calendar creates a hostile and oppressive work environment for him. But this HR action, in which I have no voice and no avenue to defend myself or debate his claim, makes this a hostile and oppressive work environment for *me*." They were unmoved. Some people just don't get irony—or else they decided that because I had been accused of an unconscionable action against poor, innocent Merdle, I *deserved* a hostile and oppressive work environment. Idiot that I am, I continued. "I feel like I should file a harassment claim against Merdle," I growled.

Dr. Hibbert, the HR warden of the workplace, shook his head. "Can't do that," he chuckled. "It's called retribution, and there are severe penalties for that."

As Joseph Heller put it, "That's some catch, that Catch-22. The best there is."

"We don't usually get any trials heard here with no hope at all."
"I am not of the same opinion," said K.
—Franz Kafka, *The Trial*

The HR rep suggested I look up the policy so I could learn for myself "what this is all about"—so of course I did. I also looked up the California state policy on harassment from which the Lockheed policy was adopted, word for word...except for one word. Where the California state harassment policy in 1992 stated that an action would have to be considered offensive by a "reasonable person," Lockheed, in adopting the policy, conveniently left out the word "reasonable"—thus negating the legal standard for judging what could and could not be considered harassment by allowing not just the judgment of a "reasonable" person, but the judgment of *any* person, no matter how unreasonable that person or their claim might be. This was clearly little more than the company's way of avoiding a potential lawsuit, where the vague standard of whether or not the accuser was, in fact, a "reasonable" person making a reasonable accusation could be debated in an objective arena—like a court. In order to squelch any possible legal action outside the company, Lockheed had simply eliminated "reasonableness" from any HR accusation. Anyone accusing any co-worker of harassment was automatically correct, reason be damned—and all in order to avoid lawsuits. If this policy isn't in itself patently unreasonable and unfair—not to mention a deliberate, willful corruption of the intention of an otherwise beneficial state law—then I don't know what is.

Capitulation is not in my nature, however. I was determined to find some loophole, or at least to express my frustration and discontent at this disturbing perversion of an otherwise useful law. I thought of several acts of revenge I could take against Merdle, like subscribing him *Hustler* magazine, or to the newsletter of NAMBLA, the North American Man/Boy Love Association, giving our work address as the delivery address. But I knew that if anything untoward happened to Merdle, I'd be the prime and primary suspect. Clearly, revenge was not worth the risk or the effort—not to mention the moral and ethical implications of stooping to Merdle's level by proving his point and actually harassing him. Ultimately I decided to take the moral high road, and settled for adopting my own version of retribution for his backstabbing behavior—the "you're dead to me" policy—and never speaking to him again.

I needed to say something to everybody else, however, so I replaced the calendar with a sign that read "The Marilyn Monroe calendar formerly occupying this space has been removed by management order following a complaint by one our your co-workers that its content is 'inappropriate in the workplace.' Failure to comply with this order could lead to termination of my employment at LMSC. I have little or no right to appeal this action. You could be next. If you have any comments or questions, see your supervisor or manager."

I hoped this message would give me the opportunity to warn my co-workers about this unreasonable, oppressive, one-sided, stacked-deck HR policy. Later, I replaced the sign with an enlargement of a cartoon panel by P.S. Mueller, entitled "Empowerment is a Two-Edged Sword"—a drawing of a little guy getting the living shit stomped out of him by a big bruiser bully, while the little guy yells, "OK! OK! You're a victim!"

ROUND ONE to HR.

Addendum: Apparently I was not alone in this specific HR action, but also apparently I was wise to not pursue it any farther than I did—like with a lawsuit. A few years after my experience, I ran across a newspaper article that mentioned that several states had heard arguments in court *specifically* about Marilyn Monroe calendars in the workplace. In every one of these cases, the calendar was deemed inappropriate for the workplace, and the defendant lost. We live in a grayer, more represssive world because of this.

A COUPLE OF BRIEF INTERLUDES

"...that's how this court does things, not only to try people
who are innocent but even to try them without
letting them know what's going on."
—Franz Kafka, *The Trial*

An alternate title for this chapter—a kinder, gentler title—was "You Can't Spell 'Horror' Without 'HR'." But I decided against that. It's not because I was never accorded any kinder, gentler treatment by HR, but because I realized that not all HR encounters are horrible. Some of them are just miserable and demeaning.

When ReplayTV decided to relocate our department from Silicon Valley to Los Angeles, for example, I went to the head of HR and explained that uprooting my household for this move caused some unintended collateral damage, in that my signify-cant other, with whom I shared a house, would also have to move. "Is there any way Replay can shake loose a few dollars to alleviate her being uprooted as well as me?" I queried.

He could have said, "No, we don't have the budget for that." He could have simply said, "No," for that matter, and I'd leave thinking, *Well, at least I tried.* But here's what he said instead: "You don't get out much, do you?"

It probably goes without saying that there would be no extra money for her move. But the enormously helpful and not at all insulting attitude of this HR department head does seem worth mentioning.

Additionally, when I joined Akimbo in 2005, the company had an HR department that consisted of a single person...and he outsourced virtually all HR tasks and paperwork. When I filled out my W2, I requested several deductions so that I would get a refund and not a tax bill. But somehow the outsourcing firm submitted my deductions as "0"—and I never noticed until early 2006, when I discovered to my horror that I owed the IRS several thousand dollars, since "I'd" submitted zero deductions.

I know, I know—I should have noticed; I should have checked. But I didn't. Like Otter says to Flounder in *Animal House*, "You fucked up. You trusted us." I fucked up. I trusted HR to be competent.

ROUND TWO:
DOES HUMOR BELONG IN THE WORKPLACE?
(Part 5 of a Nearly Infinite Series)

"[They] agreed on one thing, and that was that when ill thought-out accusations are made they are not ignored, and that once the court has made an accusation it is convinced of the guilt of the defendant and it's very hard to make it think otherwise."
"Very hard? ... It's impossible to think otherwise."
—Franz Kafka, *The Trial*

June 11, 2009

I'd been at Apple over two years by June 2009. Wednesday was meeting day, and early one afternoon that month I attended a meeting of some of my favorite iTunes co-workers. It was a small group; all whip-smart and possessing excellent senses of humor. We'd been meeting weekly for a couple of years, and we all knew we could say anything to one another without fear of offense (or of being reported to HR). But not today: today my immediate superior, Richard Zucker, decided to make an unprecedented appearance. None of the regular participants knew him very well, so we kept the meeting low-key and all business, foregoing our usual jokey camaraderie.

When we left, Zucker steered me toward a smaller conference room, explaining, "I gotta talk to you about something." Sure, whatever. A third person was waiting in the room when we arrived. I recognized him as a Human Resources rep...which should have been a giant red flag, but wasn't. It never crossed my mind that HR might have any interest or involvement in anything I'd done. I was a model employee; a living embodiment of "Apple culture"—pleasant, upbeat, hardworking, progressive, doing my best to fit in with this smart, hip population by being my smartest and hippest. I introduced myself, shook the HR rep's hand, and told him I thought he'd done a great job giving a presentation at an All Hands meeting a few weeks earlier.

"So what's going on, guys?" I asked.

HR Guy handed me a two-page typed document that turned out to be a list of grievous offenses I'd (allegedly) committed, as documented by "several" of my co-workers, he claimed (none from the meeting we'd just left, I was pleased to realize later). "There are a number of areas," the document began, "where you need to immediately improve your performance. These include improvement in your attitude which has been reflected in open criticism of your management." Well, they got me on that one. Yes, I had, in fact, pointed out to co-workers who openly wondered why I wasn't creating themed collections of movies that my management "hates that shit"—quoting Squack directly. And while I was fully aware that explaining our management's attitude in their own words (that is, hoisting them by their own petard) constituted criticism, I felt that my peers who asked had a right to know the restrictions I was working under—and my deep frustration with them. I had no idea, however, that criticizing my management was a corporate crime and a punishable offense. Especially not when it was accurate—and when they deserved the criticism.

I read through this dirty laundry list of alleged offenses with increasing incredulity. I was accused of something like a dozen different offenses, including "missing deadlines," "not answering his phone," "refusing to own up to mistakes," "telling what appear to be jokes that not everyone understands," making "inappropriate comments towards co-workers (apparently made in jest, but offensive)" and "making sarcastic remarks." (Yeah, right.) (Ah, shit—just verified that one, goddamn it!)

"Failure to show immediate significant improvement ... may result in termination," the document closed.

"This is a joke, right?" I asked Zucker and HR Guy. "I'm being *Punk'd* or something, right? No one would take any of these things seriously."

"I suggest you take it seriously," HR Guy warned. "These are serious violations of our corporate culture."

"No," I objected. "This is a list of trivia—behavior that everyone is guilty of at some point. It's full of misinterpretations and minor misunderstandings. I can prove it to you—I'm gonna go through this list point by point and explain some of these criticisms to you, so you'll see how wrong-headed and trivial most of them are."

HR Guy didn't stop me...but I discovered later that he was simply indulging me by letting me walk through this list of sins. He was under no obligation to listen to any explanation. Like the Lockheed incident with the Marilyn Monroe calendar nearly two decades earlier, once a harassment claim is filed, the accuser is automatically correct, with no discussion, no debate—and no defense for the poor sap being accused. In this case, me. "Help! I'm a victim!" these accusers claim as they bring down the sledgehammer of HR.

"Well, let's take an easy one," I said. " 'Doesn't always answer his phone.' I don't even understand that. I'm not always at my desk to answer my phone. And if someone is calling me on the phone, how does he know whether I'm at my desk or not? Makes no sense at all."

HR Guy had no response, so I moved on.

"OK," I said, "Let's take another one: Missing a deadline. What you're probably not aware of is that I have two or three deadlines *every day*. I can't meet them all without working more than the 60 hours a week I already put in—which would be illegal, not just inconvenient for someone whose minor deadline I failed to meet. I have to prioritize my deadlines so the important ones are always met, which means that occasionally, a trivial deadline is missed."

"Those deadlines aren't trivial to the person whose deadline you missed," HR Guy said. I tried to explain the difference between a "hard" deadline and a "soft" deadline, and that I'd never missed a hard deadline. He seemed unimpressed. Apparently, for his purposes, all deadlines are created equal—just like employees. Unless you complained about one. I moved on.

"It says here someone complained that I don't own up to mistakes. Did you hear that one more than once?"

HR Guy looked suspicious. "No," he admitted...at which point I knew the exact incident this charge referred to.

"That's because it only happened once," I said. "I know exactly the incident this is referring to. And I didn't 'own up' to the mistake because *I didn't make the mistake*. I tried to explain that to the guy who accused me of making the mistake, but he wouldn't believe me. I had evidence, but he wouldn't listen to it. You only heard that charge one time from one person because I *always* own up to my mistakes and correct them immediately—that's a point of personal integrity for me, as well as job responsibility. But I can tell you this: I will *never* admit to a mistake I didn't make, even if it smooths things over with a peer. That's also a point of personal integrity."

Before he could argue, I moved on. "OK, so somebody thinks I made a sarcastic remark? So what?"

"So it offended them."

"Can you give me an example?" I asked. "Otherwise, how can I know what I said that offended someone?"

HR Guy shook his head. "Can't do that," he said. "If I told you what you'd said, you might be able to identify the person objecting to what you said."

"That doesn't make any sense whatsoever," I replied, "and I think you know that. How am I supposed to correct my behavior if I have to *guess* what someone objected to?"

"Well," he suggested, "maybe you shouldn't try to be funny, since something you said offended someone."

Jesus Christ. Could he be more vague?

"It's not in my job description to protect everyone's delicate feelings," I said. "But I'll tell you this: I don't attack; I don't insult. I'm not rude or demeaning. I occasionally use sarcasm to make a point. But I'm not here to pander to some thin-skinned idiot's idea of what's funny or not. I use a lot of different types of humor around here—as a social lubricant, to make my peers feel at ease and to try to lighten up the workplace so we can enjoy our jobs more."

"It says here," he said, checking his document, "that you made insults apparently intended to be funny."

That threw me for a second, but I figured it out. "No," I said. "Absolutely not. I never insult anyone except myself. That's something I learned being on TV—if you're going to use insult humor, the only acceptable target is yourself. For instance, I once introduced myself as 'the only man on PBS who can't *spell* PBS.'"

"So you *did,* in fact, insult someone," he insisted.

"Yeah," I said. "Myself. It's called *self-deprecating humor.*"

"Well, apparently one of your co-workers found that offensive."

I had to wait a second until my mind stopped boggling. "So what you're saying," I replied slowly, "is, I make fun of myself and someone *else* is offended?"

He shrugged and pointed at the document. "Sounds that way."

I couldn't even continue down that irrational rabbit hole, so I moved on to the next point.

"I tell 'jokes some people don't understand'? Why is that my problem? How am I supposed to know what other people will or won't understand? What am I supposed to do, not say anything? Not join in while others around me are joking around and enjoying themselves?"

HR guy shrugged. "Maybe that's a good idea. Maybe you should restrict your communication to only work-related information."

"I should be the guy who has no personality?" I replied. "The guy who only talks about work?"

He shrugged again. "That might be a good idea." He had no idea that someone who exhibited no personality, who didn't share his opinions, or the details of his interests and his weekend, would be quickly ignored, if not completely ostracized, by his co-workers.

Humor had always gotten me into trouble at work, even when it was specifically requested, as in my Lockheed videos. But finally, after twenty years of asking the question, "Does humor belong in the workplace?," I received a clear and adamant answer—from HR, at least: *No*.

I soldiered on through the irritating encounter. "Maybe you should share who was involved in this complaint," I suggested, "so I have the opportunity to apologize."

He didn't take the bait. Unlike a real-world court of law, under Corporate HR Law, I had no right to face my accusers. The corporate world is not America; it's Amerikkka. But as I read through the paperwork a second time, it became clear to me exactly who filed the accusations. This was a deduction I knew I'd best keep secret; if I revealed that I knew who was involved, I'd probably be subject to even harsher HR actions. After all, the anonymity of the accuser was sacred: they could hide behind the apron strings of Mama HR and whine about how they'd been abused—how their precious feelings had been hurt—without fear of reprisal or "retribution"...but only if I didn't know who they were.

In fact, every one of the dozen charges was specific enough that I knew which co-worker was behind each of them. It wasn't any of my immediate co-workers, or anyone from our department, or any of the cubicle neighbors in my aisle; it was people in various Production departments, all of whom were housed in a building across the street from us. And the one thing they all had in common was that each of these people reported to the same Lead. I realized immediately that this was a top-down, not a bottom-up, complaint, and the scenario became crystal clear: the Lead got a bug up his ass to put me in my place, so he filed a harassment suit. But since he had no real evidence of harassment, he had to go to his direct reports for ammunition. He'd undoubtedly gone to each of his charges and asked them what sins I'd committed against them. Since he was their boss, they'd be duty-bound to come up with *something*, no matter how trivial or half-assed ("he occasionally talks about how all corporations are soulless and have no respect for their employees"). I assume he figured that if he collected enough grains of sand, he could build a castle. Evidently, he assumed correctly.

I knew who this Lead—the instigator—was as well: an insufferable, self-righteous prig who drove his co-workers crazy. (After a meeting a few months earlier, one of his peers told me angrily that he was "impossible to work with." Good thing for her she kept that opinion to herself.) This guy was a graphic artist, tall and skeletally skinny, and a hipster—non-ironically: he actually believed he pulled off that "goofy little hat and jazz beard" look. And he was covered with tattoos. He looked like the bastard offspring you'd get if a biker fucked a spider. And, not incidentally, he was gay. Not that there's anything wrong with that—but the Apple employee culture is so adamantly, insistently progressive that even a hint that one was not actively supporting every issue of the so-called Left-Coast, Liberal, Blue State agenda was seen as a shocking violation of social norms and a traitorous betrayal of the entire company employee culture. I was glad that the values of this workplace aligned with my own values, even if those values were enforced by peer pressure. As a former college semi-radical and a diehard bleeding heart social progressive, I found Apple a comfortable culture—and a complete reversal of the conservative corporate culture that I'd endured at the regressive dinosaur that was Lockheed. But when an email chain talking about Batman's suspicious sexual orientation made the rounds and I suggested that Bruce Wayne might have said to his young ward, "I'll call you Mr. Grayson, unless you prefer Dick," this apparently made Spider-Biker's homophobic Spidey-sense tingle...so he determined to teach a lesson to that offensively straight guy who singlehandedly set back gay rights a decade by making a joke he didn't appreciate: i.e., me. And so he'd coerced his co-workers into a peer-pressure pecking party—and he was the head pecker.

My absolute favorite charge, however, was that I was "argumentative." *Argumentative...* Now *there's* a loaded word! It implies someone who seeks out arguments, who goes out of his way to be contentious, whose primary method of communication is quarreling. Like most iTunes employees, I was (and am) passionate about my field—in this case, movies. Being passionate about one's field—whether music, TV, books or movies—was literally in the job description for iTunes employees. But there's a world of difference between passionately debating the merits of a band or a novel or a film and being hostile or "argumentative." HR had twisted one of the primary virtues for any iTunes employee into a vice.

Worst of all, by tweaking the language and using the word "argumentative," they had precluded any possible objection I might raise. If I disagreed with HR's assessment, they could simply point out that I was proving their point: if I wanted to argue the point, I was clearly argumentative. This insidious addition to the laundry list of offenses prohibited any opposetion, any disagreement, any defense. "He won't admit his culpability for these offenses? That's because he's argumentative. He wants —no, let's use the similar but more damning word *demands*—to explain or contradict the charges? We expected as much, since he's argumentative—look, it says so right there in our document. He wants to argue that he's *not* argumentative? Let's see him work his way out of *that* Chinese finger puzzle!" It was the addition of this single, loaded word that convinced me that HR had carefully crafted this document to close any loopholes and close any door to any possible defense. "He wants to defend himself? That's because he's argumentative." That's some catch, that Catch-22. The best there is.

We spent an hour discussing my alleged offenses, but the upshot was this: *accusation equals guilt*—and there was nothing I could do about it. I was to be placed on a type of probation called "Documented Coaching," in which Richard Zucker, my immediate superior, would be required to accompany me to all my meetings for several months, to make certain I did not say anything that could by any stretch of the imagination be considered offensive to anyone in attendance. Oh, swell. Now my boss would resent me as well, since I increased his workload. Not only was he required to attend my meetings, he was also required to monitor me, and to rat me out to HR if I slipped up and, say, made a joke that someone didn't understand.

HR Guy needed only one more thing: my signature on the document he'd brought. I debated whether I should just tear it up and walk out, but I assumed that would be construed as insubordination, and that the next HR action against me would be termination. I settled for signing it, but added under my signature the disclaimer, "Signed under duress. Signature is in no way to be interpreted as agreement." HR Guy didn't comment, but he did excuse himself and left. Time to go ruin someone else's life, I guess.

ROUND TWO to HR.

BETWEEN ROUNDS

"The trial was nothing but a big piece of business…a piece of business that concealed many lurking dangers waiting in ambush for him, as they usually did, but these dangers would need to be defended against."
—Franz Kafka, *The Trial*

In between rounds of a boxing match, the fighters head to their respective corners and, while resting, analyze what they did wrong in the previous round and what they could do to improve their performance in the upcoming round. Even though I hoped I'd never have to go another round with HR, my previous two rounds had indicated that there was simply no way to predict if or when I might be singled out again for more irrational harassment. But I decided that if this ever happened again, there would be No More Mr. Nice Victim: I would not be KO'd in the first round. I'd come out swinging.

I'd have to be a masochist to claim that I'm glad Round Two of "Me vs. HR" ever occurred. But the incident did teach me a number of valuable lessons that could ultimately serve me in any future HR fuckery. They'd inadvertently revealed enough of their SOP that I could perhaps prepare some defense in case they attacked again—a fitting blowback.

Somewhat ironically (but appropriately), for instance, I realized that HR operated like Monty Python's version of The Spanish Inquisition. That routine begins with robed Inquisitors appearing in the middle of another sketch, announcing that "No one expects...*The Spanish Inquisition!"*

The parallels are uncanny:

1) *"No one expects...The Spanish Inquisition! Our chief weapon is surprise..."*

And so it is with HR. They take you by surprise; they throw you off balance; they accost you without forewarning. They sucker punch you as a matter of Standard Operating Procedure. When you're pulled from your daily routine and confronted with their "serious" charges, they've effectively pulled the rug out from underneath you, emotionally and intellectually. Who could possibly be prepared to defend themselves against their charges on the spur of the moment? You are, in a word, ambushed.

2) *"Our chief weapon is surprise—fear and surprise..."*

Fear is a vital and indispensable part of the HR character; part of its DNA. How many times did I hear someone in an Apple meeting make a questionable or controversial remark, followed by another employee's joking response, "Uh-oh...better call HR" —followed by nervous chuckles? (Too many times; that's how many.) I can't speak for other companies, but at Apple, at least, even the joking threat of "calling HR" was enough to cast a pall over even the most convivial assembly. No one I knew at Apple ever had a pleasant—or even positive—encounter with HR. Apple's legendary culture of secrecy pales in comparison with its culture of fear—and that fear is the fear of straying from the culture of Apple and being jackboot-stomped into compliance by the SS—sorry, I meant HR. Sure I did.

3) *"Our two chief weapons: fear, surprise and ruthless efficiency..."*

As for "ruthless efficiency," I'd refer back to the Catch-22 built into my dunning notice: the claim that I was "argumentative." By including a charge (an undocumented charge at that) like this, HR insidiously undermines any attempt at defense: If you take issue with their conclusions, you're argumentative. If you contradict anything they've written, you're argumentative. If you attempt to correct any inaccuracies they might be laboring under, well…you know. They cover all potential escape routes and make it impossible to respond without fear of losing one's job. That's some catch, that Catch-22.

4) *"Er, among our chief weapons are: fear, surprise, ruthless efficiency and near-fanatical devotion to the Pope."*

The Pope, in this case, is The Company, and "fanatical devotion" translates clearly as protecting The Company against a possible lawsuit, even if it requires ignoring or denying rationality, or creating an offensive and hostile workplace for the accused in order to placate the accuser and prevent them from filing a lawsuit. In this case, the lunatics really *can* run the asylum: if a disgruntled employee files an HR suit, HR will dance to their tune in order to appease them, regardless of the rationality or sanity of their claims—solely to avoid a lawsuit.

And perhaps, in my case at least, this was precisely the point. Even though this HR action against me was classified as "harassment," there was nothing about it that would indicate any of the typical components of a serious harassment charge. There was no sexism involved; no racial prejudice; no violence or bullying; no religious intolerance. Apparently my specific sin was in transgressing against the vague and unstated "corporate culture" adhered to religiously by "good" Apple employees (or in this case, an Apple Nazi).

This revelation came as a surprise to me. I'd made my best attempt to be the Poster Boy for Apple values. I'd drunk the Kool-Aid, voluntarily. But when there are no clear guidelines, only the vague consensus of peer approval, it's virtually impossible to know when you've transgressed against the intangible. And that's when HR steps in with its Freddy Krueger/Michael Myers Response: springing from the shadows to strike fear in the hearts of powerless employees.

This, to me, is a clear and conscious perversion of policies designed to protect real victims against actual harassment. It's far easier for HR to adopt a "no exceptions" policy and ignore that some claims are complete bullshit than it is to train their personnel to apply standards of reasonableness to employee claims, and use their judgment to differentiate between serious allegations and nuisance suits. And it clearly boils down to economics: it's cheaper to use HR to squelch a potential lawsuit from an unreasonable accuser, no matter who else it affects, than it is to risk involving the Legal department and *(shudder)* Real World Courts...even in a claim so ludicrous that any real-world court would dismiss it as a nuisance suit.

Once I had this figured out, I developed a vague plan to deal with any potential future situations. Although I had no control over whether I could avoid stepping into another HR bear trap, I determined to be on High Alert and to arm myself with whatever ammunition I might need to subvert the HR playbook if and when that ever happened again. First and foremost was to adopt HR Guy's suggestion: I'd refrain from attempting to be amusing. Apple's loss. Second, I would adopt HR's "Spanish Inquisition"

SOP. They were wily, sneaky, and subversive? Well, I could do that too. I could prepare myself to fight fire with napalm.

If my minor transgressions were considered actionable in an HR sense, then I'd adopt that attitude as well. I determined to keep a secret log of any and all potentially offensive comments I heard in any meeting from that day forward. If HR ever came to me with any objections similar to those I'd recorded, I'd whip out my notebook and recount every single similarly "objectionable" remark I'd ever heard, along with the date, the meeting, and the attendees, as witnesses. They want to fuck with me? I will fuck with *everybody*. Someone took offense at something I'd said that they considered personally offensive? I'd file a countersuit against everybody who'd ever said anything someone might potentially consider offensive, and claim I was the one who was offended. They want to spank me? I'd make them spank all of iTunes. Maybe that would turn the entire division against me... although, by the rules of policy, they were not allowed to know it was me who ratted them out. But maybe this diary might provide a bargaining chip with HR: You drop these ridiculous charges against me and I won't file a nuisance suit against *everyone I've ever worked with*.

As fate would have it, I didn't have long to wait until I made the first entry in my secret Offensive Comments Log. On the Monday following my encounter with HR, I was in our weekly departmental meeting with half a dozen other employees, including Dick Zucker and his boss, Buford Squack. Squack called our L.A. studio rep; when she answered, she was clearly just waking up (even though it was 11:00 AM), and Squack decided to tease her. "You just getting out of bed?" he said. "What are you wearing?" Clear and indefensible sexual harassment, and coming from my boss's boss! Here was an Apple middle manager addressing his direct report in a sexually suggestive manner: Entry #1 in my OCL.

Four years later, I had a full dozen pages of entries, just waiting for HR to assault me again, so I could document to them the shocking—*shocking!*—systemic "harassment" prevalent in iTunes.

ROUND 3: ROTTEN TO THE CORP

"The trial will always start over again."
—Franz Kafka, *The Trial*

[Note: The following section was digested in Chapter 33, "One Bad Apple." This section includes numerous details edited out of that condensed version.]

March 31, 2013: Easter Sunday

Piph and I spent Easter Sunday at my mother's house in Gilroy, an hour south of our home in Redwood City. Even though no one in our extended family is actively Christian (least of all me, the lapsed Buddhist), Mom would take advantage of any holiday to host a buffet for the family. (She'd probably insist we all come to dinner on Passover and Ramadan if she could figure a way to justify serving bacon.) We returned home around 8 PM and prepared for a quiet evening of our own. I decided I should be a good employee and take a few minutes to check my email, if only so there were no surprises awaiting me when I logged on Monday morning.

As it happens, there was indeed a surprise awaiting me: a note from an HR representative:

"Hi Scott: I hope you are having a nice weekend. Please note I proposed [a meeting] for tomorrow morning at 10 AM in my office... I understand you work remotely from home but I'd like to ask that you come in to meet with me in person as I'd like to check-in [sic] and see how everything is going. Thanks." It was signed by a rep we'll call "HR Girl."

OK, time to play "What's Wrong with This Picture?" First off, who sends an email on a Sunday night scheduling a meeting for the first thing Monday morning? Who sends an email on a *holiday* Sunday night and expects the recipient to read it? It just seems rude, and it was only on a whim that I'd even decided to check my email that evening.

So: dilemma time. Do I just ignore her email, and respond Monday morning sometime after 10 AM, explaining that I didn't get her Sunday night email requesting a 10 AM meeting on

Monday *because it was a fucking holiday* and I was with my family, not online? No, that couldn't be the right approach (even if I left out the *fucking*)—no matter what she wanted, I didn't want to start out by being *argumentative*. God forbid! So I responded. "Unfortunately, I must decline the proposed meeting on Monday at 10 AM. I am only in the Cupertino office one day a week, so if you want to reschedule, I'd be happy to meet with you on a day I am in the office—usually Wednesdays, but this week I will be in Cupertino on Tuesday." I added the closing line, "Can you tell me the nature of this meeting?"

Tuesday, April 2

Apparently she could not, or would not, explain the nature of the meeting, as I received no reply. But when I went into "the Cupe" on Tuesday and walked into Zucker's office about 2 PM for our weekly touch-base, I was surprised to find him talking with an attractive young woman who I did not know. "Sorry," I said. "Am I interrupting?"

"No," Zucker replied. "Come in and have a seat."

I did, and he introduced his visitor as the person we're referring to as "HR Girl," my schedule-retarded correspondent. This was a surprise. She'd never responded to my email to reschedule, but here she was in Zucker's office at the time of our weekly meet. *It's almost like they were in cahoots*, I thought.

Oh dopey me. *Of course* they were collaborating. Conspiring, to be accurate.

"I asked HR Girl to be here to facilitate," Zucker stated. When I inquired what it was that needed facilitating, he brought out a document. He didn't give it to me, but I could see it was at least two pages, single-spaced. "We're concerned that some of your behavior from the past is resurfacing," he said. "I've listed several incidents here, and I'd be happy to go through them paragraph by paragraph if you'd like." I knew we'd had a couple of miscommunications lately that Zucker was upset about...but two pages? And since I had no idea what the purpose of this meeting was, I preferred to, first of all, find that out.

"No no no," I said, "I don't think we need to go through everything." Judging from the document he held, I thought it might take hours to go through everything. I said this in a casual manner; my intention was only that we not get mired in details before I knew what we were discussing. I suspected I knew at least a couple of the incidents he had written up, like a recent missed meeting (in which he changed the location and time and failed to inform me, then blamed me for "not looking for him hard enough"), and I knew that his perspective was incomplete and inaccurate, since he would never accept blame and refused to listen to my explanations. It's not like this hadn't happened before, because it had—repeatedly. I further believed that if I attempted to discuss these charges, or offer an explanation, or fill him in on facts he was missing, he would consider this "argumentative" rather than informative. It's not like this, too, hadn't happened before, because it had—repeatedly.

I turned to HR Girl. "I don't know what he's got written down on that document," I said, "but I can assure you it's only one side of the story. I guarantee you that whatever incidents he has listed on those sheets, there are alternative points of view, good explanations, different perspectives, other opinions that you're not getting."

That's when Richard Zucker made Big Mistake Number One. "Since I'm the boss," he replied, "my opinion is the only one that matters."

I was almost literally jaw-dropped. How could someone in authority make such an arrogant, inflammatory, self-incriminating statement like that at all—much less in the presence of an HR rep? His response validated in my mind that I was correct in suggesting we not go through his list paragraph by paragraph, since he clearly was not open to any explanation that might contradict his set opinion.

"Did you hear what he just said?" I asked HR Girl point-blank. "He just said, 'Since I'm the boss, my opinion is the only one that matters.' You're a witness."

She looked confused, but attempted to recover. She informed me that I was not fulfilling my responsibilities as a Level 5 employee—that I should be more "self-directed and proactive."

"What does that mean?" I said. "What is a 'Level 5' employee?"

Again, the confused look. “Fifth level Marketing personnel,” she said.

“I have no idea what the even means,” I said. “I’ve been here six years, and no one has ever referred to me as a ‘fifth level Marketing personnel.’ I’m the iTunes Movie Guru. That’s my title. That’s the title of the job I applied for six years ago. That’s what’s printed on the business cards that Apple gave me. I’ve never heard the phrase ‘fifth level Marketing personnel.’ I have no idea what that means, or what kind of performance that position entails.” I could tell that this line of argument was going nowhere—if Apple said I was a ‘fifth level Marketing’ employee, then I probably was, whether I was aware of it or not. But there was one other detail in her initial accusation that I could address—that my productivity was not up to my level.

“Well, let’s let the whole ‘Level 5’ thing slide for the moment,” I said to HR Girl. “I don’t think that label is the important thing here. The important part of what you’re saying is that my productivity is lower than expected.” She nodded. “If that’s the case—” I continued, “and I’m not admitting it *is* the case; I’m just saying that *if* that’s what I’m being accused of, then there is only one person responsible for that: Richard Zucker. For six years, I did *one job* here in iTunes: program the Movie Store. But in January, Richard Zucker decided that from now on, our junior programmer should do that job, and I should do his job. So if my productivity is less than expected, it’s solely because Richard Zucker *gave my job away* to a junior co-worker and assigned me to his task.

“I’ll tell you one other thing as well,” I continued. “Richard Zucker never mentioned to me that he thought I was underperforming. We meet one-on-one for an hour every Wednesday afternoon, and at the end of every session, I ask him directly ‘Everything good? We OK? Any problems?’ and he always answers, ‘We’re good.’ If he’s had a problem with me for longer than the last week, why did he never address me directly?”

“Well, you did miss meetings,” she accused.

“I missed *one meeting*,” I said. “And—and I’m sure this detail isn’t in your document there—I missed that meeting because Richard Zucker changed the time and the location and failed to inform me.”

She ignored my explanations, and she and Zucker took turns recounting (patently false) incidences of alleged my disobedience and other vague charges. HR Girl then reminded me that I was "very lucky," as I'd been through Documented Coaching, which seemed like a *non sequitur*. I still didn't have any idea what this was about. What did any of this have to do with my Documented Coaching? I pointed out that my Documented Coaching took place nearly five years earlier, and that every annual review I'd had since then indicated that all questionable behavior covered under the Documented Coaching had been corrected, and that there had never been another incident since. "That Documented Coaching is ancient history," I said. "I don't know why you're bringing it up now." She informed me that at Apple, an employee only gets *one* Documented Coaching opportunity. She was very emphatic about this, even holding up her index finger to emphasize the "one." She immediately proceeded to inform me (without consultation with Zucker) that I was being "involuntarily terminated."

I asked her point-blank, "Am I being fired?" She repeated that an employee only gets *one* Documented Coaching opportunity. I found this repetition peculiar, since no one had mentioned Documented Coaching or a potential second Documented Coaching.

HR Girl was undeterred by my blunt question and continued moving forward. She informed me that there were two types of involuntary termination. One was a "hard landing" in which the terminated employee was barred from ever seeking work at Apple again. She wanted to offer me the "soft landing" option. She suggested we take our meeting to another room so we could discuss my future.

I learned later that HR Girl was, in fact, there to offer me a second Documented Coaching "opportunity," although—Big Mistake Number Two—she failed to ever mention this. I can only figure that since I waived the "reading of transgressions," she took this as an indication that I was not interested in Documented Coaching—even though it had never been offered—and skipped right to termination.

I also discovered later that the conditions of this unoffered second opportunity at Documented Coaching were so restrictive as to be ludicrous. "Hourly check-in with Manager" is just one example, and there were a dozen more stipulations that were equally odious—and equally impossible to fulfill. I felt sure that this list had been carefully crafted to give the appearance of a fair chance for me to redeem my alleged bad behavior—and I was equally certain that the moment I violated any of its restrictions, Zucker would have "no choice" but to terminate me, sigh. This second Documented Coaching, with its prison-like constraints, was setting me up for inevitable and expected failure. Talk about a Catch-22!

TURNING THE CONFERENCE TABLES

"Don't make me angry. You wouldn't like me when I'm angry."
—Dr. Bruce Banner, aka The Incredible Hulk

HR Girl and I found a big empty conference room and took our seats. She informed me that "today," April second, would be my last day with Apple, and that my medical coverage would expire at midnight. She further explained that if I accepted the "soft landing" option of involuntary termination I would receive eight weeks' pay and the option of signing up for a COBRA (follow-on medical coverage). "Are there any other options?" I asked. "Could I transfer to another iTunes department, like iBooks?" She indicated that if I accepted the "soft landing" involuntary termination that I was "eligible for rehire" by another department anywhere in Apple. I took this to mean that I was, in fact, terminated, and that a transfer was not an option.

I knew the futility of attempting to debate with HR. I'd experienced that before—twice. Their word was law, and they would never give an inch. And so I said, "Well, then, let's go with the soft-landing option. I'll take the eight weeks' pay and the COBRA option." We briefly discussed the terms of this option. She told me I would receive two checks: one for eight weeks' pay, and a second as a "cash-out" of vacation time and my employee stock plan investment from the current cycle. She said she would email me some paperwork that I should fill out and return to conclude the action.

"I understand that when employees leave," I said, "they have the option of purchasing their equipment. I'd like to purchase my laptop and my iPad and my AppleTV device."

"You can just keep them," she replied, with a dismissive wave of her hand.

If I can't recall precisely what was said after that, it's partly because it seemed repetitious and trivial—and because I was struggling with my temper as she chatted brightly with me about end dates, equipment, paperwork that required signing, and so on. Until…

Now—just as an aside—one would think that an HR representative at one of the world's largest companies would have been trained in interpersonal relations. But during our conversation with Zucker, both he and HR Girl had already made at least one Big Mistake—his, of arrogance; hers, of incompetence, in failing to offer me Documented Coaching before firing me. And now she made Big Mistake Number Three, by asking me: "How do you feel about this?"

How do I *feel* about this? *How do I feel about this?* How the hell was I *supposed* to feel about this? Happy? I was reminded of those clueless, insensitive TV reporters who stick a microphone in the face of a grieving parent whose baby is trapped in a well or a tiger cage to ask them "How do you feel about this?" In a career peppered with Terminator Question moments, this was clearly a time when the only appropriate response was Arnold's Option Number 4: "Fuck you, asshole!"

But I bit my tongue. I could not, however, let this insensitive insult added to the injury of termination just slide by. If I was fired, I couldn't be more fired by expressing my bile. So I determined to be vocal about my disgust. I could have been snarky or sarcastic but instead, I was livid and decided to Hulk out and let the bile spew.

"How the hell do you *think* I feel?" I growled. "It's total bullshit! Everything Richard Zucker told you is a lie, and you won't even investigate it. This is a career-ending decision, and I deserve better. I've been a model employee for six years, but once my boss decides he doesn't like me, I'm out? I'm arguably the oldest person in iTunes—is this how you treat your older employees?"

If this had been a cartoon, I would have seen red flags popping up in HR Girl's eyes. Was I claiming age discrimination? Was I threatening a lawsuit? After all, I'd turned 62 less than two weeks earlier. At 62, I was eligible to apply for Social Security. And, at 62, I was twice the age of the average iTunes employee...and, as I pointed out, arguably the oldest employee in iTunes. I'd often wondered if I would eventually be considered an embarrassment: a guy in his 60s selling movies to tweens and teens. How could iTunes possibly be the hippest media outlet of the 21st century when they had some old codger—the age of the typical customer's *grandfather*, for fuck's sake—recommending movies and promoting the movie service?

It was at that precise moment HR Girl decided that since I felt that way, perhaps it would be a good idea to discuss my termination with her superior. "Let's just say for now that you're suspended until we can clear this up," she back-peddled.

Fine by me. She promised to set something up ASAP and send me the details. I asked if I would be walked out of the building by Security, and she dismissed the idea with another wave of her hand. "Take some time to clear out your desk of personal items," she said, "and take a few minutes to say goodbye to anyone you want to say goodbye to," then leave when I was ready. I didn't tell her I wasn't gonna be ready for about three years. But if I was being invited to wander around saying goodbye, maybe I *wasn't* being fired. If I was fired, I'd expect to be escorted out of the building by Security, if only so I didn't steal anything on the way out. Which I totally would have.

We shook hands, and I left the room believing that since termination was likely—even though we'd left it in limbo—that we had at least negotiated terms of my involuntary termination that were acceptable to both Apple and myself, and had sealed the deal with the handshake.

So I stuck my laptop in my soft leather carrying case—the same work bag I'd used at every job since Silicon Graphics nearly two decades earlier—then stuffed my few personal items in the bag. I regretted that I didn't have a bag big enough to contain my monitor and the color printer my disappeared co-worker JC had purchased out-of-pocket. And I set out to say goodbye. The only co-workers I could find to bid adieu to were

Melody (who was shocked) and Ross (who seemed resigned to think this was par for the course for Apple)—significantly, the only two co-workers with whom I would keep up any kind of communication from then on.

Once home, I had to try to explain the situation to Piph...a difficult task, since I didn't understand the situation myself. Was I fired? Laid off? Suspended? Who knew? And how would HR respond to my dropping the "age" bomb? (If they had any sense of humor whatsoever, they would reply as Cornholio would: "Are you threatening me?" So I knew that was never gonna happen.)

HR AIKIDO

"Looking at you I can almost believe that old saying,
'Having a trial like that means losing a trial like that.'"
—Franz Kafka, *The Trial*

Given a day to think through this incident, I realized several things. The first was that Dick Zucker clearly never had any intention of allowing me to concentrate on creating features for iTunes Movies. He flat-out lied to my face about that a few weeks earlier when he reorganized our department and gave my job to our junior guy on the rationale that it would "free up my time" to concentrate on my original mandate.

I deconstructed the timeline: Zucker had reorganized our department on January 9, and HR Girl had first contacted me by email on March 31st—about 11 weeks. How long would it take to begin an HR action like the one Zucker had sprung on me? How long would it take to catalog my alleged offenses, write them up with a spin that made me look like a serial offender, then get HR to discuss, debate, investigate (if they even did any investigation) and start the punishment procedure? Even if this was a rush job, let's say two weeks, minimum, maybe—which means that Zucker had given me a window of about two months to prove myself in a new position that I'd informed him would take at least two months just to plan out. Conversely, after six years of sterling service, Zucker was willing to claim I was underperforming based on only eight current weeks of activity (the first two weeks of which were spent "training my replacement" and doing his new job for him). Demoting me and then claiming I was underperforming was a great Catch-22. (As Robin Ryan, author of *Over 40 and You're Hired* put it, "You don't suddenly become a bad employee.")

The second realization was that I had—partly by design and partly by accident—been able to short-circuit HR's Standard Operating Procedure of the Surprise Attack. ("No one expects… *the Spanish Inquisition!*") I had bought myself some time to recover from the shock of an unexpected termination, and I could use that time to my advantage—calling my lawyer, for instance, and devising a strategy to deal with the upcoming interview with HR Girl's manager.

The third was that I could turn this into my own version of Captain James T. Kirk's "Kobyashi Maru" test in *Star Trek II: The Wrath of Khan.* When presented with an unwinnable situation, Kirk reprogrammed the computer that administered the test to allow for a winnable solution, which he then implemented. HR Girl was a young woman, and my guess is that she lacked any experience in actually applying her theoretical HR training to many real-life situations. The result was Zucker's Big Mistake Number Two: teaming up with an inexperienced person to "handle" this situation, presumably assuming that since she was a naïve rookie he could lie to her and manipulate her into being his hitman and executing his subversive agenda of executing me. But that approach clearly backfired on him. Ultimately, I believe it was Zucker's arrogance and HR Girl's incompetence that provided me with the leverage I needed to turn this situation to my advantage.

But two could play that game: I could take advantage of her and manipulate her to *my* benefit—or, more accurately, I could take advantage of the situation and manipulate *it* to my benefit. She wasn't expecting any pushback. But for me, this was a career-defining moment, if not a career-ending moment. I had nothing to lose by pushing back, and I determined to push back as hard as was possible without getting myself immediately terminated (no shouting; no obscene insults; no threats; no anger; no punching them in their stupid evil irrational faces. That would just be wrong). If I was going to meet with HR Girl's superior, I could spend the intervening time crafting a case against this HR action, supported by documentation I would have time to research.

I had an additional insight as well: My previous run-ins with HR over the years had in some perverse way prepared me for this Final Battle. I knew some of their tricks: the Surprise Attack; the Catch-22, Chinese Finger Puzzle charges made against their targets (like labeling the victim "argumentative," so they could automatically dismiss any objections or discussion); the adamant attitude of "guilt by accusation." And I knew some of HR's weak points, like overreaction to employee complaints, no matter how ludicrous, in order to avoid any possibility of a lawsuit. If I played my cards right, I could take advantage of this hard-won knowledge and turn HR's own playbook against them. As a further benefit, I could prove to myself that I hadn't been paranoid in obsessing over the injustices and the *techniques* of the injustices visited upon me over the years by HR, and keeping notes about them—that I was, in fact, operating under the twin principles "Know Thy Enemy" and "forewarned is forearmed." I would have no hesitation whatsoever in using HR's own underhanded machinations against them; I'd put them on the defensive when they perhaps had no defense against their own strategies. And I would feel great about it—"Revenge is a dish best served cold," as the old Klingon aphorism goes.

On a lighter note, it also occurred to me that I'd been hired by Zucker's ex-wife and fired by Zucker, proving that Apple *really is* a family!

Thursday, April 4

I didn't hear anything from HR Girl on Wednesday, but we connected on the phone early Thursday afternoon. (I had the presence of mind to take notes, so the quotes below are verbatim.) "I can tell you want some control" over this situation, she said, and that after she'd discussed our conversation on Tuesday with her colleagues, the "performance-based involuntary termination" would now "revert to a voluntary termination," with two months of paid COBRA coverage for my wife and me, and that "you can keep your computer." Friday, April 12 would now be my new last day with Apple. I asked her if I would still be receiving eight weeks' pay. Her response: "My colleagues weren't comfortable with that."

"We had a deal," I replied. "Do you not have the authority to make that deal?"

Her response was vehement: "Of course not!"

"But we agreed to the terms," I said. "We even shook on it."

Her response: "Oh, I was just shaking your hand to say good-bye!"

This brought up several questions: Who were these "colleagues," and how were they involved? If they were involved, why weren't they in our meeting? And why did they send someone to negotiate who had no authority to make a deal?

I refrained from asking these questions, but I repeated that I thought we'd struck a deal on Tuesday. She replied that there was no deal; that she was just there to "find out what you want out of this." I told her she already knew what I wanted out of this, which was exactly what we'd agreed to: involuntary termination, so I could qualify for Unemployment Insurance, the eight weeks pay she (as a representative of Apple) had offered, and two months of COBRA coverage (not just the option to purchase a COBRA they were now offering—an option that was mandated by California law). She stated that there were "obviously some miscommunications here," that I was "a special case right from the start," and that she would put me in touch with another HR representative. (No one ever explained to me why I was a "special case.")

I ended this call feeling…betrayed. (Betrayed by HR? How shocking!) They had made a deal on Tuesday, but once I agreed to the deal, it was retracted. This seemed to me to be something far beyond miscommunication—possibly even purposeful misrepresentation. I had a strong suspicion that HR was simply toying with me, and that the good-faith compromise I had made—that I will allow myself to be laid off in exchange for the agreed-upon items—was being taken advantage of by HR with their reneging on the agreement.

Further evidence of miscommunication during this action was made clear to me on Wednesday, April 3, when I finally read the document Dick Zucker was holding during our Tuesday meeting (where he'd put the papers on his desk face down, so I couldn't see what was written on them). As HR Girl and I left his office, I asked Zucker, "Can I take this with me?" and they both said yes. This document offered me the option of receiving Documented Coaching from April 2 through June 1. I was never informed that this was an option—in fact, HR Girl opened her remarks in that meeting by informing me that I was being involuntarily terminated, with no mention of Documented Coaching other than stating *twice* that Apple employees are afforded only *one* opportunity for Documented Coaching—without ever offering it to me. Once again, I felt this was clearly misinformation, and possibly even a misrepresentation of my options. When I brought this issue up with HR Girl in our Thursday phone call, she responded, "Documented Coaching was never presented to you as an option because you became argumentative with your manager when he began talking about it."

FULL RELEASE HAPPY ENDING

Since this is a chapter about HR offenses, I will forego the follow-up meetings with representatives of another department. As reported earlier (in Chapter 33, "One Bad Apple"), once my objections to HR Girl came to the attention of Employee Relations, I took a meeting with an ER representative who was tasked with investigating my apparent claim of age discrimination—a claim I'd never actually made, although my rant about being fired certainly included that possibility in my list of grievances.

And by the end of our three-hour data dump, the ER rep came away convinced of two things: first, that there was no age discrimination involved here (a conclusion with which I concurred); and second, that I had been treated unethically and subjected to a long-term plan on the part of Dick Zucker to force me out of Apple. As a result of our meeting, I was allowed to retire rather than being fired, negating Dick Zucker's clandestine plan (and HR's witting or unwitting complicity).

ROUND THREE to H— No, hang on there just a second. *I* won Round Three, goddamn it! *I* won the final and most important round.

ROUND THREE to ME! Victory!

[Note: The full account of my effort to reverse the decision to fire me and instead allow me to retire can be found in Chapter 33, "One Bad Apple."]

YOU CAN'T SPELL "HARASS" WITHOUT "HR"

Further reading and study over the following years indicated that although my experiences with HR were unusual, they were perhaps not unique (see, for example, "Round One" above). In her book *Stand Up For Yourself Without Getting Fired: Resolve Workplace Crises Before You Quit, Get Axed or Sue the Bastards,* Florida employment lawyer Donna Ballman wrote about one of the common strategies used by companies to dump older employees: "If, after years of great performance reviews, you're getting reprimanded for things everyone does, or being nitpicked for things the company didn't care about before, it's possible that the company is gearing up for what I call the 'suddenly stupid defense.' They're building a case to get rid of you for poor performance—trying to show a 'legitimate reason' other than age for firing you."

The internet has trolls; the corporate world has HR. Don't get me wrong—I'm sure there's a positive side to HR, like advocating for people in actual distress. After all, there's a positive side to everything, right? I mean, Hitler loved dogs, so how could he be a monster, right? But if there is a positive side to HR, I've rarely seen it, beyond hiring, and perhaps in Apple's Employee Relations subdivision of HR advocating on my behalf—but even then, the only reason I was granted an audience with ER was an HR rep's mistaken belief that I was claiming age discrimination, and "sending me to the ER" was HR's attempt to cover their collective ass.

My primary experience with HR, however, has been little more than incidents in which otherwise beneficial policies are blindly applied, purposefully sacrificing both reason and reasonableness, enforcing the letter of the law rather than the spirit of the law, and all for the sake of protecting the company against a potential lawsuit by an irrational or disgruntled employee. This "guilt by accusation with no exceptions for reasonableness" approach in fact invests HR with Absolute Power. And we all know that Absolute Power can never possibly corrupt. Absolutely!

It is at this point that HR moves over to the Dark Side—and the point at which I climb onto my soapbox. Any system that ignores the tenants of a free, Constitutional, democratic society and opts instead for a policy of guilt by accusation and punishment by decree, with no investigation, no trial, no opportunity to face one's accusers, no jury of one's peers, and no interest in hearing any defense from the accused, has crossed over into anti-social territory. And it's not the proverbial "slippery slope," either—it's a single step off a steep cliff.

Thus endeth the screed. I shall now endeavor to end on a positive note.

There's an old Zen parable about two monks—one a novice; the other a seasoned old veteran—on a pilgrimage to a distant village. Their particular monastery requires celibacy, to the point of prohibiting any physical contact whatsoever between the monks and any woman. At one point, these two monks reach a riverbank and encounter a woman standing there, forlorn. "I can't swim," she informs them, "but I must get across." The elder monk suggests she climb on his shoulders and he'll transport her across the river. She does, and he honors his promise. On the opposite bank, she climbs off his shoulders, thanks him, and walks away. The two monks continue their journey, but the younger monk is incensed about this transgression and stews in silence for hours. At some point, however, he simply can't contain his anger any longer and confronts his companion. "I can't believe you'd violate our doctrine prohibiting any contact with women by letting her ride on your shoulders across the river!" he cries. The older monk looks at him and smiles. "Are you still carrying that woman?" he asks. "I put her down hours ago."

The HR horror stories above have haunted me, some for decades. I've found it difficult to get over these incidents of subversion, irrationality, hypocrisy, and sheer outright malevolence, all consciously condoned in the name of corporate self-interest. But perhaps by detailing *mein kampf* against corporate duplicity, I can finally put that woman down...on paper.

Chapter 36

2020: HINDSIGHT

"And now, the hand that traces these words, falters, as it approaches the conclusion of its task; and would weave, for a little longer space, the thread of these adventures."
—Charles Dickens, *Oliver Twist*

"I'm stalling, because I didn't want to finish this book. Not that it's been so much *fun* writing it, but it did bring back memories of a few enjoyable moments that I'd like to live over again. Of course, it brought back a few unpleasant memories, too, with moments I would *not* like to live over."
—Jack Douglas,
A Funny Thing Happened to Me on My Way to the Grave

"What a long, strange trip it's been."
—The Grateful Dead, "Truckin'"

Despite the above quotes, since I began this history with a quote from *David Copperfield*, it seems only fitting that I should end with one:

"[I] bought a cottage in a hamlet on the seacoast a long way off...and was understood to live secluded, ever afterwards, in an inflexible retirement."

Or two:

"Quite a long story. Ought to end 'and they lived happily ever afterwards'; oughtn't it?"

Or three:

"And now my written story ends. I look back, once more—for the last time—before I close these leaves."

(You think *I'm* verbose? Read some Dickens!)

Now that I have some distance from the events chronicled in this...well, let's give it the benefit of the doubt and call it a book ...I also have the opportunity to include some related observations so random that they didn't fit into any chapter pigeonhole.

For instance:

I began this book by outlining what *No Plan B* isn't. I'll end by outlining what I hope it wasn't. I hope it wasn't a whiney catalog of petty indignities, micro-aggressions and overly sensitive, thin-skinned overreactions to trivial incidents. I hope it's familiar to everyone's work life, but not so similar to everyone's work life that it's dismissed as banal and boring, or ponderous and pedestrian. And since writing a book about my work life is not my life's work, I hope it's not perceived as a deep drink of a shallow mind...but then again, if that's the worst criticism leveled against this book, I'd be satisfied with that. (If nothing else, that particular criticism is at least accurate.)

Or this:

During the convoluted course of my career I've worked for companies large and small; good and evil; pleasant and hellish. And I've endured every possible variation of leaving, including being fired, laid off, downsized, ghosted and even (far too infrequently), quitting. What does that mean? Who knows.

Or this:

As an illustration of how geographically incestuous the hi-tech universe of Silicon Valley is, one of the borders of Apple's new campus is N. Tantau Ave.—the same street where I worked my first job in electronics, at ISS in 1970—not to mention that in the late '80s I lived for several years in an apartment complex at the corner of Lawrence Expressway and Homestead Road... literally across the street from the Apple Saucer.

Or how about this: Let's talk about money.

Although I was born in California (and proud of it), I spent my formative, single-digit years in the Midwest, and one of the taboos I grew up with was that you didn't talk about money—specifically how much you had, or how much you made. Talking about money was considered simply (as Captain Hook would say) "bad form." Silicon Valley, on the other hand (like Los Angeles), thrives on ostentatious displays of wealth and flaunting one's salary. One's financial worth—salary, stock, investments, and so on—is the single greatest metric by which status is obtained in an entrepreneurial culture.

My point is that I've included some salary information in this document, partly to show the ebb and flow (or, more specifically, the ebb and cash flow) of money that accompanied my rollercoaster ride to retirement. But I do so reluctantly. Out of context, these figures might appear self-serving or boastful or, more likely, pitiful and fodder for mockery ("*That's* all you made? What a tool!"). But I feel this information needs to be included in a comprehensive overview of a low-level career in hi-tech—and to put the "how I made a million dollars" of the subtitle of this book into context.

THE BEST JOB IN THE WORLD

So now I'm at that awkward age: too old for internet dating but too young for carbon dating.

I have now been retired longer than I worked at Apple—or at any job, for that matter, aside from my 13 years at Lockheed. It will be 2027 before I can claim that retirement has been my longest job—but even now I can claim it's my best job, one from which I cannot be laid off or fired, except by the Grim Reaper (who undoubtedly works for HR). Revenge (and a Lockheed pension) is incentive enough to attempt to live into my 80s, or beyond.

I am, in fact, living "in a hamlet on the seacoast a long way off, in an inflexible retirement." I spend my days in a lovely, unique, round house with an ocean view from my spacious lanai and a wife and cat who tolerate me. Paradise.

Of course, I have the same major concerns as most of my Boomer peers: *How long will my health hold out?,* for instance, and *Will a greedy, fascist government gut my Medicare and steal my Social Security?* And, of course, the most chilling and personal worry of all: *Will I outlive my money?* Even a million dollars doesn't go very far these days, especially after taxes and establishing a retirement. I often chuckle over comedian Jackie Mason's observation that "I have enough money to last the rest of my life, as long as I never buy anything"—although it's a dark, death-rattle chuckle.

FULL(ISH) DISCLOSURE, or MEA CULPA

"Most of the problems I've had during my life have been created by me. Because of boredom. I think, when things are going a little too successfully, we all have a tendency to break it up a little. I know *I* did. I also realize that sometimes I went a little overboard, too."
—Jack Douglas,
A Funny Thing Happened to Me on My Way to the Grave

One book on memoir writing insists that the memoirist must be as honest about himself as about the other people he includes in his narrative. My initial reaction to this tacit obligation is, "Yeah, right. What's the point of *that?* What's in it for *me?*" But in an attempt to fulfill this alleged requirement, I will mention a few of the numerous personal failings that have colored, aggravated and occasionally even instigated the speedbumps in my commute along the information superhighway.

Foremost among these is a character flaw over which I have little control, namely that I seem to be a polarizing personality—and apparently always have been. People like me or hate me; there's very little middle ground. I suppose I exacerbated that situation, if only by taking great delight in intentionally attempting to annoy people who find me annoying.

Second… OK, I admit it: Maybe I wasn't the world's best employee.

Was I polarizing? Without a doubt. Was I often sarcastic? Well, duh—who wouldn't be, if they had even half a brain and little tolerance for stupidity and hypocrisy? Was I anti-authoritarian? Not really—what I objected to was not authority, but *abuse* of authority. Was I a contrarian? No—I just insisted that my voice be heard, that my ideas be considered, even though they often ran against the established grain. Doormats get stepped on, and I was, after all, hired by media companies for my opinion—but I always got in trouble if my opinion contradicted that of my superiors.

Unlike others of my generation, I was never one of those salarymen who define themselves by their work—not any Plan B work, at least. I knew from Day One (technically defined as

January 12, 1981) that I didn't belong in a corporate environment, so I never invested too much stress or effort in most of my positions. They were not a career—they were jobs. I had no interest in climbing a corporate ladder and knew full well that I lacked the skills required to climb any of them anyway. Not to put too fine a point on it, I was only in it for the money. My primary (and only) goals were to further Plan A and to live a comfortable life. If I put in any extra effort, it was not because of company loyalty, but simply because of personal integrity—or because I was having fun doing it. My depth of commitment and attention to detail were in direct proportion to how interesting I found the work. I didn't mind being a C+ employee in a position about which I gave not a single shit.

Was my refusal to abandon Plan A responsible for my reluctance to fully commit to any of my jobs, since I regarded even the best of those jobs as, at best, only a second choice? Was I so obdurate and obstinate in my refusal to surrender the dream that I never woke up to the joys of honest labor—or was I so dedicated to that dream that I simply could not just "lie back and think of England" in any job? Or was it simply a native skepticism about the joys of employment, both corporate and otherwise, that held me back? I guess I may never know. Or care.

M.I.A. CULPA

But I wasn't the world's worst employee, either, goddamn it. I never once showed up to work at any job drunk or stoned, for instance. (Even after those drunken lunches at Lockheed we all went home, not back to work.) I didn't claim I was going to a meeting then go to Denny's for a second breakfast, like one Lockheed co-worker I knew. I didn't take afternoon naps in my car, like another Lockheed co-worker (but Curt shall remain nameless). I never took a single sick day from Apple, even immediately following surgery. And I was always responsible about completing my work, no matter how inane or boring it seemed. I often adopted a personal sliding scale for the relative importance of tasks, discriminating among those that required an A+ effort, those which were subject to the "Pivacek Principle" (i.e., be asked twice before you even bother to start), and those that would be acceptable at a C+ level—the kind of task in which the result is given a glance and a shrug by management and deemed "good enough for government work." As one of my first role models, *Forbidden Planet*'s Dr. Morbius, said, "In this, I shall be answerable exclusively to my own conscience and judgment."

WHAT, ME A CULPA?

"Abolish Monday mornings and Friday afternoons."
—Dire Straits, "Industrial Disease" (and its prescribed cure)

On the other hand, throughout my work life I did any number of things to assert my autonomy as an individual rather than suffer silently as a mindless corporate clone. For instance, at virtually every job I've ever had since 1976, twice a day I'd visit the men's room with a paperback book in my pocket, lock myself in a stall, and enjoy 15 minutes of uninterrupted, stress-free reading. No employer in the country begrudges their people bathroom breaks (except Amazon, it seems). I just put mine to maximum advantage, spending time in the makeshift reading room whether or not I needed to take care of business. (As an aside, this personal policy is a cousin of another Rule For Happy Employment formulated by a former co-worker: "Take all your shits on company time.")

Workplace irony alert: The one job at which I was unable to perform this activity was the Borders Bookstore in Santa Cruz. If you were caught with a book in your pocket, they would assume you were stealing it.

My Men's Reading Room activity freighted with it a few minor dilemmas, however. For one, I was restricted to paperbacks—no hardback would fit into the pocket of a pair of slacks. So any hardback books I wanted to read had to be read at home, on my own time. Fortunately, I had a massive library of paperbacks, although on occasion I had to settle for a Doc Savage pulp adventure novel, having run out of anything recent or decent. Second, the paperback could not be too big, or people could see the rectangular outline in my pocket. The Signet edition of *Don Quixote*, for instance, was off-limits, since it's two inches thick. ("Is that a box of cigars in your pocket, or are you just glad to see me?")

An additional problem was getting the book from a desk drawer into my pocket, and back again afterward. This was not difficult when I had my own cubicle, but proved a bit of a magician's challenge when I was seated in a bullpen, surrounded by co-workers. And yet despite these minimal limitations, I managed to perform this activity twice a day, every workday, for over 35 years—and no one ever noticed. Maybe it was because I was a master of the subtle, the stealthy, the surreptitious. More likely it was because people just don't pay all that much attention.

SNEAK PREVIEWS

"Let's go to the movies!"
—*Annie* (1982)

Oh, big whoop, I can hear you thinking. *So you sat in the can and read for half an hour a day. BFD. What a major blow against The System.* My response: *Yeah? Well, how about* this*:*

In late 1997, after MagiNet had been sold and the key executives (including my boss) had been relocated to the Philippines, the skeleton staff who'd agreed to stay on through the transition (in exchange for a significant bonus) came to work in the Sunnyvale office every day, doing whatever was necessary to enable the transfer of functions to the new owners. Me, I had very little to do. So for months, my routine during virtually every workday was this: Come in late. Answer some emails. Go to the movies.

At that time, Sunnyvale occupied a unique geographical location in terms of movie theaters: there were, by my count, nearly 100 screens in some 30-plus theaters within a 15-minute driving radius. The AMC 20 was five minutes away; the Century 12, just one freeway stop up the road. There was a four-screen second-run theater in a mall five minutes away (and the mall had a Togo's, so I could pick up my lunch and smuggle it in. I caught *Contact* in that theater, and was so blown away that I went back and watched it again the next day. I saw *Titanic* during work hours as well. That runs nearly four hours, and I saw it twice.) Had I so desired, I could have seen a different movie every day of the week and still been back at my desk in time to answer any emails that had come in during my "long lunch." When the cat's away...

The crowning glory of my clandestine career of going to the movies on company time, however, occurred during my years at Apple. I was hardly immune to the irony that the iTunes Movie Guru had to sneak off to see a movie during work hours...but I also knew that as hip as Apple wanted to appear, no boss in his right mind would approve of my skipping out on work and going to the movies when I should have been sitting at my desk, eyes glued to a different kind of screen, no matter what I was doing. I knew better than to ask if going to the movies on company time was OK. My mama didn't raise no dummies.

But, as documented earlier, I had very little to do on Mondays, since Programmers were actively barred from working on iTunes while other departments prepared for the weekly store update, which didn't start until 9 PM. So, following our weekly departmental staff meeting on Monday morning, my Monday afternoons were wide open. I discovered that the AMC 16 Theaters in Cupertino's nearby Vallco Mall usually had a movie I wanted to see. And I discovered that it was a 15-minute journey from lifting my butt up off the Aeron chair at my desk to plopping it down in a seat in the theater (including a snack bar popcorn stop). Furthermore, I discovered that the theater screened 15 minutes of previews before each film and that the start times listed online indicated the time the *previews* began, not the time the movie started. So the listed "screening time" became my alarm clock for the moment I'd need to get up from my desk and head for the theater. If the screen time said the show started at noon, I knew I'd have to walk out of the office at noon to catch the start of the flick (and skip the previews).

On Mondays, everyone else in our department usually left for lunch before I did, so if anyone ever asked why I was coming back from lunch so late, I could tell them I'd taken a late lunch that started long after they'd left. And if anyone ever asked what I had for lunch, I could honestly tell them: a hot dog (although when I had an extra ten minutes, I'd stop in at the Chipotle on the way and smuggle a big, quiet burrito into the theater). I did this every Monday for five years. No one ever asked where I was. No one ever knew. No one ever even suspected.

Sure, I could have gone to the movies on the weekend, like every other office worker. That schedule worked for years at Lockheed, when I'd gather a group to go see the week's newest, biggest feature film every Friday afternoon. But it's one thing to bring your own crowd, and quite another to be just another body in a crowd. I hate crowds. Besides, I had shit to do on the weekends. In summary, it's my firm belief that no job is worth having that doesn't afford the opportunity to sneak out and go to the movies once in a while.

How can I justify leaving work so often to go to the movies? Let's review several points:

1) I never missed a deadline or blew off a meeting to go to the movies.

2) My boss for most of those years, Richard Zucker, occasionally held screenings for his charges in an Apple conference room, projecting advance screener DVDs for us on company time. So there was, I believe, some precedent for watching movies on company time.

3) Everyone took a long lunch occasionally. I did it once a week—and no one ever questioned it...or even knew about it. Maybe that one long lunch per week made up for all the days when I was so busy that I had to eat lunch at my desk.

4) I was the goddamn *Movie Guru* for fuck's sake—I was *expected* to keep on top of the industry. So every trip to the movies on company time was a work-related activity, which I would claim if I'd ever been required to defend my field trips. (But I wouldn't push the envelope so far as to ask Apple to refund me for my tickets.)

5) iTunes regularly demanded that its employees keep an odd schedule—like the two or three hours we spent every Monday night turning the store, after a full 8-hour day in the office, not to mention the holiday work, and the annual all-nighter we were all forced to pull to launch new technology on the store. If they expected that kind of flexibility in my schedule, I certainly had a right to expect the same from them.

Ultimately, I don't even give a flying feces about attempting to justify my behavior. All of the above points are merely rationalizations I could have used to cover my ass if accosted. In actual fact, I felt very good about "getting away with something." (As well as seeing a lot of great movies.)

THE WORLD'S MOST VALUABLE EMPLOYEE

While I might not have much good to say about Lockheed, or Borders, or most of the startups in which I labored, I do retain warm feelings for my time at Apple. Regardless of my bitching and moaning about working conditions and my personal stresses there, I am, in fact, proud to have been a quantum of the world's most valuable company during the years when it *became* the world's most valuable company. (According to an August 2018 article in *The New York Times*, Apple was worth approximately $3 billion in 1996—and twenty-two years later, in 2018, it became the first company to be valued at one *trillion* dollars, making it the most valuable public company in the U.S., as well as the most valuable company in history.

I realize how fortunate I was to be invited to join Apple just as the company began its meteoric rise in value, and how lucky I was to have been granted enough stock that the rising tide of Apple's rise in value made retirement possible for me. And even though the impact I made at Apple is comparable to the rise in water level one could achieve by urinating in the ocean, I'm proud that my so-called career eventually took me to the highest level of employment I can conceive being capable of in the corporate community. Maybe I didn't change the world…but I helped.

WHY *NO PLAN B*? *Part 1*

Speaking of Plan A… It took three years of on-again, off-again effort to write *No Plan B*. The on-again phases came when I was reminded of the time value of the information. Frontier Village was demolished decades ago. Lockheed hasn't been just "Lockheed" since they merged with Martin Marietta in 1995 and became Lockheed Martin. Silicon Graphics is barely a footnote in Silicon Valley history, its showcase building now occupied by Google. ReplayTV? Well, DVRs never caught on, goddamn it;

in 2018, the hip tech website Gizmodo even wrote about TiVo that "most people are surprised to hear [it's] still around." Borders went belly up in 2011. Even as I write this in 2020, iTunes is being phased out, replaced by Apple Music and AppleTV+, which encompasses my old department, Movies, along with the iTunes TV store—not to mention original production. "Move fast and break things" has long been a motto of Silicon Valley startups. Mostly what they broke was spirits, but the intended point is that everything in The Valley changes at a breakneck pace. In 1981, my Lockheed friend Jeff Hopkins and I came up with a science fiction concept: "bombing peoples' past." We need hardly have bothered.

Much of the off-again downtime can be attributed to the best possible reason: my late-life revival of Plan A. I never had much of a chance to go into the details of Plan A in this book—the numerous novels and non-fiction books I've written, for instance. I could also only occasionally touch upon the "Plan A-Minus" efforts: the hundreds of articles I've published in newspapers, magazines and websites; the four plays I wrote and directed (see my book *Fourplay: A Theatrical Quartet* for scripts and details); my TV and movie appearances (check IMDb). The story of these creative efforts is content for another book (which will never be written)—and even I am shocked at how little overlap there was between the creative endeavors of Plan A and my hi-tech work life documented in *No Plan B*; the one bridge between them, perhaps, was my film guide, *Killer B's*, which played a key role as a "calling card" in my later employment.

Early in my retirement, however, after a hiatus of 30 years, I resurrected Plan A. I reformatted (and often rewrote) many of my existing books and published them as ebooks, for starters. And during the three years prior to writing and publishing *No Plan B* I've written an additional seven books and reformatted all my work for hardcopy publication through Amazon's Kindle Direct Publishing. All baker's dozen of my books are available as paperbacks from Amazon and as ebooks from Amazon, Barnes & Noble…and, oh yeah, Apple's iBooks. You should look them up, and discover some fine writing, great humor, and superb unknown movies.

WHY *NO PLAN B*? *Part 2*

"In the particular is contained the universal."
—James Joyce

What kind of egomaniacal narcissist could possibly believe that his mundane work experiences could be of any interest to anyone? Good question—not to mention a question I asked myself for years before attempting *No Plan B*, and constantly during its creation. But it is a question I will attempt to answer now.

First, *No Plan B* serves the twin goals of lauding the heroes in my career and castigating my enemies. (At one point I considered changing the title to *Revenge*, but that seemed a bit harsh—and only addressed a small percentage of the stories and people within.)

Second, while I debated whether or not to write *No Plan B*, I saw a number of similar books being published and figured *If they can pull this off, there must be some interest in a story like this...and I can certainly write a better one.* (See the note on egotism above.) It occurred to me that while there are any number of books about Silicon Valley in general and about its more famous startups and charismatic leaders, there might, just *might* be an interest in a chronicle of the experiences of an average worker simply trying to survive in the cutthroat world of hi-tech startups.

The third reason is an attempt to insert this book into a larger cultural context. (I cannot be faulted for lack of ambition.) There's an old (and almost certainly apocryphal) Chinese curse that says, "May you live in interesting times." Despite the trials and hardships documented in these pages, I am, in fact, thrilled to have lived in such an interesting place as Silicon Valley at such an interesting time in history. In conversations with peers and co-workers over the years, I've often referred to Silicon Valley as the Florence of the modern world—a place of technological renaissance that literally changed the world and Humankind. What would we give for a diary of, say, Leonardo da Vinci's gopher, or Michelangelo's janitor? Maybe my little scribblings can in some way fill in the gaps for later generations interested in day-to-day life in this New Florence as it ushered in the Digital Era. Or maybe…well, see the note on egotism above.

Finally, and perhaps most importantly, what decided me to write this account was an experience from early in life—an experience that had *nothing to do with me*. (Ignore the note on egotism above.) In 1965, a teacher named Bel Kaufman published a novel entitled *Up the Down Staircase*, a fictionalized diary about the trials and tribulations of a young high school teacher in New York. The book was an instant bestseller, and everyone loved it …except other teachers. For years afterward, every teacher I ever knew had the same grumbling criticism of this book: "I could have written that." It took me years to realize that the only appropriate response was: "Yeah. *But you didn't.*" So maybe ten thousand different hi-tech workers at a hundred different Silicon Valley companies could have written their personal equivalent of *No Plan B*. But they didn't.

EDITING 101

Since I still consider myself a novelist at heart, I considered early on writing *No Plan B* as a novel. I could have adapted these stories and incidents as a *roman à clef.* But I also realized that some of the characters, situations, conversations and events would strain credibility if framed as fiction. They were simply too unrealistic, just as real life is often too unrealistic.

Since I determined to chronicle these events as fact, it seems only appropriate to indicate where facts left off and creative editing intervened. There are at least two temp jobs that I purposefully left out of this narrative, for example. One was a short stint as a "Kelley Girl"—a temporary secretarial employee who never got any gigs after signing up for the service in 1973. Another is a week-long gig that proved so horrid that I desire never even to think of it again, much less write about it. I have attempted to make this book as funny as possible…and there was simply nothing funny about that aborted temp gig.

I will also admit that there are at least two co-workers I've excised entirely, and not just because they were peripheral to any job or incident herein, but because they betrayed me once too often to be amusing or even to warrant any mention. They have no place in my life and they have no place in this book. They are dead to me and deserve to be forgotten.

PORTÉ DISPARU ("MISSING IN ACTION")

"I've been involved with so many women, but it always ended badly...at least it always ended, which to me is synonymous."
—Philip K. Dick, *Philip K. Dick: The Dream Connection*

Freud once said that anyone in good mental health should be able to do two things well: *Lieben und Arbeiten*: "love and work."

It goes without saying that work is only one aspect of a whole life; one facet of any overall existence; one thread in the multi-hued tapestry of living, on which we try not to spill our food at the risk of pissing off mom. And since *No Plan B* concentrates on the work aspect of my life, many connected threads have by necessity been snipped—the Plan A and non-tech-oriented *arbeiten* mentioned above, for instance. But the most distressing omission is the *lieben.*

There was simply no room in this narrative to delve into or even barely mention the *lieben* side of life: the women I've loved, crushed on, chased, lusted after, befriended, admired, lived with, married, and/or lost: Laurie, Mary Kaye, Lynne, Alexandra, Patti, Narine, Phetsy, Margie, Margaret, Erika, Tricia, Dr. Sue, Dr. Suzie, Diana. They might not have played any major role in either Plan A or *No Plan B*, but their affection and friendship (and occasional returned love) was instrumental in maintaining my sanity.

Only Epiphany Jane—the one person who stuck with me through my employment rollercoaster of the past 20-plus years —appears with any regularity in this document. And even though her influence and support have been crucial to the success of Plan B, she prefers anonymity, so my nods to her have been held to a bare minimum, and included only with her reluctant approval. She was, however, the one person who not only helped me endure the failure of Plan A but who reaped the rewards by sticking with me through the exigencies of the unplanned Plan B.

THE ULTIMATE IRONY

"Persons attempting to find a motive in this narrative will be prosecuted; persons attempting to find a moral in it will be banished; persons attempting to find a plot in it will be shot."
—Mark Twain, *The Adventures of Huckleberry Finn*

"If there's no meaning in it," said the King, "that saves a world of trouble, you know, as we needn't try to find any."
—Lewis Carroll, *Alice in Wonderland*

Flakey Foont: "Mr. Natural! What does it all mean??"
Mr. Natural: "Don't mean sheeit…"
—Robert Crumb, "Mr. Natural Comix"

I was one of the lucky ones: I was granted a return to The Garden of Eden even after taking a bite of the Apple—or, in this case, *because* I took a bite of the Apple. (No one was ever banished from Paradise for drinking the Kool-Aid.)

The irony of my pinball career is not necessarily that I made a million dollars even though Plan A never panned out, and even though Plan A was my single greatest interest in life and the one facet of my existence into which I put my most determined and dedicated efforts over a forty-year period. No, the ultimate irony was that while Plan A amounted to so little over so long a time, my parallel path of hi-tech, startup-company employment made me more money than all my previous employment and all my Plan A earnings combined. In purely financial terms, I estimate that the total revenue I generated from my writing and publishing efforts over those forty years, for instance, amounts to less than a year's pay from my Apple employment alone.

Aside from my having a Plan A (which I assume most people do not have), maybe the story of my work life isn't all that unique. Maybe even my million-dollar windfall isn't all that unique either: according to a 2019 "Harper's Index" factoid, a minimum of 5,000 new Bay Area millionaires were created in 2019 from tech IPOs. While I would have much preferred to have earned my million through my own creative efforts rather than by the luck of one generous gift granted by being in the right place at the right time (and, in my defense, with the right skills and knowledge)—I can't really complain about the outcome. On ego days, I reason that motherfucking Fate owed me this windfall after all the shit She put me through (ignoring the fact that She puts everyone through a lot of shit). On the Zen days, humble and happy, I just think: *Lucky me*. I put my passion and my best effort into Plan A and received relatively little in return. I put my hard work and emotional anguish reluctantly into the accidental Plan B...and I lucked out.

Lucky me.

"We must do away with the absolutely specious notion that everybody has to earn a living. It is a fact today that one in ten thousand of us can make a technological breakthrough capable of supporting all the rest. The youth of today are absolutely right in recognizing this nonsense of earning a living. We keep inventing jobs because of this false idea that everybody has to be employed at some kind of drudgery because, according to Malthusian-Darwinian theory, he must justify his right to exist. So we have inspectors of inspectors & people making instruments for inspectors to inspect inspectors. The true business of people should be to go back to school & think about whatever it was they were thinking about before somebody came along & told them they had to earn a living."

—Buckminster Fuller

"Working for a living is shit for the birds."

—My Dad

Also Available from The Impermanent Press

Also Available From The Impermanent Press

Killer B's:
The 237 Best Movies on Video You've (Probably) Never Seen

by D. Scott Apel

The iTunes Movie Guru (Emeritus) shares his selection of the best unknown movies available on demand.

From the Introduction to Killer B's:

We live in an age of unprecedented access to movies. Too bad most of them suck. Netflix, iTunes, Amazon, Vudu, Hulu Plus... Thousands and thousands of movies are available at your fingertips. But with so many titles, the big question remains *How do you find a* good *movie?*

The answer: *Killer B's: The 237 Best Movies on Video You've (Probably) Never Seen. Killer B's* makes full use of the on demand advantage: easy access to lesser-known films. It's just as easy to find a hidden gem as a recent blockbuster...if you know what you're looking for. *Killer B's* lets you know what to look for.

Whatever you call them—buried treasures, sleepers, word of mouth movies, or "killer" B movies—these are great little films that never got the publicity, distribution or attention they needed to allow their audience to find them. Killer B's are terrific but little-known films, designed with a general audience in mind—no "cult classics," no "forgotten favorites," no "so bad they're good" flicks, just the delight of discovery.

Life's too short to watch bad films. Don't be stung by bad movies—put *Killer B's* to work for you, and find a few good movies you've (possibly) never heard of and (probably) never seen!

Now available in both ebook and print editions

Also Available From The Impermanent Press

Killer B's 2:
Son of a Killer B
237 MORE Great Movies on Demand You've (Probably) Never Seen

by D. Scott Apel

The iTunes Movie Guru (Emeritus) shares his selection of the best unknown movies available on demand.

The original *Killer B's* covered great but little-known movies released between 1980 and 1995. This sequel volume picks up where Vol. 1 left off, and includes buried treasures released between 1996 and 2016—an additional 237 superb but overlooked movies (as well as a few bingeable, overlooked TV series).

We live in an age of unprecedented access to movies. Too bad most of them suck. With instant access to so many titles, the question remains *How do you find a* good *movie?*

The answer: the *Killer B's* film guides, which make full use of the on-demand advantage: *easy access to lesser-known films*. It's just as easy to find a hidden gem as a recent blockbuster...if you know what you're looking for. *Killer B's* lets you know what to look for.

Whatever you call them—buried treasures, sleepers, word of mouth movies, or "killer" B movies—these are great little films that never got the publicity, distribution or attention they needed to allow their audience to find them. Killer B's are terrific but little-known films, designed with a general audience in mind—no "cult classics," no "forgotten favorites," no "so bad they're good" flicks, just the delight of discovery.

Life's too short to watch bad films. Don't be stung by bad movies—put *Killer B's* to work for you, and find a few good movies you've (possibly) never heard of and (probably) never seen!

Now available in both ebook and print editions

Also Available From The Impermanent Press

Killer B's: The Hive
The 487 Best Movies* On Demand You've (Probably) Never Seen
***and a few TV Shows**

by D. Scott Apel

The iTunes Movie Guru (Emeritus) shares his selection of the best unknown movies available on demand.

The Hive is where the honey is! This handy guide to the great but underseen movies available on demand brings together the contents of *Killer B's, Volume 1 (1980-1995)* and *Killer B's, Volume 2 (1996-2016),* complete in one friggin' *enormous* ebook.

Whatever you call these flicks—buried treasures, sleepers, word of mouth movies, or "killer" B movies—they are great little films that never got the publicity, distribution or attention they needed to allow their audience to find them. *You might be that audience!*

Life's too short to watch bad films. Don't be stung by bad movies—put *Killer B's* to work for you, and find a few good movies you've (possibly) never heard of and (probably) never seen!

Now available as an ebook wherever fine ebooks are sold.

Also Available From The Impermanent Press

The Infinite Mistress

by D. Scott Apel

An Alec Smart Mystery (#2)

"Fans of Donald E. Westlake's comic crime novels will love The Infinite Mistress.*"*
—ComiCaper

When a bubble-headed North Beach topless dancer hires a young Silicon Valley private eye to investigate the authenticity of her "past life memories," little does he suspect that he's about to become entangled in a plot that has repeated itself through several lifetimes—and always ends tragically for the dancer.

Or is it all just coincidence? The real question is, can he piece together the past-life clues he uncovers in time to dodge the juggernaut of karma and avoid the fated fatal finale? It's taken several lifetimes, but this time around, time is running out.

The Infinite Mistress is a fast, funny, and original twist on the mystery novel.

Now available in both ebook and print editions

Also Available From The Impermanent Press

Detective, Comics

by D. Scott Apel

Alec Smart Comic Mystery (#3)

"The heir apparent to Donald E. Westlake's comic caper novels."
—ComiCaper

When a teenage comic book magnate has a valuable book stolen from his collection, he turns to small town private eye Alec Smart to find his Batman book...and justice.

But the path to justice is a rocky road, as Alec discovers when he's forced to deal with a corrupt comic book store owner as well as the kid's estranged parents, one of whom wants him dead and one of whom wants him in bed. Not to mention his own relationship crisis: If his beloved girlfriend leaves him, will he have the fortitude to assist the kid?

The third entry in the Alec Smart comic mystery series features high stakes and low comedy, quirky characters, odd plot twists and droll dialog, as well as action, insanity...and adults running around in rented superhero costumes, trapped in a giant video-game. Yeah, you read that right.

Detective, Comics is a fresh, fast-paced and fun-filled twist on the standard detective novel formula...because formula is for babies.

Now available in both ebook and print editions

Also Available From The Impermanent Press

Philip K. Dick: The Dream Connection

Edited by D. Scott Apel

"A very impressive must-read for serious PKD readers... I literally could not put this book down. Reading the interview, you get the uncanny sensation that you're sitting in the room rapping with PKD himself."
—Science Fiction Chronicle

This exceptional anthology includes over eight hours of interviews with noted science fiction author Philip K. Dick, including the most complete and personal account of his March, 1974, "mystical experiences," plus numerous supplementary essays, including Robert Anton Wilson on PKD's mystical experiences, R. Faraday Nelson on collaborating with PKD, a rarely-seen short story in which PKD fictionalizes his mystical experiences, and much more.

"Hands down the most joyous and entertaining book on Philip K. Dick."
—Lawrence Sutin, author of Divine Invasions: A Life of Philip K. Dick.

Now available in both ebook and print editions

Also Available From The Impermanent Press

Beyond Chaos and Beyond

The Best of Trajectories, Volume II

by Robert Anton Wilson

Edited by D. Scott Apel

For over a decade (1987-1997), Robert Anton Wilson, co-author of the *Illuminatus!* trilogy and author of *The Cosmic Trigger*, published a quarterly newsletter, *Trajectories: The Journal of Futurism and Heresy*, full of original articles, unpublished fiction and outrageous opinion. The 1994 book *Chaos and Beyond* collected the best essays from the first ten issues of the newsletter; this sequel, *Beyond Chaos and Beyond*, preserves the best of the final issues, including an excerpt from RAW's unfinished sequel to *Illuminatus!,* transcripts of audio and video issues, and transcripts of the several videos featuring RAW produced specifically for his globe-girdling fan base.

Additional material includes a rare 1977 interview with RAW; a major essay on Philip K. Dick, as well as RAW's comments from a PKD documentary; transcripts of RAW's 1978 PBS appearances discussing *The Prisoner*; and a 30,000 word essay by the editor detailing his 30-plus-year association with Wilson.

Beyond Chaos and Beyond is essential reading for hardcore fans of Robert Anton Wilson's extraordinary work and life.

Now available in both ebook and print editions

Also Available From The Impermanent Press

Mein Summer Kampf

by D. Scott Apel

The most common response I get to that title is: “You think that’s funny?” The answer I’d really like to give you is the Joe Pesci answer: “Funny how? I mean, funny like I’m a clown, I amuse you?” But the answer I will give you (and Joe) is: Yes, I do, or I wouldn’t have made it the title of this collection of short humorous essays, ludicrous lists, satirical stories and even (shudder) a couple parodic poems. Yes, the answer is Yes.

There is only one other word I’d like to say about this collection: *subtle*. And that is the last time you will ever hear that word used in connection with this material. An ex-girlfriend once told me that I was like a 1,000 watt light bulb: very bright, but a little obnoxious. And I’ve been informed that my humor has a certain *“je ne sais merde.”* I prefer to believe, however, that, like the blind man whose other senses are heightened to compensate for his lack of sight, my total lack of common sense or any sense of common decency has allowed my sense of to humor expand...occasionally so far as to exceed the boundaries of comprehension or appreciation of those poor souls born without a humor gland.

But that is not you, of course, despite what they all say about you behind your back. So what the hell. Take a chance. Prove them wrong. You might just LYAO. I mean, it’s FREE, for chrissake. (Except on Amazon. They won’t let me give it away free. WTF?) What have you got to lose? I’ll answer that question, too: You know that old adage, “You get what you pay for”? This book proves it wrong: Even though it’s free, you’re still getting far less than you paid for.

Hm. That hardly sounds like a successful sales pitch, now does it? OK, try this old adage: “Ya pays yer money and ya takes yer chances.” Well, you’re not paying anything, so there’s a chance you might just get some laughs out of this collection. As a matter of fact, I guarantee you will, or your money will be cheerfully refunded. As long as you got the free version, anyway. If they made you pay 99 cents for this, then we’ll have to fall back on the new adage for internet commerce: “99 cents is the new free.”

Now available in both ebook and print editions wherever fine ebooks are sold. Or given away for free.

Made in the USA
San Bernardino, CA
03 August 2020

75793607R00363